Lecture Notes in Computer Science 10260

More information about this series at http://www.springer.com/series/7409

Flavius Frasincar · Ashwin Ittoo
Le Minh Nguyen · Elisabeth Métais (Eds.)

Natural Language Processing and Information Systems

22nd International Conference on Applications of Natural Language to Information Systems, NLDB 2017
Liège, Belgium, June 21–23, 2017
Proceedings

Editors
Flavius Frasincar
Erasmus University Rotterdam
Rotterdam
The Netherlands

Ashwin Ittoo
University of Liège
Liège
Belgium

Le Minh Nguyen
Japan Advanced Institute of Science and Technology
Nomi
Japan

Elisabeth Métais
Conservatoire National des Arts et Métiers
Paris
France

ISSN 0302-9743 ISSN 1611-3349 (electronic)
Lecture Notes in Computer Science
ISBN 978-3-319-59568-9 ISBN 978-3-319-59569-6 (eBook)
DOI 10.1007/978-3-319-59569-6

Library of Congress Control Number: 2017943005

LNCS Sublibrary: SL3 – Information Systems and Applications, incl. Internet/Web, and HCI

Printed on acid-free paper

This Springer imprint is published by Springer Nature
The registered company is Springer International Publishing AG
The registered company address is: Gewerbestrasse 11, 6330 Cham, Switzerland

Preface

Natural language processing, as a field of artificial intelligence, plays a crucial role in the way machines and humans interact. In the current digital era where a lot of text produced by humans is readable by machines, natural language processing aims to bridge the gap between human communication and digital representation. During the past few years, much attention has been given to natural language processing feeding on recent developments in machine learning (e.g., deep learning) or contributing to the emergence of new machine learning techniques (e.g., word embedding). The applications of natural processing techniques are numerous: machine translation, sentiment analysis, text classification, question answering, argumentation mining, etc., each contributing to the success of various businesses.

This volume contains the long papers, short papers, posters/demonstrations, and extended abstracts for the keynotes of the 22nd International Conference on Applications of Natural Language to Information Systems (NLDB 2017), held from June 21st to 23rd, 2017, in Liège, Belgium.

NLDB is the flagship conference for multidisciplinary research combining the fields of natural language processing and information systems. Previous editions of NLDB took place at Versailles, France (1995), Amsterdam, The Netherlands (1996), Vancouver, Canada (1997), Klagenfurt, Austria (1999), Versailles, France (2000), Madrid, Spain (2001), Stockholm, Sweden (2002), Burg, Germany (2003), Salford, UK (2004), Alicante, Spain (2005), Klagenfurt, Austria (2006), Paris, France (2007), London, UK (2008), Saarbrücken, Germany (2009), Cardiff, UK (2010), Alicante, Spain (2011), Groningen, The Netherlands (2012), Salford, UK (2013), Montpellier, France (2014), Passau, Germany (2015), and Salford, UK (2016). It is estimated that 80% of Big Data is unstructured, which highlights the deep impact that natural language processing has on processing large amounts of data and extracting signals that can be utilized in information systems. As such, the NLDB conference series helps advance research by pioneering new natural language processing techniques and their emerging applications in information systems.

The NLDB 2017 edition received 125 submissions, out of which the Program Committee selected 22 full research papers (18% acceptance rate), 19 short papers (33% acceptance rate), and 16 posters/demonstrations (46% acceptance rate). The accepted papers have been grouped into the following nine topics: Feature Engineering, Information Extraction, Information Extraction from Resource-Scarce Languages, Natural Language Processing Applications, Neural Language Models and Applications, Opinion Mining and Sentiment Analysis, Question Answering Systems and Applications, Semantics-Based Models and Applications, and Text Summarization.

The excellent program would not have been possible without the support of the many people who helped with the organization of this event. We would like to thank Satoshi Tojo (Japan Advanced Institute of Science and Technology, Japan) and Mihai Surdeanu (University of Arizona, USA), who accepted to be our keynote speakers.

We also would like to thank Manon Crélot and Kim Schouten for building and maintaining the website. We are grateful to Truong Son Nguyen and Duc Vu Tran for their help and assistance in producing the proceedings. Special thanks to Gosse Bouma, Pierre Dupont, Pierre Geurts, Farid Meziane, Michael Schyns, and Antal van den Bosch for their advice and help with the organization. In addition, we thank the reviewers for their hard work that allowed us to select the best papers to be presented at NLDB 2017. Last, but not least, we would like to thank the authors who submitted their work to this conference and all the participants who contributed to the success of this event.

June 2017

Flavius Frasincar
Ashwin Ittoo
Le Minh Nguyen
Elisabeth Métais

Organization

General Chairs

Ashwin Ittoo	University of Liège, Belgium
Elisabeth Métais	Conservatoire National des Arts et Métiers, France

Program Committee Chairs

Flavius Frasincar	Erasmus University Rotterdam, The Netherlands
Nguyen Le Minh	Japan Advanced Institute of Science and Technology, Japan

Organization Chairs

Gosse Bouma	University of Groningen, The Netherlands
Pierre Dupont	Université Catholique de Louvain, Belgium
Pierre Geurts	University of Liège, Belgium
Michael Schyns	University of Liège, Belgium
Farid Meziane	University of Salford-Manchester, UK
Antal van den Bosch	Radboud University Nijmegen, The Netherlands

Website Chairs

Manon Crélot	University of Liège, Belgium
Kim Schouten	Erasmus University Rotterdam, The Netherlands

Proceedings Chairs

Truong Son Nguyen	Japan Advanced Institute of Science and Technology, Japan
Duc Vu Tran	Japan Advanced Institute of Science and Technology, Japan

Program Committee

Witold Abramowicz	Poznan University of Economics, Poland
Jacky Akoka	Conservatoire National des Arts et Métiers, France
Hidir Aras	FIZ Karlsruhe, Germany
Guntis Arnicans	University of Latvia, Latvia
Imran Sarwar Bajwa	The Islamia University of Bahawalpur, Pakistan
Mithun Balakrishna	Lymba Corporation, USA
Pierpaolo Basile	University of Bari Aldo Moro, Italy

Nicolas Béchet	Université de Bretagne Sud, France
Gloria Bordogna	National Research Council of Italy, Italy
Gosse Bouma	University of Groningen, The Netherlands
Sandra Bringay	Université de Montpellier 3, France
Paul Buitelaar	National University of Ireland, Ireland
Cornelia Caragea	University of North Texas, USA
Christian Chiarcos	Goethe-Universität Frankfurt am Main, Germany
Raja Chiky	Institut Supérieur d'Electronique de Paris, France
Philipp Cimiano	Bielefeld University, Germany
Isabelle Comyn-Wattiau	ESSEC Business School, France
Ernesto William De Luca	Potsdam University of Applied Sciences, Germany
Antske Fokkens	Vrije Universiteit Amsterdam, The Netherlands
Vladimir A. Fomichov	National Research University Higher School of Economics, Russia
Thierry Fontenelle	Translation Centre for the Bodies of the European Union, Luxembourg
Flavius Frasincar	Erasmus University Rotterdam, The Netherlands
Andre Freitas	University of Passau, Germany
Debasis Ganguly	Dublin City University, Ireland
Ahmed Guessoum	University of Science and Technology Houari Boumediene, Algeria
Maryam Habibi	Humboldt-Universität zu Berlin, Germany
Yaakov Hacohen-Kerner	Jerusalem College of Technology, Lev Academic Center, Israel
Siegfried Handschuh	University of Passau, Germany
Sebastian Hellmann	Universität Leipzig, Germany
Michael Herweg	University of Heidelberg and IBM, Germany
Helmut Horacek	Saarland University, Germany
Dino Ienco	National Research Institute of Science and Technology for Environment and Agriculture, France
Ashwin Ittoo	University of Liège, Belgium
Paul Johannesson	Royal Institute of Technology, Sweden
Jaap Kamps	University of Amsterdam, The Netherlands
Epaminondas Kapetanios	University of Westminster, UK
Sophia Katrenko	Utrecht University, The Netherlands
Zoubida Kedad	University of Versailles, France
Eric Kergosien	University of Lille, France, France
Christian Kop	Alpen-Adria-Universität Klagenfurt, Austria
Valia Kordoni	Humboldt University Berlin, Germany
Leila Kosseim	Concordia University, Canada
Mathieu Lafourcade	Université de Montpellier, France
Els Lefever	University College Ghent and Ghent University, Belgium
Jochen Leidner	Thomson Reuters, UK
Johannes Leveling	Teckro, Ireland

Deryle W. Lonsdale	Brigham Young University, USA
Cédric Lopez	VISEO, Objet Direct, France
David Losada	University of Santiago de Compostela, Spain
John P. Mccrae	National University of Ireland, Ireland
Elisabeth Métais	Conservatoire National des Arts et Métiers, France
Marie-Jean Meurs	Université du Québec à Montréal, Canada
Farid Meziane	University of Salford, UK
Luisa Mich	University of Trento, Italy
Claudiu Mihaila	BenevolentAI, UK
Shamima Mithun	Concordia University, Canada
Marie-Francine Moens	KU Leuven, Belgium
Andres Montoyo	University of Alicante, Spain
Rafael Muñoz	University of Alicante, Spain
Ahmed Nabhan	Fayoum University, Egypt
Le Minh Nguyen	Japan Advanced Institute of Science and Technology, Japan
Jan Odijk	UIL-OTS Utrecht University, The Netherlands
Alexander Panchenko	University of Hamburg, Germany
Gabriella Pasi	Università degli Studi di Milano Bicocca, Italy
Patrick Saint-Dizier	Institut de Recherches en Informatique de Toulouse, France
Heiko Paulheim	University of Mannheim, Germany
Yulong Pei	Eindhoven University of Technology, The Netherlands
Davide Picca	Columbia University, USA
Pascal Poncelet	Université de Montpellier, France
Violaine Prince	Université de Montpellier, France
Gábor Prószéky	MorphoLogic and PPKE, Hungary
Behrang Qasemizadeh	Heinrich-Heine-Universität Düsseldorf, Germany
Shaolin Qu	Michigan State University, USA
Martin Riedl	University of Hamburg, Germany
Mathieu Roche	Cirad, TETIS, France
Mike Rosner	University of Malta, Malta
Paolo Rosso	Technical University of Valencia, Spain
Mohamad Saraee	University of Salford, UK
Bahar Sateli	Concordia University, Canada
Roman Schneider	Institut für Deutsche Sprache, Germany
Kim Schouten	Erasmus University Rotterdam, The Netherlands
Khaled Shaalan	The British University in Dubai, UAE
Max Silberztein	Université de Franche-Comté, France
Veda Storey	Georgia State University, USA
Vijayan Sugumaran	Oakland University, USA
Maguelonne Teisseire	National Research Institute of Science and Technology for Environment and Agriculture, France
Mike Thelwall	University of Wolverhampton, UK
Krishnaprasad Thirunarayan	Wright State University, USA

Dan Tufis	Institutul de Cercetari pentru Inteligenta Artificiala, Academia Romana, Romania
Antal van Den Bosch	Radboud University Nijmegen, The Netherlands
Panos Vassiliadis	University of Ioannina, Greece
Feiyu Xu	Yocoy Technologies GmbH and DFKI LT-Lab, Germany
Wlodek Zadrozny	University of North Carolina in Charlotte, USA
Fabio Massimo Zanzotto	University of Rome Tor Vergata, Italy
Kalliopi Zervanou	Utrecht University, The Netherlands
Torsten Zesch	University of Duisburg-Essen, Germany
Erqiang Zhou	University of Electronic Science and Technology of China, China

Additional Reviewers

Abdaoui Amine
Tchechmedjiev Andon
Ciro Baron
Ester Boldrini
Milan Dojchinovski
Jacques Fize
Erfaneh Gharavi
Rmy Kessler
Amit Kirschenbaum
Bettina Klimek
Stefania Marrara
Bilel Moulahi
Victoria Nebot
Armin Seyeditabari
Walid Shalaby
Borbála Siklósi
Mike Donald Tapi-Nzali
Michael Wojatzki
Seid Muhie Yimam
Sarah Zenasni
Nicola Zeni

Invited Papers

Linguistic Musicology

Satoshi Tojo

Japan Advanced Institute of Science and Technology, 1-1 Asahidai, Nomi, Ishikawa 923-1292, Japan
tojo@jaist.ac.jp

Abstract. Music and language are considered to share the common biological origin. Although the meaningful part became independent as language, why do we human beings still retain music? In this talk, we illustrate our recognition of music, where we show some examples concerning long-distance dependency in chord sequence, and we contend that there exists a tree structure in music that is realized by Chomskian context-free grammar. Referring to the issue on what is the communication, as well as our experiments on how infants acquire language, we offer an open discussion on the contents of music.

Charles Darwin said

> "As neither the enjoyment nor the capacity of producing musical notes are faculties of the least use to man in reference to his daily habits of life, they must be ranked amongst the most mysterious with which he is endowed. They are present, though in a very rude condition, in men of all races, even the most savage;" [2]

Is there any meaning in music? In the primordial era, music and language were one and the same [6]. Thereafter, its meaningful part has been extracted and became independent as languages, and the remaining part is the one now called music. If music carries some senses, are they only emotion and feeling, *e.g.*, pleasure, sorrow, anger, and so on?

Regarding this biological history, we conceive that the music seems to stay in a subordinate position to language. In the medieval ages, music had served for sacred chants in church. Then, music had often been employed to compensate the dramatic effect, lacking in the verbal sermon. In classical ages, some concrete titles were often given to music, *e.g.*, Vivaldi's *Four Seasons*, Beethoven's *Pastrale* symphony, and so on. Later, Liszt invented the term called *Programmusik* whose objective is to depict the scenary or our mental images and Wagner's *Musikdrama* became the target of criticism by Eduard Hanslick. Still later, Richard Strauss said "*there is nothing which cannot be described in music.*" Nowadays, popular music serves for their lyrics.

We are still using the diatonic scale of C-D-E-F-G-A-B, and triad/tetrad chords like C_m, F#, G_7, and so on, which were established in 17th century. Nowadays, the evolution of music seems stopped. Music as the advanced fine arts is far less popular. The current popular music itself is in a simplified style of classical music in structure, though it has now strongly connected to visual media, as idol singers and movies, and has developed as a multi-modal art. Is there any future evolution in music itself?

Digression 1: if music carries some meaning, then it implies that there should be a notion of *communication*. But, what is transferred? If you are alone in the universe, have you acquired a language? Most scientists agree to that the origin of language is for communication, but others argue that language has existed for thinking even though we are alone.

Digression 2: what is the *evolution*? We have experimented the music acquisition by the Iterated Learning Model [4], to investigate if we can obtain the framework to understand musical structure autonomously. In this work, we also discussed what is the referent of music ('Gavagai' problem of W.V. Quine) and if there are such cognitive biases that accelerate the vocabulary acquisition of infants only between 18 months and three years old.

Now, let us get back to our original interest. Heinrich Schenker [5] claimed that there were structurally important notes in music, and every music can be reduced to an *Ursatz* (basic form): tonic-dominant-tonic that supports the linear melody. In order to retrieve such basic forms, we need to hypothesize that there is a hierarchy called *vordergrund*, *mittelgrund*, and *hintergrund*, in each music piece. The Generative Theory of Tonal Music [3] is more polished and sophisticated version of Schenkerian theory, since it strongly relies on Chomskian context-free grammar. The theory consists of four parts; Grouping Analysis, Metrical Analysis, Time-span Tree, and Prolongational Tree. In this talk, we show our experience with a computer implementation of this theory, where we expound how we can retrieve tree structures, and how we should compensate the information on latent long-distance dependancy.

Finally, we close the talk by an open discussion including the questions posed by Cope [1]: "Can computers compose good music?", "Will computer composing programs replace human composers?", "Can we tell which of these works was composed by computer?", and "Does music have meaning?"

References

1. Cope, D.: Computer Models of Music Creativity. The MIT Press (2017)
2. Darwin, C.: The Descent of Men, and Selection in Relation to Sex. John Murray (1871)
3. Jackendoff, R., Lehrdahl, F.: The Generative Theory of Tonal Music. The MIT Press (1983)
4. Kirby, S.: Learning, bottlenecks and the evolution of recursive syntax. In: Linguistic Evolution Through Language Acquisition. Formal and Computational Models, pp. 173–203 (2002)
5. Schenker, H.: Harmonielehre. Neue Musikalische Theorien und Phantasien part 1. Vienna: Universal Edition (1906)
6. Wallin, N.L., et al. (ed.): The Origins of Music. The MIT Press (2000)

Using Machine Reading to Aid Cancer Understanding and Treatment

Mihai Surdeanu

University of Arizona, Tucson, Arizona, USA
msurdeanu@arizona.edu

Abstract. PubMed, a repository and search engine for biomedical literature, now indexes more than 1 million articles each year. This is clearly beyond the processing capacity of human domain experts, which hinders our capacity to truly understand many diseases. In this talk, I will introduce an effort that teaches computers to "read" millions of cancer-research publications to have a holistic understanding of the disease. Our approach extracts and assembles protein signaling pathways, which are partly responsible for causing cancer, into a large model, which allows researchers to come up with new hypotheses for understanding and treating the disease. I will show that, not only does our automated approach perform comparably with human experts at the task of reading papers, but also that the generated knowledge is able to produce new explanations for several types of cancer.

PubMed, a repository and search engine for biomedical literature[1], now indexes more than 1 million articles each year. At the same time, a typical large-scale patient profiling effort produces petabytes of data – and is expected to reach exabytes within the near future [3]. Combining these large profiling data sets with the mechanistic biological information covered by the literature is an exciting opportunity that can yield causal, predictive understanding of cellular processes. Such understanding can unlock important downstream applications in medicine and biology. Unfortunately, most of the mechanistic knowledge in the literature is not in a computable form and remains mostly hidden.

In the first part of the talk I will describe a natural language processing (NLP) approach that captures a system-scale, mechanistic understanding of cellular processes through automated, large-scale reading of scientific literature [2, 5, 4]. At the core of this approach are compact semantic grammars [6, 7] that capture mentions of biological entities (e.g., genes, proteins, protein families, simple chemicals), events that operate over these biochemical entities (e.g., biochemical reactions), and nested events that operate over other events (e.g., catalyses). This grammar-based approach is a departure from recent trends in NLP such as deep learning, but I will argue that this is a better direction for cross-disciplinary projects such as this. Grammar-based approaches are modular (i.e., errors can be attributed to a specific rule) and are easier to understand by non-NLP users. This means that biologists can actively participate in the debugging and maintenance of the overall system. Additionally, the proposed approach captures

[1] https://www.ncbi.nlm.nih.gov/pubmed.

other complex language phenomena such as hedging and coreference resolution [1]. I will highlight how these phenomena are different in biomedical texts versus open-domain language.

I will show that the proposed approach performs machine reading at accuracy comparable with human domain experts, but at much higher throughput, and, more importantly, that this automatically-derived knowledge substantially improves the inference capacity of existing biological data analysis algorithms. Using this knowledge we were able to identify a large number of previously unidentified, but highly statistically significant mutually exclusively altered signaling modules in several cancers [4], which led to novel biological hypotheses within the corresponding cancer context.

Towards the end of the talk, I will briefly review other important efforts at the intersection of biology and computer science. I will close by discussing future directions in machine reading, in particular how we can take advantage of recent developments in machine learning for natural language processing, e.g., word embeddings, while maintaining the interpretability of the models generated.

References

1. Bell, D., Hahn-Powell, G., Valenzuela-Escárcega, M.A., Hahn-Powell, G., Surdeanu, M.: An investigation of coreference phenomena in the biomedical domain. In: Proceedings of the 10th edition of the Language Resources and Evaluation Conference (LREC), pp. 177–183 (2016)
2. Hahn-Powell, G., Bell, D., Valenzuela-Escárcega, M.A., Surdeanu, M.: This before that: Causal precedence in the biomedical domain. In: Proceedings of the 2016 Workshop on Biomedical Natural Language Processing, BioNLP 2016, pp. 146–155 (2016)
3. Stephens, Z.D., Lee, S.Y., Faghri, F., Campbell, R.H., Zhai, C., Efron, M.J., Iyer, R., Schatz, M.C., Sinha, S., Robinson, G.E.: Big data: astronomical or genomical? PLoS Biol. **13**(7), e1002195 (2015)
4. Valenzuela-Escárcega, M.A., Babur, Ö., Hahn-Powell, G., Bell, D., Noriega-Atala, E., Surdeanu, M., Demir, E., Morrison, C.T.: Large-scale automated reading of scientific cancer literature can discover new cancer driving mechanisms (2017, in preparation)
5. Valenzuela-Escárcega, M.A., Hahn-Powell, G., Bell, D., Surdeanu, M.: SnapToGrid: from statistical to interpretable models for biomedical information extraction. In: Proceedings of the 2016 Workshop on Biomedical Natural Language Processing (BioNLP 2016), pp. 56–65 (2016)
6. Valenzuela-Escárcega, M.A., Hahn-Powell, G., Hicks, T., Surdeanu, M.: A domain-independent rule-based framework for event extraction. In: Proceedings of the 53rd Annual Meeting of the Association for Computational Linguistics, pp. 127–132 (2015)
7. Valenzuela-Escárcega, M.A., Hahn-Powell, G., Surdeanu, M.: Odin's runes: a rule language for information extraction. In: Proceedings of the 10th edition of the Language Resources and Evaluation Conference (LREC), pp. 322–329 (2016)

Contents

Information Extraction from Resource-Scarce Languages

Natural Language Processing Applications

Neural Language Models and Applications

Feature Engineering

Fine-Grained Opinion Mining from Mobile App Reviews with Word Embedding Features

Mario Sänger[1(✉)], Ulf Leser[1], and Roman Klinger[2]

[1] Department of Computer Science, Humboldt-Universität zu Berlin, Unter den Linden 6, 10099 Berlin, Germany
{saengerm,leser}@informatik.hu-berlin.de

[2] Institut für Maschinelle Sprachverarbeitung, Universität Stuttgart, Pfaffenwaldring 5 b, 70569 Stuttgart, Germany
klinger@ims.uni-stuttgart.de

Abstract. Existing approaches for opinion mining mainly focus on reviews from Amazon, domain-specific review websites or social media. Little efforts have been spent on fine-grained analysis of opinions in review texts from mobile smart phone applications. In this paper, we propose an aspect and subjective phrase extraction model for German reviews from the Google Play store. We analyze the impact of different features, including domain-specific word embeddings. Our best model configuration shows a performance of 0.63 F_1 for aspects and 0.62 F_1 for subjective phrases. Further, we perform cross-domain experiments: A model trained on Amazon reviews and tested on app reviews achieves lower performance (drop by 27% points for aspects and 15% points for subjective phrases). The results indicate that there are strong differences in the way personal opinions on product aspects are expressed in the particular domains.

Keywords: Sentiment analysis · Reviews · German · App reviews · Opinion mining

1 Introduction

The analysis of sentiment expressions and opinions in text gained a lot of attention within the last decade [23]. Studied types of texts include product reviews, Twitter messages or blog posts [36]. The analysis of mobile applications (also known as *apps*) and their user reviews in app stores, such as the Apple App Store[1], Google Play Store[2], BlackBerry World[3] or Windows Store[4], has only gained very limited attention so far. However, app reviews offer interesting characteristics which deserve special investigation: On the one side, they share properties with Tweets and other social media texts, *e.g.*, comparably short and

[1] https://itunes.apple.com/us/genre/ios/id36?mt=8.
[2] https://play.google.com/store/.
[3] https://appworld.blackberry.com/webstore/.
[4] https://www.microsoft.com/en-us/windows/apps-and-games.

F. Frasincar et al. (Eds.): NLDB 2017, LNCS 10260, pp. 3–14, 2017.
DOI: 10.1007/978-3-319-59569-6_1

informal language [6]. On the other side they are similar to product reviews from other domains or platforms, *e.g.*, reviews about household appliances, consumer electronics or books on Amazon, as they typically describe the user's opinion about specific aspects. In the example user review in Fig. 1, the task would be to detect for instance the aspects "game" with the evaluation "great" and "fun". It also highlights that the aspect "battery consumption" is evaluated negatively, as the word "enormous" indicates.

The game is really great and just fun. Space shortage was finally eliminated. Thanks to EA Games. Unfortunately, the game at the airport stucks sometimes. Battery consumption is really enormous since the last update. This tarnishes the whole a little. Otherwise top!!!

Fig. 1. Example of a user review for a mobile application. The review contains useful information and feedback for app developers, *e.g.* that game in general is *just fun*. However, the *battery consumption*, which is an aspect of the application, is *really enormous*.

The analysis of app reviews is also interesting from a commercial point of view. The reviews form a rich resource of information, since they hold the user's opinions about the application. Moreover the reviews often contain complaints about problems and errors of the app as well as mentions of desired features. Incorporating this feedback into the development process can have a huge influence on the success of the application [22]. However, the overwhelming amount of user reviews challenges app developers. An application can get hundreds or thousands of reviews each day, which make a manual inspection and analysis very time consuming and impractical. An automated analysis of the reviews would be beneficial for app users as well since this would enable them to analyze the advantages and disadvantages of one or multiple applications more easily. For example, they could compare two fitness trackers according to specific aspects like the accuracy of the tracked route or the visualization of the training progress.

With this paper, we present an evaluation of different features in a linear-chain conditional random field to detect aspect phrases and subjective phrases in German user reviewers from the Google Play Store. Specifically we investigate the following research questions: (1) Which performance can be achieved on German app reviews with a model which only takes textual features into account? (2) How does the performance change if training is performed on Amazon product reviews (still testing on app reviews)? (3) Under the assumption that performance in such cross-domain model application setting drops: Can the use of word embedding based features dampen the negative effect?

The rest of the paper is structured as follows: Sect. 2 highlights related work in app mining research. We present our model in Sect. 3, followed by the description of the word embedding features (Sect. 4). The evaluation of the approach is given in Sect. 5. We conclude with Sect. 6 and mention promising future steps and investigations.

2 Related Work

Recent year's work in opinion mining produced a vast number of approaches [16, 31, 34]. The majority of approaches focuses on the study of product reviews [5], Twitter messages [32] and blog posts [18]. Only very few approaches investigate mobile applications and user reviews in app stores.

A early approach is done by Harman et al. [14]. They analyze the price, customer rating and the rank of app downloads of apps in the BlackBerry App Store. Evaluation results show a strong correlation between the customer rating and the rank of app downloads. In contrast, Iacob and Harrison [17] automatically detect feature requests in app reviews. They use a corpus of 3,279 reviews from different applications in the BlackBerry App Store and manually create a set of 237 linguistic patterns (*e.g.* "*Adding <request> would be <POSITIVE-ADJECTIVE>*"). Fu et al. [8] focus on negative reviews and the identification of reasons which lead to poor ratings. For this purpose the utilize Latent Dirichlet allocation (LDA) [2] to extract topics from negative reviews and compare the main reasons for poor reviews of applications from different categories. Chen et al. [3] employ different topic models in a semi-supervised classifier to distinguish informative and non-informative reviews. A different approach to the analysis of app reviews is followed in [13]. They extract application features based on noun, verb and adjective collocations. They use SentiStrength [33], a sentence based opinion mining method, to determine the user opinions about the extracted features. Moreover, the recognized features will be combined to more general topics using LDA.

Other approaches in this area include fraud detection [9], classification of app reviews to identify bug reports and feature requests [24], and coarse-grained sentiment analysis [11, 13]. Further research investigates topic and keyword identification methods [10, 37] as well as review impact analysis [28]. Table 1 summarizes work in this area. The majority of the approaches is based on manually created English corpora which aren't available to the research community. For other languages only a few data sets exist, *e.g.* for German. Maalej and Nabil [24] make their review data available but only provide document level annotations. Sänger et al. [30] recently published a corpus of German app reviews annotated with aspects, subjective phrases and polarity. However, they only provide results for a baseline model. In this paper, we perform further experiments on this resource. To the best of our knowledge, this is the only corpus available which contains such fine-grained annotations from the domain.

The use of word embedding based features has shown considerable impact on the performance on a variety of NLP tasks, for instance chunking [4] or named entity recognition [35]. Existing approaches either use word embeddings directly [32] or derive discrete features [7] from them. For example, Guo et al. [12] perform k-means clustering to get binary feature vectors. In contrast, Turian et al. [35] utilize the intervals in which the values of the vector components lie to generate discrete features. We are not aware of any previous work that has investigated word embeddings and features based on word embeddings in the context of app reviews, especially in a cross-domain setting.

Table 1. Overview of existing work on app store review mining and analysis. For each approach the overall objective, the number of applications and reviews used as well as the app store (Apple App Store (A), Google Play Store (G) or BlackBerry World (B)) they originate from are given. All approaches use English language reviews.

Authors	Objective	Store	#Apps	#Reviews
Harman et al. [14]	Identification of correlations between price, rating and download rank	B	32,108	—
Iacob and Harrison [17]	Pattern-based detection of feature requests	B	270	137,000
Galvis et al. [10]	Identification of topics and keywords using LDA	G	3	327
Fu et al. [8]	Analysis of negative reviews and their reasons	G	171,493	13,286,706
Pagano and Maalej [28]	Analysis of the impact of app user reviews	A	1,100	1,100,000
Guzman and Maalej [13]	Extraction of application features/characteristics	A, G	7	32,210
Chen et al. [3]	Identification of informative and non-informative reviews	G	4	241,656
Vu et al. [37]	Identification of topic and keywords using topic modeling techniques	G	95	2,106,605
Maalej and Nabil [24]	Classification of app review into bugs, feature requests and simple appraisals	A, G	1,140	1,303,182

3 Baseline Model

We model the recognition of subjective phrases and application aspects as sequence labeling task, *i.e.*, every word of a review text is assigned a category label from the set $L = \{\text{O}, \text{B-Subj}, \text{I-Subj}, \text{B-Asp}, \text{I-Asp}\}$. We use a linear-chain conditional random field [21] and the MALLET toolkit [25] to implement the model. To learn the parameters of the model, the maximum likelihood method is applied. Inference is performed using the Viterbi algorithm [29].

Our baseline model takes lexical, morphological and grammatical features from each word (*e.g.* the token itself, part-of-speech tag, capitalization, 3-character pre- and suffix) into account to capture the characteristics of application aspects and evaluative phrases. The features are inspired by [19]. We further integrate negation word detection as well as smiley and emoticon recognition. For negation word detection we manually compiled a list of German terms, which imply the absence of certain matters or carry out a negation of an actual situation, and match them with the review text. We use a manually assembled list of smileys and emoticons for recognition based on the lists GreenSmilies (http://www.greensmilies.com/smilie-lexikon/) and Smiley lexicon (http://home.allgaeu.org/cwalter/smileys.html).

In addition to the textual features of the currently considered token, the characteristics of the context words are taken into account. For this purpose, all features of the words with a distance of two positions before and after the current token are added to the feature vectors. Each feature will be marked with the distance to the currently considered token. All features of our model are represented as boolean values.

4 Word Embedding Model

We generate features from word embeddings to enrich our model. We opt for derivation of discrete features to be able to gain insights about the impact and effectiveness of such features. The features are inspired by previous work [15,38].

4.1 Synonym Expansion

The first feature category that is based on embeddings represents the use of synonyms and semantically related words. More formally, for a word w up to 10 other words w' from the vocabulary V with a cosine-similarity greater than a threshold t (according to their embeddings $v(w)$ and $v(w')$) are added as synonym features.

$$\text{syn}(w) = \{w' | w' \in V \backslash \{w\} \wedge \text{sim}(v_w, v_{w'}) \geq t\}.$$

We set $t = 0.8$ empirically based on a hold out set. Similar words are likely to represent the same or similar concepts and should therefore get the same label. For instance, if the term *app* is recognized as an indicator of an aspect, it is likely that terms such as *application*, *program* or *tool* should also be considered as aspects since they describe similar concepts.

4.2 Clustering

Synonym features only model relationships implicitly between groups of similar words. To make this explicit, we perform hierarchical clustering of the word embeddings and add the index of the most similar cluster center to the current word as well as the full path and all path prefixes in the cluster hierarchy. Using the path prefixes enables the model to take varying levels of granularity into account and thus test different abstraction layers and cluster sizes.

Figure 2 shows the procedure exemplarily. As with the synonym expansion, the aim of the clustering is to check the presence of groups of words rather than individual words and thus achieve a higher recall. For example, subjective expressions like *exciting*, *fascinating* or *wonderful*, potentially used to describe the user interface of an app, should be treated equivalently and therefore should get the same label. To build the cluster tree we apply a recursive top-down approach. At the beginning all word embeddings form one cluster, which is divided into two sub-clusters using the k-means clustering algorithm and cosine similarity. Each sub-cluster is then recursively divided into two sub-clusters until a depth of 10 layers is reached.

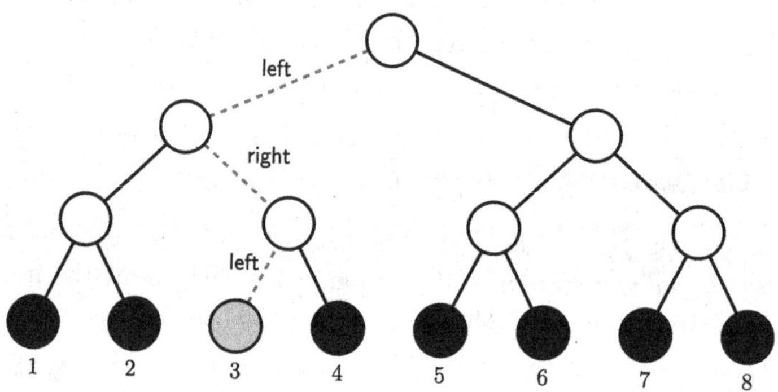

Fig. 2. Example for clustering-based feature extraction. The grey leave corresponds to the closest cluster to a considered word. Features for the path from the root are therefore *left*, *left-right*, *left-right-left*, and *cluster-id* = *3*.

5 Experiments and Results

We perform two experiments to evaluate the performance of our approach. Firstly, we conduct an in-domain experiment for app reviews. Secondly, we train on Amazon product reviews and test on the same set of app reviews. With this experiment we are able to determine the impact of the training domain on the performance of our model.

5.1 Data

As a dataset, we use the Sentiment Corpus of App Reviews (SCARE, [30]) to perform the in-domain experiment. This corpus consists of 1,760 annotated German application reviews from the Google Play Store with 2,487 aspects and 3,959 subjective phrases in total. The reviews belong to popular apps from 11 categories (*e.g.* fitness trackers, instant messengers, games and newspaper apps) and represent a variety of use-cases of mobile applications. For the cross-domain experiment, we utilize the Bielefeld University Sentiment Analysis Corpus for German and English (USAGE, [20]). The corpus contains 611 German Amazon reviews about products from eight different categories (*e.g.* coffee machines, microwaves and dishwashers) with overall 6,340 annotated product aspects and 5,086 subjective phrases. Table 2 compares the two data sets according to basic statistics. The figures especially highlight the different review text lengths (19 vs. 90 token) of the two corpora.

5.2 Experimental Setup

We first examine the baseline version of our model. Subsequently the features described in Sect. 4 and combinations of them are added. In the in-domain experiment we split the SCARE corpus by randomly sampling 1,408 reviews (80% of the corpus) as training set. The remaining reviews are used to test our model. For the cross-domain experiment we train our model on the complete USAGE corpus and evaluate on the same SCARE reviews as in the in-domain experiment. For each experiment, we report F_1 scores regarding exact and partial matches. An exact match requires that the text boundaries of a predicted subjective phrase or aspect must exactly match those of the goldstandard. When considering partial matches only an overlap of at least one token between a predicted and a goldstandard text span must exist.

As part of the evaluation of the word embedding features we make use of two different text corpora to learn the embeddings. To build general-purpose embeddings we utilize a German Wikipedia dump [1]. Moreover, we use a corpus of 800,000 app reviews we collected in [30] to learn domain-specific word embeddings. We apply the CBOW Model [26,27] with a vector size of 50. All other hyperparameters of the method are left on their default.

Table 2. Comparison of the SCARE [30] and the USAGE [20] review corpus. The SCARE corpus consists of German app reviews from the Google Play Store. In contrast, the USAGE corpus comprises Amazon product reviews about household appliances (e.g. dishwashers or coffee machines).

	SCARE (App reviews)	USAGE (Amazon reviews)
Documents	1,760	611
ø Sentences/Doc.	1.87	4.82
ø Tokens/Doc.	19.02	89.90
Subj. Phrases	3,959	5,086
ø Subj. Phrases/Doc.	2.50	8.32
Aspects	2,487	6,340
ø Aspects/Doc.	1.41	10.38

5.3 Evaluation Results

The results of our in- and cross domain experiments are given in Table 3 resp. 4.

Table 3. Evaluation results as F_1 measure of the in-domain experiment. We distinguish aspect and subjective phrase detection as well as exact and partial matches for each experiment. Furthermore, the impact of each feature according to the baseline model is given in parentheses. Bold figures mark the highest result of a column.

		Subj. Phrases		Aspects	
		Exact	Partial	Exact	Partial
	Baseline model	0.605	0.769	0.620	0.685
App review embeddings	+ Synonym expansion	0.610 (+0.8%)	0.777 (+1.0%)	0.628 (+1.3%)	**0.702 (+2.5%)**
	+ Clustering features	0.615 (+1.7%)	**0.783 (+1.8%)**	0.616 (–0.6%)	0.691 (+0.9%)
	+ All	0.615 (+1.7%)	0.782 (+1.7%)	**0.634 (+2.2%)**	0.698 (+1.9%)
Wikipedia embeddings	+ Synonym expansion	0.606 (+0.2%)	0.767 (–0.2%)	0.626 (+0.9%)	0.685 (+/–0%)
	+ Clustering features	**0.618 (+2.1%)**	0.781 (+1.6%)	0.623 (–0.5%)	0.688 (+0.4%)
	+ All	**0.618 (+2.1%)**	0.782 (+1.7%)	0.620 (+/–0%)	0.683 (–0.3%)

Our *baseline model* reaches an F_1 score of 0.62 for aspect detection and 0.61 for recognition of subjective phrases. Taking partial matches into account the recognition of subjective phrases achieves clearly better values (0.77 vs. 0.69). In general, the figures are comparable to validations results of other models in product domains [20], which proves the suitability of our approach.

To test *cross-domain*, we train our model on Amazon product reviews and test on app reviews. This decreases performance considerably. The model reaches 0.46 F_1 for subjective phrase recognition and 0.35 F_1 for aspect detection. This is a performance decrease of 24% resp. 44% in comparison to the in-domain experiment. Considering also partial matches as true positives lowers these values to 8% resp. 27%. The results indicate that there are strong differences in the way personal opinions on product aspects are expressed in the particular domains.

Performance improvements can be observed with the inclusion of *word embedding* based features. We accomplish the best overall performance by using both features, synonym expansion and clustering, based on domain-specific word embeddings in the in-domain setting. The model achieves an F_1 score of 0.62 (+1.7%) for recognition of subjective phrases and 0.63 (+2.2%) for aspects.

In the cross-domain experiment the recognition of subjective phrases can benefit from embedding features. Here, improvements up to 7.0% regarding exact matches resp. 5.5% for partial matches are reached. However, the detection of application aspects suffers from embedding features: Using the complete feature set in conjunction with the domain-specific embeddings, the performance decreases by 11.9%. That is remarkable because in the in-domain setting these embeddings show better results than the Wikipedia-based embeddings.

Table 4. Evaluation results as F_1 measure of the cross-domain experiment. We distinguish aspect and subjective phrase detection as well as exact and partial matches for each experiment. Furthermore, the impact of each feature according to the baseline model is given in parentheses. Bold figures mark the highest result of a column.

		Subj. Phrases		Aspects	
		Exact	Partial	Exact	Partial
	Baseline model	0.457	0.707	0.350	**0.504**
App review embeddings	+ Synonym expansion	0.456 (–0.2%)	0.713 (+0.8%)	**0.355 (+1.4%)**	0.497 (–1.4%)
	+ Clustering features	0.444 (–2.8%)	0.703 (–0.6%)	0.345 (–1.1%)	0.463 (–8.1%)
	+ All	0.445 (–0.7%)	**0.746 (+5.5%)**	0.316 (–9.7%)	0.444 (–11.9%)
Wikipedia embeddings	+ Synonym expansion	0.463 (+1.3%)	0.707 (+/–0%)	0.350 (+/–0%)	0.489 (–3.6%)
	+ Clustering features	**0.489 (+7.0%)**	0.718 (+1.6%)	0.337 (–3.7%)	0.485 (–3.8%)
	+ All	0.483 (+5.7%)	0.721 (+2.0%)	0.353 (+0.9%)	0.496 (–1.6%)

6 Conclusion

In this paper, we presented a fine-grained sentiment analysis model for German for app reviews from the Google play store. The model is based on conditional random fields and takes lexical, morphological and grammatical features as well as domain-specific characteristics into account to extract subjective expression and application aspects from the user review texts. To model relationships between words and groups of words we enrich our approach with discrete features based on word embeddings.

The evaluation of the model shows competitive figures according to results of similar extraction approaches developed on other product domains. Furthermore, we illustrate that the performance of our model can be improved by 2% with features based on domain-specific word embeddings. A cross-domain experiment revealed that there are clear differences in the way personal opinions and product aspects are expressed in app reviews in contrast to Amazon product reviews. This proves the necessity of domain specific models for fine-grained app review mining which take the linguisitic peculiarities of the short and informal review texts into account. Our approach represents a first step towards more detailed analysis of reviews which will support application developers as well as app customers to analyze and compare the advantages and drawbacks of one or multiple apps.

Future work will include the evaluation of the model on other sentiment data sets (*e.g.* Tweets or blog posts) as well as reviews from other languages. Moreover, we will compare the discretization of the word embeddings as done in this work with directly integrating them in our model. Another interesting research direction will be to take into account domain adaptation methods to improve the generalization of our model as well as to investigate other analysis methods (*e.g.* neural network based approaches which learn embeddings in a task specific manner). Beyond the optimization of our proposed approach the integration of further information extraction methods can improve the usefulness of the model. For example, our current model is not designed to automatically infer the polarity (positive, negative or neutral) of an subjective expression. The extraction of relations between subjective expressions and the application aspects they are actually targeting would be beneficial, too. Furthermore, the assignment of the extracted application aspects to a particular feature (group) or topic will enable further analysis of the extracted results.

Acknowledgments. We thank Christian Scheible, Peter Adolphs and Steffen Kemmerer for their valuable feedback and fruitful discussions.

References

1. Al-Rfou, R., Perozzi, B., Skiena, S.: Polyglot: distributed word representations for multilingual NLP. In: Proceedings of the Seventeenth Conference on Computational Natural Language Learning, Sofia, Bulgaria, pp. 183–192. Association for Computational Linguistics, August 2013
2. Blei, D., Ng, A.Y., Jordan, M.: Latent Dirichlet allocation. J. Mach. Learn. Res. **3**, 993–1022 (2003)
3. Chen, N., Lin, J., Hoi, S.C.H., Xiao, X., Zhang, B.: AR-miner: mining informative reviews for developers from mobile app marketplace. In: Proceedings of the 2014 International Conference on Software Engineering, Hyderabad, India, pp. 767–778 (2014)
4. Collobert, R., Weston, J., Bottou, L., Karlen, M., Kavukcuoglu, K., Kuksa, P.: Natural language processing (almost) from scratch. J. Mach. Learn. Res. **12**, 2493–2537 (2011)
5. Cui, H., Mittal, V., Datar, M.: Comparative experiments on sentiment classification for online product reviews. In: Proceedings of the Eighteenth Conference on Innovative Applications of Artificial Intelligence, Boston, MA, USA, vol. 6, pp. 1265–1270 (2006)
6. Derczynski, L., Maynard, D., Rizzo, G., van Erp, M., Gorrell, G., Troncy, R., Petrak, J., Bontcheva, K.: Analysis of named entity recognition and linking for tweets. Inf. Process. Manag. **51**(2), 32–49 (2015)
7. Faruqui, M., Tsvetkov, Y., Yogatama, D., Dyer, C., Smith, N.: Sparse overcomplete word vector representations. In: Proceedings of Association for Computational Linguistics, Beijing, China (2015)
8. Fu, B., Lin, J., Li, L., Faloutsos, C., Hong, J., Sadeh, N.: Why people hate your app: making sense of user feedback in a mobile app store. In: Proceedings of the 19th ACM SIGKDD International Conference on Knowledge Discovery and Data Mining, Chicago, USA, pp. 1276–1284. Association for Computing Machinery (2013)
9. Gade, T., Pardeshi, N.: A survey on ranking fraud detection using opinion mining for mobile apps. Int. J. Adv. Res. Comput. Commun. Eng. **4**(12), 337–339 (2015)
10. Galvis Carreno, L., Winbladh, K.: Analysis of user comments: an approach for software requirements evolution. In: Proceedings of the 2013 International Conference on Software Engineering. pp. 582–591. San Francisco, CA, USA (2013)
11. Gu, X., Kim, S.: What parts of your apps are loved by users? In: Proceedings of the 30th IEEE/ACM International Conference on Automated Software Engineering. pp. 760–770. IEEE, Lincoln, USA (2015)

12. Guo, J., Che, W., Wang, H., Liu, T.: Revisiting embedding features for simple semi-supervised learning. In: Proceedings of the 2014 Conference on Empirical Methods in Natural Language Processing, Doha, Qatar, pp. 110–120 (2014)
13. Guzman, E., Maalej, W.: How do users like this feature? A fine grained sentiment analysis of app reviews. In: Proceedings of the 22nd International Requirements Engineering Conference, Karlskrona, Sweden, pp. 153–162 (2014)
14. Harman, M., Jia, Y., Zhang, Y.: App store mining and analysis: MSR for app stores. In: Proceedings of the 9th IEEE Working Conference on Mining Software Repositories, Zurich, Switzerland, pp. 108–111 (2012)
15. Hintz, G., Biemann, C.: Delexicalized supervised German lexical substitution. In: Proceedings of GermEval 2015: LexSub, Essen, Germany, pp. 11–16 (2015)
16. Hutto, C.J., Gilbert, E.: Vader: a parsimonious rule-based model for sentiment analysis of social media text. In: Eighth International AAAI Conference on Weblogs and Social Media, Ann Arbor, MI, USA (2014)
17. Iacob, C., Harrison, R.: Retrieving and analyzing mobile apps feature requests from online reviews. In: Proceedings of the 10th IEEE Working Conference on Mining Software Repositories, San Francisco, CA, USA, pp. 41–44 (2013)
18. Jakob, N., Gurevych, I.: Extracting opinion targets in a single-and cross-domain setting with conditional random fields. In: Proceedings of the 2010 Conference on Empirical Methods in Natural Language Processing, Stroudsburg, PA, USA, pp. 1035–1045. Association for Computational Linguistics (2010)
19. Klinger, R., Cimiano, P.: Joint and pipeline probabilistic models for fine-grained sentiment analysis: extracting aspects, subjective phrases and their relations. In: IEEE 13th International Conference on Data Mining Workshops, Dallas, TX, USA, pp. 937–944 (2013)
20. Klinger, R., Cimiano, P.: The usage review corpus for fine grained multi lingual opinion analysis. In: Proceedings of the Ninth International Conference on Language Resources and Evaluation, Reykjavik, Iceland, pp. 2211–2218 (2014)
21. Lafferty, J., McCallum, A., Pereira, F.: Conditional random fields: probabilistic models for segmenting and labeling sequence data. In: Proceedings of the 18th International Conference on Machine Learning. Morgan Kaufmann, Williamstown, MA, USA (2001)
22. Liang, T.P., Li, X., Yang, C.T., Wang, M.: What in consumer reviews affects the sales of mobile apps: a multifacet sentiment analysis approach. Int. J. Electron. Commer. **20**(2), 236–260 (2015)
23. Liu, B.: Sentiment analysis: mining opinions, sentiments, and emotions. Cambridge University Press (2015)
24. Maalej, W., Nabil, H.: Bug report, feature request, or simply praise? On automatically classifying app reviews. In: Proceedings of the IEEE 23rd International Requirements Engineering Conference, pp. 116–125. IEEE, Karlskrona, Sweden (2015)
25. McCallum, A.: Mallet: a machine learning for language toolkit (2002). http://mallet.cs.umass.edu. Accessed 08 Feb 2017
26. Mikolov, T., Chen, K., Corrado, G., Dean, J.: Efficient estimation of word representations in vector space. In: Proceedings of Workshop at International Conference on Learning Representations, Scottsdale, AZ, USA (2013)
27. Mikolov, T., Sutskever, I., Chen, K., Corrado, G., Dean, J.: Distributed representations of words and phrases and their compositionality. In: Advances in Neural Information Processing Systems, South Lake Tahoe, NV, USA, pp. 3111–3119 (2013)

28. Pagano, D., Maalej, W.: User feedback in the appstore: an empirical study. In: Proceedings of the 2013 21st IEEE International Requirements Engineering Conference, pp. 125–134. IEEE, Rio de Janeiro (2013)
29. Rabiner, L.: A tutorial on hidden Markov models and selected applications in speech recognition. Proc. IEEE **77**(2), 257–286 (1989)
30. Sänger, M., Leser, U., Kemmerer, S., Adolphs, P., Klinger, R.: SCARE - the sentiment corpus of app. reviews with fine-grained annotations in german. In: Proceedings of the Tenth International Conference on Language Resources and Evaluation (LREC 2016). Portorož, Slovenia (2016)
31. Täckström, O., McDonald, R.: Discovering fine-grained sentiment with latent variable structured prediction models. In: Clough, P., Foley, C., Gurrin, C., Jones, G.J.F., Kraaij, W., Lee, H., Mudoch, V. (eds.) ECIR 2011. LNCS, vol. 6611, pp. 368–374. Springer, Heidelberg (2011). doi:10.1007/978-3-642-20161-5_37
32. Tang, D., Wei, F., Yang, N., Zhou, M., Liu, T., Qin, B.: Learning sentiment-specific word embedding for twitter sentiment classification. In: Proceedings of the 52nd Annual Meeting of the Association for Computational Linguistics, Baltimore, MD, USA, pp. 1555–1565 (2014)
33. Thelwall, M., Buckley, K., Paltoglou, G., Cai, D., Kappas, A.: Sentiment strength detection in short informal text. J. Am. Soc. Inf. Sci. Technol. **61**(12), 2544–2558 (2010)
34. Titov, I., McDonald, R.: A joint model of text and aspect ratings for sentiment summarization. In: Proceedings of 46th Annual Meeting of the Association for Computational Linguistics: Human Language Technologies, Columbus, OH, USA (2008)
35. Turian, J., Ratinov, L., Bengio, Y.: Word representations: a simple and general method for semi-supervised learning. In: Proceedings of the 48th Annual Meeting of the Association for Computational Linguistics, Uppsala, Sweden, pp. 384–394 (2010)
36. Vinodhini, G., Chandrasekaran, R.: Sentiment analysis and opinion mining: a survey. Int. J. **2**(6), 282–292 (2012)
37. Vu, P.M., Nguyen, T.T., Pham, H.V., Nguyen, T.T.: Mining user opinions in mobile app reviews: a keyword-based approach. In: Proceedings of the 30th IEEE/ACM International Conference on Automated Software Engineering, pp. 749–759. IEEE, Lincoln, NE, USA (2015)
38. Yu, M., Zhao, T., Dong, D., Tian, H., Yu, D.: Compound embedding features for semi-supervised learning. In: Proceedings of Human Language Technologies: Conference of the North American Chapter of the Association of Computational Linguistics, Atlanta, GA, USA, pp. 563–568 (2013)

Feature Selection Using Multi-objective Optimization for Aspect Based Sentiment Analysis

Md Shad Akhtar[1(✉)], Sarah Kohail[2], Amit Kumar[1], Asif Ekbal[1], and Chris Biemann[2]

[1] IIT Patna, Bihar, India
{shad.pcs15,amit.mtmc14,asif}@iitp.ac.in
[2] Universität Hamburg, Hamburg, Germany
{kohail,biemann}@informatik.uni-hamburg.de

Abstract. In this paper, we propose a system for aspect-based sentiment analysis (ABSA) by incorporating the concepts of multi-objective optimization (MOO), distributional thesaurus (DT) and unsupervised lexical induction. The task can be thought of as a sequence of processes such as aspect term extraction, opinion target expression identification and sentiment classification. We use MOO for selecting the most relevant features, and demonstrate that classification with the resulting feature set can improve classification accuracy on many datasets. As base learning algorithms we make use of Support Vector Machines (SVM) for sentiment classification and Conditional Random Fields (CRF) for aspect term and opinion target expression extraction tasks. Distributional thesaurus and unsupervised DT prove to be effective with enhanced performance. Experiments on benchmark setups of SemEval-2014 and SemEval-2016 shared tasks show that we achieve the state of the art on aspect-based sentiment analysis for several languages.

Keywords: Sentiment analysis · Aspect based sentiment analysis · MOO

1 Introduction

The number of internet users in social media platforms has increased exponentially during the last few years and so does the amount of user written reviews about a product or service. Feedback available through reviews is useful to manufactures for upgrading or enhancing the quality of their products as well as for the users to take informed decisions. However, due to a large number of user reviews, it is quite in-feasible to scroll through all the reviews.

Sentiment analysis is the area of study that target to identify the sentiments (positive, negative or neutral) of the users based on the opinions and emotions expressed in the reviews written either for a particular product or service or any of its aspects (or feature/attribute). Classification of sentiment at document or

F. Frasincar et al. (Eds.): NLDB 2017, LNCS 10260, pp. 15–27, 2017.
DOI: 10.1007/978-3-319-59569-6_2

sentence level may not always satisfy the need of user's requirement. They might need more precise information *i.e.* sentiment related to a particular aspect (or feature) of any product or service. Aspect-level analysis [15] is concerned with finding sentiment on fine-grained levels: aspects are features of the product or service that has been discussed in any user review. A common benchmark set up for ABSA was introduced in SemEval 2014 shared task 4 [24], and then subsequently extended in SemEval 2016 shared task 5 [23].

SemEval-2014 ABSA: The two tasks of SemEval-2014 of our interest in the work are (a) *aspect term extraction* and (b) *sentiment with respect to aspect terms.* The first task deals with the identification of all the aspect terms present in the review, while the second task predicts sentiment polarity for aspects. For example, in the review below there are two aspect terms (or opinion target expression, OTE), *Pasta* and *waiter.* Sentiment towards these two aspect terms are contrasting in nature. For the first aspect term (*Pasta*) it has positive sentiment while the second aspect term (*waiter*) conveys negative sentiment.

"***Pasta*** *was good but the* ***waiter*** *was rude.*"

SemEval-2016 ABSA: In 2016, the task was modified and extended to three subtasks i.e. (a) *aspect category detection*, (b) *opinion target expression (OTE) identification* and (c) *sentiment towards aspect category and OTE tuple.* Aspect category can be seen as the generalization of the aspect terms. The goal of aspect category detection task is to find the pre-defined set of *entity#attribute* pairs towards which the opinion is expressed in a review. The second task i.e. OTE is same as aspect term extraction of SemEval-2014. The sentiment classification task (third task) tries to predict the polarity for each aspect category and OTE tuple. As an example, in the following review category (i.e. *entity#attribute pair*) is *FOOD#QUALITY* while the OTE is *Food.* The opinion towards the *<entity#attribute, OTE>* tuple is negative.

"***Food*** *was okay, nothing great.*"

In our current work, we target to solve both the tasks of SemEval-2014 and the last two tasks (i.e. OTE and sentiment classification) of SemEval-2016 for ABSA.

Literature shows that most of the existing works in sentiment analysis focused primarily on document [27] and sentence [12] level. Some of the earlier approaches for aspect term extraction are based on frequently used noun and noun phrases [4,11,25]. In [11], the authors proposed the method which identifies frequently present noun phrases from the text based on association rule mining. This type of approach works well when frequently occurring terms are strongly co-related with certain types (e.g. noun), but many times fail when frequency of terms, which used as the aspects are very low. Supervised machine learning techniques [21,31] are being widely used with the emergence of various labeled datasets. Some other techniques for extracting aspect terms include manually specified subset of the Wikipedia category [9] hierarchy, semantically motivated technique [27] and unsupervised clustering technique [25]. Phrase dependency tree [29] is also helpful in aspect term extraction. Recently, a detailed survey on the aspect based sentiment analysis has been presented in [26].

The performance of any classifier is influenced by the feature set used to represent the train and test dataset. Feature selection [16,17] is the technique of automatically selecting a subset of relevant features for a classifier. By removing the irrelevant and redundant set of features, we can construct a classifier with reduced computational costs. In the present work we pose the problem of feature selection in machine learning model with respect to optimization framework. In particular we use evolutionary optimization based algorithms for finding the most optimized features set. Some of the prior works that made use of evolutionary optimization techniques can be found in [7,8], in which the authors focused on named entity recognition task in multiple languages.

One of the novel contributions of the proposed technique is to study the effectiveness of unsupervised pre-processing steps to the target task. The major problems in applying machine learning algorithms for solving different problems is the non-availability of large annotated corpus, which results in issues with vocabulary coverage.

We explore possibilities arising from the use of unsupervised part-of-speech (PoS) induction [1] and lexical expansion [19]. Unsupervised PoS induction [1] is a technique that induces lexical-syntactic categories through the statistical analysis of large, raw text corpora. As compared to linguistically motivated PoS-tags, the categories are usually more fine-grained, i.e. the linguistic class of nouns is split into several induced classes that also carry semantic information, such as days of the week, professions, mass nouns etc. As shown in [2], these induced categories as features results in improved accuracies for a variety of NLP tasks. Since the induction of PoS is entirely language independent and sensitive to domain vocabulary as shown in [1], we expect further improvements when combining these features with MOO.

While unsupervised PoS tagging primarily targets syntactic categories, we utilize lexical expansion [19] to explore semantic characteristics. Lexical expansion is also an unsupervised technique that needs a large corpus for the induction, and is based on the computation of a distributional thesaurus (DT) [14].

2 Method

In this section at first, we briefly introduce multi-objective optimization (MOO), and then discuss the approach of feature selection for the tasks. Finally, we discuss the feature sets which we use for the different tasks.

2.1 Brief Overview of MOO

In our daily life we have to face the situations where we have to deal with more than one objectives. MOO focuses on optimization of more than one objectives simultaneously in contrast to single objective optimization where algorithm focuses on only one objective. Many decision problems have been solved using the concept of MOO. Mathematically, a general MOO [5] can be defined as follows:

$$\begin{aligned} \text{Minimize/Maximize}\, f_m(x), m = 1, ..., M \\ \text{subject to}\, g_j(x) \geq 0, j = 1, ..., J; \\ h_k(x) = 0, k = 1, ..., K; \\ x_i^L \leq x_i \leq x_i^U, i = 1, ..., N \end{aligned}$$

The solution of above general equation is x, a vector $(x_1, x_2...., x_N)^T$ of size N, where $x_i; i = 1, ..., N$ represents the decision variables. The above specified optimization problem has J number of inequality constraints and K number of equality constraints. $g_i(x)$ and $h_k(x)$ represent the constraint functions.

2.2 Non-dominated Sorting Genetic Algorithm-II (NSGA-II)

We use the non-dominated sorting genetic algorithm (NSGA-II) [5] as the optimization technique to develop our models. This algorithm uses the search capability of GA and tries to minimize the fitness functions (*i.e.* objective functions). It starts with creating the parent population P_0 of size N. Each of the candidates in the population is called chromosome. For each of the chromosome, the fitness function is computed. By applying binary tournament selection, crossover and mutation operators on parent population P_0, a child population Q_0 of size N is created. In t^{th} iteration, a combined population of parent and child population $R_t = P_t + Q_t$ is formed. All the candidates of R_t are sorted according to non-dominated sorting algorithm thus producing non-dominated sets F_1, F_2, .. F_n with decreasing fitness values. We then select N chromosomes from these sets. In case of selecting a subset of chromosomes of equal fitness value we apply crowding distance operator as in NSGA-II [5] to break the deadlock. Crowding distance prefers chromosomes that lies in the less dense regions. Above sequence of steps runs until either the specified number of generation or the stopping criteria is met.

We use NSGA-II due its following positive points: (i) Low computation cost $O(MN^2)$, where no. of objective functions $= M$ and Population size $= N$; (ii) High elitism property, where in each iteration best individuals from the parent and child populations are preserved; (iii) Diversity in population without having to specify any parameter manually; and (iv) Easy to use.

2.3 Problem Formulation

Performance of any classifier highly depends on the feature set what we use. Generally, we use heuristics based approach to select a subset that optimized the fitness function. This process is very time consuming. On the other hand, an automated method of feature selection might be able to identify the most relevant features.

For a given set of features F and classification quality measures, we aim to determine the feature subset f of F *i.e.* $f \subseteq F$, which optimize all of the fitness functions. In our case we use precision, recall, F1-measure, accuracy and number of features as the objective functions. For each of the tasks we build two frameworks as follows:

- **Framework 1:** In this framework we optimize two objective functions i.e. *number of features* (minimize) and *F-measure* (maximize) for aspect term extraction or OTE. For sentiment classification objective function are *number of features* and *accuracy*.
- **Framework 2:** Here for aspect term and OTE extraction tasks, we use two objective functions: *precision* and *recall*. For sentiment classification, we optimize *accuracy of each class* as the fitness function. We maximize all of the fitness values.

2.4 Problem Encoding

If total number of features are N, then the length of chromosome will be N. All bits are randomly initialized to 0 or 1 and each represents one features. If the ith bit of a chromosome is 1 then the ith feature participates in constructing the framework otherwise not. Each chromosomes in the population (P) are initialized in the same way.

2.5 Fitness Computation

To determine the fitness value of a chromosome, following procedures are executed. Let F is the number of 1's present in the chromosome. We develop the model by training CRF for aspect and opinion term expression extraction and SVM for sentiment classification on selected features i.e. F. The motive is to optimize the values of objective functions using the search capability of NSGA-II. To evaluate the objective functions we perform 5-fold cross validation.

2.6 Features

We identify and implement a variety of features for aspect term and opinion target expression (OTE) extraction tasks. The set of features that we use in this work along with their descriptions are presented in Table 2. For sentiment classification, Table 1 lists set of features we use for the datasets of SemEval-2014 shared task. For SemEval-2016 shared task we use unigram, bigram and expansion scores based on the prior works reported in [13] as features for English. For Dutch language we use unigram, bigram and expansion score as features.

3 Experiments and Analysis

3.1 Datasets

For experiments we use the benchmark datasets of SemEval-2014 [24] and SemEval-2016 [23] shared tasks on ABSA. SemEval-2014 datasets belongs to English only covering laptop and restaurant domains while SemEval-2016 datasets contains reviews from different languages i.e. English, Spanish, Dutch and French.

Table 1. Feature set for sentiment classification for SemEval-2014 dataset.

Feature	Description
Sentiment Classification	
Aspect term and context:	We convert the actual forms of aspect terms in lower case character and use it as a feature along with the actual aspect terms. The polarity orientation of aspect term heavily depends on local context words where it appears. We include succeeding five and preceding five terms of aspect term to provide contextual information.
Lexicon:	Sentiment lexicons are the useful resources, which provide important information for predicting the sentiment. For computing lexicon sentiment score we consider the preceding five and following five tokens of the aspect term. We use following set of lexicons. – **MPQA:** We take the help of MPQA subjectivity lexicon [28] which contains a list of words denoting the negative, positive and neutral sentiments. – **Bing Liu lexicon:** For each token in training and test set we define the values in the following way: -1 for negative; 1 for positive and 2 for those do not appear in Bing Liu lexicons [6]. Then, we define two features: 1. We calculate sum of sentiment score of all the words that appear in context of target aspect term and use as a feature. 2. We also compute the sum of the sentiment scores of only those words which have *direct dependency relation* with the target aspect term. – **SentiWordNet lexicon:** This is one of the most widely used lexicons for sentiment analysis. We compute sentiment score of all words that appear in surrounding context (previous-5 and next-5) of the target aspect term. – **Other lexicons:** Apart from above mentioned lexicons we also use AFINN [22], NRC Hashtag, Sentiment 140 [30] and NRC Emotion [20] lexicons for calculating the score and use them as features.
Domain-Specific Words:	We hand-made a list of words from general intuition and web that describes domain-specific information. For e.g. *yummy, over cooked* etc. are some of the sentiment bearing words for restaurant domain. We assign score 1, -1 and 2 to each positive, negative and words that are missing in the list respectively. We compute the feature value based on local context [-5..5] of the aspect term.

3.2 Results and Analysis

We perform various experiments with different feature combinations for all the languages and domains. We divide our feature sets in two category: Standard features (Std.Fea) and Non-standard features (i.e. DT based features). Standard features correspond to the features as mentioned above *except* DT, Unsupervised POS tag and expansion score in case of aspect term and OTE extraction. For sentiment classification standard features denote the features mentioned above *except* the expansion scores. Results of aspect term and OTE extraction are reported in Table 3a. This shows how DT based features help in improving the performance. Feature selection based on MOO aids in achieving better performance. This shows how effectively MOO selects the most relevant sets of features for each domain and language. The system attains better performance with a smaller set of features compared to the scenario where the exhaustive feature set is used. Results for sentiment classification on SemEval 2014 and SemEval 2016 datasets are reported in Table 3b and c, respectively. We perform several experiments and observe that by adding the expansion score, we do not get much increment in English, but for Dutch this feature is very effective. It is also observed that after applying MOO, performance of the system improves significantly. With a much smaller number of features we obtain the increments of

Table 2. Feature set for aspect term and OTE extraction

Feature	Description
	Aspect Term Extraction
Word, local context & PoS	Word and local context play a significant role in determining the aspect term and opinion target expression. We use the current token, its lower case form and local context [-5..5] as features. Part-of-speech (PoS) information is useful to capture the syntactic property, thus we use PoS information of current and context tokens [-2..2] as features.
Head word and PoS	Generally, aspect terms belong to the category of noun phrase. The head word of the noun phrase along with its PoS tags are used as the feature.
Prefix and suffix	Suffix and prefix of fixed length character sequences are trimmed from each token and used as the features for our model. Here, we use prefix and suffix of current and context tokens [-1,0,1] as the features.
Frequent aspect term	We generate a list of frequently (more than 4) occurring OTEs from the training set. We define a binary feature for the presence or absence of extracted OTEs.
Dependency Relation	Here we define two features: i. when the current token is governor via relations nsubj, amod or dep and ii. when the current token is dependent via relations nsubj, dobj or dep. For example in the review below food is the dependent on *lousy* via relation nsubj. However, *food* is a governor of *the* via relation det. Therefore, for the token *food*, we use the relation 'nsubj' as the first feature and *null* for the second. *The food was lousy.*
Character n-grams	Character n-gram is a contiguous sequence of n character extracted from a given token. We extract character bigram, trigram and four-gram of the current token and use them as features in our model.
Orthographic feature	Many of the aspect terms start with the capital letter. We define a feature which checks whether the current token starts with the capitalized letter or not.
Semantic Orientation (SO) Score:	*SO* score [10] is the measurement of negative or positive sentiment expressed in a phrase. *SO* score of each token is computed with Point wise mutual information (PMI) as follows: $SO(w) = PMI(w, prev) - PMI(w, nrev)$ Here PMI is measurement of association of token w with respect to negative $nrev$ or positive $prev$ reviews.
DT features	Distributional thesaurus (DT) gives the lexicon expansion of the token based on similar context. In [3], the authors have used it for lexical expansion of text by virtually expanding every content word in the text with the list of most similar words from the DT. It is very helpful in unseen texts. We obtain top 5 DTs of current token and top 3 DTs of context tokens [-2,-1,1,2] as the features.
Expansion score	OTEs and aspect terms have opinions around them. Opinions are regularly lexicalized with words found in sentiment lexicons. We compute sentiment score based on induced lexicons as computed in [13] by considering the window size of 10 (preceding 5 and following 5 of the current token). We use expansion score of context tokens [-2..2] as the features in our model.
Unsupervised PoS tag	In [1], the authors implement a system which takes a reasonable amount of tokenized and unlabeled text without PoS information mentioned as input and induces number of word clusters. We use the tag of context tokens [-2..2] as the features in our system.
We additionally extract the following set of features only for English language.	
Chunk information	A text can have multi-word aspect term or OTE. To identify the boundaries of these multi-words, we use chunk information of context tokens[-1,0,1] as features.
Lemma	Lemmatization trims the inflectional forms and derivationally related forms of a token to a common base form. We use lemma of the current token as the feature.
WordNet	Tokens from the same lexical category are grouped into synsets in WordNet [18]. We extract top four noun synsets of each token and use as feature. This feature can be helpful in clustering tokens with identical sense, thus assist the system in finding the unseen aspect terms more accurately. For example, senses *lunch* and *dinner* are related to the sense *meal* in the WordNet hierarchy. So for the scenario where aspect term *lunch* appears in the test set but was unseen in the train set, this feature will guide the system to identify it as an aspect term more accurately.
Named entity information	We extract named entity information of the current token with Stanford CoreNLP tool, and use the NER sequence labels as features.

4.76% and 3.66% in restaurant (38 vs. 20) and laptop (38 vs. 12) domain, respectively. For SemEval-2016 data, we perform sentiment classification for English and Dutch. Since the number of features for this task is too little, we do not apply MOO.

Table 3. Results: (a) aspect term and OTE extraction. (b) sentiment classification SemEval-2014, (c) sentiment classification SemEval-2016. M1 and M2 corresponds to framework 1 and framework 2 of Sect. 2.3. Std.Fea refers to feature set of Sect. 2.6 except DT, Unsupervised PoS and expansion score.

Datasets	Parameters	Feature sets			After MOO	
		Std.Fea	Std.Fea + DT	Std.Fea + DT + UnPos	M1	M2
Restaurant (SemEval-2014)	No.of Fea	68	83	88	43	-
	Precision	82.29	83.09	83.30	-	83.78
	Recall	75.39	76.27	76.10	-	76.98
	F1-mea	78.69	79.54	79.53	79.92	-
Laptop (SemEval-2014)	No.of Fea	69	84	89	24	-
	Precision	82.79	84.26	83.36	-	83.76
	Recall	62.53	62.23	62.84	-	64.67
	F1-mea	71.25	71.59	71.66	70.56	-
English (SemEval-2016)	No.of Fea	63	78	83	24	-
	Precision	74.40	75.60	75.54	-	75.84
	Recall	60.78	61.76	62.58	-	62.09
	F1-mea	66.90	67.98	68.45	68.21	-
French (SemEval-2016)	No.of Fea	47	62	67	11	-
	Precision	70.64	71.81	70.85	-	70.91
	Recall	67.38	68.61	68.46	-	66.76
	F1-mea	68.97	70.18	69.64	67.85	-
Spanish (SemEval-2016)	No.ofFea	47	62	67	26	-
	Precision	71.84	76.23	76.85	-	74.28
	Recall	66.19	62.55	63.81	-	69.28
	F1-mea	68.90	68.72	69.73	70.33	-
Dutch (SemEval-2016)	No.ofFea	47	62	67	15	-
	Precision	64.88	64.22	66.10	-	66.57
	Recall	61.93	61.12	62.73	-	62.46
	F1-mea	63.37	62.63	64.37	65.01	-

(a)

Datasets	Parameters	Feature sets		After MOO	
		Std.Fea	Std.Fea + Exp.score	M1	M2
Restaurant (SemEval-2014)	No.ofFea	37	38	20	-
	Positive	88.59	88.73	-	89.56
	Negative	54.59	54.08	-	60.20
	Neutral	34.69	32.65	-	39.79
	Conflict	14.28	14.28	-	0.00
	Overall	72.48	72.13	76.89	-

Datasets	Parameters	Std.Fea	Std.Fea + Exp.score	M1	M2
Laptop (SemEval-2014)	No.ofFea	37	38	12	-
	Positive	76.83	76.53	-	78.29
	Negative	64.84	64.84	-	70.31
	Neutral	32.54	31.95	-	40.82
	Conflict	06.25	06.25	-	12.50
	Overall	61.31	61.01	64.67	-

(b)

	English		Dutch	
	Std. Fea	Std.Fea + Exp.Score	Uni + Bi-gram	Uni + Bi + Exp.Score
Positive	88.70	88.54	82.92	83.73
Negative	76.47	76.96	68.72	70.61
Neutral	11.36	11.36	03.03	03.03
Overall	81.83	81.84	73.73	74.87

(c)

3.3 Comparisons

As explained in previous section, we perform experiments on SemEval-2014 and SemEval-2016 datasets. We compare the performance of our proposed systems with those submitted in the shared tasks. Results are shown in Table 4. In non-English languages we are at first position among all the teams. In these languages for aspect terms extraction, we are 3.18%, 4.87% and 13.24% ahead in Spanish, French and Dutch respectively compared to the other top teams who participated in the challenge. The performance that we achieve for sentiment classification is also satisfactory.

3.4 Feature Selection: Analysis

Performance of any classification problem fully depends on the features used for solving the problem. Here we show the set of features selected for each of the languages English, French, Spanish and Dutch. Results are reported in Tables 5, 6 and 7 for aspect term extraction, OTE and sentiment classification respectively.

Table 4. Comparisons with other teams

Datasets	Task	Rank	Diff. from top team
Restaurant (SemEval-2014)	Aspect Ext	3/28	3.78
Laptop (SemEval-2014)	Aspect Ext	3/27	1.56
English (SemEval-2016)	OTE	3/19	3.89
Spanish (SemEval-2016)	OTE	1/4	-
French (SemEval-2016)	OTE	1/2	-
Dutch (SemEval-2016)	OTE	1/2	-
Restaurant (SemEval-2014)	Senti	5/31	4.06
Laptop (SemEval-2014)	Senti	6/31	5.04
English (SemEval-2016)	Senti	8/27	6.28
Dutch (SemEval-2016)	Senti	4/4	2.94

Table 5. Features selected for aspect term extraction: SemEval-2014. M1 and M2 corresponds to framework 1 and framework 2 of Sect. 2.3. Here ✓ represents that feature has been selected. Number denotes the context of current token. Example:- (-3..1) represents that context token from previous 3 upto next 1 have been selected.

Domains	Framework	Features																													
		Word&Context	Char n-grams (2,3,4)	Chunk	Dependency	Dependency (Head)	Dependency (Modifier)	Ortho (digit)	DT (-2..2)	Freq. Aspect List1	Freq. Aspect List2	HeadWord	HeadWord PoS	Lemma	LowerCase	NER (-1..1)	PMI	Rounded PMI (-1..1)	PoS (-2..2)	1-Char Prefix(-1..1)	2-Char Prefix(-1..1)	3-Char Prefix(-1..1)	Expansion score (-2..2)	RoundExpansion score (-2..2)	SentiWordNet (-2..2)	Round SentiWord (-2..2)	Stopword	1-Char suffix (-1..1)	2-Char suffix (-1..1)	3-Char suffix (-1..1)	Noun synset	Unsupervised PoS (-2..2)
Restuarant	M1	-3,-1..3	2,3	0,1	-	✓	✓	-	-2..0	-	✓	-	-	-	-	0	-	-1	-2..0	1	-	-	✓	-	0,2	-2,2	✓	✓	-1,0	✓	✓	-1,2
	M2	-3,-1..1,3	4	-1,1	✓	✓	✓	-	-2,0,2	✓	✓	-	✓	-	✓	-	✓	0	-2,0	-1,1	-1	1	✓	0,2	-2..0,2	0,2	✓	✓	-1	-1,0	✓	-1..2
Laptop	M1	-1,0,3	2,4	✓	-	-	✓	✓	0	-	✓	-	✓	-	-	-1	0,1	1	-2,1	-	-	-1	2	1	-	-1	-	-	-	-	-	-
	M2	2	✓	✓	✓	✓	✓	✓	-2,0	-	✓	-	✓	-	-	-1,0	0,1	-1,1	-2..1	0	-	0	-1,1	0,2	-1,2	-	-	0	-	-1,0	✓	2

Table 6. Features selected for OTE: SemEval 2016.

Language	Framework	Features																											
		Word and Context	Char n-gram(2,3,4-gram)	Chunk information(-1,0,1)	Dependency (Head)	Dependency (Modifier)	Distri. Thesaurus(-2,-1,0,1,2)	Frq. Aspct List1	Freq. Aspct List2	Head Word	Head Word POS	Lemma	Lower Case	NER	Ortho	POS (-2,-1,0,1,2)	1-Char Prefix(-1,0,1)	2-Char Prefix(-1,0,1)	3-Char Prefix(-1,0,1)	4-Char Prefix	Expansion score(-2,-1,0,1,2)	Round. Exp.Score(-2,-1,0,1,2)	SentiWord(-2,-1,0,1,2)	Round. SentiWord(-2,-1,0,1,2)	1-Char Suffix(-1,0,1)	2-Char Suffix(-1,0,1)	3-Char Suffix(-1,0,1)	4-Char Suffix	Noun Synset	Unsupervised POS(-2,-1,0,1,2)
English	M1	0,3,4	2..4		✓		-2..1						✓		✓	-2,0,2	0,1		-1			-1,1,2		2	-1					
	M2	-4..-2,1,2,4,5	4	0,-1	✓		-2..0,2	✓				✓		✓	✓	-1..2	0,1	✓	0,1	✓	-1,1,-2	-1,1	1	-2	✓	0	✓		✓	-2,0,2
Dutch	M1	-1,1		-			-1,0					-		-		-2,-1			-1,0	✓	-2	-2	-	-		-1	1		-	-1,0
	M2	-4,-2,-1,1		-	✓		-2..0			✓	✓	-	✓	-	✓	-2,0,1		0,1	1	✓	-2,-1,1	-2	-	-	0,1	✓	1		-	-1,0
Spanish	M1	-5,-1,0	2,3	-		✓	-1,0	✓	✓			-		-	✓	-2..0	0	1	-1	✓	-1	-2,1	-	-	0	1	-1		-	-1,0
	M2	-4,-3,5	✓	-			-1		✓			-	✓	-	✓	-2,-1	0,1	-1	-1,0	✓	-1,0	-2,-1,1	-	-	0,1	1	0		-	-1..1
French	M1	-3,-1		-			-2,0					-		-		-2,-1	1	0,1				2	-	-		-1			-	
	M2	-5,-3..0,2	2,3	-		✓	-1,0		✓	✓	✓	-		-		-2,-1,1	✓	0	-1,0		-2,1,2	-2..0	-	-	-1	-1		✓	-	-1

Table 7. Feature selection of sentiment classification - 2014

Features	Restaurant		Laptop	
	Model 1	Model 2	Model 1	Model 2
Word and Context	-4..3	-4,-2..1	-4,-2..3,5	-5,-2..4
Bi-gram	2		2	-2,2
Bing Lexicon	✓	✓	✓	✓
Bing Direct Lexicon	✓	✓	✓	✓
SentiWord	✓	✓		✓
PMI	✓	✓		✓
MPQA	✓	✓	✓	✓
Domain Specific Word	✓	✓	-	-
Sentiment-140 lexicon (Unigram,Bigram)	✓	Unigram		
NRC Hashtag lexicon (Unigram,Bigram)	✓	Bigram		
AFINN lexicon				
NRC Emotion	✓		✓	
Expansion Score		✓		

4 Error Analysis

In subsequent subsections, we present analysis of error encountered by the proposed method. Due to space constraints we only show analysis for SemEval-2016 datasets.

4.1 OTE

1. Long OTEs (more than two tokens) are often not correctly identified by our system. For instance, the 4-token aspect term in the below example is completely ignored by the proposed method.

   ...with delectable ***creamed Washington russet potatoes*** *and crisp...*

2. Many times our system identifies the two OTEs which is associated with 'and' as single OTE. For example, ***server*** and ***food*** are the two aspect terms in the following review but our system predict ***server and food*** as an aspect term due to the presence of 'and' in between the two.

   ...our wonderful ***server*** *and* ***food*** *made the experience a very positive one...*

3. The proposed method faced difficulties in identifying opinion target which contains special characters (e.g. ', -). For example

   The ***pizza's*** *are light and scrumptious.*

4. Some instances of the OTE that form the last token in the text are not classified by our system. For e.g. opinion target term ***pepperoni*** appears at the end of the review, which is not identified by the proposed system.

   ...big thick ***pepperoni****.*

4.2 Sentiment Classification

1. Presence of negative term like *n't, never, but* etc. always change the polarity orientation in the text but our system fails to capture such orientation on few instances specially with smaller sentences. For e.g. *"Not good !"*. It should be classified as negative but our system classifies it as positive.
2. In many cases our system is biased to a particular review. It means if a review has more than one OTE, our system assigns same class to all of them, even it is different.

   ...the ***fish*** *is unquestionably fresh,* ***rolls*** *tend to be inexplicably bland.*

   Here for *fish* and *rolls*, we have positive and negative review respectively. But, our system classifies positive in both cases.

5 Conclusion

In this paper, we reported on experiments for improving the quality of aspect-based sentiment analysis (ABSA) and its subtasks. We have discussed two contributions in detail: (1) the use of features from unsupervised lexical acquisition and (2) the use of multi-objective optimization (MOO) for feature selection. Experimental results on three subtasks of ABSA for six languages and several domains show consistent improvements in all experiments for unsupervised lexical acquisition features. MOO was able to improve the classification/extraction accuracy in some cases, but always resulted in a much more compact model.

The strength of our approach is the combination of unsupervised features and feature selection: Since unsupervised features do not require language-specific processing, they apply to all natural languages where sufficient raw corpora are available. However, unsupervised acquisition necessarily retains a certain amount of noise. The MOO feature selection mechanism counterbalances this by only retaining features (of any kind), which contribute to a good performance. This, we are able to afford the experimentation with more features and feature combinations since this setup allows us to over-generate features and have them selected automatically.

In future work, we would like to further automatize the process by extending our approach to several base classifiers, making their selection and their ensemble also subject to automatic optimization techniques.

References

1. Biemann, C.: Unsupervised part-of-speech tagging in the large. Res. Lang. Comput. **7**(2–4), 101–135 (2009)
2. Biemann, C., Giuliano, C., Gliozzo, A.: Unsupervised part-of-speech tagging supporting supervised methods. In: Proceedings of RANLP, Borovets, Bulgaria, vol. 7, pp. 8–15 (2007)

3. Biemann, C., Riedl, M.: From global to local similarities: a graph-based contextualization method using distributional thesauri. In: Proceedings of the 8th Workshop on TextGraphs in Conjunction with EMNLP, Seattle, USA, pp. 39–43 (2013)
4. Blair-Goldensohn, S., Hannan, K., McDonald, R., Neylon, T., Reis, G.A., Reynar, J.: Building a sentiment summarizer for local service reviews. In: WWW Workshop on NLP in the Information Explosion Era, Beijing, China, vol. 14, pp. 339–348 (2008)
5. Deb, K.: Multi-objective Optimization using Evolutionary Algorithms, vol. 16. Wiley, Chichester (2001)
6. Ding, X., Liu, B., Yu, P.S.: A holistic lexicon-based approach to opinion mining. In: Proceedings of the 2008 International Conference on Web Search and Data Mining, New York, USA, pp. 231–240 (2008)
7. Ekbal, A., Saha, S.: Multiobjective optimization for classifier ensemble and feature selection: an application to named entity recognition. Int. J. Doc. Anal. Recogn. (IJDAR) **15**(2), 143–166 (2012)
8. Ekbal, A., Saha, S.: Simulated annealing based classifier ensemble techniques: application to part of speech tagging. J. Inf. Fusion **14**(3), 288–300 (2013)
9. Fahrni, A., Klenner, M.: Old wine or warm beer: target-specific sentiment analysis of adjectives. In: Proceedings of the Symposium on Affective Language in Human and Machine, AISB, Aberdeen, Scotland, pp. 60–63 (2008)
10. Hatzivassiloglou, V., McKeown, K.R.: Predicting the semantic orientation of adjectives. In: Proceedings of the Eighth Conference on European Chapter of the Association for Computational Linguistics, Madrid, Spain, pp. 174–181 (1997)
11. Hu, M., Liu, B.: Mining and summarizing customer reviews. In: Proceedings of the Tenth ACM SIGKDD International Conference on Knowledge Discovery and Data Mining, Seattle, USA, pp. 168–177 (2004)
12. Kim, S.M., Hovy, E.: Determining the sentiment of opinions. In: Proceedings of the 20th International Conference on Computational Linguistics, Geneva, pp. 1367–1373 (2004)
13. Kumar, A., Kohail, S., Kumar, A., Ekbal, A., Biemann, C.: IIT-TUDA at SemEval-2016 Task 5: beyond sentiment lexicon: combining domain dependency and distributional semantics features for aspect based sentiment analysis. In: 10th International Workshop on Semantics Evaluation (SemEval-2016), San Diego, USA, pp. 311–317. ACL (2016)
14. Lin, D.: Automatic retrieval and clustering of similar words. In: Proceedings of the 17th International Conference on Computational Linguistics, Stroudsburg, vol. 2, pp. 768–774 (1998)
15. Liu, B.: Sentiment Analysis and Opinion Mining, vol. 5. Morgan & Claypool Publishers, San Rafael (2012)
16. Liu, H., Motoda, H.: Feature Selection for Knowledge Discovery and Data Mining, vol. 454. Springer Science & Business Media, Norwell (2012)
17. Liu, H., Yu, L.: Toward integrating feature selection algorithms for classification and clustering. IEEE Trans. Knowl. Data Eng. **17**(4), 491–502 (2005)
18. Miller, G.A.: Wordnet: a lexical database for English. Commun. ACM **38**(11), 39–41 (1995)
19. Miller, T., Biemann, C., Zesch, T., Gurevych, I.: Using distributional similarity for lexical expansion in knowledge-based word sense disambiguation. In: Proceedings of COLING, Mumbai, India, pp. 1781–1796 (2012)
20. Mohammad, S.M., Turney, P.D.: Crowdsourcing a word-emotion association lexicon. Comput. Intell. **29**(3), 436–465 (2013)

21. Mukherjee, A., Liu, B.: Aspect extraction through semi-supervised modeling. In: Proceedings of the 50th Annual Meeting of the Association for Computational Linguistics: Long Papers, Jeju Island, Korea, vol. 1, pp. 339–348 (2012)
22. Nielsen, F.Å.: A new ANEW: evaluation of a word list for sentiment analysis in microblogs. In: Proceedings of the ESWC 2011 Workshop on 'Making Sense of Microposts': Big Things Come in Small Packages, Heraklion, Greece, pp. 93–98 (2011)
23. Pontiki, M., Galanis, D., Papageorgiou, H., Androutsopoulos, I., Manandhar, S., Al-Smadi, M., Al-Ayyoub, M., Zhao, Y., Qin, B., Clercq, O.D., Hoste, V., Apidianaki, M., Tannier, X., Loukachevitch, N., Kotelnikov, E., Bel, N., Jimnez-Zafra, S.M., Eryiit, G.: Semeval-2016 Task 5: aspect based sentiment analysis. In: Proceedings of the 10th International Workshop on Semantic Evaluation (SemEval 2016), San Diego, USA, pp. 19–30 (2016)
24. Pontiki, M., Galanis, D., Pavlopoulos, J., Papageorgiou, H., Androutsopoulos, I., Manandhar, S.: Semeval-2014 Task 4: aspect based sentiment analysis. In: Proceedings of the 8th International Workshop on Semantic Evaluation (SemEval 2014), Dublin, pp. 27–35 (2014)
25. Popescu, A.M., Etzioni, O.: Extracting product features and opinions from reviews. In: Proceedings of the Conference on Human Language Technology and Empirical Methods in Natural Language Processing, Stroudsburg, USA, pp. 339–346 (2005)
26. Schouten, K., Frasincar, F.: Survey on aspect-level sentiment analysis. IEEE Trans. Knowl. Data Eng. **28**(3), 813–830 (2016)
27. Turney, P.D.: Thumbs up or thumbs down?: Semantic orientation applied to unsupervised classification of reviews. In: Proceedings of the 40th Annual Meeting on Association for Computational Linguistics, Philadelphia, USA, pp. 417–424 (2002)
28. Wiebe, J., Mihalcea, R.: Word sense and subjectivity. In: Proceedings of the 21st International Conference on Computational Linguistics and the 44th Annual Meeting of the Association for Computational Linguistics, Sydney, Australia, pp. 1065–1072 (2006)
29. Wu, Y., Zhang, Q., Huang, X., Wu, L.: Phrase dependency parsing for opinion mining. In: Proceedings of the 2009 Conference on Empirical Methods in Natural Language Processing, Singapore, vol. 3, pp. 1533–1541 (2009)
30. Zhu, X., Kiritchenko, S., Mohammad, S.M.: NRC-Canada-2014: recent improvements in the sentiment analysis of tweets. In: Proceedings of the 8th International Workshop on Semantic Evaluation (SemEval 2014), Dublin, Ireland, pp. 443–447 (2014)
31. Zhuang, L., Jing, F., Zhu, X.Y.: Movie review mining and summarization. In: Proceedings of the 15th ACM International Conference on Information and Knowledge Management, Virginia, USA, pp. 43–50 (2006)

Feature Selection and Class-Weight Tuning Using Genetic Algorithm for Bio-molecular Event Extraction

Amit Majumder[1](✉), Asif Ekbal[2], and Sudip Kumar Naskar[3]

[1] Academy of Technology, Kolkata, India
jobamit48@yahoo.co.in
[2] IIT Patna, Bihta, India
asif@iitp.ac.in
[3] Jadavpur University, Jadavpur, India
sudip.naskar@cse.jdvu.ac.in

Abstract. In this paper we present an efficient method for event extraction in bio-medical text. Event extraction deals with finding more detailed biological phenomenon, which is more challenging compared to simple binary relation extraction like protein-protein interaction (PPI). The task can be thought of as comprising of the following sub-problems, *viz.*, trigger detection, classification and argument extraction. Event trigger detection and classification deal with identification of event expressions from text and classification of them into nine different categories. We use Support Vector Machine (SVM) as the base learning algorithm, which is trained with a diverse set of features that cover both statistical and linguistic characteristics. We develop a feature selection algorithm using Genetic Algorithm (GA) for determining the most relevant set of features. Experiments on benchmark datasets of BioNLP-2011 shared task datasets show the recall, precision and F-measure values of 48.17%, 65.86% and 55.64% respectively.

Keywords: Event extraction · Trigger detection · Edge detection · Dependency graph · Support Vector Machine (SVM) · Class-weight tuning

1 Introduction

Huge amount of electronic biomedical documents, such as molecular biology reports, genomic papers or patient records are generated daily. These contents need to be organized in a more principled way so as to enable advanced search and efficient information retrieval. Success of text mining (TM) is evident from the organization of different shared-task evaluation campaigns, such as those organized in the MUC [1], TREC [2], ACE[1] etc. The bulk of research in the field of biomedical natural language processing (BioNLP) have mainly focused

[1] http://www.itl.nist.gov/iad/mig/tests/ace/.

F. Frasincar et al. (Eds.): NLDB 2017, LNCS 10260, pp. 28–33, 2017.
DOI: 10.1007/978-3-319-59569-6_3

on the extraction of simple binary relations. Some of the very popular bio-text mining evaluation challenges include the TREC Genomics track [2], JNLPBA[2], LLL [3] and BioCreative [4]. There is a recent trend for fine-grained information extraction from text [5]. This was addressed in three consecutive text mining challenges such BioNLP-2009 [6], BioNLP-2011 [7] and BioNLP-2013 [8]. In this paper we propose an interesting technique for information extraction (more specifically, event extraction) at the more finer level. This is known as event extraction where the focus is to extract events and their different properties that denote detailed biological phenomenon. This can be thought of as comprising of three steps, *viz.* event trigger detection, trigger classification and argument extraction.

2 Major Steps for Event Extraction

In this section we describe our major steps for event extraction. For all the tasks, i.e. trigger detection, trigger classification and argument extraction, we use supervised classifier, namely Support Vector Machine (SVM) [9]. The output of SVM is further improved by tuning the confidence score of each class using the weight factor. We also propose a SVM based technique to find the correct combination of arguments for an event. For our experiments we make use of some modules from an existing bio-molecular event extraction system named TEES [10–12] which was the best performing system in BioNLP-2009 [5].

2.1 Event Trigger Extraction

In this step we identify even trigger from text and classify them into nine predefined event types. As a classification framework we use Support Vector Machine (SVM) [9], which performs both identification and classification together. We employ a Genetic Algorithm [13] based feature selection technique to determine the most relevant features.

Class-Weight Tuning for Performance Improvement: For each instance of the test data, SVM generates confidence score for each class. Confidence score of each class is multiplied by a weight produced by a GA based approach. The class which receives the highest score is considered as the final predicted class label for the corresponding instance. The class label for an instance E is determined based on the following Eq. 1 where C refers to the set of classes.

$$\hat{c}_E = argmax_{c_i \in C}\{ConfidenceScore^E_{c_i} * Weight^E_{c_i}\} \tag{1}$$

Here, $ConfidenceScore^E_{c_i}$ represents confidence score of class label c_i for the instance E and $Weight^E_{c_i}$ represents the weight value chosen for class label c_i. The problem is encoded in term of chromosome as shown in Fig. 1. In the figure, C_0 to C_{N-1} denote the n class labels. The value in each cell represents the weight of the corresponding class label.

[2] http://www.geniaproject.org/shared-tasks/bionlp-jnlpba-shared-task-2004.

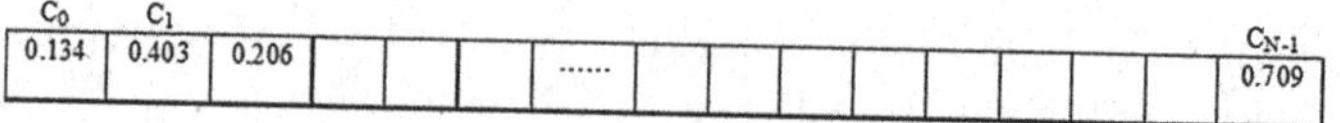

Fig. 1. Chromosome representation.

Fitness Computation: We combine the classifiers using these weight combinations as represented by chromosome. The combined classifier is evaluated on the development set[3]. We consider F-measure as the fitness of the respective chromosome.

2.2 Argument Extraction by Edge Detection

In this step, we find the arguments of triggers as detected in the previous step (i.e. trigger detection). An argument can be either a protein or another trigger. The training instances of SVM are generated by considering all possible pairs of trigger and trigger/protein.

Improvement in accuracy of edge detection by tuning class-weight: This step is employed to improve the accuracy of edge detection. For each instance of the test data, SVM generates confidence score for each class. Confidence score is multiplied by a weight which is produced by GA. The class which receives the highest score is considered as the final predicted class label for the corresponding instance. The class label for an instance E is predicted using the method as shown in Eq. 2 where C refers to the set of classes.

$$\hat{c}_E = argmax_{c_i \in C}\{ConfidenceScore^E_{c_i} * Weight^E_{c_i}\} \tag{2}$$

Here, $ConfidenceScore^E_{c_i}$ represents confidence score of class label c_i for the instance E and $Weight^E_{c_i}$ represents the weight value chosen for the class label c_i.

In edge detection, we identify arguments of a trigger words detected in trigger detection step. GA [13] has been used only for tuning the class-weight. As the number of arguments is not fixed in case of binding and regulatory events we need to apply post-processing to find out the correct combination of arguments.

3 Features

We use content, contextual and syntax features to find out event expressions from text. The features which have been used in our experiment denote surface wordforms, stem, PoS, chunk, Named Entity, Bag-of-Words (BOW), bi-gram, tri-gram features along with other features as mentioned below.

1. Linear Features: Linear features are generated by marking token with a tag that denotes their relative positions in the linear order. This feature is defined with respect to a context window. If i is a position (i.e. index) of the

[3] We optimize weights using development set.

token under consideration, then the linear features are calculated from the words with indices $i-3$ to $i+3$. In our experiments the word token itself along with its PoS tag is used to generate the linear features.

2. Upper_case_start, upper_case_middle, has_digits, has_hyphen: These features are defined based on the orthographic constructions: whether the token starts with an uppercase character, or it has any uppercase character in the middle, or has any digit(s) or hyphen inside it.

3. Dependency Path Features: Dependency features [14,15] are very useful in extracting events from text. To generate dependency path features we use Charniak-McCloskey parser [15] to find out the dependency graph from a sentence. Edge labels in the shortest path between two nodes are used as feature value.

4 Experimental Results and Analysis

In this experiment, we use the BioNLP-ST-2011 datasets and evaluation frameworks[4]. We tune the system on the development set, and use the configurations obtained for final evaluation. SVM is used as the training algorithm for event trigger detection and classification. Here, we perform both detection and classification at the same time. We determine the best fitting feature set using a GA based feature selection technique. We set the following parameter values for GA: Population size = 30, Number of generations = 40, Selection strategy = tournament selection, Probability of mutation = 0.125, Probability of crossover = 0.9. In Table 1, we show the evaluation results. For evaluation we use event expression matching technique known as Approximate Span/Approximate Recursive method[5] as defined in the BioNLP-2011 Shared Task. Comparisons show that we achieve significant performance improvement using the reduced set of features as determined by the feature selection technique.

In order to gain more insights we analyze the outputs to find the errors and their possible causes. We perform quantitative analysis in terms of confusion matrix, and qualitative analysis by looking at the outputs produced by the systems. For trigger detection and classification we can see that the system performs satisfactorily for gene_expression and phosphorylation types. However, the

Table 1. Experimental results. Here, *FS* indicates Feature Selection, *CWT* indicates Class-Weight Tuning and *Dev* denotes the development set

Dataset	Experiment	Gold (match)	Answer (match)	Recall	Precision	F-measure
Dev	Without FS and CWT	3243 (1561)	2392 (1560)	48.13	65.22	55.39
Dev	With FS and CWT	3243 (1614)	2366 (1613)	49.77	68.17	57.54
Test	Without FS and CWT	4457 (1966)	3003 (1966)	44.11	65.47	52.71
Test	With FS and CWT	4457 (2147)	3260 (2147)	48.17	65.86	55.64

[4] http://weaver.nlplab.org/~bionlp-st/BioNLP-ST/downloads/downloads.shtml.

[5] http://www.nactem.ac.uk/tsujii/GENIA/SharedTask/evaluation.shtml.

classifier does not show convincing results for regulation type events, which are in general difficult to identify and classify. One of the reasons may be the less number of training instances of regulatory events. Classifier finds it difficult to disambiguate the cases when any particular instance belongs to more than one types.

4.1 Comparison with Existing Systems

For bio-molecular event extraction, the state-of-the-art system is TEES [10], which ranked first place in BioNLP-ST-2009. Our experimental results show recall, precision and F-measure values of 49.77%, 68.17% and 57.54% respectively on development dataset, whereas official scores attained by TEES [10] are 52.45%, 60.05% and 55.99%, respectively. As compared to the official scores of TEES (recall: 49.56%, precision: 57.65% and F-measure: 53.30%), our system achieves recall, precision and F-measure values of 48.17%, 65.86% and 55.64%, respectively on the test dataset. Hence, our system performs better with more than 2.34% points. The performance that we achieve is very close to the best performing system, FAUST [16] (recall: 49.41%, precision: 64.75% and F-measure: 56.04%) and better than the second ranked system, UMass [17] (recall: 48.49, precision: 64.08 and F-measure: 55.20) in BioNLP-2011 [7]. A recently developed system named as EventMine [18], which made use of co-reference resolution obtains significant performance improvement with recall, precision and F-measure of 51.25%, 64.92% and 57.28%, respectively. Our event extraction process is different from the existing system as we make use of GA based feature selection and class-weight tuning. Though our system demonstrates comparatively lower performance on the test data in comparison with the recently developed best system, we expect it to be more effective by incorporating co-reference resolution.

5 Conclusion

In this paper we have proposed an efficient technique for event extraction that concerns event trigger detection, event classification and argument extraction. Experiments show that feature selection along with class-weight tuning improves overall performance significantly (3% F-measure points). As a base learning algorithm we used SVM that made use of a diverse set of features at each step. Experiments on benchmark datasets of BioNLP 2011 shared tasks show recall, precision and F-measure values of 48.17%, 65.86% and 55.64%, respectively. Comparisons with the other existing techniques show that this is at par the state-of-the-art performance. Overall evaluation results suggest that there are many ways to further improve the performance. In our future work, we would like to investigate distinct and more effective set of features for trigger detection and edge detection. In our future work, in every stage we would like to generate multiple classifiers using different set of features and apply class-weight tuning on multiple classifiers. We would also like to apply co-reference resolution to check whether performance of system improves or not. Another interesting direction of future work will be to investigate deep learning methods for the tasks.

References

1. Chinchor, N.: Message understanding conference (muc-7) proceedings. In: Overview of MUC-7/MET-2 (1998)
2. Voorhees, E.: Overview of TREC 2007. In: Sixteenth Text REtrieval Conference (TREC 2007) Proceedings (2007)
3. Nedellec, C.: Learning language in logic-genic interaction extraction challenge. In: Proceedings of the 4th Learning Language in Logic Workshop (LLL05), pp. 31–37 (2005)
4. Lynette Hirschman, M.K., Valencia, A.: Proceedings of the second biocreative challenge evaluation workshop. In: CNIO Centro Nacional de Investigaciones Oncologicas (2007)
5. Kim, J.-D., Ohta, T., Pyysalo, S., Kano, Y., Tsujii, J.: Overview of BioNLP'09 shared task on event extraction. In: Proceedings of the Workshop on BioNLP, BioNLP 09, pp. 1–9 (2009)
6. Lee, H.-G., Cho, H.-C., Kim, M.-J., Lee, J.-Y., Hong, G., Rim, H.-C.: A multiphase approach to biomedical event extraction. In: Proceedings of the Workshop on BioNL, BioNL 09, pp. 107–110 (2009)
7. Kim, J.-D., Sampo Pyysalo, T., Kim, M.-J., Lee, J.-Y., Hong, G., Rim, H.-C.: Overview of bionlp shared task 2011. In: Proceedings of BioNLP Shared Task 2011 Workshop, pp. 1–6, June 2011
8. Li, L., Yiwen Wang, D.H.: Improving feature-based biomedical event extraction system by integrating argument information. In: Proceedings of the BioNLP Shared Task 2013 Workshop, pp. 109–115, August 2013
9. Corinna Cortes, V.V.: Support-vector networks. In: Machine Learning, pp. 273–297 (1995)
10. Björne, J.: Biomedical event extraction with machine learning. Ph.D. thesis, University of Turku (2014)
11. Bjorne, J., Salakoski, T.: Generalizing biomedical event extraction. In: Proceedings of BioNLP Shared Task 2011 Workshop, June 2011
12. Jari Bjrne, T.S.: Tees 2.2: biomedical event extraction for diverse corpora. BMC Bioinform. **16**, s4 (2015)
13. Deb, K., Pratap, A., Agarwal, S., Meyarivan, T.: A fast and elitist multiobjective genetic algorithm: NSGA-II. IEEE Trans. Evol. Comput. **6**(2), 181–197 (2002). Velingrad
14. David McClosky, M.S., Manning, C.D.: Event extraction as dependency parsing for BioNLP 2011. In: Proceedings of BioNLP Shared Task 2011 Workshop, pp. 41–45, June 2011
15. McClosky, D.: Any domain parsing: automatic domain adaptation for parsing. Ph.D. Thesis (2010)
16. Riedela, S., David McCloskyb, M., Surdeanu, M., McCallum, A., Manning, C.D.: Model combination for event extraction in BioNLP 2011. In: Proceedings of BioNLP Shared Task 2011 Workshop, pp. 51–55 (2011)
17. Riedel, S., McCallum, A.: Robust biomedical event extraction with dual decomposition and minimal domain adaptation. In: Proceedings of BioNLP Shared Task 2011 Workshop, pp. 46–50 (2011)
18. Miwa, M., Pyysalo, S., Ohta, T., Ananiadou, S.: Wide coverage biomedical event extraction using multiple partially overlapping corpora (2013)

Automated Lexicon and Feature Construction Using Word Embedding and Clustering for Classification of ASD Diagnoses Using EHR

Gondy Leroy(✉), Yang Gu, Sydney Pettygrove, and Margaret Kurzius-Spencer

University of Arizona, Tucson, AZ, USA
{gondyleroy,ygu,mkurzius}@email.arizona.edu, sydneypsed@u.arizona.edu

Abstract. Using electronic health records of children evaluated for Autism Spectrum Disorders, we are developing a decision support system for automated diagnostic criteria extraction and case classification. We manually created 92 lexicons which we tested as features for classification and compared with features created automatically using word embedding. The expert annotations used for manual lexicon creation provided seed terms that were expanded with the 15 most similar terms (Word2Vec). The resulting 2,200 terms were clustered in 92 clusters parallel to the manually created lexicons. We compared both sets of features to classify case status with a FF\BP neural network (NN) and C5.0 decision tree. For manually created lexicons, classification accuracy was 76.92% for the NN and 84.60% for C5.0. For the automatically created lexicons, accuracy was 79.78% for the NN and 86.81% for C5.0. Automated lexicon creation required a much shorter development time and brought similarly high quality outcomes.

Keywords: Word embedding · Natural language processing · NLP · Electronic health records · EHR · Autism spectrum disorders · Clustering · Classification

1 Introduction

Over the last decades, the prevalence of Autism Spectrum Disorders (ASD) has increased. In the United States, the Centers for Disease Control and Prevention coordinate national ASD surveillance, which entails review of thousands of electronic health records (EHR). We are developing a system that can automatically extract the individual diagnostic criteria (component 1: parser) and assign case status (component 2: classifier). As part of the parser development, we created lexicons containing diagnostically relevant terms. We report here on the use of these lexicons as features for case status classification. We compare them with automatically created features using word embedding.

Word embedding, e.g., Word2Vec [1], is increasingly used in medicine to prepare features for classification or for similarity measures and clustering. For example, for classification at the document level, Zheng et al. [2] combined Word2Vec term features with others, such as ICD-10 codes, to identify Type 2 Diabetes in EHR. At the

F. Frasincar et al. (Eds.): NLDB 2017, LNCS 10260, pp. 34–37, 2017.
DOI: 10.1007/978-3-319-59569-6_4

predicate level, Wang et al. [3] used word embedding to provide features to their neural network and classify 19 biomedical events. Their approach outperformed the baselines without any manual feature encoding. Word embedding is also used because it provides similarity measures. Fergadiotis [4] successfully used it to recognize semantic similarities and differences between terms to classify paraphasic errors. Minarro-Gimenez [5] trained Word2Vec on PubMed and Wikipedia texts. They compared similarity between terms with an established ontology with mixed results.

2 Manual and Automated Creation of Lexicons as Features

In this work, we evaluate the use of lexicons as features for ASD case status classification. As part of prior work, we created diagnostically relevant lexicons for a parser by reviewing EHR containing clinical annotations that correspond to a diagnostic criterion. Table 1 shows examples of diagnostic criteria and text snippets in the EHR.

Table 1. Example annotations (Diagnostic Statistical Manual on Mental Disorders (DSM))

DSM diagnostic rule	EHR sentence fragment
Marked impairment in the use of multiple nonverbal behaviors such as eye-to-eye gaze, facial expression, body postures, and gestures to regulate social interaction (Rule A1a)	Though he was noted to not smile
	Poor eye contact with the examiner

Using 43 EHR (4,732 sentences), we grouped terms from the annotations according to their meaning, e.g., body parts or nonverbal behaviors. We added synonyms, hypernyms, hyponyms and spelling variants as well as related terms. For example, the term 'brother', extracted in the context of "no social interaction between the patient and his brother," would be combined with brothers, sister, sisters, sibling, siblings, step-brother, half-brother … The result of this process was the creation of 92 lexicons containing a total of 1,787 terms. We test these lexicons as features for classification.

Because manually creating lexicons is labor intensive, we investigate automated creation of lexicons. First, we collected all terms from the annotations in the 43 EHR. There were 1,126 unique terms. Of these, 649 appeared more than once and these were used as seed terms. Instead of dictionary lookup, these terms were automatically expanded using a vocabulary created by training Word2Vec (using the Skip-Gram Model, https://deeplearning4j.org/) on 4,480 EHR (9,387,476 tokens). We trained Word2Vec using 200 embedding dimensions, a window size of 10 and a minimum token frequency of 5. The outcome of training the model was a vocabulary containing 17,057 tokens. Then, we expanded each seed term with the 15 most similar terms. To keep our process as automated as possible, we blindly accepted all expansion terms if their Word2Vec cosine similarity with the seed term exceeded 0.55. To ensure maximum comparability with our manually created lexicons, we created 92 clusters using k-means.

3 ASD Case Status Classification

Dataset: 4,480 EHR with 'ASD' (N = 2,303) or 'Not ASD' (N = 2,177). The majority baseline is 51.4%. We used the lexicons as features for classification. Each EHR was parsed and counts of terms that occurred in the lexicons were the input features.

Classifiers: We compare a feedforward backpropagation neural network (NN) and decision trees (C5.0 with adaptive boosting) using R. The decision tree was chosen because it provides visually understandable output, which may be preferred by clinicians using the final system. The NN was chosen as a baseline for later comparisons with deep learning. For the NN, we tested different sizes for the hidden units and decay variable. For C5.0, we tested different levels of boosting and with/without winnowing.

Results: All EHR (N = 4,480) were classified. We calculated accuracy using 10-fold cross validation. Accuracy is well above the majority baseline (see Table 2). With manually created lexicons, the NN achieved between 72% and 77% accuracy. The best results were achieved with 10 hidden units and decay of 0.6, resulting in 76.92% accuracy. C5.0 performed slightly better, with accuracy between 76% and 85%. The best result was achieved with 12 trials of boosting and winnowing of variables, resulting in 84.75% accuracy.

Table 2. Classification results

Model	Parameters		Accuracy (%)	
			Manual Lex	Automated Lex
FF\BP NN	Model = 2	Decay = 0.5	72.80	78.12
	Model = 4		74.24	78.37
	Model = 6		74.84	78.50
	Model = 8		76.32	78.08
	Model = 10		76.32	78.93
	Model = 2	Decay = 0.6	76.32	77.25
	Model = 4		72.14	78.92
	Model = 6		74.89	78.01
	Model = 8		76.14	**79.78**
	Model = 10		**76.92**	79.58
C5.0 with boosting	Trials = 1	No Winnowing	76.83	79.91
	Trials = 5		82.79	85.29
	Trials = 10		84.42	86.61
	Trials = 12		**84.75**	**86.81**
	Trials = 15		84.73	86.52
	Trials = 1	With Winnowing	76.27	79.91
	Trials = 5		82.28	84.29
	Trials = 10		84.42	86.25
	Trials = 12		84.60	86.65
	Trials = 15		84.60	86.70

Similar results were found with automatically created lexicons. The NN achieved between 78% and 87% accuracy. The best performance of 79.78% accuracy was achieved with 8 hidden units and a decay of 0.6. The decision tree algorithm again achieved slightly better results, with accuracy between 79% and 87%. The best result was 86.81% accuracy without winnowing and 12 trials of boosting.

4 Conclusion

We set out to evaluate whether manually created lexicons could be replaced with automatically created lexicons for use as features in a clinical text classification task. EHR classification accuracy was high with both the manual and automated approaches. The decision tree algorithm consistently performed better than the neural network. The classification results were better with the automatically created lexicons. When looking at the accuracy results, winnowing variables resulted in better performance for the manually created lexicons. In our applications, this means that some of the lexicons were excluded from the decision tree. This was not the case with the automatically created lexicons, where the best results were found without winnowing.

Acknowledgements. The EHR were collected by the Centers for Disease Control and Prevention Autism and Developmental Disabilities Monitoring (ADDM) Network. Pettygrove and Kurzius-Spencer received support from CDC Cooperative Agreement Number 5UR3/DD000680. The conclusions presented here are those of the authors and do not represent the official position of the Centers for Disease Control and Prevention.

References

1. Mikolov, T., Chen, K., Corrado, G., Dean, J.: Efficient Estimation of Word Representations in Vector Space. *CoRR*, vol. abs/1301.3781 (2013)
2. Zheng, T., Xie, W., Xu, L., He, X., Zhang, Y., You, M., Yang, G., Chen, Y.: A machine learning-based framework to identify type 2 diabetes through electronic health records. Int. J. Med. Inform. **97**, 120–127 (2017)
3. Wang, J., Zhang, J., An, Y., Lin, H., Yang, Z., Zhang, Y., Sun, Y.: Biomedical event trigger detection by dependency-based word embedding. BMC Med. Genomics **9**, 123–133 (2016)
4. Fergadiotis, G., Gorman, K., Bedrick, S.: Algorithmic classification of five characteristic types of paraphasias. Am. J. Speech Lang. Pathol. **25**, S776–S787 (2016)
5. Minarro-Gimenez, J.A., Marín-Alonso, O., Samwal, M.: Exploring the application of deep learning techniques on medical text corpora. Stud. Health. Technol. Inform. **205**, 584–588 (2014)

Multi-objective Optimisation-Based Feature Selection for Multi-label Classification

Mohammed Arif Khan[1(✉)], Asif Ekbal[1], Eneldo Loza Mencía[2], and Johannes Fürnkranz[2]

[1] Department of Computer Science, Indian Institute of Technology Patna, Patna, India
{arif.mtmc13,asif}@iitp.ac.in
[2] Knowledge Engineering Group, Technische Universität Darmstadt, Darmstadt, Germany
{eneldo,juffi}@ke.tu-darmstadt.de

Abstract. In this short note we introduce multi-objective optimisation for feature subset selection in multi-label classification. We aim at optimise multiple multi-label loss functions simultaneously, using label powerset, binary relevance, classifier chains and calibrated label ranking as the multi-label learning methods, and decision trees and SVMs as base learners. Experiments on multi-label benchmark datasets show that the feature subset obtained through MOO performs reasonably better than the systems that make use of exhaustive feature sets.

Keywords: Multi-label classification · Multi-objective optimisation · Feature subset selection

1 Introduction

Multi-label classification [5] is concerned with categorising instances into multiple classes (labels), while the associated classes are not exclusive. Each associated class of an instance is called a label. There are two types of approaches for multi-label classification, algorithm adaptation methods and problem transformation methods [6]. Algorithm adaptation methods tackle the problem by adapting popular learning techniques to deal with multi-label data directly. A problem transformation method transforms a multi-label classification problem into one or more single-label problems.

Unlike in conventional classification, multi-label classification problems can be evaluated with a multitude of quality measures, often conflicting in nature. Multi-objective optimisation (MOO) aims at handling such problems by allowing to optimise more than one objective function simultaneously.

Feature selection techniques allow to determine the most relevant subset of features in order to reduce the dimensionality of the problem, and thereby reducing the complexity of the model. Moreover, feature selection often increases prediction accuracy because a reduction in the number of features helps to avoid

F. Frasincar et al. (Eds.): NLDB 2017, LNCS 10260, pp. 38–41, 2017.
DOI: 10.1007/978-3-319-59569-6_5

overfitting. However, most feature subset selection techniques aim at mimimizing a single objective, whereas our work uses multi-objective optimization in order to find a balanced feature subset. In the following, we briefly summarize our work, a detailed version of this paper is available as [3].

2 Multiobjective Feature Subset Selection

The goal of multi-objective optimisation (MOO) [2] is to find the vectors

$$x^* = [x_1^*, x_2^*, ..., x_N^*]^T \tag{1}$$

of decision variables that simultaneously optimise a set of $M \leq N$ objective functions

$$\{f_1(x), f_2(x), ..., f_M(x)\} \tag{2}$$

while satisfying additional constraints, if any.

In our case, we look at the problem of finding a subet F of available features, which optimizes a pair of multi-label loss functions. Such measures include Hamming loss, subset accuracy, and micro-averaged F_1-measure [5].

We solve this MOO problem using genetic algorithms. Chromosomes are binary strings, where 1(0) denotes the presence (absence) of the corresponding feature for constructing the classifier. We perform fitness computation (using 5-fold cross validation), binary tournament selection [2], crossover and mutation operations.

3 Experimental Setup

We use two datasets for conducting experiments with multi-label sentiment classification. The data sets were obtained from Mulan's dataset collection.[1] The *Emotion* dataset contains a total of 593 instances, 72 features and 6 labels. *CAL500* has a total of 502 instances, 174 labels and 68 features.

As base classifiers, we use the LibSVM [1] implementation for SVM and the J48 implementation for decision trees [4]. Along with these base learners, label powerset (LP), binary relevance (BR), classifier chains (CC), and calibrated label ranking (CLR) are used as multi-label classifiers. Model evaluation using cross validation provides the objectives (Hamming loss, subset accuracy, micro-averaged F-measure etc.), which are supplied to NSGA-II, where NSGA-II's operations viz. tournament selection, mutation, population decoding, population evaluation and non-dominated sorting [2] are used. We use grid search to tune the parameters of LibSVM and J48.

[1] http://mulan.sourceforge.net/datasets-mlc.html.

4 Results

Figure 1 shows the best obtained solutions. Here, CLR provides minimum Hamming loss while the best value of subset accuracy is obtained for LP for both the base learner. We select the two best solutions from the best population, one corresponding to Hamming loss and another corresponding to subset accuracy for each multi-label learner. Table 1 shows that if we require the solution with minimum Hamming loss then (21.12, 25.25, 38) is the best (near) optimal value for (Hamming loss, subset accuracy, number of features) obtained by CLR with SVM.

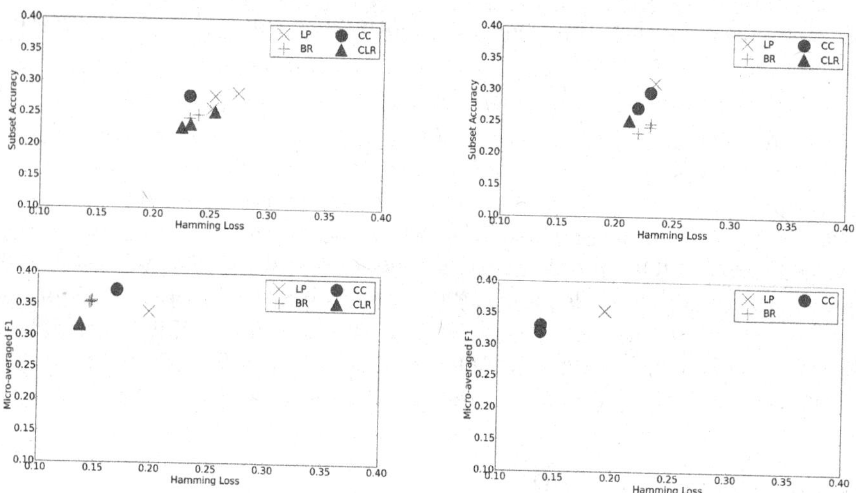

Fig. 1. Best population representation for different pairs of objective functions for Emotion (J48), Emotion (SVM), CAL500 (SVM), CAL500 (J48) (left to right clockwise)

Table 1. Results on emotion (top) and CAL500 (bottom) data

Base Classifier	ML learner	Best Solution 1 (HL, SA, NoF)	Best Solution 2 (HL, SA, NoF)	Solution S72 (HL, SA, NoF)	% Improvement	
					HL	SA
Decision tree	LP	(25.08, 25.74, 37)	(27.39, 28.22, 39)	(30.20, 22.28, 72)	05.12	05.94
	BR	(23.10, 24.26, 38	(23.84, 24.75, 32)	(25.99, 12.87, 72)	02.89	11.88
	CC	(23.10, 27.72, 32)		(28.96, 16.34, 72)	05.86	11.38
	CLR	(22.44, 22.77, 34)	(25.33, 25.25, 38)	(26.32, 12.87, 72)	03.88	12.38
SVM	LP	(23.35, 31.19, 39)		(31.35, 23.27, 72)	08.00	07.92
	BR	(21.86, 23.27, 39)	(23.02, 24.75, 34)	(26.49, 14.36, 72)	04.63	10.39
	CC	(21.86, 27.23, 39)	(22.94, 29.70, 38)	(26.49, 14.36, 72)	04.63	15.34
	CLR	(21.12, 25.25, 38)		(26.57, 15.84, 72)	05.45	09.41

Base Classifier	Multi-label learner	Best Solution 1 (HL, MAF, NoF)	Best Solution 2 (HL, MAF, NoF)	Solution S68 (HL, MAF, NoF)	% Improvement	
					HL	MAF
Decision tree	LP	(19.79, 33.91, 35)		(19.94, 32.69, 68)	00.15	01.22
	BR	(14.48, 35.28, 26)	(14.73, 35.62, 30)	(16.15, 33.96, 68)	01.67	01.66
	CC	(16.93, 37.22, 25)	(16.96, 37.34, 26)	(17.60, 36.68, 68)	00.67	00.66
	CLR	(13.67, 31.73, 26)	(13.68, 31.95, 24)	(13.85, 28.69, 68)	00.18	03.26
SVM	LP	(19.29, 35.40, 27)	(19.32, 35.41, 28)	(19.59,35.05, 68)	00.30	00.36
	BR	(13.61, 32.63, 26)	(13.66, 33.35, 29)	(13.66, 33.09, 68)	00.05	00.26
	CC	(13.70, 32.03, 37)	(13.74, 33.10, 36)	(13.76, 32.69, 68)	00.06	00.41

LP = Label Powerset, BR = Binary Relevance, CC = Classifier Chains, CLR = Calibrated Label Ranking, HL = Hamming Loss, MAF = Micro-averaged F-measure, NoF = Number of Features

Here 'Solution S72' represents the performance of classifiers on a exhaustive feature set of 72 features. In all experiments, we obtain better accuracies compared to the accuracies that we obtain for 'Solution S72'. Maximum improvement of 8% in Hamming loss is obtained for LP with SVM and maximum improvement of 15.34% in subset accuracy is obtained for CC with SVM. Results show that our proposed feature selection technique finally determines only 39 features (obtained by LP with SVM) and 38 features (obtained by CLR with SVM), which are very less compared to the exhaustive feature sets.

After getting convincing results on Emotion data set, we use the same MOO framework on another data set (CAL500). Results are also presented in Table 1.

If we closely analyse the behaviours of the algorithms, we observe that with the change of domain and learner, different objective functions were shown to be effective. For both the base learners in emotion data set, minimum Hamming loss is achieved by CLR while maximum subset accuracy is achieved in LP. While in CAL500 data set, minimum Hamming loss is achieved by CLR and BR; and maximum micro-averaged F-measure is achieved by CC and LP for decision tree and SVM, respectively. This shows that different algorithms optimise different objectives while using the same MOO algorithm.

5 Conclusion

In this work, we have proposed an effective technique that introduces the concept of multi-objective optimization to multi-label classification. We developed a feature selection technique based on MOO that reduces the features significantly, and showed the efficacy of our proposed algorithms. In future work, we would like to optimise the parameters of base learners along with the feature selection as MOO problem for multi-label sentiment analysis.

References

1. Chang, C.C., Lin, C.J.: LibSVM: a library for support vector machines. ACM Trans. Intell. Syst. Technol. **2**(3) (2011). Article No. 27
2. Deb, K.: Multi-objective Optimization Using Evolutionary Algorithms. Wiley, Chichester (2001)
3. Khan, M.A., Ekbal, A., Loza Mencía, E., Fürnkranz, J.: Multi-objective optimisation-based feature selection for multi-label classification. Technical report TUD-KE-2017-01, Knowledge Engineeering Group, TU Darmstadt (2017)
4. Quinlan, J.R.: C4.5: Programs for Machine Learning. Morgan Kaufmann Publishers Inc., San Francisco (1993)
5. Tsoumakas, G., Katakis, I.: Multi-label classification: an overview. Int. J. Data Warehouse. Mining **3**, 1–13 (2007)
6. Tsoumakas, G., Katakis, I., Vlahavas, I.P.: Mining multi-label data. In: Data Mining and Knowledge Discovery Handbook, 2nd edn., pp. 667–685 (2010)

Information Extraction

WikiTrends: Unstructured Wikipedia-Based Text Analytics Framework

Michel Naim Gerguis(✉), Cherif Salama, and M. Watheq El-Kharashi

Computer and Systems Engineering Department, Ain Shams University, Cairo 11517, Egypt
michel.naim.naguib.gerguis@gmail.com,
{cherif.salama,watheq.elkharashi}@eng.asu.edu.eg

Abstract. WikiTrends is a new analytics framework for Wikipedia articles. It adds the temporal/spatial dimensions to Wikipedia to visualize the extracted information converting the big static encyclopedia to a vibrant one by enabling the generation of aggregated views in timelines or heat maps for any user-defined collection from unstructured text. Data mining techniques were applied to detect the location, start and end year of existence, gender, and entity class for 4.85 million pages. We evaluated our extractors over a small manually tagged random set of articles. Heat maps of notable football players' counts over history or dominant occupations in some specific era are samples of WikiTrends maps while timelines can easily illustrate interesting fame battles over history between male and female actors, music genres, or even between American, Italian, and Indian films. Through information visualization and simple configurations, WikiTrends starts a new experience in answering questions through a figure.

Keywords: Data mining · Entity analytics · Entity classification · Fine-grained classification · Text analytics · Text classification · Text understanding · Wikipedia

1 Introduction

Steve Jobs once said: "You cannot connect the dots looking forward; you can only connect them looking backwards". Recently, digital humanities is gaining more attention to modeling and summarizing history. Michel et al. [18] introduced Culturomics. They conducted quantitative analysis on Google Books to study changes over around 200 years. An interesting observation raised our concerns, that people rise to fame only to be forgotten. They highlighted the increasing tendency to forget the old. We believe that history is an experienced instructor that everyone should learn from. Sometimes you may need to look thoroughly at the history in order to be able to understand the present and even to predict the future.

Au Yeung and Jatowt [4] conveyed the same message through Google news archive. Past time references were collected in country-centric views to define

F. Frasincar et al. (Eds.): NLDB 2017, LNCS 10260, pp. 45–57, 2017.
DOI: 10.1007/978-3-319-59569-6_6

automatically why the past was remembered. Also, Huet et al. [10] analyzed Le Monde archive and Hoffart et al. [9] mined news sources in real time. Both approaches leveraged the power of linking entity mentions to a knowledge base, YAGO. To the best of our knowledge, WikiTrends is the first framework to target text analytics from Wikipedia unstructured content. WikiTrends implicitly assumes that any entity is famous/important if it finds its way to Wikipedia in one or more languages. Consequently, the most famous ones are the ones that are found in all Wikipedia languages.

WikiTrends plugged in a set of extractors to add meta tags for every Wikipedia article. Consequently, every entity page was tagged with a start and end year of existence, and a location/nationality whenever possible. The time and location references act as the basic information units in WikiTrends to start building timelines and heat maps. Then, two more extractors were added to complete our story in which we can visualize, using heat maps and timelines, any type of extracted information. A gender tag was added to every person page or neutral if not applicable. Also, a types extractor adds several fine and coarse grained types, entity classes, to each page. The combined view of this information could be used to generate lots of reports based on simple configurations to align with the users' interest.

We define the novelty of WikiTrends in combining lots of different simple methods mentioned in various previous tasks in Wikipedia to build such a framework to visualize the extracted information from the unstructured content. We believe that the main extractors which add the temporal/spatial dimensions to every article are now in place to convert Wikipedia to a vibrant encyclopedia. The framework is designed to be easily extended. More extractors could be easily integrated in order to scale to new information types not only gender and entity types. Hence, the same experience of information visualization, using timelines and heat maps, could be leveraged. Now, in a simple figure, without any description, you can answer complicated questions like what was the leading country in producing movies in the nineties? Or what was the distribution of memorable people in the world before and after the world war? And many more.

We can summarize our main contributions as follows: (1) WikiTrends, a generic Wikipedia-based analytics framework that can be easily configured and extended and (2) Hybrid systems for time, location, gender, and entity type extraction from Wikipedia articles. WikiTrend's implementation and the data set are made available for the research community upon request. The paper is organized as follows: In Sect. 2, we summarize previous efforts. The main WikiTrends modules are discussed in Sect. 3. Section 4 presents our evaluation and results. Finally, we conclude and we discuss some future work in Sect. 5.

2 Related Work

There is a huge amount of previous efforts in text/news analytics that inspired us. Previous work could be classified into two categories: static and real time. Static analytics is based on some corpora like Google Books or any news archive.

WikiTrends relies on Wikipedia so, it can be classified in the static analytics group. Real time analytics encompasses all approaches that tackles a vibrant environment like news RSS feeds or Twitter streams. Another possible classification is that some efforts were timeline-centric, whereas others were map-centric. Some systems, including WikiTrends, combined both flavors [5]. One can also, classify analytics based on the adopted extraction techniques.

N-grams frequency is a widely used technique to address analytics, which requires a further step to select out of the huge database of n-grams what to preview. Due to the simplicity of n-grams frequency technique, it was considered in many languages [21] and also many specific studies like tracking universities' rankings [26], individualistic words and phrases [31], emotion words [1], changes in beliefs about old people [19], marketing evolution [14], and changes in topics in ACM articles [24]. Using language modeling techniques in a predefined timeline, Kestemont et al. [13] automatically extracted the spikes. N-grams frequency technique relies on collecting data first and then, searching, whereas language modeling techniques typically relies on specifying the needed information first to learn instantaneously. Both flavors are supported in WikiTrends.

Twitter and RSS feeds also, attracted a good traffic of efforts due to their vibrant environment like tracking the public adoption of scientific terms [32], summarizing Wold Cup matches [2]. Using a microblogging environment like Twitter could enable such systems to collect more scattered data acting as a random set of the whole world's opinion. Chen et al. [6] aggregated RSS feeds after extracting spatial and temporal mentions to add a new exploring experience based of two dimensions. Using simple text mining methods, Martins et al. [17] displayed extracted information out of RSS feeds on timelines and maps. No language barriers there [22] except if one view representing the whole world is targeted. Methods of translation could help achieving this. Unfortunately, both systems did not produce real time analytics. WikiTrends lacks the real time flavor due to relying on an encyclopedia. Real representation of the whole world could be achieved through Wikipedia language versions.

More advanced techniques entered the game. Named entity extraction and entity linking were also introduced in the analytics task rather than using n-grams counts [9]. However, the scalability of such systems to any type or even any language is limited by the availability of corresponding entity extractors. A reasonable compromise was made possible by collecting entities from a knowledge base then, matching in the text [10]. Sentiment/Opinion mining [15] and also, topic modeling [4] had a share in some analytics methods. WikiTrends tackled analytics out of entity classes and gender after stamping time and location references for the whole Wikipedia.

Takahashi et al. [29], Hoffart et al. [8], and Strötgen and Gertz [27] share the same playground, Wikipedia, with us. Takahashi et al. evaluated the significance of each entity based on its spatio-temporal effect. The more the entity can influence others far temporally and spatially, the more it can be considered significant. WikiTrends is more about groups significance rather than individuals. Hoffart et al. introduced YAGO2 in which they added temporal and spatial dimensions to Wikipedia articles in YAGO. Strötgen and Gertz used spatial and temporal dimensions to build document profiles. They built the document profiles out of the time and location mentions in the sentences not summarizing the whole document to one location and one or two points in the timeline like WikiTrends.

3 The WikiTrends Framework

This section presents the main building blocks of WikiTrends (Fig. 1). WikiTrends consists of three main modules: a parser, a bunch of extractors, and the analytics generator.

3.1 WikiTrends Parser

The main objective of WikiTrends parser is to convert the raw form of Wikipedia XML dump to a clean one. The parser also cleans HTML tags and irrelevant specific markups like files, images, media references, tables, comments, and many more. Moreover, it resolves hyperlinks, categories, headings and some templates. Also, the parser runs through a pipeline of NLP components, sentence breaker, tokenizer, stemmer, and a part-of-speech tagger in order to prepare the articles content for WikiTrends extractors.

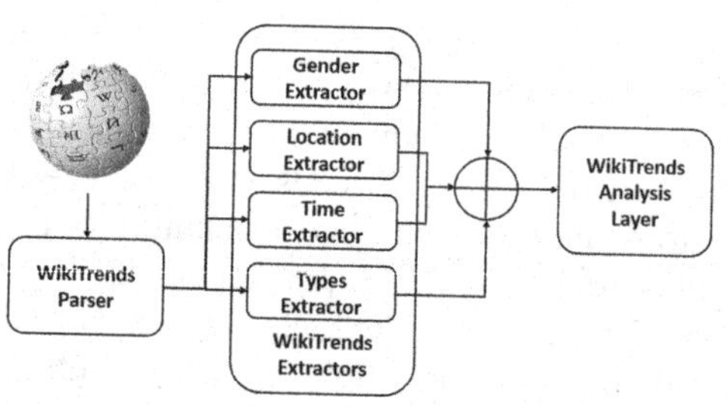

Fig. 1. WikiTrends block diagram.

3.2 WikiTrends Extractors

The extractors are the core WikiTrends components. Currently, WikiTrends consists of four extractors. Lots of extractors could be easily integrated to increase WikiTrends usability. The Gender extractor assigns each page a gender, male, female, or neutral. The location extractor aims to pinpoint each page on a map by extracting its origin. The origin could be the nationality for person pages or the location of some entity types like universities, rivers, villages, and stadiums. Other types like novels, paintings, or albums could leverage the nationality of the artist/band released them. The third extractor is the time extractor which tries to map the existence of each page on a timeline by pinpointing the start and end year of existence. Some entity types have start and end like persons and events while others can have only one point on the timeline like poems, games, or books. Finally, the types extractor assigns as much tags, entity classes, as possible. Tags could be song, guitarist, rock album, or horror film. WikiTrends is an easily extended framework in the way that new data types could be integrated through new extractors from unstructured data or adjusting the schema of some structured resources.

Gender Extractor. To assign the gender for each Wikipedia article, we experimented with four different techniques. Finally, we built a hybrid layer to leverage them all to increase the coverage.

1. From Categories: A short precise list of keywords was collected to detect male and female pages out of their categories. The unique list of Wikipedia categories then presented to these two matchers to assign a male or female tag. The matching process resulted in 7,686 male and 7,635 female categories out of 931,719 unique ones. Only 5 categories matched both tags so we ignored them favoring the precision. Finally, we propagated the tag to each article in the category. This propagation resulted in multiple tags per article as each article in Wikipedia potentially has more than one category. Majority voting was used to decide the final tag.

2. From List Pages: The same method using the previous keywords applied for a unique collection of Wikipedia list pages. The list page simply collects similar pages like "List of universities in South Sudan" or "List of Spanish films of 1950". List pages can be easily fetched using the "List of" marker. The matching process resulted in 269 male and 412 female list pages out of 70,062 unique ones. Also, majority voting was used after propagating the tag from list pages.

3. From Page Text: Pronouns were used to detect the gender of any Wikipedia article [20,33]. We built three lists for male, female, and neutral. Male list consists of he, him, his, and himself while the female one contains she, her, hers, and herself. The neutral list has it, its, and itself. The extractor counts the occurrences of any matching using the three lists within the whole article. The largest count determines the tag.

4. From First Paragraph: Using the same technique and keywords' lists, we reduced the search space to the first paragraph only. Relying that the first Wikipedia paragraph is the abstract of the whole article which should lead to precise extraction.

5. Hybrid System: We implemented a hybrid layer after reviewing the accuracy and coverage of each one of the extractors (Sect. 4.2). The hybrid system is based on majority voting.

Location Extractor. In order to tackle the location extractor, we collected a list of nationalities from Wikipedia categories. The list contains 265 nationalities which covers countries as well as colonies and other territories. We experimented with three different approaches and a hybrid layer on top of them.

1. From Categories: The same keywords matching technique was adopted using the nationalities list. Each category was assigned a nationality or more, if possible. The matching process assigned 166,488 categories some nationalities (18%). Then, the tags were propagated to the articles.

2. From List Pages: Using the same nationalities list, we matched against the list pages to propagate the labels to corresponding pages. 9,672 list pages were classified (14%).

3. From Definition Sentences: Kazama and Torisawa [12] previously defined the Wikipedia definition sentence to be the noun phrase after a copula in the first sentence. The definition sentence for Viktor Simov is: "was a

Russian painter and scenographer". We extracted the definition sentence and then matched it against the list.

4. Hybrid System: The location extractor extracts as much nationalities as possible mentioned in the definition sentence, list pages and categories. So, the resultant unique list could be a long list of four or five ones. We set a limit to only two to favor the precision. As a result, if our extractors produced more than two nationalities for any article, we would deem them buggy extractions and ignore them all. After we evaluated each of the three extractors (Sect. 4.3), we decided on how to implement the hybrid layer. The hybrid layer here is simply collecting the nationalities from each extractor ranking them by frequency. Also, we set the maximum number of possible extractions to two in the hybrid layer to favor the precision.

Time Extractor. The time extraction module aims to add the temporal dimension to our framework. Mapping the existence of entities is a tricky task. Some entity classes could be mapped using 2 points in the timeline, a starting point and an ending one, like persons through birth and death dates. One point could be sufficient to map other entity classes like films, novels, and songs through the release date. We propose a simplification to this task in which we define the start date and the end date by years only. As lots of Wikipedia categories have time mentions, we decided to rely on Years categories [29].

First, we collected all categories with a sequence of digits and analyzed the top frequent 2,000. We encountered some cases in which there is a potential mention but it is not specified by a year like 1920s short films and 4th-century Christian saints. We decided to ignore non concisely specified years. Then, we replaced every digit sequence by a marker to cluster the similar categories together ordering them by frequency. Category "2007 Copa America players" after normalization becomes "NUM Copa America players". All patterns with frequency greater than 200 were analyzed. Finally, we concluded a list of patterns to extract the start/end years. Samples of the start year patterns are: "NUM establishments", "NUM births", and "opened in NUM". "NUM disestablishments" and "NUM .+ endings" are samples of end year patterns. Another group could be used in both sides like: "NUM elections", "NUM .+ films", and "NUM .+ singles". Those patterns mainly target single point entities on the timeline. The patterns succeeded in extracting start years from 71,530 categories (8%) and end years from 29,764 categories (3%). After propagating the years to articles, we ignored the extractions if the same article has more than one start or end year. Evaluation process detailed in Sect. 4.4.

Types Extractor. The role of the types extractor is defined as: collect as much entity classes as possible. Wikipedia has lots of potential resources, semi-structured or unstructured, for the types whether to be fine or coarse grained. The extractor adds every tag with a specific marker to distinguish the source it comes from. The resources we used as types are: (1) Page category, (2) Category head noun stemmed [12], (3) List page names after trimming "list of" marker, (4) List page head noun stemmed, (5) Definition sentence, (6) Definition sentence head noun [28], and (7) Infobox title.

3.3 WikiTrends Analysis Layer

After extracting all of the needed pieces of information, WikiTrends analysis layer can start generating lots of aggregated views through timelines or heat maps. One key aspect is that the reports leverage head entities, entities which anyone could think of searching for. A heat map of the number of football players per country, a timeline comparing famous males and females across the history of humanity, the dominance of occupations over history, aggregated view of people representing each country and many more could be generated in WikiTrends. We claim that WikiTrends is an easily configured framework and this claim is tightly coupled with its analytics layer. By configurations, we mean: (1) whether to use timelines or heatmaps? (2) whether to include gender or not? (3) whether to specify a period of time, leave it open at one side or both sides, or to ignore the time? (4) whether to use some selected locations, all possible ones, or disable location? (5) whether to specify entity types to be fine grained or coarse grained or to ignore them? The following subsections will present just samples of what the analysis layer can generate.

Types Tracking Timelines. By combining the data from the time extractor and the types one, WikiTrends can generate lots of reports to illustrate trending types on a timeline. The module accepts as inputs: (1) a start year, (2) an end year, and (3) a set of entity types to track, each represented by a positive keywords list for structured search. If the start or the end years or both were not specified, the module collects all the data without boundaries in time.

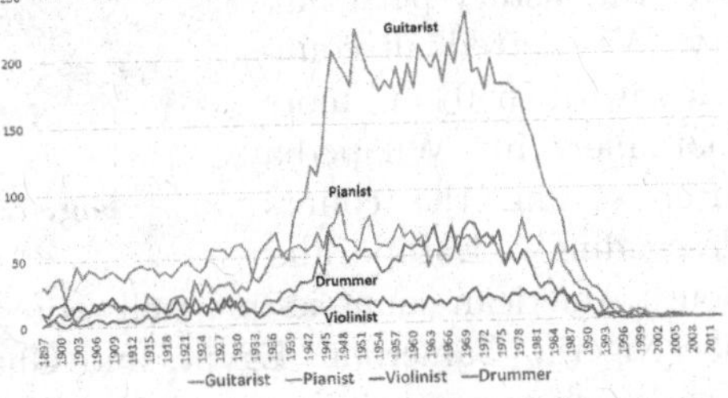

Fig. 2. Count of musicians per instrument over years.

Trending Musical Instrument. We tracked musical instruments by tracking musicians relying on WikiTrends fine-grained entity classes. Figure 2 summarizes the musical instruments' battle. Recently, guitar seems to be the most trending instrument while piano proved to be the classic one. Drums gained more interest in mid 1940s while the violin positioned as the instrument with the least adopters.

Trending Film Genre. We then, tracked a set of film genres (Fig. 3). The two competitors are drama and comedy films while drama won most of the rounds. Romance films scored their peak in 2013. Science fiction could be considered a recent genre as it first appeared in mid 1950s. Horror films gained more interest in the 21st century. A good deal of correlation is found between our timeline and the streamgraph of the most popular IMDB [11] keywords attached with movies [25].

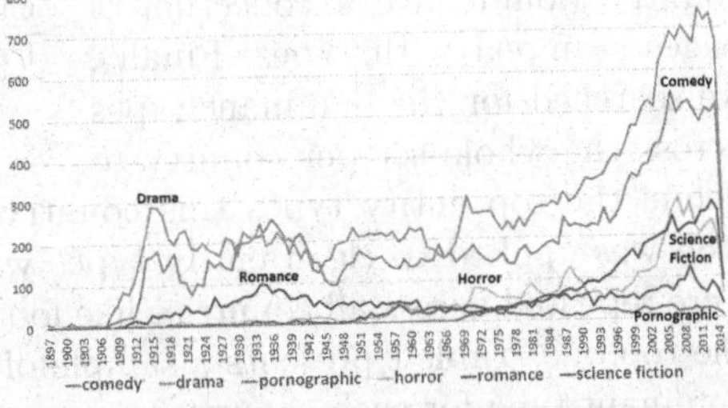

Fig. 3. Count of films released per genre over years.

Types Tracking Heat Maps. Like we tracked the entity types with timelines, we adjusted the data to be country-centric through the location pin points we extracted. Bing maps were adopted to plot our heat maps while circle notations were preferred over color gradients for readability. The configuration of the tracking heat maps is an easy task. The module accepts: (1) a set of locations to work on and (2) one entity type that can be represented by a list of positive matching keywords and another negative one. If the first input, the locations, was not set, the module assumes that its scope is open for all countries. We just represent a sample of the heat maps that could be generated out of the module.

Footballers Heat Map. Across humanities, what are the top countries presented famous footballers? Figure 4 summarizes a world view of the footballers' count in Wikipedia over the history per country. We plotted all countries with 350 or more footballer in Wikipedia after sorting the counts descendingly. Europe and South American countries are well represented. Few African countries are there like Nigeria, Cameroon, Egypt, and Ghana correlating with the real ranking. Two glitches appeared in the United States and Australia because of American and Australian football.

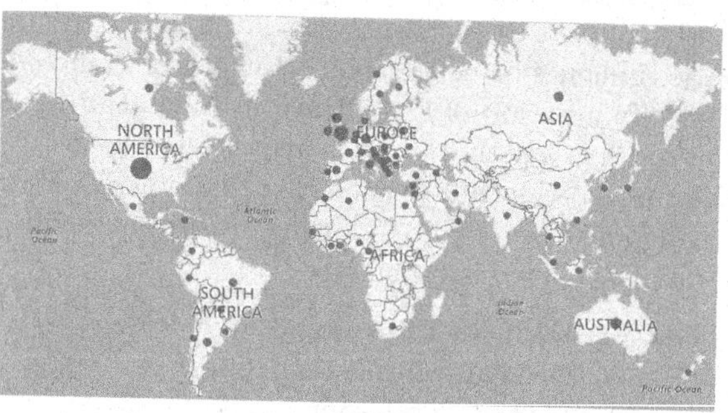

Fig. 4. Count of footballers over countries.

Country-Centric Unforgettable Additions To Humanity. We were interested to find out the unforgettable additions for each country to the humanity. First, we combined the data from the location and types extractors. Then, we divided the set to be country-centric so that each country would have a collection of pages stamped with types. Finally, we searched for the dominant types across the whole set per country to define the top entity types this country is distinguished for. A last filtration step was applied to clean entity types with low information gain, entities that were repeated across all countries like footballers, politicians, and films, to select the top one. Table 1 presents a sample of WikiTrends findings for assigning the dominant type for each country.

Table 1. Sample of unforgettable additions to humanity per country.

Country	Type	Country	Type
England	Albums	Hong Kong	Companies
Egypt	Saints	Austria	Composers
Ethiopia	Runners	South Africa	Cricketers
Italy	Painters	Mongolia	Wrestlers
France	Writers	Luxembourg	Cyclists
China	Games	Cook island	Birds
Ireland	Hurlers	Venezuela	Telenovelas

4 Evaluation

In this section, we present our efforts to evaluate each one of the extractors. Ultimately, we aim precise extractors with good coverage.

4.1 Test Set

A random collection of 100 Wikipedia articles were sampled and tagged manually.

We tagged the gender (male, female, or neutral). Zero or more locations or nationalities were added when applicable. We had to accept that a single page could have multiple origins to address persons with more than one nationality or birds originated in many countries. Finally, we tagged the start/end years of existence. In some cases, only the start or the end year was available. In other cases, the year was not stated concisely (e.g., 1940s or 19th century) so we tagged it as None. Entity types were out of the evaluation scope as we adopted a search technique. For the dominance of each tag in our test set, we have managed to tag 83% of the test set with locations, 25% with genders, 43% with start dates, and 29% with end dates.

Table 2. WikiTrends extractors evaluation.

Technique	P	R	F1
Gender: Categories	100%	40%	57%
Gender: List Pages	100%	4%	8%
Gender: Page Text	73%	96%	83%
Gender: First Parag	82%	56%	67%
Gender: Hybrid	73%	96%	83%
Location: Categories	93%	95%	94%
Location: List Pages	99%	99%	99%
Location: Def. Sent	99%	99%	99%
Location: Hybrid	92%	94%	93%
Time: Start Year	97%	74%	84%
Time: End Year	95%	69%	80%

4.2 Gender Extractor Evaluation

We implemented four extractors to tackle the gender extraction problem. Although Nguyen et al. [20] and Wu and Weld [33] reported using pronouns to anchor the primary entity in any Wikipedia article, no formal evaluation for the heuristic was reported. We evaluated our four gender extractors and the hybrid one over the labeled test set. Table 2 reports the precision, recall, and f1-score for each extractor. After running the gender extractors over the whole English dump, we report the success rate of each extractor separately and also the hybrid one (Table 3). Although the precision and recall numbers of the hybrid system are the same as the page text gender extractor, the coverage of the hybrid is somehow better.

Table 3. Gender extraction coverage.

Technique	Male	Female
Categories	0.15M (3.1%)	0.12M (2.5%)
List Pages	0.01M (0.1%)	0.02M (0.4%)
Page Text	1.39M (28.5%)	0.30M (6.3%)
First Parag	0.70M (14.4%)	0.17M (3.5%)
Hybrid	1.42M (29.3%)	0.34M (6.9%)

4.3 Location Extractor Evaluation

Hoffart et al. tackled the same problem by adding a spatial dimension to Wikipedia in YAGO2. They used the co-ordinate template, available as a structured data in some articles. We implemented a quick extractor to identify the number of articles with coord template to find only 14.4% out of the whole English dump. We relied on three approaches to extract WikiTrends's spatial dimension which successfully tagged 44% of the articles with locations. YAGO2 reported 95% accuracy by manually judging a random sample out of the extracted information.

As the evaluation was performed on a selected sample of the output, there is a limitation on calculating the recall. Dbpedia [7] also, attaches spatial data to their KB but no evaluation numbers were reported due to the human intervention in the tagging process. Table 2 summarizes our evaluation of the location extractors. Also, the coverage of each extractor over the entire English dump is presented in Table 4. We decided not to eliminate the categories-based extractor in the hybrid system for more coverage while preserving an acceptable precision level.

Table 4. Location extraction coverage.

Technique	1 Location	1 or more
Categories	1.44M (29.7%)	1.80M (37.2%)
List Pages	0.37M (7.7%)	0.44M (9.1%)
Def. Sent	1.02M (21.0%)	1.06M (21.9%)
Hybrid	1.76M (36.3%)	2.14M (44.0%)

4.4 Time Extractor Evaluation

YAGO2 and Dbpedia shared the same task in adding temporal dimension for Wikipedia entities. YAGO2 relied on infoboxes and categories. Random selection was used to evaluate the accuracy. For Dbpedia, no results were reported, to the best of our knowledge. We evaluated separately the start extractor and the end one (Table 2). The propagation of the tagged categories with time mentions to Wikipedia articles resulted in around 1 million articles stamped with both tags. The numbers of articles stamped with only one and more than one start/end markers are summarized in Table 5. Although the ratios of more than one time mention are ignorable, those articles could be considered for revision. In many cases, we found a mismatch between categories' and definition sentence's time mention. So we decided to reject every article that contains more than one start or end year.

Table 5. Time extraction coverage.

Technique	1 time mention	More than 1
Start Year	1.93M (39.9%)	0.07M (1.4%)
End Year	1.01M (20.8%)	0.02M (0.5%)

5 Conclusion and Future Work

WikiTrends created a new analytics layer out of a source of semi-structured and unstructured data. WikiTrends can generate any mix of data to present a new understating of the world through timelines and heat maps. More and more information types could be easily added. Simply to add new ingredients, we just need to implement a new extractor, give it a run over Wikipedia, register the data in the loading phase, and provide a new API for the new view. In order for the analysis layer to be faster, we used a batch processing mode in mining the data rather than extracting on the fly. Presented analytics reports seem to be similar to lots of previous efforts, but WikiTrends presents a tool for anyone to simply configure and use anytime. Although lots of projects started to build analytics out of Dbpedia [23], each one is an independent project in which data is fetched from KB, prepared, and then presented while WikiTrends can be configured to produce same reports in only one generic framework.

For the extension of this effort, lots of information types could enrich WikiTrends by either implementing new extractors from scratch or relying on structured or semi-structured sources like DBpedia. Our concern is that, it provides the information using lots of relations that need to be unified based on our definition. Not only entities but also, relations could be a potential extension to apply analytics on. We need to experiment with semi-structured data from Wikipedia Infoboxes. The infoboxes were potential sources but we found that only 51% of the articles have infoboxes so we did not want to lose half of the data power. Another issue is that there is no unified schema for the infoboxes because any author can create, edit, or change the templates so we preferred the reported techniques. WikiTrends visualized lots of data only in aggregated views. Extending the experience for individual articles could be of great value [3,30]. Holistic view of the world could be achieved by leveraging Wikipedia in multiple languages to address local entities and language/country specific uniqueness values [16]. Also, the world could be compared from different perspectives.

References

1. Acerbi, A., Lampos, V., Garnett, P., Bentley, R.A.: The expression of emotions in 20th century books. PloS One **8**(3), e59030 (2013)
2. Alonso, O., Shiells, K.: Timelines as summaries of popular scheduled events. In: 22nd International Conference on World Wide Web, pp. 1037–1044. ACM (2013)
3. Althoff, T., Dong, X.L., Murphy, K., Alai, S., Dang, V., Zhang, W.: Timemachine: timeline generation for knowledge-base entities. In: 21th ACM SIGKDD International Conference on Knowledge Discovery and Data Mining, pp. 19–28 (2015)
4. Au Yeung, C.M., Jatowt, A.: Studying how the past is remembered: towards computational history through large scale text mining. In: 20th ACM International Conference on Information and Knowledge Management, pp. 1231–1240 (2011)
5. Bautin, M., Ward, C.B., Patil, A., Skiena, S.S.: Access: news and blog analysis for the social sciences. In: 19th International Conference on World Wide Web, pp. 1229–1232. ACM (2010)

6. Chen, Y.F.R., Di Fabbrizio, G., Gibbon, D., Jora, S., Renger, B., Wei, B.: Geotracker: geospatial and temporal RSS navigation. In: 16th International Conference on World Wide Web, pp. 41–50. ACM (2007)
7. Dbpedia. http://wiki.dbpedia.org/. Accessed 1 June 2017
8. Hoffart, J., Suchanek, F.M., Berberich, K., Weikum, G.: YAGO2: a spatially and temporally enhanced knowledge base from wikipedia. Artif. Intell. **194**, 28–61 (2013)
9. Hoffart, J., Milchevski, D., Weikum, G.: Aesthetics: analytics with strings, things, and cats. In: 23rd ACM International Conference on Conference on Information and Knowledge Management, pp. 2018–2020 (2014)
10. Huet, T., Biega, J., Suchanek, F.M.: Mining history with Le Monde. In: 2013 Workshop on Automated Knowledge Base Construction, pp. 49–54. ACM (2013)
11. IMDB. http://www.imdb.com/. Accessed 1 June 2017
12. Kazama, J.I., Torisawa, K.: Exploiting wikipedia as external knowledge for named entity recognition. In: 2007 Joint Conference on Empirical Methods in Natural Language Processing and Computational Natural Language Learning (EMNLP-CoNLL), pp. 698–707 (2007)
13. Kestemont, M., Karsdorp, F., Dring, M.: Mining the twentieth centurys history from the time magazine corpus. In: European Chapter of the Association for Computational Linguistics, EACL, vol. 62 (2014)
14. Kumar, N., Sahu, M.: The evolution of marketing history: a peek through google ngram viewer. Asian J. Manag. Res. **1**(2), 415–426 (2011)
15. Leetaru, K.: Culturomics 2.0: forecasting large-scale human behavior using global news media tone in time and space. First Monday **16**(9) (2011)
16. Mahdisoltani, F., Biega, J., Suchanek, F.: YAGO3: a knowledge base from multilingual wikipedias. In: 7th Biennial Conference on Innovative Data Systems Research, CIDR (2014)
17. Martins, B., Manguinhas, H., Borbinha, J.: Extracting and exploring the geo-temporal semantics of textual resources. In: 2008 IEEE International Conference on Semantic Computing, pp. 1–9 (2008)
18. Michel, J.B., Shen, Y.K., Aiden, A.P., Veres, A., Gray, M.K., The Google Books Team, Pickett, J.P., Hoiberg, D., Clancy, D., Norvig, P., Orwant, J., Pinker, S., Nowak, M.A., Aiden, E.L.: Quantitative analysis of culture using millions of digitized books. Science **331**(6014), 176–182 (2011)
19. Ng, R., Allore, H.G., Trentalange, M., Monin, J.K., Levy, B.R.: Increasing negativity of age stereotypes across 200 years: evidence from a database of 400 million words. PloS One **10**(2), e0117086 (2015)
20. Nguyen, D.P., Matsuo, Y., Ishizuka, M.: Relation extraction from wikipedia using subtree mining. In: National Conference on Artificial Intelligence, vol. 22, no. 2, p. 1414 (2007)
21. Phani, S., Lahiri, S., Biswas, A.: Culturomics on a Bengali newspaper corpus. In: 2012 International Conference on Asian Language Processing (IALP), pp. 237–240. IEEE (2012)
22. Sasahara, K., Hirata, Y., Toyoda, M., Kitsuregawa, M., Aihara, K.: Quantifying collective attention from tweet stream. PloS One **8**(4), e61823 (2013)
23. SeeAlso. http://seealso.org/. Accessed 1 June 2017
24. Soper, D.S., Turel, O.: Who are we? Mining institutional identities using n-grams. In: 45th Hawaii International Conference on System Science (HICSS), pp. 1107–1116. IEEE (2012)
25. Sreenivasan, S.: Quantitative analysis of the evolution of novelty in cinema through crowdsourced keywords. arxiv preprint arXiv:1304.0786 (2013)

26. Stergiou, K.I., Tsikliras, A.C.: Global university reputation and rankings: insights from culturomics. Ethics Sci. Environ. Politics **13**(2), 193–202 (2013)
27. Strtgen, J., Gertz, M.: TimeTrails: a system for exploring spatio-temporal information in documents. VLDB Endowment **3**(1–2), 1569–1572 (2010)
28. Suchanek, F.M., Kasneci, G., Weikum, G.: YAGO: a core of semantic knowledge. In: 16th International Conference on World Wide Web, pp. 697–706. ACM (2007)
29. Takahashi, Y., Ohshima, H., Yamamoto, M., Iwasaki, H., Oyama, S., Tanaka, K.: Evaluating significance of historical entities based on tempo-spatial impacts analysis using wikipedia link structure. In: 22nd ACM Conference on Hypertext and Hypermedia, pp. 83–92 (2011)
30. Tuan, T.A., Elbassuoni, S., Preda, N., Weikum, G.: Cate: context-aware timeline for entity illustration. In: 20th International Conference Companion on World Wide Web, pp. 269–272. ACM (2011)
31. Twenge, J.M., Campbell, W.K., Gentile, B.: Increases in individualistic words and phrases in american books, 1960–2008. PloS One **7**(7), e40181 (2012)
32. Uren, V., Dadzie, A.S.: Relative trends in scientific terms on twitter. In: Altmetrics Workshop Held in Conjunction with the ACM 3rd International Conference on Web Science (2011)
33. Wu, F., Weld, D.S.: Open information extraction using wikipedia. In: 48th Annual Meeting of the Association for Computational Linguistics, pp. 118–127 (2010)

An Improved PLDA Model for Short Text

Chaotao Chen and Jiangtao Ren(✉)

School of Data and Computer Science, Sun Yat-sen University, Guangzhou, China
chencht3@mail2.sysu.edu.cn, issrjt@mail.sysu.edu.cn

Abstract. The boost of short texts is increasing demands for short text classification. Feature extraction based on topic models, especially those utilizing label information, such as Partially Labeled Dirichlet Allocation (PLDA), has been widely employed in normal text classification. However, the application of topic models in short text classification is still an open challenge due to the shortness and sparse nature of short texts. In this paper, we propose a topic model called Short Text PLDA (ST-PLDA) based on PLDA for short text classification. In ST-PLDA, each short text is restricted to one label and assumed to be generated from a single topic associated with its label and a background topic shared by all texts. Thus, ST-PLDA is expected to discover more compact and discriminative topic representations. Extensive experiments are conducted on real-world short text collections and the promising results demonstrate the superiority of ST-PLDA compared with other state-of-the-art methods.

Keywords: Topic model · Short text classification

1 Introduction

With the rapid development of e-commerce, online publishing, instant messaging and social media, short texts including tweets, search snippet, blog posts and product reviews are now everywhere in our daily life. As a result, there is an increasing demand for short text classification, such as sentiment analysis in tweets, offensive content detection in comments and news categorization. However, because of word sparseness, lack of context information and informal sentence expression in short texts, traditional text mining methods have limitations in automatic classification for short texts.

Latent topic models [2,5,6,12] have been widely used in text mining to discover the thematic contents of documents. The basic idea of topic models is to learn the topics from document collections under the assumption that each document is generated from a multinomial distribution over topics, where a topic is a multinomial distribution over words. Compared with traditional text features such as TF-IDF word features, the features induced by topic models can alleviate the problem of sparsity and provide more semantic information, which improves the performance of text classification. Several topic models have been proposed to make use of label information for text classification, such as labeled

F. Frasincar et al. (Eds.): NLDB 2017, LNCS 10260, pp. 58–70, 2017.
DOI: 10.1007/978-3-319-59569-6_7

LDA [9] and PLDA [10]. Specifically, for texts annotated with labels, PLDA can discover the hidden topics within each label, as well as background topics not associated with any label, which further enhances classification performance.

Although topic models have gained success in normal text classification, topic models for short text classification are still a challenging problem. In real applications, a short text may be bound up with a small number of topics that often have no relation to others due to its length restriction. Therefore, the direct application of conventional topic models like PLDA in short texts may not work well. Given that a tweet usually involves one single topic, Twitter-LDA [14] assumes that a tweet can be generated from only one topic chosen from the user's topic distribution and one background topic shared by all tweets. Although Twitter-LDA is suitable for short texts, it does not make use of label information, and therefore is less competitive in solving the problems of short text classification.

Motivated by the researches on probabilistic topic models above, we propose a new model, Short Text PLDA (ST-PLDA) based on PLDA and Twitter-LDA, which makes use of label information and topic restriction in short texts. Similar to PLDA, we assume the existence of latent topics within each label as well as background topic class shared by all texts. In most case, short texts contain little semantic information, and as a result, they do not cover many labels and topics. So we assume that each short text has only one label and restrict it to be generated from only two topics, one from the topic class associated with its label, and the other from background topic class shared by all texts. Such a restriction is consistent with the nature of short texts, and it improves the compactness of the derived topics, which further contributes to classification performance. Extensive experiments on three real-world short text datasets demonstrate that the proposed model is superior to some state-of-the-art baseline models.

The contribution of this paper lies in that we propose a model that not only exploits label information to discover latent topics within each label, but also restricts the number of topics in each text to adapt to the nature of short text, so that discriminative topic features can be produced for short text classification.

The remainder of this paper is organized as follows: Sect. 2 discusses related works. Section 3 introduces the proposed topic model and elaborates the inference and classification methods. Section 4 presents the experiment results and analysis, and we conclude this paper in Sect. 5.

2 Related Works

One of the main challenges for text classification is the high dimensionality of feature space which not only results in high computational complexity but also is prone to overfitting problems. In recent years, feature extraction based on topic models has been widely employed in text classification. In general, topic models assume that a document is presented as a mixture of topics, where a topic is a multinomial distribution over words [2]. Then each document can be represented using topic distribution inferred by topic models, which can be combined with traditional classifier such as Support Vector Machine to achieve document classification [2,7].

Recently, several topic models, namely, sLDA [1], Labeled LDA [9] and PLDA [10], have been proposed to extract more discriminative topics for text classification, by taking advantage of document tags or labels. Labeled LDA assumes that each document is annotated with a set of observed labels, and that these labels play a direct role in generating the document's words from per-label distributions over words. However, Labeled LDA does not assume the existence of any latent topics (neither global nor within a label) [10]. Unlike Labeled LDA, PLDA assumes that each document contains several latent topics of the same class, and each is associated with one or more of the document's labels. In particular, PLDA introduces one class (consisting of multiple topics) for each label in the label set, as well as one latent class optionally applied to all documents. Obviously, PLDA is more flexible, and it can extract more semantic topics within each label for text classification.

Although topic model is suitable for normal text representative learning, it may not work well for short texts due to the sparsity of words. Some previous studies have tried to enrich the short texts with external repository to get more features. Phan et al. [8] use implicit topics derived from an external corpus to expand text features. Chen et al. [3] propose a multi-granularity topic model to generate multi-granularity topics features for short texts.

However, an appropriate external corpus is not always available or just too costly to collect. Thus, in recent years more efforts have been put on designing customized topic models for short texts. Biterm topic model (BTM) [13] is among the earliest works, which directly models word pairs (i.e. biterms) extracted from short texts. By switching from sparse document-word space to dense word-word space, BTM can learn more coherent topics than LDA. According to the observation that a single tweet is usually related to a single topic, Twitter-LDA [14] assumes that each tweet is associated with only one topic based on the user's topic distribution, and each word in a tweet is generated either from the chosen topic or a background topic shared by all tweets. Based on these prior works, we propose ST-PLDA, which combines PLDA and Twitter-LDA to make use of the label information and adapt to the nature of short texts, so as to produce more discriminative topic features for short text classification.

3 Model and Algorithms

3.1 Notation

Similar to PLDA, we formally define the following terms. Consider a collection of labeled short texts $\mathbb{D} = \{(\boldsymbol{w}_1, l_1), \ldots, (\boldsymbol{w}_D, l_D)\}$, each containing a multi-set of words $\boldsymbol{w}_d$ from a vocabulary $\mathbb{V}$ of size V and an observed single label l_d from a set of labels $\mathbb{L}$ of size L. In this work, we try to find a topic model for corpus $\mathbb{D}$ that can discover a set of discriminative topics by using label information, so that we can classify the short texts with their topic distribution representations in an effective manner.

3.2 ST-PLDA Model

A good topic representation is crucial to achieve high classification performance by topic models. Models such as sLDA, Labeled LDA and PLDA show the great enhancement of topic quality by utilizing label information in topic learning. Specifically, PLDA is more flexible and promising, since it can learn the structure of latent topics within the scope of labels. By introducing high-level constraints on latent topics to make them align with the provided labels, PLDA improves interpretability of the resulting topics and correlation with similarity judgments, and reduces running time [10]. However, PLDA is designed for normal texts and will suffer from word sparsity problem in short texts.

To overcome this problem, we borrow the idea from Twitter-LDA. In the context of short texts, e.g., Twitter, a single tweet usually involves only one topic due to its length restriction [14]. So based on PLDA, we further assume that each short text only contains one label and one topic associated with the label. This constraint is consistent with the length restriction of short texts and improves the compactness of the derived topics, which helps produce more discriminative topic representation for classification. In addition to label topics, we also need to cover the common semantics. Actually not all words in a short text are closely related to its label, and some are background words commonly used in a corpus. For example, time-related words like "Monday" and "Tuesday", which express common semantic meaning in news texts, might occur in most documents. These common words are less discriminative, so classification will be disturbed if they are assigned to a label topic. Therefore, we introduce a background topic class shared by all texts just like PLDA does, but we restrict each short text to only one background topic. As a result, each short text in ST-PLDA model is assumed to involve only one label, one topic associated with its label and one background topic.

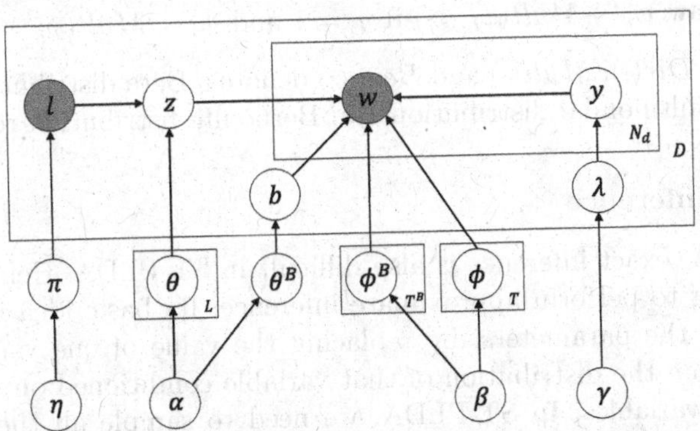

Fig. 1. Graphical model for ST-PLDA model. (Because each document's label l_d is observed, the multinomial distribution π and its prior η are unused)

Formally, ST-PLDA assumes the existence of a set of L labels in the short texts collection, as well as a background topic class. In particular, we assume that each topic takes part in exactly one label, and the total number of label topics and background topics are T and T^B, respectively. Label topic-word distributions ϕ and background topic-word distributions ϕ^B are both drawn from a symmetric Dirichlet prior β for simplicity. Label-topic distributions θ and background-topic distributions θ^B are both drawn from a symmetric Dirichlet prior α. Let z denote the label topic assignment for each short text, b denote the background topic assignment for each short text, and y denote the indicator variable for each word. The graphical model for ST-PLDA is illustrated in Fig. 1. Each short text d is generated by first picking a label l_d from corpus-wide label distribution π. Then a label topic z_d and a background topic b_d for this document are drawn from the corresponding label-topic distribution θ_{l_d} and background-topic distribution θ^B, respectively. A Bernoulli distribution λ_d that governs the choice between label words and background words is also drawn from a Beta prior γ. Each word w in document d is generated by first drawing an binary indicator variable y from λ_d, and then a word w from ϕ_{l_d,z_d} if $y = 1$ or a word w from $\phi^B_{b_d}$ if $y = 0$. The generative process for ST-PLDA is summarized as follows:

1. For each label $l \in \{1, \ldots, L\}$, draw $\theta_l \sim Dir(\alpha_l)$, where α_l is a T_l dimensional prior vector of θ_l.
2. Draw $\theta^B \sim Dir(\alpha^B)$, where α^B is a T^B dimensional prior vector of θ^B.
3. For each topic $t \in \{1, \ldots, T\}$, draw $\phi_t \sim Dir(\beta)$, where β is a V dimensional prior vector of ϕ_t.
4. For each topic $t \in \{1, \ldots, T^B\}$, draw $\phi^B_t \sim Dir(\beta)$.
5. For each document $d \in \{1, \ldots, D\}$:
   (a) Draw $z_d \sim Mult(\theta_{l_d})$.
   (b) Draw $b_d \sim Mult(\theta^B)$
   (c) Draw $\lambda_d \sim Beta(\gamma)$, where γ is a scalar prior for λ_d.
   (d) For each word $i \in \{1, \ldots, N_d\}$:
      (i) Draw $y_i \sim Bern(\lambda_d)$.
      (ii) Draw $w_i \sim Mult(\phi_{l_d,z_d})$ if $y_i = 1$ and $w_i \sim Mult(\phi^B_{b_d})$ if $y_i = 0$.

where $Beta(\cdot)$, $Dir(\cdot)$, $Mult(\cdot)$ and $Bern(\cdot)$ denote a Beta distribution, Dirichlet distribution, multinomial distribution and Bernoulli distribution respectively.

3.3 Model Inference

Similar to LDA, exact inference is also difficult in ST-PLDA. Hence, we adopt Gibbs sampling to perform approximate inference. Its basic idea is to alternatively estimate the parameters, by replacing the value of one variable with a value drawn from the distribution of that variable conditioned on the values of the remaining variables. In ST-PLDA, we need to sample all the eight types of latent variables z, b, y, ϕ, ϕ^B, θ, θ^B and λ. However, with the technique of collapsed Gibbs sampling [5], ϕ, ϕ^B, θ, θ^B and λ can be integrated out because of the conjugate priors α, β and γ. Therefore, we just need to sample the label topic assignment z and background topic assignment b for each document and also the indicator variable y for each word from their conditional distribution given the remaining variables.

We use $\boldsymbol{w}$ to denote all words observed in the corpora, $\boldsymbol{l}$ to denote all label observed in each document, and $\boldsymbol{y}$, $\boldsymbol{b}$ and $\boldsymbol{z}$ to denote all hidden variables. To perform Gibbs sampling, we first randomly choose initial states for the Markov chain. Then we calculate the conditional distribution $P(z_d|\boldsymbol{z}_{\neg d}, \boldsymbol{b}, \boldsymbol{y}, \boldsymbol{w}, \boldsymbol{l})$ and $P(b_d|\boldsymbol{z}, \boldsymbol{b}_{\neg d}, \boldsymbol{y}, \boldsymbol{w}, \boldsymbol{l})$ for each document d and $P(y_{d,i}|\boldsymbol{z}, \boldsymbol{b}, \boldsymbol{y}_{\neg d,i}, \boldsymbol{w})$ for each word $w_{d,i}$ in document d, where $\boldsymbol{z}_{\neg d}$ and $\boldsymbol{b}_{\neg d}$ denote the label topic assignments and background topic assignments for all documents except document d, respectively, and $\boldsymbol{y}_{\neg d,i}$ denotes the indicator variable assignments for all words except word $w_{d,i}$. By applying the chain rule to the joint probability of the whole data, we can easily obtain the conditional probability for z_d and b_d:

$$P(z_d = t|\boldsymbol{z}_{\neg d}, \boldsymbol{b}, \boldsymbol{y}, \boldsymbol{w}, \boldsymbol{l})$$
$$\propto I[t \in \{1, \ldots, T_{l_d}\}]\frac{c_t^{D_{l_d}} + \alpha}{c^{D_{l_d}} + T_{l_d}\alpha}\left(\frac{\Gamma(c^t + V\beta)}{\Gamma(c^t + n^t + V\beta)}\prod_{v=1}^{V}\frac{\Gamma(c_v^t + n_v^t + \beta)}{\Gamma(c_v^t + \beta)}\right) \quad (1)$$

$$P(b_d = t|\boldsymbol{z}, \boldsymbol{b}_{\neg d}, \boldsymbol{y}, \boldsymbol{w}, \boldsymbol{l})$$
$$\propto I[t \in \{1, \ldots, T^B\}]\frac{c_t^B + \alpha}{c^B + T^B\alpha}\left(\frac{\Gamma(c^t + V\beta)}{\Gamma(c^t + n^t + V\beta)}\prod_{v=1}^{V}\frac{\Gamma(c_v^t + n_v^t + \beta)}{\Gamma(c_v^t + \beta)}\right) \quad (2)$$

Here $c_t^{D_{l_d}}$ is the number of documents with observed label l_d assigned to label topic t, and $c^{D_{l_d}}$ is the total number of documents with observed label l_d and T_{l_d} is the number of topics in label l_d. c_t^B is the number of documents assigned to background topic t, while c^B is the total number of documents and T^B is the number of background topics. c_v^t is the number of times that word v is assigned to topic t, and c^t is the number of times that any word is assigned to topic t. All the counts above exclude the current document d. n_v^t is the number of times that word v is assigned to topic t in document d, and n^t is the number of times that any word is assigned to topic t in document d. Specifically, $I[t \in \{1, \ldots, T_{l_d}\}]$ denotes that only those topics in label l_d may be sampled and $I[t \in \{1, \ldots, T^B\}]$ denotes that only background topics may be sampled. Then given the assignment of z_d and b_d, the conditional probability for indicator variable $y_{d,i}$ is:

$$p(y_{d,i} = 0|\boldsymbol{b}, \boldsymbol{z}, \boldsymbol{y}_{\neg d,i}, \boldsymbol{w}) \propto \frac{c_{w_{d,i}}^{b_d} + \beta}{c^{b_d} + V\beta} \cdot \frac{c_0^d + \gamma}{c^d + 2\gamma} \quad (3)$$

$$p(y_{d,i} = 1|\boldsymbol{b}, \boldsymbol{z}, \boldsymbol{y}_{\neg d,i}, \boldsymbol{w}) \propto \frac{c_{w_{d,i}}^{z_d} + \beta}{c^{z_d} + V\beta} \cdot \frac{c_1^d + \gamma}{c^d + 2\gamma} \quad (4)$$

where $c_{w_{d,i}}^{b_d}$ is the number of times that word $w_{d,i}$ is assigned to background topic b_d, c^{b_d} is the number of times that any word is assigned to background topic b_d, $c_{w_{d,i}}^{z_d}$ is the number of times that word $w_{d,i}$ is assigned to label topic z_d, c^{z_d} is the number of times that any word is assigned to label topic z_d, c_0^d is the number of words assigned as background words in document d, c_1^d is the number of words assigned as label words in document d and c^d is the total number of words in document d.

Finally, according to the counters of topic assignments of documents, indicator variable assignments of words, and words occurrences, we can easily estimate the label topic-word distribution ϕ, background topic-word distribution ϕ^B, label-topic distribution θ and background-topic distribution θ^B as:

$$\phi_{v|t} = \frac{c_v^t + \beta}{c^t + V\beta}, \theta_{t|l} = \frac{c_t^{D_l} + \alpha}{c^{D_l} + T_l\alpha}, \phi_{v|b}^B = \frac{c_v^b + \beta}{c^b + V\beta}, \theta_b^B = \frac{c_b^B + \alpha}{c^B + T^B\alpha} \quad (5)$$

where c_v^t is the number of times that word v is assigned to label topic t, c^t is the number of times that any word is assigned to label topic t, c_v^b is the number of times that word v is assigned to background topic b, c^b is the number of times that any word is assigned to background topic b, $c_t^{D_l}$ is the number of documents with observed label l assigned to label topic t, c^{D_l} is the total number of documents with observed label l, T_l is the total number of topics in label l, c_t^B is the number of documents whose background topic is assigned to topic b, c^B is the total number of documents. A summary of the Gibbs sampling procedure is shown in Algorithm 1.

3.4 Classification

In ST-PLDA model, we first learn the topic-word distributions ϕ, ϕ^B, and the topic distribution of training texts based on training data, and then infer the topic distribution of testing data. After obtaining the topic distribution representation of training and testing data, we can use traditional classification model such as Support Vector Machine and Naive Bayes to train a classifier and test its performance. In the following experiments, we use Random Forest Classifier.

Algorithm 1. Gibbs sampling algorithm for ST-PLDA

Input: a corpus including totally V unique words and L unique labels, the expected number of topics T_l for each label l, the expected number of background topics T^B and hyperparameters α, β, γ.

Output:
label-topic distribution θ,
background-topic distribution θ^B,
label topic-word distribution ϕ and
background topic-word distribution ϕ^B.

initialize label topic assignments z and background topic assignments b for all documents and indicator variable y for all words randomly.
repeat
  for document $d = 1 : D$ **do**
    draw z_d and b_d from Eq. (1) and Eq. (2), respectively.
    for word $i = 1 : N_d$ **do**
      draw $y_{d,i}$ from Eqs. (3) and (4).
    end for
  end for
until convergence
compute the parameters ϕ, ϕ^B, θ and θ^B in Eq(5).

---

4 Experiment Analysis

4.1 Data Sets

We perform experiments on three short text collections described as follows: **News.** This dataset[1] contains 32,604 pieces of English news extracted from RSS feeds of three popular newspaper websites (nyt.com, usatoday.com, reuters.com). Categories are: sport, business, U.S., health, sci&tech, world and entertainment. All news descriptions are retained since they are typical short texts. **Comments.** This dataset consists of 15,414 Chinese text comments from the Internet. They are the posts responding to different kinds of hotspots, such as Gaming, Entertainments, News, Sciences, Sports and so on. These comments are labeled by either "offensive" or "normal". Comments with "offensive" label refer to offensive contents with profanities and abuse, sexual contents or advertisements. **Tweets.** A large set of tweets are collected and labeled by Go et al. [4]. Each tweet is labeled by its sentiment polarity (negative and positive). This dataset consists of around 104k labeled tweets and total of 39,605 tweets are sampled in our experiments. After pre-processing, the datasets of **News**, **Comments** and **Tweets** contain 12774, 8143 and 6078 distinct words and the average number of words in each text are 15.7, 12.6 and 6.1, respectively.

4.2 Classification Performance

The performance of ST-PLDA in short text classification is examined. In order to make comparisons among the classification results of different models, for each train-test partition, we first compute precision, recall and F1-score for each class and then macro-average the results across all classes.

We take four typical topic models as baseline methods: LDA, Twitter-LDA, BTM and PLDA. For LDA and PLDA, we use Stanford Topic Modeling Toolbox[2] for experiments. For BTM, we use its open-source implementation[3]. We implement Twitter-LDA and ST-PLDA with Java.

On all datasets, we randomly divide the short texts into training set and test set at the ratio of 4 : 1. For all methods, we use fixed hyperparameters of $\alpha = 0.1$ and $\beta = 0.01$, since LDA with weak priors performs better in short texts. We also set $\gamma = 20$ for ST-PLDA and Twitter-LDA the same as [15]. In all methods, Gibbs sampling is run for 1,000 iterations to guarantee convergence and the final samples are used to estimate model parameters. With the topic-word distributions acquired in training phrase, we infer the topic distribution of each text by Gibbs sampling. Then, the short texts are classified using RandomForestClassifier module of scikit-learn package[4]. For each trained topic model, we perform five-fold cross-validation on datasets. After several trials, the total number of topics is set to 36, 14, 13 on **News**, **Comments** and **Tweets** dataset,

[1] http://acube.di.unipi.it/tmn-dataset/.
[2] http://nlp.stanford.edu/software/tmt/tmt-0.4/.
[3] https://github.com/xiaohuiyan/BTM.
[4] http://scikit-learn.org/stable/index.html.

Table 1. Classification results of short text corpora.

		LDA	Twitter-LDA	BTM	PLDA	ST-PLDA
News	Recall	70.1 ± 0.4	69.9 ± 1.0	71.9 ± 0.2	74.9 ± 0.7	76.2 ± 0.7
	Precision	72.8 ± 0.5	72.9 ± 0.8	74.8 ± 0.2	77.3 ± 0.8	77.9 ± 0.6
	F1-score	71.4 ± 0.4	71.4 ± 0.9	73.3 ± 0.2	76.0 ± 0.8	77.0 ± 0.7
Comments	Recall	78.8 ± 0.8	81.2 ± 0.8	80.3 ± 1.1	85.2 ± 0.5	88.5 ± 0.3
	Precision	78.8 ± 0.8	81.2 ± 0.8	80.3 ± 1.1	85.3 ± 0.5	88.5 ± 0.4
	F1-score	78.9 ± 0.7	81.3 ± 0.7	80.4 ± 1.1	85.3 ± 0.5	88.5 ± 0.3
Tweets	Recall	64.9 ± 0.5	64.1 ± 0.5	66.2 ± 0.3	70.0 ± 0.1	72.3 ± 0.4
	Precision	65.0 ± 0.5	64.1 ± 0.5	66.3 ± 0.4	70.0 ± 0.1	72.3 ± 0.4
	F1-score	64.9 ± 0.5	64.1 ± 0.5	66.3 ± 0.4	70.0 ± 0.1	72.3 ± 0.4

respectively. And the number of background topics is set to one, because we find that one background topic is enough for these datasets. But for larger corpus, it's appropriate to set a larger value. In ST-PLDA and PLDA, the numbers of topics in the same label class are also kept consistent.

We adopt macro precision, recall and F1-score as the evaluation criteria, and list the experiment results in Table 1, with the best results highlighted in bold. As can be seen in Table 1, the best results of the three datasets are all obtained by ST-PLDA. This demonstrates the outstanding performance of ST-PLDA against baselines in learning semantic topic features for short text classification. Specifically, the notable improvement of our methods over Twitter-LDA suggests that label information contributes greatly to discovering more discriminative latent topics within each label, which further enhances classification performance. ST-PLDA also consistently outperforms PLDA on all datasets, which indicates the assumption that short text is generated from only one topic associated with its label and one background topic is feasible.

4.3 Evaluation of Topics

To further evaluate the topics learned by ST-PLDA, we analyze the latent topics quantitatively and empirically. First, we use the coherence measure C_V recommended in [11] to evaluate the quality of discovered topics. Given a set of top words (most probable words) in a topic, the measure averages the Normalized Pointwise Mutual Information (NPMI) and cosine similarity for every pair of top words within a sliding window of size 110 on an external corpus (i.e. Wikipedia). A higher C_V score implies a more coherent topic. We submit the top ten words in each discovered topics to the online Palmetto[5] topic quality measuring tool provided by [11] and record the corresponding C_V score. As Palmetto does not support Chinese currently, we only evaluate the topics discovered in **Tweets** and

[5] http://palmetto.aksw.org/palmetto-webapp/.

Table 2. Average topic coherences in **Tweets** and **News** datasets.

	LDA	Twitter-LDA	BTM	PLDA	ST-PLDA
Tweets	0.378 ± 0.008	0.386 ± 0.008	0.384 ± 0.014	0.380 ± 0.005	0.391 ± 0.005
News	0.419 ± 0.003	0.436 ± 0.003	0.428 ± 0.004	0.426 ± 0.005	0.438 ± 0.004

News datasets and summarize the results in Table 2. Obviously, our ST-PLDA gives the highest C_V scores in both **Tweets** and **News** datasets.

Another typical method to evaluate the quality of topic is to judge its top words by experience. We examine the topics discovered by ST-PLDA in **News** dataset. Table 3 shows three discovered topics under two labels (*sport* and *world*) and background topic, with each topic represented by the 13 most probable words. As we can see, in each topic, the probable words are semantically consistent with each other. And the discovered topics within each label basically describe some relevant topics, such as topics *tennis*, *football* and *basketball* in the label *sport*, topics *Death of Osama bin Laden*, *Libya conflict* and *Egypt conflict* in the label *world*, which is consistent with our understanding and expectations. Moreover, the background topic captures shared structure in news, including time-related words (e.g. Monday, Thursday) and number (e.g. one, two, first).

Table 3. Examples of topics discovered from **News** dataset by ST-PLDA.

Label	Top words
Background	said new wednesday tuesday year one two monday thursday friday first last years
Sport	open round world french masters final first championship nadal title win victory
	nfl players league team lockout sports world day football new season soccer fifa
	points game heat nba miami dallas scored mavericks season victory bulls james win
World	killed laden bin osama pakistan people al qaeda killing security officials forces police
	president forces libyan muammar government libya gaddafi leader security city rebels
	president government right bahrain egypt political police protests state human former

We also compare the topics learned by different methods. Table 4 shows an example of similar topics learned from **News** dataset by different methods. Obviously, this is a topic about Fukushima Daiichi nuclear disaster under the label *world*. The red tags are the words considered to be less correlated to the topic.

Table 4. An example of topics discovered from the **News** dataset by different methods.

Model	Top words
ST-PLDA	nuclear japan said radiation plant health food crippled earthquake levels world power water tsunami experts radioactive around fukushima
PLDA	japan nuclear radiation plant said food health day mother crippled tsunami around experts levels earthquake people power wednesday
BTM	nuclear japan plant power earthquake said tsunami crisis radiation japanese crippled fukushima tokyo friday tuesday disaster water monday
Twitter-LDA	nuclear japan plant power said radiation earthquake space crisis japanese tsunami fukushima water crippled shuttle tokyo government gas
LDA	japan nuclear power earthquake plant said tsunami japanese crisis safety radiation gas energy motor water production disaster natural

For example, "monday" is relevant to *time*, "shuttle" is relevant to *aerospace* and "production" is relevant to *industry*. As we can see, the top words learned by ST-PLDA model is more relevant to the event of Fukushima Daiichi nuclear disaster than those learned by other methods. These results above demonstrate that ST-PLDA can learn better semantic and coherence topics from short texts.

4.4 Sensitivity Analysis

The topic number plays an important role in different topic models. Due to space limitation, we only demonstrate the experiment results of **Tweets** dataset with varying topic number from 3 to 40 in Fig. 2. It is noticed that the classification performance of all methods get better as the topic number grows and converge when topic number is large. Specifically, ST-PLDA always dominates other methods regardless of the topic number. Due to the utilization of label information, ST-PLDA and PLDA can obtain better classification performance when their topic number is small, and they are less sensitive to the number of topics. These all indicate the superiority and robustness of ST-PLDA.

In contrast to LDA and PLDA, in ST-PLDA there is one more important parameter, the Beta prior γ, which controls the assignments between label topics and background topics. To examine the impact of Beta prior γ on ST-PLDA, we try different values of γ and evaluate the corresponding F1 score in classification on the three datasets. The influence of different choices of γ is illustrated in Fig. 3. As we can see, the performance increases as γ grows but becomes stable when γ is large enough ($\gamma > 10$ in this experiment). This result also indicates the robustness of our topic model with respect to the Beta prior γ.

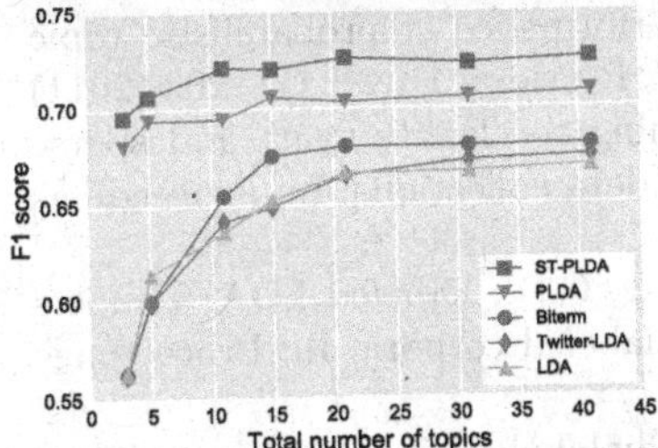

Fig. 2. Classification results of varying topic numbers in **Tweets** dataset.

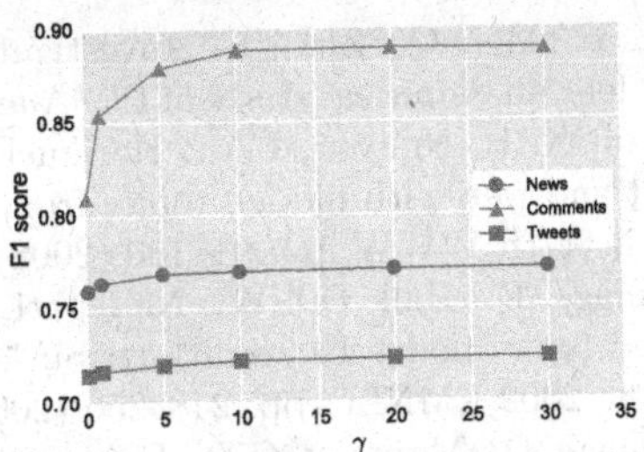

Fig. 3. Classification results of varying Beta prior γ.

5 Conclusions

Short text classification has increasingly become an important task due to the prevalence of short texts on the Internet. Although feature extraction based on topic models has been widely employed in long text classification, it is still an open problem in short text classification. In this paper, we propose a topic model called ST-PLDA, which combines PLDA and Twitter-LDA to generate good topic features for short texts. By leveraging the label information and adapting to the length restriction of short texts, ST-PLDA can be applied to discover more discriminative topic features for short text classification. Extensive experiments on real-world short texts collections demonstrate the superiority of ST-PLDA to some state-of-the-art methods, and sensitivity analysis also show the robustness of the proposed topic model.

Acknowledgments. This work was supported by the Natural Science Foundation of Guangdong Province [grant number 2015A030313125].

References

1. Blei, D.M., McAuliffe, J.D.: Supervised topic models. In: Proceedings of the 21st NIPS, pp. 121–128 (2007)
2. Blei, D.M., Ng, A.Y., Jordan, M.I.: Latent Dirichlet allocation. J. Mach. Learn. Res. **3**, 993–1022 (2003)
3. Chen, M., Jin, X., Shen, D.: Short text classification improved by learning multi-granularity topics. In: Proceedings of the 22nd IJCAI, pp. 1776–1781 (2011)
4. Go, A., Bhayani, R., Huang, L.: Twitter sentiment classification using distant supervision. CS224N project report, Stanford 1(12) (2009)
5. Griffiths, T.L., Steyvers, M.: Finding scientific topics. Proc. Natl. Acad. Sci. **101**(suppl 1), 5228–5235 (2004)
6. Hofmann, T.: Probabilistic latent semantic indexing. In: Proceedings of the 22nd International Conference on Research and Development in Information Retrieval, pp. 50–57 (1999)

7. Lu, Y., Mei, Q., Zhai, C.: Investigating task performance of probabilistic topic models: an empirical study of PLSA and LDA. Inf. Retrieval **14**(2), 178–203 (2011)
8. Phan, X.H., Nguyen, L.M., Horiguchi, S.: Learning to classify short and sparse text and web with hidden topics from large-scale data collections. In: Proceedings of the 17th WWW, pp. 91–100 (2008)
9. Ramage, D., Hall, D.L.W., Nallapati, R., Manning, C.D.: Labeled LDA: a supervised topic model for credit attribution in multi-labeled corpora. In: Proceedings of the 2009 EMNLP, pp. 248–256 (2009)
10. Ramage, D., Manning, C.D., Dumais, S.T.: Partially labeled topic models for interpretable text mining. In: Proceedings of the 17th SIGKDD, pp. 457–465 (2011)
11. Röder, M., Both, A., Hinneburg, A.: Exploring the space of topic coherence measures. In: Proceedings of the 8th WSDM, pp. 399–408 (2015)
12. Rosen-Zvi, M., Griffiths, T.L., Steyvers, M., Smyth, P.: The author-topic model for authors and documents. In: Proceedings of the 20th UAI, pp. 487–494 (2004)
13. Yan, X., Guo, J., Lan, Y., Cheng, X.: A biterm topic model for short texts. In: Proceedings of the 22nd WWW, pp. 1445–1456 (2013)
14. Zhao, W.X., Jiang, J., Weng, J., He, J., Lim, E., Yan, H., Li, X.: Comparing twitter and traditional media using topic models. In: Advances in Information Retrieval, pp. 338–349. Springer, Heidelberg (2011)
15. Zhao, W.X., Jiang, J., Weng, J., He, J., Lim, E.-P., Yan, H., Li, X.: Comparing Twitter and traditional media using topic models. In: Clough, P., Foley, C., Gurrin, C., Jones, G.J.F., Kraaij, W., Lee, H., Mudoch, V. (eds.) ECIR 2011. LNCS, vol. 6611, pp. 338–349. Springer, Heidelberg (2011). doi:10.1007/978-3-642-20161-5_34

Mining Incoherent Requirements in Technical Specifications

Patrick Saint-Dizier(✉)

IRIT - CNRS, Toulouse Cedex, France
stdizier@irit.fr

Abstract. Requirements are designed to specify the features of systems. Even for a simple system, several thousands of requirements produced by different authors are often needed. It is then frequent to observe overlap and incoherence problems. In this paper, we propose a method to construct a corpus of various types of incoherences and a categorization that leads to the definition of patterns to mine incoherent requirements. We focus in this contribution on incoherences (1) which can be detected solely from linguistic factors and (2) which concern pairs of requirements. These represent about 60% of the different types of incoherences; the other types require extensive domain knowledge and reasoning.

Keywords: Linguistics of requirements · Incoherence analysis

1 Motivations and Objectives

Requirements (or business rules) form a specific class of documents with specific functions: they are designed to describe a task, a regulation or any kind of situation in a sound way. A requirement may be composed of a conclusion alone or be associated with one or more supports that justify it (these supports are usually called the rationale' of the requirement). In some specifications, warnings describe the consequences of not following requirements, while advice describe optional requirements that may improve e.g. the result of a task. Both warnings and advice are specific forms of arguments [1]. Requirements state in a declarative way e.g. the features a product should have, the way an organization should be managed via rules, etc. Even for a small product, several thousands of requirements are often necessary.

In spite of numerous authoring guidelines, unclear, ambiguous, incomplete or poorly written requirements are relatively frequent. This results in a significant waste of time to understand a specification, in difficulties to update, trace and re-use these specifications, and, more importantly, in risks of misconceptions by users or manufacturers leading to incorrect realizations or exposure to health or ecological risks. Controlling how requirements are written, independently of whether guidelines are followed or not, is a high and fast return-on-investment activity. For example, in the maintenance sector, poorly written requirements can entail extra costs up to 80% of the initial product development costs.

F. Frasincar et al. (Eds.): NLDB 2017, LNCS 10260, pp. 71–83, 2017.
DOI: 10.1007/978-3-319-59569-6_8

The different protagonists involved in requirement production is a source of mismatches, inconsistencies and redundancies: stakeholders, technical writers, validators, users and manufacturers may all play different roles and have different views on the requirements. This is developed in e.g. [4,13–15,17]. Most industrial sectors have now defined authoring recommendations, methods and tools (e.g. Doors), to elaborate, structure and write requirements of various kinds, e.g. for easier traceability, control and update. However, our experience shows that those recommendations, in spite of the existing tools, cannot strictly be observed in particular for very large sets of requirements. Authoring tools have emerged two decades ago, e.g. one of the first investigated at Boeing [16], then at IBM with Acrolink and Doors, and, more recently, Attempto [2] that has some reasoning capabilities. [3] among many others developed a number of useful methodological elements for authoring technical documents. A synthesis of controlled language principles and tools is presented in [7,8]. Most of these principles and tools have been customized to requirement authoring, based on general purpose or domain-dependent norms (e.g. INCOSE, IREB or ISO26262).

Several road-maps on requirement elicitation and writing (e.g. [17]) show the importance of having consistent and complete sets of requirements, and rank it as a priority. However, no concrete solution so far, to the best of our knowledge, has been developed to characterize the coherence problem. Projects such as [6] aim at finding contradictions between lexico-syntactic patterns in Japanese, including spatial and causal relations. This is however quite different from the problem that is addressed here, since inconsistencies may have very diverse forms (Sect. 4). One of our main aim is indeed to characterize these forms w.r.t. requirement authoring principles. In [9], the limits of textual entailment as a method to detect inconsistencies is shown, corpora is developed from which a typology of contradictions is constructed. The need of a very fine granularity in the data is advocated to avoid errors.

Finding out incoherences in specifications is recognized by requirement authors to be a crucial and a very hard problem. Of interest is the site: www.semanticsimilarity.org that offers several tools for measuring similarities in texts. The use of SAT solvers (satisfiability solvers, running efficiently and in a sound way on very large sets of propositions) can be foreseen but this means translating requirements into propositional logic or into Horn clauses. Both of these translations fail to capture several facets of requirements, in particular complex VPs, modals and the discourse structure. Our goal is rather to develop specific linguistic patterns that can identify incoherences between requirements. These patterns could be viewed, possibly, as instantiated SAT templates.

In this article, we first show how a corpus of incoherent requirements can be constructed and annotated. This corpus leads us to develop a categorization of inconsistencies based on linguistic considerations. This contribution opens new perspectives (1) on new forms of incoherence mining in texts and (2) on mining incoherent requirements and arguments more generally. The construction of this corpus is extremely challenging: large volumes of requirements are necessary, that experts are not ready to share. Furthermore, incoherent requirements are in general not adjacent in a text and involve various textual and discourse structures.

2 Construction of a Corpus of Incoherent Requirements

Constructing a corpus of incoherent requirements is very challenging, it is difficult (1) to get real and substantial specifications from companies and (2) to extract pairs of incoherent requirements which are relatively sparse and may appear in remote sections or chapters of a specification.

Incoherence between two requirements may be partial: they may include divergences without being completely logically opposed. Next, incoherence may be visible linguistically, or may require domain knowledge and inferences to be detected and characterized. We focus in this research on incoherences which can be detected from a linguistic and general semantic analysis: these incoherences are domain and style independent and therefore mining them is simpler and probably re-usable over domains. Finally, we focus on incoherences between pairs of arguments, leaving aside incoherences which may arise from larger sets of requirements. It would obviously be more interesting and useful to consider more complex configurations: requirement compared to a sequence of requirements, or chains of requirements, but this involves more language complexity, e.g. the taking into account of discourse, co-text, titles, etc. A gradual approach to such complex forms, based on use-cases will probably be developed in the future.

2.1 Corpus Compilation Method

Our analysis of requirement incoherences is based on a corpus of requirements coming from 5 companies in three different critical industrial sectors (energy, transportation and telecommunications). Companies have requested to be anonymous; named entities (e.g. equipment and process names) in these texts have been replaced by meaningless constants. Specification documents need to be relatively long (above 100 pages) to allow the detection of various forms of incoherences; short documents are easier to manually control and have much less incoherence problems. Most specification documents, even for a simple equipment can be very long, which motivates our project.

Our documents are in French or in English. Our corpus contains about 1200 pages extracted from 7 documents, where only the requirement parts of these documents have been kept (leaving aside e.g. introductions, summaries, contexts and definitions, but also diagrams and formula). The requirement part of each document is between 150 and 200 pages long, i.e. between 3000 and 4000 requirements in each document. This is not very large, but seems to be sufficient to carry out this first analysis. A total of about 26000 requirements are considered. Most documents do not follow very accurately the norms for writing requirements, nor do they follow the guidelines imposed by their company. Reasons are not investigated here.

The main features considered to validate our corpus are the following, where diversity of form and contents captures the main linguistic features of requirements:

- requirements correspond to various professional activities, and have been written by different types of authors, over a relatively long time span (about a year),
- requirements correspond to different conceptual levels, from abstract considerations to technical specifications,
- requirements have been validated and are judged to be in a relatively 'final' state,
- requirements follow various kinds of authoring norms imposed by companies, including predefined patterns (boilerplates).

2.2 Extraction of Incoherent Requirements

It is almost impossible to manually extract incoherent arguments over large texts since this means memorizing with great precision several thousands of requirements. Specification authors can intuitively, via their knowledge of the domain, identify a very limited number of incoherences when proofreading texts, but they know that there are more incoherences, and that these may have important consequences.

The hypothesis we consider to mine incoherent requirements is that they deal with the same precise topic, but they differ on some significant element(s) which leads to the incoherence. Since requirements should a priori follow strict authoring guidelines (no synonyms, limited syntactic forms), dealing with the same precise topic means that two requirements which are potentially incoherent have a relatively similar syntactic structure and a large number of similar words, but differ on a few words. This can be illustrated by the two following requirements found in two different chapters of a specification, concerning the same software:

REQ12-7 A minimum of 10 simultaneous requests must be allowed.
REQ34-5 At least 20 simultaneous requests must be allowed.

Our strategy to mine potentially incoherent arguments is the following:

(1) In a specification, identify requirements among other types of statements such as definitions. Requirements are often labeled. If this is not the case, a grammar is used that identifies requirements based on a few specific clues such as the use of modals [5].
(2) Mine pairs of requirements which are potentially incoherent based on the two metrics developed below.
(3) Process the discourse structure of mined requirements. This is realized via the TextCoop discourse processing platform [11]. Of much interest are conditionals, circumstances, goals, purposes, illustrations and restatements. These structures are tagged in each requirement. For example: *<circumstance> when the temperature is below* 2°C, *</circumstance> the engines must not be switched off <purpose> to avoid any icing </purpose >*.
(4) Finally, manually inspect the results to identify, for each requirement pair that has been mined, if they are incoherent or not.

Mining pairs of potentially incoherent requirements is based on two metrics:

(1) a similarity metrics, since incoherent requirements deal with the same precise topic and therefore have very close linguistic contents, and
(2) a dissimilarity metrics to characterize differences.

Since, at this stage, the form of incoherent requirement pairs is unknown, we developed two metrics with general purpose constraints in order to mine a large diversity of situations, the noise being discarded manually in a later stage (step 4 above).

(a) The Similarity Metrics. Requirements follow style guidelines: requirements are short (in principle they must be smaller than 20 words, but in practice 30 words are frequently encountered), synonym terms are not allowed, the syntactic structure is very regular (passives are not allowed), negation must be avoided, adjectives and adverbs are limited to a few, fuzzy terms are not allowed, etc. Therefore, a similar content can be characterized, in a first experiment, by a large set of similar words shared by two requirements. Only the words that have a topical content are included in the metrics, to form the *content requirement signature* S. They are: nouns, proper nouns, numbers, verbs, symbol names, and boolean or scalar adjectives. Their identification is based on WordNet resources. The other terms, which mostly play a grammatical role, are not used in the metrics, they include: prepositions, adverbs, determiners, modals, auxiliaries if they are not the main verb, negation, connectors, coordination and pronouns. They may play a role in the incoherence analysis, but do not convey the topic of the requirement.

For example, in *the maximum length of an imaging segment must be 300 km*, the words that are considered in the metrics are: maximum, length, imaging, segment, be, 300 km. These form the *content requirement signature* of that requirement, composed of 7 terms. The similarity metrics considers the *content requirement signatures* S_1 and S_2 of two requirements R_1 and R_2 and computes their intersection I and union U, considering the noninflected forms of words. The similarity rate is: I/U.

Requirements have in general between a total of 6 and 40 words, with an average size of 22 words. In this initial experiment, after some tuning from a small sample of requirements, it turns out that two requirements are in a similarity relation, if:

- between a total of 6 and 12 words long, the similarity rate is greater or equal to 80%,
- between a total of 13 and 22 words long, the similarity rate is greater or equal to 70%,
- above a total of 22 words long, similarity rate is greater or equal to 65%.

Indeed longer requirements often include peripheral information which means that the threshold for the similarity weighted rate should be lower. This 3 level tuning can still be slightly improved, depending on the authoring style of the requirements, the domain via its terminology and the conceptual complexity.

(b) The Dissimilarity Metrics. The dissimilarity metrics considers those terms which are different independently of the discourse structure. It parallels the similarity metrics, searching for terms which introduce a clear difference. Intuitively, differences may be characterized by the main following situations:

- use of different values for the same statement, with a difference of at least 10% to be significant,
- use of different arithmetical operators and constraints,
- use of different named entities,
- use of antonym prepositions or connectors, e.g.:*before/after*, *neutral/after*, etc.
- use of contrasted modals: e.g.: *must/recommended*,
- presence of typical structures such as manner or temporal adverbs in a requirement and not in the other,
- presence of two main clauses (two events) in one requirement and a single main clause in the other (single event),
- presence of a conditional or a circumstance structure in one the of the requirements and not in the other one.

Provided that two requirements have been ranked as similar by the similarity metrics, the presence of at least one of these criteria in a pair of requirements entails that they may be incoherent. More than one criteria reinforces the risk of incoherence, however, there is no dissimilarity rate at this level.

These two metrics used jointly have been tested on our 7 texts separately since they deal with different topics. A total of 204 pairs of requirements have been mined as potentially incoherent. Then, from this corpus, via a manual analysis, 83 requirement pairs (on average 41%) that have been mined indeed show some form of incoherence. This is not a very high number of incoherent arguments: this confirms expert intuitions that incoherences are relatively sparse, but there are probably more incoherences. 18 pairs have been found in the same text section (i.e. among between about 80 to 150 requirements), while 65 pairs are more distant in the text and couldn't have probably been identified without a tool.

Even if it is small, this sample of 83 requirement pairs allows us to develop an analysis of incoherence among requirements, and then to develop relatively generic templates that go beyond these observations that should be able to mine a higher number of incoherent requirement pairs. Finally, a side effect of this analysis is to also mine coherent duplicates or very closely related requirements which could be eliminated. Via the similarity metrics used alone, with a threshold of 90%, our corpus contains at least 368 requirements which are very closely related and could be analyzed as duplicates.

3 Annotating Incoherence in Requirements

The next stage of our analysis is to identify more precisely the various forms incoherence takes in requirements. For that purpose, we defined a set of annotations. The discourse processing used to mine requirement pairs provides a first level of annotations as illustrated in the previous section. Annotations are made manually by the author, some confirmation were given by requirement authors, but their availability is often very limited.

The annotations we add are those that characterize the string of words which differ between the elements of a pair and the nature of the difference(s). This task allows to categorize errors (Sect. 4) and to define templates to mine incoherent arguments in specifications. Incoherences are specified informally as an attribute of the main tag <incoherence>. Here are a few examples that illustrate the method and the difficulties. Examples 1 and 2 are relatively straightforward whereas Examples 3 and 4 are much more complex to annotate and to characterize. Differences are between <diff> tags, <req> identifies a requirement, and <event> tags the events in requirements that contain two or more explicit events.

Example 1. <incoherence type = "numerical variation" incoherence = "300 ≠ 100">
<req> the maximum length of an imaging segment is <diff> 300 </diff> km. </req>
<req> the maximum length of an imaging segment is <diff> 100 </diff> km. </req>
</incoherence>

Example 2. <incoherence type = "arithmetical expression divergence" incoherence = "(<30) ≠ 50">
<req> In S, the probe X30 shall be preheated <diff> up to 30 </diff> degrees <circumstance> <diff> before doing</diff> E. </circumstance> </req>
<req> the probe X30 in S shall be preheated <diff> to 50 </diff> degrees <purpose> <diff> to realize </diff> E. </purpose></req> </incoherence>
In this example, while the arithmetical expression introduces the incoherence, the distinction between circumstance and purpose must be made flexible so that the synonymy between 'doing' and 'to realize' can be identified.

Example 3. English gloss of French example: *at flight level 30 in normal flight conditions, the maximal* 20° *flap extension speed is* 185 kts versus *at flight level 30 in normal flight conditions, extend flaps to* 20° *and then reduce speed below* 185 kts:
<incoherence type = "event synchronization with mismatches" incoherence = "(< kts) ≠ unknown">
<req> <circumstance> A FL 30 ASL et dans les conditions normales </circumstance>, la vitesse <diff> maximale de </diff> sortie des volets à 20° <diff> est </diff> 185 kts. </req>
<req> <circumstance> A FL 30 ASL et dans les conditions normales </circumstance>, <event> sortir les volets à 20° </event> puis <event> <diff> réduire la vitesse en dessous de </diff> 185 kts. </event> </req> </incoherence>
In this example, a general rule (first requirement) is contrasted with a requirement that describes a procedure composed of two events. In the second requirement, the temporal connector 'puis' (then) suggests that the constraint stated in the first requirement is split into two consecutive parts, with the risk that the

constraint is not met as it should, e.g. flaps are extended at an unknown speed, which is then reduced to 185 kts.

Example 4. <incoherence type = "incompatibility between events" incoherence = "(stop every 24 h) ≠ (no stop during the entire update)">
<req> the system S administrator must make sure <diff> to stop the system S every 24 h <purpose> for maintenance. </purpose> </diff> </req>
<req> the system S administrator must make sure <diff> that the update of system S database is not interrupted. </diff></req> </incoherence>.

In this example, a potential incoherence may arise if the system is stopped for maintenance while its associated database is being updated. The terms 'stop' and 'not interrupted' are opposed and may create the incoherence.

These annotations remain informal, in particular for the 'type' attribute. Incoherences are very diverse and do not lend themselves easily to a simple characterization. The goal is to have a first level of analysis, before implementing templates that would mine incoherent pairs of requirements. The examples given above are composed of independent statements. Connecting these statements via e.g. conditional statements could improve their global coherence.

4 A Preliminary Categorization of Incoherence in Requirements

From our sample of 83 requirement pairs which are incoherent, a preliminary categorization of incoherence types can be elaborated on a linguistic and conceptual basis. This categorization shows that incoherence has multiple facets, and that some pairs that have been mined may be a symptom of a form of incoherence. This categorization leads to the definition of templates and lexical resources to mine pairs of incoherent requirements. The examples below are direct corpus samples (translated into English for French examples). They are numbered Ri a/b where i numbers examples and a and b are the 2 elements of an incoherent pair.

4.1 Partial or Total Incompatibilities Between Expressions

The most direct and simple type of incoherence is composed of 'local' divergences:

- incompatible numerical values or arithmetical expressions, with more than 10% difference:
  R1a- Make sure to preheat the probe X30 to a maximum of 30°.
  R1b- The probe X30 must be preheated at at least 50°.
  R'1a- The maximum length of an imaging segment is 300 km.
  R'1b- The minimum length of an imaging segment is 30 km.

- incompatibility between various types of temporal, spatial or instrumental restrictions expressed as verb complements:
  R2a- Service D must be available only from the screen.
  R2b- Service D must be available in any configuration.
  A domain ontology is necessary to detect most of these incompatibilities. However, the fact that a different term is used can be identified as a potential incompatibility source, since in technical writing synonyms are not allowed.
- incompatible temporal structures or temporal organization between events:
  R3a- Update data marking when transferring data.
  R3b- Update data marking before transferring data.
- modal variation, involving e.g. a different critical level:
  R4b- It is recommended to stop the engine before E.
  R4b- The engine shall be stopped before E.
- adverbial incompatibilities or discrepancies in particular in manners: *carefully/quickly*, etc.
- some specific quantification aspects such as the difference between *every/each, most/all.*

Among these various forms of incoherences, the three first cases are the most frequent. Adverbial uses and quantification are less frequent: they are strongly controlled in requirement authoring because they often introduce underspecified or fuzzy expressions. Our corpus includes 33 cases that fall in this category, among which 24 belong to the three first cases.

4.2 Incompatible Events

In this category fall pairs of requirements that describe events which show some form of incoherence. Such incoherences often require some domain dependent knowledge, but a number of them remain at a 'surface' level and can be detected solely on a linguistic basis. Examples 3 and 4 in Sect. 3 are typical incoherent statements:

R5a- The system S must be stopped every 24 h *for maintenance.* versus
R5b- The update of the database via the system S must not be interrupted.
is a type of situation that is difficult to predict besides the antonym *stop/not interrupted.*
R6a- the maximum 20° *flap extension speed is* 185 kts. versus
R6b- extend flaps to 20° *and then slow down to* 185 kts.
is a typical business error that any domain expert should be able to avoid. R6a is a general rule which should be preferred to R6b which is a procedural statement.

4.3 Contextual Incompatibilities

This category includes various types of discourse structures (e.g. condition, circumstance, goal, illustration, etc.) associated with the main body of two similar requirements which could induce forms of incompatibility:

R7a- during the project specification phase, both on-line and off-line access must be available.
R7b- during the project implementation, both on-line and off-line access must be available.
R8a- a rule includes facts and its critical.
R8b- a rule includes facts and a description.

R7 illustrates a case where the context (circumstance) is different but expects the same behavior. One may expect a negation in one of the two main propositions 'must not be available' to motivate these two requirements or may want to merge the two circumstances to avoid any doubt. R8 shows two enumerations which are different and should probably be adjusted. R8 is a frequent case where enumerations are either incomplete (not recommended in requirement guidelines), or manipulate objects at different levels of abstraction.

4.4 Terminological Variations and Other Discrepancies

In this category, requirements which largely overlap are considered. Their slight differences may however be symptomatic of an partial inconsistency. These cases are relatively frequent and typical of documents produced either by several authors or over a long time span (where e.g. equipment names may have changed). Typical examples are:
R8a- the up-link frequency, from earth to space, must be in the s band.
R8b- the down-link frequency, from space to earth, must be in the s band.
R9a- those tests aim at checking the rf compatibility of the ground stations used during the mission and the tm/tc equipment on board.
R9b- those tests aim at checking the rf compatibility of the ground stations used during the mission and the on board equipment.
R10 is somewhat ambiguous and contains implicit knowledge which makes the identification of the incoherence slightly more challenging:
R10a- the upper attachment limit must not exceed 25 GB.
R10b- It must be possible to specify a maximum limit for the storage capacity of an attachment.

Indeed, either the limit is set to 256 GB or it can be specified, but R10b may be understood as saying that it can be specified but always below 256 GB.

4.5 Category Synthesis

The distribution observed on our corpus is the following, it remains indicative because of the small size of our corpus:

The implementation of these categories could possibly produce slightly different results. Most of the incoherences in these categories can be detected on the basis of linguistic analysis and general purpose lexical semantics data, in particular antonyms e.g. for prepositions, temporal connectors, arithmetical operators.

Category	nb of occurrences and rate
(1) incompatibilities between expressions	33, about 40%
(2) incompatible events	11, about 13%
(3) contextual incompatibilities	27, about 33%
(4) variations between requirements	12, about 14%

5 Analysis of Errors in the Incoherence Analysis

The main challenge is now the definition of templates to mine incoherent pairs of requirements, with their associated linguistic resources. The 41% accuracy of the current mining is not sufficient: a rate of 75% is the minimum acceptable accuracy for requirement authors. This means refining both metrics and analyzing the reasons of the noise to reduce it. For that purpose, a first step is to analyze why some requirement pairs have been incorrectly recognized as incoherent. The main reasons are the following:

(1) **Description of complex cases via several coherent requirements:** requirements are often detailed descriptions of a precise case within a given context. For complex cases, a set of closely related requirements may be produced where a few terms, dealing with the different cases, may be different, yet requirements remain coherent.

(2) **Different forms for a similar content:** two requirements may deal with the same point using slightly different expression means, e.g. for values. For example, values+units may be different, intervals or arithmetical constraints may be used instead of a single value, but these expressions remain globally equivalent. For example, these two requirements are equivalent according to the similarity metrics: R11a- *the A320 neo optimal cruise altitude is FL380 in normal operating conditions* versus R11b- *the A320 neo optimal cruise altitude is between FL 360 and 380, depending on weather conditions.* R11b is just more precise.

(3) **Use of more generic terms:** it is also frequent that two requirements differ only in a general purpose term or a business term where one is more generic than the other, or with a language level that is different. Detecting this situation requires a domain ontology.

(4) **Two or more differences between two requirements:** when two requirements have more than two groups of terms which are different, it turns out that in most cases they deal with different aspects of a given topic. The dissimilarity analysis should be revised so that the case of several observed differences is constrained, for example manner or temporal adverbs and different values or arithmetical expressions as advocated in 2.2(b) can co-exist, but not two groups of different values.

(5) **Presence of negative terms:** the negation, although not recommended in technical writing, or negatively oriented terms (verbs, adjectives) may appear in one requirement and not in the other, but these requirements are in fact similar to a large extent. For example R12a- *Acid A must not be thrown in*

any standard garbage versus R12b- *Acid A must be thrown in a dedicated garbage.*

(6) Influence of the co-text: requirements dealing with a given activity are often grouped under a title, subtitle, an enumeration or in a chart. Two arguments that belong to two different groups may seem to be incoherent, but if the context, given by the title or by the enumeration introduction head is different, then these two requirements may deal with different cases as in (1) and may not be incoherent. Co-text aspects are crucial in incoherence, but quite difficult to take into account because the link between a co-text and the requirement needs to be analyzed at the discourse level.

In terms of silence, two requirements have not been detected as incoherent because of:

(7) implicit elements: this is the case in the pair R10 (detected in a different way) where the implicit 'for the storage capacity' expression is unexpressed in pair a. The same situation is observed with pronouns, although their use should be very limited in technical authoring. Missing information prevents the similarity metrics from mining requirements dealing with the same precise topic.

(8) an external context: Similarly to (6) above, but in the other direction, two requirements may be exactly identical but incoherent if the sections in which they appear have titles which are opposed in some way. The incoherence may then be 'external' to the requirements. However the case structure evoked in (1) may also be considered here.

More observations are probably necessary before a model and an implementation for the detection of incoherent requirement pairs can be carried out. However, a few simple remarks can be made at this stage. Category 1 in Sect. 4 should be relatively simple to implement, with a base of antonyms, various forms of divergence expression, and a limited syntactic analysis for verb complements. Some elements that fall in category 3 should also be relatively simple to implement, after a discourse analysis of the requirements, but this category may include more complex cases than those given as illustrations. Categories 2 and 4 are much more challenging and probably the most interesting ones from a scientific point of view.

The similarity metrics clearly needs to be refined: a simple word to word match and count is obviously not accurate enough, even if it allowed us to investigate the incoherence problem from scratch. Several problems such as pronominal references, the use of more generic terms, and implicit terms, and ellipsis must be taken into account in some way.

6 Conclusion and Perspectives

We have presented in this paper the construction of a corpus of incoherent requirements and a preliminary categorization. We have restricted ourselves to incoherences which can be detected on a linguistic basis. Mining incoherences is really challenging as shown by the analysis provided for each category. Modeling and implementation is ongoing, but requires more data.

This contribution opens new perspectives (1) on new forms of incoherence in texts and (2) on mining incoherent requirements, and arguments more generally. Our corpus examples show that incoherence may take a large diversity of forms.

A major difficulty is evaluation. Since it is not possible to have a test corpus where incoherent requirements have been identified manually, it is only possible to evaluate noise, but not silence. Both dimensions are important to evaluate the accuracy and also the linguistic adequacy and soundness of templates. In addition, requirement authors certainly do not want to be bothered by getting alerts about pairs of requirements which are not incoherent, they also wish to have an estimate of what the system found.

References

1. Fontan, L., Saint-Dizier, P.: Analyzing the explanation structure of procedural texts: dealing with advices and warnings. In: STEP Conference, Venice (2008)
2. Fuchs, N.E.: First-order reasoning for attempto controlled English. In: Rosner, M., Fuchs, N.E. (eds.) CNL 2010. LNCS, vol. 7175, pp. 73–94. Springer, Heidelberg (2012). doi:10.1007/978-3-642-31175-8_5
3. Grady, J.O.: System Requirements Analysis. Academic Press, Orlando (2006)
4. Hull, E., Jackson, K., Dick, J.: Requirements Engineering. Springer, London (2011)
5. Kang, J., Saint-Dizier, P.: Discourse structure analysis for requirement mining. Int. J. Knowl. Content Dev. Technol. **3**(2), 43–65 (2013)
6. Kloetzer, J., De Saeger, S.: Two-stage method for large-scale acquisition of contradiction pattern pairs using entailment. In: Proceedings EMNLP 2013 (2013)
7. Kuhn, T.: A principled approach to grammars for controlled natural languages and predictive editors. J. Logic Lang. Inf. **22**(1), 33–70 (2013)
8. Kuhn, T.: A survey and classification of controlled natural languages. Comput. Linguist. **40**(1), 121–170 (2014)
9. De Marneffe, M.C., Rafferty, A.N.: Manning CD finding contradictions in text. In: ACL-HLT 2008 (2008)
10. O'Brien, S.: Controlling controlled English–an analysis of several controlled language rule sets. School of Applied Language and Inter-cultural Studies, Dublin City University (2003)
11. Saint-Dizier, P.: Processing natural language arguments with the <TextCoop> platform. J. Argumentation Comput. **3**(1), 49–82 (2012)
12. Saito, M., Yamamoto, K., Sekine, S.: Using phrasal patterns to identify discourse relations. In: ACL 2006 (2006)
13. Schriver, K.A.: Evaluating text quality: the continuum from text-focused to reader-focused methods. IEEE Trans. Prof. Commun. **32**, 238–255 (1989)
14. Unwalla, M.: AECMA simplified English (2004). http://www.techscribe.co.uk/ta/aecma-simplified-english.pdf
15. Weiss, E.H.: How to Write Usable User Documentation. The Oryx Press, Westport (1991)
16. Wojcik, R.H., James, E.H.: Controlled languages in Industry, in survey of the state of the art in human language technology, Chap. 7 (1996). http://www.lt-world.org/hlt-survey/ltw-chapter7-6.pdf
17. Wyner, A., Angelov, K., Barzdins, G., Damljanovic, D., Davis, B., Fuchs, N., Hover, S., Jones, K., Kaljurand, K., Kuhn, T., Luts, M., Pool, J., Rosner, M., Schwitter, R., Sowa, J.: Properties and prospects. http://wyner.info/research/Papers/CNLP&P.pdf

Enriching Argumentative Texts with Implicit Knowledge

Maria Becker[(✉)], Michael Staniek, Vivi Nastase, and Anette Frank

Institute for Computational Linguistics, Heidelberg University,
Leibniz Science Campus Empirical Linguistics
and Computational Language Modeling, Heidelberg, Germany
{mbecker,staniek,nastase,frank}@cl.uni-heidelberg.de

Abstract. Retrieving information that is implicit in a text is difficult. For argument analysis, revealing implied knowledge could be useful to judge how solid an argument is and to construct concise arguments. We design a process for obtaining high-quality implied knowledge annotations for German argumentative microtexts, in the form of simple natural language statements. This process involves several steps to promote agreement and monitors its evolution using textual similarity computation. To further characterize the implied knowledge, we annotate the added sentences with semantic clause types and common sense knowledge relations. To test whether the knowledge could be retrieved automatically, we compare the inserted sentences to Wikipedia articles on similar topics. Analysis of the added knowledge shows that (i) it is characterized by a high proportion of generic sentences, (ii) a majority of it can be mapped to common sense knowledge relations, and (iii) it is similar to sentences found in Wikipedia.

Keywords: Argumentation · Implicit knowledge · Annotation process · Textual similarity · Semantic clause types · Common sense knowledge · Wikipedia

1 Introduction

It is agreed, at least since the work of Grice [7], that overt communication relies on a large body of knowledge that both the speaker and the listener share, such that only part of the message conveyed by the speaker needs to be expressed in words, while the rest can be filled in by the hearer. The assumption of mutually shared knowledge could be a source of misunderstanding, when the knowledge implied by the speaker is different from what the hearer fills in. Omitting weak supporting information could also be used as a manipulation device, to make a weak argument seem sound. In an argumentative framework, it would then be beneficial to reconstruct this implied information to be able to rate the soundness and validity of an argument.

Retrieving implied information that is not explicitly mentioned in a text is difficult – when asked, different people may have different ideas of what exactly

F. Frasincar et al. (Eds.): NLDB 2017, LNCS 10260, pp. 84–96, 2017.
DOI: 10.1007/978-3-319-59569-6_9

and how detailed such information should be. In this work, we describe the process we designed to elicit high-quality annotations of implied knowledge in the form of simple natural language sentences, for a concise argumentation dataset – the Microtext corpus [10]. We structure the annotation process in such a way that annotators working in parallel on the same data set have to review each other's annotations, encouraging them to understand the other's point of view, and adjust their own to gradually reach agreement.

Apart from initial instructions we did not interfere in the annotation process, but we did monitor the *evolution of annotator agreement* by measuring the similarity between the added annotations.

To learn more about the nature and (linguistic) characteristics of the added information, we further annotate the data with two specific semantic information types: semantic clause types [6] and ConceptNet knowledge relations [8,15]. Previous work [1] has shown that argumentative texts are characterized by a specific distribution of *abstract linguistic clause types* [6] that distinguish them from other text genres. We will test whether the provided implied information shares these characteristics, by having it labeled with these categories. To complete the picture in terms of the type of knowledge expressed by the inserted sentences, they will be annotated with *common sense knowledge relations*, using the inventory of 28 relation types of ConceptNet [8,15]. In addition, we compare the inserted knowledge with sentences from Wikipedia, to assess the difficulty of automatically harvesting missing knowledge in natural language arguments.

In summary, the contributions of this work are: (i) high-quality annotations of implicit knowledge on the argumentative Microtext corpus, in terms of natural language sentences; (ii) characterization of the specific nature of these sentences in terms of semantic clause types and common sense knowledge relations; (iii) design of an annotation process for a difficult task that promotes agreement between annotators by having them review each other's work; (iv) an approach to monitor the annotation process – in particular, the increase in agreement – using textual similarity techniques.

This annotated data will be made public as an extension to the Microtext corpus [10], to support further research in argument analysis.

2 Related Work

Relatively little attention has been devoted so far to the task of finding and adding implicit knowledge in arguments, which is closely related to the task of enthymeme reconstruction. Enthymemes – arguments with missing propositions – are common in natural language and particularly in argumentative texts [11]. [12] present a feasibility study on the automatic detection of enthymemes in real-world texts and find that specific discourse markers (e.g. *let alone, therefore, because*) can signal enthymemes. Using these as trigger words, they reconstruct enthymemes from the local context, while [11] retrieve and fill missing propositions in arguments from similar or related arguments. Another method is the utilization of shared knowledge [3], which is related to our approach. [1,2] show that argumentative texts are rich in generic and generalizing sentences, which often express common knowledge. We will show that large portions of implied knowledge in argumentative texts are naturally stated using these clause types. In their attempt to reconstruct implicit knowledge, [4] find that the claims that users make in online debate platforms often build on implicit knowledge and that the reconstruction of implicit premises supports claim detection. They release a dataset with human-provided implicit premises based on data from online debate platforms, consisting of 125 claim pairs annotated with the premises that connect them, yielding a total of 500 gap-filling premises set. In contrast to our approach they asked the annotators to provide the premises without giving any further instructions, resulting in a substantial variance in the average number of premises and words in premises as well as a low word overlap (32%).

These studies suggest that a substantial amount of knowledge is needed for the interpretation and analysis of argumentative texts. In this work we report on an annotation method designed to encourage agreement, and through which we acquire high-quality annotations for implicit knowledge in arguments.

3 Annotating Implicit Knowledge in Arguments

3.1 The Microtext Corpus

The basis for our work is the argumentative Microtext corpus [10], which consists of 112 microtexts in German. Each microtext is a short, dense argument written in response to a question on a potentially controversial issue (e.g., *Should all universities in Germany charge tuition fees?*). Writers were asked to include a direct statement of their main claim as well as at least one objection to that claim. The texts, each of which contains roughly 5 argumentative segments, were written in German and professionally translated into English. An example together with its argument structure graph is given in Fig. 1.

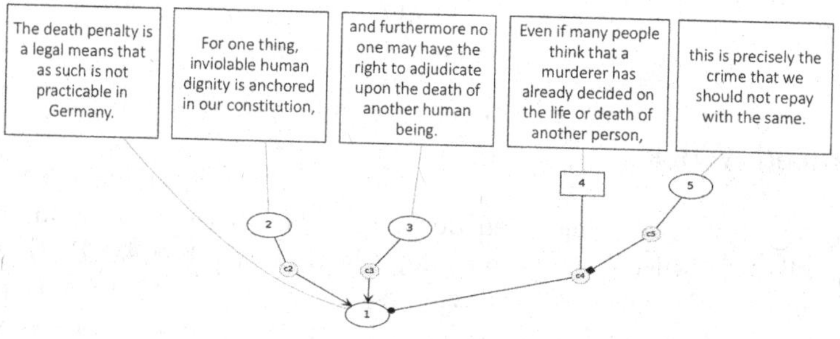

Fig. 1. Argumentation graph from the Microtext Corpus (micro/b006)

The produced microtexts were manually annotated according to a scheme based on Freeman's theory of the macro-structure of argumentation [5] for representing text-level argumentation structure. For this, each text was segmented into elementary units of argumentation which present either a conclusion or a premise. Each unit corresponds to a node in the argument graph. Nodes with outgoing pointed arrows are *proponent nodes*, while those with outgoing square-headed arrows mark *opponent nodes*. The arcs are labeled with *argumentative functions* [10]. The most frequent functions are: (a) *support*: a premise supports a conclusion or another premise; (b) *rebuttal*: a premise attacks a conclusion or premise by challenging its acceptability, or (c) *undercut*: a premise attacks the acceptability of an argumentative relation between two propositions.

3.2 Task I: Revealing Implicit Knowledge in Argumentative Texts

The aim of our annotation is to reveal implicit knowledge that connects superficially disconnected, but semantically coherent premises in argumentative texts. Being able to make this implicit information explicit could help assess the strength of an argument, apart from the benefit of making the underlying logics of the argument transparent for both humans and computational systems.

Figure 2 shows an example of the desired annotations, with a main claim *a* supported by statement *b*. While the knowledge underlying the argumentative function is not explicitly conveyed, we believe the reader has no trouble understanding why the argumentative relation holds: it is made explicit in *c*.

(a) ***Alternative treatments should be subsidized just like conventional treatments***
(b) ***since both methods can lead to the prevention, mitigation or cure of illness.***
(c) ***Treatments are subsidized if they lead to the prevention, mitigation or cure of illness.***

Fig. 2. Example: Explicating implicit knowledge that connects related premises

The difficulty of eliciting such implicit knowledge in an annotation task is that intuitions about what the implied connection is may be different between annotators. Even if their intuitions match, the phrasing chosen by the annotators may be different, structurally or in terms of lexical choice. This makes it hard to enforce agreement and to assess the quality of the annotations. We will address these challenges in two ways:

(i.) by designing an **multi-step annotation process** where annotators are asked to review and potentially revise each other's annotations and

(ii.) by **measuring the dynamic evolution of agreement** during this process using computational measures of **semantic textual similarity (STS)**.

Annotation process. The annotations are performed on sentence pairs from the Microtext corpus (the original German version)[1], that stand in an argumentative relation according to the argumentation graph. There are 464 such sentence pairs in the 112 texts in the corpus, i.e., approx. 4 pairs per microtext. The annotation process is illustrated in Fig. 3. We use 5 human judges (H1 .. H5), all of them native German speakers with a linguistic background.

[1] All examples are shown in English for convenience.

Step 1: $H1$ and $H2$ produce initial annotations **A1** and **A2**. The annotators are asked to add the minimal amount of information that makes the connection between the two sentences explicit by: (1) adding as few sentences as possible and (2) making the inserted sentences as simple as possible so that they ideally only contain one fact per sentence. Through these instructions we intend to avoid long and too detailed explanations, and in consequence, to support better agreement between the judges. If the annotators think that no information is missing (i.e., the connection between sentences is explicit), this is labeled correspondingly.

Step 2: $H1$ and $H2$ review each other's annotations, producing corrected versions: $H1(\mathbf{A2})=\mathbf{A2^c}$, $H2(\mathbf{A1})=\mathbf{A1^c}$.

Step 3: To avoid biases arising from the correction phase, two different judges $H3$ and $H4$ independently perform merges of $\mathbf{A1^c}$ and $\mathbf{A2^c}$, producing annotations **A3** and **A4**, respectively. They are allowed to select one annotation, combine them into a novel statement, or to produce a new annotation. Formally, annotator Hk produces for each sentence pair (i):

$$\mathbf{Ak_i} = merge(\mathbf{A1^c_\mathit{i}}, \mathbf{A2^c_\mathit{i}}) = \begin{cases} \mathbf{A1^c_i} & \text{if } Hk \text{ confirms } \mathbf{A1^c_i} \\ \mathbf{A2^c_i} & \text{if } Hk \text{ confirms } \mathbf{A2^c_i} \\ \mathbf{A1^c_i}/\mathbf{A2^c_i} & \text{if } Hk \text{ combines parts of } \mathbf{A1^c_\mathit{i}} \text{ and } \mathbf{A2^c_i} \\ \mathbf{Ak_i} & \text{if } Hk \text{ produces a new annotation} \end{cases}$$

Step 4: A final annotator $H5$ produces the gold standard based on **A3** and **A4** following the merge process described above, with the difference that for this final step we allow two versions of the inserted information if both of them fill the gap. This decision was inspired by the observation that in many cases **A3** and **A4** provide the same information expressed slightly differently:
(1) *People of higher age have more experience.*
(2) *People in retirement age are considered more experienced.*

Measuring the evolution of agreement using semantic textual similarity. To trace the evolution of agreement between annotators we quantify the distance between their respective annotations – i.e. added sentences – using the Word Mover's Distance [9] as implemented in *gensim*[2]. The Word Mover's Distance (WMD) (Eq. 1) measures the dissimilarity between two documents as the aggregated minimum distance in an embedding space that the (non-stopword) words of one document need to "travel" to reach the (non-stopword) word of another document. For two documents d_1 and d_2 with vocabulary of size n, the WMD is computed using the embeddings for each word i (with embedding x_i) from document d_1 and word j (with embedding x_j) from d_2 as the solution of the optimization problem:

$$WMD(d_1, d_2) = min_{T \geq 0} \sum_{i,j=1}^{n} T^{\star}_{ij} \|x_i - x_j\|_2 \tag{1}$$

[2] https://radimrehurek.com/gensim.

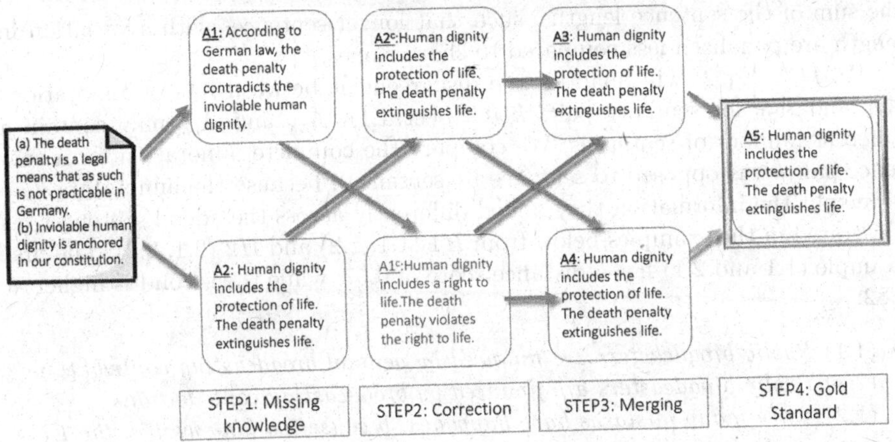

Fig. 3. Annotation pipeline illustrated with an example

$$T^{\star}_{ij} = \begin{cases} \frac{freq(i)}{\sum_{x=1}^{n} freq(x)} & \text{if } j = argmin_j \|x_i - x_j\|_2 \\ 0 & \text{otherwise} \end{cases}$$

The WMD method has two main components: the word embeddings used and the scoring function, and we adjusted these to our language and task.

Word Embeddings. The WMD relies on word embeddings that map similar words to close regions in embedding space. From several pretrained word embeddings for German, we chose those that yielded the highest correlation with human scores on four word similarity datasets:[3] 100-dimensional word2vec embeddings trained on a German "meta-corpus" of 116 million sentences (that combines several German corpora) using Skip-Gram mode with 5 negative samples [13].

Scoring function. Generally, a short text subsumed by a larger text would warrant a low distance score. In our case, however, since we aim to quantify how strongly the annotators agree and to which degree their inputs are similar, differences in length should be penalized by increasing the distance score. We therefore add a *length difference penalty* score (LDP) (3) to the WMD (2):

$$WMD'(d_1, d_2) = WMD(d_1, d_2) + LDP(d_1, d_2) \tag{2}$$

$$LDP(d_1, d_2) = \frac{|length(d_1) - length(d_2)|}{\frac{length(d_1)+length(d_2)}{2}} \tag{3}$$

LDP increases the distance score if there is a large difference in length between the sentences. The length difference is normalized by the average of

[3] Spearman correlation results on the German version of the MC30: 0.76; RG65: 0.79; wordsim353: 0.69; ZG222: 0.42. https://dkpro.github.io/dkpro-similarity/wordpairsimilarity/.

the sum of the sentence lengths, such that longer sentences with a variation in length are penalized less compared to shorter ones.

WMD' (Eq. 2) will quantify the disagreement between sets of annotations A_{xk} and A_{yk} for sentence pairs k (cf. Sect. 4.1). A_{xk} and A_{yk} may contain a different number of sentences. We compare the complete annotation for a sentence pair k (as opposed to sentence by sentence), because the annotators may have split the information they added differently across the added sentences, as illustrated in the examples below from $H1$ (1.1, 1.2) and $H2$ (2.1, 2.2). The first example (1.1 and 2.1) has a distance score of 0.57, while the second is higher at 3.82:

(1.1) *Public broadcasters are financed by general broadcasting contributions.*
(2.1) *Public broadcasters are financed by broadcasting contributions.*
(1.2) *Since many mistakes have happened, because too long waited, the EU is to interfere very quickly this time.*
(2.2) *Interference can prevent war.*

3.3 Task IIa: Situation Entity Types Annotations

We asked the annotators to characterize the inserted sentences by labeling them with *situation entity types*. The distribution of these clause types is distinctive for argumentative texts compared to other genres [2], showing particularly high ratios of generic and generalizing sentences. For the inventory of SE types we adopt the most frequent types in [6]:

states describe specific properties of individuals:
(e1) *Waste separation is a form of environmental protection.*
events are things that happen or have happened:
(e2) *Edward Snowden revealed information.*
generic sentences are predicates over classes or kinds:
(e3) *Health insurance funds take over the payment of medicine.*
generalizing sentences describe regularly occurring events or habits:
(e4) *The broadcasting fee is paid by all citizens alike.*

The annotations are performed independently by two trained annotators. They assign SE type labels at the clause level. The segmentation is performed automatically with DiscourseSegmenter [14], a python package offering both rule-based and machine-learning based discourse segmenters.

3.4 Task IIb: Concept Net Relations Annotations

To gain further insight into the type of knowledge covered by the provided sentences, we annotate them with ConceptNet relation *types* such as *PartOf*, *Causes* or *IsA*. ConceptNet [8,15] is a semantic network that contains common sense facts about the world. The knowledge is collected from volunteers over the Internet (via templates, free text, games etc.) and is represented as tuples

<left term, relation, right term>, terms (words/short phrases) are nodes, and the relations between them are edges – e.g. <dogs, *IsA*, animals>.

The annotation was performed by two annotators in parallel. They were asked to label each inserted sentence, if applicable (irrespective of whether or not the relation *instance* is covered in ConceptNet). Examples of annotated relation types are presented in Sect. 4.3.

3.5 Task III: Retrieving Similar Sentences from a Wikipedia Corpus

The annotations of implied knowledge represent a gold standard that should be obtainable automatically, whether in their exact form or as approximations. We test whether the implied knowledge that the annotators made explicit through the provided sentences can be found in a textual corpus.

We collect a corpus of Wikipedia sentences from articles that match the topics of the microtexts in the Microtext corpus. Each microtext was elicited with a query, e.g. *Should Germany introduce the death penalty?*. We match this query to German Wikipedia article titles and extract the introduction section of the article, if it exists, or the first 10 sentences. From all 18 queries used in to produce the corpus, we find matches for 50 related topics such as *tuition fees* or *waste separation*, resulting in a corpus of 874 sentences.

To test whether we can find sentences in Wikipedia that match sentences in the inserted information set, we use the distance formula WMD' (Eq. 2).

4 Analysis of the Annotations

4.1 Task I: Data Statistics and Evolution of Annotator Agreement

The annotators were provided with 464 sentence pairs from the Microtext Corpus. The annotations of Situation Entity types and ConceptNet relations were done on the sentences inserted at step 2 of the annotation process ($A1^c$-$A2^c$). $A1^c$ includes 750 sentences (1.62 sents/gap on average) and $A2^c$ 720 sentences (1.55 sents/gap on average) in total.

Only 44 (9%) of the 464 sentence pairs were labeled as *no information missing* at step 2 of the annotation process, indicating that coherence among statements strongly relies on implicit knowledge.

Evolution of annotator agreement. To compare two complete annotations, we compute the average and standard deviation of their dissimilarity with WMD' (Table 1) and plot histograms of the disagreement scores (Fig. 4).

Columns 1 and 2 in Table 1 measure the amount of editing $H1$ and $H2$ performed on the other's annotations. A2 (3.69) was edited more than A1 (0.71). Columns 3, 4 and 5 show how inter annotator agreement improves after each annotation step – smaller numbers mean lower distance and therefore higher similarity. Mutual reviewing improves the agreement between $H1$ and $H2$. The distance decreases again with the third annotation step where $H3$ and $H4$ merge

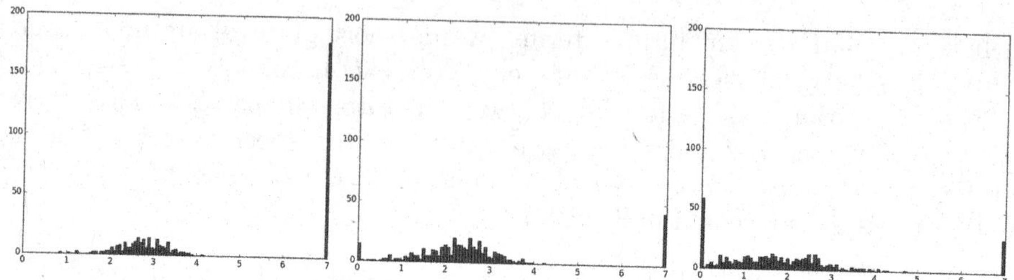

Fig. 4. WMD' histogram for (1) A1-A2, (2) A1^c-A2^c and (3) A3-A4. A shift towards 0 from one step of the annotation process to the next indicates an increase in agreement. 7 is the maximum distance score and was assigned when one annotator labeled a sentence pair with *no information missing*, while the other inserted information.

A1^c and A2^c, producing A3 and A4 with a semantic distance of 1.91. The evolution towards agreement is illustrated in Fig. 4, through the shift towards 0 in the distance between annotations from one step of the process to the next.

New solutions from annotators. High distance scores in step 3 are often assigned to annotations (i) that provide different information, (ii) where one annotator assigned *no information missing* while the other inserted missing information or (iii) when one annotator provides the information in finer-grained steps than the other. The reason for (i) is very often that one/both annotators provide a new solution to fill the gap that is different from the annotations A1^c and A2^c (and also from what the other annotator inserted at that step). Thus, *H*3 and *H*4 did not only select from existing annotations, but produced statements based on their own intuitions.

Word overlap. Compared to [4], who report a word overlap of 32% for the premises inserted by their annotators (they don't report which similarity coefficient they applied), we obtain an averaged word overlap score of 57% (Dice)/ 47% (Jaccard) for A3-A4, while only 36% (Dice)/26% (Jaccard) for A1^c-A2^c and 10% (Dice)/6% (Jaccard) for A1-A2, showing again improved agreement of the annotations along the process.

Comparison of annotations across different annotation steps. The averaged distance scores between annotations produced in early vs. later stages show an evolution towards agreement: the averaged distance score from the second

Table 1. Evolution of annotator agreement measured by WMD'.

	A1 ↓ A1^c	A2 ↓ A2^c	A1 ↓ A2	A1^c ↓ A2^c	A3 ↓ A4	A1^c ↓ A3	A1^c ↓ A4	A2^c ↓ A3	A2^c ↓ A4	A3 ↓ A5	A4 ↓ A5
WMD	0.71	3.69	4.62	2.71	1.91	2.06	1.79	2.00	1.71	1.52	1.49
SD (σ)	1.90	8.03	4.67	1.69	1.69	1.76	1.95	1.77	2.01	1.47	1.32

Table 2. Distribution of SE types among different genres (expressed as percentages)

Genre	Generic	Generaliz.	State	Event
Inserted information	0.81	0.08	0.10	0.01
Microtexts	0.48	0.12	0.32	0.08
Report	0.03	0.04	0.54	0.39

annotation step ($A1^c$ and $A2^c$) compared to those in the third step (A3 and A4) (columns 6–9 in Table 1) is 1.89; the averaged distance score between annotations from the third step to the fourth step (columns 10–11) is 1.51.

Gold standard. In the last step an expert annotator (*H*5) merges A3 and A4. *H*5 is allowed to accept both A3 *and* A4 as part of the final gold standard if both provide the required information to fill the gap. In 68% of cases A3 and A4 are accepted as equivalent, in 25% either A3 or A4 are picked, and in 7% of cases, *H*5 supplies a new solution, indicating high quality of the annotations.

4.2 Task IIa: Analysis of Situation Entity Types Annotations

The annotator agreement is 0.44 (Cohen's Kappa) for the Situation Entity type annotations on the missing information set. The gold standard was obtained by reannotating the disputed segments. Table 2 shows the distribution of SE types (gold) on the missing information set compared to other genres [1]. The sentences inserted as missing information are characterized by a very high proportion of generics (81%) and very few events (1%), while reports, for example, contain a high proportion of states (54%) and events (39%) [1]. The proportion of generics within the inserted information is significantly higher than the already high one in microtexts (48%). This suggests that the knowledge captured by generic sentences plays an important role with respect to implicit information, and we can use this tendency for acquiring such missing information automatically.

4.3 Task IIb: Analysis of ConceptNet Relation Type Annotations

ConceptNet provides an inventory of 28 relation types, from which our annotators used 20 relations to label the inserted sentences. We measure a relatively low annotator agreement of 0.30 (Cohen's Kappa) and produce a gold standard done by an expert annotator (one of the authors) which provides the basis of our final analysis. Here, 1163 out of 1470 sentences (79%) are labeled with ConceptNet relations. Examples of the relations (taken from our data) and the distribution of relation types are shown in Tables 3 and 4. The most frequently occurring relation is *Causes* (16%) followed by *HasProperty* (12%), *IsA* (8%) and *CapableOf* (8%), while there is a relatively high amount of rarely annotated relation types. 21% of sentences could not be assigned an existing ConceptNet relation.

Table 3. ConceptNet relations, with examples from the inserted sentences

CN relation	Example tuple	Example sentence
Causes	(Penalties, change in behavior)	Penalties lead to a change in behavior
HasProperty	(Control data, expensive)	Control data are expensive
CapableOf	(Camera, snapshots)	The camera can take snapshots
IsA	(Olympic disciplines, sports)	Olympic disciplines are sports

Table 4. Proportion of ConceptNet relation types in annotated data

CN rel type		CN rel type		CN rel type		CN rel type	
N.A.	0.21	CapableOf	0.08	Desires	0.04	ReceivesAction	0.02
Causes	0.16	UsedFor	0.06	PartOf	0.03	MotivatedByGoal	0.02
HasProperty	0.12	HasSubevent	0.04	HasA	0.02	DefinedAs	0.02
IsA	0.08	HasPrerequisite	0.04	AtLocation	0.02	Others	0.04

4.4 Task III: Aligning Knowledge Annotations with Wikipedia

To test whether we can find sentences in Wikipedia that match inserted information sentences, for each sentence in the inserted information set we find the most similar sentence in the Wikipedia corpus using WMD' (Eq. 2) as distance score. For example, the most similar sentence for the inserted sentence *The death penalty extinguishes life* in Wikipedia is *The death penalty is the killing of a person as a punishment for a criminal offense.* The averaged distance between $A1^c$ and Wikipedia is 2.60, very similar to $A2^c$ and Wikipedia (2.66) or A5 and Wikipedia (2.58). These distance scores are also close to $A1^c$-$A2^c$ (cf. Table 1), the distance of the annotations by $H1$ and $H2$ after the first correction round.

We take this as a strong indication that Wikipedia can in fact be a useful source for retrieving information that is missing in arguments. While we did not perform a deeper analysis of the retrieved most similar sentences, we will release them, together with the extracted Wikipedia subcorpus as a background textual knowledge resource to the Microtext corpus[4].

5 Conclusion

In this paper we present a multi-step annotation method through which we acquire high-quality annotations for implicit knowledge in argumentative texts.

Eliciting implicit knowledge in argumentative texts is a highly complex and subjective task, and formulating such knowledge in natural language sentences adds to the challenge of assessing the quality of the data. We rely on views of 5 human judges who provide, review, select or revise annotations or state novel solutions. With this process we observe continuous evolution towards increased

[4] http://www.cl.uni-heidelberg.de/english/research/downloads/resource_pages/NLDB2017_data.shtml.

similarity of the annotations, using textual similarity computation, and confirm the high quality of the data set in the final annotation step.

The acquired sentences enrich the argumentative microtexts with carefully curated implicit information. Additional annotation of semantic clause types and common sense knowledge relations further characterize the elicited implicit knowledge: a majority of the inserted sentences are generic. This tendency could be deployed for acquiring such knowledge automatically. A large majority of the sentences can be mapped to common sense knowledge relations as defined in ConceptNet. Thus, knowledge repositories could play an important role in future work on argument analysis. We finally show that the inserted sentences are similar to sentences found in Wikipedia, which suggests that the missing knowledge can be found in textual sources. We thus consider Wikipedia as a valuable textual knowledge resource for automatically acquiring knowledge that is needed to fill gaps in arguments. Future research needs to investigate how the exact knowledge provided by humans can be extracted from such sources.

We release our data set as an extension to the Microtext corpus, to facilitate future research on argument analysis and implicit knowledge acquisition. While the data set size is small, we expect it to be useful for the community as a gold standard for automatically filling knowledge gaps in arguments.

Acknowledgments. This work has been conducted within the Leibniz ScienceCampus "Empirical Linguistics and Computational Modeling", funded by the Leibniz Association under grant no. SAS-2015-IDS-LWC and by the Ministry of Science, Research and Art (MWK) of the state of Baden-Württemberg. We thank our annotators Sabrina Effenberger, Jesper Klein, Sarina Meyer and Rebekka Sons for their contribution.

References

1. Becker, M., Palmer, A., Frank, A.: Argumentative texts and clause types. In: Proceedings of the 3rd Workshop on Argument Mining. pp. 21–30 (2016)
2. Becker, M., Palmer, A., Frank, A.: Clause Types and Modality in Argumentative Microtexts. In: Workshop on Foundations of the Language of Argumentation (in conjunction with COMMA), pp. 1–9. Potsdam, Germany (2016)
3. Black, E., Hunter, A.: A relevance-theoretic framework for constructing and deconstructing enthymemes. J. Logic Comput. **1**(22), 55–78 (2012)
4. Boltuzic, F., Snajder, J.: Fill the Gap! Analyzing Implicit Premises between Claims from Online Debates. In: Proceedings of the 3rd Workshop on Argument Mining. pp. 124–133 (2016)
5. Freeman, J.B.: Argument Structure: Representation and Theory. Springer, Netherlands (2011)
6. Friedrich, A., Palmer, A.: Automatic prediction of aspectual class of verbs in context. In: Proceedings of the ACL 2014 (2014)
7. Grice, H.P.: Logic and conversation. **1975**, 41–58 (1975)
8. Havasi, C., Speer, R., Pustejovsky, J., Lieberman, H.: Digital intuition: Applying common sense using dimensionality reduction. IEEE **4**(24), 24–35 (2009)
9. Kusner, M.J., Sun, Y., Kolkin, N.I., Weinberger, K.Q.: From Word Embeddings To Document Distances. In: Proceedings of the 32nd International Conference on Machine Learning (ICML). pp. 957–966 (2015)

10. Peldszus, A., Stede, M.: An annotated corpus of argumentative microtexts. In: Proceedings of the First European Conference on Argumentation (2015)
11. Rajendran, P., Bollegala, B., Parsons, S.: Contextual stance classification of opinions: A step towards enthymeme reconstruction in online reviews. In: Proceedings of the 3rd Workshop on Argument Mining (2016)
12. Razuvayevskaya, O., Teufel, S.: Recognising enthymemes in real-world texts. In: Workshop on Foundations of the Language of Argumentation (2016)
13. Reimers, N., Eckle-Kohler, J., Schnober, C., Kim, J., Gurevych, I.: Germeval-2014: Nested Named Entity Recognition with neural networks. In: Proceedings of the 12th Edition of the KONVENS Conference, pp. 117–120 (2014)
14. Sidarenka, U., Peldszus, A., Stede, M.: Discourse Segmentation of German Texts. J. Lang. Technol. Comput. Linguist. 30(1) (2015)
15. Speer, R., Havasi, C.: Representing General Relational Knowledge in ConceptNet. In: Proceedings of LREC (2012)

Technical Aspect Extraction from Customer Reviews Based on Seeded Word Clustering

Jean-Marc Davril(✉), Tony Leclercq, Maxime Cordy, and Patrick Heymans

PReCISE Research Center, University of Namur, Namur, Belgium
{jean-marc.davril,tony.leclercq,maxime.cordy,patrick.heymans}@unamur.be

Abstract. Online reviews are an important source of information that customers use to make more informed purchase decisions. Attribute-centric reviews, in which the author supports her opinion with comments on the technical attributes of the product, are particularly insightful because they present deeper discussions about how technical specifications can meet the expectations of customers. However, as the number of available reviews grows, it becomes increasingly cumbersome to manually locate attribute-centric reviews as they get lost within a flood of less informative reviews. We propose a word clustering approach that uses the technical specifications of products to identify technical discussions in online reviews. Each output cluster represents a technical aspect of the products and can be used to extract its related attribute-centric reviews. We evaluate our approach by modeling technical aspects for 21,846 reviews for cameras and show that our approach can extract and rank relevant technical comments.

1 Introduction

Consumer reviews for products are increasingly available online. They have become an essential source of information that customers of shopping websites consult to make better purchase decisions. Previous research shows the positive impact of reviews on both customer trust and product sales [5–8,18,21].

Studying the impact of online reviews on customer decisions requires to distinguish between *search products* and *experience products* [15,16]. Search products are characterised by functional attributes, on the basis of which customers can objectively evaluate the products before purchasing them. Cameras and other electronics are examples of such products. On the contrary, *experience products* cannot be described with such concrete characteristics and are instead evaluated mainly through experience. Music, wine and recreational activities fall into this category.

In a qualitative study involving 250 students, Park et al. show that, for search products, the customers' level of technical expertise affects the perceived value of reviews [17]. They observe that informed customers with more expertise draw more value from *attribute-centric reviews* (i.e. focused on technical specifications), while the others are more likely to rely on *benefit-centric reviews*

F. Frasincar et al. (Eds.): NLDB 2017, LNCS 10260, pp. 97–109, 2017.
DOI: 10.1007/978-3-319-59569-6_10

(i.e. focused on a subjective interpretation of the product benefits without relying on technical arguments).

Park et al. also report that informed customers can settle for only a few attribute-centric reviews to decide whether or not they should buy a product, whereas non-informed customers rely on a large number of benefit-centric reviews to derive collective cues such as the popularity of the product. This suggests that informed customers would make faster purchase decisions should they be presented with appropriate reviews.

However, the total number of available reviews for a set of products can grow so large that it rapidly becomes tedious for informed customers to locate the attribute-centric reviews that address the particular product aspects they are interested in. As an illustration, in the subsequent sections of the paper we refer to a dataset of 21,486 reviews for 53 cameras from a large e-commerce website. The average number of reviews for a product is 405.4 and 7 products have received more than a thousand reviews.

E-merchants are aware of the difficulty for customers to identify helpful reviews under such conditions. They generally address the problem by allowing customers to vote for the quality of reviews. For instance, customers on Amazon.com can vote for reviews they judge to be helpful. The website then ranks the reviews according to their number of votes and makes more visible the higher-ranked reviews. However, as highlighted by Liu et al. [13], this approach introduces two biases. First, due to the *early bird bias*, reviews posted earlier tend to accumulate more votes as they were exposed for a longer time. Second, the *winner circle bias* makes high-ranked reviews more likely to draw additional votes as those are made more visible. Figure 1 illustrates these biases in our dataset. The left chart shows that on average, half of the votes are given to reviews written within the first two months. The right chart shows that on average, more than one third of the votes are given to the two most-voted reviews.

These biases, combined with the fact that vote-based systems do not take into account the level of expertise of users, constitute a strong obstacle to making relevant attribute-centric reviews visible for the informed customers. To address

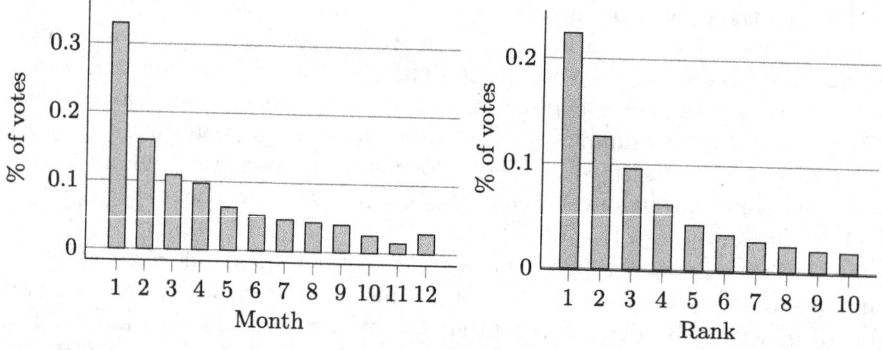

Fig. 1. The biases of the vote-based system illustrated on 21,486 reviews for cameras.

this problem, we propose a text-mining approach to identify attribute-centric reviews and extract the technical aspects (i.e. attribute-centric aspects) they deal with. This research paves the way for a system that would not only present to informed customers attribute-centric reviews lost within the current vote-based systems, but also allow them to search for reviews that discuss the specific aspects in which a given customer is interested.

Our approach consists in three steps. First, we collect a set of words that appear in the technical product specifications and we feed them into an unsupervised algorithm that computes a *technical score* for each word that occurs in the reviews. Second, we cluster together words with high technical scores that are semantically related to each other. Each resulting cluster corresponds to one technical aspect. Third, we analyze the frequencies of cluster words in the reviews to extract relevant technical comments from them.

The remainder of the paper is structured as follows. Section 2 discusses related work. Section 3 describes the identification of technical words. Section 4 describes the creation of technical word clusters. Section 5 presents an evaluation of our approach. Section 6 concludes and proposes ideas for future work.

2 Related Work

Aspect extraction techniques for reviews can be classified into four categories: (1) **Grammatical patterns**, where part-of-speech tagging and grammatical dependencies must be specified to identify aspects [19,23]. However this approach yields false positives when non-aspects in the reviews match the patterns. (2) **Supervised learning**, with models such as hidden markov models [10] or conditional random fields [11], which require the availability of labeled data to be trained. (3) **Topic modeling**, where aspects are represented by topic models which are statistical distributions over the words in the reviews [4,14,22,24]. While topic modeling techniques such as Latent Dirichlet Allocation (LDA) [3] are easy to apply because they are unsupervised, the lack of supervision also often causes the output topics to lack coherence and to fail to make sense to humans. (4) **Term frequency analysis**, where aspects are represented with frequently co-occurring words. Hu et al. [9] and Liu et al. [12] use association rule mining between nouns to discover frequent item sets as candidate aspects. In [20], Scaffidi et al. use contrastive search to identify aspects by detecting words that are significantly more frequent in product reviews than in general English texts.

Our work comes closest to the fourth category. However, instead of looking for frequently co-occurring words as candidate aspects, we use a seeded clustering algorithm where clusters represent aspects. Each cluster is first manually initialized with a small set of seed words that are representative of an aspect. We then augment each cluster c with frequently co-occurring words. In other words, we model aspects by specifying a small number of semantically representative seed words, we then automatically complete each aspect representation with words that are considered semantically related because they appear in the same contexts.

Unlike LDA-based topic modeling techniques, our approach is not fully automated as its results depend on the manual specification of the seed words. However, the seed words provide an initial direction for the algorithm that favors the creation of coherent clusters that are understandable for humans. Additionally, because this is a clustering algorithm, the process remains unsupervised.

Bagheri et al. [1,2] have also proposed to keep aspect extraction unsupervised by initializing aspect representations with seed data and incrementally augmenting them with word candidates. Their search for word candidates is based on Pointwise Mutual Information (PMI) between word co-occurrences at the document level whereas we measure the relevance of a word w for each aspect with the conditional probabilities between w and the aspect words in a context window that contains all words located 6 tokens around the occurrences of w. Another specificity of our work is the computation of technical scores for words, which enables to differentiate between technical aspects and non-technical aspects.

3 Computing Word Technicality

In this section, we present an unsupervised learning algorithm to identify which words are more likely to occur in attribute-centric reviews. To each word w in the reviews, we want to assign a technical score $t(w) \in [0, 1]$ that gives its level of technicality. The higher the technical score, the more w is considered to be frequently featuring in attribute-centric reviews.

After removing stop words and rare words (occurring in less than 10 different reviews) we arbitrarily choose a set of seed words considered to be technical. These words are typically found in product specifications provided by the vendors. All the seed words are assigned an initial score of 1 whereas all other words are assigned a score of 0. Then, we iteratively update the scores of all words on the basis of a mutually recursive definition of technical score for words and technical score for reviews. Basically, reviews are more technical as they contain more technical words. Technical words are words that are present in the lists of product specifications published by vendors or words that frequently appear in technical reviews.

Formally, on the one hand, the *technical score of a review d* is given by

$$t(d) = \frac{\sum_{i=1}^{N_d} t(w_i)}{N_d} \tag{1}$$

where $t(w_i)$ is the technical score of a word w_i occurring in d, and N_d is the total number of words in d. On the other hand, the *technical score of a word w* is given by

$$t(w) = \frac{\sum_{i=1}^{M_w} t(d_i)}{M_w} \tag{2}$$

where $t(d_i)$ is the technical score of a review d_i in which w occurs, and where M_w is the number of reviews in which w appears at least once.

Before repeating these steps, we apply min-max normalization to scale the scores between 0 and 1. That is, we set the score of each word w to

$$t^*(w) = \frac{t(w) - t_{min}}{t_{max} - t_{min}} \tag{3}$$

where t_{min} and t_{max} are respectively the lowest and highest word scores.

Finally, we repeatedly apply these equations until the average differences between current scores and previous scores is under a predefined threshold ϵ.

4 Word Clustering

Now that a technical score has been computed for each word, our next objective is to cluster together semantically related words with high technical scores, such that each cluster contains a set of words representative of a distinct technical aspect.

4.1 Constructing the Technical Semantic Space

As before, we first remove stop words and rare words. Let $\{w_1, \ldots, w_n\}$ be the set of remaining words. For each w_i, we build its *context vector* $v_i = (v_{i1}, \ldots, v_{in})$ such that v_{ij} represents a co-occurrence likelihood of w_i and w_j in reviews where w_i occurs, that is:

$$v_{ij} = \frac{p(w_i, w_j)}{p(w_i)} \tag{4}$$

where $p(w_i)$ is the number of occurrences of w_i in the reviews and $p(w_i, w_j)$ is the number of times that w_i co-occurs with w_j. Note by co-occurrence, we mean that w_j appears in a K-token context window around w_i. Also, the $n \times n$ *context matrix* $M = ({v_1}^T, \ldots, {v_n}^T)^T$ made of all context vectors is not symmetric. Indeed, M_{ij} represents the conditional co-occurrence of w_j on w_i, and may not be equal to M_{ji} if w_i and w_j do not always occur in the same reviews.

The context matrix M defines the *semantic space*. It allows us to compute which words are likely to occur together and which words tend to be surrounded by the same contextual words. This statistical information can be used to discover semantic similarities between words.

As we are interested in computing technical term clusters, we compute a *technical semantic space*, which can be seen as a reduction of the *overall semantic space*. The technical semantic space is represented by the matrix M^* obtained by pruning M from the rows and columns corresponding to words whose technical score is under a certain threshold θ_{tech}. M^* is thus of dimensions $m \times m$, with $m = \#\{w_i : t(w_i) > \theta_{tech}\}$.

4.2 Seeded Word Clustering

Before clustering the words, we must decide which product aspects should be extracted. Their selection always depends on the particular use case at hands. However, because our approach is meant to extract technical aspects, the selected aspects should be related to the technical specifications of the products.

Initially, each aspect of interest is represented by a cluster containing arbitrarily chosen words (typically according to some domain expert knowledge). Then, to each cluster c, we add words that are closely related to the words in c on the basis of the co-occurrence information contained in M^*. The words added to c are the *most dependent* word and the *most similar* word.

We consider a word w to be **dependent** on a cluster c if, when w occurs in a review, the words in c frequently co-occur in the context window of w. At iteration $k+1$ of the construction of a cluster c, the most dependent word on c can thus be added to c by using the technical context-matrix M^* as follows:

$$c^{k+1} = c^k + \arg\max_{w_i \notin c^k} \sum_{w_s \in c^k} M^*_{is} \tag{5}$$

We consider a word w to be **similar** to a cluster c if w has similar co-occurrence values in M^* as the words in c. To compute the similarity between context vectors, we rely on the cosine similarity measure. At iteration $k+1$ of the construction of a cluster c, the most representative word of c can thus be added by using the technical context vectors as follows:

$$c^{k+1} = c^k + \arg\max_{w_i \notin c^k} \sum_{w_s \in c^k} \frac{{M_s}^* \cdot {M_i}^*}{\|{M_s}^*\| \|{M_i}^*\|} \tag{6}$$

where ${M_j}^*$ is the j-th line of M^*.

We repeat these operations for all clusters until they reach a desired size.

5 Evaluation

In this section we describe three evaluations. In the first evaluation, we assess whether the algorithm presented in Sect. 3 assigns high technical scores to words that are truly technical and low scores to common words. In the second evaluation, we measure the coherence of the clusters. In the third evaluation, we evaluate the usefulness of technical clusters to extract relevant technical comments from reviews.

5.1 Technical Scores

We performed two evaluations for the measurement of technical scores presented in Sect. 3. Their objectives is to respectively assess whether our algorithm assigns high scores to technical words, and low scores to non-technical words.

We collected 21,846 reviews for cameras that contain at least 200 characters each. During pre-processing we removed stop words as well as words that do not occur in at least 20 different reviews. We chose 66 seed words from product specifications. The seed words are words that appear either in product attribute names, such as `aperture` and `sensor`, or in attribute values such as `megapixels` and `ISO`.

During the first evaluation, we assessed the assignment of a high score to technical words. We performed a 5-fold cross-evaluation during which 80% of the technical seed words were used at each fold, and the threshold ϵ was set to 0.05. At the end of each fold, we measured the average technical scores resulting from our algorithm for three distinct sets of words: (1) the 80% of the seed words, (2) the 20% of the seed words that were left out, and (3) all the non-seed words. After repeating the 5-fold cross-evaluation 500 times, we obtained an average score of 0.575 for all the non-seed words, **0.711** for the left-out seed technical words, and **0.717** for the seed technical words.

The difference between the scores for left-out seed words and for used seed words is lower than one percent, which shows that our approach is capable of assigning high scores to technical words that were unspecified prior to the running of the algorithm.

For the second evaluation, we measured the performance of our approach when noise is introduced in the seed words. To do so, we added non-technical words to the seed words by randomly selecting 6 words from the seed technical words, and replacing them with 6 words randomly selected from 60 non-technical words. The non-technical words are either words we did not consider to be representative of attribute-centric discussions such as `vacations` and `fantastic`, or words denoting product attributes that are familiar to novice customers, such as `battery` or `flash`.

Table 1. Averaged technical scores for non-technical seed words

vacations: **0.363**, purchase: **0.437** satisfied: **0.457**
disappointed: **0.466**, beautiful: **0.488**, digital: **0.524**
enjoy: **0.529** problem: **0.547** battery: **0.557**
fantastic: **0.559** color: **0.588** flash: **0.623**

Table 1 shows the average scores for 12 of the 66 non-technical words after we repeated the random word selection and the evaluation 1,000 times. Even though the non-technical words were used as seed words, their final scores reflect their non-technicality. While some of the words have scores exceeding 55%, none of them reaches the score of technical seed words. We also consider the score of 62% for the word `flash` to reflect the fact that it is both a popular word and a word representative of an aspect likely to be discussed in more depth in attribute-centric reviews. Overall, the substituted non-technical words were assigned an average score of 0.511. As for the technical words, the 6 replaced words were assigned an average score of 0.733 and the 60 seed words a score of 0.739.

5.2 Technical Clusters

To evaluate the clustering algorithm described in Sect. 4, we measure the coherence of the clusters discovered in the camera dataset. The purpose of a coherence measure is to estimate how interpretable the clusters are to humans. Since we discovered the clusters by using M^*, the goal of this evaluation is to analyze how the coherence of the clusters measured on M^* compares to their coherence measured on M. If the coherence decreases from M^* to M, this would indicate that the clusters we have discovered in the technical semantic space lose of their coherence when they are confronted to the overall semantic space.

To illustrate our approach, we selected five seed clusters for the camera dataset as shown in Table 2 and we ran five cluster constructions for each seed cluster. During each of the 25 runs, 10,000 reviews were randomly selected, and we set the size of the context window to 6 to define their context matrix M and their technical context-matrix M^*. We selected the words to be represented in M^* with a technical threshold θ_{tech} of 0.68. The M^* matrix was also augmented with the vectors of the initial seed words, regardless of their technical score.

Table 2. Examples of technical clusters computed for the camera dataset. For each cluster, the first words in the right column are the seed words, the **bold** words are the added dependent words, and the underlined words are the added similar words.

Low light performance	Light, noisy, sensor, megapixels, **APS**, **CMOS**, **Sensitivity**, **DIM**, performance, ISO, 6400, 12800
Viewfinder	Screen, viewfinder, **tilting**, **diopter**, **OLED**, **articulating**, tilt, rear, EVS, angles
Video	Video, shoot, shooting, **1920 × 1080**, **30p**, **24p**, **60p**, AVCHD, fps, 4k, mp4
Zoom	Zoom, close, **4×**, **50 mm**, **lever**, **optically**, mp4, 24 mm, 25 mm, equivalent
Wide-angle	Wide, large, angle, landscape, **24 mm**, **28 mm**, **wider**, **tele**, barrel, distortion, 25 mm, vignetting

Each run consisted of eight iterations. For the first four iterations, the clusters were augmented with their most dependent word (Eq. 5) and for the last four iterations, the clusters were augmented with their most similar word (Eq. 6). Each added word was computed on the basis of the technical vectors in M^*. Table 2 shows an example of a technical cluster constructed for each of the 5 seed clusters.

We estimated the coherence c_{cen} of each cluster wrt. M and M^* by averaging the cosine similarity between the context vectors of the words in the cluster and their centroid $\boldsymbol{v_c}$:

$$\boldsymbol{v_c} = \sum_{w_i \in t} \boldsymbol{v_i} \tag{7}$$

$$c_{cen}(t) = \frac{1}{|t|} \sum_{w_i \in t} cos(\boldsymbol{v_i}, \boldsymbol{v_c}) \tag{8}$$

Table 3 shows the average coherence measures for each cluster. The left column shows the coherence computed with the technical vectors from M^* and the right column shows the coherence computed with the matrix M. We can see that while the construction of the cluster was based on the vectors in M^*, the coherence of the clusters is higher when it is computed with the vectors in M.

Table 3. Average cluster coherences over the technical semantic space and the overall semantic space.

Cluster	Cluster coherence	
	M^*	M
Low light performance	0.495	0.567
Viewfinder	0.500	0.569
Video	0.588	0.592
Zoom	0.512	0.572
Wide-angle	0.468	0.563

This means that by clustering together words that appear in similar technical discussions, we actually selected words that co-occur even more similarly with the words in the entire vocabulary of the reviews.

5.3 Information Extraction

In the third part of our evaluation, we assess the usefulness of the technical clusters to extract technical comments from reviews. We want to evaluate whether a cluster can be used to measure two properties of the technical comments: (1) their relevance wrt. the aspect corresponding to the cluster and (2) their technical depth.

Given document d and cluster c, which represents an aspect a, we test the two following hypotheses:

H1 The ratio between (1) the number of occurrences of words from c in d and (2) the total number of technical words in d is an indicator of the **relevance** of d wrt. to a. We refer to this ratio as the *technical ratio*.

H2 The number of distinct words from c occurring in d is an indicator of the **technical depth** of d wrt. to a.

To evaluate the two hypotheses, we extract technical comments from the reviews for each cluster c shown in Table 2. One group of sentences is extracted from each review containing at least one word from c. In each review we identify the sentence s containing the largest number of words from c and we extract it from the review with its previous and next sentences when they featured at least 20% as many words from c than s.

For H1, we selected 20 extractions for each aspect a with a technical ratio uniformly spread between 0 and 1. We asked two judges with technical knowledge about cameras to classify the 20 extractions into 4 classes based on their relevance to the aspect a. Class 1 corresponds to extractions that strictly relate to a. Class 2 is for extractions that relate to a, but also covers other aspects than a while a remains the main aspect. Class 3 is for extractions that relate to a, but also cover other aspects than a and a is not the main aspect. Class 4 is for extractions that do not relate to a. Table 4 shows the technical ratios averaged over the four classes and the two judges for each aspect.

Table 4. Average technical ratios.

	Class 1	Class 2	Class 3	Class 4
Low light performance	0.864	0.532	0.285	0.326
Viewfinder	0.747	0.638	0.246	0.167
Video	0.784	0.708	0.311	0.075
Zoom	0.791	0.545	0.427	0.247
Wide-angle	0.755	0.792	0.573	0.234

For H2, we selected 20 extractions for each aspect with a number of distinct cluster words uniformly spread between the maximum and minimum observed numbers of distinct cluster words. Each extraction also has a technical ratio above 0.6. We asked the two judges to rate the extractions on a range from 1 to 4 based on the their technical depth, score 1 being for extractions that offer in-depth technical discussions of product specifications, and score 4 being for extractions that are not technical at all. Table 5 shows the numbers of distinct occurring cluster words averaged over the four classes and the two judges.

Table 5. Average numbers of distinct occurring cluster words.

	Class 1	Class 2	Class 3	Class 4
Low light performance	6.75	5.42	2.93	1.9
Viewfinder	4.42	3.52	2.97	2.17
Video	6.42	4.17	3	1.62
Zoom	4.875	4.875	2.93	1.7
Wide-angle	6.58	5.07	3.17	2.25

The results presented in Table 4 and in Table 5 show that the frequencies of cluster words in product reviews can be used to rank extractions based on their

Table 6. Agreements and disagreements between judges.

	Agreements	1-class disagr.	2-classes disagr.	3-classes disagr.
H1 task	79	19	2	0
H2 task	75	25	0	0

relevance and technical depth wrt. technical aspects. The numbers significantly vary from one aspect to another, which suggests that ranking strategies should be adjusted to each one of them.

As for the degree of agreement between the two judges, Table 6 shows the number of agreements and disagreements over the 100 extractions of each task. The judges only disagreed twice with a 2-classes difference (e.g. class 1 and class 3) and never with a 3-classes difference.

6 Conclusion and Future Work

The main contribution of this paper is an approach to create word clusters that represent technical product aspects in online reviews. After an initial set of seed words is provided, the approach is unsupervised. The algorithm first associates technical scores to the words appearing in the reviews in order to identify which ones are likely to be representative of technical comments. Words with a high technical score are then clustered together based on the frequency of their co-occurrences in the reviews. Each resulting cluster contains a set of words that are semantically related to a technical aspect.

The other main contribution is a set of three evaluations of our algorithm. The first shows that it can effectively differentiate technical words from common words. The second shows that the technical scores can be used to discover semantically related technical words. We measured the coherence of the clusters and saw that it is preserved in the overall semantic space. The third shows the usefulness of technical clusters to extract technical comments from reviews.

In this paper, we applied the approach to a set of reviews for cameras. We argue that it is suitable for other product lines that are also characterized by a list of technical specifications.

As explained in the introduction, our ultimate goal is to design effective front-ends to search for, and rank, relevant reviews from large sets. In this paper, we focused on the computational linguistic treatments required to achieve that. The graphical user interface design and its evaluation are our next goals. That part of the work will include a user study which will provide a wider perspective on the relevance and speed of the extractions.

A current limitation of this work is that we have yet to address the level of expertise required from web customers to fully exploit the content of the identified reviews. Some technical reviews are more accessible to novices than others, e.g. when their authors explain the benefits of the technical attributes and how they relate to the usage of the product in layman terms. Others assume their readers are already familiar with the technical terms and go straight to the point. Therefore, while technical reviews help customers make better purchase decisions, improving their accessibility to novice customers remains an important issue. To address this problem, we will investigate the use of text-mining techniques to measure the degree of pedagogy in technical reviews. This ability could enable to (1) present novices with the most pedagogical reviews, and (2) automatically augment less pedagogical reviews with explanations about the product attributes they cover.

References

1. Bagheri, A., Saraee, M., De Jong, F.: Care more about customers: unsupervised domain-independent aspect detection for sentiment analysis of customer reviews. Knowl.-Based Syst. **52**, 201–213 (2013)
2. Bagheri, A., Saraee, M., Jong, F.: An unsupervised aspect detection model for sentiment analysis of reviews. In: Métais, E., Meziane, F., Saraee, M., Sugumaran, V., Vadera, S. (eds.) NLDB 2013. LNCS, vol. 7934, pp. 140–151. Springer, Heidelberg (2013). doi:10.1007/978-3-642-38824-8_12
3. Blei, D.M., Ng, A.Y., Jordan, M.I.: Latent dirichlet allocation. J. Mach. Learn. Res. **3**(Jan), 993–1022 (2003)
4. Brody, S., Elhadad, N.: An unsupervised aspect-sentiment model for online reviews. In: Human Language Technologies: The 2010 Annual Conference of the North American Chapter of the Association for Computational Linguistics (2010)
5. Chen, P.Y., Dhanasobhon, S., Smith, M.D.: All reviews are not created equal: the disaggregate impact of reviews and reviewers at amazon. com (2008)
6. Chevalier, J.A., Mayzlin, D.: The effect of word of mouth on sales: online book reviews. J. Mark. Res. **43**(3), 345–354 (2006)
7. Cui, G., Lui, H.K., Guo, X.: The effect of online consumer reviews on new product sales. Int. J. Electron. Commer. **17**(1), 39–58 (2012)
8. Ghose, A., Ipeirotis, P.G.: Designing ranking systems for consumer reviews: the impact of review subjectivity on product sales and review quality. In: Proceedings of the 16th Annual Workshop on Information Technology and Systems (2006)
9. Hu, M., Liu, B.: Mining and summarizing customer reviews. In: Proceedings of the Tenth International Conference on Knowledge Discovery and Data Mining (2004)
10. Jin, W., Ho, H.H., Srihari, R.K.: Opinionminer: a novel machine learning system for web opinion mining and extraction. In: Proceedings of the 15th ACM SIGKDD International Conference on Knowledge Discovery and Data Mining. ACM (2009)
11. Li, F., Han, C., Huang, M., Zhu, X., Xia, Y.J., Zhang, S., Yu, H.: Structure-aware review mining and summarization. In: Proceedings of the 23rd International Conference on Computational Linguistics (2010)
12. Liu, B., Hu, M., Cheng, J.: Opinion observer: analyzing and comparing opinions on the web. In: Proceedings of the 14th International Conference on World Wide Web, pp. 342–351. ACM (2005)
13. Liu, J., Cao, Y., Lin, C.Y., Huang, Y., Zhou, M.: Low-quality product review detection in opinion summarization. In: EMNLP-CoNLL, vol. 7, pp. 334–342 (2007)
14. Lu, Y., Zhai, C., Sundaresan, N.: Rated aspect summarization of short comments. In: Proceedings of the 18th International Conference on World Wide Web (2009)
15. Nelson, P.: Information and consumer behavior. J. Polit. Econ. **78**(2), 311–329 (1970)

16. Nelson, P.: Advertising as information. J. Polit. Econ. **82**(4), 729–754 (1974)
17. Park, D.H., Kim, S.: The effects of consumer knowledge on message processing of electronic word-of-mouth via online consumer reviews. Electron. Commer. Res. Appl. **7**(4), 399–410 (2009)
18. Park, D.H., Lee, J., Han, I.: The effect of on-line consumer reviews on consumer purchasing intention: the moderating role of involvement. Int. J. Electron. Commer. **11**(4), 125–148 (2007)
19. Qiu, G., Liu, B., Bu, J., Chen, C.: Opinion word expansion and target extraction through double propagation. Comput. Linguist. **37**(1), 9–27 (2011)
20. Scaffidi, C., Bierhoff, K., Chang, E., Felker, M., Ng, H., Jin, C.: Red opal: product-feature scoring from reviews. In: Proceedings of the 8th ACM Conference on Electronic Commerce, pp. 182–191. ACM (2007)
21. Sparks, B.A., Browning, V.: The impact of online reviews on hotel booking intentions and perception of trust. Tourism Manage. **32**(6), 1310–1323 (2011)
22. Titov, I., McDonald, R.: Modeling online reviews with multi-grain topic models. In: Proceedings of the 17th International Conference on World Wide Web (2008)
23. Wu, Y., Zhang, Q., Huang, X., Wu, L.: Phrase dependency parsing for opinion mining. In: Proceedings of the 2009 Conference on Empirical Methods in Natural Language Processing, vol. 3 (2009)
24. Zhao, W.X., Jiang, J., Yan, H., Li, X.: Jointly modeling aspects and opinions with a MaxEnt-LDA hybrid. In: Proceedings of the 2010 Conference on Empirical Methods in Natural Language Processing, pp. 56–65. ACM (2010)

Event Detection for Heterogeneous News Streams

Ida Mele(✉) and Fabio Crestani

Faculty of Informatics, Università della Svizzera Italiana, Lugano, Switzerland
{ida.mele,fabio.crestani}@usi.ch

Abstract. In this paper we tackle the problem of detecting events from multiple and heterogeneous streams of news. In particular, we focus on news which are heterogeneous in length and writing styles since they are published on different platforms (i.e., Twitter, RSS portals, and news websites). This heterogeneity makes the event detection task more challenging, hence we propose an approach able to cope with heterogeneous streams of news. Our technique combines topic modeling, named-entity recognition, and temporal analysis to effectively detect events from news streams. The experimental results confirmed that our approach is able to better detect events than other state-of-the-art techniques and to divide the news in high-precision clusters based on the events they describe.

Keywords: Event detection · News clustering · Heterogeneous news streams

1 Introduction

Topic Detection and Tracking (TDT) is an important research area which has attracted a lot of attention especially in information analysis for discovering newsworthy stories and studying their evolution over time. The main challenge of TDT is to group news that are about some specific events (e.g., Ecuador earthquake) and tracking their evolution over time. In this paper, we focus on the problem of event detection from multiple and heterogeneous streams of news, namely, news reported by different channels (e.g., BBC, CNN) on different publishing platforms (e.g., Twitter, RSS portals, and news websites)[1].

In the past, event detection has received a lot of attention, but most of the approaches presented in the literature focus on one stream of text or tackle the problem of event detection in news articles and in tweets, separately [4,6,7,15]. This could be a limitation when we deal with heterogeneous news coming from multiple streams, since techniques that are effective for long text (e.g., news articles) are known to give poor performance when applied to short text (e.g., tweets). On the other hand, considering event detection from multiple streams

[1] The words *channel* and *stream* are used interchangeably in this paper, and we use the general term *news* to refer to a news article, an RSS feed, or a tweet.

F. Frasincar et al. (Eds.): NLDB 2017, LNCS 10260, pp. 110–123, 2017.
DOI: 10.1007/978-3-319-59569-6_11

as a single task, which is irrespective of the document type, can take advantage of cross-linking the news.

To address the problem of TDT in multiple and heterogeneous streams, we developed an approach which leverages topic models, named-entity recognition, and temporal analysis of bursty features. As we will see in Sect. 5, our approach overcomes traditional techniques for event detection [4,15] and document clustering [3]. It captures crisp events, divides the news in high-precision clusters and is document independent in the sense that it can be used for different types of news (e.g., short tweets as well as long news articles). It is also query-less which means that we do not need predefined queries and this is beneficial especially for independently discovering emerging topics or for analyzing events for which we have limited background knowledge. In addition, our approach relies on features, such as named entities and event phrases, providing a short but understandable description of the event. Finally, the size of an event's window is automatically mined from the data.

The contributions of this paper are the following:

1. we present an approach which detects events by applying topic mining, named-entity recognition, and temporal analysis of bursty features on news;
2. we cluster the news based on the events they describe;
3. we compare different methodologies for event detection and text clustering focusing on TDT in multiple and heterogeneous streams of news.

The rest of the paper is structured as follows: we review related work in Sect. 2. Section 3 describes our methodology for event detection and news clustering. We discuss the characteristics of the approach in Sect. 4 and present the experimental results in Sect. 5. Finally, Sect. 6 concludes the paper.

2 Related Work

Topic Detection and Tracking (TDT) is a wide research area which includes several tasks ranging from event segmentation of news streams to event detection and tracking. Event detection is based on monitoring streams of news and automatically organizing the news by the events they describe. Research works on event detection can be divided into two categories: *document-pivot* and *feature-pivot* approaches. The former focuses on clustering documents related to the same event and then extracting the event-based features from the discovered clusters [1]. The latter is based on finding hidden features and then clustering these features in order to identify the events from the news [4,6,15].

Fung et al. [4] addressed the problem of detecting *hot bursty event features.* Their technique finds a minimal set of features representing the events in a specific time window. They first identify bursty features by statistically modeling the frequency of each unigram with a binomial distribution. Then, they group these features into events and use time series analysis to determine the hot period of an event. The extraction of bursty features based on statistics may result in a prohibitive number of features, especially when unigrams are used. Moreover, describing the detected events using a set of single words may be not intuitive and difficult for human interpretation.

He et al. [6] treat signals as features and apply Discrete Fourier Transformation (DFT) on them. Their approach builds a signal for each feature using the *document frequency - inverse document frequency* (df × idf) scheme along with the time domain. Then, it applies DFT to transform the signal from the time domain to the frequency domain. A spike in the frequency domain indicates a corresponding high-frequency signal source. Such bursty features are then grouped into events by considering both the features' co-occurrences and their distributions in the time domain. This approach has scalability issues due to the application of DFT which can be computationally prohibitive.

In the last few years, research works focused on detecting events in Twitter. The challenge is that traditional approaches developed for formal text (e.g., news articles) cannot be applied directly to tweets, which are short, noisy, and published at a high-speed rate. One of the main problems in microblogging systems is to distinguish the newsworthy events from trends or mundane events which attract attention from fans and enthusiasts. In [2] the authors present an approach for separating real-world events from non-event tweets based on aggregated statistics of temporal, topical, social, and Twitter-centric features. Another approach consists in finding the hashtag *#breakingnews* to identify news in Twitter [10]. In our research, we do not consider these techniques since we monitor news channels, hence their tweets are *all* newsworthy. We rather analyze the streams of tweets to detect the events and divide the tweets into clusters based on the events they describe. A similar problem was addressed by [14] for detecting crime or disasters from tweets. Analogously, Popescu et al. [11] used an entity-based approach for event detection where a set of tweets containing a target entity are processed and machine learning techniques are applied to predict whether the tweets constitute an event regarding the entity or not. The drawback of these approaches is that the events must be known a priori and be easily represented by well-defined keyword queries (e.g., "earthquake") or named entities (e.g., "Obama"). Ritter et al. [13] tried to overcome this limitation by designing an open-domain system for extracting a calendar of categorized events.

Other popular approaches for event detection in Twitter are: *Twevent* [7] and Event Detection with Clustering of Wavelet-based signals (*EDCoW*) [15]. *Twevent* clusters tweets representing events and provides a semantically meaningful description of the clusters. It segments the tweets relying on statistics from Microsoft Web N-Gram service and Wikipedia [8]. Then, bursty segments are detected by analyzing the tweet frequency and user frequency. The assumption is that if a segment is related to an event, then it is present in many tweets which are posted by many different users. *EDCoW* applies measurements to see how signals (unigrams) change over time and uses wavelet analysis to spot high-energy signals which are then treated as event features.

In this paper we do not focus on just one type of document (e.g., tweets), we rather propose a technique for event detection from streams of heterogeneous documents. In Sect. 5 we will compare our approach against [4,15] since they are general and do not need any predefined queries. To the best of our knowledge this is the first work that tackles the problem of event detection from multiple and heterogeneous streams of news. Other works have analyzed multiple news streams but for other purposes, e.g., analyzing the newswires' timeliness [5].

3 *EDNC*: Event Detection and News Clustering

In this section we describe our approach which is called Event Detection and News Clustering (*EDNC*). It allows to detect events from multiple and heterogeneous news streams and to divide the news into corresponding event clusters.

We assume to have n streams of news $N = \{N_1, N_2, ..., N_n\}$, where $N_i = \{n_{i,1}, n_{i,2}, ..., n_{i,m}\}$ is the stream i consisting of m news. We want to analyze the news in order to identify a set of popular events, $E = \{e_1, e_2, ...\}$ that appear in them. Each event, $e_j \in E$, is represented by $\langle w_{e_j}, F_{e_j} \rangle$ where w_{e_j} is the time window of the event and F_{e_j} are variable-length phrases, called *event features*, which give crisp information about the event. In Sect. 5 we will provide some examples of event features. *EDNC*'s steps are summarized in Fig. 1.

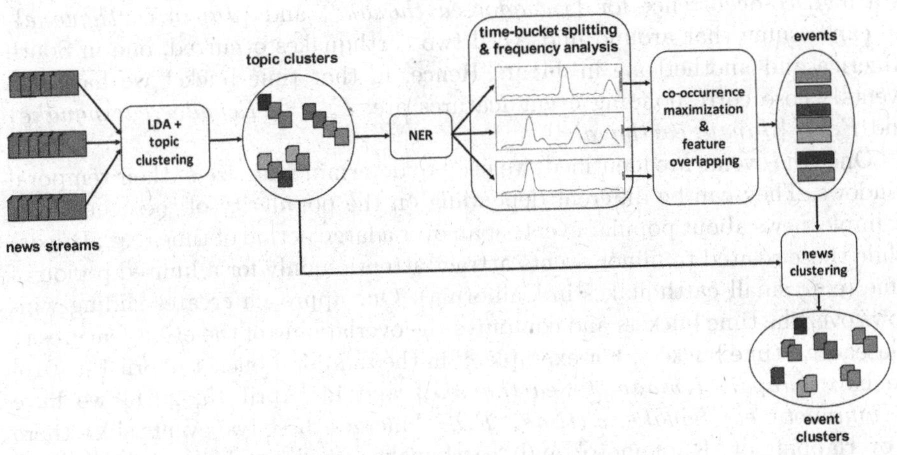

Fig. 1. A diagram showing the main steps of *EDNC* approach.

3.1 Event Detection

Our event-detection methodology first applies LDA to detect general topics and to create topic clusters of news. News are firstly divided into broad topic clusters by applying the approach described in [9], which treats each LDA topic as a cluster. In particular, a document is interpreted as a distribution vector of topics, $\boldsymbol{\theta}$, and it is assigned to the cluster x if $x = argmax_j(\theta_j)$. Although assigning the news to one topic may seem a limitation, it is actually a reasonable solution especially if we think that news are usually about one specific event. Moreover, other studies on topic modeling proved that this approach is effective especially for short text (i.e., RSS feeds and tweets) [16].

As second step, the approach analyzes the frequency of named entities and other representative event phrases over time. To do this, we apply a *named-entity recognition* tool [12] which finds out the named entities and event phrases in a document collection. Then, the news streams are sorted by time and divided into time buckets of fixed size (e.g., 24 h). *EDNC* computes the frequencies of detected named entities and event phrases in each time bucket. The most frequent named entities and event phrases (e.g., the top-10%) are retained as *event features*, $F_{e_j} = \{f_1, f_2, ...\}$. Note that these are variable-length sequences of words (e.g., "Barack Obama," "tropical storm Colin," "earth shakes") and not just single words. Since these features are very frequent in a time bucket, they can be used to semantically describe the popular events.

3.2 Estimating the Temporal Windows of Events

Maximizing the co-occurrences of the event features, we can divide the events and determine their time span. As an example, in the time bucket [April 17, 2016] if we observe $F = \{Japan, Ecuador, earthquake\}$ as frequent features and there is a high co-occurrence for $\{Ecuador, earthquake\}$ and $\{Japan, earthquake\}$, we can assume that around mid April two earthquakes occurred, one in South America and another one in Japan. Hence, in that time bucket we have two events whose corresponding event features are: $F_{e_1} = \{Ecuador, earthquake\}$ and $F_{e_2} = \{Japan, earthquake\}$.

Once the events are identified, we need to determine the size of their temporal windows. They can be different depending on the popularity of the events. For example, news about popular events span over a large period of time (e.g., Brexit) while those related to minor events attract attention only for a limited period of time (e.g., small earthquakes in California). Our approach creates sliding windows over the time buckets and computes the overlapping of the event features in consecutive time buckets. For example, if in the temporal bucket [April 14, 2016] we have $\{Japan, Kumamoto, earthquake\}$ and in [April 15, 2016] we have $\{Kumamoto, earthquake, victims\}$, *EDNC* merges these two events since there is overlapping of "Kumamoto" and "earthquake." Such overlapping depends on a parameter which specifies the percentage of shared keywords in the event features, and it can be tuned to get more defined events. In particular, bigger values of the feature-overlapping percentage (e.g., 70%) are used for identifying crisp events. *EDNC* uses consecutive buckets because if two time slots are characterized by similar keywords but they are distant (i.e., the buckets in the middle do not present any of the monitored event features), they should be considered as separated events. For example, if we observe in the time buckets [March 11, 2016] and [April 14, 2016] event keywords like $\{Japan, tsunami, earthquake\}$ and $\{Japan, Kumamoto, earthquake\}$, we can assume that they are two distinct events. Indeed, the former is about the 5th anniversary of the tsunami which devastated Japan in March 2011, while the latter is about the earthquake which hit the South of Japan in April 2016.

3.3 Event-Based Clustering of News

We created clusters of news based on the events they describe. Each cluster is identified by the event features and the temporal window.

For creating the clusters we used a traditional IR approach which retrieves the news and rank them based on their similarity to the event features. We first filter out all the news that are not within the event's temporal window, then the news are sorted by their content similarity with the event's features. In particular, we applied the cosine similarity between the news N and the list of keywords in the event features F:

$$\cos(\mathbf{N},\mathbf{F}) = \frac{\mathbf{N}\cdot\mathbf{F}}{\|\mathbf{N}\|\|\mathbf{F}\|} = \frac{\sum_{i=1}^{n} N_i\, F_i}{\sqrt{\sum_{i=1}^{n} N_i^2}\sqrt{\sum_{i=1}^{n} F_i^2}}$$

where $\mathbf{N}$ and $\mathbf{F}$ are two vectors representing the news and the event features, respectively.

4 Characteristics of *EDNC*

As explained in Sect. 1 we aim at detecting events from multiple and heterogeneous streams of news, and, for this reason, our event-detection tool fulfills the following desiderata:

1. **Document independent.** We focus on different publishing platforms, so the approach works for different types of documents (news articles, RSS feeds, and tweets), while the approaches presented in [7,10] are suitable only for tweets. In particular, they use hashtags as well as retweet popularity (i.e., the number of times the users (re)tweet the news) and such information is not available for news articles and RSS feeds.
2. **Query-less.** We assume that professional users (e.g., journalists and news analysts) would like to *discover* the events without any or limited knowledge of what is going on in the world. Hence, our technique does not need input keywords to retrieve relevant news, while other state-of-the-art approaches detect the events that match some predefined search keywords or named entities [8,11].
3. **Flexible time windows.** Having time windows with variable size allows to cluster together news about popular events which tend to span over a large period of time (e.g., earthquakes, Brexit) as well as minor events which attract attention only for a limited period of time (e.g., 5th anniversary of tsunami in Japan).
4. **Semantically significant description of events.** Our approach can be used to semantically describe the identified events, hence to label the news clusters. The event descriptions are variable-length lists of words (e.g., named entities and event phrases), making the understanding of the event easy even with limited background knowledge about it.

5 Experimental Results

In this section we present the experimental setup and results. In order to evaluate the effectiveness of our approach we collected data from different newswires and different platforms to create a heterogeneous dataset of news documents. We then used this collection for event detection and for clustering the news based on the detected events.

5.1 Dataset

For our experiments we created a dataset of heterogeneous news published by different newswires on different platforms. In particular, we collected news articles, RSS feeds, and tweets published by 9 newswire channels (ABC, Al Jazeera, BBC, CBC, CNN, NBC, Reuters, United Press International, and Xinhua China Agency) for several months. For the experiments reported in this paper, we used the English news published during 4 months (from March 1 to June 30, 2016), for a total of around 140K news documents. Each news document has a title (optional), content, link (optional), timestamp, and channel. The optional fields are present in news articles but may be not available for tweets and RSS feeds.

Since some of the techniques used for event detection are not time efficient, analyzing the whole dataset would be time consuming. So, we subsampled the dataset by selecting 10 topics which were related to some important events that happened in the 4 months of our data, such as terror attacks, Brexit, and earthquakes. News relevant to these topics form broad clusters (i.e., the news are about different, although related, events). For example, the cluster corresponding to the topic *terror attacks* includes several events, such as a bomb at an airport checkpoint in Somalia, shootings at hotels in the Ivory Coast, bomb explosions in Belgium, etc. Some of them can be also connected and interleaved. Consider, for example, the terror attacks that have recently happened in Europe. At the beginning of March, some suspects were arrested in Belgium, followed by suicide bombings in Brussels on March 22, 2016, then at the end of April one of the terrorists was handed over French authorities. Our technique aims at distinguishing these low-granularity events from the topic clusters to create the corresponding smaller event-based clusters of news.

5.2 Event Detection Evaluation

We now describe the methodology we used for the evaluation of the event detection task and the corresponding experimental results.

Evaluation Methodology. We applied *EDNC* for discovering the events reported in the news documents. To evaluate the effectiveness of our approach, we also considered two alternative approaches for event detection which are based on co-occurrences of unigrams (*Unigram Co-Occurrences*) [4] and on wavelet analysis (*EDCoW*) [15]. The former detects the events by analyzing the co-occurrences of bursty features (unigrams) in non-overlapping time windows. The latter is called Event Detection with Clustering of Wavelet-based signals (*EDCoW*). It creates a signal for each individual word, then it applies *wavelet transformation* and *auto-correlation* to measure the bursty "energy" of the words. Words with high energies are retained as event features and using *cross-correlation* the similarity between pairs of events is measured. Event detection is done by creating a graph consisting of words with high cross-correlation and partitioning it based on the modularity. Both approaches have fixed time windows whose length must be specified as a parameter of the program. We tried different values from 3 to 10 days, and we could observe better results with time windows of 7 days.

Results. Some of the events identified by our methodology are reported in Table 1. We analyzed the corresponding news to provide a short description and help the reader to understand the event features. As we can see, our methodology was able to spot popular events such as Brexit, Obama's visit to Cuba, terror attacks in Brussels, and earthquakes in Asia and South America. It could also detect some minor events such as the hijacking of an Egyptian aircraft and wildfires in Canada.

Table 2 shows the events detected by the other two state-of-the-art approaches (*Unigram Co-Occurrences* and *EDCoW*) with windows of 7 days. As we can see, *Unigram Co-Occurrences* detected more events compared to *EDCoW* which found no events in some of the time windows. Both approaches have two main drawbacks: (1) the event keywords are oftentimes general and difficult to interpret without a manual inspection of the news in the dataset; (2) the size of the temporal window is fixed and must be estimated up front. Moreover, in *EDCoW* the computation of wavelet transformation and auto-correlation is computationally complex and time consuming. Using cross-correlation as similarity measure can result in noisy grouping of events that may have happened in the same period of time just by chance. For example, in w_0: "cuba, damage, and vatican" are grouped together but they refer to different events. In particular, "cuba" probably refers to the news on preparations in Cuba for Obama's future visit, "damage" to the damages caused by the earthquake in Indonesia, and "vatican" to the scandal that involved some Catholic priests in Australia.

5.3 News Clustering

News clustering consists in dividing the news based on the event they report. We now present the evaluation methodology and the experimental results obtained for news clustering.

Evaluation Methodology. Once we detected the events in the collection, we divided the news into event-based clusters. To do so, our methodology computes the cosine similarity between the news documents and the event features as explained in Sect. 3.3.

Since we aim at capturing news stories reporting the same event, it is crucial to have clusters whose news are truly related to the event. So we focused on

Table 1. Some of the events detected by the *EDNC* approach in the period of time from March 1 to June 30, 2016. For each event we report the event features plus a short description and the indicative date of the event.

Event features	Description and indicative date
rome, pell, cardinal, cover, abuse, denies	Cardinal Pell's testimony at the child-abuse commission (Mar. 1)
indonesia, quake-strikes, sumatra, tsunami	Earthquake in Sumatra caused tsunami warning in Indonesia (Mar. 2)
anniversary, remember, tsunami, japan, 5-years-ago	Japan marked the 5th anniversary of the 2011 tsunami (Mar. 11)
brussels, captured, paris, salah-abdeslam	Police arrested one of the Paris' terror attacker (Mar. 18)
castro, cuba, havana, obama, visit	Obama visited Cuba (Mar. 21)
attack, brussels-airport, isis, maelbeek-metro	Terror attacks happened in Brussels (Mar. 22)
argentina, mauricio-macri, obama, tango	Obama visited Mauricio Macri in Argentina (Mar. 23)
cyprus, egyptair, hijacking, surrendered	An Egyptair flight was diverted to Cyprus (Mar. 29)
easter, pope, ritual, washed	Pope celebrated the Catholic Easter (Mar. 25)
referendum, dutch, ukraine, eu	Dutch referendum on the Ukraine-EU Association Agreement (Apr. 6)
japan, kumamoto, earthquake, damage, victims	Earthquake hit Kumamoto province in Japan (Apr. 14)
earthquake, ecuador, strikes	Earthquake devastated Ecuador (Apr. 16)
nairobi, kenya, building, collapses, death	A building collapsed in Nairobi, Kenya (Apr. 30)
miami, first, cruise, passengers, cuba	New cruise set sails from Miami to Havana (Apr. 30)
canada, alberta, wildfire, fort-mcmurray, fire	Fort McMurray was evacuated due to wildfires in Alberta (May 4)
crash, disappears, egyptair, flight-ms804	Egyptair plane crashed into the Mediterranean Sea (May 19)
boxing, died, louisville, muhammad-ali	The boxing champion Muhammad Ali died (Jun. 3)
funeral, memorial, muhammad-ali, remembered	Funeral of Muhammad Ali (Jun. 10)
christina-grimmie, singer, voice, orlando, shot	The singer Christina Grimmie was shot during her concert (Jun. 10)
nightclub, orlando, shooting, victims	Several people were killed at a nightclub in Orlando (Jun. 13)
britain, brexit, european, leave-vote, referendum	Brexit referendum in UK (Jun. 23)
virginia, floods, killed, homeland-security, devastating	Flooding in Virginia caused by the heavy rain (Jun. 23)

Table 2. Events detected by *Unigram Co-Occurrences* and *EDCoW* approaches using time windows of 7 days, in the period of time from March 1 to June 30, 2016.

Time window	Unigram Co-Occurrences	EDCoW
w_0 Mar. 1–7	pell, abuse tsunami, quake	cuba, damage, killed, told, vatican
w_1 Mar. 8–14	louisiana, flooding	cuba, left, meet louisiana, rain, white house
w_2 Mar. 15–21	abdeslam, paris obama, cuba	–
w_3 Mar. 22–28	brussels, attacks police, abaaoud	meet, obama, visit francis, pope
w_4 Mar. 29–Apr. 4	plane, hijacker	–
w_5 Apr. 5–11	ukraine, dutch	–
w_6 Apr. 12–18	quake, japan ecuador, earthquake	affected, left, reported, struck damage, death toll, hit, missing, working
w_7 Apr. 19–25	obama, british	–
w_8 Apr. 26–May 2	cuba, cruise building, kenya	–
w_9 May 3–9	mcmurray, fire tornado, oklahoma	fire, fort-mcmurray, started
w_{10} May 10–16	lightning, bangladesh	fire, flooding, rain, reported
w_{11} May 17–23	flight, egyptair everest, summit	–
w_{12} May 24–30	vietnam, obama	–
w_{13} May 31–Jun. 6	boxing, ali germany, lightning	funeral, kentucky, muhammad-ali, vietnam
w_{14} Jun. 7–13	grimmie, christina ali, service	–
w_{15} Jun. 14–20	orlando, mateen	gun control
w_{16} Jun. 21–27	britain, brexit	–
w_{17} Jun. 28–30	virginia, emergency	–

Table 3. Examples of news clustered by *EDNC* based on the events.

Event Features	Time Window	News/Tweets
anniversary, remember, tsunami, japan, 5-years-ago	[Mar. 09–11]	Mar. 11: Japan marks fifth tsunami anniversary Mar. 11: Five years ago giant earthquake tsunami hit northeast Japan Mar. 11: Remembering Japan's 2011 tsunami disaster
castro, cuba, havana, obama, visit	[Mar. 18–26]	Mar. 20: Obama heads to Havana for historic visit Mar. 20: Barack Obama's visit to Cuba raises hopes Mar. 20: #Cuba to welcome Obama
argentina, mauricio-macri, obama, tango	[Mar. 21–27]	Mar. 23: Obama meets Argentine leader Mar. 23: Obama and family arrive in Argentina Mar. 24: Watch the Obamas dance the tango in Argentina
cyprus, egyptair, hijacking, surrendered	[Mar. 29–30]	Mar. 29: EgyptAir Jet Hijacked, Diverted to Cyprus Mar. 29: Hijacker forces EgyptAir flight to land in Cyprus Mar. 30: 'What should one do?'-#EgyptAir hijacker
japan, kumamoto, earthquake, damage, victims	[Apr. 14–21]	Apr. 16: At least 24 killed after Japan jolted by pair of deadly earthquakes Apr. 16: Consecutive, deadly earthquakes rock southern Japan Apr. 17: Japan quakes: Dozens killed; rescue efforts hampered
earthquake, ecuador, strikes	[Apr. 17–26]	Apr. 17: An #earthquake jolts #Ecuador's Pedernales Apr. 17: Strong quake hits off coast of Ecuador, tsunami waves possible Apr. 18: #Ecuador quake toll likely to rise 'in a considerable way'

the precision of the clusters rather than the recall. The precision is defined as the number of news that are relevant to the event over the number of news in the event cluster, where *relevant* means that the news content is about the event. For annotating the news with respect to their relevance to an event, we randomly selected some of the events and used CrowdFlower[2] to collect labels on the relevance of the news to the events. For each news-event pair we collected 3 judgements, and to ensure high-quality evaluation, we removed those news-event pairs for which the evaluators' confidence was less than 2/3.

We compared the news clustering obtained with our methodology against *k-means* [3] and a temporal-aware version of it. The unsupervised clustering algorithm, *k-means*, applies cosine similarity to find similar news and group them into clusters. We run *k-means* with different values of k and observed a good trade-off between precisions and cluster sizes with $k = 500$. The resulting clusters do not have any label describing the news in them, so we had to manually check the content of the clusters to figure out the corresponding events and create a short description of it to show together with the news to the CrowdFlower's evaluators. Since *k-means* per se is unaware of the timestamps of the news documents, we implemented the *k-means+time* approach which applies *k-means* and then filters out news that are not within the temporal window of the event.

Results. Examples of news clusters obtained with our approach are shown in Table 3. For each event we also report the time window. We can notice that the time-window length can vary depending on the events and some of them can span for long periods of time (e.g., earthquakes were popular for about 10 days).

Table 4. Average precision of the event clusters obtained with different methodologies.

	k-means	k-means+time	EDNC
Avg. Precision	0.51	0.83	**0.93**

Table 4 shows the average precisions achieved by the different clustering approaches. Results show that *k-means* has low precisions compared to our approach. In particular, it tends to group similar events that happened in different time windows. For example, it does not separate the news about the Japan's recent earthquake from the ones about the tsunami's 5th anniversary or the wildfires in California from the one in Canada. To filter out these noisy news, we implemented the clustering techniques called *k-means+time* which removes the news whose timestamps do not belong to the time intervals of interest. We could observe that when the time windows are taken into account the precision improves, but still there are more false positives compared to our approach.

On the other hand, *EDNC* has a low number of false positives and, consequently, a good value of precision. We noticed that false positives are caused by less popular events and overlapping of event features. For example, news like "Cuban concerns over Venezuela's economic woes..." and "Cuba's combat rappers fight for the country's youth..." were wrongly grouped with the news about

[2] https://www.crowdflower.com/.

Obama's visit to Cuba. This was probably due to the fact that less popular events (e.g., represented by few news in the dataset) are not captured, hence their news are clustered together with the next most similar ones. Other news about Ecuador earthquake were clustered with the news on Japan earthquake, and the manual assessors considered these as false positives. Inspecting the data, we could notice that in these news articles there is the word "Japan" because the two earthquakes happened in the same days and there were discussions on the possibility that they were somehow connected. *EDNC* considered these news relevant to both earthquakes because of the keywords "Ecuador" and "Japan."

6 Conclusions and Future Work

In this paper we propose a technique for event detection and news clustering. Our approach extracts real-world events from heterogeneous news streams and divides the news based on the events they report.

As future work, we would like to analyze the evolution of the events and how they are connected (e.g., the immigration crisis followed by the Pope speech about welcoming immigrants looking for asylum, or the slaughter in Orlando followed by the Obama's visit to the families of the victims). We also plan to explore other applications of this methodology, such as news summarization.

Acknowledgement. This research was partially funded by the Secrétariat d'Etat à la formation, à la recherche et à l'innovation (SEFRI) under the project AHTOM (Asynchronous and Heterogeneous TOpic Mining).

References

1. Allan, J., Papka, R., Lavrenko, V.: On-line new event detection and tracking. In: 21st International ACM SIGIR Conference on Research and Development in Information Retrieval, pp. 37–45. ACM, New York (1998)
2. Becker, H., Naaman, M., Gravano, L.: Beyond trending topics: real-world event identification on Twitter. In: International AAAI Conference on Web and Social Media (2011)
3. Ding, C., He, X.: K-means clustering via principal component analysis. In: 21st International Conference on Machine Learning, pp. 29–38. ACM, New York (2004)
4. Fung, G.P.C., Yu, J.X., Yu, P.S., Lu, H.: Parameter free bursty events detection in text streams. In: 31st International Conference on Very Large Data Bases, pp. 181–192. VLDB Endowment (2005)
5. Gwadera, R., Crestani, F.: Mining and ranking streams of news stories using cross-stream sequential patterns. In: 18th ACM Conference on Information and Knowledge Management, pp. 1709–1712. ACM, New York (2009)
6. He, Q., Chang, K., Lim, E.P.: Analyzing feature trajectories for event detection. In: 30th International ACM SIGIR Conference on Research and Development in Information Retrieval, pp. 207–214. ACM, New York (2007)
7. Li, C., Sun, A., Datta, A.: Twevent: segment-based event detection from tweets. In: 21st ACM International Conference on Information and Knowledge Management, pp. 155–164. ACM, New York (2012)

8. Li, C., Weng, J., He, Q., Yao, Y., Datta, A., Sun, A., Lee, B.S.: TwiNER: named entity recognition in targeted Twitter stream. In: 35th International ACM SIGIR Conference on Research and Development in Information Retrieval, pp. 721–730 ACM, New York (2012)
9. Lu, Y., Mei, Q., Zhai, C.: Investigating task performance of probabilistic topic models: an empirical study of PLSA and LDA. Inf. Retr. **14**(2), 178–203 (2011)
10. Phuvipadawat, S., Murata, T.: Breaking news detection and tracking in Twitter. In: 2010 IEEE/WIC/ACM International Conference on Web Intelligence and Intelligent Agent Technology, vol. 3, pp. 120–123. IEEE Computer Society, Washington, DC (2010)
11. Popescu, A.M., Pennacchiotti, M., Paranjpe, D.: Extracting events and event descriptions from Twitter. In: 20th International Conference Companion on World Wide Web, pp. 105–106. ACM, New York (2011)
12. Ritter, A., Clark, S., Mausam, Etzioni, O.: Named entity recognition in tweets: an experimental study. In: Conference on Empirical Methods in Natural Language Processing, pp. 1524–1534. Association for Computational Linguistics, Stroudsburg (2011)
13. Ritter, A., Mausam, Etzioni, O., Clark, S.: Open domain event extraction from Twitter. In: 18th ACM SIGKDD International Conference on Knowledge Discovery and Data Mining, pp. 1104–1112. ACM, New York (2012)
14. Sakaki, T., Okazaki, M., Matsuo, Y.: Earthquake shakes Twitter users: real-time event detection by social sensors. In: 19th International Conference Companion on World Wide Web, pp. 851–860. ACM, New York (2010)
15. Weng, J., Lee, B.S.: Event detection in Twitter. In: International AAAI Conference on Web and Social Media (2011)
16. Yan, X., Guo, J., Lan, Y., Cheng, X.: A biterm topic model for short texts. In: 22nd International Conference Companion on World Wide Web, pp. 1445–1456. ACM, New York (2013)

Twitter User Profiling Model Based on Temporal Analysis of Hashtags and Social Interactions

Abir Gorrab[1(✉)], Ferihane Kboubi[1], Ali Jaffal[2], Bénédicte Le Grand[2], and Henda Ben Ghezala[1]

[1] RIADI Laboratory, National School of Computer Science (ENSI), University of Manouba, Manouba, Tunisia
{Abir.Gorrab,Ferihane.Kboubi, henda.benghezala}@riadi.rnu.tn

[2] Centre de Recherche En Informatique, University Paris1 Panthéon Sorbonne, Paris, France
Ali.jaffal@malix.univ-paris1.fr, Benedicte.le-grand@univ-paris1.fr

Abstract. Social content generated by users' interaction in social networks is a knowledge source that may enhance users' profiles modeling, by providing information on their activities and interests over time. The aim of this article is to propose several original strategies for modeling profiles of social networks' users, taking into account social information and its temporal evolution. We illustrate our approach on the Twitter network. We distinguish interactive and thematic temporal profiles and we study profiles' similarities by applying various clustering algorithms, by giving a special attention to overlapping clusters. We compare the different types of profiles obtained and show how they can be relevant for the recommendation of hashtags and users to follow.

Keywords: User profile · Temporality · Social interactions · Hashtags · Similarity

1 Introduction

With the success of social networks, the integration of social information has become strategic. In this paper, we investigate strategies to build profiles of Twitter users that exploit social information, which is heterogeneous and evolves over time. Our final goal is to use these profiles to cluster users with similar profiles in order to suggest new hashtags and users to follow. In addition, thematic content reflects users' interests and is then prominent in analyzing their preferences. The temporal aspect of social content is also used in social works in order to track the evolution of users' social behaviors. With this in mind and inspired by studies of time-sensitive social profiles, we propose a new social user profile construction strategy and analysis.

The rest of this paper is organized as follows. Section 2 reviews related work. We detail in Sect. 3 our proposal including temporal social interactions' and temporal hashtags' analysis, social profiles' construction and users' clustering. In Sect. 4,

F. Frasincar et al. (Eds.): NLDB 2017, LNCS 10260, pp. 124–130, 2017.
DOI: 10.1007/978-3-319-59569-6_12

we analyze and discuss the effectiveness of our model on a dataset of tweets. Finally, Sect. 5 concludes the paper and introduces future work.

2 Related Work

In this section, we expose some related works on temporal information exploitation. We then review works on user profiles similarity. Temporal characteristics have been investigated in various research works, but for different purposes. In [3], authors proposed a time-aware user profile model based on social relations, by measuring freshness and importance of social users' interests. In [1], a language model document prior is proposed that uses social and temporal features to estimate documents' relevance. A wide range of researchers have focused on measuring the similarity of social user profiles. In [9], authors propose a social user profiling model and use it in an Information Retrieval system. They also propose a new process of search results' classification. Besides, diffusion kernels are exploited in [10] to calculate tags similarities, by connecting users based on social similar preferences. Furthermore, authors in [7] analyze Twitter profiles, by calculating their similarities using TF-IDF, after applying an indexation algorithm with Lucene.

What distinguishes our work from the existing approaches is the strategy of social profiles' constitution and analysis of users' clusters obtained, with a focus on overlapping clusters.

3 Proposed Model

Our methodology of social users' profiling comprises three main steps, as shown in Fig. 1. The first step consists in information preprocessing, by collecting and filtering social information. The input data consists, for each user, of a set of tweets written during a time interval. We differentiate six features: the user ID, the number of tweets he wrote, the list and the number of hashtags contained in each tweet, their timestamps and the number of followers. In a second step, we build interactive and thematic social and temporal user profiles. In fact, we use our generic social user profile model proposed in [6] to instantiate and build original social and temporal profiles. The third step exploits these profiles to build users' clusters. Clustering interactive and temporal user profiles allow us to regroup similar users based on social properties like activity and popularity and study their temporal evolution.

In Sect. 3.1, we detail our methodology for social and temporal user profiles construction. In Sect. 3.2, we describe users' clustering process.

3.1 Social and Temporal Profiles' Construction

To build social profiles, we distinguished two social information types, notably social interactions which include the number of followers, the number of tweets and also the number of hashtags contained in each tweet; and the thematic hashtags.

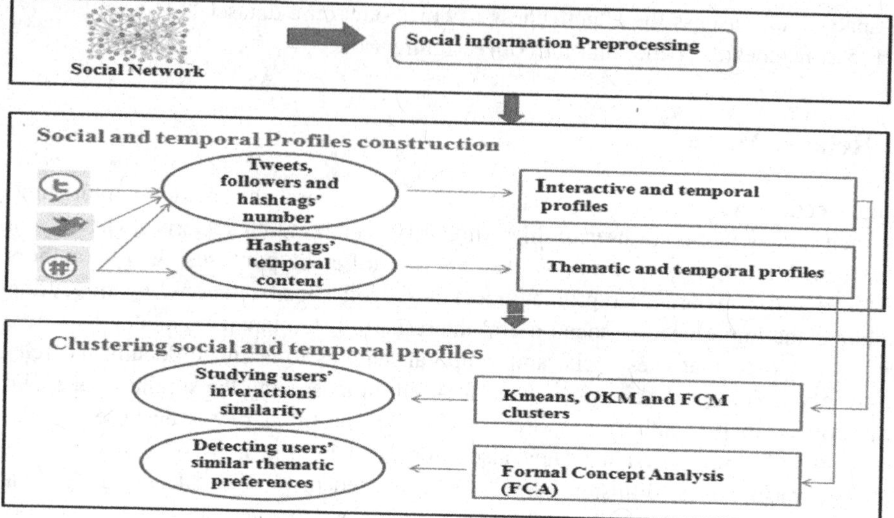

Fig. 1. Our methodology for building and exploiting social and temporal user profiles

3.1.1 Interactive and Temporal User Profiles' Construction

The number of followers of a given user, the number of his tweets published in a given time interval and the number of hashtags contained in each tweet provide a clear vision of this user's social activity and popularity. We set a time variable t that determines the duration of the social interactions considered, where $t \in [t_O \ldots t_{current}]$; with t_O is the timestamp of the oldest tweet in the dataset. We then calculate the number of tweets written by the user in this time interval, and also the number of hashtags contained in his tweets. Considering the number of followers, we always consider the latest update of the followers list.

3.1.2 Thematic and Temporal User Profiles' Construction

We distinguish three types of hashtags' lists that could be used to characterize user profiles. The difference between them results from tweets' temporality and frequency.

- **Historical profile (P_H):** We consider all the tweets of the user since the initial time.

$$P_H = \{H_i(t)\} \tag{1}$$

- **History and frequency based profile (P_{HF}):** In this case, we use all the social content starting from t_O. We then remove unfrequent hashtags from the user profile, unless they are recent. TF measure is used here to calculate hashtags' frequency in each user model.

$$P_{HF} = \{H_i(t)\} \backslash \{H(NF_i)(t))\} \tag{2}$$

- **Instantaneous profile (P_I):** We consider only the hashtags from the most recent tweet sent by the user.

$$P_I = \{H_i(t_{current})\} \tag{3}$$

$\forall i \in [1 \ldots N]$; $\forall t \in [t_0 \ldots t_{current}]$; Where N is the total number of hashtags in the tweets sent by the user, *Hi (t)* corresponds to the ith hashtag at instant *t*; and *H(NF$_i$)(t)* is the ith unfrequent hashtag at instant *t*. A hashtag is considered unfrequent if its appearance frequency in the user model does not exceed a threshold $\theta \in [0 \ldots 1]$.

3.2 Users' Clustering Based on Social and Temporal Profiles

To cluster users according to the similarity of their social interactions, we apply Kmeans, OKM [4] and FCM [2] algorithms to each component, notably the number of followers, tweets and hashtags in order to emphasize the significance of each social feature. To cluster users according to their thematic and temporal profiles, we construct a similarity matrix. We then apply the same clustering algorithms to the similarity matrix obtained and compare resulting clusters. Our aim is to track the level of users' belonging to the various clusters, based on their hashtags' temporal similarities. Furthermore, we apply another approach to cluster users based on their thematic profiles similarities: Formal Concept Analysis (FCA) developed in [8]. FCA builds overlapping clusters with native labels, by constructing conceptual graphs called Galois lattices. This approach takes as input a set of objects characterized by attributes called formal context. In our case study, the objects represent the ids of twitter users and the attributes are the hashtags associated to these users. From each formal context, FCA groups objects (users) into clusters according to their common attributes (hashtags). These clusters are called formal concepts.

From each clustering result obtained, we can provide various recommendations of hashtags or users to follow. We can provide a given user with common hashtags in the cluster to which he belongs, users having the same interactive properties or thematic similarities, and even users from other clusters that are very active or popular.

4 Experimental Illustration

We conducted a series of experiments on a Twitter dataset, used in [5]. From this dataset, we extracted a significant sample of tweets corresponding to 1050 users, notably 4000 tweets. We chose users with different values of social features, i.e. different numbers of tweets, followers and hashtags.

4.1 Illustration of Clustering Based on Social Interactions

In these experiments, we study the interactive profiles considered from initial time.

We compared the number of profiles contained in each cluster corresponding to the three dimensions of the interactive and temporal profile, and respectively to each dimension. The results are shown in Fig. 2, where Nfollows, Ntweets and Nhashtags denote respectively the number of followers, tweets and hashtags. C1, C2 and C3 are respectively cluster 1, 2 and 3. We notice that the number of users in each cluster changes according to the features that have been considered. If we consider the number of followers, the number of profiles is reduced in C1 and C2, but it is higher in C3. When compared in terms of tweets number, the number of users is the highest in C2 and less important in C1 and C3.

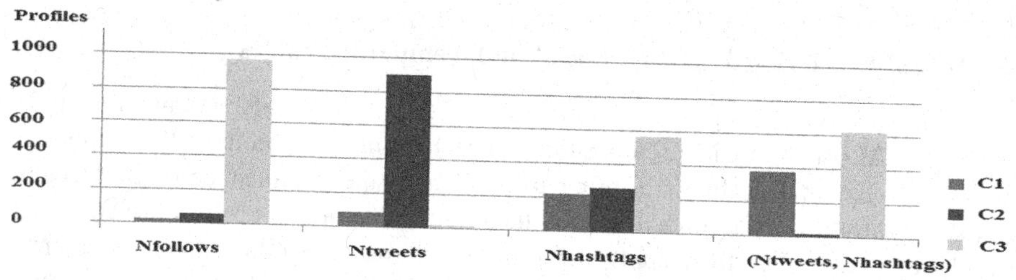

Fig. 2. Comparative graph of users' numbers by cluster

For Nhashtags, the number of users varies from 220 in C1 to 260 in C2, and reaches 570 in C3. The number of profiles in each cluster gives a valuable indication of the quantitative aspect of user's social activity.

4.2 Illustration of Clusters Based on Thematic Profiles

To study the impact of thematic user profiles on clustering results, we start by choosing the adequate value of θ. We choose $\theta = 0.25$ to eliminate the most unfrequent hashtags. Therefore, we analyze tweets starting from the initial instant t_0. We analyze then the three profiles types: P_H, P_{HF} and P_I. We also eliminate from our dataset the users who have only one tweet, since they stay invariant in all the strategies.

We summarize the results of OKM clustering. For each type of user profiles, we show the list of overlapping clusters and the relative number of profiles they contain. For P_H profiles, there are three overlapping clusters that contain respectively 59, 7 and 1 profile. That means that 59 users belong simultaneously to both clusters 1 and 2, 7 users are in clusters 1, 2 and 3 and one user belongs to clusters 1, 2, 3 and 4. P_{HF} profiles are also formed of three overlapping clusters of 24, 23 and 16 users, while with the P_I profiles, 28 users belong to both clusters 1 and 2, and 10 users are in clusters 1, 2 and 3 simultaneously, with different membership degrees. We can use these clusters to recommend users, considering each type of thematic profiles. A limit of this approach is the lack of cluster's labeling. This is where the contribution of FCA appears, as it facilitates clustering results' interpretation.

4.3 Formal Concept Analysis of Temporal Thematic Profiles

From the lattice, we calculate the conceptual similarity; defined in our previous work [8]; between users and between hashtags. Users are conceptually similar if they belong to the same concepts; which means that they use the same hashtags as other users in different concepts. This similarity is defined by Eq. (4).

$$\text{Conceptual similarity}(ui, \text{uj}) = \frac{\text{Nb concepts containing } ui \text{ and uj}}{\text{Nb concepts containing ui or uj}} \quad (4)$$

Table 1 presents the pairs of most similar users based on the P_H profile. The pair of most similar users is (374; 231) with a conceptual similarity of 60%. These results are relevant and can be exploited to recommend hashtags of similar users, since users who present a high similarity level are likely to be interested in similar topics.

Table 1. Users' similarities percentage for the historical profile P_H

(456;514):40%	(456;363):40%	(363;456):40%	
(1242;235):50%	(235;1242):50%	(1008;514):50%	(738;374):50%
(514;903):57%	(903;514):57%		
(374;231):60%	(231;374):60%		

5 Conclusion and Future Work

In this work, we conducted a deep study to investigate the efficiency of the temporal strategy of deriving social user profiles and its impact on users' clustering. We built interactive and thematic temporal social profiles, formed respectively by users' social interactions and hashtags' content. Thematic profiles are differentiated by the history taken into account and also the frequency of hashtags in each profile. The formula of deriving profiles was proved so useful to similarities' calculation and clusters' construction. To go further, we will integrate these analysis in hashtags and users' recommender system, taking into account user's preferences and the clusters to which he belongs.

References

1. Badache, I., Boughanem, M.: Document priors based on time-sensitive social signals. In: ECIR (2015)
2. Bezdek, J.C., Trivedi, M., Ehrlich, R., Full, W.: Fuzzy clustering: a new approach for geostatistical analysis. Int. J. Syst. Meas. Decis. **1**(2), 13–24 (1981)
3. Canut, M.F., On-At, S., Péninou, A., Sèdes, F.: Time-aware egocentric network-based user profiling. In: ASONAM (2015)
4. Cleuziou, G.: A generalization of k-means for overlapping clustering. Technical report, 54 (2007)

5. Danisch, M., Dugué, N., Perez, A.: On the importance of considering social capitalism when measuring influence on Twitter. In: Behavioral, economic, and socio-cultural computing (2014)
6. Gorrab, A., Kboubi, F., Le Grand, B., Ghezala, H.B: Towards a dynamic and polarity-aware social user profile modeling. In: AICCSA (2016)
7. Hannon, J., Bennett, M., Smyth, B.: Recommending twitter users to follow using content and collaborative filtering approaches. In: RecSys, pp. 199–206 (2010)
8. Jaffal, A., Le Grand, B.: Towards an automatic extraction of smartphone users' contextual behaviors. In: RCIS (2016)
9. Nathaneal, R., Andrews, J.: Personalized search engine using social networking activity. Indian J. Sci. Technol. **8**(4), 301–306 (2015)
10. Wang, X., Liu, H., Fan, W.: Connecting users with similar interests via tag network inference. In: Proceedings of the 20th ACM International Conference on Information and Knowledge Management, pp. 1019–1024 (2011)

Extracting Causal Relations Among Complex Events in Natural Science Literature

Biswanath Barik[(✉)], Erwin Marsi, and Pinar Öztürk

Department of Computer and Information Science,
Norwegian University of Science and Technology, Trondheim, Norway
{biswanath.barik,emarsi,pinar}@idi.ntnu.no

Abstract. Causal relation extraction is the task of identifying and extracting the causal relations occurring in a text. We present an approach that is especially suitable for extracting relations between complex events – which are assumed to be already identified – as found in natural science literature, supporting literature-based knowledge discovery. The approach is based on supervised learning, exploiting a wide range of linguistic features. Experimental results indicate that even with a limited amount of training data, reasonable accuracy can be obtained by using a pipeline of classifiers, optimising hyper-parameters, down-weighting negative instances and applying feature selection methods.

Keywords: Causal relation · Relation extraction · Information extraction · Knowledge discovery · Text mining

1 Introduction

Automatic extraction of causal relations from text has many applications, e.g., in search, question-answering and text summarization. Here we address the task of extracting causal relations from natural science literature, more specifically, from journal articles in marine science, which includes marine biology, marine chemistry, marine ecology, physical oceanography and many other fields. Chains of causal relations among events play a crucial role in our understanding of global problems such as climate change and their impacts. For example, the increase of CO_2 in the atmosphere causes increased uptake of CO_2 by the oceans, which in turn causes increased ocean acidification (decreasing pH of the ocean water). Acidification has harmful consequences for marine organism like corals and plankton, which in turn ultimately effects the whole marine food chain, including humans. Although some of these causal chains are well-known, others are latent in the literature, waiting for researchers to make the right connection between hitherto unrelated events. However, discovery of such causal chains is hampered by at least two factors. First, the steadily growing number of scientific publications makes it hard for individual researchers to keep up with the literature, even in their own area of expertise. Second, the inherently interdisciplinary nature of global problems such as climate change, which requires connecting

F. Frasincar et al. (Eds.): NLDB 2017, LNCS 10260, pp. 131–137, 2017.
DOI: 10.1007/978-3-319-59569-6_13

knowledge from distant scientific disciplines and their sparsely connected literatures. Computational tools supporting automatic extraction of causal chains from huge and diverse collections of scientific literature are therefore urgently needed.

Causal relation extraction has been addressed in various works in the NLP and text mining communities. Approaches range from rule/pattern-based causal relation extraction [6,8,9] to supervised learning [2,5] and co-occurrence-based unsupervised methods [3,4]. Almost all approaches assume that causal relations hold among atomic entities – typically between nominals – as in "*cigarettes cause cancer*" [7]. In our domain, however, causal relations connect events which can be arbitrarily large and complex structures [1], which poses problems for existing approaches. Here we describe a new approach tailored for extracting causal relations between such complex events.

2 Data Set

Our dataset is an extension of the pilot corpus described in [11], intended to initiate and facilitate work on text mining of natural science literature. It contains annotations for variables, events and relations, following a revised version of the annotation guideline of [11]. *Variables* are things that are changing[1], ranging from simple things like "*global temperature*" to complex things like "*timing and magnitude of surface temperature evolution in the Southern Hemisphere in deglacial proxy records*". Variables can be involved in three types of *events*: an *Increase* means a variable is changing in a positive direction, a *Decrease* means it is changing in a negative direction, while a *Change* leaves the direction unspecified. Events can in turn be related in three ways: *Causation*, *Correlation* or *Feedback*. We will ignore the latter two here, as well as annotations involving referring expressions. Causation is only annotated if the text contains an explicit trigger, that is, a clear textual cue such as a verb (*leads to*) or adverb (*therefore*). In addition, variables and events can be joined into complex structures using *And* (conjunction) or *Or* (disjunction). An example annotation is given in Fig. 1. This illustrates that variables and events in the our domain are often complex rather than atomic and expressed as noun phrases containing multiple modifiers. The distance between change triggers and their variables can be large, making events syntactically complex units.

The dataset contains abstracts and full-text of selected articles from marine science journals: 327 documents, 4449 sentences, 2646 events (events embedded in larger events are discounted) and 520 causal relations. Texts were annotated by several annotators, without overlap. To estimate inter-annotator agreement, we selected five new documents containing at least one causal relation. All were annotated by two annotators, both computational linguists and familiar with the domain. Agreement on causal relations (ignoring agreement on causal triggers)

[1] Originally only so-called *quantitative variables* were annotated. This constraint has since been dropped.

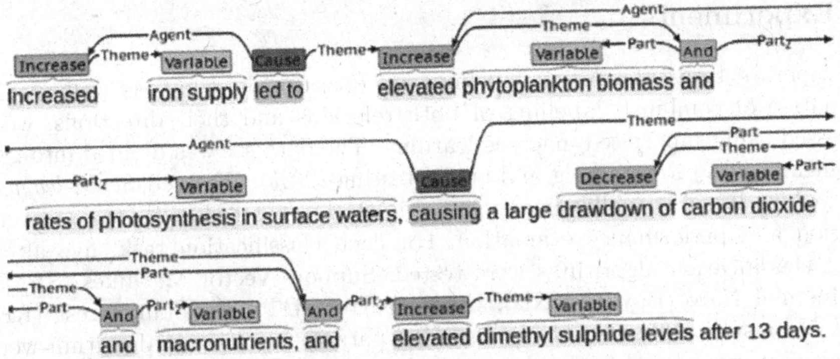

Fig. 1. Annotation example with complex event structures

has an average precision of 59.4, recall of 84.6 and F_1 of 69.8. The *kappa* score is 0.459. Disagreements were mostly due to differences in change events.

3 Task

The input consists of text with annotated events [12] and the task is to extract any causal relations among the given events. For this, only top-level events are considered, no embedded events. For instance, in Fig. 1, the three candidate events for causal relations are "*Increased iron supply*", "*elevated phytoplankton biomass and rates of photosynthesis in surface waters*" and "*large drawdown of carbon dioxide and macronutrients and elevated dimethyl sulphide levels after 13 days*". Causal relations across sentences are not considered, as it requires resolving referring expressions. The task can be framed as a three-way classification task on the exhaustive pairwise combination of ordered top-level events in a sentence. For every pair e_i, e_j where $e_i < e_j$, $Cause(e_i, e_j)$ is a function mapping an event pair to a class label in domain $\{1, 0, -1\}$ such that $Cause(e_i, e_j) = 1$ if e_i causes e_j, $Cause(e_i, e_j) = -1$ if e_j causes e_i and $Cause(e_i, e_j) = 0$ in all other cases. Alternatively, the task can be decomposed into a sequence of two subtasks: (1) *relation labelling* classifies event pairs as either causally related or not, regardless of the direction of the relation; (2) *direction labelling* classifies a established causal relation as either forward or backward.

The task formulation above has the disadvantage that 0 (non-causal) is by far the most frequent class. This skewed class distribution is problematic for most learners. A solution is to limit the number of possible event combinations in a sentence. In fact, 93% of the causally-related events in our data are adjacent, with only 6.5% having one intervening event and merely 0.05% having two. Therefore, by limiting the task to adjacent events only, we ignore unlikely causal instances and counteract the skewed class distribution.

4 Experiments

The separate tasks of relation labeling and direction labeling, as well as the alternative of combined labelling of both relations and their directions, were addressed using supervised machine learning. The data set was divided into 261 documents (80%) for training and 66 for testing (20%). We used *Scikit-learn* – the machine learning toolkit implemented in Python – for classification, feature selection and performance evaluation. For each classification task, five alternative classification algorithms were tested: Support Vector Machines (SVM), Multinomial Naive Bayes (MNB), Decision Tree (DT), Random Forest (RF) and k-Nearest Neighbours (kNN). Training parameters of each algorithm were optimized using group-based cross validation with random shuffling on training instances. In addition, the causal and non-causal class weights (w, 1.0 - w) were optimized.

Feature extraction relies on linguistic analysis through the Stanford CoreNLP toolkit [10] for sentence splitting, tokenisation, lemmatisation, part-of-speech (POS) tagging and dependency parsing. We systematically extracted features from events, the context between event pairs, and various dependency and binary features in and around the event pair and its context. To illustrate the feature extraction process, consider the syntactic dependency structure in Fig. 2. There are two events, e_1 = '$\updownarrow$ (pH of the surface ocean)' and e_2 = '$\uparrow$ (atmospheric CO_2)', which are causally related by the causal trigger '*result of*'. In event e_1, the head word of the variable is '*pH*'. The head of the causality trigger is '*changing*', which also serves as the head of the change event. Similarly, in event e_2, the variable head is 'CO_2'. The trigger head is '*increase*', which is also the head of the event e_2. The in-between context of event pair e_1, e_2 is '*as a result of*' with head '*result*'. On the basis of this analysis, the most important feature sets extracted are:

1. Features from events: (1) *event head (EH)* information including word, lemma & POS; (2) *variable head (VH)* information including word, lemma & POS; (3) *trigger head (TH)* information including word, lemma & POS; (4) *dependency relation* between *VH* and *EH*, *TH* and *EH*.
2. Features from in-between context: (1) *dependency head* of the context - word, lemma and POS; (2) *bag-of-word features* - uni-gram and bi-gram of word,lemma & POS; (3) *combination* of word and POS; (4) *selected prepositional relation* of head like 'by', 'to', 'from', 'in' etc.; (5) *causal triggers* [13] present in the context or not.
3. Features from event pairs: (1) *common head* of two events - lemma and POS; (2) *distance* between the heads of two events in dependency path; (3) *dependency relation* between context head and event head; (4) *number* of intervening events.
4. Features from before & after context: *bag-of-word* & *dependency* features with a certain window.

Three feature selection algorithms were tested. *χ^2-based feature selection* (XS) selects the k highest scoring features based on χ^2 statistics. *Tree-based* *feature selection* (TF) uses forests of trees to evaluate the importance of features by using their inter-tree variability. *Recursive feature elimination* (FE) uses an external estimator (SVM) to assign feature weights, iteratively removing a certain number (or percentage) of features, ultimately resulting in a minimal feature set with highest importance.

5 Results

Relation labeling scores are shown in the left half of Table 1. The top half of the table present the scores for the five different classifier types when using all features, along with their best parameter setting. The bottom half of the table presents the scores with feature selection methods. Feature selection yields a substantial improvement in scores, with XS as the most successful approach, where SVM in combination with XS performs best on relation labeling.

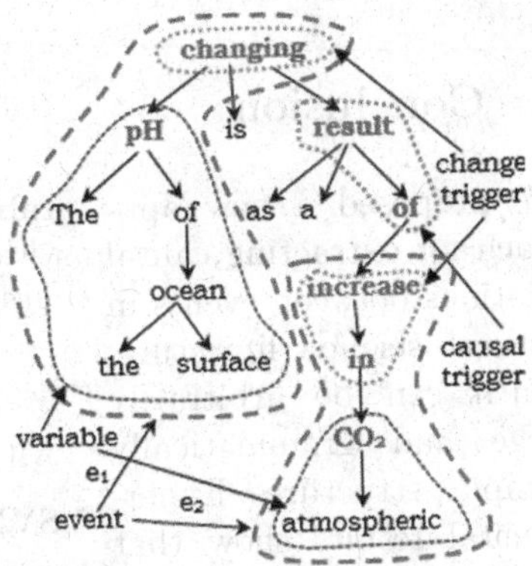

Fig. 2. Variables, triggers and events in a dependency structure

Direction labeling scores are shown in the right half of Table 1 in terms of macro average over *forward* and *reverse* classes. Evidently this subtask is easier and the scores appear to be relatively high. DT gives the best results, also showing more balanced precision and recall. Feature selection does not yield any improvement and therefore is not considered in direction labeling.

Table 1. Scores on the test data for relation labeling (on positive class) and direction labeling (macro average over *forward* and *reverse* classes)

Method	Relation labeling				Direction labeling			
All feats.	Params	Pr	Re	F_1	Parameters	Pr	Re	F_1
SVM	$C=0.01$, $w=0.65$	0.62	0.58	0.60	$C=10.0$, $w=0.95$	0.77	0.79	0.78
DT	$split=6$, $w=0.6$	0.61	0.48	0.54	$split=12$, $w=0.90$	0.82	0.83	**0.82**
RF	$n=10$, $w=0.95$	0.65	0.62	**0.64**	$n=10$, $w=0.65$	0.81	0.82	0.81
MNB	$alpha=0.35$	0.54	0.51	0.53	$alpha=1.0$	0.76	0.77	0.76
*k*NN	$N=2$, $weight=$ dist	0.66	0.26	0.37	$N=2$, $weights=$ unif	0.70	0.70	0.70
Feat. Sel.	Classifier (#feats)	Pr	Re	F_1				
XS	SVM (2300)	0.71	0.63	**0.66**	SVM (910)	0.83	0.79	0.81
TF	MNB (1600)	0.65	0.55	0.59	DT (480)	0.78	0.80	0.79
FE	SVM (3100)	0.51	0.67	0.58	DT (630)	0.77	0.82	0.79

Combined labeling with a single classifier yields the scores in Table 2. As expected, scores are lower than on the individual subtasks. Again the combination of SVM of XS performs best.

Combined labeling with a pipeline of classifiers was carried out by successive application of the best performing classifiers on the individual subtasks. This yields a precision of 0.59, a recall of 0.56 and an F-score of 0.57. These results are thus substantially better than with the single classifier approach. Apparently the disadvantage of error propagation in a pipeline system is out-weighted by the ability to tune classifiers and feature sets for each subtask.

6 Conclusion

We proposed a new approach for extracting causal relations between events in natural science literature, which can be arbitrarily large and grammatically complex structures. Experimental results show that reasonable accuracy can be obtained by (1) restricting causality to adjacent events (2) applying supervised learning from a relatively small number of manually annotated texts (3) using a pipeline of separate classifiers for relation and direction labeling (4) exploiting a wide range of linguistic features, ranging from shallow word-level features to dependency structures (5) applying automatic feature selection (6) and optimizing hyperparameters.

Table 2. Scores on test data for combined labeling with a single classifier (macro average over *forward* and *reverse* classes)

Method	Combined labeling			
All feats	Parameters	Pr	Re	F_1
SVM	$C = 0.1$, $w = 0.65$	0.51	0.46	**0.48**
DT	$split = 4$, $w = 0.7$	0.31	0.31	0.31
RF	$n = 6$, $w = 0.6$	0.69	0.38	**0.48**
MNB	$alpha = 0.35$	0.55	0.31	0.40
*k*NN	$N = 4$, $weights = \text{dist}$	0.67	0.30	0.40
Feat. Sel	Classifier (#feats)	Pr	Re	F_1
XS	SVM (3100)	0.56	0.44	**0.49**
TF	DT (4900)	0.41	0.57	0.47
FE	SVM (800)	0.88	0.29	0.39

References

1. Barik, B., Marsi, E., Öztürk, P.: Event causality extraction from natural science literature. Res. Comput. Sci. **117**, 97–107 (2016)
2. Beamer, B., Girju, R.: Using a bigram event model to predict causal potential. In: Proceedings of the CICLing, pp. 430–441 (2009)
3. Chang, D.-S., Choi, K.-S.: Causal relation extraction using cue phrase and lexical pair probabilities. In: Su, K.-Y., Tsujii, J., Lee, J.-H., Kwong, O.Y. (eds.) IJCNLP 2004. LNCS (LNAI), vol. 3248, pp. 61–70. Springer, Heidelberg (2005). doi:10.1007/978-3-540-30211-7_7

4. Do, Q.X., Chan, Y.S., Roth, D.: Minimally supervised event causality identification. In: Proceedings of the EMNLP, Edinburgh, UK, pp. 294–303. (2011)
5. Blanco, E., Castell, N., Moldovan, D.: Causal relation extraction. In: Proceedings of LREC. ELRA, Marrakech, Morocco (2008)
6. Girju, R., Moldovan, D.I.: Text mining for causal relations. In: Proceedings of FLAIRS, pp. 360–364 (2002)
7. Hendrickx, I., et al.: Semeval-2010 task 8: Multi-way classification of semantic relations between pairs of nominals. In: Proceedings of SemEval, pp. 33–38 (2010)
8. Kaplan, R.M., Berry-Rogghe, G.: Knowledge-based acquisition of causal relationships in text. Knowl. Acquisition **3**(3), 317–337 (1991)
9. Khoo, C.S.G., Chan, S., Niu, Y.: Extracting causal knowledge from a medical database using graphical patterns. In: Proceedings of ACL, Hong Kong, pp. 336–343 (2000)
10. Manning, C., Surdeanu, M., Bauer, J., Finkel, J., Bethard, S., McClosky, D.: The stanford CoreNLP natural language processing toolkit. In: Proceedings of ACL: System Demonstrations, Baltimore, Maryland, pp. 55–60 (2014)
11. Marsi, E., et al.: Towards text mining in climate science: extraction of quantitative variables and their relations. In: Proceedings of BioTxtM, Reykjavik, Iceland (2014)
12. Marsi, E., Öztürk, P.: Extraction and generalisation of variables from scientific publications. In: Proceedings of the EMNLP, Lisbon, Portugal, pp. 505–511 (2015)
13. Mirza, P.: Extracting temporal and causal relations between events. CoRR abs/1604.08120 (2016)

Supporting Experts to Handle Tweet Collections About Significant Events

Ali Hürriyetoğlu[1(✉)], Nelleke Oostdijk[2], Mustafa Erkan Başar[2], and Antal van den Bosch[2,3]

[1] Statistics Netherlands, P.O. Box 4481, 6401 CZ Heerlen, The Netherlands
a.hurriyetoglu@cbs.nl
[2] Centre for Language Studies, Radboud University, P.O. Box 9103, 6500 HD Nijmegen, The Netherlands
n.oostdijk@let.ru.nl, ebasar@science.ru.nl
[3] Meertens Institute, Amsterdam, The Netherlands
antal.van.den.bosch@meertens.knaw.nl

Abstract. We introduce Relevancer that processes a tweet set and enables generating an automatic classifier from it. Relevancer satisfies information needs of experts during significant events. Enabling experts to combine automatic procedures with expertise is the main contribution of our approach and the added value of the tool. Even a small amount of feedback enables the tool to distinguish between relevant and irrelevant information effectively. Thus, Relevancer facilitates the quick understanding of and proper reaction to events presented on Twitter.

Keywords: Social media · Text mining · Machine learning · Twitter

1 Introduction

Tweet collections comprise a relatively new document type. The form, motivation behind their generation, and intended function of the tweets are more diverse than traditional document types such as essays or news articles. Understanding this diversity is essential for extracting relevant information from tweets. However, the Twitter platform does not provide any kind of infrastructure other than hashtags, which is limited by the number of users who know about it, to organize tweets. Thus, collecting and analyzing tweets introduces various challenges [4]. Using one or more key terms and/or a geographical area to collect tweets is prone to cause the final collection to be incomplete or unbalanced [5], which in turn decreases our ability to leverage the available information.

In order to alleviate some of the problems that users experience, we developed Relevancer which aims to support experts in analyzing tweet sets collected via imprecise queries in the context of high-impact events.[1] Experts can define their information need with up-to-date information in terms of automatically detected information threads [1], and use these annotations to organize unlabeled tweets.

[1] https://bitbucket.org/hurrial/relevancer.

F. Frasincar et al. (Eds.): NLDB 2017, LNCS 10260, pp. 138–141, 2017.
DOI: 10.1007/978-3-319-59569-6_14

The main observations and contributions that are integrated in Relevancer to help experts to come to grips with event-related event collections are: (i) almost every event-related tweet collection comprises tweets about similar but irrelevant events [1]; by taking into account the temporal distribution of the tweets about an event it is possible to achieve an increase in the quality of the information thread detection and a decrease in computation time [2]; and the use of inflection-aware key terms can decrease the degree of ambiguity [3].

Section 2 outlines the main processing stages and Sect. 3 describes a use case that demonstrates the analysis steps and the performance of the system. Finally, Sect. 4 concludes this paper with a brief summary, some remarks on the system's performance, and directions for future development.

2 System Architecture

Relevancer consists of the following components:

Filtering. We handle frequent hashtags and users separately. Upon presenting them to the expert for annotation, each of these is represented by five related sample tweets. If the expert decides that a user or a hashtag is irrelevant, tweets that contain this hashtag or were posted by this particular user are kept apart. The remaining tweets are passed on to the next step.

Pre-processing. The aim of the pre-processing is to convert the collection to more standard text without loosing any information. An expert may choose to apply all or only some of the following steps. As a result, the expert is in control of any bias may arise due to preprocessing.

RT Elimination. Any tweet that starts with a 'RT @' or that in its meta-information has an indication of it being a retweet is eliminated.

Normalization. User names and URLs in a tweet text are converted to 'usrusr' and 'urlurl' respectively.

Text cleaning. Text parts that are auto-generated, meta-informative, and immediate repetitions of the same word(s) are removed.

Duplicate elimination. Tweets that after normalization have an exact equivalent in terms of tweet text are excluded from the collection.

Near-duplicate elimination. A tweet is excluded, if it is similar to another tweet, i.e. above a certain threshold in terms of cosine-similarity.

Clustering. We run KMeans on the collection recursively in search of coherent clusters using tri-, four- and five-gram characters. Tweets that are in the automatically identified coherent clusters are kept apart from the subsequent iterations of the clustering. The iterations continue by relaxing the coherency criteria until the requested number of coherent clusters is obtained.

Annotation. Coherent clusters are presented to an expert in order to distinguish between the available information threads and decide on a label for them. Next, if the expert finds the cluster coherent, she attaches the relevant label to it. Otherwise she marks it as incoherent[2]. The cluster annotation speeds the labeling process in comparison to individual tweet labeling.

Classifier Generation. For training, 90% of the labeled tweets are used, while the rest is used to validate a Support Vector Machine (SVM) classifier.

3 Experiments and Evaluation

We demonstrate the use and performance of the Relevancer on a set of 229,494 Dutch tweets posted between December 16, 2010 and June 30th, 2013 and containing the key term 'griep' (EN: flu). After the preprocessing, retweets (24,019), tweets that were posted from outside the Netherlands (1,736), clearly irrelevant (158), and exact duplicates (8,156) were eliminated.

Our use case aims at finding personal flu experiences. Tweets in which users are reporting symptoms or declaring that they actually have or suspect having the flu are considered as relevant. Irrelevant tweets are mostly tweets containing general information and news about the flu, tweets about some celebrity suffering from the flu, or tweets in which users empathize or joke about the flu.

The remaining 195,425 tweets were clustered in two steps. First we split the tweet set in buckets of ten days each. The bucketing method increases the performance of and decreases the time spend by the clustering algorithm [2]. We set the clustering algorithm to search for ten coherent clusters in each bucket. Then, we extract the tweets that are in a coherent cluster and search for ten other clusters in the remaining, un-clustered, tweets. In total, 10,473 tweets were put in 1,001 clusters. Since the temporal distribution of the tweets in the clusters has a correlation of 0.56 with the whole data, aggregated at a day level, we consider that the clustered part is weakly representative of the whole set.

We labeled 306 of the clusters: 238 were found to be relevant (2,306 tweets), 196 irrelevant (2,189 tweets), and 101 incoherent (985 tweets). The tweets that are in the relevant or irrelevant clusters were used to train the SVM classifier. The performance of the classifier on the held-out 10% and unclustered part are illustrated in the Table 1.

The baseline of the classifier is the prediction of the majority class in the test set, in which the precision and recall of the minority class is undefined. Therefore, we compare the generated classifier and the baseline, which have 0.67 and 0.56 accuracy respectively.

The results show that Relevancer can support an expert to manage a tweet set under rather poor conditions. The expert can create a tweet set using any key word, label automatically detected information threads, and have a classifier

[2] The label definition affects the coherence judgment. Specificity of the labels determines the required level of the tweet similarity in a cluster.

Table 1. Classifier performance on the validation and 255 unclustured tweets

	Validation set				Unclustered			
	Precision	Recall	F1	Support	Precision	Recall	F1	Support
Relevant	.95	.96	.96	237	.66	.90	.76	144
Irrelevant	.96	.94	.95	213	.75	.39	.51	111
Avg/Total	.95	.95	.95	255	.70	.68	.65	255

that can classify the remaining (unclustered) tweets or new tweets. A classifier generated as a result of this procedure will perform between 0.67 and 0.95 accuracy when applied straightforwardly.

4 Conclusion

We described our processing tool that enables an expert to explore a tweet set, to define labels for groups of tweets, and to generate a classifier. At the end of the analysis process, the experts understands the data and is able to use his understanding in an operational setting to classify new tweets. The worst case performance of the classifier is significantly better than a majority class based baseline. The tool is supported by a web interface that can potentially be used to monitor and improve the performance in a particular use-case in real time.

In further research, we will integrate visualization of the tweet and cluster distributions, add additional interaction possibilities between the tweet set and the expert, refine clusters based on their inter-cluster distance distribution from the cluster center, and improve the flexibility of the bucketing for the clustering.

Acknowledgments. COMMIT, Statistics Netherlands, and Floodtags supported our work.

References

1. Hürriyetoğlu, A., Gudehus, C., Oostdijk, N., Bosch, A.: Relevancer: finding and labeling relevant information in tweet collections. In: Spiro, E., Ahn, Y.-Y. (eds.) SocInfo 2016. LNCS, vol. 10047, pp. 210–224. Springer, Cham (2016). doi:10.1007/978-3-319-47874-6_15
2. Hürriyetoğlu, A., van den Bosch, A., Oostdijk, N.: Using relevancer to detect relevant tweets: the Nepal earthquake case. In: Working Notes of FIRE 2016 - Forum for Information Retrieval Evaluation, Kolkata, India, December, 2016. http://ceur-ws.org/Vol-1737/T2-6.pdf
3. Hürriyetoğlu, A., van den Bosch, J.W.A., Oostdijk, N.: Analysing the role of key term inflections in knowledge discovery on twitter. In: Proceedings of the 1st International Workshop on Knowledge Discovery on the WEB, Cagliari, Italy, September, 2016. http://www.iascgroup.it/kdweb2016-program/accepted-papers.html
4. Imran, M., Castillo, C., Diaz, F., Vieweg, S.: Processing social media messages in mass emergency: A survey. ACM Comput. Surv. (CSUR) **47**(4), 1–38 (2015). http://doi.acm.org/10.1145/2771588
5. Olteanu, A., Castillo, C., Diaz, F., Vieweg, S.: CrisisLex: A lexicon for collecting and filtering Microblogged communications in crises, pp. 376–385. The AAAI Press (2014)

Named Entity Classification Based on Profiles: A Domain Independent Approach

Isabel Moreno[1(✉)], M.T. Romá-Ferri[2], and Paloma Moreda[1]

[1] Department of Software and Computing Systems, University of Alicante, Alicante, Spain
{imoreno,moreda}@dlsi.ua.es

[2] Department of Nursing, University of Alicante, Alicante, Spain
mtr.ferri@ua.es

Abstract. This paper presents a Named Entity Classification system, which uses profiles and machine learning based on [6]. Aiming at confirming its domain independence, it is tested on two domains: general - CONLL2002 corpus, and medical - DrugSemantics gold standard. Given our overall results (CONLL2002, F1 = 67.06; DrugSemantics, F1 = 71.49), our methodology has proven to be domain independent.

Keywords: Named Entity Classification · Profile · Domain independent

1 Introduction

The goal of Named Entity Recognition and Classification (NERC) is to recognize the occurrences of names in text (known as NER) and assign them a category (denoted as NEC) [4]. NERC is a prerequisite for many tasks, such as general language generation [9] or question answering [4]. Nevertheless, NERC systems are typically focused on a specific domain. When a NERC tool needs to be adapted to a new domain, with different constraints and a new set of entities, considerable effort is required [4].

Although NERC research has attracted considerable attention [4], few NERC studies are specifically designed to be applied in several domains. Experiments on several textual genres from OntoNotes were done by [8]. In the best case, this method achieved a F1 greater than 70%; while at worst, F1 is less than 50%. Kitoogo and Baryamureeba [2] chose 2 corpora from journalism and law domains. Their proposal obtained a difference in terms of F1 of more than 20 points between overall law results (F1 = 92.04%) and global journalism performance (F1 = 70.27%). As a result, these approaches are not domain independent at all.

Taking this into account, our aim is to develop a NERC system domain independent. To that end, the purpose of this paper is to develop a domain independent NEC system, assuming the output of a "perfect NER" so as to avoid any bias. The implemented NEC is based on profiles, on the basis of the NERC proposed in [6]. This work is evaluated on two different Spanish

F. Frasincar et al. (Eds.): NLDB 2017, LNCS 10260, pp. 142–146, 2017.
DOI: 10.1007/978-3-319-59569-6_15

domains: CONLL2002 [7] (general) and DrugSemantics [5] (pharmacotherapeutic) datasets. Our hypothesis is that profile-based entity classification is domain independent and performance among domains will be stable.

Next our approach is described (Sect. 2). Then, it is evaluated (Sect. 3). Last, conclusions are drawn (Sect. 4).

2 Method: Named Entity Classification Through Profiles

Our approach for NEC is based on [6], who adapted previous work from [3]. In [3], profiles were generated from a concept extractor system to compute similarity, with their own formula, to categorize supervisors in scientific texts. Whereas [6] recognized whether noun phrases are active ingredients or not using machine learning and profiles derived from lemmas of content bearing words in a training corpus. A more detailed description of our method can be found in [6], but here a brief description is provided. This profile-based method has two stages:

Profile Generation phase, whose aim is to train the system in five steps. First, the annotated corpus is sentece-splitted, tokenized, lemmatized and POS-tagged. Second, the training corpus is divided in target (positive instances, e.g. is Organization) and constrasting sets (negative instances, e.g. not an Organization). Third, from both sets, we extract lemmas of nouns, verbs, adjectives and adverbs, in a window of size W[1] and their frequency (called top and common descriptors). W is determined empirically between 20 or 40 descriptors. Fourth, each descriptor receives a relevance index based on the *term frequency, disjoint corpora frequency (TFDCF)* and the *relevance common index* [3]. This step produces a profile for each entity type (e.g. Organization) that is composed of two lists (top and common lists). Each item in this lists is a pair representing a descriptor and its relevance index. The length of the profile (P) is the number of descriptors belonging to top and common lists. P has been determined empirically between: (i) 20000: 10000 descriptors from each list, as [6]; (ii) 100: the 50 descriptors most frequent for both lists, as [3]; and (iii) 50: the 50 descriptors most frequent from top list and none from common list, to determine its necessity. Fifth, each entity type trains is own classifier with the Voted Perceptron algorithm [1] using profiles as features (i.e. the value is its relevance index).

Profile Application phase, whose aim is to classify entities detected by a NER. To that end, each entity identified by a NER fills its profile, following the same restrictions as in the generation phase. Then, this one is compared against the ones generated from training data to compute similarity. Last, the one with the highest similarity will determine the final entity type.

Last, it should be noted that **Domain Adaptation** is direct, since there is no need to change the NEC system. It only requires a training corpus previously annotated with the target entities and the tag set employed in this corpus. This data allows to generate profiles to train the new NEC for this new domain.

[1] $\frac{W}{2}$ words after and before the entity.

3 Evaluation

Here evaluation measures, corpus and results for both domains are presented.

Measures: For each entity, a weighted arithmetic mean of Recall (Rw), Precision (Pw) and F-measure$_{\beta=1}$ (F1w) are calculated, combining positive (+) and negative class (−) according to the number of instances. Overall results are *Macro-averaged* (PM, RM, F1M) as the arithmetic-mean for n entities. Formulas for F1 (F1M, F1w) can be found in Eq. 1. The others follow the same logic.

$$F1w = \frac{F1_{+} \cdot n_{+} + F1_{-} \cdot n_{-}}{n_{+} + n_{-}} \qquad F1_{M} = \frac{\sum_{i=1}^{n} F1w_i}{n} \tag{1}$$

Data sets: Spanish corpora from two different domains are employed:

CONLL2002 dataset [7] is a collection of news articles. This work uses person, organization and location entities. Miscellaneous is discarded, since it has no practical application [4]. ML models are inferred on the training set and these are assessed on the test set.

DrugSemantics gold standard [5] is a collection of 5 Spanish Summaries of Product Characteristics (SPC) manually annotated. This work uses the most frequent entities from this gold standard: disease, drug and unit of measurement. Evaluation uses 5-fold cross-validation (i.e. 4 SPCs to train and one to evaluate).

Table 1. CONLL2002 (left) and DrugSemantics (right) weighted Precision (Pw), Recall (Rw) and F$_{\beta=1}$ (F1w) results with different window (W) and profile (p) sizes

Entity	W	p	Pw	Rw	F1w	Entity	W	p	Pw	Rw	F1w
Organization	20	20000	61.10	62.34	61.20	Disease	20	20000	73.95	72.88	71.63
Person	20	20000	73.42	78.50	74.03	Drug	40	100	70.21	73.62	70.51
Location	20	20000	66.72	70.24	65.94	Unit	40	50	72.40	76.88	72.34
Macro-average			67.08	70.36	67.06	**Macro-average**			72.18	74.46	71.49

Results and discussion: Table 1 shows overall results and for each entity type. Our NEC system has a small difference between domains, in terms of F1 (F1M in Eq. 1), that is 4.43 points (Macro-average row, columns F1 in Table 1: 67.06% versus 71.49%). Thus confirming its domain independence.

Regarding general domain, Person entity obtains the highest results (F1 = 74.03%), but it can be seen that all entities required the same configuration. Concerning medical domain, Unit of Measurement achieves the best results (F1 = 72.34%), but window size was the greatest and the profile size, the smallest. Hence, for almost all entities the inclusion of common descriptors seems to provide more accurate results.

A factor affecting our results is the imbalanced nature of our data, since training data was binary divided (target and contrasting): e.g. only 23% of the training set from CONLL2002 belongs to Person entity, whereas the negative class (i.e. contrasting set) represents the remaining 77%. Hence, the effect of techniques to overcome the imbalance problem should be tested.

Comparing our results to other domain independent NERC is not free of certain limitations (e.g. different data sets and entities are used). But still, a comparison is made to outline the relevance of our work. The difference between domains in previous works is greater than 20 points in terms of F1 [2,8], but in our case is smaller (less than 5 points). Thus, our results are encouraging.

4 Conclusions and Future Work

In this paper, a domain independent Named Entity Classification system based on profiles is presented. Domain adaptation only requires a new annotated training corpus and its associated tag set. As a result, this system, whose methodology is based on [6], has been easily converted to 6 entities from two different domains thanks to an unsupervised feature generation and weighting from the training data. Without traditional knowledge resources from any domain (such as dictionaries), it was evaluated on two Spanish data sets from general and medical domains: CONLL2002 shared task [7] corpus and DrugSemantics corpus [5]. Our methodology has proven to be domain independent (CONLL2002, F1 = 67.06; DrugSemantics, F1 = 71.49).

Although the results are encouraging, there is still room for improvement. As future work, our methodology needs to be further studied on other corpora to prove whether this approach is language independent. Besides, we plan to apply techniques to overcome the imbalance problem.

Acknowledgments. This paper has been supported by the Spanish Government (TIN2015-65100-R; TIN2015-65136-C02-2-R), Generalitat Valenciana (PROMETEOII/2014/001) and BBVA Foundation (FUNDACIONBBVA2-16PREMIOI).

References

1. Freund, Y., Schapire, R.E.: Large margin classification using the perceptron algorithm. Mach. Learn. **37**(3), 277–296 (1999)
2. Kitoogo, F., Baryamureeba, V.: Towards domain independent named entity recognition. In: Strengthening the Role of ICT in Development, pp. 84–95 (2008)
3. Lopes, L., Vieira, R.: Building and applying profiles through term extraction. In: X Brazilian Symposium in Information and Human Language Technology, Natal, Brazil, pp. 91–100 (2015). https://aclweb.org/anthology/W/W15/W15-5613.pdf
4. Marrero, M., Urbano, J., Sánchez-Cuadrado, S., Morato, J., Gómez-Berbís, J.M.: Named entity recognition: fallacies, challenges and opportunities. Comput. Stan. Interfaces **35**(5), 482–489 (2013)
5. Moreno, I., Moreda, P., Romá-Ferri, M.T.: Reconocimiento de entidades nombradas en dominios restringidos. In: Actas del III Workshop en Tecnologías de la Informática, Alicante, Spain, pp. 41–57 (2012)
6. Moreno, I., Moreda, P., Romá-Ferri, M.T.: An active ingredients entity recogniser system based on profiles. In: Proceedings of 21st International Conference on Applications of Natural Language to Information Systems, pp. 276–284 (2016)

7. Tjong Kim Sang, E.F.: Introduction to the CoNLL-2002 shared task. In: Proceedings of the 6th Conference on Natural Language Learning (2002)
8. Tkachenko, M., Simanovsky, A.: Selecting features for domain-independent named entity recognition. In: Proceedings of KONVENS 2012, pp. 248–253 (2012)
9. Vicente, M., Lloret, E.: Exploring flexibility in natural language generation throughout discursive analysis of new textual genres. In: Proceedings of the 2nd International Workshop FETLT (2016)

Information Extraction from Resource-Scarce Languages

Does the Strength of Sentiment Matter? A Regression Based Approach on Turkish Social Media

Ali Mert Ertugrul[1(✉)], Itir Onal[2], and Cengiz Acarturk[1]

[1] Graduate School of Informatics, Middle East Technical University, Ankara, Turkey
{alimert,acarturk}@metu.edu.tr
[2] Department of Computer Engineering, Middle East Technical University, Ankara, Turkey
itir@ceng.metu.edu.tr

Abstract. Social media posts are usually informal and short in length. They may not always express their sentiment clearly. Therefore, multiple raters may assign different sentiments to a tweet. Instead of employing majority voting which ignores the strength of sentiments, the annotation can be enriched with a confidence score assigned for each sentiment. In this study, we analyze the effect of using regression on confidence scores in sentiment analysis using Turkish tweets. We extract hand-crafted features including lexical features, emoticons and sentiment scores. We also employ word embedding of tweets for regression and classification. Our findings reveal that employing regression on confidence scores slightly improves sentiment classification accuracy. Moreover, combining word embedding with hand-crafted features reduces the feature dimensionality and outperforms alternative feature combinations.

Keywords: Sentiment analysis · Regression · Word embedding · Word2vec

1 Introduction

Sentiment analysis of social media has gained intense research interest recently [11,12]. It is challenging due to lack of context and limited number of characters of posts. These challenges have led to difficulties in interpreting the polarity of the posts by humans. A tweet may be perceived as positive by some readers and negative by the others. Although majority voting can be employed, it is a weak method in terms of the consistency of the assignments. This can be partially resolved using confidence scores. For a tweet, confidence score of a sentiment is the percentage of raters assigning the corresponding sentiment to the tweet. Confidence scoring has the potential for introducing a gradual representation of the sentiment of tweets, instead of discrete classification based on direct labeling.

Our major goal is to investigate whether employing the confidence scores has a significant role in the classification or not. For this, we first build regression

F. Frasincar et al. (Eds.): NLDB 2017, LNCS 10260, pp. 149–155, 2017.
DOI: 10.1007/978-3-319-59569-6_16

models to estimate the confidence scores of each sentiment separately. Then, we assign the sentiment, whose confidence score is maximum among others to the tweet. We apply our methods on a set of collected tweets in Turkish, which is an underrepresented language in the domain of sentiment analysis. Turkish is an agglutinative and highly inflectional language which presents challenges for traditional natural language processing (NLP) due to its complex morphology.

2 Related Work

Tweets may contain specific micro-blogging elements such as hashtags and emoticons, which are used for sentiment analysis [1,5]. Researchers found out algorithms that can learn representations of the data and extract useful information rather than extracting the features of the text only [2]. They have explored deep learning methods based on word embeddings. Tang et al. [14] developed a framework by concatenating the sentiment-specific word embedding features with the hand-crafted features. Moreover, Ren et al. [13] proposed to learn topic-enriched multi-prototype word embeddings for Twitter sentiment classification.

Sentiment analysis has been also at the focus of NLP research in Turkish, recently. Coban et al. [3] used Bag-of-Words and N-gram models to classify Turkish tweets as positive or negative. Kulcu et al. [6] performed sentiment analysis on tweets related to the news items. To our knowledge, word embeddings have not been used for sentiment analysis of social media in Turkish.

In the literature, there are a few studies employing regression for sentiment analysis [9]. The study of Liu [7] consisted of studies which perform regression in sentiment analysis. However, most of them performed regression using discrete labels. Moreover, Onal et al. [10] investigated the effect of using regression on confidence scores in sentiment analysis of tweets in English using only hand-crafted features. To our knowledge, no previous study has examined the role of using regression on sentiment analysis by employing word embeddings and hand-crafted features. This study aims to address this gap by analyzing tweets in Turkish.

3 Data Collection and Preprocessing

In this study, we conduct sentiment analysis using Turkish tweets that are related to the *seasons*. We first collected Turkish tweets, including keywords related to the topic *seasons* via Twitter Search API. We eliminated duplicates, truncated tweets, and tweets having only one word. This resulted in a total of 1030 tweets in the sample dataset. Moreover, we collected 2.1M Turkish tweets via Twitter Streaming API to create a corpus for learning continuous word representations.

We specified four classes, namely *positive*, *negative*, *neutral*, and *irrelevant*. The *irrelevant* class was used for tweets containing the keywords related to the *seasons* topic, yet not in the intended sense of the *seasons* concept. We collected sentiments for each tweet from at least seven native Turkish speakers.

Since social media data have different characteristics compared to newspaper or book texts, there is a need for a preprocessing step. First, we discarded the tweets which are Foursquare-related check-ins. We removed the words having less than two characters except numbers, the ones that involved mentions, hashtags, links and *"RT"* keyword. We also filtered out Turkish stop words, emoticons and punctuation marks. Then, we fixed misspelled words and parsed the fixed words to obtain their word stems. We separated suffixes from stems using *Zemberek API*[1] for both datasets. In this operation, we divided each word into the form of its word stem, its derivational affixes and its inflectional suffixes. We extracted derived words by omitting inflectional suffixes and keeping the derivational ones.

4 Features Extracted from Tweets

4.1 Lexical Features

We extracted word unigrams, word bigrams, part-of-speech (POS) tags and word negation as lexical features. We found derived-word unigrams in our dataset and each derived word corresponded to a feature in our representation. We considered the presence of a word in a tweet so that unigram features can take only binary values. We also employed derived-word bigrams as features, in a similar way. We obtained negation suffixes using Zemberek and employed the presence of a negation suffix as a feature. In addition, we identified the part-of-speech (POS) tags of each word using Zemberek. We identified 14 predefined POS tags of Turkish. Moreover, if a words POS tag could not be identified, it was assigned to the *null* category. We scored the presence of the POS tags so that the POS tag features could take only binary values. Finally, we considered the presence of an exclamation mark (!) and a question mark (?) as additional lexical features.

4.2 Emoticons

In the preprocessing step, we removed the emoticons from the tweets. However, we kept the presence of positive and negative emoticons as two binary-valued features. Positive emoticons are { :) , :D , =) , :-) , =D , (: , :p , D= , (= , D: , p: , :-) , :d , d: } and negative emoticons are { :(, :-(, =(, :/ ,): ,)-: ,)= , /: }.

4.3 Features Based on Sentiment Scores

We assigned a *happiness score* to a tweet, based on the happiness scores of words within it using the LabMT [4]. We first translated each word into English using Yandex Translate API[2]. Then, we found the happiness score of the corresponding word in the LabMT word list. We calculated the average happiness score of a tweet using only the scores of words existent in LabMT list and used this score as a continuous feature. Finally, if Yandex Translate API returned multiple outputs

[1] https://code.google.com/p/zemberek/.

[2] Yandex Translate API https://tech.yandex.com/translate/.

for a single word, we calculated the mean of the happiness scores of multiple English words, and assigned the mean score to that Turkish word.

We also used the output of a framework [15], which is a lexicon-based polarity prediction framework for Turkish. This framework produces positive and negative sentiment scores ranging between $[1 - 5]$ and $[-1, -5]$, respectively. We employed these two scores as *SentiStrengthTR* features in our experiments.

4.4 Word Embedding

In this study, we obtained a continuous vector representation for each word in the tweets using *word2vec* [8]. We followed the *skip-gram* approach, to estimate the neighboring words using only the corresponding word. Due to the character limitation in tweets, we set the window size to 2 to estimate neighboring (context) words. Therefore, we trained the model with 1.5M tweets having more than 4 words in the corpus dataset. We empirically specified the length of the vectors as $n = 150$ and set the number of randomly selected negative samples to 10.

Let $\boldsymbol{w}^{(i)} = [w_1^{(i)}, w_2^{(i)}, \ldots, w_n^{(i)}]$ represent the embedding of the ith word of the corresponding tweet learned using word2vec, where n denotes the dimension of word embedding. Also, N represents the number of the words in the corresponding tweet. We obtained the normalized continuous vector representation of a tweet $\boldsymbol{w}'$ in terms of the words it includes as $\boldsymbol{w}' = \frac{1}{N}\sum_{\forall i}^{N} \boldsymbol{w}^{(i)}$.

5 Experiments and Results

We extracted word unigrams ($\boldsymbol{f_1}$), word bigrams ($\boldsymbol{f_2}$), POS tag unigrams ($\boldsymbol{f_3}$), presence of negation suffix ($\boldsymbol{f_4}$), exclamation mark ($\boldsymbol{f_5}$) and question mark ($\boldsymbol{f_6}$), emoticons ($\boldsymbol{f_7}$), average happiness score ($\boldsymbol{f_8}$), SentiStrengthTR ($\boldsymbol{f_9}$) and word2vec features ($\boldsymbol{f_{10}}$). Using their combinations, we performed classification by Support Vector Machines (SVM) and regression by Support Vector Regression (SVR). Since word embedding contains semantic relationship information among words, we used it instead of N-grams and compared their results.

Assume that, three of five raters assigned positive sentiment and two of them assigned neutral sentiment to a tweet. Then, we obtained 0.6 *positive* score, 0.4 *neutral* score and 0 for other sentiments for that tweet. During classification, we labeled each training tweet with the sentiment having the highest confidence score. Then, we trained an SVM classifier using the training feature matrix and discrete class labels. The classifier directly assigned a sentiment to a new test tweet. During regression, we trained separate regressors for each sentiment using the training feature matrix and confidence score of the corresponding sentiment. In order to estimate the sentiment of a test tweet, we separately tested it with the regressors trained for each sentiment. Each regressor assigned a score to that test tweet and we assigned the sentiment with the maximum score to that tweet.

We performed 4-class (positive, negative, neutral, irrelevant), 3-class (positive, negative, neutral) and 2-class (positive, negative) classification and regression experiments. In the 4-class, 3-class and 2-class classification experiments, majority class classification performances were 35.92%, 42.38% and 54.9%, respectively. We performed 10-fold cross validation to optimize the cost parameter $C \in [0.005, 0.01, 0.05, 0.1, 0.5, 1, 5, 10, 50, 100]$ of SVM and SVR.

Table 1 shows that combination of $\boldsymbol{f_1}$, $\boldsymbol{f_7}$ and $\boldsymbol{f_9}$ gives the best 4-class classification performance with both SVM and SVR. In 3-class experiment, combination of $\boldsymbol{f_1}$, $\boldsymbol{f_2}$, $\boldsymbol{f_7}$, $\boldsymbol{f_9}$ and all feature combinations lead to the best accuracy with SVR (69.89%) and SVM (68.96%), respectively. Moreover, combination of $\boldsymbol{f_1}$, $\boldsymbol{f_2}$, $\boldsymbol{f_7}$ and $\boldsymbol{f_9}$ gives the best accuracy for 2-class experiment with both SVM (85.03%) and SVR (86.57%). Results reveal that using regression on confidence scores gives a slightly better or equal accuracy compared to classification on discrete labels. We observe that, $\boldsymbol{f_1}$, $\boldsymbol{f_2}$, $\boldsymbol{f_7}$ and $\boldsymbol{f_9}$ carry significant information about sentiment while other hand-crafted features do not bring extra information.

Table 1. Performances (%) obtained using combinations of hand-crafted features

Feature Combinations	SVM 4-class	SVR 4-class	SVM 3-class	SVR 3-class	SVM 2-class	SVR 2-class
$\boldsymbol{f_1}$	46.5	46.3	49.95	49.55	65.04	65.97
$\boldsymbol{f_1}, \boldsymbol{f_2}$	46	46.5	50.96	50.34	65.63	67.16
$\boldsymbol{f_1}, \boldsymbol{f_3}$	48.6	47.7	52.18	52.05	63.98	66.12
$\boldsymbol{f_1}, \boldsymbol{f_4}$	45.5	46.1	49.71	50.8	64.9	66.42
$\boldsymbol{f_1}, \boldsymbol{f_5}, \boldsymbol{f_6}$	46.1	46.3	50.26	49.77	65.18	67.01
$\boldsymbol{f_1}, \boldsymbol{f_7}$	60.5	61.2	68.5	68.41	82.48	83.88
$\boldsymbol{f_1}, \boldsymbol{f_8}$	46.2	45.6	50.75	50	64.28	66.87
$\boldsymbol{f_1}, \boldsymbol{f_9}$	55.7	56	61.93	61.82	77.94	78.36
$\boldsymbol{f_1}, \boldsymbol{f_2}, \boldsymbol{f_7}$	61.6	61.1	68.48	67.95	82.62	83.28
$\boldsymbol{f_1}, \boldsymbol{f_2}, \boldsymbol{f_9}$	54.9	55.7	62.03	60.57	77.36	78.36
$\boldsymbol{f_1}, \boldsymbol{f_7}, \boldsymbol{f_9}$	**61.7**	**61.7**	68.47	68.86	83.99	85.37
$\boldsymbol{f_1}, \boldsymbol{f_2}, \boldsymbol{f_7}, \boldsymbol{f_9}$	60.9	61.2	68.93	**69.89**	**85.03**	**86.57**
$\boldsymbol{f_1} - \boldsymbol{f_9}$	61.5	60.5	**68.96**	68.64	84.57	85.22

Table 2 shows that combination of $\boldsymbol{f_7}$, $\boldsymbol{f_9}$, $\boldsymbol{f_{10}}$ and combination of all features ($\boldsymbol{f_3} - \boldsymbol{f_{10}}$) lead to the best accuracy for 4-class experiment with SVM (62%) and SVR (62.2%), respectively. 3-class and 2-class classification results reveal that combination of $\boldsymbol{f_7}$, $\boldsymbol{f_9}$, $\boldsymbol{f_{10}}$ gives the best accuracy with both SVM and SVR. We can conclude that, regression on class confidence scores gives a slightly better performance compared to the classification based solely on discrete labels. Moreover, by comparing the results in Table 1 and Table 2 we can infer that replacing the unigram and bigram features with word embedding results in both slightly better performance and reduced feature dimensionality.

Table 2. Performances (%) obtained using combinations of word embedding with various hand-crafted features

Feature Combinations	SVM 4-class	SVR 4-class	SVM 3-class	SVR 3-class	SVM 2-class	SVR 2-class
f_{10}	47.8	48.4	53.88	54.55	69.08	67.31
f_{10}, f_3	49.4	47.4	54.57	54.09	65.94	67.01
f_{10}, f_4	47.4	47.6	53.07	53.3	68.01	67.61
f_{10}, f_5, f_6	47.7	47.6	53.66	53.75	68.63	66.87
f_{10}, f_7	61.8	62	**70.99**	70.11	85.77	86.27
f_{10}, f_8	48.5	48.4	54.2	54.77	68.03	66.42
f_{10}, f_9	55.4	55.2	63.99	62.61	79.41	79.55
f_{10}, f_7, f_9	**62**	62	**70.99**	**71.14**	**86.05**	**87.01**
$f_3 - f_{10}$	61.7	**62.2**	69.61	69.43	85	86.42

6 Conclusion

In this study, we employed various features to classify sentiments of Turkish tweets and we analyzed the effect of using regression on confidence scores of sentiments. Our main finding is that employing regression on confidence scores slightly boosts the accuracy, compared to classifying tweets based on their discrete class labels. We also found out that employing word embedding instead of N-gram features leads to a low-dimensional and better representation of tweets for sentiment analysis. As future work, we will analyze our method on larger-length datasets and extract word embedding from sentences and paragraphs.

References

1. Agarwal, A., Xie, B., Vovsha, I., Rambow, O., Passonneau, R.: Sentiment analysis of twitter data. In: Proceedings of the Workshop on Languages in Social Media. pp. 30–38 (2011)
2. Bengio, Y., Courville, A., Vincent, P.: Representation learning: a review and new perspectives. IEEE TPAMI **35**(8), 1798–1828 (2013)
3. Çoban, Ö., Özyer, B., Özyer, G.T.: Sentiment analysis for turkish twitter feeds. In: SIU, pp. 2388–2391 (2015)
4. Dodds, P.S., Harris, K.D., Kloumann, I.M., Bliss, C.A., Danforth, C.M.: Temporal patterns of happiness and information in a global social network: hedonometrics and twitter. PloS ONE **6**(12), e26752 (2011)
5. Go, A., Bhayani, R., Huang, L.: Twitter sentiment classification using distant supervision. CS224N Proj. Rep. Stanford 1(12) (2009)
6. Kulcu, S., Dogdu, E.: A scalable approach for sentiment analysis of turkish tweets and linking tweets to news. In: ICSC, pp. 471–476 (2016)
7. Liu, B.: Sentiment analysis and opinion mining. Synth. Lect. Hum. Lang. Technol. **5**(1), 1–167 (2012)

8. Mikolov, T., Sutskever, I., Chen, K., Corrado, G.S., Dean, J.: Distributed representations of words and phrases and their compositionality. In: Advances in Neural Information Processing Systems. pp. 3111–3119 (2013)
9. Onal, I., Ertugrul, A.M.: Effect of using regression in sentiment analysis. In: SIU, pp. 1822–1825 (2014)
10. Onal, I., Ertugrul, A.M., Cakici, R.: Effect of using regression on class confidence scores in sentiment analysis of twitter data. In: ACL 2014, 136 (2014)
11. Pang, B., Lee, L., Vaithyanathan, S.: Thumbs up?: sentiment classification using machine learning techniques. In: Proceedings of the ACL-02 Conference on Empirical Methods in Natural Language Processing, vol. 10. pp. 79–86 (2002)
12. Pang, B., Lee, L., et al.: Opinion mining and sentiment analysis. Foundations and Trends®. Inf. Retrieval **2**(1–2), 1–135 (2008)
13. Ren, Y., Zhang, Y., Zhang, M., Ji, D.: Improving twitter sentiment classification using topic-enriched multi-prototype word embeddings. In: AAAI, pp. 3038–3044 (2016)
14. Tang, D., Wei, F., Qin, B., Liu, T., Zhou, M.: Coooolll: a deep learning system for twitter sentiment classification. In: SemEval 2014, pp. 208–212 (2014)
15. Vural, A.G., Cambazoglu, B.B., Senkul, P., Tokgoz, Z.O.: A framework for sentiment analysis in turkish: application to polarity detection of movie reviews in turkish. In: Computer and Information Sciences III, pp. 437–445 (2013)

AL-TERp: Extended Metric for Machine Translation Evaluation of Arabic

Mohamed El Marouani(✉), Tarik Boudaa, and Nourddine Enneya

Laboratory of Informatics Systems and Optimization,
Faculty of Sciences, Ibn-Tofail University, Kenitra, Morocco
mohamed.elmarouani@gmail.com,
tarikboudaa@yahoo.fr, enneya@uit.ac.ma

Abstract. This paper presents AL-TERp (Arabic Language Translation Edit Rate - Plus) an extended version of machine translation evaluation metric TER-Plus that supports Arabic language. This metric takes into accounts some valuable linguistic features of Arabic like synonyms and stems, and correlates well with human judgments. Thus, the development of such tool will bring high benefits to the building of machine translation systems from other languages into Arabic that its quality remains under the expectations, specifically for evaluation and optimization tasks.

Keywords: MT evaluation · TER · TER-plus · Arabic MT

1 Introduction

Evaluation in machine translation is a challenging task that determines how much our system responds to the user requirements in term of translation quality. Apart from human evaluation, several automatic methods and tools have been developed by the research community. These methods are based on the comparison of a hypothesis to translation references, and are precision-oriented, recall-oriented or error-oriented. BLEU [1], TER [2] and METEOR [3] are the most known and used tools. Other tools and extensions have been created in order to well correlate with the human judgment and integrate specificities of target languages.

TER-Plus [4] (notated as TERp henceforth) is a tunable extension of TER that integrates flexible matching like synonyms, stems, and paraphrases substitutions. TERp doesn't support Arabic as a target language for automatic evaluation. We note that machine translation into Arabic language, especially English-to-Arabic, does not provide a high quality output in comparison to other closed languages pairs. This low quality is due among others to the complex morphology of Arabic [5]. Hence, we believe that adaptation of TERp in order to support Arabic can bring important improvement to the MT into Arabic because a good evaluation metric has a crucial role in the comparison of different MT systems' outputs and in parameters tuning of ours systems.

In this paper, we present AL-TERp an adaptation of TERp which supports the Arabic language and is more faithful to the human judgment. The Sect. 2 presents the metrics TERp, TER, METEOR and AL-BLEU. In the Sect. 3, we describe the

F. Frasincar et al. (Eds.): NLDB 2017, LNCS 10260, pp. 156–161, 2017.
DOI: 10.1007/978-3-319-59569-6_17

adaptations brought to TERp in order to support Arabic language. The Sect. 4 reports results of experiments. The Sect. 5 concludes the paper with brought contributions and some perspectives of improvement.

2 Related Work

Since the manual evaluation of machine translation results is, practically, not possible because of its high cost, researchers have designed automatic evaluation metrics trying to align with the basic evaluation criteria, like adequacy or fluency. We are concerned in this work, especially, by present the state-of-the-art of the metrics treating the particularities of morphologically complex languages like Arabic, and representing a high correlation with human judgment. In the remaining subsections, we present TER metric and how TERp improves on it. We also discuss METEOR and AL-BLEU metric dedicated for Arabic.

2.1 TER and TER-plus

For a hypothesis sentence, Translation Edit Rate (TER) is defined as the minimum edit distance over all references, normalized by the average reference length. These edits can be: word insertion, word deletion, word substitution and block movement of words called shifts. In contrast to BLEU, TER is an error measure. So, the lower it scores, the higher the metric is better.

TERp is an extension of TER aimed to better correlate with human judgment. In this perspective, TERp improves the metric via, among others, the following mechanisms: (i) TERp uses, in addition to the edit operations of TER, three new relaxing edit operations: stem matches, synonym matches, and phrases substitutions. (ii) The cost of each edit is optimized according to human judgments data set.

Stems are identified in TERp by application of Porter stemming algorithm [6], and synonyms using Wordnet [7]. Phrase substitutions are determined by looking up in a pre-computed phrases table of phrases and its paraphrases. With the exception of phrase substitutions, all edit operations used by TERp have fixed cost edits, i.e., the edit cost does not depend on the used words, and the optimization of its parameters is doing via a hill-climbing search algorithm [8]. Experiments led by [4] demonstrate that TERp achieves significant gains in correlation with human judgments over other MT evaluation metrics (TER, METEOR, and BLEU).

TERp doesn't support Arabic given since it does not have an Arabic synonyms provider, Arabic stemmer and a pre-computed paraphrase table. Also, the edit costs depend deeply on the evaluated language that is English.

2.2 METEOR and AL-BLEU

To respond to one of the BLEU drawbacks, METEOR introduced a recall in the calculation of its score. It takes into account, like TERp, flexible matching such as synonyms, stems and paraphrases. Its score's calculus formula is much more complicated than other metrics. Actually, METEOR doesn't support Arabic using all of its features, because we cannot get the word stems with Porter stemmer and synonyms with the standard Wordnet.

Despite that BLEU is still the most used metric for MT evaluation, it doesn't take into account the richness of morphology of some languages like Arabic. To respond to its shortcomings, Bouamor et al. [9] have developed an extension of BLEU (AL-BLEU) that extends the exact n-gram matching of BLEU to morphological, syntactic and lexical levels with optimized partial credits.

AL-BLEU weights are optimized in a hill-climbing search fashion in order to be well correlated with a human judgments data set. The obtained results show a significant improvement of AL-BLEU against BLEU and a competitive improvement against METEOR. Then, the performances realized by AL-BLEU give more confidence in the ability of automatic MT evaluation metrics improvement by the introduction of linguistic knowledge. Hence, one of the motivations of our work described the following section.

3 AL-TERp

Aiming to bring into the research community an MT evaluation tool that takes into account the linguistic specificities of Arabic, to adopt the error-oriented approach and to correlate better with human judgments, we have adapted TERp tool in order to support this language – this tool is called henceforth AL-TERp. The main proposed adaptations are summarized in the following subsections.

3.1 Normalization

The text normalization is a set of pre-processing operations that prepares our inputs to perform our task which is MT evaluation. We have replaced TERp normalizer by a handcrafted one dedicated for Arabic language. This component transforms hypothesis and reference inputs into pre-processed sentences by applying a set of treatments such as: removing non Arabic tokens and diacritics, standardization and tokenization of punctuation, converting of Arabic number digits and normalization of some Arabic characters like Hamza or Alif maqsura.

3.2 Arabic WordNet

The Arabic WordNet (AWN) [10] is a lexical database of the Arabic language following the development process of Princeton English WordNet and Euro WordNet. Our need in the context of building AL-TERp is to know if two words are synonyms or not. The available tools don't provide an integrated API which deal with this requirement. Thus, we have developed under AWN a layer verifying if two words are synonyms and to check if a word is a stopword.

3.3 Stemming

TERp uses Porter stemmer to provide stems of each English word in the reference and hypothesis sentences. Given that stemmers are language dependent, this stemmer doesn't support Arabic language. So, in order to construct our baseline MT evaluation metric AL-TERp we have picked in the first stage the simplest stemmer of Khoja [11].

3.4 Paraphrase Database

We have used Arabic paraphrases database provided by [12]. Each entry in the paraphrases database contains a set of features added to the phrase and its paraphrase. In our case, we use only $p(e|f)$ which is the probability of the paraphrase given the original phrase (in negative log value) and the reciprocal probability $p(f|e)$.

3.5 Edit Costs Optimization

The principal strength point of TERp is the possibility of optimization of its edit costs in regard to human judgment datasets. The module of optimization is then adapted to modify the set of edit costs of the metric in a process of a hill-climbing algorithm trying to obtain high correlation in terms of Kendall coefficients between AL-TERp scores and a range ranking given by a human annotator for outputs of a set of MT systems.

4 Experiments and Results

4.1 Data and Performance Criteria

To the best of our knowledge, the unique data set of human judgment of MT into Arabic has been developed by [9] in the project of creation of AL-BLEU metric.

The data set used in our experiments is composed of 1383 sentences selected from two subsets: (i) the standard English-Arabic NIST 2005 corpus, commonly used for MT evaluations and composed of political news stories; and (ii) a small dataset of translated Wikipedia articles. The corpus contains annotations that assess the quality of five systems, by ranking their translation candidates from best to worst for each source sentence in the corpus by two annotators. We have segmented our dataset in two partitions: the first one of 1000 sentences is used for parameters' optimization of our system (OPT), and the remained partition of 383 for testing purpose (TEST).

The optimization algorithm is adapted to take into account our dataset based on MT systems ranking. Besides, the correlation scores are calculated following the Kendall tau coefficient [13]. The tau coefficient of Kendall is calculated at the corpus level using the Fisher transformation [14]. This method allows us to find the average correlation of a corpus using correlations at the sentence level.

4.2 Results

The preliminary work required in these experiments is to determine the set of parameters maximizing the correlation between human ranking of OPT subset and scores produced by AL-TERp. Afterward, we have carried out for TEST subset a comparative study of correlations between human judgments and scores obtained by execution of 5 automatic evaluation metrics: BLEU, AL-BLEU, METEOR, TER and AL-TERp. METEOR is used in its universal mode but without using paraphrasing, which would require compiling a paraphrase database using a parallel corpus with Arabic in one side. The averaged correlations in the dataset level are presented in Table 1.

Table 1. Corpus-level correlation with human rankings (Kendall's τ) for BLEU, ALBLEU, METEOR, TER and AL-TERp

MT system	Kendall's tau
BLEU	0.2011
AL-BLEU	0.2085
METEOR	0.1782
TER	0.2619
AL-TERp	**0.3242**

4.3 Discussion

We observe a strong improvement of AL-TERp value correlation against all other metrics even with AL-BLEU which is constructed especially for Arabic language. Furthermore, the lowest correlation is realized by METEOR which is very likely due to the using of a version without all its components. BLEU and AL-BLEU correlation are similar. Also, TER performs better than others metrics and is closer to AL-TERp which we drive to verify and argue if scores offered by errors-oriented metrics correlate well with human judgments.

This baseline version of AL-TERp, that uses a surface stemmer of a morphologically rich language like Arabic and doesn't introduce other linguistic features, provides promising results: +11% against AL-BLEU and +6% against TER. These results are encouraging to improve the metric in order to take into account the specificities of Arabic language. On other hand, AL-TERp metric's optimization under large scale corpora with high quality manual annotation, in the future, can enhance MT evaluation of Arabic as a target language. Optimization towards a specific type of human judgments like adequacy or fluency is also possible if a specific MT output is desired.

5 Conclusions

We presented AL-TERp which is a baseline metric for Arabic MT error-oriented evaluation. This metric is optimized via a middle-size human judgment dataset. Performances realized in term of Kendall correlation exceeds by 6% the best one realized by TER metric.

In our ongoing work, we plan to enhance this metric in order to improve its performance by introduction of other linguistic features, and increasing of human judgment correlation by utilization of efficient optimization algorithms. In this perspective, we believe that the metric will bring also important benefits for MT systems tuning and for errors analysis.

Acknowledgments. We would like to thank Houda Bouamor for her grateful helping by providing us the dataset used in this work and for her comments and recommendations.

References

1. Papineni, K., Roukos, S., Ward, T., Zhu, W.-J.: BLEU: a method for automatic evaluation of machine translation. In: Proceedings of the 40th Annual Meeting on Association for Computational Linguistics, pp. 311–318. Association for Computational Linguistics (2002)
2. Snover, M., Dorr, B., Schwartz, R., Micciulla, L., Makhoul, J.: A study of translation edit rate with targeted human annotation. In: Proceedings of Association for Machine Translation in the Americas (2006)
3. Banerjee, S., Lavie, A.: METEOR: an automatic metric for MT evaluation with improved correlation with human judgments. In: Proceedings of the ACL Workshop on Intrinsic and Extrinsic Evaluation Measures for Machine Translation and/or Summarization, pp. 65–72 (2005)
4. Snover, M., Madnani, N., Dorr, B.J., Schwartz, R.: Fluency, adequacy, or HTER?: exploring different human judgments with a tunable MT metric. In: Proceedings of the Fourth Workshop on Statistical Machine Translation, pp. 259–268. Association for Computational Linguistics (2009)
5. Habash, N.Y.: Introduction to Arabic Natural Language Processing (2010)
6. Snowball: A language for stemming algorithms. http://snowball.tartarus.org/texts/introduction.html
7. Miller, G.A., Fellbaum, C.: WordNet then and now. Lang Resour. Eval. **41**, 209–214 (2007)
8. Russell, S., Norvig, P.: Artificial Intelligence: A Modern Approach (2009)
9. Bouamor, H., Alshikhabobakr, H., Mohit, B., Oflazer, K.: A human judgement corpus and a metric for arabic MT evaluation. In: Proceedings of the 2014 Conference on Empirical Methods in Natural Language Processing (EMNLP), pp. 207–213. Association for Computational Linguistics, Doha, Qatar (2014)
10. Elkateb, S., Black, W., Rodríguez, H., Alkhalifa, M., Vossen, P., Pease, A., Fellbaum, C.: Building a wordnet for arabic. In: Proceedings of The fifth international conference on Language Resources and Evaluation (LREC 2006), pp. 22–28 (2006)
11. Shereen, K.: Stemming Arabic Text. http://zeus.cs.pacificu.edu/shereen/research.htm
12. Ganitkevitch, J., Callison-Burch, C.: The multilingual paraphrase database. In: LREC, pp. 4276–4283 (2014)
13. Kendall, M.G.: A new measure of rank correlation. Biometrika **30**, 81–93 (1938)
14. Clayton, N., Dunlap, W.P.: Averaging correlation coefficients: should Fisher's z transformation be used? J. Appl. Psychol. **72**, 146–148 (1987)

A Morphological Approach for Measuring Pair-Wise Semantic Similarity of Sanskrit Sentences

Vaishakh Keshava(✉), Mounica Sanapala, Akshay Chowdlu Dinesh, and Sowmya Kamath Shevgoor

Department of Information Technology,
National Institute of Technology Karnataka, Surathkal, India
kvaishakhnambiar@gmail.com, smounica9@gmail.com, akshaychowdlu10@gmail.com, sowmyakamath@nitk.edu.in

Abstract. Capturing explicit and implicit similarity between texts in natural language is a critical task in Computational Linguistics applications. Similarity can be multi-level (word, sentence, paragraph or document level), each of which can affect the similarity computation differently. Most existing techniques are ill-suited for classical languages like Sanskrit as it is significantly richer in morphology than English. In this paper, we present a morphological analysis based approach for computing semantic similarity between short Sanskrit texts. Our technique considers the constituent words' semantic properties and their role in individual sentences within the text, to compute similarity. As all words do not contribute equally to the semantics of a sentence, an adaptive scoring algorithm is used for ranking, which performed very well for Sanskrit sentence pairs of varied complexities.

Keywords: Morphological analysis · Semantic similarity · NLP

1 Introduction

Semantic measures are central elements of a large variety of Natural Language Processing applications and knowledge-based systems, and have therefore been subject to intensive and interdisciplinary research efforts during past decades. The process of semantic similarity measurement evaluates the depth of the semantic relationship between various constituent entities of the natural language under consideration, which is then examined at multiple levels to finally express the level of similarity numerically, for purposes such as ranking and scoring.

Sentence-level similarity measures focus on analyzing a word and its association with other words. The semantics of a sentence is determined by the agents, experiencers, instruments, location, verb etc., used in expressing the writers intent, which represent different thematic relations. The *tense* also contributes to the semantics, while *prefixes* tend to alter the meaning of a word, and

F. Frasincar et al. (Eds.): NLDB 2017, LNCS 10260, pp. 162–169, 2017.
DOI: 10.1007/978-3-319-59569-6_18

so should also be taken into account. Hence, each word has its own contribution to the semantics of the sentence, and each contribution is different.

Current methods for capturing semantic similarity are more geared towards the English language and focus towards Sanskrit is comparatively quite low. Existing semantic similarity computation methods can be categorized into two groups - those based on measuring path distance between concepts (dictionary/thesaurus based) and, those which use the information content of a concept (corpus-based). Hybrid methods have also been tried in certain contexts. Some approaches to determine similarity use a variety of computational models that implement distributional semantics based techniques like Latent Semantic Analysis [2] and semantic nets [7], syntax or dependency-based models [9,14], random indexing and grammar patterns [10].

Recent work in the field of Natural Language Processing for Indian Languages has attempted to deal with the problem of parsing. Huet et al. [7] applied computational linguistics techniques to Sanskrit Language. Goyal et al. [3] applied an analysis using semantic relations and parsing in Sanskrit text for understanding meaning. Grammar based approach towards the development of language tools for Sanskrit [1,4,8] are followed due to its well defined grammar. Hellwig et al. [6] used statistical approaches for building these tools with a small manually tagged corpus as a boot-strap. Kulkarni et al. [12] followed a combination of the grammar based approach with statistical evidences to push the most likely solution to the top. Sanskrit is a classical language with an ancient history. Sanskrit grammar (called *Vyakarana*) is culminated in Panini's monumental work 'Ashtadhyayi' [11]. To represent Sanskrit text in a machine processable form, a transliteration scheme called the WX notation [5] was used. Figure 1 illustrates the notations used in the WX scheme for representing vowels, phonetic sounds and consonants for the Devanagari script (used to write Sanskrit). The Sanskrit WordNet [13] is a linked lexical knowledge that captures the synonyms, provides *gloss* (an example of usage) which can be used for word sense disambiguation, and also indicates the *category* (noun, verb, adverb or adjective context) of the word. As most Dravidian languages are rooted in Sanskrit, any techniques developed for Sanskrit can easily be extended to other Indian languages. In this paper, a system that computes the semantic similarity of two Sanskrit texts by considering the core properties and surface structure of the Sanskrit language is presented. The rest of the paper is organized as follows. Section 2 presents the proposed methodology devised for semantic similarity computation. Section 3 presents the experimental results, followed by conclusion and references.

अ a	आ A	इ i	ई I	उ u	ऊ U	ऋ q	ॠ Q	ऌ L	ए e	ऐ E	ओ o	औ O	अं M	अः H	क् k	ख् K	ग् g	घ् G	ङ् f	च् c	छ् C	ज् j	झ् J
ञ् F	ट् t	ठ् T	ड् d	ढ् D	ण् N	त् w	थ् W	द् x	ध् X	न् n	प् p	फ् P	ब् b	भ् B	म् m	य् y	र् r	ल् l	व् v	श् S	ष् R	स् s	ह् h

Fig. 1. The scheme used in WX notation

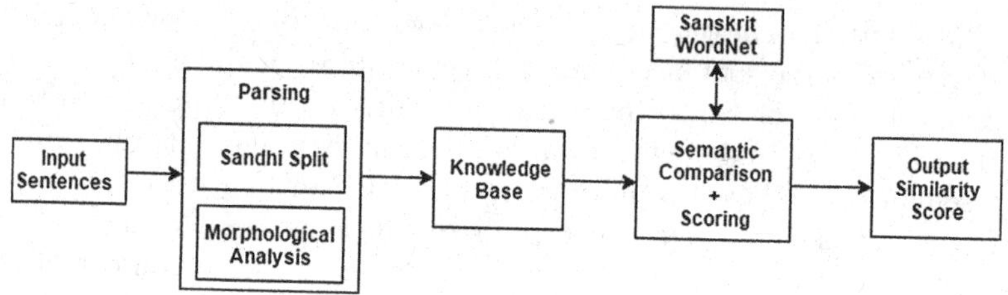

Fig. 2. Proposed Methodology

2 Proposed Methodology

The overall methodology designed for processing two Sanskrit sentences semantically for computing their similarity is depicted in Fig. 2. The system takes two Sanskrit sentences as input in WX notation. The input sentences are parsed to get the morphological properties. Parsing also involves performing Sandhi splitting and also helps in resolving real time ambiguities in the sentences. During morphological analysis phase, the morphology, i.e. the identification, analysis and description of the structure of a given languages (Sanskrit) morphemes and other linguistic units, such as root words, affixes, parts of speech, intonations and stresses, or implied context is determined. In the fusional language form of Sanskrit, compound words are likely to occur. During the sandhi splitting process, a compound word is split into its individual morphemes, which enables a clear analysis of morphemes in the sentences. The properties of each token obtained from the morphological analysis are used to create a knowledge base. This knowledge base stores the details about the agent, object, instrument, location, possession etc. of each sentence. Next, the semantics of both the sentences are compared using the extracted properties stored in the knowledge base. The Sanskrit WordNet is used at this stage to take care of synonyms. The karaka relationships in the sentences help in identifying the doer, action, place of action etc., which gives semantic information of the sentence. Separate scoring algorithms for nouns, verbs are other words are also incorporated, after which the percentage similarity between the two sentences is computed and displayed.

2.1 Implementation

Parsing: The Sanskrit tools available at *The Sanskrit Heritage Site*[1] were used for performing morphological analysis and parsing. These tools can resolve the real time ambiguities as well. The full parser [8] which takes sentences which contains Sandhis, i.e. compound words, was used for evaluation.

For example, consider two words *prawyupakAraH* and *prawi sahAyam*. Without a sandhi split, *prawyupakAraH*, there will not be any match *prawi sahAyam* in WordNet. Upon sandhi split, we get *prawyupakAraH* = *prawi* + *upakAraH*.

[1] Available at http://sanskrit.inria.fr/.

Table 1. Word attributes

Property	Description
Statement	Statement number
Word	Morpheme from sentence
Form	Noun/Verb/Other word
Gender	Male/Female/Neutral
Tense	One of the 10 tenses
Case	One of the 7 cases
Person	First/Second/Third
Number	Singular/Dual/Plural
Base form	Root/First form

Table 2. Word relations

Property/case	Description
Nominative	Subject of a verb
Accusative	Direct object of a verb
Instrumental	Object used to perform action
Dative	Indirect object of a verb
Ablative	Movement from something
Genitive	Possession
Locative	Location
Verb	Action or Event
Other words	Other than nouns/verbs

sahAyam is a synonym of *upakAraH.* So now we get *prawyupakAraH* = *prawi* + *sahAyam.* Now, the system understands that both mean the same and is able to return a better similarity score. This is why the process of Sandhi split is crucial.

Knowledge Base Creation: During parsing, the morphological properties of the words are obtained, which are stored as attributes as shown in Table 1. The root forms or base forms of each word are stored as per their category. If the word is a noun, it is further categorized into 7 cases (Vibhakti). Verbs can be found under 'Verb' column. If it is neither a noun nor a verb, it is stored in 'Other Words' column (Table 2).

Similarity Scoring: *Scoring for verbs:* Let X = $\{x_1, x_2, ...x_n\}$ be the set of verb roots in sentence 1 and Y = $\{y_1, y_2, ...y_m\}$ be the set of verb roots in sentence 2. Let $|X|$ and $|Y|$ be the size of set X and Y respectively. Let the synsets of a word be stored in a set S. Let SV[m] be an array to store the score initialized to 0. The proposed scoring mechanism gives more weight to the root (which determines the action) followed by the tense. Since the *Person* and *Number* is also determined by the noun, it is given lesser weight in verb scoring part. It is observed that when multiple attributes match, the similarity is more due to the dependency between the word attributes. So, a component $floor(count/2)$ is added to the score at the end. Algorithm 1 illustrates the process of scoring verbs.

Algorithm 1. Scoring Verbs

```
for each x_i , i from 1 to n do
    S = Synonyms of x_i;
    for each y_j, j from 1 to m do
        score = count = 0;
        if (y_j in S) then
            score = score + 4;
            count + +;
            if (Tense matches) then
                score = score + 2;
                count + +;
            end
            if (Number matches) then
                score = score + 1;
                count + +;
            end
            if (Person matches) then
                score = score + 1;
                count + +;
            end
            score = score + floor(count/2);
            if (score > SV[j]) then
                SV[j] = score;
            end
        end
    end
end
V_score = Σ_{i=1}^{m} (SV[i]);
V_score_max = (10 * max(|X|, |Y|));
```

Scoring Nouns of a Particular Vibhakti: Like in the case of verbs let X and Y be the set of nouns (of a particular case in its base form) of sentence 1 and sentence 2 respectively. $SN[m]$ be an array to store the score. A score of 5 is given in case the root matches and a score of 2 in case the number *matches.* Like in the case of verb a component $floor(count/2)$ is added to the score, where $N_{score} = \sum_{i=1}^{m}$ $(SN[i])$ and $N_{score_{max}} = (8 * \max(|X|, |Y|))$.

Scoring of Other Words: Let X and Y be the set of other words in sentence 1 and sentence 2 respectively. $SO[m]$ be an array to store the score. For other words, we give a score of 5 if the exact same word (or its synonym) is present in both the sentences. Accordingly, we get $O_{score} = \sum_{i=1}^{m} (SO[i])$ and $O_{score_{max}} = (5 * \max(|X|, |Y|))$. Overall similarity score between the two sentences is given by,

$$\frac{(V_{score} + N_{score} + O_{score})}{(V_{score_{max}} + N_{score_{max}} + O_{score_{max}})} * 100 \tag{1}$$

where, V_{score}, N_{score} and O_{score} is the total verb, noun and other word score respectively. $V_{score_{max}}$, $N_{score_{max}}$ and $O_{score_{max}}$ are the maximum verb, noun and other-word scores respectively.

3 Experimental Results

To evaluate the effectiveness of the proposed approach for similarity measurement, sentence pairs of various complexity levels were used. These were considered as different testcases, categorized into classes of successively increasing complexity. Six such levels were considered and for each testcase, sentence pairs which were *perfectly similar*, *partially similar* and *perfectly dissimilar* were used to assess the similarity score calculation performance and accuracy. A total of 180 sentence pairs (30 of each level) were used for the evaluation. Table 3 shows the accuracy of the proposed system for all class of sentences.

Table 3. Experimental results for all the levels of sentences

Level	Class	Sentence type	Correct	Incorrect	Avg. accuracy
Level 1	Noun+verb	Perfectly similar	10	0	96.66%
		Partially similar	9	1	
		Dissimilar	10	0	
Level 2	Actor+object+verb	Perfectly similar	10	0	93.33%
		Partially similar	9	1	
		Dissimilar	9	1	
Level 3	Prefixes	Perfectly similar	9	1	90%
		Partially similar	9	1	
		Dissimilar	9	1	
Level 4	Active and passive voice	Perfectly similar	8	2	83.33%
		Partially similar	9	1	
		Dissimilar	8	2	
Level 5	Complex - 1	Perfectly similar	7	3	80%
		Partially similar	9	1	
		Dissimilar	8	2	
Level 6	Complex - 2	Perfectly similar	7	3	80%
		Partially similar	9	1	
		Dissimilar	8	2	
Overall Accuracy					**87.22%**

As an example, consider a sentence pair which has more than one noun or verb. These can categorized as level 5 based on its complexity.

1. *rAmaH sIwayA saha vipinam acalaw* (Rama went to forest with Sita)
2. *rAmaH vanam calawi* (Rama goes to forest)

In these sentences, the actor is 'Rama', the act is 'to go' and the destination is 'forest' (vipinam, vanam). Sentence 1 is in past tense while sentence 2 is in present tense. Also in sentence 1, the actor 'Rama' is accompanied by 'Sita' to forest. Due to this, the system computed similarity score can be considered appropriate at 66%.

It can be seen that the proposed approach was quite effective and was able to handle increasing levels of complexity in Sanskrit sentences very well. The overall accuracy of the system considering all the six levels was about 87.22%.

4 Conclusion and Future Work

A morphological analysis based technique for measuring semantic similarity between two Sanskrit sentences of varied morphological characteristics was discussed in this paper. The latent properties of words in a sentence are captured and used by the scoring algorithm, that associates different weights to various components of the sentence. Cases like active/passive voice, prefixes and words other than noun/verb that contribute to semantics to some extent were also addressed. Experimental evaluation showed that our approach works very well for sentence pairs of varying complexity levels. For improving our model further, we intend to apply the Word2Vec model to capture other related words in addition to synsets obtained from WordNet. The model could be further enhanced by addressing compound sentence similarity and also by extending support to other Dravidian languages.

References

1. Ambati, B., Gadde, P., Jindal, K.: Experiments in Indian language dependency parsing. In: ICON09 NLP Tools Contest: Indian Language Dependency Parsing (2009)
2. Deerwester, S., Dumais, S., et al.: Indexing by latent semantic analysis. J. Am. Soc. Inf. Sci. **41**(6), 391 (1990)
3. Goyal, P., Arora, V., Behera, L.: Analysis of Sanskrit text: parsing and semantic relations. In: Huet, G., Kulkarni, A., Scharf, P. (eds.) ISCLS 2007-2008. LNCS, vol. 5402, pp. 200–218. Springer, Heidelberg (2009). doi:10.1007/978-3-642-00155-0_7
4. Goyal, P., Huet, G.: Completeness analysis of a Sanskrit reader. In: 5th International Symposium on Sanskrit Computational Linguistics, pp. 130–171 (2013)
5. Gupta, R., Goyal, P., Diwakar, S.: Transliteration among Indian languages using WX notation. In: KONVENS, pp. 147–150 (2010)
6. Hellwig, O.: Extracting dependency trees from Sanskrit texts. In: Kulkarni, A., Huet, G. (eds.) ISCLS 2009. LNCS, vol. 5406, pp. 106–115. Springer, Heidelberg (2008). doi:10.1007/978-3-540-93885-9_9
7. Huet, G.: Shallow syntax analysis in Sanskrit guided by semantic nets constraints. In: International Workshop on Research Issues in Digital Libraries, p. 6. ACM (2006)
8. Huet, G.: Formal structure of Sanskrit text: requirements analysis for a mechanical Sanskrit processor. In: Huet, G., Kulkarni, A., Scharf, P. (eds.) ISCLS 2007-2008. LNCS, vol. 5402, pp. 162–199. Springer, Heidelberg (2009). doi:10.1007/978-3-642-00155-0_6
9. Husain, S.: Dependency parsers for Indian languages. In: ICON09 NLP Tools Contest: Indian Language Dependency Parsing (2009)
10. Chang, J., et al.: Using grammar patterns to evaluate semantic similarity for short texts. In: Computing Technology & Information Management (ICCM) (2012)
11. Katre, S.M., et al.: Astādhyāyī of Pāini. Motilal Banarsidass Publisher, Delhi (1989)

12. Kulkarni, A., Pokar, S., Shukl, D.: Designing a constraint based parser for Sanskrit. In: Jha, G.N. (ed.) ISCLS 2010. LNCS, vol. 6465, pp. 70–90. Springer, Heidelberg (2010). doi:10.1007/978-3-642-17528-2_6
13. Kulkarni, M., Dangarikar, C., et al.: Introducing Sanskrit Wordnet. In: 5th Global Wordnet Conference (2010)
14. Padó, S., Lapata, M.: Dependency-based construction of semantic space models. Comput. Linguist. **33**(2), 161–199 (2007)

Word-Level Identification of Romanized Tunisian Dialect

Chaima Aridhi[1(✉)], Hadhemi Achour[2], Emna Souissi[1], and Jihene Younes[2]

[1] Université de Tunis, ENSIT, 1008 Montfleury, Tunisia
chaima.aridhi@gmail.com, emna.souissi@ensit.rnu.tn
[2] Université de Tunis, ISGT, LR99ES04 BESTMOD, 2000 Le Bardo, Tunisia
ademy.achour@isg.rnu.tn, jihene.younes@gmail.com

Abstract. In the Arabic-speaking world, textual productions on social networks are often informal and generally characterized by the use of various dialects, which can be transcribed in Latin or Arabic characters. More specifically, electronic writing in Tunisia is characterized in large part by a mixture of Tunisian dialect with other languages and by a margin of individualization giving users the freedom to write without depending on orthographic or grammatical constraints. In this work, we address the problem of the automatic Tunisian dialect identification within the electronic writings that are produced on social networks using the Latin alphabet. We propose to study and experiment two different identification approaches. Our experiments show that the best performance is obtained using a machine learning based approach using Support Vector Machines.

Keywords: Language identification · Tunisian dialect · Informal text · Social web · N-grams · Machine learning · SVM · Natural language processing

1 Introduction

Language identification consists in automatically assigning a language to a textual unit, supposed to be monolingual [1]. The problem has been dealt with several years ago, and numerous identification approaches have been proposed in the literature. The problem is considered as relatively well solved when dealing with long and well written texts, especially in European languages. However, new challenges have emerged with short and informal textual contents that are widespread on the social web [2, 3]. These productions are indeed, characterized by an informal writing that does not conform to particular spelling rules and may combine linguistic productions from different origins. This is, for example, the case of the Arabic dialects that are widely used in Arabic social networks and which differ in a significant way from the MSA (Modern Standard Arabic). Indeed, dialectal textual productions include several linguistic phenomena, such as the use of both Arabic and Latin writing systems, the use of digits, abbreviations. But above all, they may be multilingual, including words from different other languages, mainly, English and French, depending on the historical and geographical nature of the countries.

F. Frasincar et al. (Eds.): NLDB 2017, LNCS 10260, pp. 170–175, 2017.
DOI: 10.1007/978-3-319-59569-6_19

In this paper, we focus on the Tunisian dialect (TD). We address in particular, the problem of its automatic identification within the electronic writings that are produced on social networks, using the Latin alphabet, since these informal textual productions tend to be highly multilingual, generally composed of a mixture of TD and other languages. This identification step can be, very useful for the automatic construction of TD linguistic resources and is, even crucial for various applications such as topic detection and tracking on social web, opinion mining and sentiment analysis, machine translation, etc.

In this work, we are concerned with short textual messages transcribed in the Latin alphabet and TD identification is performed at a word level. Our purpose is tó automatically categorize a given word as a TD or a non TD word. To this end, we propose to study and experiment two different TD identification approaches based on N-gram language modeling: the first uses the "Cumulative Frequency Addition" method, and the second is a machine learning based approach, using Support Vector Machines (SVMs).

2 Related Work

Several works have focused on the automatic language identification and proposed various solution approaches. In [4], we distinguish three main families of approaches in the language identification: linguistic approaches, statistical and probabilistic approaches, and approaches based on general classification methods (neural networks, SVM, etc.). The linguistic approaches are generally based on a linguistic knowledge which is defined beforehand [5–7]. Statistical and probabilistic approaches use large corpora of texts for each language, in order to detect some of its formal regularities using statistical or probabilistic models [8–10]. Several works have used models based on N-grams for the language identification of written texts [2, 11, 12]. Classification methods using machine learning algorithms were also used to identify languages such as Naive Bayes [3], SVM [4, 13], Neural Networks [14], and CRF [15].

With regard to the identification works on Arabic dialects, Cotterell and Callison-burch [16], exploited the comments written by the readers of several Arabic online newspapers to realize an identification system, distinguishing Arabic dialects from each other, and based on an N-gram extraction method with the combination of the two learning algorithms: SVM and the Naive Bayes classifier. The research carried out by Darwish et al. [17], was specifically focused on the Egyptian dialect in order to distinguish it from the MSA, by exploiting some of its specific linguistic (lexical, morphological, phonological and syntactic) features. Fewer works have been carried out on the identification of the Tunisian dialect, among which we can cite [18] who focused on automatically identifying the messages extracted from the social web by using a lexicon-based approach in order to distinguish the Tunisian dialect written text. Another work was proposed by Hassoun and Belhadj [19] who resorted to an N-gram method to perform a language identification in order to categorize three languages (Tunisian Arabish[1], French and English).

[1] Arabic dialect written with Latin alphabet.

3 Tunisian Dialect Identification

3.1 TD Identification Using N-Gram Based Cumulative Frequency Addition

The first approach for automatically identifying TD words we are proposing to experiment uses a simple and fast method which is the N-gram based Cumulative Frequency Addition method, proposed in [12]. We propose to apply this method to a word-level identification of TD, in order to build a system able to decide if an input word is a TD word or not. For this purpose, we use a pre-established corpus that is extracted from real world social web textual messages and formed by TD and non TD words transcribed in the Latin alphabet. N-grams of characters are extracted from each word belonging to this corpus. The N-gram proposed model can be defined as follows:

- *T*: a training corpus composed by a list of words manually annotated by a Tunisian annotator. Each word is assigned the corresponding language (TD/ Non TD).
- *TDNgrams:* set of non-redundant N-grams, extracted from TD words of *T*, with their occurrence frequency.
- *NTDNgrams:* set of non-redundant N-grams, extracted from Non TD words of the corpus *T*, with their occurrence frequency.
- *w*: input word to be identified. *w* is represented by a set of N-grams.

To identify the word *w* language, our system computes for each N-gram in *w*, its internal frequency in the TD and Non TD language. The internal frequency of a given N-gram in a given language, is obtained by dividing its frequency by the sum of the frequencies of all N-grams of the considered language. The cumulative sum of internal frequencies of the N-grams contained in the word *w* is then calculated in both TD and Non TD languages. The language of the word *w* is thus, identified by comparing the two obtained sums and choosing the language with the maximal sum.

3.2 TD Identification Using Support Vector Machines

Support Vector Machines [20] are commonly used for classification problems. They are in particular, largely used for text classification, for which they seem to be well adapted [21, 22]. In this work and in order to automatically identify the romanized Tunisian dialect, we propose, a binary SVM classification model based on N-grams, that classifies each new input word, into two potential classes: +1 (TD word); −1 (Non TD word). In this model, the different N-grams extracted from the training corpus are considered as features describing a given word. Indeed, each word is represented by a vector *V* of N-grams, whose dimension corresponds to the size of the total list of distinct corpus N-grams. Each element *fi* of the vector *V* consists of a value associated to the ith N-gram, describing its occurrence in the considered word. A given word *w* is thus, represented by a vector $V = (f_1, f_2, \ldots, f_n)$, where:

n is the total number of the corpus N-grams,

fi is a value associated to the ith feature (i^{th} N-gram) for the word *w*. We propose to consider and combine 3 potential values for *fi*.

f_{1i}: occurrence frequency of the N-gram in *w*.
f_{2i}: N-gram location in *w* (at the beginningin the middle, at the end).
f_{3i}: the existence of one or more digits in the N-gram.

Considering these features, in the learning phase, the classification algorithm learns and constructs a model for predicting classes to assign to new input words in the test phase. We experimented different combinations of feature values (f_1, f_2, f_3) in order to seek the best performance reached by our system, using the SVMPerf[2] tool. Experiments and results are presented in the next section.

4 Experiments and Results

To experiment the two proposed models in the previous section, we used the TD corpus constructed by [18] consisting in a set of user-generated TD messages, extracted from social web (mainly, Facebook Tunisian pages). We annotated a portion of this corpus by associating with each word its corresponding tag: "TD" for the words belonging to the Tunisian dialect, and "NTD" for the foreign words. The annotated data was then randomly split into a training set (85%) and a test set (15%). The characteristics of the used corpora are described in Table 1.

Table 1. Used corpus description

Corpus	%	#Total words
Global	100%	86,940
Training	85%	73,899
Test	15%	13,041

Results obtained from the conducted experimentations to test the two proposed TD identification approaches, are reported in the following Table 2 in terms of accuracy, recall, precision and F-measure.

Table 2. Performance measures

		N-gram	Accuracy	Recall	Precision	F-measure
N-gram CSIF		1-gram	77.09%	68.71%	70.58%	69.63%
		2-gram	84.34%	75.26%	86.30%	80.40%
		3-gram	90.22%	84.08%	90.96%	87.38%
SVM	f_3	1-gram	87.03%	88.96%	76.97%	82.53%
	$f_2 * f_3$	2-gram	90.57%	**91.12%**	83.70%	87.25%
	$f_1 * f_2 * f_3$	**3-gram**	**93.57%**	86.04%	**95.05%**	**90.32%**

[2] https://www.cs.cornell.edu/people/tj/svm_light/svm_perf.html.

The results reported in Table 2 show that, for both proposed identification approaches, 3-gram based models lead to a significantly better performance than those obtained using 1-gram and 2-gram models.

As can be seen from this table, all the obtained results with the SVM classifier are generally better than those obtained with the first classification approach. According to the conducted experiments, the most performant TD identification model is the 3-gram based SVM model combining together the three features f_1 (N-gram frequency), f_2 (N-gram location) and f_3 (digits presence in N-gram), with an accuracy reaching 93.57% and an F-measure exceeding 90%.

5 Conclusion

This work addresses the problem of Tunisian dialect automatic identification. We have focused in particular, on the Romanized electronic written form of TD, since it is the most used on the social web. We proposed to implement and experiment two N-gram based approaches. The first approach uses a simple and fast identification method based on cumulative N-gram frequency addition. The second one uses an SVM classifier. Our experiments show that SVMs perform better regardless the size of N-grams, reaching 93.6% of classification accuracy with a 3-gram based model.

We consider this work as a preliminary study of the Tunisian dialect identification that needs to be extended and enhanced. Indeed, we plan to carry on more experiments using N-gram models with $N > 3$. Other identification approaches using different machine learning techniques may be experimented for the case of TD identification. We aim in particular, experimenting with approaches based on sequential labeling techniques (such as MEMM, CRF, etc.), in order to classify words within a text, into TD vs. non TD language, taking into account their context.

In a next step, we wish to move to the study of a more challenging task which is the automatic identification of the Arabic transcribed written form of TD. This task presents important difficulties mainly due to the high overlapping between TD and MSA (Modern Standard Arabic) languages [18], and will require identification approaches able to resolve the ambiguity of common words according to their context of use.

References

1. Jalam, R.: Apprentisage Automatique et Catégorisation de Textes Multilingues. Ph.D. thesis, Université Lumière, Lyon (2003)
2. Tromp, E., Pechenizkiy, M.: Graph-based n-gram language identification on short texts. In: Proceedings of the 20th Machine Learning conference of Belgium and The Netherlands, The Hague (2011)
3. Winkelmolen, F., Mascardi, V.: Statistical language identification of short texts. In: Proceedings of the 3rd International Conference on Agents and Artificial Intelligence, Rome (2011)

4. Jalam, R., Teytaud, O.: Simplified Identification de la Langue et Catégorisation de Textes basées sur les N-grams. In: Journées Francophones d' extraction et de gestion de connaissances, Montpellier (2002)
5. Dunning, T.: Statistical identification of language. In: Computing Research Laboratory Technical Memo MCCS 94–273, New Mexico State University, New Mexico (1994)
6. Giguet, E.: Méthode pour l'analyse automatique de structures formelles sur documents multilingues. Ph.D. thesis, Université de Caen, Normandy (1998)
7. Lins, R.D., Gonçalves, P.: Automatic language identification of written texts. In: Proceedings of the 2004 ACM Symposium on Applied Computing, Nicosia (2004)
8. Souter, C., Churcher, G., Hayes, J., Hughes, J., Johnson, S.: Natural language identification using corpus-based models. Hermes - J. Lang. Commun. Bus. **13**, 183–203 (1994)
9. Martino, M.J., Paulsen, R.C.: Natural language determination using partial words. Google Patents (2001)
10. Grefenstette, G.: Comparing two language identification schemes. In: Proceedings of the 3rd International Conference on the Statistical Analysis of Textual Data (JADT 1995), Rome (1995)
11. Cavnar, W.B., Trenkle, J.M.: n-Gram-based text categorization. In: Proceedings of SDAIR-94, 3rd Annual Symposium on Document Analysis and Information Retrieval, Las Vegas (1994)
12. Ahmed, B., Cha, S.H., Tappert. C.: Language identification from text using n-Gram based cumulative frequency addition. In: Proceedings of Student/Faculty Research Day, CSIS, New York (2004)
13. Bhargava, A., Kondrak, G.: Language identification of names with SVMs. In: Proceedings of HLT 2010 Human Language Technologies: The 2010 Annual Conference of the North American Chapter of the Association for Computational Linguistics, California (2010)
14. Simões, A., Almeida, J.J., Byers, S.D.: Language identification: a neural network approach. In: 3rd Symposium on Languages, Applications and Technologies (SLATE 2014), Bragança (2014)
15. Chittaranjan, G., Vyas, Y., Bali, K., Choudhury, M.: Word-level language identification using CRF: code-switching shared task report of MSR India system. In: Proceedings of the First Workshop on Computational Approaches to Code Switching, Doha (2014)
16. Cotterell, R., Callison-Burch, C.: A multi-dialect, multi-genre corpus of informal written Arabic. In: 9th International Conference on Language Resources and Evaluation, Reykjavik, pp. 241–245 (2014)
17. Darwish, K., Sajjad, H., Mubarak, H.: Verifiably effective Arabic dialect identification. In: Proceedings of the 2014 Conference on Empirical Methods in Natural Language Processing (EMNLP), Doha (2014)
18. Younes, J., Achour, H., Souissi, E.: Constructing linguistic resources for the Tunisian dialect using textual user-generated contents on the social web. In: Daniel, F., Diaz, O. (eds.) Current Trends in Web Engineering: 15th International Conference, ICWE 2015 Work-shops, (NLPIT), Rotterdam (2015)
19. Hassoun, M., Belhadj, S.: Les nouveaux défis du TAL Exploration des médias sociaux pour l'analyse des sentiments: Cas de l'Arabish. In: Actes du colloque de Ghardaïa (2014)
20. Cortes, C., Vapnik, V.: Support-vector networks. Mach. Learn. **20**, 273–297 (1995)
21. Vinot, R., Grabar, N., Valette, M.: Application d'algorithmes de classification automatique pour la détection des contenus racistes sur l'Internet. In: Proceedings of the 10th Annual Conference on Natural Language Processing TALN, Batz-sur-Mer (2003)
22. Joachims, T.: Text categorization with support vector machines. In: Proceedings of the 10th European Conference on Machine Learning, Chemnitz (1998)

Named Entity Recognition in Turkish: Approaches and Issues

Doğan Küçük[1], Nursal Arıcı[1], and Dilek Küçük[2](✉)

[1] Gazi University, Ankara, Turkey
{dogan.kucuk,nursal}@gazi.edu.tr
[2] TÜBİTAK Energy Institute, Ankara, Turkey
dilek.kucuk@tubitak.gov.tr

Abstract. In this paper, we provide a review of the literature on named entity recognition in Turkish together with pointers to related open research problems. Unlike well-studied languages such as English and Spanish; Turkish is an agglutinative, morphologically-rich, and non-configurational language with limited language processing resources, tools, data sets, and guidelines. Hence, we believe that this paper will serve as a significant reference for computational linguists working on Turkish, those working on languages with similar structural characteristics to Turkish, and also for those working on resource-scarce languages.

Keywords: Named entity recognition · Information extraction · Turkish · Survey · Literature review

1 Introduction

Named entity recognition (NER) is defined as the task of extracting and classifying the names of people, locations, and organizations (so-called the *basic named entity types* or *PLOs*) in addition to other significant names in natural language texts [15]. With the recent advent of research topics like opinion mining and social network analysis, other named entity types like product and brand names have gained interest, and informal text types like micro-blog texts have started to replace well-studied formal text types like news articles as the target domain of NER research.

In this paper, we present a review of the literature on NER in Turkish. We also elaborate outstanding issues which basically hinder NER research in Turkish. Turkish is an agglutinative and non-configurational language from the Turkic language family and is structurally different from well-studied languages like English and Spanish. Considering natural language processing (NLP) research on Turkish, there are limited publicly available resources, tools, and data sets, which applies to the NER research as well. Therefore, we believe that this review paper will be an important reference for NER researchers working on Turkish, for those working on structurally-similar languages, and also for those studying

F. Frasincar et al. (Eds.): NLDB 2017, LNCS 10260, pp. 176–181, 2017.
DOI: 10.1007/978-3-319-59569-6_20

resource-scarce languages. The rest of the paper is organized as follows: Sect. 2 presents an overview of the writing rules governing the basic named entities in Turkish texts and related phenomena. In Sect. 3, a review of the literature on NER in Turkish is provided. Section 4 presents a list of open research issues regarding NER in Turkish, and finally Sect. 5 concludes the paper.

2 Named Entities in Turkish

The main rules governing named entities of type person, location, and organization names in Turkish are provided below [4]:

- The initial letters of all tokens of the named entities are capitalized. Examples include *Orhan Pamuk* (a person name), *Kuzey İrlanda* ('*Northern Ireland*'), and *Boğaziçi Üniversitesi* ('*Boğaziçi University*').
- The sequence of inflectional suffixes added at the ends of the named entities are separated from them with an apostrophe, like the ablative case marker (*-dan*) added to the end of the city name in *Ankara'dan* ('*from Ankara*') [4].

Significant named entity-related phenomena in Turkish are listed below where several of these apply to named entities in other languages as well.

- Prevalent person names in Turkish are homonymous to common names which makes their recognition difficult [8]. Example names which can be used as forenames or surnames include *Barış* ('*peace*'), *Onur* ('*honour*'), *Deniz* ('*sea*').
- In social media texts such as tweets, unlike formal texts, the following peculiarities exist [7,10]:
  - The capitalization rule and the use of apostrophes in named entities are often neglected.
  - The named entities are modified to stress or show affection. Contracted forms and neologisms are common, in addition to instances of hypocorism which are rare in formal texts.
  - Turkish characters with diacritics (*ç, ğ, ı, ö, ş, ü*) are often replaced with their non-accentuated versions (*c, g, i, o, s, u*) in names.

3 A Review of Named Entity Recognition Studies

To the best of our knowledge, in the first study presenting NER results on Turkish texts, a language-independent NER algorithm is described which employs a bootstrapping approach with contextual and morphological patterns, and the trie data structure [1]. It achieves an F-Measure of 53.04% on a Turkish data set with 203 entities while the corresponding results for English, Greek, Hindi, and Romanian are 54.30%, 55.32%, 41.70%, and 70.47%, respectively [1].

In [21], a statistical name tagger, based on Hidden Markov Models (HMMs), that extracts PLOs in Turkish is presented. The system is trained and evaluated on news article data sets where the raw texts of the sets are from METU Turkish Corpus [17] (henceforth referred to as MTC). Their training and test data sets include 37,277 and 2,197 named entities, respectively, and the best performance of this system is 91.56% in F-Measure [21].

In [11], a rule based named entity recognizer is described which targets at PLOs and date/time and money/percent expressions, basically following the specifications of the Message Understanding Conference (MUC) series [5]. It is mainly proposed for news articles and is based on a set of lexical resources and patterns bases. It achieves an F-Measure of 78.7% on news articles (from MTC), 69.3% on child stories, and 55.3% on historical texts, where these data sets have 1,591, 1,028, and 1,132 entities, respectively. Since the recognizer is engineered for news articles, it achieves lower performance rates on the other text genres, suffering from the *porting problem* [11]. In a recent study [9], the named entity annotations on the news article set are revised and made publicly available.

A hybrid successor to this rule-based recognizer [11] is presented in [13]. The hybrid system has a simplistic learning module which memorizes common named entities in annotated corpora and adds them to the lexical resources of the recognizer. It performs better than its predecessor and is evaluated on a financial news article corpus in addition to a larger news data set compiled again from MTC, and on the aforementioned child stories and historical text sets [13].

This hybrid recognizer [13] is used within a semantic news video indexing and retrieval system, where the extracted entities are utilized as semantic annotations for videos [12]. In this system, the recognizer is evaluated on automatically extracted (noisy) video texts (with a word-error-rate of 8.93%) and manually-transcribed video texts. The F-Measure rates on these noisy and clean texts are 82.78% and 87.93%, respectively [12].

An automatic rule learning approach for the recognizing PLOs and date/time expressions is presented in [19]. The approach generates recognition rules utilizing a rule learning strategy based on inductive logic programming. It is evaluated on a set of terrorism-related news articles of about 54,500 tokens and 5,692 annotated entities. The system attains an F-Measure of 91.08% using 10-fold cross validation [19].

There are several studies that use conditional random fields (CRFs) for NER in Turkish [16,18,22], all of which consider only PLOs. In the most recent of these studies [18], the CRF-based approach is reported to achieve a performance rate of 95% in terms of the MUC-style F-Measure formula and 92% in terms of CoNLL F-Measure formula. This approach makes use of morphological features and gazetteers. The HMM-based system [21] and two CRF-based systems [18,22] use the same training and test sets which make their results comparable.

In [14], the authors test the use of association measures like point-wise mutual information and mutual dependency in addition to their new association measure proposal to extract named entities comprising two words. They provide discussions on the convenience of these measures with their evaluations [14].

In [6], it is shown that Wikipedia article titles can be used as lexical resources for NER in Turkish. A subset of the titles is first annotated as PLOs and next, the remaining titles are classified into these types using the k-nearest neighbor algorithm [6]. In another study [8], Java Wikipedia Library (JWPL) [23] and

Wikipedia's category structure are exploited to compile a list of about 55,000 person names in Turkish and a high-precision person name extraction system is built using this list.

More recently, tweets are considered as the target text genre for NER in Turkish. The CRF-based NER system [18] is evaluated on a number of informal texts including tweets [2] where the best performance that the system achieved on tweets is 19.28% using the CoNLL F-Measure metric. In [7], a tweet data set in Turkish is presented where PLOs, and date, time, money, percent expressions are annotated in addition to movie/song names, and the annotations are made publicly available. In [10], the rule-based recognizer [11] is tested on the two tweet sets in [2,7] and the performance results are lower compared to the results on news articles. To tailor the recognizer to tweets: (i) the capitalization constraint is relaxed, (ii) the lexical resources are expanded based on diacritics, (iii) tweets are normalized [10]. Lastly, a CRF-based approach is used for NER on Turkish tweets in [3], similar to [2].

In Tables 1 and 2, we provide the classifications of the reviewed studies with respect to their approaches and the types of test data sets, respectively.

Table 1. The Breakdown of the studies with respect to the employed approaches

Approach	Studies
CRFs	[2,3,16,18,22]
Gazetteer-learning (with kNN)	[6]
HMMs	[21]
Hybrid	[13]
Rule-based	[7,8,10,11]
Rule-learning	[19]
Using association measures	[14]

Table 2. The Breakdown of the studies with respect to the types of the test sets

Type(s) of the test data set(s)	Studies
Generic news only	[14,18,21,22]
Terrorism-related news only	[19]
Tweets only	[3,7,10]
E-mail texts only	[16]
Generic news + tweets	[7]
Transcribed text + tweets + online forum texts	[2]
Generic news + financial news + historical texts	[6]
Generic news + financial news + historical texts + child stories	[11]
Generic news + financial news + historical texts + tweets	[8]
Generic news + financial news + historical texts + child stories + video speech transcriptions	[13]

4 Outstanding Issues

In order to make objective comparisons of different proposals, annotated data sets should ideally be publicly available. Though some comparison results are given in different studies, comparisons of the same two systems on different data sets may lead to contradictory results in different studies (see [6, 18]). To the best of our knowledge, there are only two studies that describe publicly available annotated corpora for NER in Turkish: the first study presents an annotated tweet corpus [7], and the second study presents an annotated news corpus [9].

A second related issue is the standardization of the annotation guidelines to be used when creating the data sets. There are different approaches employed by different studies regarding this issue. For instance, in [11] MUC's SGML tags are used both to create the annotated sets and to format the system output. In [3, 18], IOB2 scheme [20] is used to format the output. On the other hand, some systems consider the apostrophes and the sequence of suffixes attached to named entities as part of these entities while others like [6, 11] exclude the suffixes during annotation.

Lastly, there is a need for diversity of the text genres targeted by the NER systems. Most of the systems are proposed for news articles while several of them are tested on other text types as well (see Table 2). In order to extend the scope of these systems, data sets from other domains, like the humanities archives and medical texts, can be considered.

5 Conclusion

In this paper, we present a review of the literature on NER in Turkish which is an agglutinative and non-configurational language. The approaches of the related studies include rule-based, machine learning-based, and hybrid ones. We have also discussed the related issues including the scarcity of publicly available data sets, and the need for diversity of the data sets and for the standardization of the annotation guidelines. This paper will hopefully help promote NER research in Turkish as well as in structurally similar and resource-scarce languages.

References

1. Cucerzan, S., Yarowsky, D.: Language independent named entity recognition combining morphological and contextual evidence. In: Joint SIGDAT Conference on Empirical Methods in Natural Language Processing and Very Large Corpora (1999)
2. Çelikkaya, G., Torunoğlu, D., Eryiğit, G.: Named entity recognition on real data: a preliminary investigation for Turkish. In: 7th International Conference on Application of Information and Communication Technologies (2013)
3. Eken, B., Tantuğ, A.C.: Recognizing named entities in Turkish tweets. In: International Conference on Computer Science, Engineering and Applications (2015)
4. Göksel, A., Kerslake, C.: Turkish: A Comprehensive Grammar. Routledge, London (2005)
5. Grishman, R., Sundheim, B.: Message understanding conference-6: a brief history. In: International Conference on Computational Linguistics (1996)

6. Küçük, D.: Automatic compilation of language resources for named entity recognition in Turkish by utilizing wikipedia article titles. Comput. Stand. Interfaces **41**, 1–9 (2015)
7. Küçük, D., Jacquet, G., Steinberger, R.: Named entity recognition on Turkish tweets. In: Language Resources and Evaluation Conference (2014)
8. Küçük, D., Küçük, D.: High-precision person name extraction from Turkish texts using Wikipedia. In: Biemann, C., Handschuh, S., Freitas, A., Meziane, F., Métais, E. (eds.) NLDB 2015. LNCS, vol. 9103, pp. 347–354. Springer, Cham (2015). doi:10.1007/978-3-319-19581-0_31
9. Küçük, D., Küçük, D., Arıcı, N.: A named entity recognition dataset for Turkish. In: Signal Processing and Communications Applications Conference (2016)
10. Küçük, D., Steinberger, R.: Experiments to improve named entity recognition on Turkish tweets. In: EACL Workshop on Language Analysis for Social Media (2014)
11. Küçük, D., Yazıcı, A.: Named entity recognition experiments on Turkish texts. In: Andreasen, T., Yager, R.R., Bulskov, H., Christiansen, H., Larsen, H.L. (eds.) FQAS 2009. LNCS, vol. 5822, pp. 524–535. Springer, Heidelberg (2009). doi:10.1007/978-3-642-04957-6_45
12. Küçük, D., Yazıcı, A.: Exploiting information extraction techniques for automatic semantic video indexing with an application to Turkish news videos. Knowl. Based Syst. **24**(6), 844–857 (2011)
13. Küçük, D., Yazıcı, A.: A hybrid named entity recognizer for Turkish. Expert Syst. Appl. **39**(3), 2733–2742 (2012)
14. Metin, S.K., Kışla, T., Karaoğlan, B.: Named entity recognition in Turkish using association measures. Adv. Comput. Int. J. **3**, 43–49 (2012)
15. Nadeau, D., Sekine, S.: A survey of named entity recognition and classification. Lingvisticae Investigationes **30**(1), 3–26 (2007)
16. Özkaya, S., Diri, B.: Named entity recognition by conditional random fields from Turkish informal texts. In: Signal Processing and Communications Applications Conference (2011)
17. Say, B., Zeyrek, D., Oflazer, K., Özge, U.: Development of a corpus and a treebank for present-day written Turkish. In: International Conference of Turkish Linguistics (2002)
18. Şeker, G.A., Eryiğit, G.: Initial explorations on using CRFs for Turkish named entity recognition. In: International Conference on Computational Linguistics (2012)
19. Tatar, S., Çicekli, I.: Automatic rule learning exploiting morphological features for named entity recognition in Turkish. J. Inf. Sci. **37**(2), 137–151 (2011)
20. Tjong Kim Sang, E.F.: Text chunking by system combination. In: Workshop on Learning Language in Logic and the Conference on Computational Natural Language Learning (2000)
21. Tür, G., Hakkani-Tür, D., Oflazer, K.: A statistical information extraction system for Turkish. Nat. Lang. Eng. **9**(2), 181–210 (2003)
22. Yeniterzi, R.: Exploiting morphology in Turkish named entity recognition system. In: ACL Student Session (2011)
23. Zesch, T., Müller, C., Gurevych, I.: Extracting lexical semantic knowledge from wikipedia and wiktionary. In: Language Resources and Evaluation Conference (2008)

Natural Language Processing Applications

Simplified Text-to-Pictograph Translation for People with Intellectual Disabilities

Leen Sevens(✉), Vincent Vandeghinste, Ineke Schuurman, and Frank Van Eynde

Centre for Computational Linguistics, KU Leuven,
Blijde Inkomststraat 13, 3000 Leuven, Belgium
{leen.sevens,vincent.vandeghinste,ineke.schuurman,
frank.vaneynde}@kuleuven.be
http://ccl.kuleuven.be/

Abstract. In order to enable or facilitate online communication for people with Intellectual Disabilities, the Text-to-Pictograph translation system automatically translates Dutch written text into a series of Sclera or Beta pictographs. The baseline system presents the reader with a more or less verbatim pictograph-per-word translation. As a result, long and complex input sentences lead to long and complex pictograph translations, leaving the end users confused and distracted. To overcome these problems, we developed a rule-based simplification system for Dutch Text-to-Pictograph translation. Our evaluations show a large improvement over the baseline.

Keywords: Syntactic simplification · Text-to-Pictograph translation · Augmented and alternative communication · Social media

1 Introduction

In today's digital age, it is challenging for people with Intellectual Disabilities (ID) to partake in online activities such as email, chat, and social media websites. Not being able to access or use information technology is a major form of social exclusion. There is a need for digital communication interfaces that enable people with ID to contact one another.

Vandeghinste et al. [1] developed a Text-to-Pictograph translation system for the WAI-NOT[1] communication platform. WAI-NOT is a Flemish non-profit organisation that gives people with communication disabilities the opportunity to familiarise themselves with the Internet. Their safe website environment offers an email client that makes use of the Dutch pictograph translation solutions. The Text-to-Pictograph translation system automatically augments written text with Beta[2] or Sclera[3] pictographs. It is primarily conceived to improve the comprehension of textual content.

[1] http://www.wai-not.be/.
[2] https://www.betasymbols.com/.
[3] http://www.sclera.be/.

F. Frasincar et al. (Eds.): NLDB 2017, LNCS 10260, pp. 185–196, 2017.
DOI: 10.1007/978-3-319-59569-6_21

The baseline Text-to-Pictograph translation system presents the reader with an almost verbatim pictograph-per-content word translation and it does not use any deep syntactic knowledge during pre-processing. Hands-on sessions with our users revealed that the pictograph translations would often be too difficult to understand.[4] For instance, participants were quick to notice that long and complex input sentences resulted in long and complex pictograph translations.

Section 2 presents an overview of related work on the topic of syntactic simplification methods for natural languages. Section 3 discusses our objectives for pictograph simplification. Section 4 introduces the simplification module. This module can be activated optionally by the user if deemed necessary. The results of our evaluations are presented in Sect. 5. Section 6 concludes.

2 Status Quaestionis

Text simplification is the process of reducing the linguistic complexity of a text, while still retaining the original information content and meaning of the text [2]. There are two types of simplification. *Lexical simplification* is concerned with the substitution of difficult or uncommon words or expressions by simpler synonyms. *Syntactic simplification* is concerned with the simplification of long and complicated sentences into equivalent simpler ones [3]. Since our system already uses pictographs as a means to support lexical items, we will focus on syntactic simplification. Note that, while syntactic simplification for pictograph translation has not yet been explored in the literature, there are some very strong similarities to be found with simplification for less resourced languages.

Various approaches toward automatic text simplification have been proposed: rule-based systems, Machine Translation approaches, and compression methods.

Chandrasekar et al. [4] were the first to explore **rule-based methods** to automatically transform long and complicated sentences into simpler sentences, with the objective of reducing sentence length as a pre-processing step for Natural Language Processing applications. Early simplification systems had to make disambiguation decisions without using parsers, and therefore raised more issues than they addressed [5]. Carroll et al. [6] use a probabilistic bottom-up parser for analysing complex input sentences, and handcrafted rules for the transformation stage. However, the system only manages to simplify two constructs, namely coordinated clauses and the passive voice. The PorSimples simplification system for Brazilian Portuguese-speaking people with low literacy skills [7] comprises seven operations and manages to simplify a total of 22 syntactic constructs, including sentence splitting, transformation into active voice, Subject-Verb-Object ordering, and changing the discourse markers. The bottleneck of this system, however, is the time needed to simplify sentences. Bott et al. [8] opt for a hybrid approach which largely relies on rule-based components. Their

[4] Note that our users were already familiar with (at least one of) the pictograph sets. Beta and Sclera pictographs are often used in schools, daycare centres, and sheltered workshops in Belgium, primarily to depict activities or the daily menu on printed schedules, or to provide step-by-step instructions for people with ID.

system covers the splitting of relative clauses, coordinated clauses, and participle constructions. Siddharthan [5] notes that hand-crafted systems are limited in scope to lexical simplification, but adds that syntactic rules can indeed successfully be written by hand.

The **monolingual Machine Translation (MT) approach** to syntactic simplification is a two-stage process. The first step is alignment of the source and target sentences, resulting in a phrase table that contains aligned sequences of words in the source and target language, along with probabilities. The second step is decoding. Siddharthan [2] notes that phrase-based MT can only perform a small set of simplification operations, such as lexical substitution and simple paraphrases. They are not well suited for reordering or splitting operations.

Sentence **compression** is a research area that aims to shorten sentences, thus focussing on deletion operations, for the purpose of summarising. In this framework, transformation rules are learned from parsed corpora of sentences, which are aligned with their manually compressed versions [9]. A notable example of sentence compression for Dutch are the systems described by Daelemans et al. [10] and Vandeghinste and Pan [11]. Interestingly, to our knowledge, these are also the only systems that have ever been developed for the simplification (or, in this case, compression) of Dutch. They were developed in order to automatically produce subtitles for television programmes on the basis of written transcripts.

While most of the methods described above certainly have many merits, not all of them are appropriate for the task of translating Dutch sentences into simplified pictograph sequences. MT methods require parallel data. The corpus that we need for our simplification task would have to consist of Dutch sentences (or their pictograph translations) on the source language side, and simplified Dutch sentences (or their pictograph translations) on the target language side. Not only does such a corpus, to our knowledge, not exist,[5] this approach would not be effective if we want to learn real, strong simplifications, like those performed with the specific needs of our target population in mind. Problems like splitting, for instance, require very complex copying operations.

Rule-based simplification systems, on the other hand, do not necessarily require parallel data, which makes them more suitable for our task. Without syntactic parsers, hand-crafted systems are not able to deal with the richness of natural languages. Today, this argument does not apply anymore. We opt for a hand-crafted simplification system that makes use of syntactic parsing.

3 Objectives

Based on the problems that our users experience when using the Text-to-Pictograph translation system and a number of guidelines, such as the checklist of Klare Taal "Clear Language" for user-adapted communication,[6] we made a

[5] With the exception of a corpus for sentence compression for Dutch subtitles [9]. However, as we already remarked, compression is not the same as simplification, and this corpus was not developed for people with Intellectual Disabilities.

[6] www.klaretaalrendeert.be/files/Checklist%20duidelijk%20geschreven%20taal.pdf.

Table 1. Syntactic phenomena to be treated by the syntactic simplification module for pictograph translation.

	Phenomenon	Operations
(a)	Coordinated sentence	- Split into two or multiple sentences - Identify the antecedent (subject) if subject is covert (in case of ellipsis)
(b)	Subordinate clause	- Detach from the main clause
(c)	Clause order	- Determine the subordinate clause's temporal or logical position with respect to the main clause
(d)	Participial phrase	- Detach from the main clause - Identify the antecedent (subject)
(e)	*(om) te "to"* + infinitive clause	- Detach from the main clause - Identify the antecedent (subject)
(f)	Relative clause	- Detach from the main clause - Identify the antecedent (subject, direct object, or indirect object)
(g)	Embedded appositive clause	- Place the verb *to be* in front of the apposition - Identify the antecedent (subject)
(h)	Adverbial phrase or prepositional phrase in theme position	- Move to the back of the sequence
(i)	Covert subjects or objects in the newly created independent clause	- Place all the antecedents at their appropriate positions within the clause
(j)	Non subject-verb-object order	- Convert to subject-verb-object order - Cluster all the verbs at the verb position
(k)	Passive voice	- Place the agent at the patient's position and vice versa

list of objectives that the simplification system should attain. Keep in mind that the system is not developed for generating textual output, but for generating pictograph output, with simplified text as an intermediary step. The pictograph language has very few grammatical properties (no number, no tense, very few function words, etc.), which leads to a number of decisions. Table 1 summarises the syntactic phenemena to be treated. We present a number of concrete examples below. The parenthesised letters refer to the identifiers of the operations in Table 1. Only Sclera examples are shown.

Pictograph sequences should **not be too lengthy**. This can be achieved by splitting coordinated sentences into multiple, shorter clauses **(a)**. This operation increases text length, as there will be more sentences, but also decreases the length of the sentences (see Fig. 1(a) and (b)).

Original input sentence	Simplified pictograph translation
Ik ben woensdag een lieve baby gaan bezoeken en ik heb hem een papfles gegeven. *"On Wednesday I went to visit a cute baby and I gave him the bottle."*  (a)	**Read as:** *"I visited a cute baby on Wednesday. I gave him the bottle."*  (b)
Ik moest naar mijn oma gaan die in het het ziekenhuis ligt. *"I had to go to my grandmother who lies in the hospital."*  (c)	**Read as:** *"I had to go to my grandmother. Grandmother lies in the hospital."*  (d)
Ik moest douchen nadat we gegeten. hebben. *"I must take a shower after we had dinner."*  (e)	**Read as:** *"We have had dinner. I must take a shower."*  (f)
Ik hoorde dat je gepest wordt door die jongen. *"I heard you are being bullied by that boy."*  (g)	**Read as:** *"I'm hearing. That boy bullies you."* 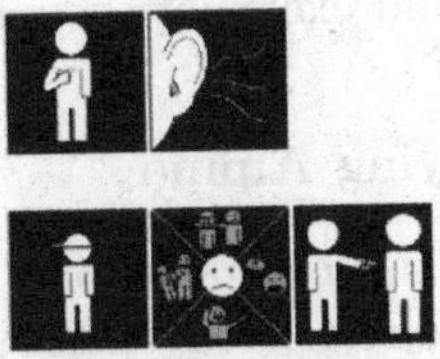 (h)

Fig. 1. Examples of simplified pictograph translations.

The presence of subordinate clauses **(b)**, participial phrases **(d)**, *(om) te "to"* + infinitive clauses **(e)**, relative clauses **(f)**, and appositions **(g)** can seriously hamper the understanding of the pictograph message. For that reason, we will **split complex sentences** into multiple, shorter clauses. Each one of these clauses will henceforth be considered as and behave like an independent clause. In order to achieve this, we must **identify the antecedents** of any covert subjects or objects that the newly created clause may contain, and insert them at their appropriate position **(i)** (see Fig. 1(c) and (d), where the complex sentence is split, and the antecedent *grandmother* is retrieved and repeated).

The translation system works on the sentence level. Global sentence ordering on the message level will currently not be considered in our approach. Nevertheless, we do take the **temporal and logical ordering of individual clauses** into account **(c)**. As subordinate conjunctions, for which no pictographs are available, will be deleted, the (chrono)logical placement of the clauses will henceforth aid the reader in understanding the order of the events described (see Figs. 1(e) and (f), where temporal re-ordering took place).

Word order in Dutch varies across clause types. We will display the pictograph sequences consistently as **SVO-type sequences (j)**, with a complete verb cluster located at the V position, and **convert passive constructions into active ones (k)**. Fixed pictograph order compensates for the loss of function words or grammatical markers. Adverbs and prepositional phrases that are located in front of the subject will be detopicalised **(h)** (see Fig. 1(g) and (h), where the original subordinate clause is converted into an SVO-type clause, and the passive construction is transformed into an active one).

4 System Description

In this section, we describe the syntactic simplification module.

4.1 Pre-processing

In the pre-processing step, all quotation marks and emoji are removed from the message, as they will not be converted into pictographs. The input message may consist of one or multiple sentences. As the syntactic parser works on the sentence level, the sentences are split based on punctuation signs (period, question mark, semicolon, and exclamation mark).

4.2 Applying Alpino

Alpino [12] is a computational analyser of Dutch which aims at full, accurate parsing of unrestricted text. Alpino incorporates both knowledge-based techniques, such as a Head-Driven Phrase Structure (HPSG) grammar and a lexicon, which are both organised as inheritance networks, and corpus-based techniques. Based on the Part-of-Speech categories that are assigned to words and word sequences, and a set of grammar rules compiled from the HPSG grammar,

Alpino's left-corner parser finds all parses for a given input sentence, and stores this set compactly in a packed parse forest. All parses are rooted by an instance of the *top* category. If there is no parse covering the complete input, the parser finds all parses for each substring. A best-first search algorithm is applied in order to select the best parse from the parse forest.

We run Alpino on the input sentences and create an Alpino Treebank, which contains the full parses of all sentences. If parsing takes too long, a time-out will occur, and shallow linguistic analysis will be performed instead.

4.3 Syntactic Simplification

If the parse succeeded, the simplification module can start processing the Alpino Treebank. In our approach, every clause in the original sentence, be they a main clause or not, will henceforth correspond to a new *sentence.* Every sentence will eventually be translated into a pictograph sequence, and followed by a line break.

The syntactic simplification for pictograph translation consists of two steps. First, the Treebank is processed and the sentences are created (operations **(a)** to **(g)**). A sentence consists of a multiple-level hierarchy of *phrases* and *words.* Phrases, such as noun phrases or prepositional phrases, may embed even more phrases (recursively) and/or words. For example, the prepositional phrase *in de boom "in the tree"* consists of a word *in "in"* and noun phrase *de boom "the tree"*. Whereas the original Text-to-Pictograph translation tool would convert the input message into a flat array of words, linguistic analysis is now no longer shallow. At this stage, the simplification module will also mark the original clause type (such as *appositive clause* or *relative clause*), indicate interrogation and passivity, and identify the head and the grammatical function of the antecedents. The latter operation is necessary in the case of ellipsis, appositive clauses, relative clauses, and *(om) te "to"* + infinitive clauses, where either the subject or one of the objects is covert or undefined and must be restored in order to create an independent clause. *To be* is added for appositive clauses, in order to allow for the noun phrase to be equated with its antecedent. We made a list of Dutch subordinate conjunctions expressing either concession (such as *hoewel "although"*) or temporal priority (such as *voordat "before"*) with respect to the events in the main clause. If the simplification system finds a subordinate clause that starts with any of these conjunctions, we will move that clause in front of the main clause.

The second step consists of re-ordering the syntactic constituents and placing the antecedents in their correct positions (subject or object position) within the newly created sentences. Prepositional phrases and adverbs that are located at the beginning of the sentence, in front of the subject, are detopicalised and moved to the back of the sentence **(h)**. The system gathers all verbs that occur within the sentence, deletes them from their original positions, and put them together into a new verb cluster. At this point, the antecedents that were retrieved in the previous step, as well as the newly created verb cluster, must be inserted at their appropriate positions within the sentence to create an SVO-type clause (operations **(i)** and **(j)**). For sentences that carry the *passive* feature, we first

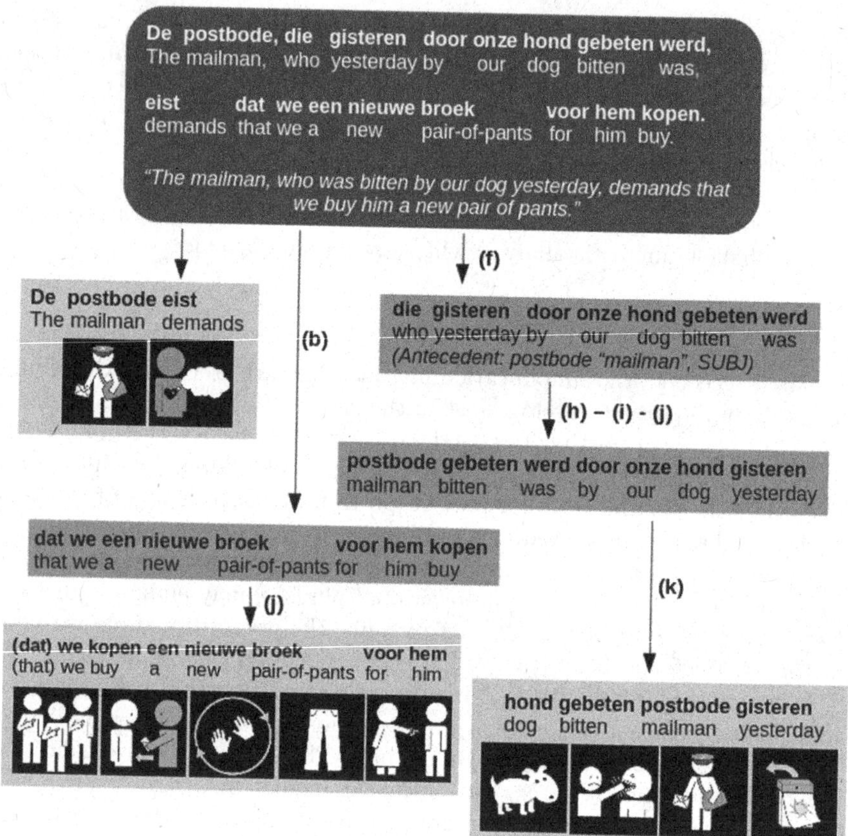

Fig. 2. Syntactic simplification of a Dutch input sentence that contains a subordinate clause, a relative clause, a topicalised adverb, and a passive construction.

check if the agent is overtly expressed by means of a prepositional phrase. If this is the case, the agent is moved to the beginning of the sentence, and the patient is moved behind the verb cluster **(k)**.

Note that the order of the simplification operations is not chosen arbitrarily. One sentence may contain several phenomena that could be simplified. Candido et al. [7] apply their operations in cascade. At each iteration, the system verifies the various phenomena to be simplified in order. When a phenomenon is identified, its simplification is executed. The resulting simplified sentence is re-parsed and goes through a new iteration. Re-parsing slows down the simplification system considerably. In our system, the input sentences are only parsed once. Processing the Treebank by means of recursion and loops allow us to deal with all syntactic phenomena to be simplified in an efficient way.

The order of the operations that we apply to the output of the Alpino parser is the one that is shown in Table 1. This order was determined logically, based on the idea that some operations are needed as a prerequisite to make certain other operations work. For instance, for the conversion of passive voice into active voice, the patient and the agent, if any, will switch places. In most cases, this operation is self-evident. However, if the passive construction would be located within a relative clause, we must first identify the antecedent of the covert patient before this transformation can take place. Therefore, the identification of the antecedents and their correct placement within the newly created sentence should happen before the conversion of passive constructions into active ones (Fig. 2).

5 Evaluation

We perform two types of evaluations. The first evaluation uses newspaper text from De Standaard,[7] a Flemish newspaper. We will not evaluate the actual translation into pictographs, as De Standaard presents a lot of jargon or words that are difficult to translate, and because the pictograph translation system was not developed for this type of text in the first place. However, given that the text presents a considerable number of complex syntactic phenomena, it is an interesting corpus for putting the simplification pre-processing module to the test. The second automated evaluation uses email messages from WAI-NOT.

We automatically simplified 100 sentences (1942 words an average of 19.42 words a sentence) from the newspaper De Standaard, and we post-edited the output according to the simplification objectives that we set out earlier.[8] We compare these reference translations to the system's output using BLEU [13], NIST [14], Position-Independent Word Error Rate (PER), and Human-Targeted Translation Error Rate (HTER[9]) [15] scores (see Table 2). The lower bound condition is the one that does not syntactically analyse, nor simplify the input text. On the other hand, the simplification condition uses the simplification module.

Table 2. Evaluation of the syntactic simplification module on 100 sentences from De Standaard. $^{*}p < 0.05$, $^{**}p < 0.01$.

System	BLEU	NIST	PER	HTER
Lower bound	0.3187	6.7565	19.3253	35.3905
Simplification	0.9496^{**}	10.7357^{**}	1.3494	1.9971

* p ¡ 0.05 (statistically significant),
** p ¡ 0.01 (statistically very significant)

[7] http://www.standaard.be/.

[8] We did not evaluate using manually simplified reference translations, because multiple acceptable simplifications are possible, especially with respect to the order of the syntactic constituents.

[9] HTER is the minimum edit distance between the machine translation and its manually post-edited version.

Table 3. Analysis of the complex syntactic phenomena that occur within the 100 sentences from De Standaard and 50 messages from WAI-NOT.

	De Standaard		WAI-NOT	
	Cases	Correct	Cases	Correct
Split coordinated sentences	37	36	97	90
Detach subordinate clauses	51	50	18	17
Change clause order (when temporality or a logic relation is expressed)	1	1	1	1
Detach participial phrases	0	0	3	3
Detach *(om) te "to"* + infinitive clauses	25	25	0	0
Detach relative clauses	31	31	0	0
Detach appositive clauses	16	15	0	0
Move adverbial clauses or Prepositional Phrases in theme position to the back	27	26	4	4
Insert any covert subjects or objects in the newly created independent clause, at the correct position	89	73	3	3
Convert non subject-verb-object order into subject-verb-object order	153	147	49	49
Convert passive voice into active voice	9	9	1	1
Total	**439**	**413**	**176**	**168**

Fine-grained results are presented in Table 3. We must note that the system does not oversimplify on this test set: it does not perform any unnecessary simplification operations. The results reveal that most errors are made when the antecedents of the covert subjects and objects are identified and must be inserted at a correct position within the newly created independent clause. However, we found that these errors were the result of simplifying a syntactic parse that was erroneous in the first place.[10] For instance, relative clause attachment can be ambiguous, and the parser's erroneous decisions are propagated. Nevertheless, the results look promising. In particular, non-SVO order occurs a lot, but the system manages to deal appropriately with this particular phenomenon in most cases. Additionally, nearly all complex and coordinated sentences were split correctly. The recall of the system on this test set is 100%. The precision is 94.1%.

We automatically simplified our test set of 50 WAI-NOT email messages (a total of 84 clearly delimited sentences or 980 words) and we analysed the syntactic phenomena to be simplified. These emails were written by people with disabilities, with limited writing skills. The WAI-NOT emails differ from newspaper text in many ways (see Table 3). First, there is a relatively large number of coordinated sentences to be found. In fact, many sentences are chained together like one long flow of thoughts, without the presence of punctuation signs or

[10] We refer to van Noord et al. [16] for an evaluation of the Alpino parser.

conjunctions. In many cases, the Alpino parser is able to convert these messages into multiple, fully grammatical sentences. However, this explains why the splitting of coordinated sentences does not always work perfectly on this type of text. The users' input is not always grammatical, and these particular cases can form an obstacle for the system. There is a rather small number of complex constructions. This can be attributed to the fact that people with low literacy skills experience problems with all kinds of advanced syntactic constructions. However, we can still expect these constructions to appear on social media websites, where the users will be able to read their family members' status updates and subscribe to fan pages. Finally, the presence of non-SVO order is primarily caused by inversion in interrogative sentences. The recall of the system on this test set is 100%. The precision is 95.5%.

6 Conclusion

We described a syntactic simplification system for Text-to-Pictograph translation, the first of its kind. It is also the first step toward the creation of a fully-functioning simplification tool for the Dutch language, which does not yet exist. With no parallel data available, and given that parsers have become fast and reliable, we opt for a rule-based approach that makes use of syntactic parsing. By using recursion and applying the simplification operations in a logical way, only one syntactic parse is needed per message. Promising results are obtained.

Evaluations in the literature tend to be on a small scale and are done either by automatic metrics or manually by fluent readers. There have been few user studies to date that evaluate text simplification systems with real users. Future evaluations of our system, within the framework of the Able to Include project,[11] will involve the elicitation of human judgements. Target users will be included. Our goal is to measure the improvements in the understandability of the simplified sentences when translated into pictographs, as compared to the baseline system.

Additionally, deep syntactic analysis paves the way for other improvements in the Text-to-Pictograph translation system, such as automatically generating temporality indicators for future or past.

Acknowledgments. We would like to thank the Agentschap Innoveren & Ondernemen and the European Commissions CIP for funding Leen Sevens doctoral research and Able-To-Include, which allows further development and valorisation of the tools. We also thank the people from WAI-NOT for their valuable feedback and the integration of the tools on their website. Finally, we would like to thank our users.

References

1. Vandeghinste, V., Sevens, I.S.L., Van Eynde, F.: Translating Text into Pictographs. Nat. Lang. Eng. **23**, 217–244 (2015)

[11] http://able-to-include.com/.

2. Siddharthan, A.: A survey of research on text simplification. Recent Adv. Autom. Readability Assess. Text Simplification **165**(2), 259–298 (2014)
3. Medina Maestro, M., Saggion, H., Schuurman, I., Sevens, L., O'Flaherty, J., De Vliegher, A., Daems, J.: Towards integrating people with intellectual disabilities in the digital world. In: Proceedings of WISHWell 2016, London, UK, pp. 1–10 (2015)
4. Chandrasekar, R., Doran, C., Srinivas, B.: Motivations and methods for text simplification. In: Proceedings of COLING 1996, vol. 2, pp. 1041–1044. Association for Computational Linguistics, Copenhagen (1996)
5. Siddharthan, A.: Syntactic simplification and text cohesion. Res. Lang. Comput. **4**(1), 1–195 (2004)
6. Carroll, J., Minnen, G., Pearce, D., Canning, Y., Devlin, S., Tait, J.: Simplifying text for language-impaired readers. In: Proceedings of EACL 1999, pp. 1–2. Association for Computational Linguistics, Bergen (1999)
7. Candido, Jr., A., Maziero, E., Gasperin, C., Pardo, T., Specia, L., Aluisio, S.M.: Supporting the adaptation of texts for poor literacy readers: a text simplification editor for Brazilian Portuguese. In: Proceedings of BEA4 (NAACL-HLT 2009 Workshop), pp. 34–42. Association for Computational Linguistics, Boulder (2009)
8. Bott, S., Saggion, H., Mille, S.: Text simplification tools for Spanish. In: Proceedings of LREC 2012, pp. 1665–1671. European Language Resources Association, Marrakech (2012)
9. Vandeghinste, V., Tjong Kim Sang, E.: Using a parallel transcript/subtitle corpus for sentence compression. In: Proceedings of LREC 2004. European Language Resources Association, Lisbon (2004)
10. Daelemans, W., Höthker, A., Tjong Kim Sang, E.: Automatic sentence simplification for subtitling in Dutch and English. In: Proceedings of LREC 2004, pp. 1045–1048. European Language Resources Association, Lisbon (2004)
11. Vandeghinste, V., Pan, Y.: Sentence compression for automated subtitling: a hybrid approach. In: Text Summarization Branches Out (ACL 2004 Workshop), pp. 89–95. Association for Computational Linguistics, Barcelona (2004)
12. van Noord, G.: At last parsing is now operational. In: Proceedings of TALN 2006, pp. 20–42. Leuven University Press, Leuven (2006)
13. Papineni, K., Roukos, S., Ward, T., Zhu, W.: BLEU: a method for automatic evaluation of machine translation. In: Proceedings of ACL 2002, Philadelphia, pp. 311–318 (2002)
14. Doddington, G.: Automatic evaluation of machine translation quality using N-gram co-occurrence statistics. In: Proceedings of HLT 2002, San Diego, pp. 138–145 (2002)
15. Snover, M., Dorr, B., Schwartz, R., Micciulla, L., Makhoul, J.: A study of translation edit rate with targeted human annotation. In: Proceedings of AMTA 2006, Massachusetts, pp. 223–231 (2006)
16. van Noord, G., Bouma, G., Van Eynde, F., de Kok, D., van der Linde, J., Schuurman, I., Tjong Kim Sang, E., Vandeghinste, V.: Large scale syntactic annotation of written Dutch: lassy. In: Peter, S., Odijk, J. (eds.) Essential Speech and Language Technology for Dutch: Resources, Tools and Applications, 147–164. Theory and Applications of Natural Language Processing. Springer, Heidelberg (2013)

What You Use, Not What You Do: Automatic Classification of Recipes

Hanna Kicherer[1], Marcel Dittrich[2], Lukas Grebe[2], Christian Scheible[1], and Roman Klinger[1](✉)

[1] Institut Für Maschinelle Sprachverarbeitung, Universität Stuttgart, Pfaffenwaldring 5b, 70569 Stuttgart, Germany
{hanna.kicherer,christian.scheible,roman.klinger}@ims.uni-stuttgart.de
[2] Chefkoch GmbH, Rheinwerk 3, Joseph-Schumpeter-Allee 33, 53227 Bonn, Germany
{marcel.dittrich,lukas.grebe}@chefkoch.de

Abstract. Social media data is notoriously noisy and unclean. Recipe collections built by users are no exception, particularly when it comes to cataloging them. However, consistent and transparent categorization is vital to users who search for a specific entry. Similarly, curators are faced with the same challenge given a large collection of existing recipes: They first need to understand the data to be able to build a clean system of categories. This paper presents an empirical study on the automatic classification of recipes on the German cooking website Chefkoch. The central question we aim at answering is: Which information is necessary to perform well at this task? In particular, we compare features extracted from the free text instructions of the recipe to those taken from the list of ingredients. On a sample of 5,000 recipes with 87 classes, our feature analysis shows that a combination of nouns from the textual description of the recipe with ingredient features performs best (48% F_1). Nouns alone achieve 45% F_1 and ingredients alone 46% F_1. However, other word classes do not complement the information from nouns. On a bigger training set of 50,000 instances, the best configuration shows an improvement to 57% highlighting the importance of a sizeable data set.

Keywords: Recipe · Cooking · Food · Classification · Multi-label · Text mining

1 Introduction

In 2012, 63.7% of Germans used the Internet as source of inspiration for cooking [1]. One popular cooking website is *Chefkoch*[1], where every user can contribute to a common database of recipes and discussions. The result of this social network approach is a large data set of diverse and potentially noisy information.

Commonly, a recipe consists of at least three major parts, exemplified in Fig. 1: the *list of ingredients*, whose entries consist of an ingredient type, an

[1] http://www.chefkoch.de (all URLs in this paper: last accessed on 2017-01-31).

F. Frasincar et al. (Eds.): NLDB 2017, LNCS 10260, pp. 197–209, 2017.
DOI: 10.1007/978-3-319-59569-6_22

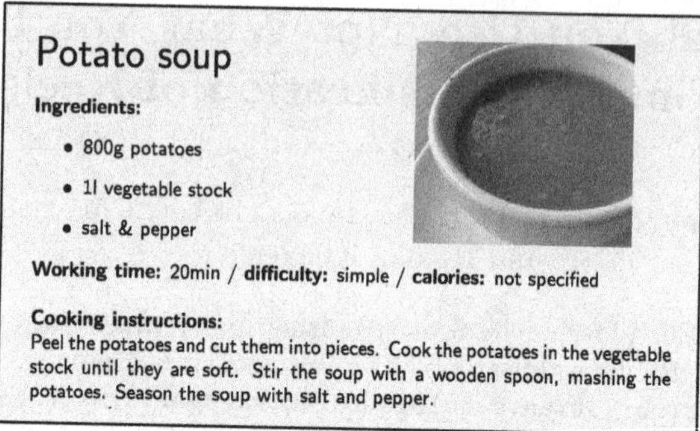

Fig. 1. Example recipe

amount, and a unit; the *cooking instructions* wherein the steps for preparing the dish using the ingredients is described in natural language; and *meta data* which supplies for instance information about the preparation time and difficulty. Each recipe is assigned to a number of categories, for instance of subtypes *regional* (*e.g.*, *Germany, Malta, USA and Canada*), *seasonal* (*e.g.*, *Christmas, spring, winter*), or *course* (*e.g.*, *vegetables, pork, dessert*) (see http://www.chefkoch.de/rezepte/kategorien/). When submitting new recipes, both users and curators may not understand the full range and structure of the category system. Thus, each new recipe may introduce additional noise into the database. Therefore, contributors would benefit from automatic support in choosing appropriate categories for a recipe.

In this paper, we estimate a statistical model of category assignments based on recipes in the Chefkoch database. This model will be beneficial for database completion, adjustment and consolidation of existing recipes and will help users and curators by suggesting categories for a new recipe. Our main contributions are experiments to investigate the performance of the model: (1) We compare logistic regression classification models taking into account different types of information from the ingredient list and textual description. In particular, we make use of ontological information to generalize over specific ingredients and we investigate different subtypes of word classes. (2) Our evaluation of different feature sets shows that nouns are more important than verbs and the order of ingredients in the list is only of limited importance for classification. (3) We provide a visualization of the recipes with using dimensionality reduction to contribute to a better understanding of the data. This also highlights which subset of categories are specifically challenging.

2 Related Work

Recipes have been the subject of several previous studies. We focus on text-oriented research here, a counter-example is classification on image data [2]. Most related to this paper is prior work on recipe classification on the Japanese recipe platform *Rakuten* (http://recipe.rakuten.co.jp) by Chung et al. [3]. They estimated the relatedness of an ingredient to a recipe category using frequency measures. In experiments on *Allrecipes* (http://allrecipes.com), Kim et al. [4] found that rare ingredients are more important to characterize a recipe. They employed entropy-based measures to set up a similarity network and clustered to group by cuisine. Similarly, Ghewari et al. predicted the geographical origin of recipes on *Yummly* (http://www.yummly.com) with 78% accuracy using ingredient information [5]. Similarly to our work, they ranked features for each cuisine by pointwise mutual information. Naik et al. [6] performed classification with different models and principle component analysis on *Epicurious* (http://epicurious.com) and *Menupan* (http://menupan.com) and reached 75% accuracy. Recent work by Hendrickx et al. [7] predicted wine features from reviews.

Next to the automatic analysis of recipe data, previous work attempted to build formal representations of recipes as ontologies. Xie et al. [8] state that such domain knowledge is a prerequisite to model the semantics of a recipe correctly. The *cooking ontology* [9] is such a formalization, specializing in ingredients, condiments, kitchen tools, and movements while cooking and contains lexical variants in Japanese. Other food related ontologies are for instance the *BBC Food Ontology* (http://www.bbc.co.uk/ontologies/fo) and the *LOV Food Ontology* (http://lov.okfn.org/dataset/lov/vocabs/food). In this paper, we will make use of *WikiTaaable* [10,11]. It contains lexical variants for English, French, German, and Spanish and includes a recipe and an ingredient ontology (2875 food items, 540 in German), among other parts. The ontology represents food items hierarchically, and contains their nutritional values and compatibility with dietary restrictions.

To automatically extract relationships between ingredients, Gaillard et al. [12] developed an interactive adaptation knowledge model to substitute ingredients of a given recipe. They extract ingredient choices in recipes (*e.g.*, "500g butter or margarine") from the *WikiTaaable* recipe ontology as their knowledge base. Mota et al. [13] extend this approach by using a food ontology. Sidochi et al. [14] extract substitutes in recipes from *Ajinomoto* (http://park.ajinomoto.co.jp) by taking into account process information. Teng et al. [15] consider ingredients replaceable when they regularly co-occur with the same ingredients in other recipes from *Allrecipes*.

Aiming at understanding the internal structure of recipes, Greene et al. [16,17] segment each entry of the ingredients list in recipes from a database of the New York Times into *name*, *unit*, *quantity*, *comment*, and *other* using sequential prediction with linear-chain conditional random fields. Similarly, Jonsson [18] split textual descriptions from *Allrecipes* into *ingredient*, *tool*, *action*, *intermediate product*, *amount*, *unit* and *other* and detect relations between these classes.

Wang et al. [19] developed a system to teach cooking, which includes pointing out potential problems that may arise while preparing a dish and offering solutions, based on action or flow graph structures [20,21] and predicate-argument structures [22–24]. Based on such graph structures, the similarity as well as specific characteristics of recipes can be calculated [25].

Few works exists on German recipe data. Wiegand et al. [26,27] analyze on *Chefkoch* whether a food item can be substituted by another, whether it suits a specific event, and whether it is mentioned as an ingredient of a specific dish. Reiplinger et al. [28] applied distant supervision for the estimation of relation extraction models.

Features in our multi-label classification approach are inspired by these previous approaches. We discuss these in the following.

3 Feature Sets for Recipe Classification

We frame the task of automatically categorizing a recipe as a multi-label classification problem. Each recipe is represented as a high-dimensional feature vector which is the input for multiple binary prediction models, one for each category. The output of each model corresponds to an estimate of the probability of the recipe being associated with this category. Throughout this paper, we report our results with binary logistic regression models [29] which outperformed decision trees [30], in all configurations using more than one feature. The inputs to each of these models are different feature sets and their combinations described below.

From the cooking instructions, we extract bag-of-words features without changing case from the textual description (abbreviated as WORDS) as a baseline (changing case does not lead to performance differences). In the example recipe in Fig. 1, these are all words from the cooking instructions (*e.g.*, "Peel", "the", "potatoes"). To investigate which word classes are relevant, we use the subsets of VERBS (*e.g.*, "Peel", "cut") and NOUNS (*e.g.*, "potatoes", "pieces", "spoon"). We perform POS tagging with the Stanford Core NLP [31] with the German model.

Based on the ingredient list, we use a variety of features, with the bag of INGREDIENTS ("potatoes", "vegetable stock", "salt & pepper") being the most fundamental one. We introduce generalization by expanding this feature to INGREDIENT CLASSES (IC), adding all parents as defined in the WikiTaaable ontology (adding *vegetable* for *potato*). We encode the order of the list through INGREDIENT RANKS features for the first and second position in the list (IR, e.g., *potatoes@1* and *vegetable-stock@2*).

The feature set UNIT TYPE (UT) adds binary features for each combination of ingredient and unit (*potatoes-weight_unit*, *vegetable_stock-volume_unit*) as an approximation for ingredient amounts. As a motivating example, if flour is specified in kilograms, it is likely to be used to create dough for baking. In contrast, an amount given in table spoons could indicate its use in soup. We restrict this feature to mg, g, kg, ml, cl, dl, l, and spoons, tea-, table spoon, level or heaped.

Similarly to the ingredient rank feature, we assume the ingredient with the highest amount (HIGH. A. INGR., HAI) to be important (note that this feature requires unit normalization). In the example in Fig. 1, the feature *vegetable-stock_highest-amount* holds. The template INGREDIENT NUMBER generates a binary feature for each possible count. We expect it to be of value for low counts which occur more frequently (in the example, the feature *3-ingredients* holds).

All features above consider information from the recipe text or from the ingredient list independently. To combine information from both sources, we introduce the feature sets CONTEXT WORDS (CW), CONTEXT VERBS (CV), and CONTEXT NOUNS (CN). For each ingredient in the list, all occurrences in the recipe text are detected. All combinations of each word, verb, or noun, respectively, with the ingredient in the same sentence form another feature. For instance for verbs, the first sentence of our example yields features "peel-potato" and "cut-potato".

As the only feature from the meta data, we add the PREPARATION TIME (PT) as stacked bins (in the example, *Preparation* > *5 min* and *Preparation* > *15 min* hold). We sum preparation time, cooking or baking time, and resting time.

4 Results

4.1 Experimental Setup

We use a database dump of 263,854 Chefkoch recipes from June 2016. The minimum number of ingredients in any recipe is 1, the maximum 61, the average is 9.98. The overall number of unique ingredients is 3,954. The number of recipes varies across categories (on average 7,825.3, however, the median is only 1,592). The categories on Chefkoch are structured hierarchically with up to four levels. Recipes are associated with leaf categories and then automatically belong to all parent categories. This leads to a total of 182 categories, out of which 162 are leaves. The minimum number of categories assignment to a recipe is 0, the maximum 36, the mean is 4.8. The category with the fewest recipes is "Malta", which contains 30 entries. "Baking" is the largest category, containing 67,492 recipes.

We use a random sample of 20% (52,771) of the recipes as our test set. As our main goal of this paper is to develop a model which is suitable for database consolidation, we omit all categories which occur fewer than 500 times in this test set (≈1%). This leads to 87 categories we work with[2]. Note that with this step, we do not omit any recipes due to the multi-label classification setting. The comparison of feature sets and their impact is performed on a training set of 5,000 instances. The best model configuration is then trained on 50,000 and tested on the same test set for further analyses.

4.2 Classification Results

Comparison of Feature Sets Table 1 shows macro-averaged F_1 over all categories (we do not report accuracy values due to the unbalancedness of the data) with different feature sets. The left column shows the individual contributions of each feature set. Considering only information from the instruction text, we find that the model using all WORDS yields 46% F_1. Using only NOUNS performs

[2] Listed at http://www.ims.uni-stuttgart.de/data/recipe-categorization.

Table 1. Precision, recall and F1 measures in percent for recipe classification with 5000 training instances and different feature combinations. The left table shows feature classes in isolation. The right table shows combinations of feature classes.

Feature combination	Features	P	R	F_1
WORDS (Baseline)	19,942	63	36	46
NOUNS	11,176	58	37	45
VERBS	3,580	46	25	32
INGREDIENTS	1,448	58	34	43
INGR. CLASSES (IC)	61	23	19	21
INGR. RANKS (IR)	1,302	42	21	28
HIGH. A. INGR. (HAI)	633	14	24	18
UNIT TYPE (UT)	1,548	24	30	27
INGR. NUMBER (IN)	32	10	00	00
PREP. TIME (PT)	9	03	02	05
CONTEXT WORDS (CW)	194,042	41	25	31
CONTEXT NOUNS (CN)	71,311	39	24	30
CONTEXT VERBS (CV)	41,269	29	24	26

Feature combination	Features	P	R	F_1
INGR & IC	1,509	60	34	44
INGR & IR	2,750	58	35	44
INGR & UT	2,996	56	35	43
INGR & HAI	2,081	58	35	44
INGR & WORDS	21,390	64	39	48
INGR & NOUNS	12,624	61	40	48
INGR & VERBS	5,028	58	38	46
INGR & CW	195,490	63	27	38
INGR & CN	72,759	62	29	39
INGR & CV	42,717	60	29	39
INGR & IC & IR	2,813	58	36	44
INGR & IR & HAI	3,391	58	36	45
INGR & IC & IR & HAI	3,452	58	37	45

comparably well, albeit at a loss of precision compensated for by higher recall. In contrast, VERBS in isolation lead to a drop by 14% points. Information about *entities* involved in the preparation process is much more important than information about *activities*.

The INGREDIENTS feature alone yields an F_1 of 43%, which is comparable to the instructions-based results above. Most other features in this group (IC, IR, HAI, UT) perform relatively poor. IN and PREPARATION TIME provides no useful signal. Using CONTEXT WORDS , CONTEXT NOUNS , and CONTEXT VERBS instead of their standalone counterparts leads to losses of up to 15% points. We suspect that the main reason is sparsity due to large feature set sizes.

The right column of Table 1 shows combinations of feature sets. First, note that any combination of the INGREDIENTS feature with other features based either on the instructions or the list of ingredients yields an improvement. Conversely, combinations with the CONTEXT WORDS , CONTEXT NOUNS , and CONTEXT VERBS lead to drops, which is another indicator for sparsity – the CONTEXT WORDS features vastly outnumber the INGREDIENTS features.

Combinations of more than two feature sets do not lead to further improvements. Our overall best model makes use of INGREDIENTS and NOUNS, performing at 48% F_1. In order to determine whether performance improves with the availability of a larger training set, we re-run the experiment for this setting with a sample of 50,000 training instances. We find a considerable improvement in precision (67%), a recall (49%), and F_1(57%).

Comparison of Categories. The comparison of macro-F_1estimates above provides only a coarse analysis as it summarizes over a total of 87 categories. As we are unable to provide a full results listing due to space constraints,

Table 2. The 10 best (left) and 10 worst (right) categories with INGREDIENTS and NOUNS feature combination.

Category	P	R	F_1	Category	P	R	F_1
Backen (baking)	89	88	88	**Kalorienarm** (low-calorie)	36	11	17
Pasta & Nudel (pasta)	88	87	87	**Resteverwertung** (leftover meals)	36	11	17
Kuchen (cake)	85	85	85	**Dünsten** (steaming)	32	10	15
Brot/Brötchen (bread)	87	78	82	**Studentenküche** (students' cuisine)	35	10	15
Kekse & Plätzchen (cookies)	86	78	82	**Camping** (camping)	33	9	14
Fisch (fish)	84	76	80	**Spezial** (Special)	22	10	14
Rind (beef)	81	78	80	**Beilage** (side dish)	28	8	13
Torten	82	73	77	**Frankreich** (France)	32	6	11
Vegetarisch (vegetarian)	77	76	76	**Raffiniert & preiswert** (clever & cheap)	22	4	7
Dessert (dessert)	80	71	75	**Geheimrezepte** (secret recipes)	09	01	2

we highlight those categories where our model performs best and worst, respectively, in Table 2. For this comparison, we make use of the results using the training set of size 50,000 introduced above. This analysis is based on the best-performing model, INGREDIENTS and NOUNS.

The category for which our model performs best is "baking" with an F_1 measure of 88%. A large amount of the remaining top 10 categories are defined by certain ingredients (henceforth *defining ingredients*) of the dish, such as "pasta", "beef", or "fish". In contrast, the 10 categories where performance is worst mostly center around abstract ideas or processes. For instance, the most difficult category is "secret recipes" with only 2% F_1. This and other categories such as "cheap & clever", "camping", or "students' cuisine" require world knowledge beyond what can be learned from the recipes alone. Overall, among the 87 categories considered in this experiment, 41 categories have an F_1 above 50%. The remaining 46 categories score lower. Table 3 reports the mean results for leaves in specific subtrees in the hierarchy. The model performs best for leaves under the inner node "baking & desserts" – which is the largest category by recipe count – with an F_1 of 79%. Next is "course" with 65% F_1. "regional" (22% F_1) is the most challenging category, followed by "special" (42% F_1).

Overall, we find that there are certain types of categories, in particular those that have defining ingredients, where our model performs particularly well. This results suggest that more complex features may be necessary in order to fully capture more abstract ideas such as the purpose or cultural origin of a dish.

4.3 Visualization

One hypothesis as to why some categories are more difficult to predict than others is that the conceptual definition and distinction between them is unclear. To investigate this in more detail, we visualize randomly selected subsets of 5,000

Table 3. Macro evaluation scores for feature combination *Ingredients*, *Ingredient Classes*, *Ingredient Ranks* and *Highest Amount Ingredient* over all categories of a superclass of he hierarchy.

Category class	Precision	Recall	F1
Backen & süßspeisen (Baking & desserts)	83	75	79
Menärt (Course)	71	60	65
Zubereitungsarten (Preparation methods)	68	53	60
Saisonal (Seasonal)	57	34	43
Spezielles (Special)	58	33	42
Regional (Regional)	39	16	22

recipes by projecting the feature matrix with INGREDIENTS features into two dimensions via t-SNE [32]. Figure 2 shows plots of the resulting spaces for six different root categories. Each point represents a recipe of a specific leaf category. "Overlap" denotes recipes that belong to more than one leaf. We find that some categories seem to be comparably easy to separate from others after projection, for example "dessert" in "course", or "baking" in "preparation methods". Other categories have recipes located as single cluster but are subsumed by other categories, *e.g.*, "cookies" in "baking & desserts" and "Christmas" in "seasonal".

Another phenomenon is that the recipes of a category are spread across the whole plot but with varying density (like "quick and easy" in "special"). Some categories do not form clusters, such as "cake". This pattern is particularly noticeable for "special" where most categories (except for "quick and easy") are indistinguishable. This result suggests that some categories are more difficult to distinguish than others. This may be caused either by inaccurate category definitions or by inadequate feature representations.

4.4 Feature Analysis

To understand the problem structure of the classification task, we generate lists of features ranked by pointwise mutual information. The complete list of most relevant features is available as download[3]. Here, we limit ourselves to an exemplifying discussion of the categories "pork" and "vegetarian". Interestingly, the ingredient "pork" does not appear in the list of typical features for the category "pork". This is in line with previous results on wine reviews [7]. In contrast, the most relevant features are "yellow pepper", "fried pepper", "orange mustard", and "barbecue sausages". For other categories with defining ingredients such as "eggs", we see a similar pattern: The defining ingredient is often not among the most typical features. This is presumably because eggs occur in many dishes and are therefore not precise enough to distinguish egg recipes from non-egg recipes. Putting eggs into focus happens by cooccurrence with other specific ingredients.

[3] http://www.ims.uni-stuttgart.de/data/recipe-categorization.

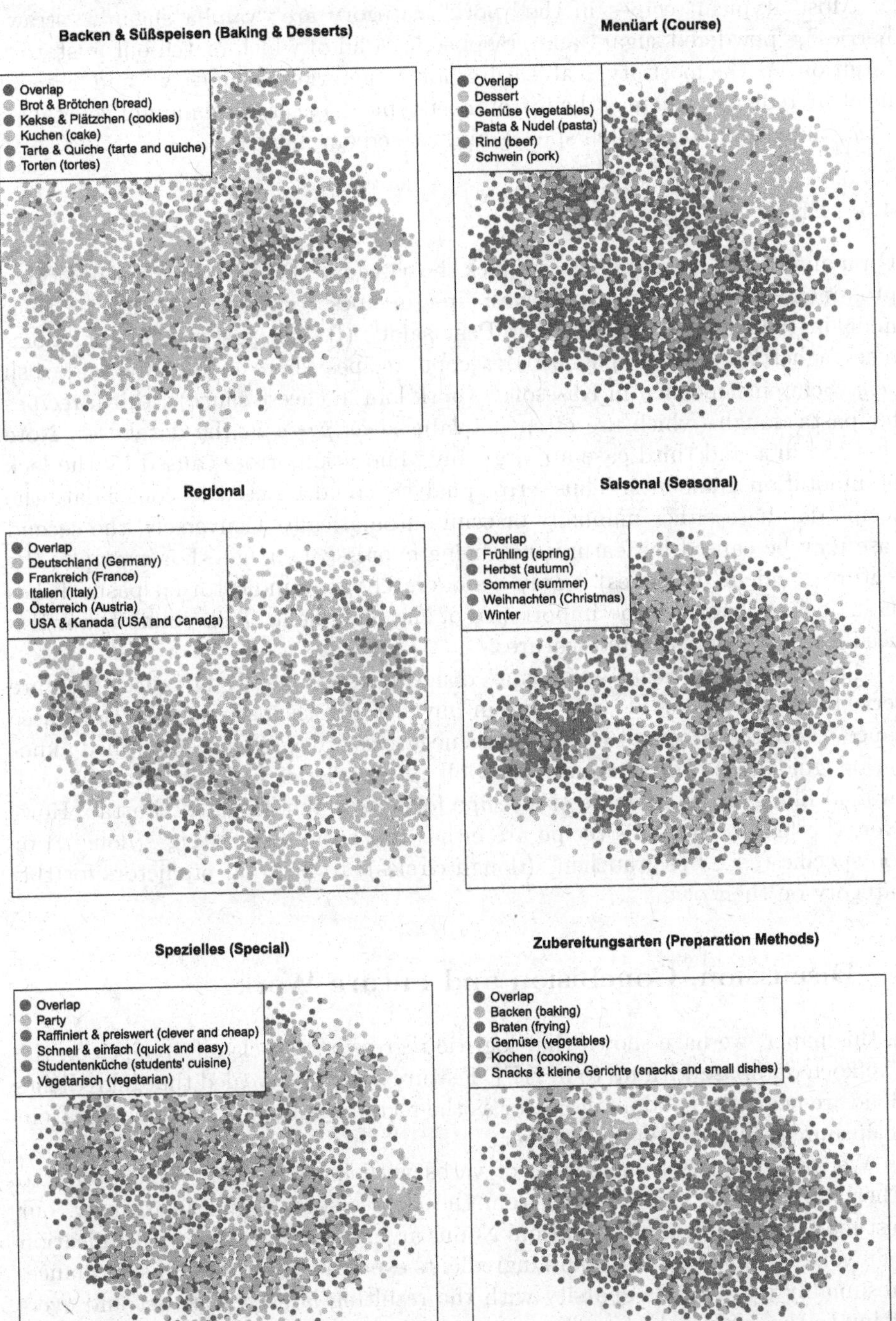

Fig. 2. Visualization of categories based on INGREDIENTS with t-SNE.

Most atypical recipes in the "pork" category are "vanilla sugar", "strawberries", "powdered sugar" and "raspberries", all of which match our gustatory intuition. As the most atypical features for "vegetarian" recipes, we find fish and meat ingredients, whereas the list of most typical features are mainly vegetables (*e.g.*, tomatoes, flour, green spelt grain, rice cream, falafel).

4.5 Error Analysis

For a qualitative error analysis, we pick the category "Pasta". We identified three prominent classes of false positives: first, recipes containing noodles as their main ingredient (*e.g.*"Italienischer Pastasalat" (Italian pasta salad) or "Sommerspaghetti" (summer spaghetti)); second, recipes where noodles are a side dish (*e.g.*"Schweinelendchen in Käsesoße" (pork loin in cheese sauce)); third, recipes for pasta dough (which are often not labeled as *pasta* in the database). Note that the first and third case are arguably annotation errors caused by the lack of annotation guidelines. Thus, error analysis could be used to consolidate the recipe database either manually or semi-automatically. Conversely, the second case may be caused by features not being expressive enough. For example, the feature "Nudeln" (noodles) is only a moderately good indicator for pasta dishes as it does not capture the importance of the ingredient. This points towards a need for more sophisticated features.

The set of false negative "Pasta" dishes consists mainly of sauces that are served with pasta but do not contain any noodles themselves (*e.g.*"Bolognese sauce"). Another frequent cause of false negatives are again underspecified annotation guidelines. For instance, "Ravioli mit zweierlei Füllung" (ravioli with twofold filling) is an example of a recipe for dough annotated as "Pasta". However, the features for this recipe are either too basic (e.g., "Teig" (dough)) or too specific (e.g., "Teigrädchen" (dough circles)) to be good predictors for this category on their own.

5 Discussion, Conclusion and Future Work

In this paper, we have shown that logistic regression can classify recipes on the Chefkoch database with up to 57% F_1. Feature analysis revealed that ingredients alone are nearly as good an indicator as the recipe description. Information from both sources complement each other.

We expected the combination of verbs with ingredients to be superior to other word classes and features from the classes separately. Surprisingly, our best model contradicts our intuition: Nouns are more important for classification than verbs. Combining verbs and ingredients even causes a drop in performance, presumably due to data sparsity with the resulting large feature set and overfitting to the comparably small number of training instances. We conclude that nouns are more important than activities in the description. Our error analysis revealed that many classification mistakes arise due to inconsistencies in the dataset. This suggests the applicability of our model to curate the database as well as to support users in finding appropriate categories.

Visualization of our recipe feature spaces highlights the difficulty of the task. For some categories, classification is comparably simple, while for others it remains challenging. This is, at least partially, due to the selection of our feature sets – for instance the visualization based on ingredients suggests that subcategories of baking and desserts are difficult to distinguish. However, features which take into account the process of preparation may be able to measure the difference between, for instance, tortes and cake.

For future work, we will investigate the use of our statistical model for supporting manual database curation. After correcting part of the database, we can retrain the model to spot new inconsistencies. This leads to an iterative cleaning process. For further feature engineering, we suggest two routes: On the one hand, we can enrich the textual description through structured information extraction; this includes more sophisticated grounding to ontological concepts and semantic role labeling. On the other hand, we suggest to develop embeddings of both ingredients and activities into a joint vector space. These will enable generalization over different substitutes and preparation procedures. Such an approach might also be helpful to learn what differentiates a defining ingredient from others. Another route of future work is the use of structured learning approaches to also make use of relations between different categories. Methods to be employed will include probabilistic graphical models.

References

1. Media, T.F.: Wenn Sie kochen, woher beziehen Sie Anregungen für Ihre Gerichte? (2012) (inGerman). https://de.statista.com/statistik/daten/studie/305898/umfrage/umfrage-in-deutschland-zu-den-rezept-quellen-fuer-selbstgekochte-gerichte/
2. Cadene, R.: Deep learning and image classification on a medium dataset of cooking recipes (2015). http://remicadene.com/uploads/summer-internship-2015.pdf
3. Chung, Y.: Finding food entity relationships using user-generated data in recipe service. In: CIKM (2012)
4. Kim, S.D., Lee, Y.J., Kang, S.H., Cho, H.G., Yoon, S.M.: Constructing cookery network based on ingredient entropy measure. Indian J. Sci. Technol. vol. 8, no. 23 (2015)
5. Ghewari, R., Raiyani, S.: Predicting cuisine from ingredients (2015). https://cseweb.ucsd.edu/~jmcauley/cse255/reports/fa15/029.pdf
6. Naik, J., Polamreddi, V.: Cuisine classification and recipe generation (2015). http://cs229.stanford.edu/proj2015/233_report.pdf
7. Hendrickx, I., Lefever, E., Croijmans, I., Majid, A., van den Bosch, A.: Very quaffable and great fun: applying NLP to wine reviews. In: Proceedings of the 54th Annual Meeting of the Association for Computational Linguistics, Berlin, Germany, Association for Computational Linguistics, vol. 2, pp. 306–312, August 2016
8. Xie, H., Yu, L., Li, Q.: A hybrid semantic item model for recipe search by example. In: IEEE International Symposium on Multimedia (2010)
9. Nanba, H., doi, Y., Tsujita, M., Takezawa, T., Sumiya, K.: Construction of a cooking ontology from cooking recipes and patents. In: UbiComp Adjunct (2014)

10. Ribeiro, R., Batista, F., Pardal, J.P., Mamede, N.J., Pinto, H.S.: Cooking an ontology. In: Euzenat, J., Domingue, J. (eds.) AIMSA 2006. LNCS (LNAI), vol. 4183, pp. 213–221. Springer, Heidelberg (2006). doi:10.1007/11861461_23
11. Cordier, A., Lieber, J., Molli, P., Nauer, E., Skaf-Molli, H., Toussaint, Y.: WIKITAAABLE: A semantic wiki as a blackboard for a textual case-based reasoning system. In: SemWiki 2009, ESWC (2009)
12. Gaillard, E., Nauer, E., Lefevre, M., Cordier, A.: Extracting generic cooking adaptation knowledge for the TAAABLE case-based reasoning system. In: Cooking with Computers Workshop, ECAI (2012)
13. Mota, S.G., Agudo, B.D.: ACook: recipe adaptation using ontologies, case-based reasoning systems and knowledge discovery. In: Cooking with Computers workshop, ECAI (2012)
14. Shidochi, Y., Takahashi, T., Ide, I., Murase, H.: Finding replaceable materials in cooking recipe texts considering characteristic cooking actions. In: Workshop on Multimedia for Cooking and Eating Activities, CEA (2009)
15. Teng, C.Y., Lin, Y.R., Adamic, L.A.: Recipe recommendation using ingredient networks. In: WebSci (2012)
16. Greene, E.: The New York Times Open Blog: Extracting structured data from recipes using conditional random fields (2015). https://open.blogs.nytimes.com/2015/04/09/extracting-structured-data-from-recipes-using-conditional-random-fields/. Accessed 20 June 2016
17. Greene, E., McKaig, A.: The New York Times Open Blog: Our tagged ingredients data is now on GitHub (2016). https://open.blogs.nytimes.com/2016/04/27/structured-ingredients-data-tagging/. Accessed 31 Jan 2016
18. Jonsson, E.: Semantic word classification and temporal dependency detection on cooking recipes Thesis, Linköpings universitet (2015)
19. Wang, L., Li, Q.: A personalized recipe database system with user-centered adaptation and tutoring support. In: SIGMOD 2007 Ph.D. Workshop on Innovative Database Research (2007)
20. Wang, L., Li, Q., Li, N., Dong, G., Yang, Y.: Substructure similarity measurement in chinese recipes. In: WWW (2008)
21. Maeta, H., Sasada, T., Mori, S.: A framework for recipe text interpretation. In: UbiComp Adjunct (2014)
22. Kiddon, C., Ponnuraj, G.T., Zettlemoyer, L., Choi, Y.: Mise en place: Unsupervised interpretation of instructional recipes. In: EMNLP (2015)
23. Mori, S., Sasada, T., Yamakata, Y., Yoshino, K.: A machine learning approach to recipe text processing. In: Cooking with Computers workshop, ECAI (2012)
24. Mori, S., Maeta, H., Yamakata, Y., Sasada, T.: Flow graph corpus from recipe texts. In: LREC (2014)
25. Yamakata, Y., Imahori, S., Sugiyama, Y., Mori, S., Tanaka, K.: Feature extraction and summarization of recipes using flow graph. In: Jatowt, A., Lim, E.-P., Ding, Y., Miura, A., Tezuka, T., Dias, G., Tanaka, K., Flanagin, A., Dai, B.T. (eds.) SocInfo 2013. LNCS, vol. 8238, pp. 241–254. Springer, Cham (2013). doi:10.1007/978-3-319-03260-3_21
26. Wiegand, M., Roth, B., Klakow, D.: Web-based relation extraction for the food domain. In: Bouma, G., Ittoo, A., Métais, E., Wortmann, H. (eds.) NLDB 2012. LNCS, vol. 7337, pp. 222–227. Springer, Heidelberg (2012). doi:10.1007/978-3-642-31178-9_25
27. Wiegand, M., Roth, B., Klakow, D.: Data-driven knowledge extraction for the food domain. In: KONVENS, pp. 21–29 (2012)

28. Reiplinger, M., Wiegand, M., Klakow, D.: Relation extraction for the food domain without labeled training data – is distant supervision the best solution? In: Przepiórkowski, A., Ogrodniczuk, M. (eds.) NLP 2014. LNCS, vol. 8686, pp. 345–357. Springer, Cham (2014). doi:10.1007/978-3-319-10888-9_35
29. Cox, D.R.: The regression analysis of binary sequences. J. Roy. Stat. Soc. Ser. B (Methodological) **20**(2), 215–242 (1958)
30. Quinlan, J.R.: C4.5: Programming for Machine Learning. Morgan Kauffmann, CA (1993)
31. Manning, C.D., Surdeanu, M., Bauer, J., Finkel, J., Bethard, S.J., McClosky, D.: The Stanford CoreNLP natural language processing toolkit. In: ACL Demo (2014)
32. Maaten, L.V.D., Hinton, G.: Visualizing data using t-SNE. J. Mach. Learn. Res. **9**, 1–48 (2008)

Constructing Technical Knowledge Organizations from Document Structures

Sebastian Furth[1(✉)] and Joachim Baumeister[1,2]

[1] denkbares GmbH, Friedrich-Bergius-Ring 15, 97076 Würzburg, Germany
{sebastian.furth,joachim.baumeister}@denkbares.com
[2] Institute of Computer Science, University of Würzburg,
Am Hubland, 97074 Würzburg, Germany

Abstract. Semantic Search emerged as the new system paradigm in enterprise information systems. These information systems allow for the problem-oriented and context-aware access of relevant information. Ontologies, as a formal knowledge organization, represent the key component in these information systems, since they enable the semantic access to information. However, very few enterprises already can provide technical ontologies for information integration. The manual construction of such knowledge organizations is a time-consuming and error-prone process. In this paper, we present a novel approach that automatically constructs technical knowledge organizations. The approach is based on semantified document structures and constraints that allow for the simple adaptation to new enterprises and information content.

Keywords: Concept hierarchies · Ontology engineering · Document components · Information extraction

1 Introduction

In the past, the technical service maintained and repaired machines by simply using *service documentation* such as repair manuals, diagnostic handbooks, or a spare parts catalog. Nowadays, *Semantic information systems* [5] started to replace standard document information systems in order to better manage the still growing complexity and size of service documentation. Semantic systems promise advantages that are realized by employing an ontology that describes the technical breakdown of the machinery and their inter-relations, i.e., the *technical knowledge organization.* The development of the ontology describing the machinery, however, is a application-specific, time-consuming and error-prone task and often is done manually by human experts. Therefore, we propose a novel approach for automatically learning technical knowledge organizations.

2 Formalized Document Components

In the semantic publishing community the representation of document components by ontology vocabularies is well-established. Such vocabularies typically

F. Frasincar et al. (Eds.): NLDB 2017, LNCS 10260, pp. 210–213, 2017.
DOI: 10.1007/978-3-319-59569-6_23

comprise structural components (e.g. paragraphs, sections, sentences) [3,4] and rhetorical elements (e.g. discourse elements/sections like “Motivation”, “Problem Statement” or “Discussion”) [2,4]. Important structural elements for technical documents [7] are `:Book`, `:Article`, `:Chapter` or block elements like `:Paragraph`, `:Procedure` or `:Figure`. Common rhetorical elements in technical documents comprise `:Description`, `:Operation`, `:Repair`, `:FaultIsolation` or `:Parts`.

Interweaving structural and rhetorical representations gives access to the most important aspects of technical documents—*Core Documentation Entities*. A common example for a Core Documentation Entity is a component overview that can typically be found in a section describing the machine or in the spare part information. Component overviews typically consist of an exploded-view drawing and an associated list of labels, product numbers etc.

3 Constraint-Based Construction of Technical Knowledge Organizations

For the construction of technical knowledge organizations from document components we propose a process comprising the following tasks: partial hierarchy extraction from document components, entity unification, constraint problem generation and constraint resolution.

3.1 Extracting Partial Hierarchies from Document Structures

Given a semantically represented corpus of technical documents (see Sect. 2) the direct access to *Core Documentation Entities* like repair instructions or component overviews is possible. In order to build up an extensive technical knowledge organization partial hierarchies need to be extracted from all relevant document components. The extraction task itself can be realized as a simple query over the semantically represented corpus of technical documents.

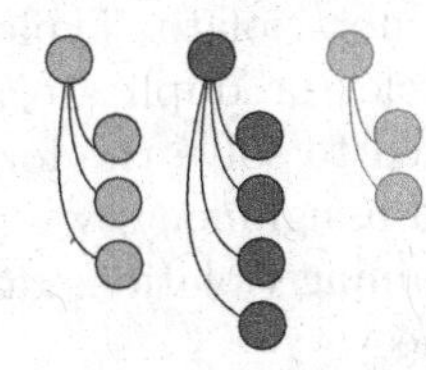

Fig. 1. Partial hierarchies.

3.2 Unification of Concept Candidates

In technical documents it is common practice that descriptions of components are iteratively detailed or spread over several paragraphs, e.g. because of different views revealing varying subsets of sub-components and their function. This typically results in duplicate occurrences of concept candidates in the extracted partial hierarchies. These duplicates need to be semantically unified (see Fig. 2). The unification of duplicate concept candidate occurrences is a classical ontology matching [6] task.

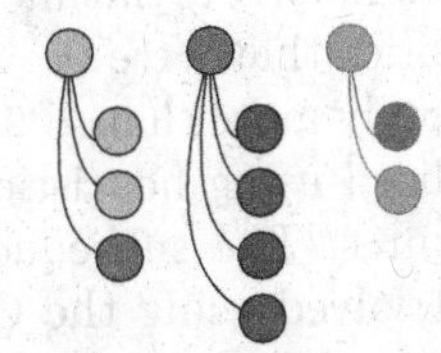

Fig. 2. Unified concepts. (Color figure online)

3.3 Constraint-Based Hierarchy Construction

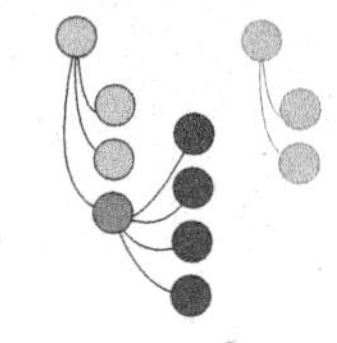

Fig. 3. Concept hierarchy.

Now, given partial hierarchies with unified concept candidates the task is to construct a complete hierarchy. However, the scenario depicted in Fig. 2 shows that simply connecting unconnected nodes (e.g. the root of the reddish tree) to a unified occurrence in another partial hierarchy is not possible. In the depicted scenario two possible unified occurrences exist for the respective node. Thus, in this paper we propose a constraint-based approach for the construction of a complete technical knowledge organization. Therefore, the partial hierarchies including the already computed unifications are used to formulate a constraint-based planning problem.

We formally define a set of unified concept candidates as $C = \{c_1, c_2, \ldots, c_n\}$. An identity relation is defined as a tuple $i = (parent, child)$ with $parent \in C$ and $child \in C$ and serves as planning entity. The *child* element in the relation serves as planning variable, i.e., the element that will be switched while solving the planning problem. The set of all identity relations $I = \{i_1, i_2, \ldots, i_n\}$ defines the potential search space of the planning problem. A solution of the planning problem is a child assignment for each identity relation $i \in I$.

In order to construct a complete and consistent technical knowledge organization a set of constraints is defined which a solution has to fulfil. The constraints define the conditions that the child assignments of all identity relations $i \in I$ must not violate. Typical examples of such constraints comprise the avoidance of cycles or duplicate assignments. Standard optimization algorithms can be utilized to solve the formulated constraint satisfaction problem. From all computed assignments we choose the solution which violates the least constraints. Remaining violations can be reviewed and corrected by a human expert/ontology engineer.

4 Application and Implementation Remarks

The presented approach for constructing technical knowledge organizations has already been employed to construct ontologies for different special purpose machinery. Partial hierarchies have been extracted from Core Documentation Entities that were previously derived from large corpora of technical documents (usually more than 10,000 pages). The unification of concept candidates has been realized using heuristic scoring rules operating upon a set of concept similarity features. The subsequent constraint satisfaction problem has been formulated and solved using the OptaPlanner[1] framework. Computed solutions have been exported to the open source ontology engineering tool KnowWE[2] [1]. The export comprised explicit representations of computed identity relations and allowed for

[1] https://www.optaplanner.org.
[2] https://www.d3web.de.

reviewing and correcting constraint violations. The resulting ontology comprises more than 1,000,000 triples.

5 Conclusion

In this paper, we presented a novel approach for the automatic construction of technical knowledge organizations from corpora of technical documents. The presented approach relies on a novel semantic representation for technical documents that makes Core Documentation Entities directly accessible. The representation of these Core Documentation Entities is based on the interweaving of existing structural and rhetorical elements. A three-stage construction process extracts partial hierarchies from Core Documentation Entities, unifies concept candidates, and builds up a complete hierarchy based on constraints. Implementation remarks and real-world usage scenarios show the practical applicability of the presented approach. Future work comprises the introduction of a self-critic component based on potential constraint violations and usability improvements concerning the manual correction of constraint violations.

Acknowledgments. The work described in this paper is supported by the German Bundesministerium für Wirtschaft und Energie (BMWi) under the grant ZIM ZF4170601BZ5 "APOSTL: Accessible Performant Ontology Supported Text Learning".

References

1. Baumeister, J., Reutelshoefer, J., Puppe, F.: KnowWE: a semantic wiki for knowledge engineering. Appl. Intell. **35**(3), 323–344 (2011). http://dx.doi.org/10.1007/s10489-010-0224-5
2. Constantin, A., Peroni, S., Pettifer, S., Shotton, D., Vitali, F.: The document components ontology (DoCO). Semant. Web **7**, 167–181 (2015)
3. Di Iorio, A., Peroni, S., Poggi, F., Vitali, F.: Dealing with structural patterns of XML documents. J. Assoc. Inf. Sci. Technol. **65**(9), 1884–1900 (2014)
4. Groza, T., Handschuh, S., Möller, K., Decker, S.: SALT - semantically annotated LaTeX for scientific publications. In: Franconi, E., Kifer, M., May, W. (eds.) ESWC 2007. LNCS, vol. 4519, pp. 518–532. Springer, Heidelberg (2007). doi:10.1007/978-3-540-72667-8_37
5. Guha, R., McCool, R., Miller, E.: Semantic search. In: Proceedings of the 12th International Conference on World Wide Web, pp. 700–709. ACM (2003)
6. Isaac, A., Meij, L., Schlobach, S., Wang, S.: An empirical study of instance-based ontology matching. In: Aberer, K., Choi, K.-S., Noy, N., Allemang, D., Lee, K.-I., Nixon, L., Golbeck, J., Mika, P., Maynard, D., Mizoguchi, R., Schreiber, G., Cudré-Mauroux, P. (eds.) ASWC/ISWC - 2007. LNCS, vol. 4825, pp. 253–266. Springer, Heidelberg (2007). doi:10.1007/978-3-540-76298-0_19
7. Şah, M., Wade, V.: Automatic metadata extraction from multilingual enterprise content. In: Proceedings of the 19th ACM International Conference on Information and Knowledge Management, pp. 1665–1668. ACM (2010)

Applications of Natural Language Techniques in Solving SmartHome Use-Cases

Parnab Kumar Chanda(✉), Nitish Varshney, and Ashok Subash

Samsung R&D Institute India, Bangalore, India
{p.chanda,nitish.var,ashok}@samsung.com

Abstract. This paper demonstrates approaches in solving use-cases arising in smart home scenarios which includes activity discovery and routine recommendation for home automation using principles that essentially applies to the field of natural language processing. We have developed methods and built a prototype system to address such use-cases. All the components are built using state of the art natural language techniques and the results are shown to be meaningful when applied in context of addressing smart home use-cases.

1 Introduction

Recent advancements in the field of Sensor technologies and Internet Of Things (IoT) has enabled building of sophisticated smart environments. The prime focus of such smart environments is to open avenues and new research areas whereby lifestyle of the human beings centered around such environments can be improved. With the plethora of devices available, it is getting increasingly possible to capture human activities in great detail. Furthermore, applying existing machine learning techniques it is also possible to enhance the experience of the user by automating, prompting and recommending actions thereby improving the adoption of Smart Home systems in the mass market.

We have focused on Natural Language techniques and explored the possibility of its applicability in solving some important use cases that will arise when such smart environments will be popular with increasing adoption rates. In this paper, we have demonstrated a system which discovers routine for a user using unsupervised techniques by mining temporal sensor data and further recommend the user with the most likely sequence of events for automation.

2 Methods

The system diagram in Fig. 1 shows stages through which historical sensor data is analyzed to create routines. The first stage, Activity Segmentation, splits continuous temporal data to generate segments such that significant portions of user activities are captured within it. KCAR [1] showed that sequence of events can be segmented by considering temporal and conceptual similarity between two sensors. While KCAR used static ontology for measuring the conceptual

F. Frasincar et al. (Eds.): NLDB 2017, LNCS 10260, pp. 214–217, 2017.
DOI: 10.1007/978-3-319-59569-6_24

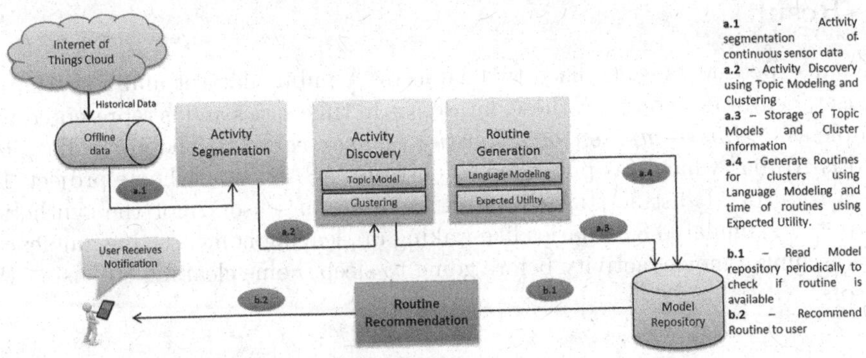

Fig. 1. System architecture

similarity of two sensors, we measure it based on their relative triggering pattern. Conceptual similarity of two sensors are computed as the cosine similarity of their word2vec[1] feature vectors.

In the second stage, the segments are passed to Activity Discovery module which utilizes Topic Modeling followed by Segment Clustering to discover the recurrent patterns within the various segments. Since human tends to do the same activity with variations, the generated segments will have captured variations of the same activity. Using Topic Modeling on these segments allows us to assign similar topic distribution to segments that captures variations of the same activity. For Topic Modeling, we use the well known Latent Dirichlet Allocation (LDA) [2]. From the context of Topic Modeling, each segment is considered as a document and the sensor events within the segment as words in the document. Additionally, to keep some context of the order in which sensors are triggered, we generate bi-grams of the words and consider them as part of the same document(segment) as well. Next, we need to discover the significant activities that are captured in these segments. For this, we require a clustering mechanism that will group together all segments capturing the same activity. To this end, we employ a hierarchical clustering algorithm where similarity of two segments is measured as the symmetric KL-divergence of their corresponding topic distributions. The appropriate number of clusters, which in turn relates to the distinct user activities is determined by Silhouette Coefficient.

Finally, Routines capturing the most likely sequence of actions for doing an activity, is generated using Language Modeling(LM). We train a 3-gram LM for each activity cluster using the segments that were assigned to it. We collect the unique sensor events for each activity cluster and generate possible routines using permutations of these sensor events. The sequence for which the language model gives the highest probability is recommended as a routine for that activity. Further, we compute for each routine the most probable time of the day of occurrence utilizing the Expected Utility approach as given by [3].

[1] https://deeplearning4j.org/word2vec.

3 Results

For our experiments we utilized two datasets; A public dataset and a synthetic dataset. Sensor data on both these datasets is in time series and is represented by a tuple as $< timestamp, sensorid, location, sensor\_value >$. The public dataset used is Aruba[2] which was published as part of CASAS[3] smart home project. It has a total of 11 distinct tagged activities using 39 sensors. For the synthetic dataset, we simulated 8 scenarios like waking up, leaving home, setting ambience for watching a movie, activity before going to sleep, home cleaning etc. using 15 sensors.

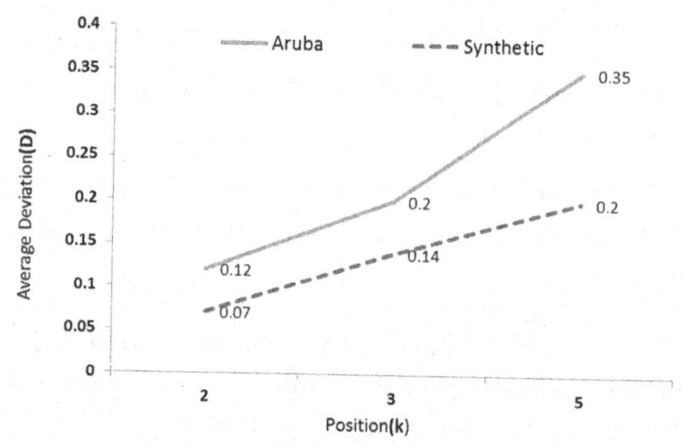

Fig. 2. Average deviation at k=2,3,5 for the relevant routines

The effectiveness of our Activity Discovery mechanism was evaluated using standard metrics used for reporting results of clustering. The intuition is that an effective Activity Discovery technique should be able to cluster data segments across the dataset that captures similar activities. We report Adjusted Rand Index(RAND-INDEX) and Cluster Purity as the metrics for clustering. The results are reported in Table 1.

We evaluate the recommended routines based on the following criteria.

- **Routine Relevance:** A recommended routine is considered a relevant routine if it effectively captures an actual user activity. In Table 2, we report the results on relevance of the routines suggested.
- **Goodness of Routine:** For each relevant routine, we measure its goodness based on the order of the actions that are recommended to be automated. We report the goodness of each relevant routine in terms of average deviation from the ideal routines. We measure the deviation at position 2, 3 and 5 given by $D@k$ for $k = 2, 3, 5$. For a routine, the deviation at k is given by:

$$D(S_r, I_r, k) = \frac{Dist(S_{r(k)}, I_{r(k)})}{k} \quad (1)$$

[2] http://ailab.wsu.edu/casas/datasets/aruba2.zip.
[3] http://ailab.wsu.edu/casas/about.html.

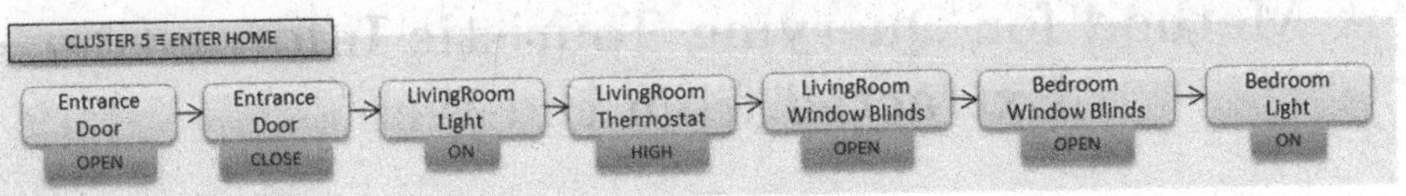

Fig. 3. Synthetic dataset - routines from activity clusters

Table 1. Evaluation of Activity Discovery. Value close to 1 indicate perfect clustering.

Dataset/Metric	Cluster purity	Adjusted - RAND
Aruba	0.93	0.88
Synthetic	0.89	0.86

Table 2. Evaluation of routine suggestion.

Dataset	Actual number of activities	Routines recommended	Relevant routines
Aruba	11	13	8
Synthetic	8	10	7

where, $S_{r(k)}$ and $I_{r(k)}$ are the top k events in the recommended and ideal routines respectively and $Dist(S_{r(k)}, I_{r(k)})$ is the edit distance between the string representation of event sequences of $S_{r(k)}$ and $I_{r(k)}$. A value of $D@k$ closer to 0 indicates a better match with the ideal routine. The average $D@k$ for the relevant routines are shown in the Fig. 2. A sample routine recommended by the system corresponding to an activity is shown in Fig. 3.

4 Conclusion

In this paper we have demonstrated that existing Natural Language Processing methodologies like Topic Modeling and Language Modeling can be seamlessly applied to solve certain interesting use-cases of smart homes. As a part of our work, we have presented a system and developed methods to solve two core issues in smart homes like Activity Discovery and Routine Identification. We believe that the core modules developed as part of our system can be extended to address use-cases in smart buildings, ambient assisted living and connected cars as well.

References

1. Ye, J., Stevenson, G., Dobson, S.: KCAR: a knowledge-driven approach for concurrent activity recognition. Pervasive Mob. Comput. **19**, 47–70 (2015)
2. Blei, D.M., Ng, A.Y., Jordan, M.I.: Latent dirichlet allocation. J. Mach. Learn. Res. **3**, 993–1022 (2003)
3. Rashidi, P., Cook, D.J.: Keeping the resident in the loop: adapting the smart home to the user. Trans. Syst. Man Cyber. Part A **39**, 949–959 (2009)

A Method for Querying Touristic Information Extracted from the Web

Ermelinda Oro(✉) and Massimo Ruffolo

National Research Council (CNR), Via P. Bucci 7/11C, 87036 Rende, CS, Italy
{linda.oro,massimo.ruffolo}@icar.cnr.it

Abstract. In this paper, we define a method that enables to: (i) exploit ontologies and terminology to represent concepts into specific domains, (ii) extract information from deep web pages, and opinions from social and community networks, (iii) semantically query information by using natural language interface. The method has been applied to query the touristic domain. This use case has shown the effectiveness of the method that can be easily extended to other domains.

Keywords: Natural language interface · Web data extraction · Ontology · Linked data · Question answering · Tourism domain

1 Introduction

Tourism is one of the most dynamic and web-based industries worldwide. It is an information-intensive market where tourists can use and leverage a plethora of sources having heterogeneous formats. To plan and organize touristic travels tourists navigate e-commerce web sites and social networks for accommodation and reservation, forums and blogs, holiday resort and points of interest web sites, comments on topics related to tourism. But searching and querying such a Big Data by standard search engines may result unsatisfactory, especially on mobile systems, whereas, by using formal languages results too complex for end-users. In this scenario, the usage of natural language interface for querying the web and existing knowledge bases offers opportunity to bridge the technological gap between end-users and systems that make use of formal query languages.

Several researchers and practitioners are working on the definition of algorithms and systems capable to translate natural language questions into formal languages able to query structured data. Question Answering systems (QAs) have attracted extensive attentions in both NLP [4,5] and database communities [6,7]. Different surveys are presented in literature [1,2]. But only few approaches worked on the tourism domain and defined a complete approach from the knowledge representation, data acquisition and information extraction, to the natural language processing and question answering.

In this paper, we present a method that enables to query, in natural language, knowledge bases populated by touristic information extracted from the web. This use case has shown the effectiveness of the proposed method that can be easily extended to other domains.

F. Frasincar et al. (Eds.): NLDB 2017, LNCS 10260, pp. 218–221, 2017.
DOI: 10.1007/978-3-319-59569-6_25

2 Proposed Method

This section describes a method for querying in natural language knowledge bases populated by using information extracted from the web. The proposed method is tailored to be flexible, scalable and general. It is constituted by three phases: (i) Definition of the ontology and terminology representing concepts into the specific domain. (ii) Extraction of information from deep web pages, from social and community networks. (iii) Semantic querying by using natural language processing, ontologies, and the Semantic Web tools. Figure 1 shows modules of the proposed method.

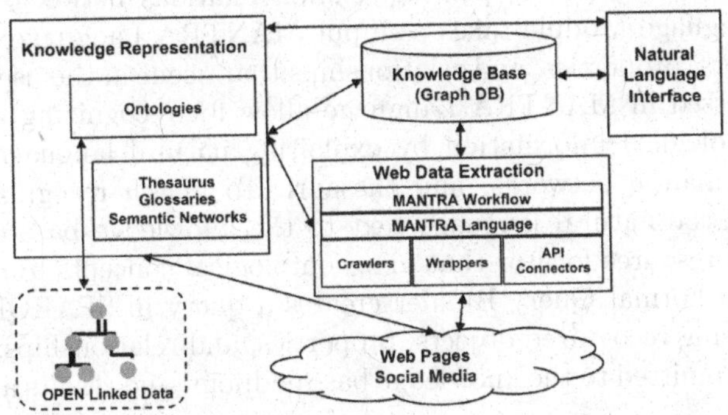

Fig. 1. Architecture of the proposed method

Knowledge Representation. The knowledge of the target domain can include ontologies, as well as thesauri, dictionaries and semantic networks. In our tourism domain, we created all such instruments by observing information existing on the Web and by including concepts from existing open linked data and by using top-level ontologies. The implemented ontology describes classes and properties of places (Places), objects and events (e.g. Facility, PointOfInterest, and Event). It includes extracted and computed reputation information (SocialObject). It maintains data about sources where the information has been extracted in order to be able to compute the reliability of the obtained information.

Web Data Extraction. Instances of the knowledge base are dynamically created by monitoring and extracting semi- and unstructured information (such as data, descriptions and comments about accommodations) by connecting to APIs of social networks, or by implementing smart crawlers and wrappers of deep web pages. To extract data from booking websites (e.g. booking.com, venere.it, and tripAdvisor), we modeled wrappers by using a visual interface[1] that records navigation actions performed by users into websites. In order to process comments and analyze opinions we implemented the sentiment analyzer writing rules in the MANTRA Language [3]. The MANTRA Language represents grammar-based

[1] MANTRA Web Extractor (MWE) http://mwe.altiliagroup.com/.

programs combined with logic predicates to identify concepts and their relations belonging to specific knowledge domains, and to compute sentiment polarities and opinion-targets. We can monitor websites and social networks scheduling workflows that populate the knowledge base (e.g. a graph database).

Natural Language Querying. We created a Natural Language Interface (NLI) that allows users to query knowledge bases through natural language expressions that are dynamically translated into formal queries (e.g. SPARQL and Cypher Query) to exploit various knowledge bases (i.e. ontologies and graph databases). Users write questions expressed in natural language by using a web-based GUI, shown in Fig. 2. The query in natural language is preprocessed to recognize linguistic constructs (such as, pos-tag, chunk, relations between chunk). The MANTRA Language Module takes as input MANTRA Language Programs to identify concepts, properties, and relationships that occur in the users questions. Patterns expressed in MANTRA Language allow for recognizing in a bottom-up fashion ontological information by exploiting natural language constructs, dictionaries, semantic networks, and thesauri. To match recognized concepts extracted from the natural language text to the knowledge base concepts, we use an external resource locator that maps ontological concepts to specific URI. The submodule Formal Query Builder creates a query in SPARQL or Cypher Language by using recognized objects, properties, and relationships. The formal query is then submitted to the knowledge base endpoint and results are visualized to users.

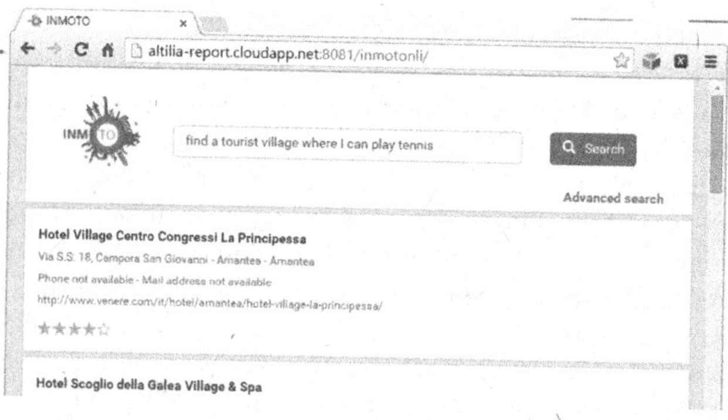

Fig. 2. Web-based graphical user interface for natural language querying

3 Discussion and Conclusion

In this paper, we presented a modular method that enables to query information extracted from the web. The main contribution of this paper consists in the definition of a proposed method that enables to: (i) exploit ontologies and terminology to represent concepts of specific domains; (ii) extract information and opinions from deep web pages, social and community networks; (iii) semantically query information by using a natural language interface. The modular method enables to easily create specific domain solutions. We tested our method for querying tourism information. More in detail, we focused on extracting and querying both descriptive data and opinions about accommodations. In particular, we collected descriptive data from booking websites, user ratings and comments from both booking websites and social networks. In our test, we extracted more than 3000 Italian hotels offering more than 20 different types of services from booking.com and venere.it. In addition, we monitored more than 5000 comments from around 1600 users. We collected 100 different questions written by a group of heterogeneous persons in Italian or English natural language. Questions adopted in the test considered services, nearby points of interest and opinions about the hotel. Example of questions are: "I would like to eat in a very good restaurant of an hotel in Cosenza" "I'm looking for a 4 star hotel in Amantea with free parking, swimming pool and elevator. Furthermore, I'd like to play tennis and read some books in a library." We compared obtained results with the computed Ground Truth obtaining precision 1. This approach works well for domain specific knowledge, like the considered touristic domain. Experimental applications, involving real user questions on touristic domain, demonstrate that our system provides high-quality results. In the future, we intend to evaluate our approach on a larger scale, and we plan to conduct an intensive usability study. In addition, our goal is to provide robust question answering interface that exploits some innovative algorithms based on deep neural networks.

References

1. Dwivedi, S.K., Singh, V.: Research and reviews in question answering system. Procedia Technol. **10**, 417–424 (2013)
2. Mishra, A., Jain, S.K.: A survey on question answering systems with classification. J. King Saud Univ. Comput. Inf. Sci. **28**(3), 345–361 (2016)
3. Oro, E., Ruffolo, M.: Using apps and rules in contextual workflows to semantically extract data from documents. In: Proceedings of the 17th International Conference on Information Integration and Web-based Applications & Services (2015)
4. Unger, C., Bühmann, L., Lehmann, J., Ngonga Ngomo, A.C., Gerber, D., Cimiano, P.: Template-based question answering over RDF data. In: Proceedings of the 21st International Conference on World Wide Web, pp. 639–648. ACM (2012)
5. Yahya, M., Berberich, K., Elbassuoni, S., Ramanath, M., Tresp, V., Weikum, G.: Natural language questions for the web of data. In: Proceedings of the 2012 Joint Conference on Empirical Methods in Natural Language Processing and Computational Natural Language Learning, pp. 379–390. Association for Computational Linguistics (2012)
6. Yahya, M., Berberich, K., Elbassuoni, S., Weikum, G.: Robust question answering over the web of linked data. In: Proceedings of the 22nd ACM International Conference on Information & Knowledge Management, pp. 1107–1116. ACM (2013)
7. Zou, L., Huang, R., Wang, H., Yu, J.X., He, W., Zhao, D.: Natural language question answering over RDF: a graph data driven approach. In: Proceedings of the 2014 ACM SIGMOD International Conference on Management of Data, pp. 313–324. ACM (2014)

Towards Generating Object-Oriented Programs Automatically from Natural Language Texts for Solving Mathematical Word Problems

Sourav Mandal[1(✉)] and Sudip Kumar Naskar[2]

[1] Haldia Institute of Technology, Haldia, India
sourav.mandal@hithaldia.in
[2] Jadavpur University, Kolkata, India
sudip.naskar@cse.jdvu.ac.in

Abstract. This paper proposes a novel technique for generating object-oriented computer program automatically from natural language text input containing a mathematical word problem (MWP) to produce the final answer. The system identifies all the entities like owners, items, cardinal values from the MWP texts and the arithmetic operations by understanding the verb semantics. Successively, it generates a complete object oriented program using JAVA language. The proposed system can solve addition-subtraction type MWPs and produced an accuracy of 90.48% on a subset of the AI2 Arithmetic Questions (http://allenai.org/data.html) dataset.

1 Introduction

The objective of the work presented here is to generate computer programs automatically from MWP texts which when executed will produce the desired answers. For example, "*Tom has 6 apples. He lost 3 apples. How many apples does he have now?*" is a word problem. In object oriented programming (OOP)[1] approach, we define a class 'Person' with the data members like *name*, *item_name* and *item_count*, and a method *evaluate_result*(), and declare an object 'obj' of this class for solving the MWP. Here, *obj.name = Tom*, *obj.item_name = apple* and *obj.item_count = 6*. The operation associated with the verb 'has' is assignment (observation) and can be coded as *obj.item_count = 6*. Similarly, the verb 'lost' represents subtraction (i.e., decrement) and can be coded as *obj.item_count = obj.item_count - 3*.

2 Related Work

The development of formal language models from natural language text has been studied by researchers for various domains among which [2,3,5,6] are relevant to our work. Mihalcea et al. [6] first proposed a system that attempts to convert

[1] http://docs.oracle.com/javase/tutorial/java/concepts/.

F. Frasincar et al. (Eds.): NLDB 2017, LNCS 10260, pp. 222–226, 2017.
DOI: 10.1007/978-3-319-59569-6_26

Table 1. Equation formation based on verb category and schema information

Category(Operator)	Examples	Schema entry	Equations
(Null) Observation('=')	Tom has 6 green apples	[Tom, null, apple green, 6]	Tom-apple-green.count = 6
Increment('+')	Harry gathered 10 red marbles in the drawer	[Harry, drawer, marble, red, 10]	Harry-marble-red.count = Harry-marble-red.count + 10 and drawer-marble-red = drawer-marble-red + 10
Decrement('−')	Joan lost 12 seashells	[Joan, null, seashells, null, 12]	Joan-seashell-null.count = Joan-seashell-null.count - 12
Positive Transfer('+' & '−')	Sam bought 8 of Mike's baseball cards	[Sam, Mike, card, baseball, 8]	Sam-card-baseball.count = Sam-card-baseball.count + 8 and Mike-card-baseball.count = Mike-card-baseball.count - 8
Negative Transfer('−' & '+')	John gave 7 red balloons to Mary	[John, Mary, balloon, red, 7]	John-balloon-red.count = John-balloon-red.count - 7 and Mary-balloon-red.count = Mary-balloon-red.count + 7

natural language texts directly into computer programs in 'PERL' language. Alongside, many researchers recently developed various models to solve word problems using different techniques [1,4,8].

3 System Description

First we studied the verbs appearing in the dataset (cf. Sect. 4) for verb categorization and equation formation. Analyzing the predicates and arguments from the output of semantic role labelling (SRL), similar types of verbs were manually grouped together into 5 categories based on their arithmetic operational connotation. SRL techniques are mainly used to semantically process texts to define role(s) of each word present in a text and to identify predicates and arguments of the verb(s). Table 1 presents the verb categories along with the associated arithmetic operations and the targeted equation statements. The schema entry contains information about [*primary_owner*, *secondary_owner*,

Table 2. Generating executable program statements in JAVA

Owner-Item-Attribute/Objects	Item_count(x)	Verb_lemma	Operation	Equation statements	State no./Sentence no.
Tom-seashell-null/obj[0]	12	Find	Assignment	obj[0].x = 12	1/1
John-seashell-null/obj[1]	6	Has	Assignment	obj[1].x = 6	1/2
Tom-seashell-null/obj[0]	4	Give	−	obj[0].x = obj[0].x − 4	2/3
John-seashell-null/obj[1]	4	Give	+	obj[1].x = obj[1].x + 4	2/3

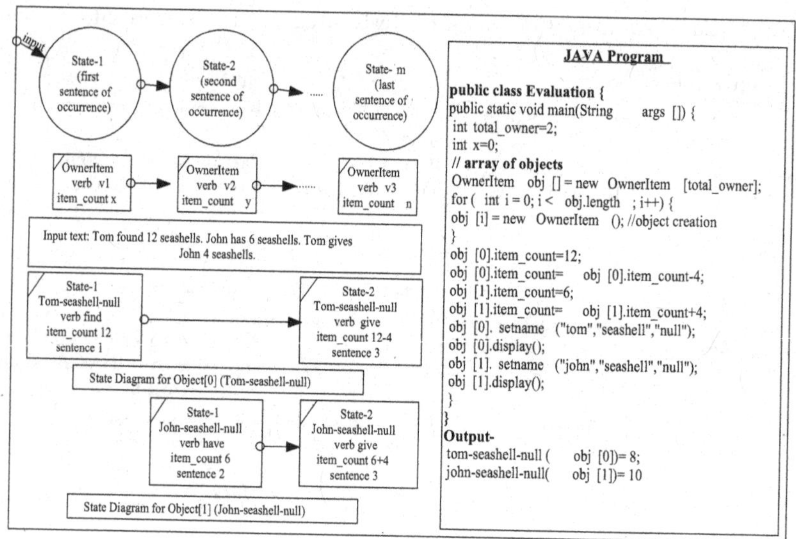

Fig. 1. State diagrams of the 'OwnerItem' objects and final JAVA program

item_name, item_attribute, item_quantity] which are extracted from each sentence of the MWP text. For information extraction(IE) from sentences which is template based, we used the output of an SRL tool – Mateplus[2] [7]. The system stores the extracted information in the 'Sentence' and 'Verb' templates. Successively, the system identifies each unique 'Owner-Item-Attribute'(OIA) triplet such that at least one component is unique and fills the 'OIA' templates with relevant information. For object creation and program statements generation, the identified unique OIA combinations are represented as real 'Objects' using OOP. E.g., if the input text is "*Tom found 12 seashells. John has 6 seashells. Tom gave 4 seashells to John.*", the system identifies 2 unique OIA combinations – 'tom-seashell-null' and 'john-seashell-null' represented as 'obj[0]' and 'obj[1]' (cf. Table 2) by instantiating the class 'OwnerItem' (cf. Figure 1) which resembles an 'OIA' templates. Both the verbs, 'find' and 'have', generate the assignment statements. The verb 'give' belongs to the 'negative transfer' category; hence it generates the decrement operation ('−') statement with the primary_owner 'Tom' (i.e. obj[0]) and increment operation ('+') statement with the secondary_owner 'John' (i.e. obj[1]). By matching and replacing the triplets with the respective actual objects in the 'equations' (cf. 'Equations' column in Table 1), the actual executable JAVA programming statements are created. Figure 1 demonstrates a simple forward state transition diagram for all 'OwnerItem' objects and the generated program for the example mentioned earlier. A sentence in the input text, where an 'OwnerItem' object exists, is treated as a 'state' for that 'OwnerItem' object in the diagram. Based on the operations performed on them, their item quantities are updated and finally the last

[2] https://github.com/microth/mateplus.

sentential state corresponding to the object about which the question has been asked holds the answer to the MWP. The program statements are placed sequentially according to the sequence of events (i.e., predicates) in the MWP, in a predefined program skeleton written using 'JAVA' programming language with additional program statements to display the answer by analyzing the question sentence (not shown in Fig. 1). The program is compiled and executed by the JAVA compiler (JVM) itself to generate the final answer.

4 Dataset, Results and Discussions

There are no standard references or datasets available for this kind of work. We selected 189 word problems from the MA1, MA2 datasets which are subsets of the 'AI2 Arithmetic Questions' dataset [1]. The proposed method achieved an accuracy of 90.48% on our testset. We did not consider the IXL dataset having more information gaps and 66 problems of MA1 and MA2 containing "missing information" and "irrelevant information"[3] as solving these problems involve complex reasoning and presently the system does not have the capabilities to handle them.

5 Conclusions

This paper makes an effort to build a bridge between natural language and formal (object oriented) language for solving mathematical word problems. Any event-driven scenario can be modelled using the object-oriented approach. The proposed model can be augmented to help automatic code generation from the viewpoint of software engineering. As an immediate extension we would like to extend the system to solve word problems involving multiplication and division along with automatic verb classification.

References

1. Hosseini, M.J., Hajishirzi, H., Etzioni, O., Kushman, N.: Learning to solve arithmetic word problems with verb categorization. In: Proceedings of the 2014 Conference on Empirical Methods in Natural Language Processing, EMNLP, Doha, Qatar, A Meeting of SIGDAT, A Special Interest Group of the ACL, 25–29 October 2014, pp. 523–533 (2014)
2. Kate, R.J., Wong, Y.W., Mooney, R.J.: Learning to transform natural to formal languages. In: Proceedings, the Twentieth National Conference on Artificial Intelligence and the Seventeenth Innovative Applications of Artificial Intelligence Conference, Pittsburgh, Pennsylvania, USA, 9–13 July 2005, pp. 1062–1068 (2005)

[3] The dataset is available at: https://sites.google.com/site/nlautoprogramming/ with explanation of "missing information", "irrelevant information" and errors.

3. Kushman, N., Barzilay, R.: Using semantic unification to generate regular expressions from natural language. In: Human Language Technologies: Conference of the North American Chapter of the Association of Computational Linguistics, Proceedings, Westin Peachtree Plaza Hotel, Atlanta, Georgia, USA, 9–14 June 2013, pp. 826–836 (2013)
4. Kushman, N., Zettlemoyer, L., Barzilay, R., Artzi, Y.: Learning to automatically solve algebra word problems. In: Proceedings of the 52nd Annual Meeting of the Association for Computational Linguistics, ACL, Baltimore, MD, USA, 22–27 June 2014, vol. 1, pp. 271–281 (2014). Long Papers
5. Liu, H., Lieberman, H.: Metafor: visualizing stories as code. In: Proceedings of the 2005 International Conference on Intelligent User Interfaces, San Diego, California, USA, 10–13 January 2005, pp. 305–307 (2005)
6. Mihalcea, R., Liu, H., Lieberman, H.: NLP (natural language processing) for NLP (natural language programming). In: Computational Linguistics and Intelligent Text Processing, 7th International Conference, CICLing 2006, Mexico City, Mexico, 19–25 February 2006, Proceedings, pp. 319–330 (2006)
7. Roth, M., Lapata, M.: Context-aware frame-semantic role labeling. TACL **3**, 449–460 (2015)
8. Roy, S., Roth, D.: Solving general arithmetic word problems. In: Proceedings of the 2015 Conference on Empirical Methods in Natural Language Processing, EMNLP 2015, Lisbon, Portugal, 17–21 September 2015, pp. 1743–1752 (2015)

Authorship Attribution System

Oleksandr Marchenko[1(✉)], Anatoly Anisimov[1], Andrii Nykonenko[2], Tetiana Rossada[1], and Egor Melnikov[3]

[1] Taras Shevchenko National University of Kyiv, Kiev, Ukraine
omarchenko@univ.kiev.ua

[2] International Research and Training Center for IT and Systems, Kyiv, Ukraine

[3] Phase One: Karma LTD, London, UK

Abstract. A new effective system for identification and verification of text authorship has been developed. The system is created on the basis of machine learning. The originality of the model is caused by a suggested unique profile of the author's style features. Together with the use of the Support Vector Machine method, this allows us to achieve the high accuracy of the authorship detection. Proposed method allows the system to learn styles for a large number of authors using small amount of data in a training set.

Keywords: Machine learning · Support Vector Machine · Authorship detection

Identification of authorship is a unique and extremely demanded task. This is due to the huge variety of it's applications in different fields of human activity including plagiarism control, detecting the authorship of anonymous texts, investigations in criminalistics, and many others. The task is very complicated due to the fundamental problem of defining and assessing style features inherent to a particular author. Until now, a large quantity of authors texts in a training set was the mandatory precondition for the high-quality performance of all existing authorship detection systems.

The authors of this presentation have developed an authorship attribution system being able to accurately operate even with a minimal set of texts for each author in a training set (from 5 Kbytes of text per author) as well as with a number of authors amounting up to 20. Our results can be compared with values achieved by the Local Histograms of Character N-grams model [2], that was trained on a subset of RCV1 (Reuters Corpus Volume I) [1] and demonstrated the accuracy score between 49.2%–86.4% for 10 authors. Another work [3] reports the accuracy between 39.0%–80.8% on RCV1, authors use a set of tensor space models to attribute 10 authors.

Among recent works it was reported 90% accuracy on fragments of Ph.D. theses for 10 authors, using stylometry and machine learning [4]. Usage of character-level and multi-channel Convolutional Neural Networks [5] gives average F1 between 43.6%–73.4% depending on the amount of authors and a test dataset.

F. Frasincar et al. (Eds.): NLDB 2017, LNCS 10260, pp. 227–231, 2017.
DOI: 10.1007/978-3-319-59569-6_27

1 Method

The system has a two-level structure. At the first level, a set of classifiers calculates probabilities of authorship of the input text for each given author (choosing from the set of authors the system was trained on). At the second level, based on the analysis of decisions made by first-level classifiers the system finds out one author of a text.

Our model examines each text separately and collects information for hypotheses. Some hypotheses are transferred to a machine learning module as is, other information is averaged for each author to obtain attributes peculiar to each author style. Averaging gives us ability to receive smooth statistics due to more diversified data. Increased confidence interval allows the system to attribute authorship with a far better accuracy. Any collected statistical information (e.g., average amount of letters in a word) becomes independent from the text style and better displays the authors pattern.

The result of the input data processing is a set of vectors for each individual author. At the training stage, the first level of the model chooses coefficients for each vector position. The second level of the model chooses coefficients for each author's classifier. After that, the model is considered to be trained and able to classify new texts.

2 Implementation

From the perspective of machine learning, the problem of authorship detection is reduced to the problem of text classification.

Linear support vector machine (linear SVM) is used as a basic machine learning algorithm for training classifiers.. For the implementation Python programming language, scikit-learn(http://scikit-learn.org/stable/) and numpy (http://www.numpy.org/) packages were used. The stage of selecting informative features was the most difficult one, the features mentioned in [1–5] were implemented as a basic feature set. Some of these features appeared to be ineffective for the considered task. For example, analysis of mistakes, word N-grams, as well as features like vocabulary richness and vocabulary size did not work. We assume that such features can work effectively only in the case of authors writing in one fixed topic, and not in the case when texts are taken from the news corpus. For the same reasons, features like word/sentence length, typical first/last letter in a word/sentence, frequency of word combinations did not prove to be effective.

Features like dependency triplets and k-ee subtree pattern were left out due to the insignificant increase of the precision while having high computational complexity.

Finally, the set of features for authorship attribution included the following:

- punctuation features (punctuation signs, their means and standard deviation);
- morphological features (statistics of letter combinations and letters);

Table 1. List of datasets

Dataset name	Author count	Text count	Total size, B	Avg. size, KB
Dataset0	15	37	107.788	From 4 to 9
Dataset1	15	191	542.732	From 24 to 58
Dataset2	15	848	2.533.525	From 130 to 197
Dataset3	15	1.554	5.107.210	From 300 to 388
Dataset4	15	2.440	8.156.620	From 504 to 593

- lexical features (statistics of stopwords, universal words, and author's words, etc.);
- syntactical features (N-grams of parts of speech, frequency of syntactical connections, frequency of rewriting rules (Chomsky grammar), etc.);
- complicated features based on vector representation of word usage statistics.

After the training stage ends (each classifier recognizes its personal author), the second stage follows, where the selection of coefficients-weights is made in order to resolve conflicts. A conflict happens when several classifiers simultaneously consider the text as the one that belongs to its authors. Special method OVR (one-vs-rest) solves a number of optimization problems related to the selection of priority weights for classifiers to minimize the number of authorship attribution errors (Table 1).

3 Test Methodology

When selecting a system assessment method, the factors like reproducibility and assessment comprehensiveness played a crucial role. The goal was to create a single text corpus where all researchers can verify the accuracy of our system operation, measure and compare the results of their systems using the same set of texts.

RCV1 dataset was applied for evaluating. To ensure a comprehensive evaluation, RCV1 was sorted according to authors, and then 5 separate datasets were generated.

Creating these 5 datasets allows us to provide a comprehensive assessment of the system accuracy, starting from 2–3 articles per author up to thousands.

The accuracy of any machine learning algorithm depends on how the data is partitioned into training and test sets. The cross-validation algorithm called Leave One Out (LOO) always provides consistently same results on a data set. An essential drawback of LOO is its high computational complexity: for each sample of data it is necessary to train the model on all other data and only after that to test the model on a given sample. The result, close to LOO, is provided by the method called Simplified LOO.

Simplified LOO converts all the texts into features vectors that form a features matrix at the very beginning of the work and does not calculate them again. Afterwards, each vector is sequentially selected from the features matrix and used as a test sample; the rest of the matrix data is used for training the model. Simplified LOO may cause an overfitting, because the constructed system contains complex features that use statistics collected from the whole corpus. For large corpora, the influence of this factor is insignificant. Hence Simplified LOO provides relatively close results to LOO.

4 Results of Experiments

The results of the developed model can be seen in Table 2.

Table 2. Perfomance of the authorship attribution system

		20-fold cross validation			Cross validation LOO			Simplified LOO		
		P	R	F1	P	R	F1	P	R	F1
$Dataset_0$	G	0.7297	0.7297	0.7297	0.7297	0.7297	0.7297	0.9189	0.9189	0.9189
	C	0.6789	0.7222	0.6849	0.6844	0.7222	0.6881	0.9333	0.9222	0.92
$Dataset_1$	G	0.7068	0.7068	0.7068	0.7120	0.7120	0.7120	0.7120	0.7120	0.7120
	C	0.7218	0.7014	0.6937	0.7355	0.7081	0.6992	0.8139	0.7955	0.7918
$Dataset_2$	G	0.7205	0.7205	0.7205	0.7252	0.7252	0.7252	0.7547	0.7547	0.7547
	C	0.7185	0.7107	0.7062	0.7238	0.7168	0.7127	0.7533	0.7477	0.7442
$Dataset_3$	G	0.7394	0.7394	0.7394	0.7413	0.7413	0.7413	0.7606	0.7606	0.7606
	C	0.7385	0.7361	0.7210	0.7384	0.7380	0.7223	0.7596	0.7580	0.7432
$Dataset_4$	G	0.7680	0.7680	0.7680				0.7725	0.7725	0.7725
	C	0.7761	0.7656	0.7619				0.7805	0.7702	0.7667

To calculate test results, three methods are used: K-fold crossvalidation, Simplified LOO, and LOO. It was decided to use the value of K which would be larger than the number of authors. The value K = 20 does not fully prevent from the case when an author is not presented in a training set at all, but gives a close approximation. For partitioning data sets in K-fold Crossvalidation, the KFold function (n_folds = 20, shuffle = True, random_state = 1) from the scikit-learn package was used.

In Table 2 the line G (Global) contains F1 evaluation calculated using the total number of true positives, false negatives, and false positives. The line C (Class-Based) contains F1 evaluation calculated as an average for F1 assessments of each author.

5 Conclusion

The paper describes the development of a unique English text authorship attribution system. The system operates on text corpora containing articles of a large number of authors (15–20) and demonstrates high accuracy of text authorship attribution. The system does not require a large training set for each author. The minimum set may contain only 5 Kbytes of text per author. Using machine learning models and developing a unique profile of author's style features allows reaching the results at a new state-of-the-art level. In the future we plan to test the model on PAN's competition data.

Acknowledgments. The authors of the article are grateful to Phase One: Karma LTD company, especially to the Unplag team for the support in research and considerable assistance in the development, testing and implementation of the authorship attribution method.

References

1. Lewis, D., Yang, Y., Rose, T., Li, F.: RCV1: a new benchmark collection for text categorization research. J. Mach. Learn. Res. **5**, 361–397 (2004)
2. Escalante, H., Solorio, T., Montes-y-Gomez, M.: Local histograms of character N-grams for authorship attribution. In: Proceedings of the 49th Annual Meeting of the Association for Computational Linguistics: Human Language Technologies, vol. 1, June 2011
3. Plakias, S., Stamatatos, E.: Tensor space models for authorship identification. In: Darzentas, J., Vouros, G.A., Vosinakis, S., Arnellos, A. (eds.) SETN 2008. LNCS, vol. 5138, pp. 239–249. Springer, Heidelberg (2008). doi:10.1007/978-3-540-87881-0_22
4. Ramnial, H., Panchoo, S., Pudaruth, S.: Authorship attribution using stylometry and machine learning techniques. In: Berretti, S., Thampi, S.M., Srivastava, P.R. (eds.) Intelligent Systems Technologies and Applications. AISC, vol. 384, pp. 113–125. Springer, Cham (2016). doi:10.1007/978-3-319-23036-8_10
5. Ruder, S., Ghaffari, P., Breslin, J.: Character-level and Multi-channel Convolutional Neural Networks for Large-scale Authorship Attribution. CoRR (2016)

Neural Language Models and Applications

Estimating Distributed Representations of Compound Words Using Recurrent Neural Networks

Natthawut Kertkeidkachorn[1(✉)] and Ryutaro Ichise[1,2]

[1] SOKENDAI (The Graduate University for Advanced Studies), Tokyo, Japan
[2] National Institute of Informatics, Tokyo, Japan
{natthawut,ichise}@nii.ac.jp

Abstract. Distributed representations of words play a crucial role in many natural language processing tasks. However, to learn the distributed representations of words, each word in the text corpus is treated as an individual token. Therefore, the distributed representations of compound words could not be directly represented. In this paper, we introduce a recurrent neural network (RNN)-based approach for estimating distributed representations of compound words. The experimental results show that the RNN-based approach can estimate the distributed representations of compound words better than the average representation approach, which simply uses the average of individual word representations as an estimated representation of a compound word. Furthermore, the characteristic of estimated representations of compound words are closely similar to the actual representations of compound words.

1 Introduction

Representations of words play a crucial role in many models of natural language processing tasks such as part of speech tagging [4] and parsing [18]. Conventionally, a word as an atomic unit of language is transformed to a vector by the one-hot encoder as its representation. However, such representations are presented in the high-dimensional space, which leads to the curse of the dimensionality [1]. To overcome the curse of the dimensionality, the concept of distributed representation was proposed [1]. Distributed representation of a word uses a dense real-value vector to represent the word in the low-dimensional vector space. Since the representation is projected to the low-dimensional vector space, this representation does not encounter with the curse of the dimensionality problem. Also, both synthetic and semantics of words are encoded into their representation [15].

Recently, many studies [1,13,14,16] focus on modelling the distributed representation of words. One of the prominent approaches is word2vec [13,14]. By leveraging the shallow neural network model trained over the unlabeled text corpus, words in the corpus are embedded as the distributed representations [13,14]. Based upon the hypothesis of the distributional occurrence of context words, words sharing similar meaning occur in similar context words. Under this

F. Frasincar et al. (Eds.): NLDB 2017, LNCS 10260, pp. 235–246, 2017.
DOI: 10.1007/978-3-319-59569-6_28

hypothesis, the neural network model can learn the distributed representations of words, which can capture both the function and the meaning of the words. However, to learn the distributed representations of words, each word in the text corpus is treated as an individual token. Consequently, the distributed representations of compound words, which typically consist of two or more tokens, could not be represented directly.

In order to cope with the problem of compound words, many approaches [11,14] have been proposed. These approaches detect compound words by a statistical strategy and replace compound words by unique tokens. Such approaches can learn the actual representations of compound words; however, some representations of compound words may not be able to learn because we may not be able to detect all compound words. Furthermore, some detected compound words may appear infrequently; in consequence, the representations of such compound words cannot be learned. Estimating the distributed representation of a compound word by using its individual words is the promising solution, because we usually can learn the representations of the words in the compound word. For example, given the compound word "Hida Station", we may not be able to learn the actual representation of the compound word "Hida_Station". However, we can learn each representation of the words "Hida" and "Station", since these words, in particular "Station", appear frequently. Our assumption is that the representation of the compound word "Hida_Station" could be estimated by the representations of "Hida" and "Station". In this study, we want to estimate the distributed representations of compound words by using their individual word representations. Currently, the widely-used workaround for estimating the distributed representation of a compound word is to average vector representations of individual words in the compound word. Although many studies [7,17,19] utilized average distributed representations of words, the meaning of a compound word is not simple composition of the individual words [14].

In this paper, we therefore introduce the recurrent neural network (RNN)-based approach for estimating distributed representations of compound words by their word representations. In the RNN-based approach, distributed representations of words in a compound word are given to the model in order to estimate the distributed representation of the compound word.

The rest of the paper is structured as follows. We describe the background of the neural network language model and formalize the problem in Sect. 2. Section 3 discusses related works. In Sect. 4, we introduce the RNN-based approach for estimating distributed representations of compound words. Experiments and results are reported in Sect. 5. In Sect. 6, we conclude our work and discuss the future direction.

2 Distributed Representation of Compound Words

In this section, we briefly give the background of the neural network language model. Then, the problem of compound word representations is defined.

2.1 Neural Network Language Model

The neural network language model is introduced in the study [1]. The idea is to learn representations of words by using the neural network architectures. Typically, there are two general architectures: (1) Continuous Bag of Words (CBOW) model and (2) Skip-Gram model [1,13,14]. The concept of the CBOW model is to predict the target word by the context words, while the idea of the Skip-Gram model is to predict the context words by the target word. More specifically, given a sequence of training words $w_1, w_2, w_3, .., w_N$ and a context window c, the learning function of the CBOW model is to maximize the following average log probability

$$\frac{1}{N}\sum_{t=1}^{N} log\ p(w_t|w_{t-c}, ..., w_{t-1}, w_{t+1}, ..., w_{t+c}) \tag{1}$$

where

$$p(w_t|w_{t-c}, ..., w_{t-1}, w_{t+1}, ..., w_{t+c}) = \frac{exp(\bar{v} \cdot v_{w_t})}{\sum_{w=1}^{|V|} exp(\bar{v} \cdot v_w)}$$

Here, v_w is the distributed representation of the word w, $\bar{v}$ is an average distributed representation of words in the context c and V is the set of vocabulary of all words. Inversely, the Skip-Gram model is to maximize the following log probability

$$\frac{1}{N}\sum_{t=1}^{N} \sum_{-c \leq i \leq c, i \neq 0} log\ p(w_{t+i}|w_t) \tag{2}$$

where

$$p(w_{t+i}|w_t) = \frac{exp(v_{w_{t+i}} \cdot v_{w_t})}{\sum_{w=1}^{|V|} exp(v_w \cdot v_{w_t})}$$

Here, v_w is the distributed representation of the word w and V is the set of vocabulary of whole words.

2.2 Problem Definition

As shown in Eqs. (1) and (2), these two models treat each word in the word sequence as a token. Consequently, they cannot handle a compound word straightforwardly. In this section, we formally define the definition of a compound word and then formalize the problem of estimating distributed representation of a compound word by its sequence.

Definition 1. *A compound word w_{cp} is a sequence of words ($w_{cp\_1}, w_{cp\_2} w_{cp\_3}$, ..., w_{cp_n}), where the words are put together to create the meaning of w_{cp}.*

Distributed Representations of Compound Words. The objective is to model the function $f : (v_{w_{cp\_1}}, v_{w_{cp\_2} w_{cp\_3}}, ..., v_{w_{cp\_n}}) \to \bar{v}_{w_{cp}}$, where $v_{w_{cp\_i}}$ is the distributed representation of the i^{th}word of the compound word w_{cp} and $\bar{v}_{w_{cp}}$ is the estimated distributed representation of the compound word w_{cp}.

3 Related Work

Recently, many studies [5,11,14] proposed learning distributed representation of compound words. Mikolov et al. proposed the statistical-based approach for replacing compound words with unique tokens [14]. In their approach, the co-occurrence of words is used to determine whether such group of words is compound words or not. In the study [11], the Doc2Vec approach was proposed. The concept of Doc2Vec is to learn distributed representation of sentences and paragraphs with the context words. Although this approach can learn the distributed representation of larger chunk of words, the predefined tokens are still required in the learning process. Consequently, both studies [11,14] cannot directly estimate the distributed representations of new compound words by using distributed representation of words. Later, Dima et al. proposed a method to estimate distributed representations of the compound noun by using the deep neural network architecture [5]. The approach can interpret the distributed representations of compound words by their words. However, their architecture is limited to handle two consecutive words as a compound word. Consequently, it cannot deal with the dynamic length of compound words.

In contrast to other studies [5,11,14], the workaround for estimating the distributed representation of a compound word by using their individual words is to average distributed representations of individual words in the compound words. This method can directly estimate the distributed representation of the compound word and solve the dynamic length of compound words. However, as reported in the study [14], the meaning of a compound word is not a simple composition of the individual words. Consequently, estimating the distributed representation of a compound word by average representations might not be a good representation.

To avoid the dynamic length of compound words and to better estimate the representations of compound words, we therefore introduce the RNN-based approach for this task.

4 Methodology

In this section, we describe the method to learn the distributed representations of words in compound words and then introduce the RNN-based model for estimating the distributed representation of a compound word.

4.1 Learning Distributed Representation of Words

In the learning process, if a sequence of words contains compound words, we create a new sequence and replace any compound words in the sequence with a unique token. For example, given the sequence "San Francisco is located in United State of America", the new sequence "San_Francisco is located in United_State_of_America" is created. Both sequences are used to learn the representations of words. After learning the distributed representation of words, the distributed representation of the compound word, e.g. "San_Francisco", and individual words, e.g. "San" and "Francisco", are acquired. The distributed representations of compound words and individual words are given to our RNN-based approach so that our RNN-based approach can later learn to estimate the representations of compound words.

4.2 Recurrent Neural Networks

Recurrent neural networks (RNNs) are circular neural networks, which are typically used for modelling a sequence of arbitrary length. Formally, given a sequence of input $x_1, x_2, x_3, ..., x_n$, the RNN model learns to map the given sequence to a sequence of output $y_1, y_2, y_3, ..., y_n$, where each input and output at time t are corresponded. At any time t, the RNN model learns the current latent state with the input data at t and the previous latent state at time $t-1$. Then, the current latent state is used to predict the output. Based on this concept, the most basic RNN [6] is derived as the following equation:

$$h_t = f(W_{i,h}x_t + W_{h,h}h_{t-1} + b_h) \tag{3}$$

$$y_t = g(W_{h,y}h_t + b_y) \tag{4}$$

where x_t is the input vector at time t, h_t is the vector of hidden layer at time t, y_t is the prediction vector at time t, $W_{i,h}, W_{h,h}, W_{h,y}$ are parameter matrices, b_h, b_y are the bias parameters for the network and f, g are the activation function, e.g. sigmoids. Although the RNN model can deal with the sequential data, long-term dependencies cannot be captured due to the vanished and exploding gradient [2]. Recently, more advanced RNN models, e.g. long short-term memory (LSTM) [8] and gated recurrent unit (GRU) [3], are proposed to handle long-term dependencies. In this study, we focus on the GRU unit, which had been reported that it provides better performances than the LSTM unit in many datasets [3]. The GRU unit in our approach is descried as follows:

$$z_t = f(W_z x_t + U_z h_{t-1} + b_z) \tag{5}$$

$$r_t = f(W_r x_t + U_r h_{t-1} + b_r) \tag{6}$$

$$h_t = g(W_h x_t + U_h(r_t \circ s_{t-1}) + b_h) \tag{7}$$

$$s_t = z_t \circ s_{t-1} + (1 - z_t) \circ h_t \tag{8}$$

where z_t is the update gate vector at time t, r_t is the reset gate vector at time t, h_t, h_{t-1} is the vector of hidden layer at time t and $t-1$, s_t is the output vector at time t, x_t is the input vector at time t, W and U are parameter matrices, b is the bias parameters, f and g are the activation function and $\circ$ represents the Hadamard product operation.

In our study, we only use the output from the last state as the distributed representation of a compound word as shown in Fig. 1. Given a sequence of representations of the compound word w_{cp} $(v_{w_{cp\_1}}, v_{w_{cp\_2}w_{cp\_3}}, ..., v_{w_{cp\_n}})$, the RNN-based approach calculates the estimated distributed representation of the compound word w_{cp} from the last state as follows.

$$\bar{v}_{w_{cp}} = z_{Last} \circ s_{Last-1} + (1 - z_{Last}) \circ h_{Last} \tag{9}$$

where $\bar{v}_{w_{cp}}$ is the estimated representation of the compound word w_{cp}, z_{Last}, r_{Last} and h_{Last} are the update gate vector, the reset gate vector and the hidden layer vector at the last sequence respectively and h_{Last-1} is the hidden layer vector before the last state. In the learning process, the idea is that we want to minimize the error between the estimated representation and the actual representation of the compound word. Therefore, the objective of the whole network learning is to minimize the following function:

$$\mathcal{L}(v_{w_{cp}}, \bar{v}_{w_{cp}}) = \|v_{w_{cp}} - \bar{v}_{w_{cp}}\|_2^2 \tag{10}$$

where $v_{w_{cp}}$ is the actual representation of the compound word w_{cp}, learned by replacing the compound word w_{cp} in the sequence with the unique token (as described in Sect. 4.1), and $\bar{v}_{w_{cp}}$ is the estimated representation of the compound word w_{cp} by the RNN-based approach.

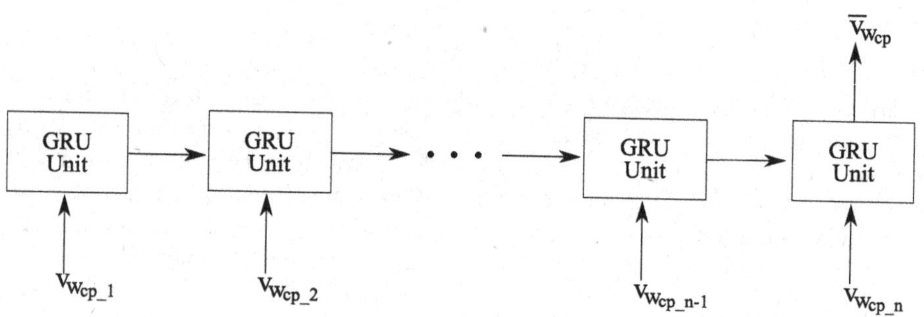

Fig. 1. The RNN-based approach for estimating distributed representation of a compound word by its word sequence

5 Experiments

In this section, we present experiments for evaluating the performance of the RNN-based approach. The objectives of the experiments are two-fold: (1) investigating the improvement of the estimated representations of compound words and (2) assessing the quality of representations of compound words.

5.1 Experimental Setup

We start with describing the text corpus, which is used to learn the distributed representations of individual words and compound words. We then provide the details of the dataset for estimating distributed representations of compound words. After that, the implementation of the RNN-based approach and the network training are presented.

Corpus. To learn the distributed representations of individual and compound words, all Wikipedia articles as sequences are used as mentioned in Sect. 4.1. Still, there is the problem regarding locating compound words in the sequence. In order to address this problem, we utilize tags provided by Wikipedia. We assume that a sequence of words in any tag is a compound word. For example, given the sentence [Barack Obama] was [the U.S. president], where [ ] denotes a tag, e.g. a hyperlink tag, we can form two sequences: (1) Barack Obama was the U.S. president and (2) Barack_Obama was the_U.S._president. The implementation of extracting tags and identifying compound words are followed Wiki2Vec[1].

Based upon the text corpus above, we create the pair between a compound word and its individual words as the **dataset**for experiments. From the above example, we can create the (Barack_Obama, Barack Obama) and (the_U.S._pres ident, the U.S. president). The statistic of the dataset is as follows. The number of pairs between compound words and their individual words is 16,369,076 pairs and the average length of the compound words is 3.06 tokens. This dataset is used as the input of the RNN-based approach.

Implementation. The implementation and the details of the network training are as follows. To learn the distributed representations of words and compound words, we use the python version of word2vec[2]. Most of the parameters are set by the default. Note that, in this setting all words that appear less than 25 times are ignored. However, since we use the text corpus, in which most sequences are duplicated, as the training set, we set the words that appear less than 50 times are discarded. Also, since the dimension of vector and the length of the window size directly affect representations of words, these two parameters are varied in the experiments to investigate their effects. Furthermore, to handle the out of vocabulary problem, words that appear less than 50 times are replaces by the token "UNK".

In our RNN-based approach, we implemented the networks by using tensorflow[3]. The GRU unit is selected as the unit in the RNN model. One hidden layer network is used and a number of nodes in the hidden layer is set at 128. The Adam algorithm [10] is used as the optimization method due to its computational efficiency. The learning rate is set at 0.01. The dataset is fed as the mini-batch, whose size is 50,000 samples. We set the number of the iteration at 5,000, which is enough to reach the convergence.

5.2 Experiment 1

Experiment 1 is to investigate the improvement of compound word representations estimated by their individual words using the RNN-based approach. In this experiment, the distributed representations of compound words estimated by the RNN-based approach are compared with the average representations. The

[1] https://github.com/idio/wiki2vec.

[2] https://radimrehurek.com/gensim/models/word2vec.html.

[3] https://www.tensorflow.org/.

average representation is computed by averaging the distributed representations of all individual words in the compound words. To evaluate the improvement, the location and the direction of estimated distributed representations of compound words are considered. The idea to measure the location is that the closer the location to the actual compound word representation, the better it is, while the idea to evaluate the direction is that the more similar the angle to the actual compound word representation, the better it is. Note that the actual compound word representation is the distributed representation of the compound words as a single token, e.g. San_Francisco, learned during the word embedding process. Based on these intuitions, two evaluation metrics: (1) the proportion of the improvement of the Euclidean distance, which measures the closeness of the location, and (2) the proportion of the improvement of the cosine similarity, which measures the similarity of the direction, are defined as follows.

$$Location = \frac{\sum_{i=1}^{N} d_{Loc}(v_{w_{cp_i}}, \bar{v}_{w_{cp_i}}, \bar{\bar{v}}_{w_{cp_i}})}{N} \times 100\% \quad (11)$$

$$d_{Loc}(v_{w_{cp}}, \bar{v}_{w_{cp}}, \bar{\bar{v}}_{w_{cp}}) = \begin{cases} 1, & \text{if } \|v_{w_{cp}} - \bar{v}_{w_{cp}}\| < \|v_{w_{cp}} - \bar{\bar{v}}_{w_{cp}}\| \\ 0, & \text{otherwise} \end{cases} \quad (12)$$

$$Direction = \frac{\sum_{i=1}^{N} d_{Dir}(v_{w_{cp_i}}, \bar{v}_{w_{cp_i}}, \bar{\bar{v}}_{w_{cp_i}})}{N} \times 100\% \quad (13)$$

$$d_{Dir}(v_{w_{cp}}, \bar{v}_{w_{cp}}, \bar{\bar{v}}_{w_{cp}}) = \begin{cases} 1, & \text{if } \frac{v_{w_{cp}} \cdot \bar{v}_{w_{cp}}}{\|v_{w_{cp}}\| \|\bar{v}_{w_{cp}}\|} > \frac{v_{w_{cp}} \cdot \bar{\bar{v}}_{w_{cp}}}{\|v_{w_{cp}}\| \|\bar{\bar{v}}_{w_{cp}}\|} \\ 0, & \text{otherwise} \end{cases} \quad (14)$$

where $v_{w_{cp}}$ is the actual representation of the compound word w_{cp}, $\bar{v}_{w_{cp}}$ is the estimated representation of the compound word w_{cp} by the RNN-based approach, $\bar{\bar{v}}_{w_{cp}}$ is the average representation of the compound word w_{cp} and N is a number of compound words.

In this experiment, the dimension of vector representations and the length of window size are varied to investigate their effects because both are the major factors that directly influence the representations of compound words. For observing the effect of the dimension of vector representations, we set the dimension size at 100, 200, 300, 400 and 500, while the length of the window size is fixed at 5. For inspecting the effect of the length of the window size, we set the window size at 5,10, 15 and 20, while the dimension of vector representations is fixed at 200. Also, we conduct the experiment with CBOW and Skip-Gram in order to investigate any influence caused by the models. In the experiment, we conduct the experiment by using the 10-fold cross validation technique.

The results of this experiment are listed in Table 1. The results show that most of compound words can be better estimated by using the RNN-based approach in both location and direction aspects. Also, the results indicate that the parameters, the dimension of vector representation and the length of the window size, slightly affect the results. However, for the CBOW setting with larger length of window size, the changes are clearly observed. In this case, only around 86%–88% of compound words can better be estimated by using the RNN-based

Table 1. The results of the improvement in aspects of location and direction of estimation in Experiment 1

# Dimension	# Window size	CBOW		Skip-Gram	
		Location	Direction	Location	Direction
100	5	97.98%	96.70%	99.01%	98.61%
200	5	98.58%	97.14%	99.18%	98.76%
300	5	98.79%	97.16%	99.10%	98.60%
400	5	98.82%	96.92%	98.79%	98.08%
500	5	98.13%	94.84%	98.12%	97.00%
200	10	98.67%	96.50%	99.19%	98.77%
200	15	88.01%	59.74%	99.06%	98.60%
200	20	86.26%	58.10%	98.88%	98.30%

approach in the location aspect, while around 58%–59% of compound words can better be estimated by using the RNN-based approach in the direction aspect. Nevertheless, the improvement of the estimated representations by the RNN-based approach over average representations still can be observed. Therefore, the RNN-based approach can do better to estimate the representations of compound words than the average representation approach.

Although the RNN-based approach shows the improvement over the average representation method, to learn the RNN-based approach, the training pairs are still required. Therefore, we analyzed the number of training pairs used in the experiment to achieve the result in Table 1 by plotting the learning curve. We used 10% of the data for testing the improvement in the location and direction aspects, while the rest of the data are used as the training data. The number of training example pairs are gradually increased. To plot the learning curve, the standard parameter setting (see Footnote 2) is set. Figure 2 shows the learning curve of the RNN-based approach. The learning curve shows after the training size is larger than 10,000 pairs, more than 90% of compound words can be estimated better the aspect of location and direction by the RNN-based approach than the average method in both CBOW and Skip-Gram models.

5.3 Experiment 2

Experiment 2 is to evaluate the quality of the estimated representations of compound words by the RNN-based approach. This experiment is to further understand how much improvement of the estimated representations of the compound words we achieved. In this experiment, the experiment setting is the same as Experiment 1 and the average representation method is used as **baseline**. However, we change the evaluation method in order to observe the quality of the estimated distributed representations of compound words. We compute the cosine similarity between the estimated distributed representations of compound words

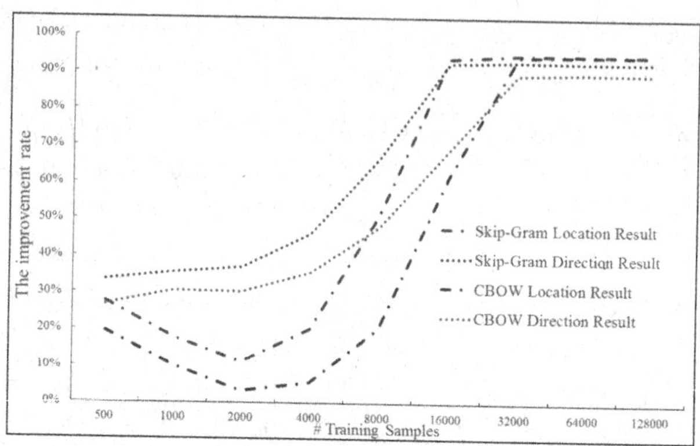

Fig. 2. Learning curve of the RNN approach by using CBOW and Skip-Gram setting with 200-dimensional vector and window size 5 in aspect of location and direction

and other word representations in the whole vocabulary. The results are ranked by their similarity score. The higher the similarity score acquire, the lower the rank is. Then, we determine the rank result of the estimated distributed representation by its pair rank. For example given the pair ("Tokyo_Station", "Tokyo" "Station"), the rank result is corresponded to the rank of "Tokyo_Station" in the rank list. In the experiment, we conduct only the ranking by the cosine similarity because many applications [9] used the cosine similarity for evaluating the similarity between representations. Since we need to compare all representations (≈968,009 words), only 1,000 pairs are sampled for testing the ranking result, while the rest are used to train the model. To measure the results, we report the mean reciprocal rank (MR), which averages the inverse of the rank and Hit@10 is the proportion of times that the rank of its pair is less than 10.

Table 2. The results of quality of the estimated representations of compound words comparing with the representations of compound words

# Dim	# Window Size	Baseline				RNN-based Approach			
		CBOW		Skip-Gram		CBOW		Skip-Gram	
		MR	Hit@10	MR	Hit@10	MR	Hit@10	MR	Hit@10
100	5	0.003	0.70%	0.001	0.10%	**0.078**	**22.42%**	0.056	15.92%
200	5	0.006	1.90%	0.002	0.10%	**0.119**	**33.63%**	0.073	21.42%
300	5	0.006	2.20%	0.002	0.40%	**0.133**	**37.54%**	0.076	22.52%
400	5	0.007	2.50%	0.002	0.40%	**0.148**	**42.24%**	0.082	24.42%
500	5	0.007	2.30%	0.002	0.20%	**0.112**	**31.23%**	0.064	17.71%
200	10	0.439	50.55%	0.785	81.48%	0.927	94.90%	**0.988**	**99.10%**
200	15	0.455	52.45%	0.767	79.78%	0.941	95.80%	**0.987**	**99.20%**
200	20	0.466	53.05%	0.784	81.58%	0.939	96.30%	**0.986**	**98.90%**

The results of this experiment are listed in Table 2. The results show that the RNN-based approach provides significant improvement of the quality of the representations than the baseline in all settings. This result confirms the hypothesis in the study [14], where representations of compound words are not simple average representations of individual words. The experimental results also indicate that the quality of the representations is robust to the length of the dimensional vector representation, while the length of the window size has significant influence. The estimated representations of compound words can be estimated better when the length of the window size becomes larger. One intuition is that the length of the window size is used to capture the long dependency of the context. Since the average length of the compound words in the **dataset** is around 3 tokens, the length of window size at 5 could not capture the whole dependency. Consequently, the quality of the estimated representations is degraded.

To further understand the representations of compound words and their estimation, the representations of compound words are projected to 2-d space by using the t-distributed stochastic neighbor embedding (t-SNE) [12]. To visualize the representations in the 2-d space, the standard parameter setting (see Footnote 2) is set. Moreover, most of the compound words are person names or location names. When plotting in the 2-d space, black color represents the compound words, which are person, while the grey color denotes the compound words, which is location as shown in Fig. 3. Figure 3 shows that the estimated representations of compound words by using the RNN-based approach are closely similar to the actual representations than using the average representation approach. Furthermore, the average representations show some ambiguity between person and location. This indicates that the average representation could falsely interpret the meaning of the compound words in the vector space.

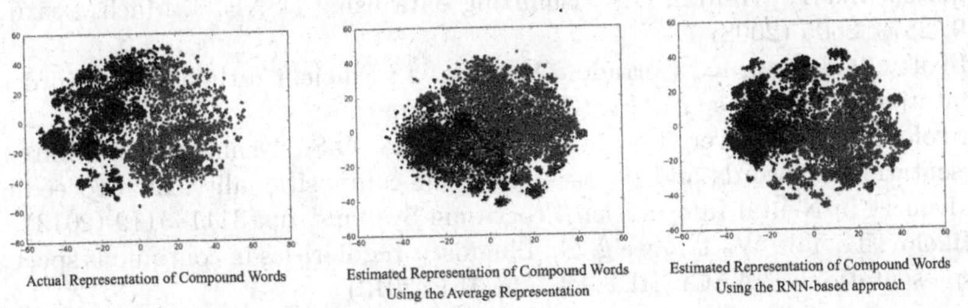

Actual Representation of Compound Words
Estimated Representation of Compound Words Using the Average Representation
Estimated Representation of Compound Words Using the RNN-based approach

Fig. 3. Scatter plot of representations of compound words by their types using CBOW with the 200-dimensional vector and the window size 5

6 Conclusion

In this paper, we introduce the RNN-based approach for estimating the representations of compound words. Based on the experimental results, we show that estimated representations by the RNN-based approach outperforms the average representations in both location and direction aspects. Also, the improvement of the quality of the estimated representations of the compound words by the RNN-based approach is greatly increased. In the future, we will further investigate semantics of estimated representations of the compound words in the analogy task and other applications.

References

1. Bengio, Y., Ducharme, R., Vincent, P., Jauvin, C.: A neural probabilistic language model. J. Mach. Learn. Res. **3**, 1137–1155 (2003)
2. Bengio, Y., Simard, P., Frasconi, P.: Learning long-term dependencies with gradient descent is difficult. IEEE Trans. Neural Netw. **5**, 157–166 (1994)
3. Chung, J., Gulcehre, C., Cho, K., Bengio, Y.: Empirical evaluation of gated recurrent neural networks on sequence modeling. In: NIPS Workshop (2014)
4. Collobert, R., Weston, J., Bottou, L., Karlen, M., Kavukcuoglu, K., Kuksa, P.: Natural language processing (almost) from scratch. J. Mach. Learn. Res. **12**, 2493–2537 (2011)
5. Dima, C., Hinrichs, E.: Automatic noun compound interpretation using deep neural networks and word embeddings. In: IWCS, p. 173 (2015)
6. Elman, J.L.: Finding structure in time. Cogn. Sci. **14**, 179–211 (1990)
7. Garten, J., Sagae, K., Ustun, V., Dehghani, M.: Combining distributed vector representations for words. In: NAACL-HLT, pp. 95–101 (2015)
8. Hochreiter, S., Schmidhuber, J.: Long short-term memory. Neural Comput. **9**, 1735–1780 (1997)
9. Kertkeidkachorn, N., Ichise, R.: T2KG: an end-to-end system for creating knowledge graph from unstructured text. In: AAAI Technical Report. AAAI Press (2017)
10. Kingma, D., Ba, J.: Adam: a method for stochastic optimization. In: ICLR (2015)
11. Le, Q.V., Mikolov, T.: Distributed representations of sentences and documents. ICML **14**, 1188–1196 (2014)
12. Maaten, L.V.D., Hinton, G.: Visualizing data using t-SNE. J. Mach. Learn. Res. **19**, 2579–2605 (2008)
13. Mikolov, T., Chen, K., Corrado, G., Dean, J.: Efficient estimation of word representations in vector space. In: ICLR (2013)
14. Mikolov, T., Sutskever, I., Chen, K., Corrado, G.S., Dean, J.: Distributed representations of words and phrases and their compositionality. In: Proceedings of Advances in Neural Information Processing Systems, pp. 3111–3119 (2013)
15. Mikolov, T., Yih, W.-T., Zweig, G.: Linguistic regularities in continuous space word representations. NAACL-HLT **13**, 746–751 (2013)
16. Pennington, J., Socher, R., Manning, C.D.: Glove: global vectors for word representation. EMNLP **14**, 1532–1543 (2014)
17. Shimaoka, S., Stenetorp, P., Inui, K., Riedel, S.: An attentive neural architecture for fine-grained entity type classification. In: AKBC (2016)
18. Socher, R., Bauer, J., Manning, C.D., Ng, A.Y.: Parsing with compositional vector grammars. In: ACL, pp. 455–465 (2013)
19. Socher, R., Perelygin, A., Wu, J.Y., Chuang, J., Manning, C.D., Ng, A.Y., Potts, C., et al.: Recursive deep models for semantic compositionality over a sentiment treebank. In: EMNLP, vol. 1631, p. 1642 (2013)

A Large-Scale CNN Ensemble for Medication Safety Analysis

Liliya Akhtyamova[1], Andrey Ignatov[2(✉)], and John Cardiff[1]

[1] Institute of Technology Tallaght, Dublin, Ireland
liliya.akhtyamova@postgrad.ittdublin.ie, john.cardiff@it-tallaght.ie
[2] ETH Zurich, Zurich, Switzerland
andrey.ignatoff@gmail.com

Abstract. Revealing Adverse Drug Reactions (ADR) is an essential part of post-marketing drug surveillance, and data from health-related forums and medical communities can be of a great significance for estimating such effects. In this paper, we propose an end-to-end CNN-based method for predicting drug safety on user comments from healthcare discussion forums. We present an architecture that is based on a vast ensemble of CNNs with varied structural parameters, where the prediction is determined by the majority vote. To evaluate the performance of the proposed solution, we present a large-scale dataset collected from a medical website that consists of over 50 thousand reviews for more than 4000 drugs. The results demonstrate that our model significantly outperforms conventional approaches and predicts medicine safety with an accuracy of 87.17% for binary and 62.88% for multi-classification tasks.

Keywords: Ensembles · Convolutional Neural Networks · Adverse Drug Reactions · Deep learning · Sentiment analysis

1 Introduction

Monitoring Adverse Drug Reactions (ADR) — unintended responses to a drug when it is used at recommended dosage levels, has a direct relationship with the public health and healthcare costs around the world. Side effects of medicines lead to 300 thousand deaths per year in the USA and Europe [1], therefore revealing adverse drug reactions is of paramount importance for the government authorities, drug manufacturers, and patients. Data from the European Medicines Agency (EMA) shows that patients are not reporting side effects adequately through official channels, making it necessary to explore some different ways of ADR monitoring.

In this case, social media provides a substantial source of information that gives unique opportunities and challenges for detecting ADR using NLP techniques. It was shown that a large population of patients are actively involved in sharing and posting health-related information in various healthcare social networks [2], and thus the latter promise to be a powerful tool for monitoring

F. Frasincar et al. (Eds.): NLDB 2017, LNCS 10260, pp. 247–253, 2017.
DOI: 10.1007/978-3-319-59569-6_29

ADR. However, the considered task still remains extremely challenging due to varying posts formats and the complexity of human language. Currently, deep neural networks have achieved impressive results on many NLP-related problems, and a particular success here have Convolutional Neural Networks. While having a large number of parameters, they demand massive datasets for efficient training, and the lack of large annotated text corpora made their application to ADR extraction task very limited. In this work, we eliminate this problem and propose an end-to-end solution for predicting drugs safety using an ensemble of CNNs.

The contributions of this paper are as follows: (i) We present a large-scale ADR extraction dataset which we make available along with this paper. (ii) We propose a CNN ensemble for tackling the problem of ADR binary and multi-classification that requires a minimal number of preprocessing steps and no hand-crafted features. (iii) Our experimental results reveal that the proposed solution significantly outperforms baseline approaches and boosts the performance of the conventional CNN-based method.

2 Related Research

The earliest work on ADR extraction was [3], where the authors investigated the potential of user comments for early detection of unknown ADR. This and the subsequent works were mainly focused on a limited number of drugs and were based on hand-designed features [4]. To tackle the problem of lack of investigation in this area some challenges were organized. One competition was Diegolab-2015, where the goal was to develop an algorithm for solving the problems of ADR classification and extraction. The teams showed competitive results on a difficult Twitter dataset, and the best performance was achieved by [5] with 59% F1-score for ADR class.

Another work contributing to the topic of ADR detection is [6], where the authors used a publicly available ADE corpus for binary medical case reports classification and achieved an F-score of 77% for documents with ADR. In [4] the authors tried to combine ADE corpus with data from social media (DailyStrength, Twitter). In a number of papers ADR detection was considered from the position of sentiment analysis. In [7] the authors extracted semantic, sentiment, and affect features from two datasets (AskaPatient and Pharma tweets) and classified them using SVM with linear kernel [8]. They split the datasets into two classes, defining ADR classification problem as a binary sentiment analysis problem, and achieved an accuracy of 78.20% and 79.73% for AskaPatient and Pharma datasets, respectively.

Though CNNs became a standard approach in many NLP-related tasks, only a few researches considered building a committee of several networks. In [9] the authors combined two separate CNNs with different architectures for the task of Twitter Sentiment Analysis. In [10] an ensemble of five CNNs was used for English to French machine translation, where it demonstrated superior results compared to a single network. In this work, we will show that larger committees can yield even better performance when a diverse set of CNNs is used.

3 Method

3.1 Input Processing

In our task, the input to the classification model has the form of a user text post **T** that is treated as an ordered sequence of words $\mathbf{T} = \{w_1, w_2, ..., w_N\}$. First, plain words are mapped to their vector representations using a pre-trained word embedding model, which in our case is word2vec. The resulting representations are stacked together to form a single sentence matrix $\mathbf{M_T}$. If the original text **T** consists of N words and the dimensionality of word embeddings is d, this results in a $d \times N$ real-valued matrix which i-th column is a vector representation of the i-th word of the sentence. This matrix is then passed to a CNN and further steps are described below.

3.2 CNN Architecture

The architecture of our baseline CNN is presented in Fig. 1. It consists of one convolutional, one pooling and two fully-connected layers. The convolutional layer contains 300 filters of size $5 \times d$, where d is the dimensionality of word embeddings or the height of the sentence matrix. The number of neurons in the fully-connected layers is 1024 and 256. We use a dropout technique in these layers with dropout rate 0.2 to avoid overfitting. The CNN is trained to minimize cross-entropy loss function which is augmented with l_2-norm regularization of CNN weights, the parameters of the network are optimized with Adam algorithm.

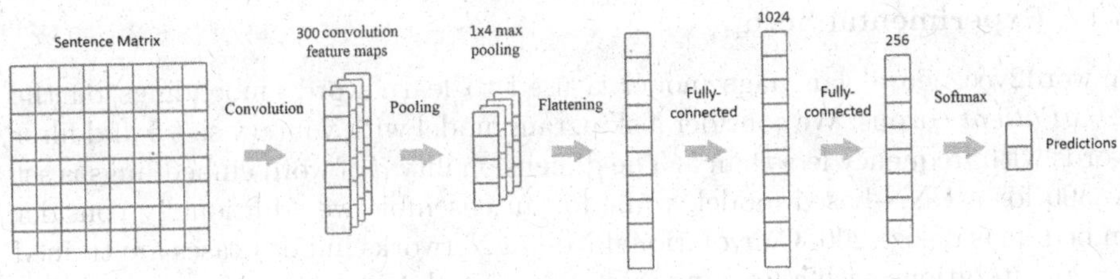

Fig. 1. The overall architecture of the proposed CNN-based model

3.3 Ensemble of CNNs

In this work we propose using a committee of up to 40 CNNs with various structural parameters that are trained on the same dataset. To guarantee the diversity of the models, we consider CNNs that have different number of convolutional filters (200–400), size of the convolutional filter (4–8) and dimension of word embeddings (200–300). The prediction of the committee is determined by a majority vote, and from the statistical viewpoint this combination of models is more powerful than a single one if sub-models are uncorrelated. If they are unbiased estimators of the true distribution, the combination will be still unbiased but with a reduced variance.

4 Dataset Construction and Preprocessing

In this paper, we present a public[1] dataset gathered from the popular health forum *AskaPatient*[2], where people share their treatment experience. Each record in this forum is left by patients and consists of the following fields: drug name, drug rating, reason for taking this medication, side effects of the medication, comments, sex, age, duration and dosage, date added. User ratings are ranged from 1 to 5. In total *AskaPatient* database contains 59912 publicly available reviews for about 4K drugs left during the last 5 years.

We consider the following two problems:

- *Binary ADR classification:* reviews with ratings 1–2 are labeled as negative (since they correspond to negative side-effects and contain ADR mention) and reviews with ratings 4–5 are labeled as positive (can be presumed as a positive medication experience). Posts with rating 3 are ignored as not truly positive, negative or neutral [7].
- *Multi-class ADR classification:* we predict all five classes listed in user ratings

Since different medical forums may not contain other fields except for explicit user comments, we use only this field in our experiments to make our system more general. We use 80% of the dataset for training and 20% for testing the model. The same proportion of train/test data is utilized for each class.

5 Experiments

5.1 Experimental Setup

A word2vec neural language model is used to learn word embeddings on the *AskaPatient* corpus. We consider a skipgram model with window size 5 and filter words with frequency less than 5. The dimensionality d of word embeddings is set to 300 for a CNN-based model, while for an ensemble we additionally consider embeddings of size 200. Convolutional Neural Networks in both cases are trained for 20K iterations with a learning rate of 5e$-$4 and l_2-regularization set to 1e$-$2.

To establish some baseline results on the presented dataset we have additionally implemented two algorithms commonly used in NLP. The first one is based on the *bag-of-words* model that takes into account only the multiplicity of the appearing words, regarding neither the word order nor grammar. The text in this model is represented by a single vector with values indicating the number of occurrences of each vocabulary word in the text. To classify the obtained vectors we use Logistic Regression and Random Forest classifiers. The second model is based on *averaged word embeddings* – instead of stacking the produced embeddings into a sentence matrix, their averaging is performed to obtain one vector of size d that is further classified using the same algorithms. We use 500 trees for Random Forest and regularization term $C = 0.01$ for Logistic Regression.

[1] Please email the authors to get access to the dataset.

[2] askapatient.com.

5.2 Results and Discussion

The summary results for our experiments are presented in Tables 1 and 2 for binary and multi-classification tasks respectively. These tables specify the predictive accuracy associated with each class of ADR for both baseline and proposed methods. As one can see, the basic CNN-based model demonstrates a notably stronger performance compared to the baseline approaches and reaches an accuracy of 85.05% and 59.11% on binary and multi-classification tasks accordingly. Using a proposed committee of 40 CNNs dramatically improves the results, outperforming a single CNN by over 2% and 3.5% of accuracy on both tasks.

Table 1. Classification results for the binary classification problem

Method	ADR accuracy %	Non-ADR accuracy %	Overall accuracy %
Avg. embeddings + Logistic Reg	74.11	76.41	75.29
Bag-of-words + Logistic Reg	75.33	77.07	76.22
Avg. embeddings + Random Forest	76.29	85.13	80.82
Bag-of-words + Random Forest	77.94	**85.19**	81.65
Single CNN	85.15	84.96	85.05
Ensemble of 20 CNNs	**89.38**	84.92	**87.17**

Table 2. Classification results for the multi-classification problem

Method	Class 1	Class 2	Class 3	Class 4	Class 5	Overall %
Avg. embeddings + Logistic Reg	79.07	2.99	22.67	16.94	57.87	43.79
Bag-of-words + Logistic Reg	73.56	7.95	24.70	28.24	56.51	45.60
Bag-of-words + Random Forest	72.26	13.22	28.17	31.63	67.37	49.59
Avg. embeddings + Random Forest	81.49	26.44	33.93	35.94	**74.09**	57.85
Single CNN	78.72	38.03	42.79	**52.34**	63.04	59.11
Ensemble of 40 CNNs	**83.86**	**38.08**	**49.25**	50.85	69.18	**62.88**

Figure 2 shows the dependency between the number of CNNs in the ensemble and its accuracy. First, the overall performance of ensemble grows as the number

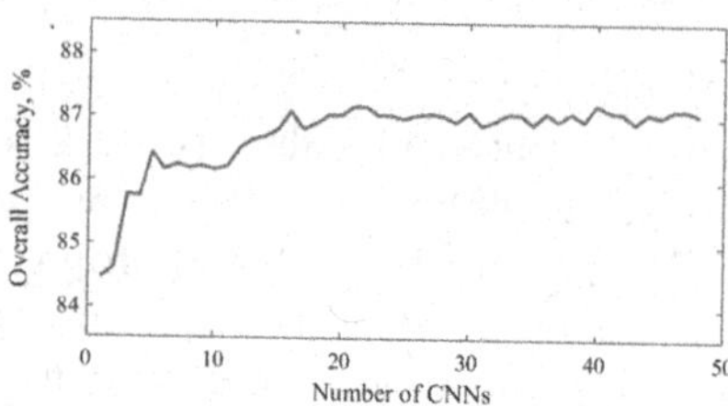

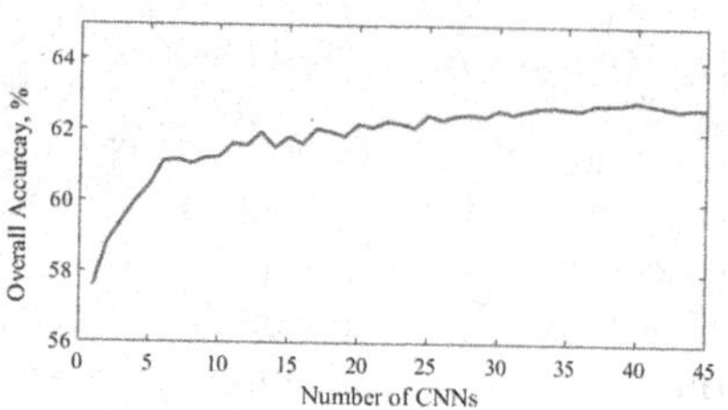

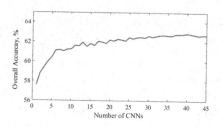

Fig. 2. Dependency between the number of CNNs in ensemble and its total accuracy for the binary [left] and multi-classification [right] problems

of CNNs increases, but then stabilizes at the threshold that is roughly equal to 20 CNNs for binary and 40 CNNs for multi-classification tasks; after this points we observe only slight fluctuations of the results.

The excellent performance of this model presumes that the proposed framework can facilitate enhanced detection of adverse drug events, with both better event recall and timelier identification. While tested in the context of adverse drug events, the framework is general to be applied to datasets from other domains, particularly when working with social media where the data volume is colossal and numerous sources of information exist. In such tasks it may significantly reduce annotation time and expenses.

6 Conclusion and Future Work

In this paper, we presented a large-scale ADR corpus crawled from a medical health forum. The corpus includes comments on drugs, user ratings and a number of other categories than can be used for a predictive model construction. We proposed an end-to-end solution that is based on a large ensemble of Convolutional Neural Networks, that in contrast to many previous works does not require any handcrafted features and data preprocessing. Our experimental findings show that the proposed model significantly outperforms baseline methods and introduces a large improvement to the standard CNN-based method.

We see several ways for the improvement of the existing solution. First of all, a wider set of models can be included in ensemble, particularly it can be reasonable to add Recurrent Neural Networks to the consideration. Secondly, a more sophisticated way of building a committee can be used, for instance bagging or boosting of the CNNs. Finally, we are planning to augment the existing dataset with data from other pharmaceutical forums and websites to create a reacher set of ADR mentions.

References

1. Businaro, R.: Why we need an efficient and careful pharmacovigilance? J. Pharmacovigil. **01**(04), (2013)

2. Chou, W.Y.S., Hunt, Y.M., Beckjord, E.B., Moser, R.P., Hesse, B.W.: Social media use in the United States: implications for health communication. J. Med. Internet Res. **11**(4), e48 (2009)
3. Leaman, R., Wojtulewicz, L., Sullivan, R., Skariah, A., Yang, J., Gonzalez, G.: Towards internet-age pharmacovigilance: extracting adverse drug reactions from user posts to health-related social networks. In: Proceedings of the 2010 Workshop on Biomedical Natural Language Processing, pp. 117–125. Association for Computational Linguistics (2010)
4. Sarker, A., Ginn, R., Nikfarjam, A., O'connor, K., Smith, K., Jayaraman, S., Gonzalez, G.: Utilizing social media data for pharmacovigilance: a review HHS public access. J. Biomed. Inform. **54**, 202–212 (2015)
5. Sarker, A., O'Connor, K., Ginn, R., Scotch, M., Smith, K., Malone, D., Gonzalez, G.: Social media mining for toxicovigilance: automatic monitoring of prescription medication abuse from twitter. Drug Saf. **39**(3), 231–240 (2016)
6. Gurulingappa, H., Mateen-Rajput, A., Toldo, L.: Extraction of potential adverse drug events from medical case reports. J. Biomed. Semant. **3**(1), 15 (2012)
7. Sharif, H., Zaffar, F., Abbasi, A., Zimbra, D.: Detecting adverse drug reactions using a sentiment classification framework. In: Proceedings of the Sixth ASE International Conference on Social Computing (SocialCom) (2014)
8. Joachims, T.: Thorsten: training linear SVMs in linear time. In: Proceedings of the 12th ACM SIGKDD International Conference on Knowledge Discovery and Data Mining-KDD 2006, New York, USA, p. 217. ACM Press, New York (2006)
9. Deriu, J., Gonzenbach, M., Uzdilli, F., Lucchi, A., Luca, V.D., Jaggi, M.: Swisscheese at semeval-2016 task 4: sentiment classification using an ensemble of convolutional neural networks with distant supervision. In: Proceedings of the 10th International Workshop on Semantic Evaluation, pp. 1124–1128 (2016)
10. Sutskever, I., Vinyals, O., Le, Q.V.: Sequence to sequence learning with neural networks. In: Ghahramani, Z., Welling, M., Cortes, C., Lawrence, N.D., Weinberger, K.Q., eds. Advances in Neural Information Processing Systems 27, pp. 3104–3112. Curran Associates, Inc. (2014)

A Feature Based Simple Machine Learning Approach with Word Embeddings to Named Entity Recognition on Tweets

Mete Taşpınar[1(✉)], Murat Can Ganiz[2], and Tankut Acarman[1]

[1] Department of Computer Engineering, Galatasaray University, Istanbul, Turkey
mtaspinar@ogr.gsu.edu.tr, tacarman@gsu.edu.tr
[2] Department of Computer Engineering, Marmara University, Istanbul, Turkey
murat.ganiz@marmara.edu.tr

Abstract. Named Entity Recognition (NER) is a well-studied domain in Natural Language Processing. Traditional NER systems, such as Stanford NER system, achieve high performance with formal and grammatically well-structured texts. However, when these systems are applied to informal and noisy texts, which have mixed language with emoticons or abbreviations, there is a significant degradation in results. We attempt to fill this gap by developing a NER system with using novel term features including Word2vec based features and machine learning based classifier. We describe the features and Word2Vec implementation used in our solution and report the results obtained by our system. The system is quite efficient and scalable in terms of classification time complexity and shows promising results which can be potentially improved with larger training sets or with the use of semi-supervised classifiers.

Keywords: Named entity recognition · Word2Vec · Word embeddings · Classification · Machine learning

1 Introduction

Extracting meaningful information from social media platforms becomes more important with ever increasing amount of available data. There are several challenges in mining microblog texts such as tweets. The enormous amount of noisy data involving abbreviations, typing errors, and special characters to indicate special terms such as hashtags or mentions makes extracting operations difficult. Due to these challenges, existing NER systems [2–6, 8, 11, 13, 14] usually do not perform well on these domains. In this study, we present a simple yet effective machine learning based classifier using some novel features including word embeddings based features for identifying different classes of named entities in tweets. In order to evaluate our approach, we use the NEEL dataset [1] for our experimental study and we evaluate our results with respect to the studies [2–4] published in NEEL 2016 Challenge. We conduct several experiments with different subsets of the features. We illustrate that the addition of word embedding features considerably increases the accuracy, and a simple machine learning classifier with word embedding features can compete with more

F. Frasincar et al. (Eds.): NLDB 2017, LNCS 10260, pp. 254–259, 2017.
DOI: 10.1007/978-3-319-59569-6_30

complicated methods such as Conditional Random Fields (CRF). The impact of this study and usability of the results is crucial for several reasons. Firstly, more advanced classifiers; possibly ensemble learning and semi-supervised approaches can be applied to improve the achieved performance. Secondly, use of machine learning based classification algorithms such as Support Vector Machines (SVM) and word embeddings algorithms such as Word2Vec [18, 19] will allow to develop highly scalable and distributed models versus the traditional models used in this domain such as CRFs. They scale well especially with the increasing amount of training set.

2 Related Work

A special Twitter implementation of GATE Natural Language Processing (NLP) framework abbreviated as TwitIE is presented in [2]. GATE NLP is based on Stanford NER classifier and uses CRF model. In [3], a feature based approach performing Stanford NER is described and ARK is used for part-of-speech (POS) tagging. Several features such as length of the mention and when the mention is capitalized are trained with the supervised classifiers such as Random Forest, Naive Bayes, k-nearest neighbour and Support Vector Machines (SVM). The standard NER system implementations such as Stanford NER, MITIE, twitter_nlp and TwitIE are studied in [4]. The dataset is trained for MITIE.

For Turkish tweets the NER software of European Media Monitor (EMM) is used in [5, 6]. 3 different Turkish datasets including tweets, a speech-to-text interface and the data taken from a Turkish hardware forum are applied to a machine learning algorithm named CRFs [6–8]. For Spanish formal documents, a rule based approach is applied in [9, 10] an unsupervised feature generation is shown to improve the stand-alone performance of the process NER. In [11], the Stanford NER system performance metric F1 is improved by 25% by re-building the part-of-speech, and chunking jobs.

3 Implementation and Feature Set

We are particularly focused on NER to present a simple, feature based machine learning approach with additional word embedding features for identifying different classes of named entities in tweets. The features used in this study are as follows; StartCapital (whether the term is capitalized or not), AllCapital (If the term is all uppercase), Hashtag (If the term starts with the letter '#'), Mention (If the term starts with the letter '@'), POS (Part-of-Speech Tag of the term), Length (number of characters in the word), VowelRatio (The ratio of number consonant over the number of vowels in the word) and SimClassCentroid[i] (Cosine Similarity between term's Word2Vec vector to the centroid Word2Vec vector of class i).

We employ a 3-term wide sliding window approach in extracting features. We use Stanford POS Tagger with 36-tag tagset. Additionally, we use Word2Vec algorithm to create vector space representations of each term in the training set. Word2vec is trained by a fairly large corpus, consist of 400 million tweets [15]. We compute class centroid vectors by averaging the term vectors belonging to a particular named entity class.

For each term in the dataset, cosine similarity to each class centroid is calculated. These are used as additional features.

4 Experimental Study

For training and testing purposes, we use the NEEL 2016 twitter dataset provided by [1]. We use Python programming language with gensim library [16] for executing word2vec as an underlying word embeddings algorithm and scikit-learn library [17] for training and testing classifiers. We use the following off-the-shelf supervised classification algorithms from scikit-learn toolkit in our experimental study: Logistic Regression, Support Vector Machine, KNeighborsClassifier (k-NN), MultinomialNB, BernoulliNB, ExtraTreeClassifier and DecisionTreeClassifier.

We conduct several experiments using different subsets of the feature set and the entity types. The dataset is annotated with seven entity types: Person, Thing, Organization, Location, Product, Event and Character. The 5 features that we extracted are StartCapital, AllCapital, Hashtag, Mention, POS (Part-of-Speech) Tag, the other features that we try did not generate good scores. We have also 7 additional word2vec based features, one for each named entity class. Evaluation results with 7 NER types and different subsets of features are given through Tables 1 to 3. In Table 1, 5 features and 7 NER types are used. A precision of 0.55 is reached and F1 is reached at level 0.49 when we use ExtraTreeClassifier algorithm. In Table 2, 7 word2vec features and 7 NER types are used and KNeighboursClassifier reaches at 0.70 precision and 0.57 F1. Combination of 5 features and 7 word2vec features slightly increases precision at 0.71 and F1 at 0.58 using Logistic Regression algorithm.

Table 1. Experiment results with 5 features and 7 NER types.

	Precision	Recall	F1	F1 (Micro avg)
Logistic Regression	0.27	0.25	0.24	0.25
SVM	0.52	0.44	0.48	0.44
ExtraTreeClassifier	**0.55**	**0.46**	**0.49**	**0.46**

We also evaluate both of 5 features and 7 word2vec features with an additional class of 'NoType', which means that a term is not a named entity. Due to the nature of natural language, an overwhelming majority of the terms in tweets are not named entities. This leads to a highly-skewed class distribution where NoType class dominates with 86%. On this dataset, two models, ExtreTreeClassifier with 5 features and Logistic Regression with 5 features +7 word2vec features can reach only 0.88 F1.

In order to get a detailed look of the results of our best performing model (Logistic Regression, 5 features +7 word2vec features, 7 NER classes), we provide confusion matrix and class based evaluation metrics. As given in Table 4, majority of the instances belong to Person and Product class (238 entities for each. We can see that "Organization" is the most confused named entity class by our models. We see from the first column that majority of the "Organization" entities (57 out of 122) are

Table 2. Experiment results with 7 word2vec features and 7 NER types.

	Precision	Recall	F1	F1 (Micro avg)
Logistic Regression	0.65	0.55	0.52	0.55
SVM	0.66	0.58	0.55	0.58
k-NN	**0.70**	**0.58**	**0.57**	**0.58**
ExtraTreeClassifier	0.58	0.52	0.49	0.52

Table 3. Experiment Results with 5 features +7 word2vec features and 7 NER Types.

	Precision	Recall	F1	F1 (Micro avg)
Logistic Regression	**0.71**	**0.56**	**0.58**	**0.56**
SVC (Support Vector Classifier)	0.63	0.56	0.58	0.56
KNeighborsClassifier	0.56	0.50	0.50	0.50
ExtraTreeClassifier()	0.54	0.51	0.49	0.51

Table 4. Confusion matrix of Logistic Regression, 5 features +7 word2vec features, 7 NER classes.

NER type	Person	Thing	Organization	Location	Product	Event	Character
Person	**209**	17	4	0	2	6	0
Thing	0	**21**	1	0	1	6	0
Org.	57	12	**37**	1	4	11	1
Location	7	2	0	**15**	0	1	0
Product	4	3	8	0	**94**	129	0
Event	0	3	2	0	0	**11**	0
Character	15	1	7	0	3	1	**0**

misclassified as "Person". Overall, the majority of the misclassifications are accumulated at the first column.

We compare our results with the three studies in the NEEL 2016 workshop [1] in Table 5. Our results are higher in comparison with respect to the algorithms using TwitIE, Stanford NER, MITIE and twitter_nlp in [2, 4]. And precision is reached at the same level in [3] using feature-based approach.

Table 5. Comparison of the performance with respect to the studies presented in NEEL 2016 workshop [1].

Study	Precision	Recall	F1
A feature based approach performing Stanford NER, [3]	0.729	0.626	0.674
Stanford NER, MITIE, twitter_nlp and TwitIE, [4]	0.587	0.287	0.386
TwitIE (CRF Model), [2]	0.435	0.459	0.447
Our approach (Logistic Regression, 5 features +7 word2vec features, 7 NER classes)	0.71	0.56	0.58

5 Conclusions

Our approach is based on extracting Tweet specific syntactic features along with word embeddings, in particular Word2Vec [18, 19] based semantic features and using them in machine learning based classifiers. Experimental results show that our system can outperform two of the three studies in the NEEL 2016 workshop [1] (please see Table 5) in terms of F1 metric and present close precision performance level (0.71 versus 0.729) while comparing with respect to the best performing study (see for instance, [3]), although the training set size is quite limited. One important advantage of our approach is the low training time complexity and scalability. In the future work, we are planning to use more advanced classifiers; possibly ensemble learning and semi-supervised approaches to improve classification performance.

Acknowledgements. The co-authors Mete Taşpınar and Murat Can Ganiz would like to thank Buğse Erdoğan and Fahriye Gün from Marmara University @BIGDaTA_Lab for their help. This work is supported in part by Marmara University BAP D type project.

References

1. Rizzo, G., van Erp, M., Plu, J., Troncy, R.: Making sense of Microposts (#Microposts2016) Named Entity rEcognition and Linking (NEEL) Challenge. In: 6th Workshop on Making Sense of Microposts (#Microposts2016), pp. 50–59 (2016)
2. Torres-Tramon, P., Hromic, H., Walsh, B., Heravi, B., Hayes, C.: Kanopy4Tweets: entity extraction and linking for twitter. In: 6th International Workshop on Making Sense of Microposts (#Microposts) (2016)
3. Ghosh, S., Maitra, P., Das, D.: Feature based approach to named entity recognition and linking for tweets. In: 6th International Workshop on Making Sense of Microposts (#Microposts) (2016)
4. Greenfield, K., Caceres, R., Coury, M., Geyer, K., Gwon, Y., Matterer, J., Mensch, A., Sahin, C., Simek, O.: A reverse approach to named entity extraction and linking in Microposts. In: 6th International Workshop on Making Sense of Microposts (2016)
5. Kucuk, D., Jacquet, G., Steinberger, R.: Named entity recognition on Turkish tweets. In: Proceedings of the Language Resources and Evaluation Conference (2014)
6. Celikkaya, G., Torunoglu, D., Eryigit, G.: Named entity recognition on real data: a preliminary investigation for Turkish. In: Proceedings of the 7th International Conference on Application of Information and Communication Technologies (2013)
7. Şeker, G.A., Eryiğit, G.: Initial explorations on using CRFs for Turkish named entity recognition. In: Proceedings of the 24th International Conference on Computational Linguistics, COLING 2012, Mumbai, India (2012)
8. Eken, B., Cüneyd Tantug, A.: Recognizing named entities in Turkish tweets. In: Proceedings of the Fourth International Conference on Software Engineering and Applications, Dubai, UAE, January 2015
9. Moreno, I., Moreda, P., Romá-Ferri, M.T.: MaNER: a MedicAl named entity recogniser. In: Biemann, C., Handschuh, S., Freitas, A., Meziane, F., Métais, E. (eds.) NLDB 2015. LNCS, vol. 9103, pp. 418–423. Springer, Cham (2015). doi:10.1007/978-3-319-19581-0_40

10. Moreno, I., Moreda, P., Romá-Ferri, M.T.: An active ingredients entity recogniser system based on profiles. In: Métais, E., Meziane, F., Saraee, M., Sugumaran, V., Vadera, S. (eds.) NLDB 2016. LNCS, vol. 9612, pp. 276–284. Springer, Cham (2016). doi:10.1007/978-3-319-41754-7_25
11. Riiter, A., Clark, S., Etzioni, M., Etzioni, O.: Named entity recognition in tweets: an experimental study. In: Proceedings of the 2011 Conference on Empirical Methods in Natural Language Processing, Edinburgh, Scotland, UK, 27–31 July 2011
12. Siencnik, S.: Adapting word2vec to named entity recognition. In: Proceedings of the 20th Nordic Conference of Computational Linguistics NODALIDA (2015)
13. Kucuk, D., Steinberger, R.: Experiments to improve named entity recognition on Turkish tweets. In: Proceedings of the 5th Workshop on Language Analysis for Social Media (LASM) @ EACL 2014, Gothenburg, Sweden, 26–30 April 2014, pp. 71–78 (2014)
14. Ek, T., Kirkegaard, C., Jonsson, H., Nugues, P.: Named entity recognition for short text messages. Procedia-Soc. Behav. Sci. **27**, 178–187 (2011)
15. Godin, F., Vandersmissen, B., De Neve, W., Van de Walle, R.: Named entity recognition for twitter microposts using distributed word representations. In: ACL-IJCNLP 2015, pp. 146–153 (2015)
16. https://pypi.python.org/pypi/gensim
17. http://scikit-learn.org/stable/index.html
18. Mikolov, T., Chen, K., Corrado, G., Dean, J.: Efficient estimation of word representations in vector space. In: ICLR Workshop (2013)
19. Mikolov, T., Yih, W.-T., Zweig, G.: Linguistic regularities in continuous space word representations. In: Proceedings of NAACL HLT (2013)

Challenges and Solutions with Alignment and Enrichment of Word Embedding Models

Cem Şafak Şahin(✉), Rajmonda S. Caceres, Brandon Oselio, and William M. Campbell

MIT Lincoln Laboratory, Lexington, MA, USA
{cem.sahin,rajmonda.caceres,brandon.oselio,wcampbell}@ll.mit.edu

Abstract. Word embedding models offer continuous vector representations that can capture rich semantics of word co-occurrence patterns. Although these models have improved the state-of-the-art on a number of NLP tasks, many open research questions remain. We study the semantic consistency and alignment of these models and show that their local properties are sensitive to even slight variations in the training datasets and parameters. We propose a solution that improves alignment of different word embedding models by leveraging carefully generated synthetic data points. Our approach leads to substantial improvements in recovering consistent and richer embeddings of local semantics.

Keywords: Word embedding · Manifold alignment · Neural network models · Dimensionality reduction

1 Introduction

Recently there has been a growing interest in continuous vector representations of linguistic entities, most often referred to as embeddings. This includes techniques relying on matrix factorization [8], as well as popular neural network methods [5, 10, 11]. These embeddings are able to capture complex semantic patterns and have shown remarkable performance improvements across various NLP tasks.

Nonetheless, continuous word representations are not well understood and evaluations of them are still nascent. Existing work has focused primarily on qualitative analysis of word similarities and semantics captured by word embeddings [4, 10]. Recent work has also considered evaluating the quality against a gold standard human-generated representation or through crowdsourcing [13, 14]. However, it is very challenging and expensive to generate comprehensive gold standard datasets capturing the variety and richness of linguistic properties.

This work was sponsored by the Defense Advanced Research Projects Agency under Air Force Contract FA8721-05-C-0002. Opinions, interpretations, conclusions, and recommendations are those of the authors and are not necessarily endorsed by the United States Government.

F. Frasincar et al. (Eds.): NLDB 2017, LNCS 10260, pp. 260–266, 2017.
DOI: 10.1007/978-3-319-59569-6_31

While word embedding models are observed to improve with more training data, overcoming the bias of the initial training dataset and incorporating new semantic knowledge requires large amounts of new training data. It is more often the case, that large training datasets are not easy to acquire due to reasons of privacy or limited access (with few exceptions such as companies like Google or Amazon that own the data). It is therefore desirable to be able to fuse the semantics captured by different *incomplete* word embedding models into richer and common representations. Manifold alignment techniques have a rich history of addressing similar challenges within the domain adaptation and transfer learning research areas [16,17], but they have primarily been applied to data sources such as images, and genomic data. In [15] manifold alignment techniques are used to discover textual logical relationships in supervised settings. We believe that there is a great opportunity to further leverage the same techniques in unsupervised settings. However, it is not clear if these techniques will easily translate to alignment of continuous vector spaces when labels are not available.

Herein we first discuss some fundamental limitations of word representations in their ability to be embedded and aligned in lower-dimensional space. We show effects of the curse of dimensionality and demonstrate that manifold learning techniques, commonly applied in other problem settings to reduce such effects, are not consistent in preserving local semantic structure. Our second contribution consists of an approach that overcomes some of the effects of artificial high dimensionality by leveraging synthetically generated neighboring points, or as we refer to them, *latent words*. Inspired by the surprising insight that in high dimensional space, semantically similar words relate to one another via simple linear operations [3,10,11], we conjecture that unseen words and word co-occurrences in the training datasets can be imputed in high dimensional space via simple local linear functions. Data imputation has been successfully used in traditional statistical analysis of incomplete datasets to improve learning and inference. The application of this concept however to improve the quality of word embedding representations is novel. Local densification of word point clouds allows us to take much better advantage of manifold embedding and alignment techniques. Additionally, we can fuse and enrich word embedding models without the need of model retraining and access to more training data.

2 Our Approach: Local Enrichment via *Latent* Words

To motivate our approach, we first highlight experimental results from our work in [12] which shows that word embedding models generate locally unstable representations. The experiment analyzes the changes in the local neighborhood of selected words across different re-runs of the same model. Even when we strategically pick more frequent words, or increase the neighborhood size, we observe that no more than about 60% of the neighborhood stays the same across the different model re-runs. Herein, our approach for embedding and aligning distributed word models is presented. Let us start by defining some necessary notation. Assume that we are given a set of word embedding models, $W^i|_{i\in[1,k]}$, where k is the total number of models. These models are different for various reasons, such as different training datasets, different learning objectives, or different random initializations of the same model. In addition, the size of vector representations may not be the same for all models. The vocabulary of W^i is denoted by V^i. $\mathbb{V}$ is a set of all vocabularies such that $\mathbb{V} = \cup_{i=1}^{k} V^i$. A word l in V^i is shown as w_l^i such that $W^i(w_l^i) \rightarrow \mathbb{R}^m$, and m is the size of the latent space. We use $[x_{l1}^i, \cdots, x_{lm}^i]$ to show the continuous vector representation of w_l^i. Let $d(.,.)$ represent the similarity function between two vector representations. We illustrate using the cosine similarity measure, defined by $d(w_l^i, w_m^i) = \frac{\vec{w}_l^i \cdot \vec{w}_m^i}{||w_l^i|| |w_m^i|}$. Since, input co-occurrence frequencies are normalized, we expect similar results if we used Euclidean distance instead. Let $n_\epsilon^i|_{w_l^i}$ be a set of words that fall in the ϵ-neighborhood of a word w_l^i, such that $n_\epsilon^i|_{w_l^i} = \{w_m^i | d(w_m^i, w_l^i) < \epsilon, w_l^i, w_m^i \in V^i\}$.

Assume that the word embedding representation lies on an underlying manifold and that this manifold is locally continuous, linear and smooth. We then leverage the property of these models to express linguistic relationships via simple linear operations. As illustrated in [11], if x, y and z are vector representations of *king*, *woman*, and *man*, respectively, then *queen* can be extrapolated by a simple linear combination of these vectors $x + y - z$. In addition to analogies, other linguistic inductive tasks such as *series completion* and *classification* can also be solved with vector operations on word embeddings [3,7].

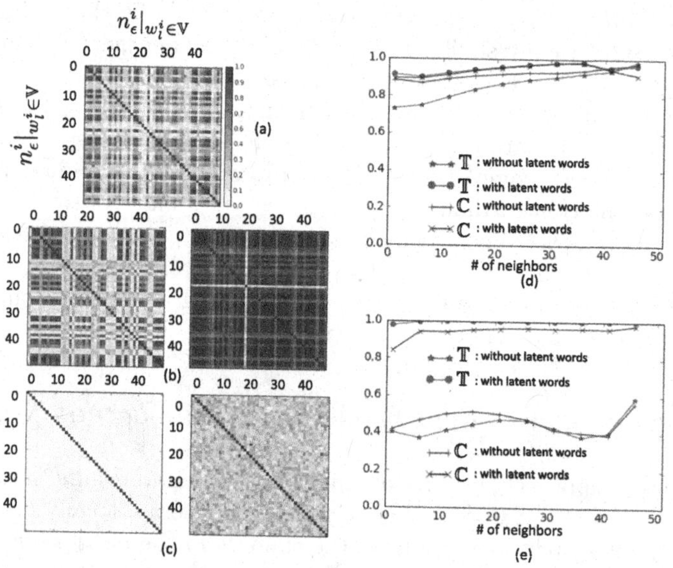

Fig. 1. $d(.,.)$ (dark green is better) for the most common word and its ϵ-neighborhood (a): embedding model in R^{200}, (b): PCA applied without (left) and with (right) latent words mapped to R^{50} and (c): LLE LLE applied without (left) and with (right) latent words mapped to R^{50}; $\mathbb{T}$ and $\mathbb{C}$ (larger numbers are better) for (d): PCA and (e): LLE. (Color figure online)

Inspired by these insights, we surmise that words can be added/subtracted to recover unobserved words. Even though, we don't have the exact generative model for semantically similar unobserved words, we assume they occur nearby the observed words and this gives us a mechanism for densifying the original neighborhoods. A latent word is generated by linear operations on the original words within an ϵ-neighborhood and is only included if it falls within this neighborhood. A latent word w_*^i can be generated by $w_*^i = \sum(\alpha_n \times w_{r_n}^i)$, where α_n is a randomly chosen integer from $[-1, +1]$ and $w_{r_n}^i \in n_\epsilon^i|_{w_l^i}$. Note that w_*^i is a valid latent word if and only if $d(w_l^i, w_*^i) < \epsilon$. These latent points are only leveraged as anchor points to help improve dimensionality reduction and alignment of the original embedding models. Furthermore, we only measure the quality of embedding and alignment with respect to only the original input words.

3 Experimental Setup and Results

We analyze the effects of local sample densification on the quality of lower-dimension embeddings and cross-model alignment using the Wikipedia dataset [1], given in [12]. We first analyze the effects of adding latent words on the quality of dimensionality reduction by using two different techniques, PCA and LLE [6].

Figure 1(a) shows pairwise distances between words in the neighborhood of the most frequent word w_l^i. Figure 1(b) shows what happens to these pairwise similarities when projected in R^{50} by PCA. On the right, we only use the original neighborhood to perform the embedding, while on the left, we have added 200 latent words. We picked what we considered to be a sufficient number of latent words based on the number of original words (50) and the dimensionality of the original space (R^{200}). We leave the rigorous analysis of the upper and lower bounds on the number of latent points for future work. We observe a stark increase of within-neighborhood pairwise similarities, indicating a much more tightly-knit neighborhood representation. Figure 1(c) shows similar results for LLE without (left) and with (right) latent words. LLE has its own local neighborhood parameter (10 neighbors in this example). LLE struggles with finding a good lower embedding when only the original data points are used, but as we show here, the addition of latent points, greatly improves its performance.

Next we discuss the quality of aligning two different models in low-dimension. As discussed previously, one of our goals is to align and fuse corresponding local neighborhoods from multiple models. Figure 1(d) and (e) demonstrate our approach can assist with stabilizing and aligning models much better. We consider two metrics to evaluate the quality of lower-dimensional embeddings: (i) trustworthiness ($\mathbb{T}$), which measures the ratio of nearest neighbors in the high-dimensional neighborhood that carries over in low dimension and (ii) continuity ($\mathbb{C}$), which measures the ratio of nearest neighbors in the high-dimensional neighborhood that are missing in low dimension (refer to [9] for exact formulas of these measures). As shown in Fig. 1(d), these metrics are really close with and without latent words for PCA. However, substantial performance improvements due to addition of latent words are observed for LLE, where $\mathbb{T}$ and $\mathbb{C}$ values are more than two times better when latent words are included (Fig. 1(e)).

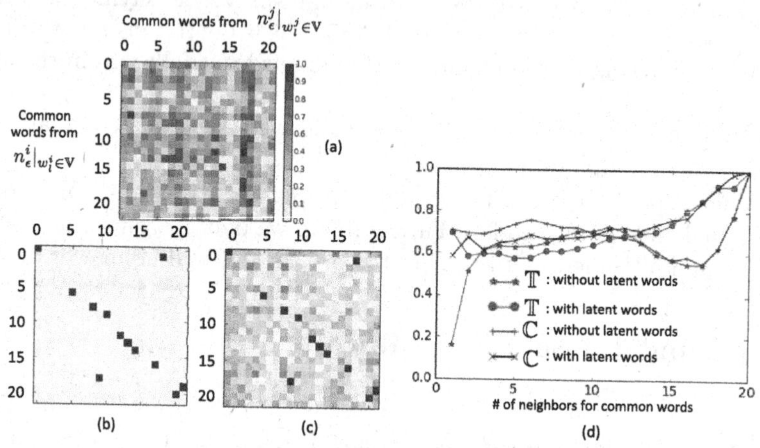

Fig. 2. $d(.,.)$ for common words in two models W^i, W^j, (a): R^{200}, (b): LRA applied without latent words to map to R^{50} and (c): LRA applied with 200 latent words mapped to R^{50} and (d): $\mathbb{T}$ and $\mathbb{C}$ for common words in $n^i_\epsilon|_{w^i_l}$ and $n^j_\epsilon|_{w^j_l}$ after finding a joint union manifold in R^{50} (larger numbers are better). (Color figure online)

Figure 2(a) presents pairwise distances between common words for $n^i_\epsilon|_{w^i_l}$ and $n^j_\epsilon|_{w^j_l}$ in two model instances, W^i and W^j. Note, however, that even though the most common words for W^i and W^j are the same, their continuous vector representations are different. Since, we are performing manifold alignment, we illustrate via a successful alignment technique, the low rank alignment (LRA) [2], which is an extension of LLE. Before alignment, the common words in $n^i_\epsilon|_{w^i_l}$ and $n^j_\epsilon|_{w^j_l}$ do not have any similarity since the diagonal is not dark green as shown in Fig. 2(a). Figure 2(b) shows $d(.,.)$ on a joint low-dimensional space where no latent words are used. The common words are mostly aligned (dark green points on diagonal), but the similarity between different word pairs is lost. When we add 200 latent words, we observe improvements in $d(.,.)$ as shown in Fig. 2(c). However, unlike the case of embedding one single model, in the case of aligning two models, the improvement of similarity scores is not uniform across all the common words in the two neighborhoods. $\mathbb{T}$ and $\mathbb{C}$ values are also analyzed for $n^i_\epsilon|_{w^i_l} \cap n^j_\epsilon|_{w^j_l}$ as presented in Fig. 2(d). These metrics are slightly better for our approach for up to 12 neighbors. Beyond this point, the addition of latent words causes considerable improvement in the alignment performance.

Lastly, we have illustrated how we can stabilize and improve the dimensionality reduction and alignment of continuous word models using the most frequent words (or common words), but we have observed similar behavior when we pick less frequent words or fewer common words across different models. We leave the careful characterization of word frequency affects and sufficiency of anchor points in different models for future work.

4 Conclusion

Although continuous word representations have been remarkably useful across various NLP tasks, characterization and careful evaluation of these representations are still nascent. In this paper, we present some fundamental limitations of word representations when it comes to their ability to be embedded and aligned in a lower-dimensional space. In order to overcome these limitations, we propose to leverage artificially created *latent* words, generated by local linear combinations of coordinates of original words. We evaluate the performance of mapping an embedding model from a high- to lower-dimensional space and show that adding latent words improves the quality of representation. We also leverage the injection of latent words to achieve better alignment of two embedding models.

Our tailored manifold alignment approach offers a platform for fusing different word embedding models and generating richer semantic representations. In this paper, we only provide results for alignment of a subset of local neighborhoods. As a future work, we plan to extend our approach to generate a holistic embedding model that optimizes alignment across all local neighborhoods.

References

1. Latest wikipedia dump. http://dumps.wikimedia.org/enwiki/latest/enwiki-latest-pages-articles.xml.bz2
2. Boucher, T., Carey, C., Mahadevan, S., Dyar, M.D.: Aligning mixed manifolds. In: Proceedings of 29th AAAI Conference on AI, pp. 2511–2517 (2015)
3. Hashimoto, T., Alvarez-Melis, D., Jaakkola, T.: Word embeddings as metric recovery in semantic spaces. Trans. Assoc. Comp. Linguist. **4**, 273–286 (2016)
4. Huang, E.H., Socher, R., Manning, C.D., Ng, A.Y.: Improving word representations via global context and multiple word prototypes. In: Proceedings of 50th Annual Meeting of ACL, vol. 1. pp. 873–882 (2012)
5. Le, Q.V., Mikolov, T.: Distributed representations of sentences and documents. CoRR abs/1405.4053 (2014)
6. Lee, J.A., Verleysen, M.: Nonlinear Dimensionality Reduction (2007)
7. Lee, L.S.: On the linear algebraic structure of distributed word representations. CoRR abs/1511.06961 (2015)
8. Levy, O., Goldberg, Y.: Neural word embedding as implicit matrix factorization. Adv. Neural Inf. Process. Syst. **27**, 2177–2185 (2014)
9. van der Maaten, L., Postma, E.O., van den Herik, H.J.: Dimensionality reduction: a comparative review (2008)
10. Mikolov, T., Chen, K., Corrado, G., Dean, J.: Efficient estimation of word representations in vector space. CoRR abs/1301.3781 (2013)
11. Mikolov, T., Sutskever, I., Chen, K., Corrado, G.S., Dean, J.: Distributed representations of words and phrases and their compositionality. Adv. Neural Inf. Process. Syst. **26**, 3111–3119 (2013)

12. Safak Sahin, C., Caceres, R.S., Oselio, B., Campbell, W.M.: Consistent alignment of word embedding model (2017). arXiv:1702.07680
13. Schnabel, T., Labutov, I., Mimno, D., Joachims, T.: Evaluation methods for unsupervised word embeddings. In: Proceedings of Conference on EMNLP, pp. 298–307 (2015)
14. Tsvetkov, Y., Faruqui, M., Ling, W., Lample, G., Dyer, C.: Evaluation of word vector representations by subspace alignment. In: Proceedings of Conference on EMNLP (2015)
15. Wang, C., Cao, L., Fan, J.: Building joint spaces for relation extraction. Relat. **1**, 16 (2016)
16. Wang, C., Mahadevan, S.: Manifold alignment without correspondence. In: Proceedings of 21st IJCAI, CA, USA, pp. 1273–1278 (2009)
17. Wang, C., Mahadevan, S.: Heterogeneous domain adaptation using manifold alignment. In: Proceedings of 22nd IJCAI, vol. 2. pp. 1541–1546 (2011)

Legalbot: A Deep Learning-Based Conversational Agent in the Legal Domain

Adebayo Kolawole John(✉), Luigi Di Caro, Livio Robaldo, and Guido Boella

Dipartimento di Informatica, Universita Di Torino,
Corso Svizzera 185, 10149 Torino, Italy
kolawolejohn.adebayo@unibo.it,
{dicaro,guido.boella}@di.unito.it

Abstract. This paper presents a deep learning based dialogue system which has been trained to answer user queries posed as questions during a conversation. The proposed system, though generative, takes advantage of domain specific knowledge for generating valid answers. The evaluation analysis shows that the proposed system obtained a promising result.

Keywords: Recurrent neural networks · Long short-term memory · Chatbot · Conversational agent

1 Introduction

Dialogue Systems (DS), a.k.a. Conversational Systems (CS), have been a subject of research since mid-60's (cf. [17]). In the domain of DS, since the work of [11], exciting results have been reported by systems which model human conversation and response with Neural Networks (NN) systems [13,14,16].

Modeling human conversation is quite challenging since it involves generating plausible and intelligible response to a message giving some contexts. Conversational systems can be either of (1) retrieval-based [6,7] and (2) machine translation-inspired generative systems [1,4,14,16]. Retrieval-based systems use a repository of predefined responses and some kind of heuristic to pick an appropriate response based on the input and context. These type of systems benefit from some clearly defined templates which could be used to limit the potential responses from which to search from. Thus, they tend to give coherent responses since they are less prone to making linguistic or grammatical mistakes [13].

Our work is more challenging since the text have longer sequences, compared to the short text employed in [13,16]. Also, our work is close to IR-based response ranking systems, except that ours is generative. Furthermore, with the exception of the work of [16], most CS systems are trained on open-end data. Because of this, the conversation tends to be off point most of the time. We introduce a more challenging corpus curated from law textbooks, providing prose answers to some basic legal questions specifically within the US jurisdiction. Thus, we deal with messages with longer sequences while also being domain specific. We

F. Frasincar et al. (Eds.): NLDB 2017, LNCS 10260, pp. 267–273, 2017.
DOI: 10.1007/978-3-319-59569-6_32

picture a machine legal advisor that is able to inform, advice and educate its users on some basic every-day legal issues. Giving our limited data, we show that our system works and that it's capable of scaling better with more training data. Our system, henceforth *legalbot*, benefits from the sequence-to-sequence (Seq2Seq) model [15] integrated with special attention scheme in order to focus on some important information between the context and response pair.

2 Conversational Systems

A conversation is made up of the context, message and response. The context is an aggregation of previous query and responses, while the message is the query which leads to the response. Conversational systems (CS) could lean towards the short text conversation [13] or the long text conversation. Our work is inspired by the recurrent neural networks (RNNs) machine translation approach in [1,4]. The authors used an encoder to transform the input into a high dimensional vector representation and then use a decoder to generate a translation from the input representation. The work described in [16] is consistent with this approach, also benefiting from *Seq2Seq* [15]. Sordoni et al. [14] incorporate word embeddings in order to capture long range dependency. Word embeddings in particular have shown to capture more semantic information with excellent result on many NLP tasks [9]. A copy-based attention RNNs was employed in [5]. The model was trained to focus on important information to transfer from the message to the response. Li et. al. [8] used the Long Short-Term Memory (LSTM) to automatically mine user information about entities in the dialogue. An intent-based attention RNN was introduced in [18], using three RNNs, each for the message, response and intention, they keep track of the structural knowledge of the conversation process. Specifically, our work is close to [18] since we also introduce an attention scheme for modeling an *intense-focus* between important words appearing in the message as well as the response. We use a variant of RNNs, -the LSTM, which is more robust to vanishing gradient problem while having the ability to retain information over longer time steps.

At each time step t, let an LSTM unit be a collection of vectors in $\mathbb{R}^d$ where d is the memory dimension: an *input gate* i_t, a *forget gate* f_t, an *output gate* o_t, a *memory cell* c_t and a *hidden state* h_t. The LSTM transition can be represented with the following equations (x_t is the an input vector at t, σ represents sigmoid activation function and $\odot$ the elementwise multiplication. The u_t is a tanh layer which creates a vector of new candidate values that could be added to the state):

$$i_t = \sigma\left(W^{(i)}x_t + U^{(i)}h_{t-1} + b^{(i)}\right),$$

$$f_t = \sigma\left(W^{(f)}x_t + U^{(f)}h_{t-1} + b^{(f)}\right),$$

$$o_t = \sigma\left(W^{(o)}x_t + U^{(o)}h_{t-1} + b^{(o)}\right),$$

$$u_t = \tanh\left(W^{(u)}x_t + U^{(u)}h_{t-1} + b^{(u)}\right),$$
$$c_t = i_t \odot u_t + f_t \odot c_{t-1},$$
$$h_t = o_t \odot \tanh c_t \tag{1}$$

Giving an input symbol in a sequence, the LSTM learns a probability distribution by being trained to predict the next symbol. Normally, the input X is paired with some outputs $Y = y_1, y_2,...,yN_y$. The softmax function is used to distribute the probability over the outputs as below:

$$\begin{aligned} p(Y|X) &= \prod_{k=1}^{N_y} p(y_k|x_1, x_2, ..., x_t, y_1, y_2, ..., y_{k-1}) \\ &= \prod_{k=1}^{N_y} \frac{exp((h_{t-1}, e_{yt})}{\sum_{y'} exp(f(h_{t-1}, e_{y'}))} \end{aligned} \tag{2}$$

where $f(h_{t-1}, e_{yt})$ is the activation function between h_{t-1} and e_{yt}). h_{t-1} is the hidden state at the time step *t* − *1*.

2.1 Encoder-Attention-Decoder

Given a set of conversation between two or more persons, we denote all the conversation as $D = C_1, C_2....C_m$ where each C_i is a sequence of some tokens. At each time step, the encoder reads the embedding vector $\vec{x_t}$ forward and converts each C_i into a fixed high dimensional representation. Equations (3) and (4) shows the forward and backward context being computed by the non-linearity function as a recurrence. The representation is taken as the final hidden state h_T (see Eq. (5)) value computed by merging the forward and backward context.

$$\vec{h_t}^{forward} = f(x_t, h_{t-1}) \tag{3}$$

$$\overleftarrow{h_t}^{backward} = f(x_{t-1}, h_{t-1}) \tag{4}$$

$$h_T = concat(\vec{h_t}^{forward}, \overleftarrow{h_t}^{backward}) \tag{5}$$

where the function f(,) in this work is a LSTM block. To instatiate our network, we used *Glove* vectors [10]. This is consistent with the approach employed by [14]. Out-of-Vocabulary (OOV) Words were assigned embedding weights initialized from random Gaussian distribution. Our choice of *Glove* is because it was trained on a huge data and it is semantically rich. Throughout the training, the weights of the embeddings remain fixed. Next, we feed the ensuing representation into another LSTM for the *intense-focus*. For clarity, the *intense focus* is achieved with a bi-directional LSTM which searches the input sequence and create attention for the important words. In our data, the message is usually of short sequences when compared to the response which can be of arbitrarily longer sequences, our idea is to identify the most semantically important words and by looking through the sequence both left and right, we capture again the relationship of this important words with their context. The decoder is also another LSTM block with the hidden state computed similarly to Eq. (5) except that it is non-bidirectional. The representation from the hidden state h_T of the *intense focus* is passed to the decoder which predicts each response/target symbol. The conditional probability is distributed by a non-linear function, in this case *softmax*. Our model maximizes the conditional log likelihood where θ is the parameter to be learned. Instead of translating the target language to the source as usually done in machine translation [1] tasks, we instead predict the likelihood of a response word, given a query word.

$$\frac{\max}{\theta} \frac{1}{N} \sum_{i=1}^{N} logp\theta(y_n|x_n) \tag{6}$$

3 Dataset

Our intention is to develop a machine advisor that is able to give simple legal advice to users. A user may want to know whether (s)he has the rights to ignore a police interrogation, for instance, when no crime has been committed. We develop a dataset which has been curated from some online law textbooks about criminal law, property rights, family, divorce and company rights. Even though the data follow the question-answer pattern in our source books, the sequences of progression in the conversation makes it suitable for a conversational system. This is more so since it exhibits a kind of phenomenon which we called *context loop*, i.e., a question leads to an answer, the answer given also leads to another question which leads to another answer and vice versa. Where necessary, we have manually adjust the tone of the conversation in order to reflect true dialog while still preserving the information it serves to pass across. We have a total of 1200 question-answer pairs formatted into dialogues, yielding a total of 2400 message and response samples. Figure 1 shows a sample conversation from the dataset.

Enquirer	Am I legally obligated to answer a police officer's questions?
Legal Advisor	No. Refusing to answer a police officer's questions is not a crime. The Fifth Amendment to the U.S. Constitution guarantees the right to silence.
Enquirer	So in that case, I can easily walk away from being questioned
Legal Advisor	Yes you can. Unless a police officer has probable cause to make an arrest, or a reasonable suspicion to conduct a stop and frisk, you have the legal right to walk away from a police officer.

Fig. 1. Sample conversation from our dataset

4 Training

We trained our model with the log-likelihood function. We used Keras[1] deep learning library. To avoid any imprecision in evaluation, we randomly select 50 context from the dataset and for each, we created identical sentences as queries. We optimized the log likelihood with ADAM optimizer. Our best model was achieved with the following configuration: batch size = 32, epochs = 700, and hidden state size = 400. We stick to our surface model since we observed no real improvement while stacking LSTMs in order to have an increased depth.

5 Evaluation

There are different metrics often used in evaluating dialogue systems. A prominent example is the perplexity score as used in [12]. However, this metric doesn't suffice in our case. Following the work of Vinyals et al. in [16], we employed human judgment as our choice evaluation approach. The goal is to present a question, the gold-standard response as well as the machine's response to 3 human judges. Each judge has to score a response using three scales of measure, i.e., acceptable (assigned score = 1), borderline (assigned score = 0.5) and unacceptable (assigned score = 0.0). The total maximum score per judge equals the total number of test samples and the maximum score obtainable is a product of the number of judges and samples. Our accuracy is obtained by a simple Formula given in Eq. 7. Our assessment aims at observing the level of acceptance of the response from our model by human users (Fig. 2).

$$Acceptance = \frac{TotalScoreObtained}{MaximumSCoreObainable} * 100 \tag{7}$$

The three judges were each assigned the 50 questions to score using our acceptance metric. Using the formula in 7, our system achieved a score of 0.48 which implies that roughly 24 out of 50 questions were within the range borderline or acceptable. Few things might have contributed to the poor performance of our model. As earlier highlighted, the sentences in the response are rather too long (66 tokens on the average) which is not so for the question which averages 15

Original Enquiry	Am I legally obligated to answer a police officer's questions?
Test sample formatted	Am I legally obliged to allow a police officer interrogate me
Original Enquiry	Given this kind of situation, how do you advise that I present my case?
Test sample formatted	Given this kind of situation, what advise do you give on how to talk to the policeman?

Fig. 2. Context conversion for test samples.

[1] https://github.com/fchollet/keras.

tokens per question. Also, we have limited amount of data since it requires significant manual effort in formatting information from our sources in order to look quite conversational. Nevertheless, the result is promising and with potential for improvement with huge amount of data. Sadly, these kind of data is quite scarce in the legal domain especially with the stringent copyright issues.

6 Conclusion

We have presented legalbot, a *Seq2Seq* conversational agent. Our model was trained on a micro dataset curated from question-answer information on some civil legal issues. Our neural network model achieved an acceptance score of 48% as evaluated by 3 human judges. The result is promising considering the nature and size of the data. Going forward, we would like to increase the samples in our data. Also, we are thinking of streamlining the number of sentences per response. For empirical evaluation, we would like to implement some existing systems and test their performance on our data while also testing our approach on available short-text conversation datasets. We plan in our future works to apply the approach presented here to our systems in legal informatics [2,3].

Acknowledgments. Kolawole J. Adebayo has received funding from the Erasmus Mundus Joint International Doctoral (Ph.D.) programme in Law, Science and Technology. Luigi Di Caro have received funding from the European Union's H2020 research and innovation programme under the grant agreement No 690974 for the project "MIREL: MIning and REasoning with Legal texts".

References

1. Bahdanau, D., Cho, K., Bengio, Y.: Neural machine translation by jointly learning to align and translate (2014). arXiv preprint arXiv:1409.0473
2. Boella, G., Di Caro, L., Graziadei, M., Cupi, L., Salaroglio, C., Humphreys, L., Konstantinov, H., Marko, K., Robaldo, L., Ruffini, C., Simov, K., Violato, A., Stroetmann, V.: Linking legal open data: breaking the accessibility and language barrier in european legislation and case law. In: Proceedings of the 15th International Conference on Artificial Intelligence and Law, pp. 171–175. ACM (2015)
3. Boella, G., Di Caro, L., Robaldo, L.: Semantic Relation Extraction from Legislative Text Using Generalized Syntactic Dependencies and Support Vector Machines. Springer, Berlin (2013)
4. Cho, K., Van Merriënboer, B., Gulcehre, C., Bahdanau, D., Bougares, F., Schwenk, H., Bengio, Y.: Learning phrase representations using RNN encoder-decoder for statistical machine translation (2014). arXiv preprint arXiv:1406.1078
5. Gu, J., Lu, Z., Li, H., Li, V.: Incorporating copying mechanism in sequence-to-sequence learning (2016). arXiv preprint arXiv:1603.06393
6. Ji, Z., Lu, Z., Li, H.: An information retrieval approach to short text conversation (2014). arXiv preprint arXiv:1408.6988
7. Kadlec, R., Schmid, M., Kleindienst, J.: Improved deep learning baselines for Ubuntu corpus dialogs (2015). arXiv preprint arXiv:1510.03753

8. Li, J., Galley, M., Brockett, C., Spithourakis, G., Gao, J., Dolan, B.: A persona-based neural conversation model (2016). arXiv preprint arXiv:1603.06155
9. Mikolov, T., Chen, K., Corrado, G., Dean, J.: Efficient estimation of word representations in vector space (2013). arXiv preprint arXiv:1301.3781
10. Pennington, J., Socher, R., Manning, C.D.: Glove: global vectors for word representation: In: EMNLP, vol. 14, pp. 1532–1543 (2014)
11. Ritter, A., Cherry, C., Dolan, W.: Data-driven response generation in social media. In: Proceedings of Empirical Methods in Natural Language Processing (2011)
12. Serban, I., Sordoni, A., Bengio, Y., Courville, A., Pineau, J.: Building end-to-end dialogue systems using generative hierarchical neural network models (2015). arXiv preprint arXiv:1507.04808
13. Shang, L., Lu, Z., Li, H.: Neural responding machine for short-text conversation (2015). arXiv preprint arXiv:1503.02364
14. Sordoni, A., Galley, M., Auli, M., Brockett, C., Ji, Y., Mitchell, M., Nie, J., Gao, J., Dolan, B.: A neural network approach to context-sensitive generation of conversational responses (2015). arXiv preprint arXiv:1506.06714
15. Sutskever, I., Vinyals, O., Le, Q.: Sequence to sequence learning with neural networks. In: Advances in Neural Information Processing Systems (2014)
16. Vinyals, O., Le, Q.: A neural conversational model (2015). arXiv preprint arXiv:1506.05869
17. Weizenbaum, J.: Eliza: a computer program for the study of NL communication between man and machine. Commun. ACM **9**(1), 36–45 (1966)
18. Yao, K., Zweig, G., Peng, B.: Attention with intention for a neural network conversation model (2015). arXiv preprint arXiv:1510.08565

Using Word Embeddings for Computing Distances Between Texts and for Authorship Attribution

Armin Hoenen(✉)

Text Technology Lab/CEDIFOR, Goethe University Frankfurt, Frankfurt, Germany
hoenen@em.uni-frankfurt.de

Abstract. In this paper, word embeddings are used for the task of supervised authorship attribution. While previous methods have for instance been looking at characters (n-grams), syntax and most importantly token frequencies, the method presented focusses on the implications of semantic relationships between words. With this instead of authors word choices, semantic networks of entities as perceived by authors may come closer into focus. We find that those can be used reliably for authorship attribution. The method is generally applicable as a tool to compare different texts and/or authors through word embeddings which have been trained separately. This is achieved by not comparing vectors directly, but by comparing sets of most similar words for words shared between texts and then aggregating and averaging similarities per text pair. On two literary corpora (German, English), we compute embeddings for each text separately. The similarities are then used to detect the author of an unknown text.

Keywords: Authorship attribution · Word embeddings · Text distance

1 Introduction

In a supervised setting, authorship attribution (AA) is the task of attributing authorship of a text, the author of which is unknown to an author from a corpus of training texts. An overview of current AA methods is given by Stamatatos [9], consider also [1,3,5]. Word choices of authors (see for instance [6]) and especially most frequent words (mfw) have played an important role in computational AA from the beginning and a performant method was invented by Burrows [2]. His method is called Delta and computes scores which are directly based on the relative frequencies of the words in a text belonging to a corpus. Each relative frequency is rescaled subtracting its mean over the whole corpus and then dividing the difference by the standard deviation leading to a value, which relative to the corpus gives a measure of how much an author favours or disfavours the term in a text. A vector of those z-transformed values for each mfw of the corpus is computed for every text and the vector distance by an established distance

F. Frasincar et al. (Eds.): NLDB 2017, LNCS 10260, pp. 274–277, 2017.
DOI: 10.1007/978-3-319-59569-6_33

measure, typically cosine distance [8] which has been shown to outperform other Delta variants [4], constitutes text pair distances.

In this paper, a new method to AA is presented, using word2vec embedding profiles [7] in order to generate neighbour similarity. Word embeddings have been applied to a variety of NLP tasks and are generally believed to capture distributional similarity with an implication to semantic similarity.

2 Corpora

We use two corpora provided by the computational stylistics group[1]: an English prose corpus and a German one. The two corpora vary in a large number of parameters such as number of texts (German 66, English 26), the number of authors (German 21, English 10), the sizes of the respective texts (for tokens $\text{mean}_{de} = 84,187$, $\text{sd} = 101,221$ with the smallest text having $13,993$, the largest $607,144$ tokens, where punctuation marks have all been discounted, $\text{mean}_{en} = 245,292$, $\text{sd} = 182,066$, $\text{min} = 41,129$, $\text{max} = 973,341$; for sentences $\text{mean}_{de}| = 5,070$ with $\text{sd} = 5,218$ and $\text{mean}_{en} = 16,501$ with $\text{sd} = 13,203$) and most of all in language. With this, the corpra are very heterogeneous but cover many famous authors in the genre at hand and represent thus a rather realistic real-world authorship attribution scenario.

3 Method

For each text, we construct word embeddings using the commandline tool word2vec.[2] The joint embedding space is not meaningful for comparing single texts within since its training is on the union of the texts. Thus, it could only be asked, which words occur in which texts, but not how their embeddings differ from text to text. Similarly, training embeddings for each text and then comparing the vectors of shared words across texts directly is not informative.

For a word in a specific text T_i being part of a corpus C, one can obtain the m most similar words according to the embeddings of this text alone, $0 < m < |T_i| - 1$. The word embedding vectors v_j for all words $w_j \in T_i$ of a specific text have a fixed number of dimensions (here 100). We choose the n most frequent words of the union of all texts in the corpus and call this set $MFW, 0 < n < \sum_{i=1}^{|C|} |T_i|, T_i \in C$. For each most frequent word $mfw_i \in MFW$, we collect the m most similar neighbours for each text T_i. If the most frequent word is not in the text, the set contains m times ϵ. Otherwise, similarity for the current most frequent word with each other word $\in T_i$ is defined through some established vector similarity (here: cosine similarity) between the word pairs' vectors, $\delta(w_j, w_k) = cos(v_j, v_k)$. Thus, for each text T_i, for each word $w_i \in MFW$, we obtain a set with m most similar neighbours in T_i. The superset containing all such sets from one text is called W_t, which is meaningfully comparable across texts. This is one of the main findings of the paper.

[1] https://sites.google.com/site/computationalstylistics/.

[2] https://code.google.com/archive/p/word2vec/, default settings, corpus lowercased and punctuation marks deleted.

Hereinfurther, we compute similarity of two texts as the aggregated Jaccard set similarities between all neighbour sets of the most frequent words for any pair of texts ($\delta(W_{t_i}, W_{t_j})$). Instead of Jaccard, one could use the Spearman rank correlation and the true neighbour ranks, which we leave to future work. For evaluation, we use an all-or-nothing scenario. Viewing each text as unknown, we compute the most similar text and increment a hit counter whenever the author of both the unknown and the most similar texts are the same person. As a baseline, we employ the Cosine Delta method.

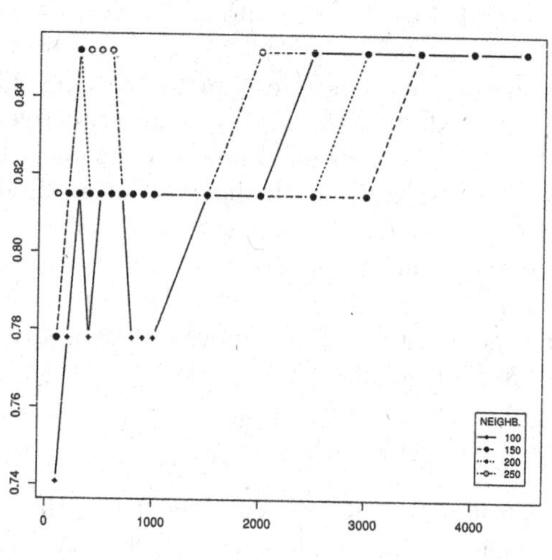

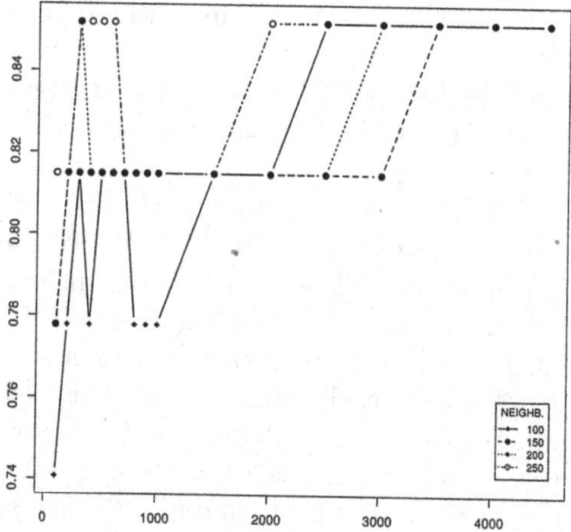

Fig. 1. Performance for German (above) and English (below). Numbers of mfw (x-axis) as well as numbers of neighbours (legend) are varied and percentages of correctly identified texts displayed (y-axis). Plateaus are not left after 4000 mfw (no texts lost again). Cosine Delta constantly performed at 0.95 for German and at 0.96 for English.

4 Results

We found the Euclidian, Manhattan and Cosine distances to perform similarly. The same goes for parameters of the word2vec tool, 100 or 300 dimensions, cbow vs. skip-gram, minCount of 1 or 5 all yielded very similar results. Although the results are far above chance, they remain below the baseline of the Cosine Delta. See Fig. 1 for the performance on the numbers of most frequent words and neighbours to be used.

5 Discussion and Conclusion

The evaluated corpora were quite heterogeneous with regard to the sizes of their texts, some being rather small. Although the result is disappointing (negative) in that it could not outperform a (comparatively strong) baseline, with larger or more balanced corpora performance could improve. Current results are to be seen as preliminary. The evaluation scenario takes into account only the one closest text, discarding information on how well the rest of texts are relatively ordered. With these restrictions, the results are just a first example showing that the method in se is feasible but not how it can be optimally applied. The texts correctly identified by the word embeddings were not always a subset of the correctly identified ones by Cosine Delta. First attempts at combining votes were occassionally successful. To conclude, the main finding is that the presented method works.

References

1. Argamon, S.: Interpreting Burrows's delta: geometric and probabilistic foundations. Literary Linguist. Comput. **23**(2), 131–147 (2008)
2. Burrows, J.: Delta: a measure of stylistic difference and a guide to likely authorship. Literary Linguistic Comput. **17**(3), 267–287 (2002)
3. Eder, M.: Does size matter? Authorship attribution, small samples, big problem. Literary Linguist. Comput. **30**(2), 167–182 (2013)
4. Evert, S., Proisl, T., Vitt, T., Schöch, C., Jannidis, F., Pielström, S.: Towards a better understanding of Burrows's Delta in literary authorship attribution. In: Proceedings of the Fourth Workshop on Computational Linguistics for Literature, pp. 79–88. Association for Computational Linguistics, Denver, Colorado, USA (2015)
5. Koppel, M., Schler, J.: Exploiting stylistic idiosyncrasies for authorship attribution. In: Proceedings of IJCAI'03 Workshop on Computational Approaches to Style Analysis and Synthesis, vol. 69, p. 72 (2003)
6. Marsden, J., Budden, D., Craig, H., Moscato, P.: Language individuation and marker words: Shakespeare and his Maxwells Demon. PLoS ONE **8**(6), 63–88 (2013)
7. Mikolov, T., Chen, K., Corrado, G., Dean, J.: Efficient estimation of word representations in vector space. In: Proceedings of Workshop at ICLR (2013)
8. Smith, P.W.H., Aldridge, W.: Improving authorship attribution: optimizing Burrows' Delta method. J. Quant. Linguist. **18**(1), 63–88 (2011)
9. Stamatatos, E.: A survey of modern authorship attribution methods. J. Am. Soc. Inf. Sci. Technol. **60**(3), 538–556 (2009)

Combination of Neural Networks for Multi-label Document Classification

Ladislav Lenc[1,2(✉)] and Pavel Král[1,2(✉)]

[1] Faculty of Applied Sciences, Department of Computer Science and Engineering, University of West Bohemia, Plzeň, Czech Republic
{llenc,pkral}@kiv.zcu.cz

[2] Faculty of Applied Sciences, NTIS - New Technologies for the Information Society, University of West Bohemia, Plzeň, Czech Republic

Abstract. This paper deals with multi-label classification of Czech documents using several combinations of neural networks. It is motivated by the assumption that different nets can keep some complementary information and that it should be useful to combine them. The main contribution of this paper consists in a comparison of several combination approaches to improve the results of the individual neural nets. We experimentally show that the results of all the combination approaches outperform the individual nets, however they are comparable. However, the best combination method is the supervised one which uses a feed-forward neural net with sigmoid activation function.

Keywords: Combination · Czech · Deep neural networks · Document classification · Multi-label · Thresholding

1 Introduction

This paper deals with multi-label document classification by neural networks. Formally, this task can be seen as the problem of finding a model M which assigns a document $d \in D$ a set of appropriate labels $l \in L$ as follows $M : d \rightarrow l$ where D is the set of all documents and L is the set of all possible document labels. In our previous work [1], we have compared standard feed-forward networks (i.e. multi-layer perceptron) and popular convolutional networks (CNNs).

The resulting F-measures of these nets were high, however these values are still far from perfect. Therefore, in this paper, we use several approaches to combine individual networks in order to improve the final classification score. The main contribution of this paper thus consists in a comparison of classifier combination methods for multi-label classification which has, to the best of our knowledge, never been done on this task before. The methods are evaluated on the documents in Czech language, being a representative of highly inflectional

This work has been supported by the project LO1506 of the Czech Ministry of Education, Youth and Sports.

F. Frasincar et al. (Eds.): NLDB 2017, LNCS 10260, pp. 278–282, 2017.
DOI: 10.1007/978-3-319-59569-6_34

Slavic language with a free word order. These properties decrease the performance of usual methods and therefore, a more sophisticated parametrization is beneficial. This evaluation is another contribution of this paper.

The rest of the paper is organized as follows. Section 2 describes the combination methods. Section 3 deals with experiments realized on the ČTK corpus and then discusses the obtained results. In the last section, we conclude the experimental results and propose some future research directions.

2 Networks and Combination Approaches

2.1 Individual Nets

We use a feed-forward deep neural network (FDNN) and a convolutional neural net (CNN) with two different activation functions, namely *sigmoid* and *softmax*, in the output layer. Our CNN is motivated by Kim [2], however we used only one-dimensional convolutional kernel. The topologies of our nets are detailed in our previous work [1].

2.2 Combination

We consider that the different nets keep some complementary information which can compensate recognition errors. We also assume that similar network topology with different activation functions can bring some different information and thus that all nets should have its particular impact on the final classification. Therefore, we consider all the nets as the different classifiers which will be further combined.

Two types of combination will be evaluated and compared. The first group does not need any training phase, while the second one learns a classifier.

Unsupervised Combination. The first combination method compensates the errors of individual classifiers by computing the average value from the inputs. This value is thresholded subsequently to obtain the final classification result. This method is called hereafter *Averaged thresholding*.

The second combination approach first thresholds the scores of all individual classifiers. Then, the final classification output is given as an agreement of the majority of the classifiers. We call further this method as *Majority voting with thresholding*.

Supervised Combination. We use another neural network of type multi-layer perceptron to combine the results. This network has three layers: $n \times 37$ inputs, hidden layer with 512 nodes and the output layer composed of 37 neurons (number of categories to classify). n value is the number of the nets to combine. This configuration was set experimentally on the preliminary results. We also evaluate and compare, as in the case of individual classifiers, two different activation functions: *sigmoid* and *softmax*. These combination approaches are hereafter called *FNN with sigmoid* and *FNN with softmax*.

3 Experiments

3.1 Tools and Corpus

For implementation of all neural-nets we used Keras tool-kit [3] which is based on the Theano deep learning library [4].

For the following experiments we used the Czech text documents provided by the ČTK. This whole corpus contains 2,974,040 words belonging to 11,955 documents. The documents are annotated from a set of 60 categories as for instance agriculture, weather, politics or sport out of which we used 37 most frequent ones. We have further created the development set which is composed of 500 randomly chosen samples removed from the entire corpus. This corpus is freely available for research purposes at http://home.zcu.cz/~pkral/sw/.

We use the five-folds cross validation procedure for all following experiments, where 20% of the corpus is reserved for testing and the remaining part for training of our models. The optimal value of the threshold is determined on the development set. For evaluation of the multi-label document classification results, we use the standard recall, precision and F-measure (*F1*) metrics. The results are micro-averaged.

3.2 Results of the Individual Networks

The first experiment (see Sect. 1 of Table 1) shows the results of the individual neural nets with sigmoid and softmax activation functions. These results demonstrates very good classification performance of all individual networks.

Table 1. Experimental results

Approach	Prec.	Recall	F1 [%]
1. Individual networks			
(a) FDNN with softmax	84.4	82.1	83.3
(b) FDNN with sigmoid	83.0	81.2	82.1
(c) CNN with softmax	80.6	80.8	80.7
(d) CNN with sigmoid	86.3	81.9	84.1
2. Unsupervised combination			
Network (a) & (c) & (d) combined by *averaged thresholding*	86.7	83.5	85.1
Network (a) & (b) & (d) combined by *majority voting with thresholding*	87.5	82.6	85.0
3. Supervised combination			
All networks combined by *FNN with softmax*	85.7	83.6	84.6
All networks combined by *FNN with sigmoid*	88.0	82.8	**85.3**

3.3 Results of Unsupervised Combinations

The second experiment shows (see Sect. 2 of Table 1) the results of *Averaged thresholding* and *Majority voting with thresholding* methods. These results confirm our assumption that the different nets keep complementary information and that it is useful to combine them to improve classification scores of the individuals networks. These results further show that the performance of both methods are comparable.

Note that due to the space limit, only the best performing combination for each method is reported in this table.

3.4 Results of Supervised Combinations

The following experiments show the results of the supervised combination method with an FNN (see Sect. 2.2). We have evaluated and compared the nets with both sigmoid and softmax (see Sect. 3 of Table 1) activation functions.

These results show that these combinations have also positive impact on the classification and that sigmoid activation function brings better results than softmax. Moreover, as supposed, this supervised combination slightly outperforms both previously described unsupervised methods.

4 Conclusions and Future Work

In this paper, we have used several combination methods to improve the results of individual neural nets for multi-label document classification of Czech text documents. We have shown that it is useful to combine the nets to improve the classification score of the individual networks. We have also proved that the thresholding is a good method to assign the document labels of multi-label classification. We have further shown that the results of all the approaches are comparable. However, the best combination method is the supervised one which uses an FNN with sigmoid activation function. The F-measure of this approach is 85.3%.

We further analyzed the final results and discovered that the classification should be still improved if the number of classes is known for every document. Therefore, the first perspective is to build a meta-classifier to provide this information. The consecutive multi-label classification will be using the class dependent thresholds. The next perspective consists in proposing a novel combination method based on deep neural network. The main challenge of this work will be to found an optimal network topology with a reasonable number of parameters to avoid the overfitting. We also would like to experiment with confidence measures to improve the final classification results.

References

1. Lenc, L., Král, P.: Deep neural networks for Czech multi-label document classification. In: 17th International Conference on Intelligent Text Processing and Computational Linguistics (CICLing 2016), Konya, Turkey. Springer (2016)

2. Kim, Y.: Convolutional neural networks for sentence classification (2014). arXiv preprint arXiv:1408.5882
3. Chollet, F.: Keras (2015). https://github.com/fchollet/keras
4. Bergstra, J., Breuleux, O., Bastien, F., Lamblin, P., Pascanu, R., Desjardins, G., Turian, J., Warde-Farley, D., Bengio, Y.: Theano: a CPU and GPU math expression compiler. In: Proceedings of the Python for Scientific Computing Conference (SciPy), Austin, TX, vol. 4 (2010)

Supporting Business Process Modeling Using RNNs for Label Classification

Philip Hake(✉), Manuel Zapp, Peter Fettke, and Peter Loos

Institute for Information Systems (IWi), German Research Center for Artificial Intelligence (DFKI) and Saarland University, Saarbrücken, Germany
{philip.hake,manuel.zapp,peter.fettke, peter.loos}@dfki.de

Abstract. Business Process Models describe the activities of a company in an abstracted manner. Typically, the labeled nodes of a process model contain only sparse textual information. The presented approach uses an LSTM network to classify the labels contained in a business process model. We first apply a Word2Vec algorithm to the words contained in the labels. Afterwards, we feed the resulting data into our LSTM network. We train and evaluate our models on a corpus consisting of more than 24,000 labels of business process models. Using our trained classification model, we are able to distinguish different constructs of a process modeling language based on their label. Our experimental evaluation yields an accuracy of 95.71% on the proposed datasets.

Keywords: Deep learning · LSTM · Neural network · Business process modeling · Natural language processing

1 Introduction

Conceptual Modeling and particularly Business Process Modeling are important and effective means for capturing and communicating the activities of a company. It is a widely-used technique in both practice and research to design, describe and analyze enterprises [1]. Furthermore, process modeling is used in research and practice to acquire process blueprints, called reference process models, which enable the development of standard software for specific domains.

Although there is a variety of process modeling languages, the different modeling languages obey a characteristic graph structure and they only differ in edge and node types representing different business semantics. The models also contain labels attached to the nodes describing process related activities, events or used resources. These labels consist of incomplete sentences, e.g. check customer invoice, and exhibit a frequent usage of abbreviation. While the syntax of a process modeling language is often strongly formalized, the syntax of the natural language contained in the labels is not restricted by this formalization.

In our approach, we exploit the characteristics of the language contained in the labels to classify a node according to its type. We aim at supporting the detection of inconsistencies between the labeling and the chosen node type in large business process model repositories. A detected inconsistency between node type and label could either

F. Frasincar et al. (Eds.): NLDB 2017, LNCS 10260, pp. 283–286, 2017.
DOI: 10.1007/978-3-319-59569-6_35

indicate an uncommon use of natural language within the process model, or refer to a faulty node type. Based on the number of detected inconsistencies the quality or maturity of a process model could be automatically assessed.

In conclusion, our work contributes to the field of conceptual modeling in the field of business process management by providing and evaluating an approach for natural language-based label classification. To support the outlined use case, we train a recurrent neural network (RNN) in order to classify the nodes according to the text contained in the labels. We empirically evaluate our approach and assess its accuracy using an extensive process model corpus covering individual process models as well as reference process models for different domains.

Our paper is structured as follows. In Sect. 2 we present the classification approach. Section 3 introduces the experimental evaluation and results analysis. Finally, we conclude our work in Sect. 4 and give an overview on potential future research.

2 Label Classification

In order to prepare our data to serve as an input for our neural network, we consecutively apply four different preprocessing operations. The following formalization describes these operations in detail.

Let Σ = {a, …, z, ü, ö, ä, A, …, Z, Ü, Ö, Ä, ß} be our alphabet where Σ* is the Kleene star. The Kleene star describes a set of all finite words, which are obtained by an arbitrary concatenation of symbols contained in the alphabet of Σ. Now we define W ⊊ Σ* as the set of all words in our input data. Furthermore, let (Σ*) * be the Kleene star of Σ*, representing the set of all possible finite word sequences. We denote $S \subsetneq (\Sigma^*)$ * as the set of all sequences contained in our input data. Furthermore, |s| defines the length of a sequence $s \,\varepsilon\, S$.

We additionally, denote *#w* as the number of occurrences of the word $w \,\varepsilon\, W$ in our input data set. To feed the words into our neural network, we translate each word to a numeric representation. Therefore, we define an injective function F that assigns each word a unique integer:

$$F : \sum\nolimits^{*} \rightarrow \mathbb{N} \tag{1}$$

The definition of the function F we use in our approach fulfills the following properties:

$$\text{Let}\, w,\, w' \,\varepsilon\, W \,\text{and}\, w \neq w',\ \text{then}\ \#w \geq \#w' \leftrightarrow F(w) < F(w') \tag{2}$$

The words contained in the word vector derived from the label are transformed into integer values. We obtain a numeric vector describing our label. The third processing step handles deviations concerning different sequence lengths.

Since the sequences *S* exhibit different lengths, we need to normalize the obtained numeric vectors in order to feed them into the neural network. Let *max* be the maximum sequence length |s| of all sequence S. We declare the function P that takes a sequence of arbitrary length and maps it to a vector of integers of the dimension max:

$$P : (\Sigma^*)^* \rightarrow \mathbb{N}^{max} \quad (3)$$

This function performs an operation that is referred to as zero-padding and is defined as follows:

$$P(w_1, \ldots, w_n) = 0^{max-n} \cdot F(w_1) \cdot \ldots \cdot F(w_n) \quad (4)$$

Applying the function P to the input dataset will return a set of numeric integer vectors having the dimension of *max*. Based on this data we train a separate neural network to learn the semantic similarity between words based on their context. Therefore, the network transforms the integer representation of a word into an n-dimensional dense numeric output vector.

These n-dimensional vectors are called word embeddings. The dimensionality n of the resulting embedding space is an important parameter of our approach. The described approach is commonly known as Word2Vec and was first described in [2]. Word2Vec is an integral building block of NLP algorithms.

The very basic feedforward neural network, also known as multilayer perceptron is not able to learn temporal information, unlike RNNs, where at least one feedback loop is introduced to the network. Introducing a feedback loop allows the network to maintain a state over time, which in turn enables the network to learn sequences. Unfortunately, recurrent neural networks involve the vanishing gradient problem, why Hochreiter and Schmidhuber [3] introduce the Long short-term memory (LSTM) network that addresses these shortcomings. The LSTM is considered an advancement of the RNN. To prevent the network from overfitting, the LSTM can be further extended by a technique called dropout [4]. The dropout defines a fraction of randomly selected neurons, which are ignored during the training process. The outputs of the described LSTM layer serves as input to a subsequent fully-connected layer with one output neuron using a sigmoid activation function.

3 Experimental Evaluation

We train our network using TensorFlow and a GPU computing platform, consisting of a Geforce GTX Titan X with 12 GB of RAM, an Intel-i7 with 4 physical cores and 16 GB memory. We implement the network according to the specifications introduced in section two. We define a batchsize and embedding space dimensionality of 32. We also apply a dropout of 0.2 to our LSTM layer to prevent an overfitting.

In deep learning applications, the success of the learning process highly depends on the quality of the training data. We decided to train and evaluate our approach on 24,523 labels (11,129 functions and 13,394 events) of German process models from the IWi process model corpus [5]. In comparison, the SAP reference models, which are widely-used for evaluation purpose, contain 9,381 event and function labels. The IWi corpus consists of a variety of Business Process Models predominantly following the modeling language Event-Driven Process Chain (EPC). In our evaluation we aim at distinguishing event nodes from function nodes based on their labels.

We measured the quality of the classification approach using the mean accuracy and mean loss of a 10-fold cross validation. Training and validating the proposed neural network on the described dataset yield a mean accuracy of 95.71%. Furthermore, we investigated the development of accuracy and loss over a training period of 250 epochs. We observed that the loss converges from epoch 180 onwards. Further adjustments of the weights, are unlikely to minimize the loss function. Therefore, additional training epochs would not result in an increased accuracy. We also observed that the mean accuracy started to converge from epoch 180 on but did not increase significantly over the remaining epochs. After 250 epochs, an accuracy of 95.71% and a loss of 0.092% were reached.

4 Conclusion

We proposed a novel approach for distinguishing process model nodes based on their label. Using Deep Learning techniques from the field of NLP, we have obtained a high accuracy in a first experimental evaluation. To further evaluate our approach and assess its classification quality, an extensive dataset containing additional modeling constructs needs to be acquired. This also applies for the support of multiple natural languages. Furthermore, to apply our techniques to model correction, consistency checks or modeling recommendations, further evaluations need to be conducted. To measure the network's capabilities concerning the detection of modeling errors requires pre-tagged datasets. In order to obtain a tagged corpus for training further machine learning approaches in the field of business process modeling, the models could be tagged semi-automatically.

Acknowledgment. We gratefully acknowledge the support of NVIDIA for the donation of the GPUs used for this research.

References

1. Fettke, P.: How conceptual modeling is used. Commun. AIS **25**, 571–592 (2009)
2. Mikolov, T., Chen, K., Corrado, G., Dean, J.: Efficient estimation of word representations in vector space. CoRR abs/1301.3 (2013)
3. Hochreiter, S., Schmidhuber, J.: Long short-term memory. Neural Comput. **9**, 1735–1780 (1997)
4. Srivastava, N., Hinton, G., Krizhevsky, A., Sutskever, I., Salakhutdinov, R.: Dropout: a simple way to prevent neural networks from overfitting. J. Mach. Learn. Res. **15**, 1929–1958 (2014)
5. Thaler, T., Dadashnia, S., Sonntag, A., Fettke, P., Loos, P.: The IWi Process Model Corpus. Publications of the Institute for Information Systems (IWi) at the German Research Center for Artificial Intelligence (DFKI), IWi-Heft, vol. 199, 10/2015 (2015)

A Convolutional Neural Network Based Sentiment Classification and the Convolutional Kernel Representation

Shen Gao[1], Huaping Zhang[1(✉)], and Kai Gao[2]

[1] College of Computer Science, Beijing Institute of Technology, Beijing 100080, China
63388@qq.com, kevinzhang@bit.edu.cn

[2] Department of Computer, Hebei University of Science & Technology, Shijiazhuang 050000, China
gaokai@hebust.edu.cn

Abstract. This paper presents a multiple layer based convolutional neural network for sentiment analysis. Word embedding is present to learn the features and representations. This paper also presents a convolutional kernel representation for textual data. In order to evaluate the performance, this paper uses short-text corpus to evaluate. Experimental results show the feasibility of the approach.

Keywords: Word embedding · Convolutional neural network · Classification · Sentiment analysis · Representation

1 Introduction

Sentiment analysis of short-text is challenging because of the unlabeled data and the limited contextual information. Some traditional approaches have handcrafted parsing programs, and many of them require labeled training data. Related works manage to obtain improved syntactic parsing results by simply replacing the linear model of a parser with a fully connected feed-forward network [1–3]. Convolutional & pooling based architecture presents promising results among document classification [4], short-text categorization [5], paraphrase identification [6], semantic role labeling [7] and question answering [8]. This paper presents a convolutional neural network (CNN) based sentiment classification and the novel convolutional kernel representation. The architecture of the proposed model includes the word embedding for pre-processing, pooling & filter layer for extracting useful features, and the decision layer for final decision. Visual kernel representation is also present.

2 Modelling on Convolutional Neural Network

Before preprocessing data, a padding operation has been done on each sentence to make it to have the same length. It is reasonable to count all the words in the whole corpus and then build a dictionary V. It is feasible to build a word embedding matrix $W \in R^{d\times|V|}$, where d denotes the dimensions of the embedding.

F. Frasincar et al. (Eds.): NLDB 2017, LNCS 10260, pp. 287–291, 2017.
DOI: 10.1007/978-3-319-59569-6_36

This paper presents a multi-layer convolutional neural network, a feed-forward neural network with max-pooling layer, to do the sentiment classification. As for the convolutional layer, this paper uses "relu" activation function. This paper uses a max-pooling layer for obtaining useful features and avoiding over-fitting. The dropout is an optional layer, which is used to prevent from over-fitting. Last, a simple approach for final decision is to train a linear classifier by logistic regression. In detail, let $x_i \in \mathbb{R}^D$ be the D-dimensional word vector corresponding to the i-th word in the sentence, $x_{i:i+j}$ refers to the concatenation of words $x_i, x_{i+1}, \ldots x_{i+j}$, a feature c_i is generated from a window of word $x_{i:i+h-1}$ by the operation $c_i = f(wx_{i:i+h-1} + b)$. The factor $b \in \mathbb{R}$ is a bias, and a non-linear activation function f to each c_i is also used.

3 Convolutional Kernel Representation for Textual Data

As the parameter of the convolutional kernel in image processing domain is usually a 3-dimensional vector parameter (i.e., representing RGB color, respectively), each kernel parameter can be viewed as a pixel based representation. It is reasonable to visualize these pixels and then the image can be used to represent the convolutional kernel parameters. Inspired by the image processing, this paper uses the corresponding training words as the convolutional kernel representation. As for the two-layer CNN, the first layer extracts some features, which are then fed into the second layer for further processing. A mapping $V \rightarrow \mathbb{R}^D$ maps a word w (from V) to a real-valued vector $\vec{w}$ in the corresponding embedding space with dimensionality D. Given a number of context around w, it needs to capture as much relevant information as possible, so this paper uses a region, and the widths equal to the dimensionality of the word vectors. The space of the word embedding is denoted as S_E (its dimension is D_E). The width of processing window is denoted as W_C (i.e., a threshold, in this paper, it is set to 3). Based on the above operation, the analyzing kernel can be denoted as a matrix $[C_1, C_2, \ldots, C_i, \ldots, C_{WC}]^T$, where C_i is a D_E-dimension vector, and the shape of the kernel parameter is $[W_C, D_E]$. Although the kernel parameter's second dimension (i.e., D_E) is the same as the dimension of the word embedding's, the vector C_i may not be aligned with any other word vector w_i in the embedding space. As some words around (or nearby to) the word vector w_i perhaps have similar semantic, it is reasonable to select those nearby vectors to denote C_i. So this paper chooses some relevant words closer to the corresponding word embedding space as the weight parameter' representation. It is also reasonable to use these words near to the kernel's weight vector as the processing corpus' features.

4 Experiments and Analysis

In order to evaluate the proposed model's performance, this paper analyzes the performance on short-text open datasets (i.e., e-commerce goods' reviews) for sentiment classification. The metrics are the precision, recall and F1, see the Eq. 1 below.

$$Precision = \frac{TP}{TP + FP} \quad Recall = \frac{TP}{TP + FN} \quad \mathrm{F1} = \frac{2 \times Precision \times Recall}{Precision + Recall} \tag{1}$$

This paper uses NLPCC open dataset, which is collected from product review web sites. The polarity of each review is binary (i.e., positive or negative). This dataset contains 10000 reviews. This paper selects 10% corpus as the test dataset randomly (Table 1). All the experiments have been finished by using TensorFlow framework.

Table 1. The proposed model's performance on NLPCC corpus

Polarity(number of reviews)	Precision (%)	Recall (%)	F1 (%)
Negative(515)	73	72	72
Positive(485)	70	72	71

In order to represent the convolutional kernel effectively, this paper presents three different schemas. Table 2 shows the representation of the kernel (translated from the Chinese terms). First, schema-1's results show that the first & third kernels' parameters are for the positive comments while the second is for negative. Second, schema-2 is the first layer's kernel parameter representation on the two-layer CNN for training epoch is set to 2000, and schema-3 is the first layer's kernel parameter representation on the two-layer CNN for training epoch is set to 5000. From the experimental results, the schema-1's result is similar to that of the schema-2's, existing some new words in schema-2. It is clear that the second layer plays some roles in semantic classification. From the kernel parameter representation, it is clear that which kernel will present a stronger activation for sentiment analysis. As analyzing Chinese, some words can't present any useful meaning, so these words are marked as "ERR".

Table 2. Kernel representation for three different schemas

Kernel parameter	Schema-1: one-layer CNN	Schema-2: two-layer CNN for less training epochs	Schema-3: two-layer CNN for more training epochs
The 1st kernel para-meter	① Recommendation ② Combination③ Roughly ④ Slight⑤ Reasonable price	① Recommendation ② Amusing③ Walk ④ Hand-feeling⑤ Towards	① Recommendation② Title③ Reasonable price④ Amusing⑤ Musical
	① Pruning② Casio③ Rise ④ Defense⑤ Children	① Split② Habit ③ Appearance④ Good ⑤ Available	① Recommend② Amazing③ Reasonable price④ Split⑤ Fitable
	① Half② Recommendation ③ Bag④ Combination ⑤ Reply	① Colorful② Portray ③ Details④ Thomas⑤ Film	①Hand-feeling ② Recommendation③ Pure④ Backwards⑤ Treasures

(continued)

Table 2. (*continued*)

Kernel parameter	Schema-1: one-layer CNN	Schema-2: two-layer CNN for less training epochs	Schema-3: two-layer CNN for more training epochs
The 2nd kernel para-meter	① Garbage② Bad③ At-all ④ Worthless⑤ Roughly	① Reasonable price② Girl friend③ Amazing④ Title ⑤ERR	① Electrify② Repeat ③ Expensive④ Male ⑤ This part
	① New year② ERR ③ Chatter④ Singing ⑤Chinese subtitle	① Sharing ② Recommendation ③ Thinking④ Three times ⑤ Towards	① Camera② Fuzzy ③ Roughly④ Uncle ⑤Badly
	① Garbage② Roughly ③Badly④ Nothing ⑤ Worthless	① Silm② Precaution ③ After dinner④ high ⑤ Bag	① Cheap② Badly ③ Roughly④ Bad ⑤ Endless
The 3rd kernel para-meter	① Recommendation ② Combination③ Roughly ④ Rendering⑤ Accident	① ERR② Folk music③ Replacement④ Insurance ⑤ Can't open	① Recommendation② Title③ Elegant④ 50% off ⑤ Musical
	① Punning② Rise③ But ④ Children⑤ Sigh	① Worthless② Badly ③ Garbage④ Retreat ⑤ Roughly	① Recommendation② Amuzing③ Blue④ Reasonable price ⑤ Hand-feeling
	① Half② Ranking③ Reply ④ PDF⑤ Majority	① Worthless② Badly ③ Garbage ④ Can't open⑤ Very bad	① Hand-feeling② Recommendation③ Pure ④ Treasure⑤ Retreat

5 Conclusions and Future Works

This paper presents a multi-layer convolutional neural network, a feed-forward neural network with max-pooling layer, to do the sentiment classification. The proposed model can learn the representations of features. Although the proposed representation can present the convolutional kernel efficiently, there are also some words whose meanings are different from the others. How to optimize it is our further work.

Acknowledgments. This work is sponsored by National Basic Research Program of China (973 Program, Grant No.: 2013CB329606). This work is also sponsored by National Science Foundation of Hebei Province (No. F2017208012).

References

1. Weiss, D., Alberti C., Collins M., Petrov, S.: Structured training for neural network transition-based parsing. In: 53rd Annual Meeting of the Association for Computational Linguistics and 7th International Joint Conference on Natural Language Processing, vol. 1, pp. 323–333. ACL Press, Beijing (2015)
2. Pei, W., Ge, T., Chang. B.: An effective neural network model for graph-based dependency parsing. In: 53rd Annual Meeting of the Association for Computational Linguistics and 7th International Joint Conference on Natural Language Processing, vol. 1, pp. 313–322. ACL Press, Beijing (2015)
3. Durrett, G., Klein, D.: Neural CRF parsing. In: 53rd Annual Meeting of the Association for Computational Linguistics and 7th International Joint Conference on Natural Language Processing, vol. 1, pp. 302–312. ACL Press, Beijing (2015)
4. Johnson, R., Zhang, T.: Effective use of word order for text categorization with convolutional neural networks. In: Conference of the North American Chapter of the Association for Computational Linguistics: Human Language Technologies, pp. 103–112. ACL Press, Colorado (2015)
5. Wang, P., Xu, J., Xu, B., Liu, C., Zhang, H., Wang, F.: Semantic clustering and convolutional neural network for short text categorization. In: 53rd Annual Meeting of the Association for Computational Linguistics and 7th International Joint Conference on Natural Language Processing, vol. 2, pp. 352–357. ACL Press, Beijing (2015)
6. Yin, W., Schutze, H.: Convolutional neural network for paraphrase identification. In: Conference of the North American Chapter of the Association for Computational Linguistics: Human Language Technologies, pp. 901–911. ACL Press, Colorado (2015)
7. Severyn, A., Moschitti, A.: Twitter sentiment analysis with deep convolutional neural networks. In: ACM SIGIR Conference on Research and Development in Information Retrieval, pp. 959–962. ACM Press, Santiago (2015)
8. Dong, L., Wei, F., Zhou, M., Xu, K.: Question answering over freebase with multi-column convolutional neural networks. In: 53rd Annual Meeting of the Association for Computational Linguistics and 7th International Joint Conference on Natural Language Processing, vol. 1, pp. 260–269. ACL Press, Beijing (2015)

Quotology - Reading Between the Lines of Quotations

Dwijen Rudrapal[1(✉)], Amitava Das[2], and B. Bhattacharya[1]

[1] NIT Agartala, Tripura, India
dwijen.rudrapal@gmail.com, babybhatt75@gmail.com
[2] IIIT Sri City, Andhra Pradesh, India
amitava.santu@gmail.com

Abstract. A quote is short eloquent sentence/s drawn from long experience. Quotes are full of poetry, abstraction in the form of restrained information, hidden significance and objective, and pragmatic twists. While a quote explanation always in elaborate form with more sentences than the quote, both of them convey the same concept or meaning. However, systematic study to understand linguistic structures and interpretation of quotes has not received much research attention till date. To this end we have developed a corpus of English quotes and their interpretations in elaborated forms. Finally, we proposed an automatic approach to recognize Textual Entailment (TE) between English quote and its explanation where quote has been considered as the text (T) and its explanation/interpretation has been considered as hypothesis (H). We have tested various linguistic features including lexical, syntactic, and semantic cues and also tried word-to-vector similarity measure using deep learning approach on quote-explanation to identify TE relation.

Keywords: Textual entailment · Semantic similarity · Deep learning · Text summarization

1 Introduction

It is a pleasure to be able to quote lines to fit any occasion...

–Abraham Lincoln

A quote is a text or spoken information represented with restrained information. Quote is associated with a specific tone, diction, mood, figurative language (metaphors, similes, imagery, alliteration, onomatopoeia, personification), while explanation includes detail significance, objectives and context of the quote. So, even though a quote explanation includes more sentences than quote, both of them express similar meaning. To the best of our knowledge there is hardly any systematic study on linguistic structure of quotes and its explanation. Having that motivation in mind we develop a QUote-Explanation Dataset (QUED) and propose a recognition of Textual Entailment (RTE) system for English quote

F. Frasincar et al. (Eds.): NLDB 2017, LNCS 10260, pp. 292–296, 2017.
DOI: 10.1007/978-3-319-59569-6_37

and its explanation where quote is considered as text (T) and its explanation/interpretation is considered as hypothesis (H). This paper is organized as follows. Section 2 discuss the related research work followed by proposed methodology in Sect. 3, experiment result and discussion in Sect. 4, and conclusion in Sect. 5.

2 Related Work

RTE task is a well defined problem in NLP domain. Since introduction of automatic RTE task by [4], several RTE challenges (RTE-1 to RTE-7) and other researches contributed state-of-the-art RTE systems ranging from lexical similarity methods to complex and extensive linguistic analysis methods. Lexical-syntactic similarity based approaches use features like n-gram, word similarity, synonym and antonyms [5], word overlap [1] of T and H to determine the existence of entailment. In the work [12], relatedness between T and H measured for RTE task using dependency graphs and Lexical chains. The system propose by [11], form sequence of transformations for T into H to make resulting T identical to H and decides entailment relation. With Lexical, syntactical measures, various machine learning approaches also introduced towards RTE problem. Those approaches use various features like WordNet and numeric expressions [6], syntactic and semantic features [2] from T and H for RTE task. Recent work [3] publish the Stanford Natural Language Inference (SNLI) corpus towards RTE task and proposes a feature-rich classifier model and a neural network model to recognize TE relation on that dataset. Another recent work [10] develops one RTE dataset from clinical text domain and proposes a classifier-based RTE system for the dataset.

3 Proposed RTE System for Quote-Explanation Pair

We proposed a RTE system for our dataset based on three features: lexical cosine similarity, semantic similarity and word-to-vector similarity based on deep learning method[1]. In this section we discuss the corpus preparation procedure and computation of above features to recognise entailed T-H pairs.

Corpus Acquisition: We developed our corpus in two Phases. In first phase, we collected explanations for 200 English quotes through Amazon Mechanical Turk[2]. In second phase, manually we collected explanations of 800 English quotes from online websites[3]. Finally, we developed a corpus of 1000 English quotes with 4012 sentences as their explanations. The corpus is pre-processed by eliminating stop words and transforming into root words.

Recognition of TE relation: We computed the score of lexical cosine similarity, semantic similarity and word-to-vector similarity for each pair of T-H. The computational process involves following steps:

[1] http://deeplearning4j.org/word2vec.html.
[2] https://www.mturk.com/mturk/welcome.
[3] http://brightdrops.com/.

- Cosine similarity is a measure of similarity between two n-dimensional vectors. We form two binary vectors (A & B) for all unique words and term-frequency in T and H to obtain their cosine similarity using Eq. 1.

$$COS\,(A, B) = \frac{|A \bigcup B|}{\sqrt{|A| \times |B|}} \tag{1}$$

- To obtain semantic similarity score for each T-H pair, we use a text to text similarity measure proposed by the work [9]. The work measures similarity between two ontology concepts based on Extended Information content (eIC). In our work we use quote, explanation as concept c1, c2 respectively in Eq. 2 to calculate their semantic similarity.

$$sim_{FaITH}(c_1, c_2) = \frac{eIC(msca(c_1, c_2))}{eIC(c_1) + eIC(c_2) - eIC(msca(c_1, c_2))} \tag{2}$$

- Vector representations of words [8] lend themselves for many state-of-the-art solutions of NLP problems. We measure relatedness of quote and its explanation from their vector representations of words by using deep-learning library Word2Vec toolkit[4]. We train Word2Vec tool with our dataset and use word similarity score in Eq. 3 to measure the relatedness of T and H.

$$w2v_{sim}(A, B) = \frac{2 * \sum_{i=0}^{i=n} max_{sim}(w_i)}{N} \tag{3}$$

For each T-H pair, we computed above three scores and compared with feature specific threshold values to recognise the pair as entailed or non-entailed. Experimentally we set the threshold for semantic, cosine and word-to-vector similarity as 0.62, 0.22 and 0.04 respectively.

4 Experiment Result and Analysis

We set up one experiment to evaluate the dataset and the performance of our proposed approach. For experiment and evaluation, we prepared 1000000 (1000 * 1000) pairs of quote-explanation by pairing each quote with all explanation. In our experiment, we include QUED and 3 more state-of-the-art entailment dataset: RTE-01 to RTE-06[5], SNLI [3], PHEME [7] and two RTE systems: one is a baseline RTE system based on Unigram, Bigram, Longest Common Subsequence (LCS) and Skip-grams and another is RTE-SDK RTE framework[6]. The detail performance result (F1 score) is reported in Table 1. The evaluation result shows that the RTE task on quote-explanation dataset is more challenging than the other standard RTE dataset. Proposed RTE system outperforms (F-measure of 48.14%) over the dataset then other 2 systems.

[4] http://deeplearning4j.org/word2vec.html.
[5] http://www.nist.gov/tac/data/RTE/index.html.
[6] https://code.google.com/archive/p/rite-sdk/.

Table 1. Performance of the proposed methodology on various entailment dataset

Approaches	Dataset								
	RTE-1	RTE-2	RTE-3	RTE-4	RTE-5	RTE-6	SNLI	PHEME	QUED
Baseline	65.16	40.5	34.8	36.4	38.46	36.5	28	39.63	28.57
RTE-SDK	48.7	48.8	49.9	49.6	49.8	48.67	49.9	48.0	43.6
Proposed approach	62.34	63.17	62.97	73.93	67.8	65.8	60.0	60.34	**48.14**

5 Conclusion and Future Works

In this research work we developed a new domain RTE corpus on English quote-explanations. We also proposed an approach for RTE on this dataset and reported the accuracy rate as 48.14%. Comparative study of evaluation shows that the RTE task on quote-explanation dataset is more challenging. Our next target is to utilize this concept in social media text summarization.

References

1. Adams, R., Nicolae, G., Nicolae, C., Harabagiu, S.: Textual entailment through extended lexical overlap and lexico-semantic matching. In: Proceedings of the ACL-PASCAL Workshop on Textual Entailment and Paraphrasing, pp. 119–124. ACL (2007)
2. Agichtein, E., Askew, W., Liu, Y.: Combining lexical, syntactic, and semantic evidence for textual entailment classification. In: TAC. NIST (2008)
3. Bowman, S.R., Angeli, G., Potts, C., Manning, C.D.: Learning natural language inference from a large annotated corpus. In: Proceedings of the 2015 Conference on Empirical Methods in Natural Language Processing, pp. 632–642. ACL (2015)
4. Dagan, I., Glickman, O.: Probabilistic textual entailment: generic applied modeling of language variability. In: Learning Methods for Text Understanding and Mining, January 2004
5. Herrera, J., Peñas, A., Verdejo, F.: Textual entailment recognition based on dependency analysis and WordNet. In: Quiñonero-Candela, J., Dagan, I., Magnini, B., d'Alché-Buc, F. (eds.) MLCW 2005. LNCS (LNAI), vol. 3944, pp. 231–239. Springer, Heidelberg (2006). doi:10.1007/11736790_13
6. Herrera, J., Rodrigo, Á., Peñas, A., Verdejo, F.: UNED submission to AVE 2006. In: Working Notes for CLEF 2006 Workshop Co-located with the 10th ECDL, Spain, 20–22 September 2006
7. Lendvai, P., Augenstein, I., Bontcheva, K., Declerck, T.: Monolingual social media datasets for detecting contradiction and entailment. In: Proceedings of the Tenth International Conference on Language Resources and Evaluation (2016)
8. Mikolov, T., Chen, K., Corrado, G., Dean, J.: Efficient estimation of word representations in vector space (2013). CoRR abs/1301.3781
9. Pirró, G., Euzenat, J.: A feature and information theoretic framework for semantic similarity and relatedness. In: Patel-Schneider, P.F., et al. (eds.) ISWC 2010. LNCS, vol. 6496, pp. 615–630. Springer, Heidelberg (2010). doi:10.1007/978-3-642-17746-0_39

10. Shivade, C.P., Raghavan, P., Patwardhan, S.: Addressing limited data for textual entailment across domains. In: Proceedings of the 54th Annual Meeting of the Association for Computational Linguistics, vol. 1: Long Papers, Germany, 7–12 August 2016
11. Stern, A., Dagan, I.: The BIUTEE research platform for transformation-based textual entailment recognition (2013)
12. Wang, R., Neumann, G.: Recognizing textual entailment using sentence similarity based on dependency tree skeletons. In: Proceedings of the ACL-PASCAL Workshop on Textual Entailment and Paraphrasing, pp. 36–41, ACL, Prague, June 2007

Opinion Mining and Sentiment Analysis

Automatically Labelling Sentiment-Bearing Topics with Descriptive Sentence Labels

Mohamad Hardyman Barawi(✉), Chenghua Lin, and Advaith Siddharthan

Computing Science, University of Aberdeen, Aberdeen, UK
{r01mhbb,chenghua.lin,advaith}@abdn.ac.uk

Abstract. In this paper, we propose a simple yet effective approach for automatically labelling sentiment-bearing topics with descriptive sentence labels. Specifically, our approach consists of two components: (i) a mechanism which can automatically learn the relevance to sentiment-bearing topics of the underlying sentences in a corpus; and (ii) a sentence ranking algorithm for label selection that jointly considers topic-sentence relevance as well as aspect and sentiment co-coverage. To our knowledge, we are the first to study the problem of labelling sentiment-bearing topics. Our experimental results show that our approach outperforms four strong baselines and demonstrates the effectiveness of our sentence labels in facilitating topic understanding and interpretation.

1 Introduction

Probabilistic topic models such as latent Dirichlet allocation (LDA) [3] capture the thematic properties of documents by modelling texts as a mixture of distributions over words, known as topics. The words under each topic tend to co-occur together and have a tight thematic relation with one another, and can therefore be used as a lens for exploring and understanding large archives of unstructured text. Since the introduction of LDA, many extensions have been proposed, an important one being the joint sentiment-topic model family that aims to mine and uncover rich opinion structures. One represented work in this area is the joint sentiment-topic (JST) model [11], which has spurred subsequent research in developing variants of sentiment topic models for a range of opinion mining tasks such as aspect-based sentiment analysis [14], contrastive opinion mining [15], and the analysis of sentiment and topic dynamics [16].

JST is a hierarchical topic model which can detect sentiment and topic simultaneously from opinionated documents. The hidden topics discovered, therefore, are essentially sentiment-bearing topics resembling opinions. This is an intrinsic difference compared to the standard topics extracted by LDA which only express thematic information. We exemplify this difference with two topic examples shown in Table 1, where each topic consists of the top 10 topic words with the highest marginal probability. By examining the topic words, we see that the terms of the LDA topic are recognisably about the theme *"computer technology"*, whereas the terms of the JST topic capture opinions relating to *"unsatisfactory online shopping experience"*.

F. Frasincar et al. (Eds.): NLDB 2017, LNCS 10260, pp. 299–312, 2017.
DOI: 10.1007/978-3-319-59569-6_38

Table 1. Examples of LDA and JST topics with nouns (unformatted), adjectives(italics) verbs (bold).

[LDA]: Computer models information data system network model *parallel* methods software
[JST]: Amazon order **return ship receive** refund *damaged disappointed* policy *unhappy*

Although sentiment topic models have become an increasingly popular tool for exploring and understanding opinions from text, existing models all share some noticeable drawbacks, which can significantly limit their usefulness and effectiveness. First, applying sentiment topic models for exploratory purposes requires interpreting the meaning of the topics discovered, which, so far, relies entirely on manual interpretation. However, it is generally difficult for a non-expert user to understand a topic based only on its multinomial distribution, especially when the user is not familiar with the source collection [13]. The second limitation lies in these models' inability to facilitate accurate opinion and sentiment understanding, which is crucial for many applications. The issue stems from the fact that, although the topic words of sentiment-bearing topics collectively express opinions, these opinions are essentially shallow. Taking the JST topic in Table 1 for example, with manual examination one can interpret that this topic expresses plausible opinions relating to *"unsatisfactory online shopping experience"*, but it is impossible to gain deep insight of the opinion, i.e. whether the sentiment *unhappy* is only targeted to the product being ordered, or it is also related to Amazon's policy.

Remarkably, there is no existing work that has formally studied the problem of automatic labelling of sentiment-bearing topics. Substantial work on automatic topic labelling exists, but has focused on labelling standard topics discovered by LDA to facilitate the interpretation of topics discovered. These works assume that standard topics mainly express thematic information [1], and thus has driven most of the existing topic labelling approaches to rank a candidate label by measuring the thematic association between the label and the topic terms. In contrast, the top terms of sentiment-bearing topics consist of a good mixture of *nouns*, *verbs*, and *adjectives* resembling opinions [6,10,11]. Therefore, existing topic labelling approaches engineered for standard LDA topic cannot be applied to labelling sentiment-bearing topics as they provide no mechanism for modelling opinion.

In this paper, we formally study the problem of automatically labelling sentiment-bearing topics extracted by the JST model [11]. Specifically, we propose a novel framework for automatically selecting sentence labels that can facilitate understanding and interpretation of multinomial sentiment-bearing topics extracted by JST. In contrast to existing approaches which generate topic labels in the form of either a single term [9], a small set of terms (e.g. the top-n topic words) [5], or phrases [1], we choose the sentence as the label modality as it has grammatically linked word structures which are suitable for expressing complete thoughts, and hence could better facilitate the task of interpreting the opinions encoded in sentiment-bearing topics. We compare the effectiveness of our sentence based topic labelling approach against four strong baselines, including two sentence label baselines and two topic labelling systems which have been widely bench-marked in the literature [1,13]. Experimental results on three real-world datasets show that the labels generated by our approach are more effective than all the baselines in terms of facilitating sentiment-bearing topic understanding and interpretation.

To summarise, our contributions in this paper are two-fold: (i) we introduce a novel mechanism which can automatically learn the relevance to sentiment-bearing topics of the underlying sentences in a corpus; and (ii) we design an effective sentence label selection criteria which jointly considers topic-sentence relevance as well as aspect and sentiment co-coverage. To our knowledge, we are the first to study the problem of labelling sentiment-bearing topics. We describe related work in Sect. 2, followed by our labelling method in Sect. 3, experimental design in Sect. 4, results in Sect. 5 and conclusions in Sect. 6.

2 Related Work

Since its introduction, LDA has become a popular tool for unsupervised analysis of text, providing both a predictive model of future text and a latent topic representation of the corpus. The latter property of topic models has enabled exploration and digestion of large text copra through the extracted thematic structure represented as a multinomial distribution over words. Still, a major obstacle to applying LDA is the need to manually interpret the topic, which is generally difficult for non-expert users. This has in turn motivated a number of works in automatically learning semantically meaningful labels for facilitating topic understanding.

Automatically Learning Topic Label from Data. In an early work, Mei et al. [13] proposed generating topic labels using either bigrams or noun phrases extracted from a corpus and ranked the relevance of candidate labels to a given topic using KL divergence. Noun phrases were ranked by their frequencies whereas bigrams were ranked using T-score. Candidate labels were then scored using relevance functions which minimised the similarity distance between the candidate labels and the topic words. Finally, the top-ranked candidate label was chosen as the topic's label. Mei's approach showed that topic labels generated using ngrams were better in general when applied to different genre of texts. Mao et al. [12] labelled hierarchical topics by investigating the sibling and parent-child relations among the topics. Their approach followed a similar paradigm to [13], which ranked candidate labels by measuring the relevance of the labels to a reference corpus using Jensen-Shannon divergence. More recently, Cano et al. [5] proposed labeling topics using labels generated based on multi-document summarisation. Basically, they measured term relevance of documents to topics and generated topic label candidates based on the summarisation of a topic's relevant documents.

Automatic Topic Labelling Leveraging External Sources. Another type of approach in automatic topic labelling leverages external sources, e.g., Wikipedia or DBpedia [7–9]. Lau et al. [9] proposed selecting the most representative term from a topic as its label by computing the similarity between each word and all others in the topic. Several sources of information were used to identify the best label, including pointwise mutual information scores, WordNet hypernymy relations, and distributional similarity. These features were combined in a re-ranking model. In a follow-up work, Lau et al. [8] generated label candidates for a topic based on top-ranking topic terms and titles of Wikipedia articles. They then built a Support Vector Regression (SVR) model for ranking the label candidates. Other researchers [7] proposed using graph centrality measures to identify DBpedia concepts that are related to the topic words as their topic labels. More recently, Aletras et al. [1] proposed generating topic labels of multiple modalities, i.e., both textual and images labels. To generate textual labels, they used the top-7 topic terms to search Wikipedia and Google to collect article titles which were subsequently chunk parsed. The image labels were generated by first querying the top-n topic terms to Bing search engine. The top-n candidate images retrieved were then ranked with PageRank and the image with the highest PageRank score was selected as the topic label. To summarise, the topic labelling approaches in the above-mentioned works were engineered for labelling standard LDA topics rather than sentiment-bearing topics, and are mostly fall into one of the following linguistic modalities: a single term [9], a small set of terms (e.g., the top-n topic words) [9], or phrases [1,8]. These linguistic modalities, while sufficient for expressing facet subjects of standard topics, are inadequate to express complete thoughts or opinions due to their linguistic constraints, i.e. lacking a subject, a predicate or both. Our goal is to address this gap and study the problem of automatically labelling sentiment-bearing topics with more appropriate and descriptive sentence labels.

3 Methodology

The goal of our work is to develop a novel approach for automatically labelling multinomial sentiment-bearing topics with descriptive sentence labels. We first briefly introduce the JST model used for extracting sentiment-bearing topics, and then proceed to describe the proposed approach for sentence label selection. It should be noted that our approach does not have any specific dependencies on the JST model, and thus it is general enough to be directly applied to any other sentiment topic model variants as long as they generate multinomial topics as output.

3.1 Preliminaries of the JST Model

The graphical model of JST is shown in Fig. 1a, in which D denotes a collection of documents, N_d a sequence of words in document d, S the number of sentiment

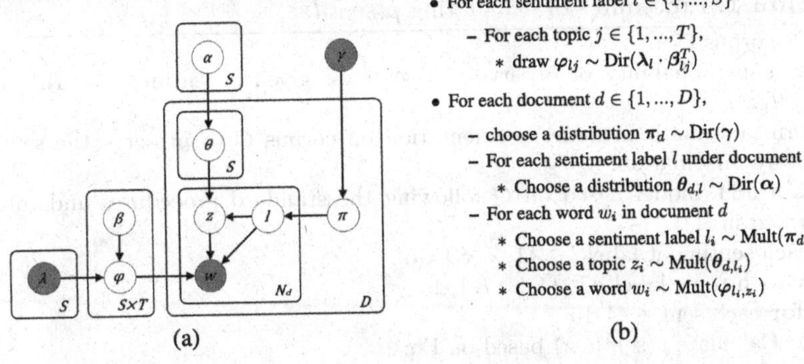

α
S
γ
θ
S
β
z
l
π
λ
φ
w
S
S×T
N_d
D
(a)
• For each sentiment label $l \in \{1, ..., S\}$
– For each topic $j \in \{1, ..., T\}$,
∗ draw $\varphi_{lj} \sim \text{Dir}(\boldsymbol{\lambda}_l \cdot \boldsymbol{\beta}_{lj}^T)$
• For each document $d \in \{1, ..., D\}$,
– choose a distribution $\pi_d \sim \text{Dir}(\boldsymbol{\gamma})$
– For each sentiment label l under document d
∗ Choose a distribution $\boldsymbol{\theta}_{d,l} \sim \text{Dir}(\boldsymbol{\alpha})$
– For each word w_i in document d
∗ Choose a sentiment label $l_i \sim \text{Mult}(\pi_d)$
∗ Choose a topic $z_i \sim \text{Mult}(\boldsymbol{\theta}_{d,l_i})$
∗ Choose a word $w_i \sim \text{Mult}(\varphi_{l_i,z_i})$
(b)

Fig. 1. (a) JST graphical model; (b) the generative process of JST.

labels, T the total number of topics, and $\{\alpha, \beta, \gamma\}$ the Dirichlet hyperparameters (cf. [11] for details). Figure 1b summarises the complete procedure for generating a word w_i in JST. First, one draws a sentiment label l from the per-document sentiment proportion π_d. Following that, one draws a topic label z from the per-document topic proportion $\boldsymbol{\theta}_{d,l}$ conditioned on sentiment label l. Finally, one draws a word from the per-corpus word distribution $\varphi_{l,z}$ conditioned on both the sentiment label l and topic label z.

The problem to be solved by the JST model is the posterior inference of the variables, which determine the hidden sentiment-bearing topic structures that can best explain the observed set of documents. Formally, a sentiment-bearing topic is represented by a multinomial distribution over words denoted as $p(w|l, z) \equiv \varphi_{w,l,z}$, where w, l, and z represent the word, sentiment label and topic label indices, respectively. In particular, the approximated per-corpus sentiment-topic word distribution is

$$\varphi_{l,z,w} = \frac{N_{l,z,w} + \beta}{N_{l,z} + V\beta}, \tag{1}$$

where V is the corpus vocabulary size; $N_{l,z,w}$ is the number of times word w appeared in topic z with sentiment label l; $N_{l,z}$ is the number of times words are assigned to z and l. Recalling that $\varphi_{w,l,z}$ is a multinomial distribution, we have $\sum_{w \in V} \varphi_{w,l,z} = 1$.

3.2 Modelling the Relevance Between Sentiment-Bearing Topics and Sentences

The original JST model can only learn topic-word and topic-document associations as it operates on bag-of-words features at the document-level, with the corpus sentence structure being ignored. Therefore, we propose a new computational mechanism that can uncover the relevance to a sentiment-bearing topic of the underlying sentences in the corpus. To achieve this, we first preserve the

Algorithm 1. Procedures of calculating $p(\text{sent}|l, z)$.

Input: A corpus C

Output: The probability of observing a sentence given a sentiment-bearing topic $p(\text{sent}|l, z)$.

Perform automatic sentence segmentation on corpus C to preserve the sentence structure information.
Train a JST model based on C following the standard procedures and settings described in [11].
for each sentiment label $l \in \{1, ..., S\}$ **do**
    for each topic label $z \in \{1, ..., K\}$ **do**
        for each sent $\in C$ **do**
            Calculate $p(\text{sent}|l, z)$ based on Eq. 2
        end for
        Normalise the probability of $p(\text{sent}|l, z)$
        Sort sentences based on the probability of $p(\text{sent}|l, z)$ in a descending order.
    end for
end for

sentence structure information for each document during the corpus preprocessing step (see Sect. 4 for more details). Second, modelling topic-sentence relevance is essentially equivalent to calculating the probability of a sentence given a sentiment-bearing topic $p(\text{sent}|l, z)$, i.e., the likelihood of a sentence (from the corpus) associating with a given sentiment-bearing topic. The posterior inference of JST, based on Gibbs sampling [11,17], can recover the hidden sentiment label and topic label assignments for each word in the corpus. Such label-word assignment information provides a means to re-assembling the relevance between a word and a sentiment-bearing topic. By leveraging the sentence structure information and gathering the label assignment statistics for each word of a sentence, we can derive the probability of a sentence given a sentiment-bearing topic as

$$p(\text{sent}|l, z) = \frac{p(l, z|\text{sent}) \cdot p(\text{sent})}{p(l, z)} \propto p(l, z|\text{sent}) \cdot p(\text{sent}), \tag{2}$$

where $p(l, z|\text{sent}) = \frac{\sum_{w \in \text{sent} \vee l'_w = l, z'_w = z} \varphi_{l',z',w}}{\sum_{w \in \text{sent}} \varphi_{l',z',w}}$, and $p(\text{sent}) = \sum_l \sum_z \prod_{w \in \text{sent}} \varphi_{l,z,w}$. Note that the per-corpus sentiment-topic word distribution $\varphi_{w,l,z}$, defined in Eq. 1, is obtained via the posterior inference using Gibbs sampling. Also $p(l, z)$ is discounted as it is a constant when comparing sentencial labels for the same sentiment-bearing topic. A summary of our mechanism of calculating $p(\text{sent}|l, z)$ is given in Algorithm 1.

3.3 Automatic Sentence Label Selection

Given a sentiment-bearing topic, one intuitive approach for selecting the most representative sentence label is to rank the sentences in the corpus according to the topic-sentence relevance probability $p(\text{sent}|l, z)$ derived in the previous section. One can then select the sentence with the highest probability as a label for the topic. We found that a high-degree of relevance, however, cannot be taken as the only criterion for label selection as it might favour selection of short sentences as labels covering limited amount of information, or risk selecting sentence labels that might cover either thematic or sentiment information alone. To address the issues and to select the most representative sentence labels covering sentiment-coupled aspects which reveal opinions, it is important to consider the occurrences of both aspect and sentiment, and the balance between them. To combat this challenge, we design the sentence label selection criteria which jointly consider two properties: sentence-topic relevance as well as aspect and sentiment co-coverage. Such criteria provide a basis for building an algorithm for ranking sentence labels in terms of how well they can describe the opinion encoded in a sentiment-bearing topic.

Formulation of Sentence Label Ranking. We now describe our sentence label ranking function contributed by the two properties of our label selection criteria. Given a sentiment-bearing topic, our objective is to select a sentence label with the highest ranking score, where the label ranking function is defined as follows

$$L(s|t_{l,z}) = \alpha \cdot Rel(s|t_{l,z}) + (1 - \alpha) \cdot Cov(s|t_{l,z}). \tag{3}$$

Here $Rel(s|t_{l,z})$ is the relevance score between a sentence s and a given sentiment-bearing topic $t_{l,z}$ as described in Sect. 3.2. $Cov(s|t_{l,z})$, the aspect and sentiment co-coverage score, encodes two heuristics: (i) sentence labels covering either sentiment or aspects information alone will be significantly down-weighted; and (ii) labels which cover salient aspects of the topic and couple with sentiment will be given high weightage. Parameter α brings out the trade-off between relevance and the co-coverage of aspect and sentiment, and was empirically set to 0.4.

Let i be a word from sentence s, a_i a binary variable that indicates whether word i is an aspect word, o_i a binary variable that indicates whether word i is a sentiment word, $w_{l,z,i}$ the importance weight of word i given topic $t_{l,z}$, and $t^i_{l,z,n}$ a binary variable which indicates the presence of word i in the top-n words of sentiment-bearing topic $t_{l,z}$. Formally, the aspect and sentiment co-coverage score is formulated as

$$Cov(s|t_{l,z}) = \frac{2 \cdot A(s|t_{l,z}) \cdot S(s|t_{l,z})}{A(s|t_{l,z}) + S(s|t_{l,z})} \tag{4}$$

$$A(s|t_{l,z}) = \sum_{i \in s} w_{l,z,i} \cdot a_{s,i} \cdot t^i_{l,z,n} \tag{5}$$

$$S(s|t_{l,z}) = \sum_{i \in s} w_{l,z,i} \cdot o_{s,i} \cdot t^i_{l,z,n}, \tag{6}$$

where the weight $w_{l,z,i}$ essentially equals to $\varphi_{l,z,i}$, i.e., the marginal probability of word i given a sentiment-bearing topic $t_{l,z}$. We identify whether word i is an

Table 2. Dataset statistics.

Dataset	Total # of doc.	avg. # of words	avg. # of sentences	Vocab. size
Kitchen	2000	25	4	2450
Electronics	2000	25	4	2317
IMDb	1383	118	13	14337

aspect word or a sentiment word as follows. In the preprocessing, we perform parts of speech (POS) tagging on the experimental datasets (detailed in Sect. 4). Words tagged as nouns are regarded as aspects words whereas sentiment words are the ones that have appeared in the MPQA sentiment lexicon[1]. Recalling that a multinomial topic is represented by its top-n words with the highest marginal probability, we further constrain that word i must also appear in the top-n topic words of sentiment-bearing topic $t_{l,z}$. This enforces that a good sentence label should cover as many important sentiment coupled aspects of a topic as possible. In the case where a sentence contains either aspect or sentiment information alone (i.e., $A(s|t_{l,z}) = 0$ or $S(s|t_{l,z}) = 0$), the resulting aspect and sentiment co-coverage score would be zero, and thus down-weighting the corresponding sentence. Finally, a sentence label $\hat{s}$ for a sentiment-bearing topic $t_{l,z}$ can be obtained from (Eq. 7)

$$\hat{s} = \underset{s}{\operatorname{argmax}}\, L(s|t_{l,z}). \tag{7}$$

4 Experimental Setup

We evaluated our topic labelling approach through an experiment where participants rated labels generated by our approach as well as two baselines and two competitor systems.

4.1 Setup

Datasets. We evaluated the effectiveness of the sentence label selected by our approach on three real-world datasets. Two datasets are publicly available, i.e., Amazon reviews for kitchen and electronic products, where each dataset contains 1000 positive and 1000 negative reviews[2] [4]. We have also collected a movie review dataset for *Internal Affairs* and *The Departed* from IMDb[3]. These two movies virtually share the same storyline but with different casts and productions: *Internal Affairs* is a 2002 Hong Kong movie, while *The Departed* is a 2006 Hollywood movie.

[1] http://www.cs.pitt.edu/mpqa/.
[2] https://www.cs.jhu.edu/~mdredze/datasets/sentiment/.
[3] http://www.imdb.com/.

Implementation Details. In the preprocessing, we first performed automatic sentence segmentation[4] on the experimental datasets in order to preserve the sentence structure information of each document, followed by parts of speech tagging on the datasets using the Stanford POS tagger [18]. Punctuation, numbers, and non-alphabet characters were then removed and all words were lowercased. Finally, we trained JST models with the preprocessed corpus following the standard procedures described in [11], with the MPQA lexicon [19] being incorporated as prior information for model learning. We empirically set the model with 2 sentiment labels and 10 topics for each sentiment label, resulting 20 sentiment-bearing topics in total for each of the three evaluation datasets.

4.2 Baselines

Top probability (Top-prob). The first baseline is to select the sentence with highest topic relevance probability $p(\text{sent}|l, z)$ according to the JST model, as described in Sect. 3.2.

Centroid. The second baseline is a centroid based sentence label. For each sentiment-bearing topic, we first construct a sentence cluster consists of the top 150 most relevant sentences for the given topic, ranked based on the topic relevance probability $p(\text{sent}|l, z)$. Next, for each of the sentence in the cluster, we compute the cosine similarity between the sentence and the remaining sentences in the cluster. Finally, the sentence with the highest cosine similarity score is picked as the topic label. This is a stronger baseline as it selects a sentence representative of multiple high probability sentences.

Phrase/Bigram Baselines. In addition to the two sentential baselines, we also compare our approach to two systems which have been widely bench-marked in the topic labelling task, namely, **Mei07** [13] and **Aletras14** [2]. Note that **Mei07** is our re-implementation which generates bigram labels, while **Aletras14** is the original implementation kindly provided by the authors which generates phrase labels. For both, we selected the top three bigrams/phrases for inclusion in the label.

4.3 Evaluation Task

For each sentiment-bearing topic, annotators were provided with the top 10 topic words with the highest marginal probability and the labels generated by each system. They were then asked to judge the quality of each label on a 4-point Likert Scale: 3-Very good label, a perfect description of the topic; 2-Reasonable label, but does not completely capture the topic; 1-Label is semantically related to the topic, but would not make a good topic label; and 0-Label is completely inappropriate, and unrelated to the topic. The most relevant review of the sentiment-bearing topic ((calculated using $p(d|l, z)$, the probability of a document given a sentiment-bearing topic) was also provided to annotators so that they can have

[4] http://www.nltk.org/.

Table 3. Human evaluation based on Top-1 average rating.

Domain	Mei07	Aletras14	Top-prob	Centroid	Sent-label
Kitchen	0.31	1.29	0.64	1.79	1.81
Electronics	0.52	2.13	0.83	1.33	2.48
IMDb	0.36	1.73	0.69	1.67	2.58
Average	0.39	1.72	0.72	1.59	2.29

Table 4. Average label length across three datasets.

	Mei07	Aletras14	Top-prob	Centroid	Sent-label
Avg. label length	6	6.8	6.83	23.8	12.3

a better context for topic understanding. To ensure there was no bias introduced in this step, we checked whether the most relevant review contains our sentence label. This only occurred in 7.5% of cases. For the remaining 92.5%, sentence labels appeared in only the second to the fifth most relevant reviews, not shown to the user. This suggest that our experience is not bias towards our system and that the most relevant review does not necessary contains the most representative sentence label.

We recruited 30 Computing Science postgraduate students to participate in the evaluation task. Recalling that 20 sentiment-bearing topics were extracted for each dataset and that there are 5 systems to compare (i.e., our proposed approach and the four baselines) and 3 datasets, the total number of labels to rate is 300. To avoid the evaluation task being overly long, we broke the evaluation task into 3 sessions carried out on different days, with each session evaluating labels from one dataset only. Completing one session took around 18 min for each participant on average.

5 Experimental Results

5.1 Human Evaluation

We report results using the Top-1 average rating [8], which is the average human rating (based on the Likert Scale) assigned to the best candidate labels selected by each of the approaches, and the higher rating will indicate a better overall quality of a label. Table 3 shows the Top-1 average ratings for each approach (with our approach denoted as **Sent-label**). The sentence labels generated by our approach outperforms all baselines significantly (two-tailed paired t-test; $p < 0.001$ in all cases). Furthermore, as shown in Table 4, the label selected by our approach also keeps a good balance of information-richness and brevity, in contrast to the other two sentential baselines that favour either very short or very long sentences. To measure inter-annotator agreement (IAA), we first calculated Spearman's ρ between the ratings given by an annotator and the average ratings

Table 5. Labelling examples for sentiment-bearing topics.

		Positive topics	Negative topics
Kitchen	Topic words	*very good well really nice price quality set little happy*	*money don't product disappointed, back waste without very worth make*
	Mei07	are very; a very; very good	the money; money on; you will
	Aletras14	prices and quality; nice guy; coin grading	food waste; zero waste; waste your money
	Top-prob	Well worth every penny	Heres why I am sorely disappointed
	Centroid	I got this for the dogs and they seem to like it	I ordered the product and when I opened the box I found that I received only the bottom piece
	Sent-label	Nice little toaster with good price	Totally dissatisfy with this product and it's damn waste of money
Electronics	Topic words	*sound headphones music ear noise cord ipod pair quality head*	*receiver slightly laser pointer green serious blocks kensington delormes beam*
	Mei07	the sound; The sound; sound is	pointer is; of this; laser pointer
	Aletras14	Noise-cancelling headphones; Previous Bose headphones; Bose headphones	Laser safety; Laser pointer; Laser diode
	Top-prob	They have very good sound quality	I made the mistake to buy the Kensington laser pointer before this one
	Centroid	I just leave the mounts in place on the windshields of both cars and move the Nuvi and power cord to whichever car I am using at the moment	I can maybe prefer a bit the ergonomy of the Kensington together with the very practical possibility to store the USB receiver inside the unit but this is probably just my taste and the hiro is quite comfortable either and lighter
	Sent-label	The output of sound quality from an ipod is amazing	The Kensington laser pointer is slightly expensive
IMDb	Topic words	*without no want clever intelligent surely play offer effective puts*	*language use vulgar blood used excessive dialog foul us realism*
	Mei07	is one; that it; that there	violence and; of violence; terms of
	Aletras14	Flying Spaghetti Monster; Expelled: No Intelligence Allowed; Prayer	Vampire: The Masquerade ? Bloodlines; Monkeys in Chinese culture; Chavacano
	Top-prob	But what would Lucifer be without his collaborators	But the story flows well as does the violence
	Centroid	The Departed is without doubt the best picture of the year and never fails to entertain	It's far too graphically violent for teenagers, including images of heads being shot and spurting blood, limbs being broken, etc.
	Sent-label	If you want to see an intelligent, memorable thriller, watch The Departed	The movie includes some overdone foul language and violent scenes

from all other annotators for the labels corresponding to the same topic. We then averaged the ρ across annotators, topics, and datasets, resulting in an average $\rho = 0.73$, a good IAA.

We want to stress that these baselines are fair. To our knowledge, we are the first to study the problem of labelling sentiment-bearing topics, so there is no directly comparable system available which can generate sentence labelling for sentiment-bearing topics. In the past, top-n topic terms have been commonly used for manually interpreting sentiment-bearing topics for a variety of sentiment-topic models (i.e., its not just exclusively used for standard topic models), and that is why we propose an automatic labelling approach here. For the phrase label baselines, they can capture a fair amount of sentiment information from sentiment-bearing topics based on the adjective/adverb phrases extracted. The sentence label baselines are also strong baselines as they both make use of the probability distributions from the JST model, with the centroid baseline further addressing the diversity issue.

5.2 Qualitative Analysis

Table 5 shows six sentiment-bearing topics for the Kitchen, Electronics and IMDb dataset extracted by JST. For each topic, we also show the top-3 labels generated by Mei07 and Aletras14, two baselines (i.e., Centroid, Top-prob), and the sentence label generated by our approach (Sent-label). It can be seen from the table that the sentence labels generated by our approach generally capture the opinions encoded in the sentiment-bearing topics quite well; whereas in quite a few cases the labels generated by Mei07 and Aletras14 either only capture the thematic information of the topics (e.g., *Noise-cancelling headphones*) or merely sentiment information (e.g., *very good*).

Our labelling approach also shows better performance than the sentential baselines. For instance, both sentential baselines were unable to adequately interpret the negative sentiment-bearing topics in the Kitchen dataset. For example, the Centroid baseline "*I ordered ... received only the bottom piece.*" captures the thematic information (i.e., *product*) but fails to capture the sentiment information (e.g., *worth*). The Top-prob baseline captures negative sentiment information (i.e., *disappointed*) but does not include any thematic information (e.g., *money, product*). A user who read the Top-prob baseline (i.e., "*Heres why I am sorely disappointed*") is likely to have some confusions in understanding what causes the disappointment in the label, e.g., whether it is due to *money* or *product.* Our approach (i.e., Sent-label) also performs better in the Electronics dataset by giving more descriptive information about products. Take the positive sentiment-bearing topics for example, the labels generated by Mei07 and Aletras14 capture two different thematic aspects i.e., *sound* and *headphones*, respectively. For the Top-prob label, it captures positive sentiment about *sound quality*, whereas the Centroid baseline label seems less relevant to the topic. In contrast, our proposed approach shows that the topic conveys the opinion of iPod sound quality being amazing.

To summarise, our experimental results show that our approach outperforms four strong baselines and demonstrates the effectiveness of our sentence labels in facilitating topic understanding and interpretation.

6 Conclusion

In this paper, we proposed a simple yet effective approach for automatically labelling sentiment-bearing topics with descriptive sentence labels. To our knowledge, we are the first to study the problem of labelling sentiment-bearing topics. The human evaluation shows that the labels produced by our approach are more effective than a range of strong baselines in facilitating sentiment-bearing topic interpretation and understanding. It should also be noted that our approach does not have any specific dependencies on the JST model, and thus it is general enough to be directly applied to any other sentiment topic model variants which generate multinomial topics as output.

In the future, we would like to extend our work for opinion summarisation. One natural way of achieving this is to summaries documents through the propagation of the document-topic and topic-sentence associations learned from our framework.

Acknowledgments. This work is supported by the awards made by the UK Engineering and Physical Sciences Research Council (Grant number: EP/P005810/1, EP/P011829/1).

References

1. Aletras, N., Baldwin, T., Lau, J., Stevenson, M.: Evaluating topic representations for exploring document collections. J. Assoc. Inf. Sci. Technol. **68**, 154–167 (2015)
2. Aletras, N., Baldwin, T., Lau, J.H., Stevenson, M.: Representing topics labels for exploring digital libraries. In: Proceedings of the 14th ACM/IEEE-CS Joint Conference on Digital Libraries, pp. 239–248. IEEE Press (2014)
3. Blei, D.M., Ng, A.Y., Jordan, M.I.: Latent Dirichlet allocation. J. Mach. Learn. Res. **3**, 993–1022 (2003)
4. Blitzer, J., Dredze, M., Pereira, F., et al.: Biographies, bollywood, boom-boxes and blenders: domain adaptation for sentiment classification. ACL **7**, 440–447 (2007)
5. Cano Basave, A.E., He, Y., Xu, R.: Automatic labelling of topic models learned from twitter by summarisation. In: Proceedings of ACL (2014)
6. He, Y., Lin, C., Gao, W., Wong, K.F.: Dynamic joint sentiment-topic model. ACM Trans. Intell. Syst. Technol. (TIST) **5**(1), 6 (2013)
7. Hulpus, I., Hayes, C., Karnstedt, M., Greene, D.: Unsupervised graph-based topic labelling using DBpedia. In: Proceedings of the Sixth ACM International Conference on Web search and Data Mining, pp. 465–474. ACM (2013)
8. Lau, J., Grieser, K., Newman, D., Baldwin, T.: Automatic labelling of topic models. In: Proceedings of ACL, pp. 1536–1545 (2011)
9. Lau, J.H., Newman, D., Karimi, S., Baldwin, T.: Best topic word selection for topic labelling. In: Proceedings of the 23rd International Conference on Computational Linguistics: Posters, pp. 605–613 (2010)

10. Li, C., Zhang, J., Sun, J.T., Chen, Z.: Sentiment topic model with decomposed prior. In: SIAM International Conference on Data Mining (SDM 2013). Society for Industrial and Applied Mathematics (2013)
11. Lin, C., He, Y., Everson, R., Rüger, S.: Weakly-supervised joint sentiment-topic detection from text. IEEE Trans. Knowl. Data Eng. (TKDE) **24**, 1134–1145 (2011)
12. Mao, X.L., Ming, Z.Y., Zha, Z.J., Chua, T.S., Yan, H., Li, X.: Automatic labeling hierarchical topics. In: Proceedings of the 21st ACM International Conference on Information and Knowledge Management, pp. 2383–2386. ACM (2012)
13. Mei, Q., Shen, X., Zhai, C.: Automatic labeling of multinomial topic models. In: Proceedings of the 13th ACM SIGKDD International Conference on Knowledge Discovery and Data Mining, pp. 490–499. ACM (2007)
14. Poria, S., Chaturvedi, I., Cambria, E., Bisio, F.: Sentic LDA: improving on LDA with semantic similarity for aspect-based sentiment analysis. In: 2016 International Joint Conference on Neural Networks (IJCNN), pp. 4465–4473. IEEE (2016)
15. Ren, Z., de Rijke, M.: Summarizing contrastive themes via hierarchical non-parametric processes. In: Proceedings of the 38th International ACM SIGIR Conference on Research and Development in Information Retrieval, pp. 93–102 (2015)
16. Si, J., Mukherjee, A., Liu, B., Li, Q., Li, H., Deng, X.: Exploiting topic based twitter sentiment for stock prediction. ACL **2**, 24–29 (2013)
17. Steyvers, M., Griffiths, T.: Probabilistic topic models. Handb. Latent Semant. Anal. **427**(7), 424–440 (2007)
18. Toutanova, K., Klein, D., Manning, C.D., Singer, Y.: Feature-rich part-of-speech tagging with a cyclic dependency network. In: Proceedings of the 2003 Conference of the North American Chapter of the Association for Computational Linguistics on Human Language Technology, vol. 1, pp. 173–180 (2003)
19. Wilson, T., Wiebe, J., Hoffmann, P.: Recognizing contextual polarity in phrase-level sentiment analysis. In: Proceedings of the Conference on Human Language Technology and Empirical Methods in Natural Language Processing, pp. 347–354 (2005)

Does Optical Character Recognition and Caption Generation Improve Emotion Detection in Microblog Posts?

Roman Klinger(✉)

Institut Für Maschinelle Sprachverarbeitung, Universität Stuttgart,
Pfaffenwaldring 5b, 70569 Stuttgart, Germany
roman.klinger@ims.uni-stuttgart.de

Abstract. Emotion recognition in microblogs like Twitter is the task of assigning an emotion to a post from a predefined set of labels. This is often performed based on the Tweet text. In this paper, we investigate whether information from attached images contributes to this classification task. We use off-the-shelf tools to extract a signal from an image. Firstly, with employ optical character recognition (OCR), to make embedded text accessable, and secondly, we use automatic caption generation to generalize over the content of the depiction. Our experiments show that using the caption only slightly improves performance and only for the emotions *fear*, *anger*, *disgust* and *trust*. OCR shows a significant impact for *joy*, *love*, *sadness*, *fear*, and *anger*.

Keywords: Emotion classification · Social media · Caption generation · Optical character recognition

1 Introduction

In natural language processing, emotion recognition is the task of associating words, phrases or documents with predefined emotions from psychological models. We consider discrete categories as proposed by Ekman [1] and Plutchik [2], namely *anger*, *fear*, *joy*, *sadness*, *surprise*, *disgust*, *love*, *shame*, and *trust*.

Emotion detection has been applied to, *e.g.*, tales [3], blogs [4], and as a very popular domain, microblogs on Twitter [5]. The latter in particular provides a large source of data in the form of user messages [6]. A common source of weak supervision are hashtags and emoticons to train classifiers. These measure the association of all other words in the message with the emotion [7]. For instance the Tweet "Be prepared for a bunch of depressing tweets guys because I am feeling it tonight. Very sad." is associated via the trigger words "depressing" and "sad" with the emotion *sadness* [8]. In this example, a standard text classification approach is likely to succeed. However, there are (at least) two cases in which the expressed emotion is not communicated in the text of the Tweet: Firstly, the main message can be hidden as text in an image which is linked to the post. This is a popular strategy, given constraints on post lengths (for instance on

F. Frasincar et al. (Eds.): NLDB 2017, LNCS 10260, pp. 313–319, 2017.
DOI: 10.1007/978-3-319-59569-6_39

Twitter to 140 characters) and to advertise a specific message or content with graphical support. In addition, some authors try to hide their message from search engines and platform curators, for instance in hate speech or fake news. Secondly, an author might show their emotion by posting a photo that depicts a particular situation. In this paper, we investigate if the recognition of emotional content of a micropost can be improved by taking into account information from linked images. To achieve this, we extract textual characterizations of the images associated with posts, using off-the-shelf tools.

Related work in this area aims, for instance, at detecting and understanding of facial expressions [9,10]. Similar techniques have also been applied to detection of specific classes of linked images, for instance fake pictures [11]. Recent research showed sentiment classification benefits from the combination of text and image information [12].

We perform experiments on a Twitter corpus with a subset of emotions. For linked emotions, we incorporate two different approaches to extract information and represent it as text: (1) We process every image linked to a Tweet with optical character recognition (OCR) and combine these textual features from the recognized text with the Tweet text. The hypothesis is that OCR text complements the Tweet text and therefore improves classification performance. (2) We process every image with a pretrained neural network-based caption generation model and combine the generated text with the Tweet. We expect that some content is more likely to be associated with specific emotions, for instance groups of people or "selfies" might be more likely to be joyful. In addition, we analyze the corpus and point out interesting future research directions. Our corpus will be publicly available at http://www.ims.uni-stuttgart.de/data/visualemotions.

2 Methods and Experimental Setup

2.1 Features

We formulate the task of emotion detection from microposts as a multiclass classification problem, *i.e.*, we assume each instance belongs to exactly one emotion; for each, we use one maximum entropy classification model. Features are drawn from three different sources: the micropost text itself, text detected by optical character recognition in a linked image, and a generated caption which describes the content of the image.

Micropost text. We represent the text from the Tweet itself as standard bag-of-words. For better reproducibility of the experiments, we only perform token normalization by disregarding all non-alphanumeric characters and the hash sign ("#"). Hashtags which denote an emotion are ignored (see Sect. 2.2). Usernames (*i.e.*, character sequences starting with @) are mapped to "@USERNAME". We refer to such features of post d as ϕ^d_{text}.

Optical Character Recognition. Each image which is linked to a Tweet is processed by an optical character recognition (OCR) system. We use Tesseract 3.04.01 [13] with default parameters and ignore all output shorter than six

Table 1. Corpus Statistics. D_{all} is sampled from all Tweets, "w/ϕ^d_{OCR}" and "w/ϕ^d_{Vis}" denote counts for subsets with OCR features and caption features. D_{OCR} and D_{Vis} are sampled from the set of all Tweets with recognized text in the image and do not contain recognized text in the image.

Emotion	D_{all}	w/ϕ^d_{OCR}	w/ϕ^d_{Vis}	D_{OCR}	D_{Vis}
joy	91,836	6,927 (8 %)	18,672 (20 %)	92,066	111,604
love	41,470	3,477 (8 %)	8,963 (22 %)	46,290	50,974
sadness	26,521	1,495 (6 %)	2,952 (11 %)	19707	14,370
fear	12,721	1,490 (12 %)	2,299 (18 %)	19,400	7,925
anger	11,902	831 (7 %)	1,384 (12 %)	10,379	5,317
shame	4,562	138 (3 %)	193 (4 %)	1,988	862
surprise	5,492	195 (4 %)	792 (14 %)	2,790	5,681
trust	5,170	561 (11 %)	886 (17 %)	7,274	3,151
disgust	326	8 (2 %)	22 (7 %)	106	116
All	200,000	15,122 (8 %)	36,163 (18 %)	200,000	200,000

bytes. Features are generated from the recognized text as bag-of-words. In addition, we add one feature which always holds if any text was recognized. We refer to this feature set as ϕ^d_{OCR}.

Caption Generation. Recently, several approaches have been proposed to generate caption-like descriptions of the content of an image [14–16]. Such methods have been shown to be robust enough to serve as off the shelf tools. In these experiments, we rely on NeuralTalk2 (https://github.com/karpathy/neuraltalk2), a deep neural network CNN and RNN architecture. We use the pretrained COCO data set [17] model which is available with NeuralTalk2. As in the OCR output, we add features using a bag-of-words scheme and one feature which indicates whether a caption was generated (*i.e.*, this feature represents only that an image is attached, not the content). We refer to these features as ϕ^d_{Vis}.

2.2 Corpus

To analyze the impact of each feature set and combination, we downloaded Tweets for a particular set of hashtags from Twitter between March and November 2016. The emotions with example hashtags are *joy* (*e.g.* #happy, #joy, #happiness, #glad), *sadness* (*e.g.* #sad, #sadness, #unhappy, #grief), *surprise* (#surprise, #surprised), *love* (#love), *shame* (#shame), *anger* (*e.g.* #anger, #rage, #hate), *fear* (*e.g.*, #fear, #scare, #worry), *disgust* (#disgust), *trust* (#trust). From this overall set $\mathcal{D}$, we subsample three corpora, each with 200,000 instances, such that empirical testing of estimated models is not affected by different training set sizes. Sizes for these sets are shown in Table 1. From these

Table 2. Results for Tweet text features alone, on different sets (Experiment 1) and for OCR features (ϕ^d_{OCR}) and caption features (ϕ^d_{Vis}) in isolation (Experiment 2).

Emotion	Experiment 1									Experiment 2					
	ϕ^d_{text}									ϕ^d_{OCR}			ϕ^d_{Vis}		
	D_{all}			D_{OCR}			D_{Vis}			D_{OCR}			D_{Vis}		
	P	R	F	P	R	F	P	R	F	P	R	F	P	R	F
joy	78	86	82	81	89	85	79	88	84	70	83	76	57	98	72
love	70	72	71	75	78	77	73	73	73	62	58	60	47	6	11
sadness	75	72	73	80	69	74	76	56	65	58	46	51	58	1	2
fear	82	70	75	86	76	81	79	60	68	84	70	76	18	0	0
anger	84	68	75	86	70	77	80	50	61	80	62	69	91	9	17
shame	89	65	75	86	52	65	63	17	27	56	40	47	0	0	0
surprise	75	48	58	65	32	43	62	31	42	53	20	29	0	0	0
trust	85	65	74	84	65	73	84	59	69	76	60	67	45	2	4
disgust	73	39	51	17	4	6	0	0	0	0	0	0	0	0	0
Macro-Av	79	65	71	73	59	65	66	48	54	60	49	53	35	13	12

subcorpora, we use 150,000 randomly sampled instances for training and 50,000 for testing.

The corpus D_{all} is sampled without any constraints. It therefore contains posts with and without image attachments. The subcorpus D_{OCR} is sampled from all instances for which the optical character recognition generated output longer than six bytes (*i.e.*, $\forall d \in D_{\text{OCR}} : \phi^d_{\text{text}} \neq \varnothing$). The subcorpus D_{Vis} is sampled from all instances for which an image was linked, but for which the optical character recognition did *not* return any output (*i.e.*, $\forall d \in D_{\text{Vis}} : \phi^d_{\text{Vis}} \neq \varnothing \wedge \phi^d_{\text{OCR}} = \varnothing$). We therefore assume that D_{OCR} consists of Tweets with images which contain text and D_{Vis} consists of Tweets with images without text.

The first three columns of Table 1 show the numbers of Tweets for each emotion, using those which contain ϕ^d_{OCR} and ϕ^d_{Vis} features, respectively. Interestingly, the amount of Tweets with text related to *fear* and *trust* is higher than for other images. Tweets which are associated with *love*, *joy*, *fear* and *trust* contain more images without text than other emotions. In general, the portion of Tweets with emotion hashtags including images is 18 %.

3 Results

In the following, we discuss three experiments: In Experiment 1, we analyze Tweet features only (ϕ^d_{text}), but on three different sets (D_{all}, D_{OCR}, D_{Vis}). The left part of Table 2 shows the results as F_1, precision and recall. We observe that, on average, Tweet text features ϕ^d_{text} are sufficient to predict emotion labels, also for Tweets which contain an image with text: The performance of

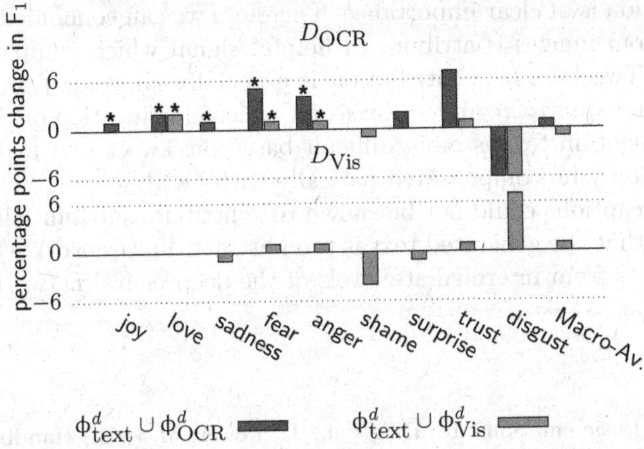

Fig. 1. Experiment 3: Complementarity of ϕ^d_{OCR} and ϕ^d_{Vis} to ϕ^d_{text}. The baseline corresponds to results with ϕ^d_{text} only as shown in Table 2. Significant differences ($\alpha = 0.01$) are denoted with a * (tested via bootstrap resampling [18]).

ϕ^d_{text} is not dramatically different on average for sets D_{all} and D_{OCR} (when the very infrequent emotion classes, especially *disgust*, are not taken into account). However, performance improves for *joy*, *love*, *sadness*, *fear*, and *anger*, while it decreases for the others. For Tweets with images without embedded text (D_{Vis}), text features are not as sufficient; we observe a clear drop in most emotions (except of *joy* amd *love*).

In Experiment 2 (also shown in Table 2), we analyze the classification performance without ϕ^d_{text}, but with ϕ^d_{OCR} alone (on ϕ^d_{OCR}) and with ϕ^d_{Vis} alone (on ϕ^d_{Vis}). For, ϕ^d_{OCR}, the performance is still good, but lower than for ϕ^d_{text}, therefore though a text image is added to the Tweet, the text of Tweet is a more important signal than the text in the recognized text in the image. The features ϕ^d_{Vis} are not sufficient for acceptable classification performance.

In Experiment 3, we analyze if ϕ^d_{OCR} or ϕ^d_{Vis} complement the information in ϕ^d_{text} in D_{OCR} and D_{Vis}. Figure 1 shows these differences; the baseline corresponds to results in Table 2. Though ϕ^d_{Vis} is not sufficient for classification alone, it contributes slightly to *fear*, *anger*, *trust*, and *disgust* on D_{Vis}, however, the positive impact is limited. The contribution of ϕ^d_{OCR} in addition ϕ^d_{text} on D_{OCR} is substantial, with up to 7 % points in F_1 for *trust*, 5pp for *fear* and 4pp for *anger*.

4 Conclusion and Future Work

In this paper, we investigated the effect of features from optical character recognition and caption generation on emotion classification from Tweets. While the caption generation does only help generalization in few cases (in which a qualitative analysis shows an actual better generalization across image content), the

OCR information is of clear importance. Therefore we can conclude that textual information from images contributes a helpful signal which complements text features from Tweets. This contribution is especially large for *fear*, *anger* and *trust*. Interesting are *shame* and *surprise*, for which classification on Tweets with images which contain text is more difficult based on Tweet text features alone. This drop can only be compensated partially with OCR.

Generated captions could not be shown to contribute substantially; one possible reason is that the generated text is too abstract. Future work will therefore focus on features from intermediate levels of the deep neural network.

References

1. Ekman, P.: Basic emotions. In: Dalgleish, T., Power, M. (eds.) Handbook of Cognition and Emotion. Wiley, Sussex (1999)
2. Plutchik, R.: The nature of emotions. Am. Sci. **89**(4), 344 (2001)
3. Alm, C.O., Roth, D., Sproat, R.: Emotions from text: machine learning for text-based emotion prediction. In: HLT-EMNLP (2005)
4. Aman, S., Szpakowicz, S.: Identifying expressions of emotion in text. In: Matoušek, V., Mautner, P. (eds.) TSD 2007. LNCS (LNAI), vol. 4629, pp. 196–205. Springer, Heidelberg (2007). doi:10.1007/978-3-540-74628-7_27
5. Dodds, P.S., Harris, K.D., Kloumann, I.M., Bliss, C.A., Danforth, C.M.: Temporal patterns of happiness and information in a global social network: hedonometrics and twitter. PloS one, vol. 6, no. 12 (2011)
6. Costa, J., Silva, C., Antunes, M., Ribeiro, B.: Concept drift awareness in twitter streams. In: ICMLA (2014)
7. Wang, W., Chen, L., Thirunarayan, K., Sheth, A.P.: Harnessing twitter "big data" for automatic emotion identification. In: SocialCom/PASSAT (2012)
8. @kezia_hunter: Be prepared for a.... Twitter (2017). https://twitter.com/kezia_hunter/status/818260781108228098
9. Bartlett, M.S., Littlewort, G., Lainscsek, C., Fasel, I., Movellan, J.: Machine learning methods for fully automatic recognition of facial expressions and facial actions. In: SMC (2004)
10. Kahou, S.E., Pal, C., Bouthillier, X., Froumenty, P., Gülçehre, C., Memisevic, R., Vincent, P., Courville, A., Bengio, Y., Ferrari, R.C., Mirza, M., Jean, S., Carrier, P.L., Dauphin, Y., Boulanger-Lewandowski, N., Aggarwal, A., Zumer, J., Lamblin, P., Raymond, J.P., Desjardins, G., Pascanu, R., Warde-Farley, D., Torabi, A., Sharma, A., Bengio, E., Côté, M., Konda, K.R., Wu, Z.: Combining modality specific deep neural networks for emotion recognition in video. In: ICMI (2013)
11. Gupta, A., Lamba, H., Kumaraguru, P., Joshi, A.: Faking sandy: characterizing and identifying fake images on twitter during hurricane sandy. In: WWW (2013)
12. Wang, Y., Wang, S., Tang, J., Liu, H., Li, B.: Unsupervised sentiment analysis for social media images. In: IJCAI (2015)
13. Smith, R.: An overview of the tesseract OCR engine. In: Ninth International Conference on Document Analysis and Recognition, ICDAR 2007 (2007)
14. Krizhevsky, A., Sutskever, I., Hinton, G.E.: Imagenet classification with deep convolutional neural networks. In: NIPS (2012)
15. Vinyals, O., Toshev, A., Bengio, S., Erhan, D.: Show and tell: a neural image caption generator. In: CVPR (2015)

16. Karpathy, A., Fei-Fei, L.: Deep visual-semantic alignments for generating image descriptions. In: CVPR (2015)
17. Lin, T., Maire, M., Belongie, S.J., Bourdev, L.D., Girshick, R.B., Hays, J., Perona, P., Ramanan, D., Dollár, P., Zitnick, C.L.: Microsoft COCO: common objects in context. CoRR abs/1405.0312 (2014)
18. Efron, B.: Bootstrap methods: another look at the Jackknife. Ann. Stat. **7**(1), 1–26 (1979)

Identifying Right-Wing Extremism in German Twitter Profiles: A Classification Approach

Matthias Hartung[1,2(✉)], Roman Klinger[2,3], Franziska Schmidtke[4], and Lars Vogel[4]

[1] Semantic Computing Group, CITEC, Bielefeld University, Bielefeld, Germany
mhartung@cit-ec.uni-bielefeld.de
[2] Semalytix GmbH, Bielefeld, Germany
[3] Institut für Maschinelle Sprachverarbeitung, University of Stuttgart, Stuttgart, Germany
klinger@ims.uni-stuttgart.de
[4] Kompetenzzentrum Rechtsextremismus, Friedrich-Schiller-Universität Jena, Jena, Germany
{franziska.schmidtke,lars.vogel}@uni-jena.de

Abstract. Social media platforms are used by an increasing number of extremist political actors for mobilization, recruiting or radicalization purposes. We propose a machine learning approach to support manual monitoring aiming at identifying right-wing extremist content in German Twitter profiles. We frame the task as profile classification, based on textual cues, traits of emotionality in language use, and linguistic patterns. A quantitative evaluation reveals a limited precision of 25% with a close-to-perfect recall of 95%. This leads to a considerable reduction of the workload of human analysts in detecting right-wing extremist users.

Keywords: Extremism monitoring · Classification · Social media

1 Introduction

Recent years have seen a dramatic rise in importance of social media as communication channels for political discourse [9]. Various political actors use different kinds of social platforms to engage directly with voters and supporter networks in order to shape public discussions, induce viral social trends, or spread political ideas and programmes for which they seek support.

With regard to extremist political actors and parties, a major current focus is on recruiting and radicalizing potential activists in social media. For instance, the American white nationalist movements have been able to attract a 600% increase of followers on Twitter since 2012 [3]. Twitter is comparably under-moderated in comparison to other platforms (*e. g.*, YouTube or Facebook[1]) and can therefore be seen as the predestinated channel for such activities [4].

[1] https://www.facebook.com, https://www.youtube.com.

F. Frasincar et al. (Eds.): NLDB 2017, LNCS 10260, pp. 320–325, 2017.
DOI: 10.1007/978-3-319-59569-6_40

Growing efforts are spent into monitoring extremist activities in social media by state institutions, platform providers or companies. Extremism monitoring aims at detecting *who* is active (possibly separating opinion leaders from followers, and discovering dynamics of network evolution), *what* they say (identifying prominent topics and possibly hate speech or fake news), and *which purpose* they pursue (revealing strategies such as mobilization or recruiting). Currently, these goals are mostly pursued in time-consuming manual work [1].

We propose a method to support the identification of extremist users in Twitter and aim at detecting right-wing extremist content in German Twitter profiles, based on lexical information and patterns of emotionality underlying language use. Our application scenario is an instance of semi-automatic knowledge base completion in that automated classification methods are applied in order to facilitate manual efforts to grow the data pool of known German right-wing extremists. We are aware that binary categorization of political attitudes is an oversimplification; yet, we consider this a valid approach for the given use case, as it is not intended to work in isolation from experts' decisions.

2 Related Work

There is only limited work with a focus on right-wing extremist detection. However, other forms of extremism have been the subject of research. As an early example, Ting et al. aimed at identification of hate groups on Facebook [15]. They build automatic classifiers based on social network structure properties and keywords. While this work focused on detection of groups, Scanlon et al. dealt with specific events of interaction, namely the recruitment of individuals [12] on specific extremist's websites. Their domain are Western Jihadists. In contrast, Ashcroft et al. identify specific messages from Twitter [2]. Similarly, Wei et al. identify Jihadist-related conversations [16].

Similar to our work is the approach of Ferrara et al., who identify ISIS members among Twitter users [6]. Kaati et al. identify multipliers of Jihadism on Twitter, as their aim is also the identification of specific profiles, for a different domain, though [7].

3 Profile Classification

Right-wing extremism is an ideology of asymmetric quality of social groups, defined by race, ethnicity or nationality, and a related authoritarian concept of society. Table 1 shows an overview of the conceptial dimensions of right-wing extremism, following Stöss [13].

Right-wing extremism is defined by adopting all or at least a majority of the attitudes in Table 1. It is, accordingly, appropriate to investigate entire Twitter profiles rather than individual Tweets. Therefore, we frame the task of detecting right-wing extremism in Twitter as supervised classification of user profiles into the target categories R (right-wing extremist) and N (non-extremist). We use support vector machines with a linear kernel [5].

Table 1. Conceptual dimensions of right-wing extremism (following Stöss [13])

Dimension	Definition
National-chauvinism	Presumed superiority and demanded homogeneity of the in-group
Xenophobia	Imagined inferiority of out-groups and potential threat to in-group
Racism	Definition of in- and out-groups strictly in terms of race
Social Darwinism	Imagined homogeneity and purity of own race; fight between races as unavoidable means to leverage survical of the strongest race
Support of dictatorship	Perception of democracy as weakening the in-group by substituting violent struggle by peaceful competition, negotiation and universal rights
National socialism	Glorification of historical national socialism by referring to its symbols (using symbolic codes) or denial of the Holocaust

Under the assumption that linguistic variables serve as informative predictors of users' underlying attitudes, we mainly focus on the vocabulary and certain semantic patterns as features of the model, as described in the following.

Lexical Features. We create a *bag-of-words frequency profile* of all tokens (unigrams and bigrams) used by an author in the entirety of all messages in their profile. Stopwords, Twitter-specific vocabulary such as "RT" (indicating re-tweets) and short links (URLs referring to websites external to Twitter) are filtered, while keeping hashtags and references to other Twitter users.

Emotion Features. We estimate a single label classification model for emotional categories, *viz.*, anger, disgust, fear, joy, love, sadness, shame, surprise, trust (motivated by Plutchik [10]) on a sample of 1.2M English and German Tweets from March until November 2016.[2] Similarly to Suttles et al. [14], we follow a weak supervision approach by utilizing emotion hashtags. As features in our downstream prediction model, we use confidence scores for each emotion as provided by this classifier.

Pro/Con Features. We use lexico-syntactic patterns capturing the main political goals or motives to be conveyed by an author in their messages:

gegen ... `<NOUN>` / against ... `<NOUN>`
`<NOUN>` ... statt ... `<NOUN>` / `<NOUN>` ... instead of ... `<NOUN>`

Social Identity Features. Based on the assumption that collective identities are constructed by means of discursive appropriation, we apply another pattern to detect real-world entities that are recurrently used in appropriation contexts:

`unser[e|en|em|er|es]? ... <NOUN> / our ... <NOUN>`

Transformation of Feature Values. The resulting feature vectors are transformed by the tfidf metric [8] in order to increase the relative impact of features that are (i) prominent in the respective profile and (ii) bear high discriminative power, *i.e.*, they occur in a relatively small proportion of all profiles in the data.

[2] All English Tweets are translated to German via Google translate (http://translate.google.com) to receive a more comprehensive training set.

4 Evaluation

4.1 Data Collection and Annotation

Annotations are provided by domain experts at the level of individual user profiles. These annotations comprise 37 *seed profiles* of political actors from the German federal state Thuringia. They are split into 20 profiles labeled as right-wing and 17 non-extremist ones. Right-wing seed profiles contain organizations as well as leading individuals within the formal and informal extremist scene as documented by Quent et al. [11]. Non-extremist seed profiles contain political actors of the governing parties and single-issue associations [11]. Using the Twitter REST API[3], entire timelines (comprising all Tweets by the respective user until December 15, 2016) are acquired for all seed profiles and their followers.

4.2 Experimental Results

We train a classification model on the seed profiles (comprising 45,747 Tweets in total, among them 15,911 of category R and 29,836 of category N) with all features described in Sect. 3.

Results of a *10-fold cross-validation on the seed profiles* can be seen from Table 2 (left part). We compare the performance of the classifier relying on all features, each feature group in isolation, and a majority baseline categorizing all profiles as "R". All feature groups turn out as reliable predictors of political orientation. Bag-of-words (BOW) lexical cues have the strongest individual contribution and cannot be outperformed by any other feature combination.

The *test set* comprises 100 randomly sampled profiles from followers of the seed users which have been annotated by one of the authors of this paper. Table 2 (right part) shows the results of this evaluation: In comparison to cross-validation on the seed profiles, the performance drops considerably, while still outperforming the baseline of categorizing all profiles as "R" by 8 points in F_1 score. Limiting the test data to profiles containing at least 100 Tweets each (*cf. Test Set*$_{>100}$ in the table) yields an improved performance of $F_1 = 0.47$.

Table 2. Classification results in detecting profiles of category R, using 10-fold cross-validation on seed profiles (left part), a held-out test set and a restricted test set comprising only profiles with at least 100 Tweets (right part)

Features	Precision	Recall	F_1 Score
all	0.87	1.00	0.93
BOW	0.91	1.00	0.95
Bigrams	0.80	1.00	0.89
Emotions	0.78	0.90	0.84
Pro/Con	0.63	1.00	0.77
Identity	0.70	0.95	0.81
Baseline	0.54	1.00	0.70

	Precision	Recall	F_1 Score
Test Set	0.25	0.95	0.40
Baseline	0.19	1.00	0.32
Test Set$_{>100}$	0.32	0.92	0.47
Baseline	0.21	1.00	0.35

[3] https://dev.twitter.com/rest/public.

Table 3. Top features from a global list of 100 features categorized in feature classes for category N and R, according to feature weights in the model.

	Category N	Category R
Words	heute, wir, beim,'s, the, uhr, geht, für_die, to, of, glückwunsch, Stellenangebot, feuerwehren, morgen, danke	d18, deutschland, #wehrdich, brd, deutsche, DTL, asylanten, Bürgerinitiative_wir, demonstration, asyl, herbstoffensive, asylbewerber, durchgeführt_!, volk, !_!
Network	nabu, ldkth, awo, mikemohring, bodoramelow, mdr_th, cdu_fraktion, naju, lmvth, der_AWO, lakoth16, DGB_Jugend, jef_de, dgb, bund_net	NPD, FN, suegida, identitäreaktion, weimarticker, sternde, spiegelonline, der_NPD, goldenerlöwe, npdde, Thüringer_NPD, agnordost, antifa, NPD-Landesverband, AB_ERFURT
Local	erfurt, in_Erfurt	hildburghausen, Jena, nordhausen, Saalfeld, Erfurt_), suhl, Webetgasse, Bauvereinstraße, Hußstraße, Gera_Zschochernstraße
Regional	Thüringen, thüringer, in_Thüringen, r2g, hochwasser, gebietsreform	kyffhäuserkreis, wir_lieben, lieben_Thüringen
National/global	TTIP, #mitredeneu, Bund, ews2014	#merkelmussweg, genozid
Emotionality	— None —	EMO_TWEETS_PROP>0.3, MOST_FREQ_EMOTION=Disgust

4.3 Qualitative Discussion

We perform a feature analysis by sorting features according to their weight in the model and manually categorize them into different semantic classes (*word* features, references to other profiles in the *network* structure, *emotionality*, and topics of *local*, *regional* or *global* geographical scope), shown in Table 3.

We find that users from category N presumably aim at promoting other users only if they share similar political orientations. Contrarily, right-wing users also follow delimitation strategies, by referring to media platforms (e.g., *sternde*) or left-wing political groups (e.g., *antifa*) in provocative or offensive ways. In general, the tonality in the language used by the right-wing authors in our data is much more aggressive (e.g., *wehr dich*/*fight back*, *Herbstoffensive*/*autumn offensive*) and characterized by emphasizing identitary contrasts (e.g., *Deutsche* vs. *Asylanten*/*Germans* vs. *refugees*) pointing into the direction of nationalism or chauvinism. Among the most discriminative features in our model are codes such as *d18*, which are indicative of a glorification of national socialism. Beyond that, we find that a substantial proportion of emotionally rich messages or messages conveying disgust are good predictors of right-wing extremism in our data. These characteristics clearly reflect aspects involved in the conceptual definition of right-wing extremism (cf. Table 1), which we consider supportive evidence in favor of the plausibility of our approach from a theoretical perspective.

5 Conclusions and Outlook

We presented a machine learning approach to identify Twitter profiles which correspond to right-wing extremism. Our work aims at supporting human experts in their monitoring activities which are currently carried out purely manually. Our classification model achieves high recall on right-wing extremist profiles such that only very few candidates are missed. At the same time, inconspicuous profiles are effectively filtered, which reduces the work load by 25%.

With its focus on discrete classification, the present study is certainly affected by an oversimplification, as the spectrum of political attitudes is more complex than only the two target categories considered. We are currently working on a ranking model based on similarity metrics in order to project unseen profiles on a continuous scale of political attitudes. In future work, we aim at developing this method further into a learning-to-rank approach. In addition, we propose the development of features that are based on deeper methods of natural language analysis in order to be able to address more fine-grained aspects in the conceptualization of right-wing extremism.

References

1. Amadeu-Antonio-Stiftung: Rechtsextreme und menschenverachtende Phänomene im Social Web (2016). https://www.amadeu-antonio-stiftung.de/w/files/pdfs/monitoringbericht-2015.pdf
2. Ashcroft, M., Fisher, A., Kaati, L., Omer, E., Prucha, N.: Detecting jihadist messages on twitter. In: Proceedings of EISIC (2015)
3. Berger, J.: Nazis vs. ISIS on Twitter. A Comparative Study of White Nationalist and ISIS Online Social Media Networks. Tech. rep., Center for Cyber and Homeland Security, George Washington University, Washington, D.C. (2016)
4. Blanquart, G., Cook, D.: Twitter influence and cumulative perceptions of extremist support. a case study of geert wilders. In: Proceedings of ACTC (2013)
5. Cortes, C., Vapnik, V.: Support-vector networks. Mach. Learn. **20**, 273–297 (1995)
6. Ferrara, E., Wang, W.Q., Varol, O., Flammini, A., Galstyan, A.: Predicting online extremism, content adopters, and interaction reciprocity (2016). arxiv: https://arxiv.org/abs/1605.00659
7. Kaati, L., Omer, E., Prucha, N., Shrestha, A.: Detecting multipliers of jihadism on twitter. In: IEEE International Conference on Data Mining Workshop (ICDMW) (2015)
8. Manning, C.D., Raghavan, P., Schütze, H.: Introduction to Information Retrieval. Cambridge University Press, Cambridge (2008)
9. Parmelee, J., Bichars, S.: Politics and the Twitter Revolution. Lexington Books, Landham, MD (2013)
10. Plutchik, R.: The nature of emotions. American Scientist (2001)
11. Quent, M., Salheiser, A., Schmidtke, F.: Gefährdungen der demokratischen Kultur in Thüringen (2016). http://www.denkbunt-thueringen.de/wp-content/uploads/2016/02/Gef%C3%A4hrdungsanalyse.pdf
12. Scanlon, J.R., Gerber, M.S.: Automatic detection of cyber-recruitment by violent extremists. Secur. Inform. **3**(1), 5 (2014)
13. Stöss, R.: Rechtsextremismus im Wandel. Friedrich-Ebert-Stiftung, Berlin (2010)
14. Suttles, J., Ide, N.: Distant supervision for emotion classification with discrete binary values. In: Gelbukh, A. (ed.) CICLing 2013. LNCS, vol. 7817, pp. 121–136. Springer, Heidelberg (2013). doi:10.1007/978-3-642-37256-8_11
15. Ting, I.H., Chi, H.M., Wu, J.S., Wang, S.L.: An approach for hate groups detection in facebook. In: Uden, L., Wang, L., Hong, T.P., Yang, H.C., Ting, I.H. (eds.) The 3rd International Workshop on Intelligent Data Analysis and Management, pp. 101–106. Springer, Netherlands (2013). doi:10.1007/978-94-007-7293-9_11
16. Wei, Y., Singh, L., Martin, S.: Identification of extremism on twitter. In: International Conference on Advances in Social Networks Analysis and Mining (2016)

An Approach for Defining the Author Reputation of Comments on Products

Carlos A. de Sa(✉), Roney L. de S. Santos, and Raimundo S. Moura

Departamento de Computação, Universidade Federal Do Piauí (UFPI), Teresina, PI, Brazil
{carlos.sa,rsm}@ufpi.edu.br, roneylira@hotmail.com

Abstract. Author reputation is a very important variable for evaluating web comments. However, there is no formal definition for calculating its value. This paper presents an adaptation of the approach presented by Sousa et al. (2015) for evaluating the importance of comments about products and services available online, emphasizing measures of author reputation. The implemented adaptation consists in defining six metrics for authors, used as input in a Multilayer Perceptron Artificial Neural Network. On a preliminary evaluation, the Neural Network presented an accuracy of 91.01% on the author classification process. Additionally, an experiment was conduced aiming to compare both approaches, and the results show that the adapted approach had better performance in classifying the importance of comments.

Keywords: Author reputation · Artificial neural networks · Fuzzy systems

1 Introduction

The inclination to interact and form groups is a characteristic pertaining to any society [1]. Currently, the Online Social Networks (OSN) such as Twitter[1] and Facebook[2] enable a great deal of social interaction among Internet users.

One of the contemporary research topics in Computer Science is the challenge of transforming non-structured texts into structured knowledge, so that the users may benefit from the large volume of data they produce [7].

During the process of buying or selling products or services online, positive evaluations help the consumer feel safe during the negotiation. On the other hand, negative evaluations may also assist in the process of choosing the right product or seller, resulting in considerable impact on the sales [2].

To identify the most relevant comments, Sousa et al. in [8], proposed the Top(x) approach to infer the best comments about products or services, that utilizes a Fuzzy System with three input variables: author reputation, number

[1] http://twitter.com.
[2] http://www.facebook.com/.

F. Frasincar et al. (Eds.): NLDB 2017, LNCS 10260, pp. 326–331, 2017.
DOI: 10.1007/978-3-319-59569-6_41

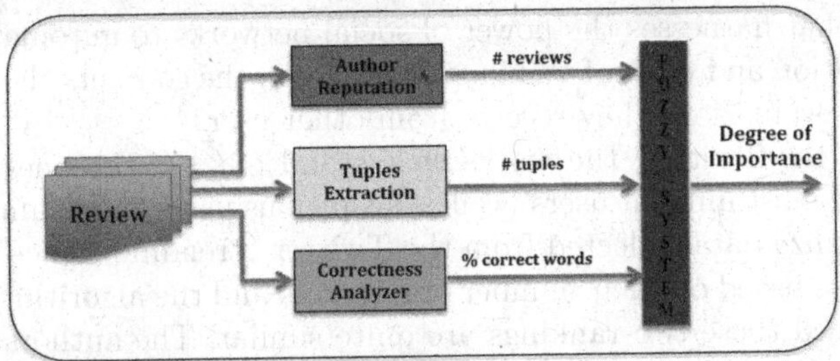

Fig. 1. Top(x) approach by Sousa et al. [8]

of tuples *<feature, quality word>* and richness of vocabulary; and one output variable: degree of importance of the comment (see Fig. 1). To define the author reputation, the authors considered only the amount of comments. So, the more comments posted by an author, the higher your reputation. It is important to observe that this hypothesis is weak, and can easily be disproved by observation, that a spammer may be considered a good author.

In the context of e-commerce, consumers are alert to the qualification and exposure of the comment's author [3]. According to Jones et al. in [4], reputation involves an estimation of character, ability and reliability of an individual.

This paper focuses on considering measures for author reputation for web opinion mining systems, exploring the various existing resources, such as: number of comments by that user, favorites, number of followers a user has, number of friends, among others. Based on those resources, an author reputation may be considered better than another's.

Aiming to improve the analysis of the author reputation variable, this work presents a study that utilizes an Artificial Neural Network Multilayer Perceptron (ANN MLP). Through this ANN MLP, it was possible to analyze a set of measures to define which of them are the most relevant in evaluating author reputation. Another aspect to be presented is the comparison between the original Top(x) approach and the new approach utilizing ANN MLP.

The remainder of this article is organized as follow: Sect. 2 presents Related Research in the field. Section 3 explores the Data Retrieval and Corpus. Section 4 discusses the Proposed Approach. Section 5 shows the results of the experiments performed. Lastly, Sect. 6 presents conclusions and future works.

2 Related Research

Several authors have been investigating about author reputation evaluation on the web, in Wikis, blogs, forums and RSOs. In Wiki environments, Wohner et al. in [9], argue that persistent contributions to the Wiki last on average 14 days without suffering any modifications, and they also classify authors as blocked, vandal or regular. Zhao et al. in [10], defined SocialWiki, a prototype

Wiki system that harnesses the power of social networks to automatically manage the reputation and trust of Wiki users, based on the contents they contribute in and on the evaluations they receive from other users

Regarding the Twitter, the works that stand out are the ones directed at identifying the most influent users, well as suspicious users and spammers. Kwak et al. in [5], utilize data collected from the Twitter "trending topics" to create a ranking of users based on their number of followers and the algorithm PageRank, and they noticed these two rankings are quite similar. The authors created yet another ranking based on the users' retweets, a mechanism in which an user forwards another user's tweet onto their own timeline.

3 Data Retrieval and Corpus Preparation

For the evaluation of our proposal, we created one Corpus with data gathered on Buscapé[3] site. Initially, a total of 2433 comments were collected and later cleaned. By the end of the filtering process, 2000 reviews remained.

After the manual evaluation, 923 of 2000 reviews were classified as positive, 602 as negative, and 141 as neutral, while 334 reviews were considered garbage.

In a first moment, to define the reputation of their own authors, a sample of 356 comments was selected, with 132 positive evaluations, 131 negative and 93 neutral evaluations, identified as **Subcorpus I**.

Table 1. Results of the manual evaluation for author reputation

Score	#Total	Score	#Total	Score	#Total	Score	#Total
0	68	3	23	6	9	9	5
1	163	4	11	7	5	10	5
2	50	5	16	8	1	-	

Table 1 shows the results of the manual evaluation of comment's importance by the specialist. The 11 different scores attributed to comments in the table were generalized for the entire universe through a ANN MLP.

In a second moment, to compare the precision of original approach by Sousa et al. (2015) with the proposal approach, 271 reviews were randomly selected of 2000 comments, divided as 100 positive, 100 negative and 71 neutral, for the evaluation of their importance, named as **Subcorpus II**.

Considering manual evaluation of importance of the comments, the specialist considered three factors in the evaluating procedure: the amount of information present in the comment, richness of vocabulary and author reputation, and four different classes: excellent, good, sufficient and insufficient. As results were: 17 excellent, 24 good, 145 sufficient and 85 insufficient.

[3] http://www.buscape.com.br.

4 Proposed Approach

An ANN MLP was applied aiming to infer the reputation of the authors of comments contained in the Corpus, as well as inform the importance of every input measure. Figure 2 shows the proposed approach, where 'a' represents the ANN output, and also the author reputation standardized to values between 0 and 10. The 'k', in turn, refers to the level of importance of the comment, as it does in the original approach.

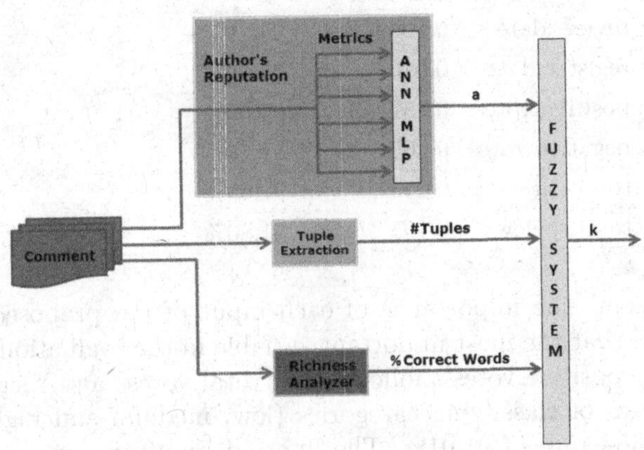

Fig. 2. Proposed approach

The proposed ANN model uses six input variables, defined as follows:

- **Review date**: This information is important because the more recent a review is, the more updated the comment will be;
- **Website register date**: This measure evaluates old authors with a better reputation than new authors;
- **Positive votes**: The more positive votes an author comment receives, the better your reputation;
- **Negative votes**: The more negative votes an author receive, the worse your reputation will be;
- **Total of votes**: The more votes an author comment has, the better the author reputation;
- **Total of reviews by the comment's author**: This information is relevant because it attests active participation of the author on the website.

5 Experiments and Results

To establish a comparison between the Top(x) approach by Sousa et al. [8] and the new approach proposed in this article, an experiment was performed by applying a ANN MLP to define author reputation on **Subcorpus I** instead of directly counting the number of comments.

Regarding the neural network topology, the input layer contains six units, representing the measures previously presented. In the hidden layer, the best adjustments consisted of eight neurons and the Hyperbolic Tangent activation function. Finally, the output layer uses one neuron for classifying the eleven possible author grades (0 to 10) and the activation function Softmax.

Table 2. The importance of the input variables

Input variable	Importance	Normalized importance
review_date	0.106	42.10%
register_date	0.086	34.40%
positive_votes	0,252	100.00%
negative_votes	0.205	81.70%
total_votes	0.245	97.60%
total_reviews	0.105	41.80%

Table 2 presents the importance of each input of the proposed network. It can be observed that the most important variable in the evaluation of an author reputation was "positive_votes", followed by "total_votes" and "negative_votes".

In the process of classifying categories (low, medium and high), our ANN obtained precision rate of 91.01%. The inferred reputation was used as single input in the Top(x) approach, replacing the previous measure (total comments), and described below in the second experiment, considering the **Subcorpus II**.

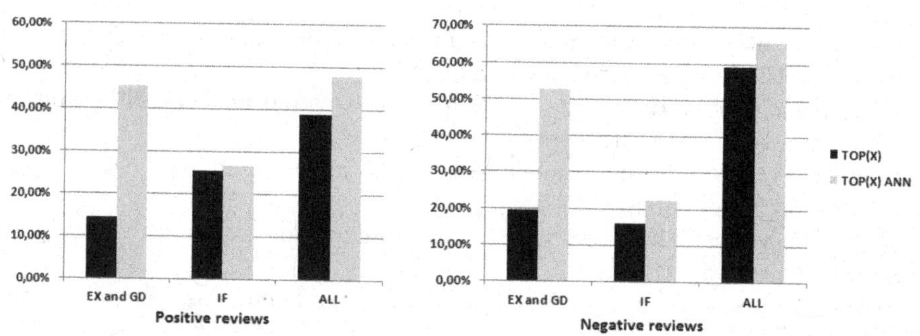

Fig. 3. Comparative graphics between positive and negative reviews

Figure 3 shows the result of the F-measure for the positive and negative reviews of both approaches: original and new using ANN. It can be observed that the Top(x) approach with the ANN MLP has superior performance in identifying excellent (EX) and good (GD) comments. For the insufficient (IF) comments the improvement is not substantial, and when all comments are used together, there is a significant increase in performance.

6 Conclusion

This paper presents a new approach to evaluating comments in products on the Web based on the Top(x) approach by Sousa et al. [8]. This paper presents a set of six measures extracted from a Corpus collected from the website Buscapé.

The results demonstrate that the new approach presents superior performance to the original approach. Another factor to be highlighted are the relevant measures, in which the positive votes, negative votes, and total of votes were considered the most important because it considers the reputation attributed by other users.

As future works, it is expected to apply this new approach on a larger Corpus; carry out a more extensive process of manual evaluations; and applying other machine learning techniques to define an author reputation. Lastly, researchers from our team are currently conducting research on other dimensions of the Top(x) approach, for example, further exploring the richness of vocabulary and working on replacing the Fuzzy System with a ANN that better identifies critical comments [6].

References

1. Castells, M.: The Rise of the Network Society, 2nd edn. Blackwell Publishers Inc., Cambridge (2000)
2. Hamilton, R., Vohs, K.D., McGill, A.L.: We'll be honest, this won't be the best article you'll ever read: the use of dispreferred markers in word-of-mouth communication. J. Consum. Res. **41**(1), 197–212 (2014)
3. Hu, N., Liu, L., Zhang, J.J.: Do online reviews affect product sales? the role of reviewer characteristics and temporal effects. Inf. Technol. Manage. **9**(3), 201–214 (2008)
4. Jones, C., Hesterly, W.S., Borgatti, S.P.: A general theory of network governance: exchange conditions and social mechanisms. Acad. Manage. Rev. **22**(4), 911–945 (1997)
5. Kwak, H., Lee, C., Park, H., Moon, S.: What is twitter, a social network or a news media? In: Proceedings of the 19th International Conference on WWW, USA, pp. 591–600 (2010)
6. de Santos, R.L., de Sousa, R.F., Rabelo, R.A.L., Moura, R.S.: An experimental study based on fuzzy systems and artificial neural networks to estimate the importance of reviews about product and services. In: 2016 International Joint Conference on Neural Networks (IJCNN), July 2016
7. SBC: Grandes desafios da pesquisa em computacao no brasil 2006–2016. Sociedade Brasileira de Computacao, Porto Alegre, RS, Brasil (2006)
8. de Sousa, R.F., Rabelo, R.A.L., Moura, R.S.: A fuzzy system-based approach to estimate the importance of online customer reviews. In: 2015 IEEE International Conference on Fuzzy Systems (FUZZ-IEEE) (2015)
9. Wöhner, T., Köhler, S., Peters, R.: Automatic reputation assessment in wikipedia. In: 32nd International Conference on Information Systems, Shanghai (2011)
10. Zhao, H., Ye, S., Bhattacharyya, P., Rowe, J., Gribble, K., Wu, S.F.: Socialwiki: Bring order to wiki systems with social context. In: Proceedings Social Informatics - Second International Conference, SocInfo 2010, Laxenburg, Austria (2010)

Quality of Word Embeddings on Sentiment Analysis Tasks

Erion Çano(✉) and Maurizio Morisio

Politecnico di Torino, Duca degli Abruzzi, 24, 10129 Torino, Italy
{erion.cano,maurizio.morisio}@polito.it

Abstract. Word embeddings or distributed representations of words are being used in various applications like machine translation, sentiment analysis, topic identification etc. Quality of word embeddings and performance of their applications depends on several factors like training method, corpus size and relevance etc. In this study we compare performance of a dozen of pretrained word embedding models on lyrics sentiment analysis and movie review polarity tasks. According to our results, Twitter Tweets is the best on lyrics sentiment analysis, whereas Google News and Common Crawl are the top performers on movie polarity analysis. Glove trained models slightly outrun those trained with Skip-gram. Also, factors like topic relevance and size of corpus significantly impact the quality of the models. When medium or large-sized text sets are available, obtaining word embeddings from same training dataset is usually the best choice.

Keywords: Word embeddings · Lyrics mood analysis · Movie review polarity

1 Introduction

Semantic vector space models of language were developed in the 90s to predict joint probabilities of words that appear together in a sequence. A particular upturn was proposed by Bengio et al. in [1], replacing sparse n-gram models with word embeddings which are more compact representations obtained using feed-forward or more advanced neural networks. Recently, high quality and easy to train Skip-gram shallow architectures were presented in [10] and considerably improved in [11] with the introduction of negative sampling and subsampling of frequent words. The "magical" ability of word embeddings to capture syntactic and semantic regularities on text words is applicable in various applications like machine translations, error correcting systems, sentiment analyzers etc. This ability has been tested in [12] and other studies with analogy question tests of the form "A is to B as C is to __" or male/female relations. A recent improved method for generating word embeddings is Glove [15] which makes efficient use of global statistics of text words and preserves the linear substructure of Skip-gram word2vec, the other popular method. Authors report that Glove outperforms other methods such as Skip-gram in several tasks like word similarity,

F. Frasincar et al. (Eds.): NLDB 2017, LNCS 10260, pp. 332–338, 2017.
DOI: 10.1007/978-3-319-59569-6_42

word analogy etc. In this paper we examine the quality of word embeddings on 2 sentiment analysis tasks: Lyrics mood recognition and movie review polarity analysis. We compare various models pretrained with Glove and Skip-gram, together with corpora we train ourself. Our goal is to report the best performing models as well as to observe the impact that certain factors like training method, corpus size and thematic relevance of texts might have on model quality. According to the results, Common Crawl, Twitter Tweets and Google News are the best performing models. Corpus size and thematic relevance have a significant role on the performance of the generated word vectors. We noticed that models trained with Glove slightly outperform those trained with Skip-gram in most of experiments.

2 Word Embedding Corpora and Models

In this section we present the different word embedding models that we compare. Most of them are pretrained and publicly available. Two of them (Text8Corpus and MoodyCorpus) were trained by us. The full list with some basic characteristics is presented in Table 1. Wikipedia Gigaword is a combination of Wikipedia 2014 dump and Gigaword 5 with about 6 billion tokens in total. It was created by authors of [15] to evaluate Glove performance. Wikipedia Dependency corpus is a collection of 1 billion tokens from Wikipedia. The method used for training it is a modified version of Skip-gram word2vec described in [7]. Google News is one of the biggest and richest text sets with 100 billion tokens and a vocabulary of 3 million words and phrases [10]. It was trained using Skip-gram word2vec with

Table 1. List of word embedding corpora

Corpus name	Training	Dim	Size	Voc	URL
Wiki Gigaword 300	Glove	300	6 B	400000	link
Wiki Gigaword 200	Glove	200	6 B	400000	link
Wiki Gigaword 100	Glove	100	6 B	400000	link
Wiki Gigaword 50	Glove	50	6 B	400000	link
Wiki Dependency	word2vec	300	1 B	174000	link
Google News	word2vec	300	100 B	3 M	link
Common Crawl 840	Glove	300	840 B	2.2 M	link
Common Crawl 42	Glove	300	42 B	1.9 M	link
Twitter Tweets 200	Glove	200	27 B	1.2 M	link
Twitter Tweets 100	Glove	100	27 B	1.2 M	link
Twitter Tweets 50	Glove	50	27 B	1.2 M	link
Twitter Tweets 25	Glove	25	27 B	1.2 M	link
Text8Corpus	word2vec	200	17 M	25000	link
MoodyCorpus	word2vec	200	90M	43000	link

negative sampling, windows size 5 and 300 dimensions. Even bigger is Common Crawl 840, a huge corpus of 840 billion tokens and 2.2 million word vectors also used at [15]. It contains data of Common Crawl (http://commoncrawl.org), a nonprofit organization that creates and maintains public datasets by crawling the web. Common Crawl 42 is a reduced version made up of 42 billion tokens and a vocabulary of 1.9 million words. Common Crawl 840 and Common Crawl 42 were trained with Glove method producing vectors of 300 dimensions for each word. The last Glove corpus is the collection of Twitter Tweets. It consists of 2 billion tweets, 27 billion tokens and 1.2 million words. To observe the role of corpus size in quality of generated embeddings, we train and use Text8Corpus, a smaller corpus consisting of 17 million tokens and 25,000 words. The last model we use is MoodyCorpus, a collection of lyrics that followed our work in [3] where we build and evaluate MoodyLyrics, a sentiment annotated dataset of songs. The biggest part of MoodyCorpus was built using lyrics of Million Song Dataset (MSD) songs (https://labrosa.ee.columbia.edu/millionsong/). As music tastes and characteristics change over time (http://kaylinwalker.com/50-years-of-pop-music), it is better to have diversified sources of songs in terms of epoch, genre etc. Thereby we added songs of different genres and epochs that we found in two subsets of MSD, Cal500 and TheBeatles. The resulting corpus of 90 million tokens and 43,000 words can be downloaded from http://softeng.polito.it/erion. Further information about public music datasets can be found at [2].

3 Sentiment Analysis Tasks

The problem of music mood recognition is about utilizing machine learning, data mining and other techniques to automatically classify songs in 2 or more emotion categories with highest possible accuracy. Different combinations of features such as audio or lyrics are involved in the process. In this study we make use of song lyrics exploiting the dataset described in [9] (here AM628). The original dataset contains 771 song texts collected from AllMusic portal. AllMusic tags and 3 human experts were used for the annotation of songs. We balanced the dataset obtaining 314 positive and 314 negative lyrics. We also utilize MoodyLyrics (here ML3K), a dataset of 3,000 mood labeled songs from different genres and epochs described in [3]. Pioneering work in movie review polarity analysis has been conducted by Pang and Lee in [13,14]. The authors released sentiment polarity dataset, a collection of 2,000 movie reviews categorized as positive or negative. Deep learning techniques and distributed word representations appeared on recent studies like [17] where the role of RNNs (Recurrent Neural Networks), and CNNs (Convolutional Neural Networks) is explored. The author reports that CNNs perform best. An important work that has relevance here is [8] where authors present an even larger movie review dataset of 50,000 movie reviews from IMBD. This dataset has been used in various works such as [5,16] etc. For our experiments we used a chunk of 10 K (MR10K) as well as the full set (MR50K). We first cleaned and tokenized texts of the datasets.

The dataset of the current run is loaded and a set of unique text words is created. All 14 models are also loaded in the script. We train a 15th (self_w2v) model using the corpus of the current run and Skip-gram method. The script iterates in every line of the pretrained models splitting apart the words and the float vectors and building {word: vec} dictionaries later used as classification feature sets. Next we prepare the classification models using tf-idf vectorizer which has been successfully applied in similar studies like [4]. Instead of applying tf-idf in words only as in other text classifiers, we vectorize both word (for semantic relevance) and corresponding vector (for syntactic and contextual relevance). Random forest was used as classifier and 5-fold cross-validation accuracy is computed for each of the models.

4 Results

In Figs. 1 and 2 we see results of 5-fold cross-validation on the 2 lyrics datasets. Top three models are crawl_840, twitter_50 and self_w2v. On AM628 (very smallest dataset), it is crawl_840 (the biggest model) that leads, followed by twitter_50. Self_w2v is severely penalized by its size and thus is at the bottom. On ML3K (large dataset) self_w2v reaches the top of the list, leaving behind twitter_50. Wikigiga, google_news and dep_based are positioned in the middle whereas MoodyCorpus and Text8Corpus end the list. Their accuracy scores drift from 0.62 to 0.75. It is interesting to see how self_w2v goes up from the last to the top, with scores edging between 0.61 and 0.83. This model is trained with the data of each experiment and depends on the size of that dataset which grows significantly (see Table 2). We see that accuracy values we got here are in line with reports from other similar works such as [6] where they use a dataset of 1032 lyrics from AllMusic to perform content analysis with text features. Accuracy scores for movie review polarity prediction are presented in Figs. 3 and 4. Again we see that crawl_840 performs very well. Google_news is also among the top whereas Twitter models are positioned in the middle of the list. Once again self_w2v grows considerably, this time from the 3rd place to the top. On MR50K it has a discrete margin of more than 0.03 from the 2nd position. Again wikigiga models are positioned in the middle of the list and the worst performing models are MoodyCorpus and Text8Corpus. Our scores on this task are somehow lower than those reported from various studies that explore advanced deep learning constructs on same dataset. In [8] for example, authors who created movie review dataset try on it their probabilistic model that is able to capture semantic similarities between words. They report a maximal accuracy of 0.88. A study that uses a very similar method is [16] where authors combine random forest with word vector average values. On movie review dataset they achieve an accuracy of 0.84 which is about what we got here.

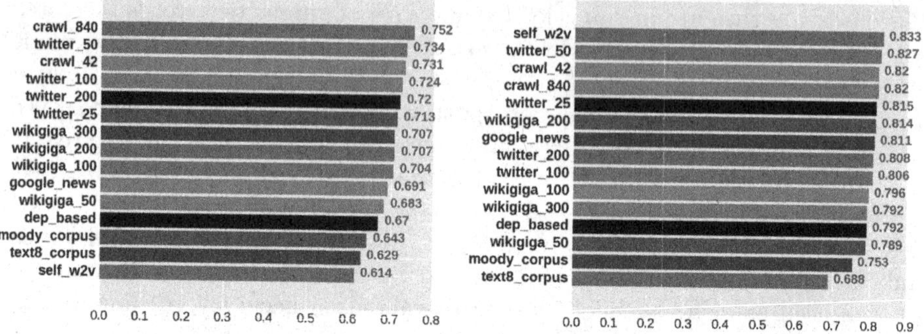

Fig. 1. Lyric accuracies on AM628

Fig. 2. Lyric accuracies on ML3K

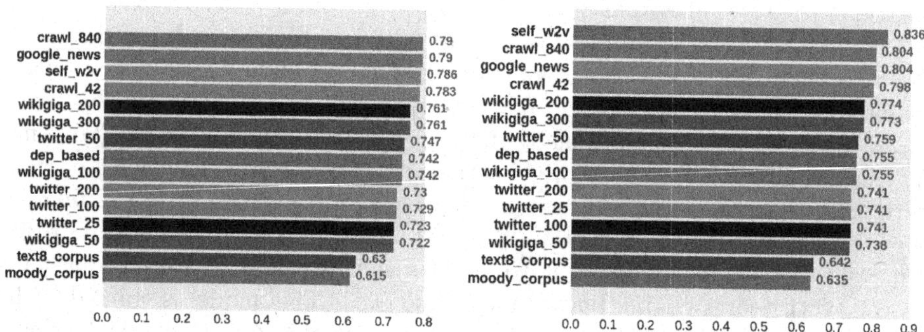

Fig. 3. Review accuracies on MR10K

Fig. 4. Review accuracies on MR50K

5 Discussion

In this paper we examined the quality of different word embedding models on two sentiment analysis tasks: Lyrics mood recognition and movie review polarity. We observed the role of factors like training method, vocabulary and corpus size and thematic relevance of texts. According to our results, the best performing models are Common Crawl, Twitter Tweets and Google News. In general, models trained with Glove slightly outperform those trained using Skip-gram, especially on lyrics sentiment analysis (Twitter and Crawl). We also notice that vocabulary richness and corpus size have a significant influence on model quality. The biggest models like crawl_840 are always among the best. Likewise self_w2v performs very well on both tasks when trained with medium or large data sizes (see Table 2). Being the smallest in sizes, MoodyCorpus and Text8Corpus are always the worst. Regarding thematic relevance, Twitter corpora perform better on lyrics sentiment analysis. They are large and rich in vocabulary with texts of an informal and sentimental language. This language is very similar to the one of song lyrics, with ***love*** being the predominant word (see word cloud in [3]). Movie

Table 2. Properties of self_w2v

Trial	Dataset	Dim	Size	Voc	Score
1	AM628	200	156699	8756	0.614
2	ML3K	200	1028891	17890	0.833
3	MR10K	300	2343641	53437	0.786
4	MR50K	300	11772959	104203	0.836

review results on the other hand, are headed by Common Crawl and Google News which are the largest, both in size and vocabulary. These models are trained with diverse and informative texts that cover every possible subject or topic. Having a look on some movie reviews we also see a similar language with comments about the movies of different categories. Furthermore, we saw that when training set is big enough, obtaining word embeddings from it (self_w2v) is the best option.

References

1. Bengio, Y., Ducharme, R., Vincent, P., Janvin, C.: A neural probabilistic language model. J. Mach. Learn. Res. **3**, 1137–1155 (2003)
2. Çano, E., Morisio, M.: Characterization of public datasets for recommender systems. In: 2015 IEEE 1st International Forum on Research and Technologies for Society and Industry Leveraging a Better Tomorrow (RTSI), pp. 249–257, September 2015
3. Çano, E., Morisio, M.: Moodylyrics: a sentiment annotated lyrics dataset. In: 2017 International Conference on Intelligent Systems, Metaheuristics and Swarm Intelligence, Hong Kong, March 2017
4. Hu, X., Downie, J.S., Ehmann, A.F.: Lyric text mining in music mood classification. In: Proceedings of the 10th International Society for Music Information Retrieval Conference, ISMIR 2009, Kobe International Conference Center, Kobe, Japan, 26–30 October 2009, pp. 411–416 (2009)
5. Johnson, R., Zhang, T.: Effective use of word order for text categorization with convolutional neural networks. In: NAACL HLT 2015, The 2015 Conference of the North American Chapter of the Association for Computational Linguistics: Human Language Technologies, Denver, Colorado, USA, 31 May–5 June 2015, pp. 103–112 (2015)
6. Lee, W.-S., Yang, D.: Music emotion identification from lyrics. In: 2013 IEEE International Symposium on Multimedia, pp. 24–629 (2009)
7. Levy, O., Goldberg, Y.: Dependency-based word embeddings. In: Proceedings of the 52nd Annual Meeting of the Association for Computational Linguistics, ACL 2014, Baltimore, MD, USA, 22–27 June 2014, pp. 302–308 (2014)
8. Maas, A.L., Daly, R.E., Pham, P.T., Huang, D., Ng, A.Y., Potts, C.: Learning word vectors for sentiment analysis. In: Proceedings of the 49th Annual Meeting of the Association for Computational Linguistics: Human Language Technologies, Portland, Oregon, USA, June 2011, pp. 142–150. Association for Computational Linguistics (2011)

9. Malheiro, R., Panda, R., Gomes, R.P., Paiva, R.P.: Emotionally-relevant features for classification and regression of music lyrics. IEEE Trans. Affect. Comput. **PP**(99), 1 (2016)
10. Mikolov, T., Chen, K., Corrado, G., Dean, J.: Efficient estimation of word representations in vector space (2013). CoRR abs/1301.3781
11. Mikolov, T., Sutskever, I., Chen, K., Corrado, G.S., Dean, J.: Distributed representations of words and phrases and their compositionality. In: Advances in Neural Information Processing Systems 26: 27th Annual Conference on Neural Information Processing Systems 2013, Proceedings of a Meeting held 5–8 December 2013, Lake Tahoe, Nevada, United States, pp. 3111–3119 (2013)
12. Mikolov, T., Yih, S.W.-T., Zweig, G.: Linguistic regularities in continuous space word representations. In: Proceedings of the 2013 Conference of the North American Chapter of the Association for Computational Linguistics: Human Language Technologies (NAACL-HLT-2013). Association for Computational Linguistics, May 2013
13. Pang, B., Lee, L.: A sentimental education: sentiment analysis using subjectivity. In: Proceedings of ACL, pp. 271–278 (2004)
14. Pang, B., Lee, L., Vaithyanathan, S.: Thumbs up? Sentiment classification using machine learning techniques. In: Proceedings of EMNLP, pp. 79–86 (2002)
15. Pennington, J., Socher, R., Manning, C.D.: Glove: global vectors for word representation. In: Moschitti, A., Pang, B., Daelemans, W. (eds.) Empirical Methods in Natural Language Processing (EMNLP), pp. 1532–1543. ACL (2014)
16. Pouransari, H., Ghili, S.: Deep learning for sentiment analysis of movie reviews. Technical report, Stanford University (2014)
17. Shirani-Mehr, H.: Applications of deep learning to sentiment analysis of movie reviews. Technical report, Stanford University (2014)

Question Answering Systems and Applications

A Hierarchical Iterative Attention Model for Machine Comprehension

Zhuang Liu[(✉)], Degen Huang, Yunxia Zhang, and Chuan Zhang

School of Computer Science and Technology,
Dalian University of Technology, Dalian, China
{zhuangliu,zhangyunxia,zhangchuangood}@mail.dlut.edu.cn,
huangdg@dlut.edu.cn

Abstract. Enabling a computer to understand a document so that it can answer comprehension questions is a central, yet unsolved goal of Natural Language Processing, so reading comprehension of text is an important problem in NLP research. In this paper, we propose a novel Hierarchical Iterative Attention model (HIA), which constructs iterative alternating attention mechanism over tree-structured rather than sequential representations. The proposed HIA model continually refines its view of the query and document while aggregating the information required to answer a query, aiming to compute the attentions not only for the document but also the query side, which will benefit from the mutual information. Experimental results show that HIA has achieved significant state-of-the-art performance in public English datasets, such as CNN and Childrens Book Test datasets. Furthermore, HIA also outperforms state-of-the-art systems by a large margin in Chinese datasets, including People Daily and Childrens Fairy Tale datasets, which are recently released and the first Chinese reading comprehension datasets.

Keywords: Machine comprehension · Hierarchical Iterative Attention · Tree-LSTM · Chinese machine comprehension · Cloze-style reading comprehension

1 Introduction

Reading comprehension is the ability to read text, process it, and understand its meaning. How to endow computers with this capacity has been an elusive challenge and a long-standing goal of Artificial Intelligence. A recent trend to measure progress towards machine reading is to test a system's ability of answering questions over the text it has to comprehend. Towards this end, several large-scale datasets of Cloze-style questions over a context document have been introduced recently which allow the training of supervised machine learning systems [6,9,10]. Cloze-style queries are representative problems in reading comprehension. Over the past few months, we have seen much progress that is utilizing neural network approach to solve Cloze-style questions.

F. Frasincar et al. (Eds.): NLDB 2017, LNCS 10260, pp. 341–352, 2017.
DOI: 10.1007/978-3-319-59569-6_43

In the past year, to teach the machine to do Cloze-style reading comprehensions, large-scale training data is necessary for learning relationships between the given document and query. Some large-scale reading comprehensions datasets have been released: the CNN/Daily Mail corpus, consisting of news articles from those outlets [9], and the Children's Book Test (CBTest), consisting of short excerpts from books available through Project Gutenberg [10]. Recently, Cui *et al.* [6] has released the first machine Chinese reading comprehension datasets, including a human-made out-of-domain test set for future research. All previous works are focusing on automatically generating large-scale training data for neural network (NN) training, which demonstrate its importance. Furthermore, the more complicated problems the more data is needed to learn comprehensive knowledge from it, such as reasoning over multiple sentences etc.

Many NN-based reading comprehension models [2,6,9,10,12,15,16,26,28] have been proposed, which utilize the attention mechanism with recurrent neural networks [17,21] to construct sentence representations considering the word order, but didn't take the syntactic structure of sentences into account yet. Recently, tree-structured models [19,24] obtained from the syntactic structures of the sentences were shown to be able to produce more robust representations and capture better semantics in certain tasks. But they have not been applied on machine reading comprehension tasks with attention mechanism.

In this paper, we propose a novel attention-based neural network model: Hierarchical Iterative Attention model (HIA), designed to study machine comprehension of text, which constructs iterative alternating attention mechanism over tree-structured. The model first construct tree-structured sentence representations for sentences from their parsing trees and estimate attention weights on different nodes of the hierarchies. Then, HIA's core module, Inference Attention Module, begins by deploying an iterative inference attention mechanism that alternates between attending query encodings and document encodings, to uncover the inferential links that exist between the document, the missing query word and the query. The results of the alternating attention is gated and fed back into the inference LSTM. After a number of steps, the weights of the document attention are used to estimate the probability of the answer.

To sum up, our contributions can be summarized as follows:

- We propose a novel end-to-end neural network models for machine reading comprehension, which combine Tree-LSTM based embeddings and an inference attention mechanism to handle the Cloze-style reading comprehension task.
- Also, we have achieved the state-of-the-art performance in public reading comprehension datasets, including English datasets and Chinese datasets.
- Our further analyses with the models reveal some useful insights for further improving the method.

Table 1. Data statistics of the CNN datasets and Children's Book Test datasets (CBTest). CBTest CN stands for CBTest Common Nouns and CBTest NE stands for CBTest Named Entites. CBTest had a fixed number of 10 options for answering each question. Statistics provided with the CBTest data set.

	CNN			CBTest CN			CBTest NE		
	Train	Valid	Test	Train	Valid	Test	Train	Valid	Test
# queries	380,298	3,924	3,198	879,450	2,000	2,500	108,719	2,000	2,500
Max# options	527	187	396	10	10	10	10	10	10
Avg# options	26.4	26.5	24.5	10	10	10	10	10	10
Avg# tokens	762	763	716	470	448	461	433	412	424
Vocab. size	118,497			53,185			53,063		

Table 2. Data statistics of People Daily datasets and Children's Fairy Tale datasets.

	People Daily			Children's Fairy Tale	
	Train	Valid	Test	Test-auto	Test-human
# queries	870,710	3,000	3,000	1,646	1,953
Max# tokens in docs	618	536	634	318	414
Max# tokens in query	502	153	265	83	92
Avg# tokens in docs	379	425	410	122	153
Avg# tokens in query	38	38	41	20	20
Vocabulary size	248,160			NA	

2 Problem Notation, Datasets

2.1 Definition and Notation

The task of the HIA is to answer a Cloze-style question by reading and comprehending a supporting passage of text. The Cloze-style reading comprehension problem [25] aims to comprehend the given context or document, and then answer the questions based on the nature of the document, while the answer is a single word in the document. Thus, the Cloze-style reading comprehension can be described as a triple:

$$(\mathcal{Q},\ \mathcal{D},\ \mathcal{A})$$

where $\mathcal{Q}$ is the query (represented as a sequence of words), $\mathcal{D}$ is the document, $\mathcal{A}$ is the set of possible answers to the query.

2.2 Reading Comprehension Datasets

Several institutes have released the Cloze-style reading comprehension data, and these have greatly accelerated the research of machine reading comprehension.

<table>
<tr><td>Document</td><td>1 ||| 人民网 1月 1日 讯 据 《纽约 时报》 报道， 美国 华尔街 股市 在 2013年 的 最后 一 天 继续 上涨， 和 全球 股市 一样， 都 以 最高 纪录 或 接近 最高 纪录 结束 本年 的 交易。
2 ||| 《纽约 时报》 报道 说， 标普 500 指数 今年 上升 29.6%， 为 1997年 以来 的 最 大 涨幅；
3 ||| 道琼斯 工业 平均 指数 上升 26.5%， 为 1996年 以来 的 最 大 涨幅；
4 ||| 纳斯达克 上涨 38.3%。
5 ||| 就 12月 31日 来说， 由于 就业 前景 看好 和 经济 增长 明年 可能 加速， 消费者 信心 上升。
6 ||| 工商 协进会 报告， 12月 消费者 信心 上升 到 78.1， 明显 高于 11月 的 72。
7 ||| 另 据 《华尔街 日报》 报道， 2013年 是 1995年 以来 美国 股市 表现 最 好 的 一 年。
8 ||| 这 一 年 里， 投资 美国 股市 的 明智 做法 是 追 着 "傻钱" 跑。
9 ||| 所谓 的 "傻钱" X， 其实 就 是 买 入 并 持有 美国 股票 这样 的 普通 组合。
10 ||| 这个 策略 要 比 对冲 基金 和 其它 专业 投资者 使用 的 更为 复杂 的 投资 方法 效果 好 得 多。</td></tr>
<tr><td>Query</td><td>所谓 的 "傻钱" X， 其实 就 是 买 入 并 持有 美国 股票 这样 的 普通 组合。</td></tr>
<tr><td>Answer</td><td>策略</td></tr>
</table>

Fig. 1. Example training sample in People Daily datasets. The "**X**" represents the missing word. In this example, the document consists of 10 sentences, and the 9th sentence is chosen as the query.

We begin with a brief introduction of the existing Cloze-style reading comprehension datasets, two English datasets and the first Chinese reading comprehension datasets recently released. Typically, there are two main genres of the English Cloze-style datasets publicly available, CNN/Daily Mail[1] [9] and Children's Book Test (CBTest)[2] [10], which all stem from the English reading materials. Also, there are the first Chinese Cloze-style reading comprehension datasets, People Daily [6] and Children's Fairy Tale (CFT)[3] [6], which are roughly collected 60K news articles from the People Daily website[4] and the Children's Fairy Tale by Cui *et al.* [6]. Figure 1 shows an example of People Daily datasets. Table 1 provides some statistics on the two English datasets: CNN/Daily Mail and Children's Book Test (CBTest). The statistics of People Daily datasets as well as Children's Fairy Tale datasets are listed in the Table 2.

3 Proposed Approach

In this section, we will introduce our Hierarchical Iterative Attention model (HIA) for Cloze-style reading comprehension task. The proposed HIA model is shown in Fig. 2.

In two recent architectures [19,24], tree-structured models obtained from the syntactic structures of the sentences were shown to be able to produce more robust representations and capture better semantics in certain tasks. So we propose to apply the Tree-LSTM to obtain the representations for the document and query. The document module computes tree-structured representations for the sentences using Tree-LSTMs. The query module on the middle left generates a query vector representation from the word sequence of the query. The model first construct tree-structured sentence representations for sentences from their parsing trees and estimate attention weights on different nodes of the hierarchies.

[1] CNN and Daily Mail datasets are available at http://cs.nyu.edu/%7ekcho/DMQA.
[2] CBTest datasets is available at http://www.thespermwhale.com/jaseweston/babi/CBTest.tgz.
[3] People Daily and CFT datasets are available at http://hfl.iflytek.com/chinese-rc.
[4] http://www.people.com.cn.

In HIA's core module, Inference Attention module, our model is primarily motivated by Chen *et al.* [2], Kadlec *et al.* [12], Sukhbaatar *et al.* [23], which aim to directly estimate the answer from the document, instead of making a prediction over the full vocabularies. But we have noticed that by just concatenating the final representations of the query RNN states are not enough for representing the whole information of query. So we propose to utilize the repeated, tight integration between query attention and document attention, which allows the model to explore dynamically which parts of the query are most important to predict the answer, and then to focus on the parts of the document that are most salient to the currently attended query components.

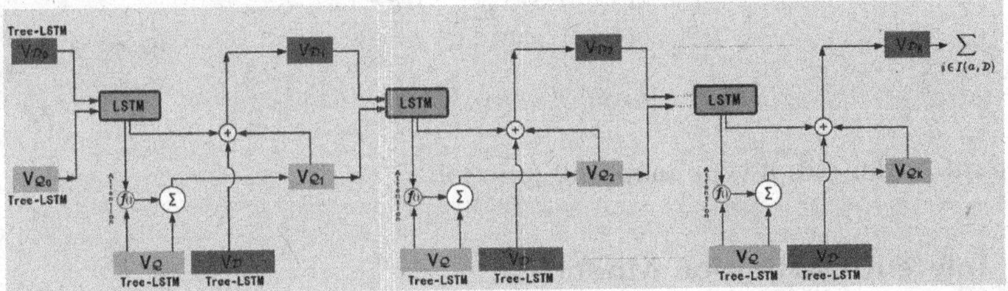

Fig. 2. Architecture of the proposed Hierarchical Iterative Attention model (HIA).

3.1 Tree-LSTM Model

The input of module includes the transcriptions of the document and the query using Tree-LSTMs. The query encodings and document encodings are represented separately as query vector $V_{\mathcal{Q}}$, document $V_{\mathcal{D}}$ in Fig. 2. Two variants of Tree-LSTM [19,24] can be used: *the Child-Sum Tree-LSTM* and the *N-ary Tree-LSTM* [8,18]. A Child-Sum Tree-LSTM over a dependency tree is referred to as a Dependency Tree-LSTM, which is used here due to its relatively compact structure. Tree-LSTM generates a vector representation for each node in the dependency tree based on the vector representations of its child nodes [3]. Each node t has a hidden state h_t as its vector representation and a set of memory cells c_t. It has the input gates i_t and output gates o_t for the memory cells, and the forget gates f_{tk} that controls the information flowing in from its child node k. It also takes an input x_t, which is the vector representation of the head word of the node. The hidden state h_t at node t is the representation for a phrase consisting of words in the subtree rooted at node t. Below is how h_t of a node t is obtained from its child nodes k. We thus propose a new variant of tree-structured LSTM that shares weight matrices Us for same-type children and also allows variable number of children. For this variant, we calculate vectors in the LSTM unit at t-th node with $C(t)$ children with following equations [8,18]. First, the hidden states of the child nodes are summed,

$$\widehat{h}_t = \sum_{k \in C(t)} h_k \tag{1}$$

where $C(t)$ denotes the set of children of node t. The representation of the head word x_t of node t and $\widehat{h}_t$ in (1) are used to control the input gates i_t and output gates o_t, and each child $k \in C(t)$ has its own forget gate f_{tk} obtained from h_k and x_t,

$$f_{tk} = \sigma(W^{(f)}x_t + U^{(f)}h_k + b^{(f)}) \tag{2}$$

Finally, the hidden state h_t and memory cells c_t are obtained as the following:

$$u_t = tanh(W^{(u)}x_t + U^{(u)}\widehat{h}_t + b^{(u)}) \tag{3}$$

$$c_t = i_t \odot u_t + \sum_{k \in C(t)} f_{tk} * c_k \tag{4}$$

$$h_t = o_t \odot tanh(c_t) \tag{5}$$

where m($\odot$) denotes a type mapping function.

3.2 Inference Attention Model

This phase aims to uncover a possible inference chain that starts at the query and the document and leads to the answer. Figure 2 illustrates inference attention module.

Query Attention Module. We use a bilinear term instead of a simple dot product [10,23] in order to compute the importance of each query term in the current time step t. This simple bilinear attention has been successfully used in [6]. We formulate a query glimpse $\mathbf{q}_t$ at time step t by:

$$q_{i,t} = \underset{i=1,\ldots,|Q|}{softmax}\, \tilde{\mathbf{q}}_i^T \mathbf{A}_q \mathbf{s}_{t-1} \tag{6}$$

$$\mathbf{q}_t = \sum_i q_{i,t}\tilde{\mathbf{q}}_i \tag{7}$$

where $q_{i,t}$ are the query attention weights and $\tilde{\mathbf{q}}_i$ are the query encodings.

Document Attention Module. Our method extends the Attention Sum Reader [12], and performs multiple hops over the input. The alternating attention continues by probing the document given the current query glimpse $\mathbf{q}_t$. The document attention weights are computed based on both the previous search state $t-1$ and the currently selected query glimpse $\mathbf{q}_t$:

$$d_{i,t} = \underset{i=1,\ldots,|D|}{softmax}\, \tilde{\mathbf{d}}_i^T \mathbf{A}_d[\mathbf{s}_{t-1}, \mathbf{q}_t] \tag{8}$$

$$\mathbf{d}_t = \sum_i d_{i,t}\tilde{\mathbf{d}}_i \tag{9}$$

where $d_{i,t}$ are the attention weights for each word in the document, and the document attention is also conditioned on $\mathbf{s}_{t-1}$, so it makes the model perform transitive reasoning on the document side. This use previously obtained document information to future attended locations, which is particularly important for natural language inference tasks [23].

Inference Attention Module. The inference is modeled by an additional LSTM [11]. The recurrent network iteratively performs an alternating search step to gather information that may be useful to predict the answer. The module performs an attentive read on the query encodings, resulting in a query glimpse $\mathbf{q}_t$ at each time step, then gives the current query glimpse $\mathbf{q}_t$, it extracts a conditional document glimpse $\mathbf{d}_t$, representing the parts of the document that are relevant to the current query glimpse. Both attentive reads are conditioned on the previous hidden state of the inference LSTM $\mathbf{s}_{t-1}$, summarizing the information that has been gathered from the query and the document up to time t, making it easier to determine the degree of matching between them. The inference LSTM uses both glimpses to update its recurrent state and thus decides which information needs to be gathered to complete the inference process.

Answer Prediction. Finally, after a fixed number of time-steps K, the document attention weights obtained in the last search step $d_{i,K}$ are used to predict the probability of the answer. We aggregate the probabilities for tokens which appear multiple times in a document before selecting the maximum as the predicted answer:

$$P(a|\mathcal{Q},\ \mathcal{D}) = \sum_{i \in I(a,\mathcal{D})} d_{i,K} \tag{10}$$

where $I(a, \mathcal{D})$ is the set of positions where token a appears in the document $\mathcal{D}$, we then use cross-entropy loss between the predicted probabilities and true answers for training.

4 Experiments

4.1 Experimental Setups

The general settings of our neural network model are detailed below.

- Embedding Layer: The embedding weights are randomly initialized with the uniformed distribution in the interval [−0.05, 0.05].
- Hidden Layer: We initialized the LSTM units with random orthogonal matrices [20].
- Vocabulary: For training efficiency and generalization, we truncate the full vocabulary (about 200K) and set a shortlist of 100K. During training we randomly shuffled all examples in each epoch. To speedup training, we always pre-fetched 10 batches worth of examples and sorted them according to the length of the document. This way each batch contained documents of roughly the same length.

Table 3. Results on the CNN news, CBTest NE (named entity) and CN (common noun) datasets. The result that performs best is depicted in bold face.

	CNN News		CBTest NE		CBTest CN	
	Valid	Test	Valid	Test	Valid	Test
Deep LSTM Reader (Hermann *et al.* [9])	55.0	57.0	-	-	-	-
Attentive Reader (Hermann *et al.* [9])	61.6	63.0	-	-	-	-
Impatient Reader (Hermann *et al.* [9])	61.8	63.8	-	-	-	-
LSTMs (context+query) (Hill *et al.* [10])	-	-	51.2	41.8	62.6	56.0
MemNN (window + self-sup.) (Hill *et al.* [10])	63.4	66.8	70.4	66.6	64.2	63.0
AS Reader (Kadlec *et al.* [12])	68.6	69.5	73.8	68.6	68.8	63.4
Stanford AR (Chen *et al.* [2])	72.4	72.4	-	-	-	-
Iterative Attention (Sordoni *et al.* [22])	72.6	73.3	75.2	68.6	72.1	69.2
GA Reader (Dhingra *et al.* [7])	73.0	73.8	74.9	69.0	69.0	63.9
EpiReader (Trischler *et al.* [26])	**73.4**	74.0	75.3	69.7	71.5	67.4
CAS Reader (avg mode)(Cui *et al.* [6]),	68.2	70.0	74.2	69.2	68.2	65.7
AoA Reader (Cui *et al.* [5])	73.1	**74.4**	**77.8**	72.0	72.2	69.4
HIA (our)	73.2	**74.4**	76.9	**72.1**	**72.4**	**70.0**

- Optimization: In order to minimize the hyper-parameter tuning, we used stochastic gradient descent with the ADAM update rule [13] and learning rate of 0.001 or 0.0005, with an initial learning rate of 0.001.

Due to the time limitations, we only tested a few combinations of hyper-parameters, while we expect to have a full parameter tuning in the future. The results are reported with the best model, which is selected by the performance of validation set. Our model is implemented with Tensorflow [1] and Keras [4], and all models are trained on Tesla K80 GPU.

4.2 Results

We compared the proposed model with several baselines as summarized below. To verify the effectiveness of our proposed model, we first tested our model on public English datasets. Our evaluation is carried out on CNN news datasets [9] and CBTest NE/CN datasets [10], and the statistics of these datasets are given in Table 3. The results on Chinese reading comprehension datasets are listed in Table 4, as we can see that, the proposed HIA significantly outperforms the most recent state-of-the-art CAS Reader in all types of test set, with a maximum.

English Reading Comprehension Datasets. In CNN news datasets, our model is on par with the AoA Reader, with 0.1% improvements in validation set. But we failed to outperform EpiReader. In CBTest CN, though there is a drop in the validation set with 0.9% declines, there is a boost in the test set

Table 4. Results on People Daily datasets and Children's Fairy Tale (CFT) datasets. The result that performs best is depicted in bold face. CAS Reader (marked with *) are the most recent works.

	People Daily		Children's Fairy Tale	
	Valid	Test	Test-auto	Test-human
AS Reader	64.1	67.2	40.9	33.1
CAS Reader (avg mode)*	65.2	68.1	41.3	35.0
CAS Reader (sum mode)*	64.7	66.8	43.0	34.7
CAS Reader (max mode)*	63.3	65.4	38.3	32.0
HIA (our)	**68.9**	**71.5**	**45.8**	**37.9**

with an absolute improvements over other models, which suggest our model is effective. In CBTest CN dataset, our model gives modest improvements over the state-of-the-art systems. When compared with AoA Reader and Iterative Attention model, our model shows a similar result, with slight improvements on validation and test set, which demonstrate that our model is more general and powerful than previous works.

Chinese Reading Comprehension Datasets. In People Daily and CFT datasets, our HIA outperforms all the state-of-the-art systems by a large margin, where a 3.7%, 3.4%, 2.8% and 2.9% absolute accuracy improvements over the most recent state-of-the-art CAS Reader in the validation and test set respectively. We have also noticed that, even we have an absolute improvement of 2.8% at least. This demonstrates that our model is powerful enough to compete with Chinese reading comprehension, to tackle the Cloze-style reading comprehension task.

So far, we have good results in machine reading comprehension, all higher than most baselines above, verifying that hierarchical iterative attention is useful, suggesting that our HIA models performed better on relatively difficult reasoning questions.

5 Related Work

Neural attention models have been applied recently to machine learning and natural language processing problems. Cloze-style reading comprehension tasks have been widely investigated in recent studies. We will take a brief revisit to the previous works.

Hermann *et al.* [9] have proposed a methodology for obtaining large quantities of ($\mathcal{Q}$, $\mathcal{D}$, $\mathcal{A}$) triples through news articles and its summary. Along with the release of Cloze-style reading comprehension dataset, they also proposed an attention-based neural network to tackle the issues above. Experimental results showed that the proposed neural network is effective than traditional baselines. Hill *et al.* [10] released another dataset, which stems from the children's books. Different from Hermann *et al.* [9]'s work, the document and query are all generated from the raw story without any summary, which is much more general than previous work. To handle the reading comprehension task, they proposed a window-based memory network, and self-supervision heuristics is also applied to learn hard-attention. Kadlec *et al.* [12] proposed a simple model that directly pick the answer from the document, which is motivated by the Pointer Network [27]. A restriction of this model is that, the answer should be a single word and appear in the document. Results on various public datasets showed that the proposed model is effective than previous works. Liu *et al.* [14] proposed to exploit these reading comprehension models into specific task. They first applied the reading comprehension model into Chinese zero pronoun resolution task with automatically generated large-scale pseudo training data. Trischler *et al.* [26] adopted a re-ranking strategy into the neural networks and used a joint-training method to optimize the neural network. Sordoni *et al.* [22] have proposed an iterative alternating attention mechanism and gating strategies to accumulatively optimize the attention after several hops, where the number of hops is defined heuristically.

6 Conclusions

In this paper we presented the novel Hierarchical Iterative Attention model (HIA) over tree-structured sentence representations, and showed it offered improved performance for machine comprehension tasks. Among the large, public Chinese and English datasets, our model could give significant improvements over various state-of-the-art baselines, especially for Chinese reading comprehension corpora, on which our model outperformed state-of-the-art systems by a large margin.

As future work, we need to consider how we can utilize these datasets (or new corpora) to solve more complex machine reading comprehension tasks (with less annotated data), and we are going to investigate hybrid reading comprehension models to tackle the problems that rely on comprehensive induction of several sentences. We also plan to augment our framework with a more powerful model for natural language inference.

Acknowledgments. We would like to thank the reviewers for their helpful comments and suggestions to improve the quality of the paper. This research is supported by National Natural Science Foundation of China (No. 61672127).

References

1. Abadi, M., Agarwal, A., Barham, P., Brevdo, E., Chen, Z., Citro, C., Corrado, G.S., Davis, A., Dean, J., Devin, M., et al.: Tensorflow: large-scale machine learning on heterogeneous distributed systems. arXiv preprint arXiv:1603.04467 (2016)
2. Chen, D., Bolton, J., Manning, C.D.: A thorough examination of the CNN/daily mail reading comprehension task. arXiv preprint arXiv:1606.02858 (2016)
3. Chen, D., Manning, C.D.: A fast and accurate dependency parser using neural networks. In: EMNLP, pp. 740–750 (2014)

4. Chollet, F.: Keras (2015)
5. Cui, Y., Chen, Z., Wei, S., Wang, S., Liu, T., Hu, G.: Attention-over-attention neural networks for reading comprehension. arXiv preprint arXiv:1607.04423 (2016)
6. Cui, Y., Liu, T., Chen, Z., Wang, S., Hu, G.: Consensus attention-based neural networks for Chinese reading comprehension. arXiv preprint arXiv:1607.02250 (2016)
7. Dhingra, B., Liu, H., Cohen, W.W., Salakhutdinov, R.: Gated-attention readers for text comprehension. arXiv preprint arXiv:1606.01549 (2016)
8. Fang, W., Hsu, J.Y., Lee, H.y., Lee, L.S.: Hierarchical attention model for improved machine comprehension of spoken content. arXiv preprint arXiv:1608.07775 (2016)
9. Hermann, K.M., Kocisky, T., Grefenstette, E., Espeholt, L., Kay, W., Suleyman, M., Blunsom, P.: Teaching machines to read and comprehend. In: Advances in Neural Information Processing Systems, pp. 1693–1701 (2015)
10. Hill, F., Bordes, A., Chopra, S., Weston, J.: The goldilocks principle: reading children's books with explicit memory representations. arXiv preprint arXiv:1511.02301 (2015)
11. Hochreiter, S., Schmidhuber, J.: Long short-term memory. Neural Comput. **9**(8), 1735–1780 (1997)
12. Kadlec, R., Schmid, M., Bajgar, O., Kleindienst, J.: Text understanding with the attention sum reader network. arXiv preprint arXiv:1603.01547 (2016)
13. Kinga, D., Adam, J.B.: A method for stochastic optimization. In: International Conference on Learning Representations (ICLR) (2015)
14. Liu, T., Cui, Y., Yin, Q., Wang, S., Zhang, W., Hu, G.: Generating and exploiting large-scale pseudo training data for zero pronoun resolution. arXiv preprint arXiv:1606.01603 (2016)
15. Liu, Y., Li, S., Zhang, X., Sui, Z.: Implicit discourse relation classification via multi-task neural networks. arXiv preprint arXiv:1603.02776 (2016)
16. Liu, Z., Huang, D., Zhang, J., Huang, K.: Research on attention memory networks as a model for learning natural language inference. In: EMNLP 2016, p. 18 (2016)
17. Mikolov, T., Karafiát, M., Burget, L., Cernockỳ, J., Khudanpur, S.: Recurrent neural network based language model. In: Interspeech, vol. 2, p. 3 (2010)
18. Miwa, M., Bansal, M.: End-to-end relation extraction using LSTMS on sequences and tree structures. arXiv preprint arXiv:1601.00770 (2016)
19. Munkhdalai, T., Yu, H.: Neural tree indexers for text understanding. arXiv preprint arXiv:1607.04492 (2016)
20. Saxe, A.M., McClelland, J.L., Ganguli, S.: Exact solutions to the nonlinear dynamics of learning in deep linear neural networks. arXiv preprint arXiv:1312.6120 (2013)
21. Schmidhuber, J.: A fixed size storage O (n3) time complexity learning algorithm for fully recurrent continually running networks. Neural Comput. **4**(2), 243–248 (1992)
22. Sordoni, A., Bachman, P., Trischler, A., Bengio, Y.: Iterative alternating neural attention for machine reading. arXiv preprint arXiv:1606.02245 (2016)
23. Sukhbaatar, S., Weston, J., Fergus, R., et al.: End-to-end memory networks. In: Advances in Neural Information Processing Systems, pp. 2440–2448 (2015)
24. Tai, K.S., Socher, R., Manning, C.D.: Improved semantic representations from tree-structured long short-term memory networks. arXiv preprint arXiv:1503.00075 (2015)
25. Taylor, W.L.: cloze procedure: a new tool for measuring readability. Journal. Bull. **30**(4), 415–433 (1953)

26. Trischler, A., Ye, Z., Yuan, X., Suleman, K.: Natural language comprehension with the epireader. arXiv preprint arXiv:1606.02270 (2016)
27. Vinyals, O., Fortunato, M., Jaitly, N.: Pointer networks. In: Advances in Neural Information Processing Systems, pp. 2692–2700 (2015)
28. Wang, S., Jiang, J.: Machine comprehension using match-LSTM and answer pointer. arXiv preprint arXiv:1608.07905 (2016)

A Syntactic Parse-Key Tree-Based Approach for English Grammar Question Retrieval

Lanting Fang[1(✉)], Luu Anh Tuan[2], Lenan Wu[1], and Siu Cheung Hui[2]

[1] School of Information Science and Engineering, Southeast University, Nanjing 210096, Jiangsu, China
{230139356,wuln}@seu.edu.cn

[2] School of Computer Science and Engineering, Nanyang Technological University, 50 Nanyang Avenue, Singapore 639798, Singapore
anhtuan001@e.ntu.edu.sg, asschui@ntu.edu.sg

Abstract. Grammar question retrieval aims to find relevant grammar questions that have similar grammatical structure and usage as the input question query. Previous work on text and sentence retrieval which is mainly based on statistical analysis approach and syntactic analysis approach is not effective in finding relevant grammar questions with similar grammatical focus. In this paper, we propose a syntactic parse-key tree based approach for English grammar question retrieval which can find relevant grammar questions with similar grammatical focus effectively. In particular, we propose a syntactic parse-key tree to capture the grammatical focus of grammar questions according to the blank or answer position of the questions. Then we propose a novel method to compute the parse-key tree similarity between the parse-trees of the question query and the database questions for question retrieval. The performance results have shown that our proposed approach outperforms other classical text and sentence retrieval methods in accuracy.

1 Introduction

English, which is widely used for international communications, is probably one of the most important languages nowadays. To learn English well, it is important to understand the concepts of English grammar with lots of practice on exercise questions. In addition, it is also important to practice questions according to grammatical usage such as pronouns, prepositions, etc. When learning English grammar, students are usually interested in finding questions with similar grammatical structure and usage for practicing. However, it is tedious and troublesome to find, identify and classify questions that have similar grammatical usage manually. As such, it is highly attractive to develop a retrieval system for English grammar questions with similar grammatical usage for students to practice and learn English grammar.

In this research, we propose a syntactic parse-key tree based approach for English grammar question retrieval. Although the proposed syntactic parse-key based retrieval approach can be easily altered to applied to other syntactic based

F. Frasincar et al. (Eds.): NLDB 2017, LNCS 10260, pp. 353–365, 2017.
DOI: 10.1007/978-3-319-59569-6_44

retrieval problem, such as example-based querying problems [1], this paper only consider the grammar question retrieval based on English multiple choice questions (MCQs), which are the most common form of English grammar questions. A MCQ question consists of a stem (i.e. a sentence with a blank position) and four choices. In the database, each question also contains the correct answer. Table 1 gives two sample English grammar questions. In the questions, the blank position is represented as '*' for the correct answer. In the retrieval system, users can submit a question query to retrieve the relevant MCQ grammar questions from the database. A sample question query can be submitted as *"The lady * you saw performing on stage is our favorite English teacher."* Note that the submitted query does not contain the question choices.

In English grammar question retrieval, it aims to find from the database the most similar grammar questions to the input query. Note that the meaning of similarity here does not refer to textual similarity but the similarity in grammatical structure and usage to the question query. For example, the sample question query is similar to question Q1 as both of them are about asking the grammatical usage on clause. Even though the question query and question Q2 share many similar words, they are in fact not similar due to the fact that question Q2 is about the grammatical usage on adjective based on the blank position.

Table 1. Sample English grammar questions

Q1	Question Stem: *The waitress * we thought deserves a Service Quality award has resigned* Choices: *A. whom B. where C. which D. when* Answer: *A. whom*
Q2	Question Stem: *My favorite teacher is my English teacher, and she is by far the * teacher that I have ever had* Choices: *A. good B. better C. best D. worst* Answer: *B. best*

Previous works on text and sentence retrieval are mainly based on statistical analysis approach and syntactic analysis approach which have been shown to be effective for many practical applications such as Web search engine and question-answering system. However, these approaches are not effective in finding relevant grammar questions with similar grammatical focus as they only capture similar textual content or syntactic sentence structure between the query and database questions. In this paper, we propose a new syntactic parse-key tree structure, to capture the grammatical structure according to the blank position of grammar questions for their grammatical focus. Based on the syntactic parse-key tree, we propose a novel method to compute the parse-key tree similarity between the question query and the database questions for question retrieval. The rest of the paper is organized as follows. Section 2 reviews the related work on text and sentence retrieval. Section 3 presents the proposed approach for English grammar question retrieval. Section 4 discusses the performance evaluation of the proposed approach. Finally, Sect. 5 concludes the paper.

2 Related Work

In information retrieval (IR), there are many existing models such as statistical analysis approach and syntactic analysis approach which are widely used for text and sentence retrieval. The statistical analysis approach relies mainly on term occurrences in documents to find relevant documents. Some classical methods such as TF-IDF [10] and BM25 [9] follow this approach.

The syntactic analysis approach exploits the linguistic information for improving the retrieval results. In particular, part-of-speech (POS) of words in sentences is commonly used in this approach. Wang et al. [14] incorporated POS into bag-of-word and Markov Random Field to strengthen the conventional IR models for biomedical information retrieval. Schubotz et al. [11] used POS based distance methods to extract identifiers to improve math information retrieval results.

Apart from POS tagging, there are some other syntactic analysis approaches which exploit the dependency structures of sentences. Carmel et al. [3] used both statistical features and syntactic features for information retrieval. They extracted three types of features include common statistical-based features, POS features and dependence features. Then they use online SVMRank to rank the documents based on extracted features. Bendersky et al. [2] proposed a retrieval framework that models dependencies between arbitrary concepts in the query rather than just query terms. In [15], syntactic roles of words were used to detect key concepts to help rank the candidate questions. Maxwell and Croft [7] showed that the retrieval performance can be improved through the use of dependency parsing techniques in the extraction of non-adjacent subsets of dependent terms. Recently, Chinkina et al. [4] developed an online information retrieval system that retrieves Web documents based on the grammatical structures they contain.

In addition to POS tagging and dependency relations, some other approaches also investigated the use of syntactic tree to help retrieve relevant sentences. Collins and Duffy [5] proposed tree kernel function to count the common subtrees between syntactic trees. Based on this work, Wang et al. [13] proposed a retrieval framework based on improved tree kernel method to find similar questions in a community based question-answering system.

3 Proposed Approach

Figure 1 shows our proposed approach for grammatical question retrieval which consists of the following three processes: Parse-key Tree Construction, Parse-key Tree Similarity and Ranking.

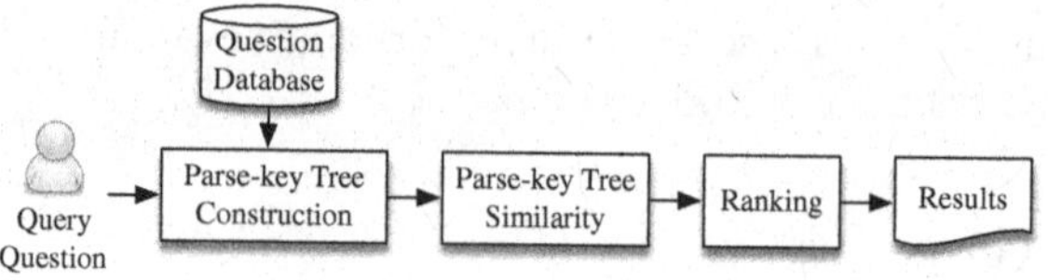

Fig. 1. Proposed approach

3.1 Parse-Key Tree Construction

The Parse-key Tree Construction process aims to construct the parse-key trees from English grammar questions. It consists of the following three steps: syntactic parsing, word-blank distance extraction and tree construction.

Syntactic Parsing. This step uses the Stanford parser [16] to generate the syntactic parse tree of a grammar question. A parse tree is an ordered, rooted syntactic tree that represents the grammatical structure of a sentence. Figure 2(a) shows the parse tree of the sample query *"The lady * you saw performing on stage is our favorite English teacher."* The leaf nodes in Fig. 2(a) are the words in the sample query. The leaf nodes' parents (i.e. pre-terminal nodes) are their part-of-speech (POS) tags, e.g. noun, verb, pronoun, etc.

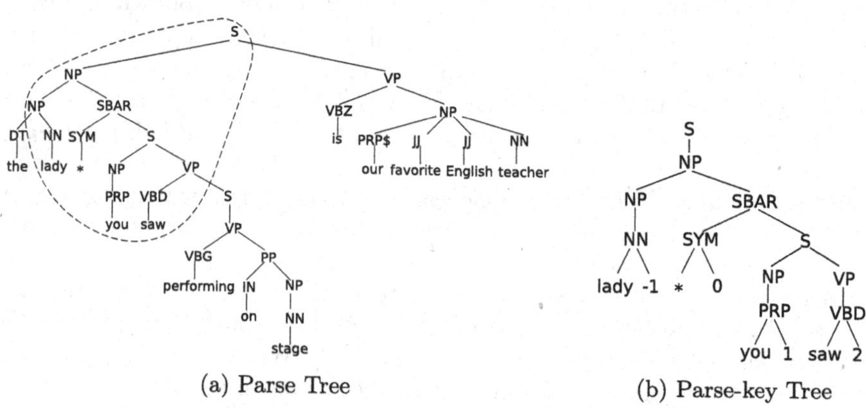

Fig. 2. Paser tree and parse-key tree for the sample query

Word-Blank Distance Extraction. The position of the blank space ('*')in the question may provide hint on the grammatical focus of the query. For example, the sample query "*The lady * you saw performing on stage is our favorite English teacher.*" has the focus on clause, while the question "*The lady whom you saw performing * stage is our favorite English teacher.*" has the focus on preposition. To identify the grammatical focus of a query or question, we define word-blank distance to capture the relative position of each word to the blank position in the query or question.

Definition 1 (Word-blank Distance). *Given a grammar question with a blank position, the word-blank distance of each word in the question is defined as the distance between the word position and the blank position.*

Specifically, we use *0* to represent the word-blank distance of the blank position, i to represent the word-blank distance of the *i-th* word after the blank position, and $-j$ to represent the word-blank distance of *j-th* word before the blank position. For example, for the question stem "*lady * you saw*", we can generate the following word-blank distance information: {"lady":−1, "*":0, "you": 1, "saw":2}. "lady" is the first word before the blank position, so its word-blank distance is −1. "you" is the first word after the blank position, so its word-blank distance is 1.

Tree Construction. The syntactic parse tree can be used to represent the grammatical structure of a question. However, based on our empirical experiments, it is not necessary to use the entire parse tree in order to find the grammatical focus of an English grammar question. Here, we incorporate the word-blank distance into the parse tree, and propose *parse-key tree* as a sub-parse tree to represent the grammatical focus of a question.

Definition 2 (Neighbor Nodes). *Given a parse tree and two integer parameters M and N, we define neighbor nodes as a set of leaf nodes with word-blank distance in the range $[M, N]$.*

Consider the parse tree of the question stem *"The lady * you saw performing on stage is our favorite English teacher."* shown in Fig. 2(a). With the parameters $M = -1$ and $N = 2$, we can extract the neighbor nodes {"lady", "*", "you", "saw"}.

Definition 3 (Parse-key tree). *Given a grammar question with a blank position, the parse-key tree is defined as a sub-parse tree, which consists of the neighbor nodes and their predecessors, together with the information on word-blank distance.*

Algorithm 1 shows the Parse-key Tree Construction process. The algorithm takes in a question stem Q_{stem} as input and returns the parse-key tree T_{PK}. First, it uses the Stanford parser to parse the question stem to obtain the parse tree (line 1). Next, it computes the word-blank distance for the words in Q_{stem} (line 2). Then, it constructs a parse-key tree from the parse tree and word-blank distances (lines 3–7). To do this, it first extracts the neighbor nodes from the parse tree and the predecessor nodes of all neighbor nodes. For example, the predecessor nodes of the neighbor node "lady" are {"S", "NP", "NP", "NN"}. The parse-key tree T_{PK} is then initialized as the sub-parse tree consisting of neighbor nodes and their predecessors. The sub-parse tree enclosed by the dotted

Algorithm 1. Parse-key Tree Construction

Input: Q_{stem}: A question stem
Output: T_{PK}: A parse-key tree

```
T ← parse tree obtained from Q_stem
Compute word-blank distances for the words in Q_stem
neighbor ← neighbor nodes extracted from T
predecessor ← predecessor nodes of neighbor nodes extracted from T
T_PK ← subtree consisting of nodes in neighbor and predecessor
for each leaf node n in T_PK do
  | Add sibling node labeled with n's word-blank distance to n
return T_PK
```

shape in Fig. 2(a) is the sub-parse tree with parameters $M = -1$ and $N = 2$ of the parse tree. Then, for each leaf node n in T_{PK}, we add a sibling node labeled with n's word-blank distance to n. For example, word-blank distance of the "lady" node is "−1", we add a sibling node labeled "−1" to "lady". Finally, the parse-key tree T_{PK} is returned. The parse-key tree of the sample query is shown in Fig. 2(b).

3.2 Parse-Key Tree Similarity

After constructing the parse-key trees of the query and each database question, we compute the similarity between them. The proposed parse-key tree similarity process consists of the following two steps: calculating structural similarity and calculating POS order similarity.

Calculating Structural Similarity. This step aims to capture the structural similarity between parse-key trees of the query and each database question. Tree kernel [5] can be used to capture the structural information from a syntactic tree [8,12,13]. However, tree kernel does not fit well into parse-key tree. Therefore, we propose a new method to calculate the structural similarity. The main idea behind structural similarity is to calculate the common tree fragments between two parse-key trees.

Definition 4 (Production). *Given a node, the production at the node is the relationship between the node and its children. It is denoted as "node* $\rightarrow$ *child*$_1 \ldots$*child*$_n$*", where child*$_1 \ldots$*child*$_n$ *are the children of the node.*

For example, consider the node "SBAR" in Fig. 2(b). The children of "SBAR" are "SYM" and "S", so its production is "SBAR→ SYM S". Note that the punctuation nodes can change the grammatical structure of a question, while word-blank distance nodes may provide hint on the grammatical focus of a query. Therefore, we define specific production to enhance the effect of such nodes.

Definition 5 (Specific Production). *Given a pre-terminal node (i.e. node that only has leaf node) called PT-node, a specific production at PT-node is the* *relationship between PT-node and one of children which is either a punctuation node, e.g. ',' or a word-blank distance node, e.g. '1'. It is denoted as "PT-node → child". The specific production at a node is empty if it is not a pre-terminal node. Two specific productions are the same only if they are equal and not empty.*

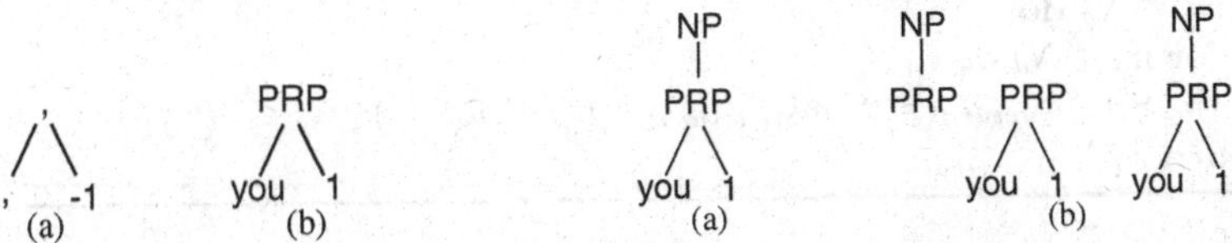

Fig. 3. An example for pre-terminal nodes

Fig. 4. An example for tree fragment

For example, consider the example in Fig. 3(a). The children of the node "," are "," and "−1". So it has two specific productions: (1) ", → ," and (2) ", → −1". Let's consider another example given in Fig. 3(b). The children of the node "PRP" are "you" and "1", so its specific production is " PRP → 1".

Definition 6 (Tree Fragment). *Given a parse-key tree, a tree fragment is a sub-graph which has more than one node and must be the entire production at the node.*

Consider the parse-key tree shown in Fig. 4(a). It has three different tree fragments, which are given in Fig. 4(b). Note that "PRP → you" is not a tree fragment, because "PRP → you" is not the entire production.

The structural similarity between two parse-key trees is based on the number of common tree fragments.

Definition 7 (Common Tree Fragments). *Given two tree fragments, they are common tree fragments if the production or any specific production at each node in the two tree fragments are the same.*

As defined earlier, a tree fragment is a subgraph of the parse-key tree. Thus, the number of common tree fragments between the two trees can effectively capture their structural similarity.

Algorithm 2 shows the structural similarity calculation method. The inputs of the algorithm are two parse-key trees T_q and T_d, and the output of the algorithm is the structural similarity which is defined as the total number of common tree fragments in the two trees. We use N_q and N_d to denote the set of non-leaf nodes in T_q and T_d, respectively (lines 1–2). The structural similarity $Sim_{structural}$ is initialized as 0 (line 3). For each node $n_q \in N_q$ and node $n_d \in N_d$, we compute the number of common tree fragments rooted at n_q and n_d, denoted by $CTF(n_q, n_d)$, and add the number to $Sim_{structural}$ (lines 3–6).

The function $CTF(n_q, n_d)$ takes nodes n_q and n_d as input and computes the number of common tree fragments rooted at n_q and n_d as output. The $CTF(n_q, n_d)$ is computed as follows:

Algorithm 2. Structural Similarity Calculation

Input: T_q: parse-key tree of query; T_d: parse-key tree of database question
Output: $Sim_{structural}$: structural similarity

$N_q \leftarrow$ all the nodes in T_q(exclude leaf nodes)
$N_d \leftarrow$ all the nodes in T_d(exclude leaf nodes)
$Sim_{structural} = 0$
for $n_q \in N_q$ **do**
  for $n_d \in N_d$ **do**
    $Sim_{structural} = Sim_{structural} + CTF(n_q, n_d)$
return $Sim_{structural}$;

1. If the production and the specific production at n_q and n_d are both different, then $CTF(n_q, n_d) = 0$.
2. If the production or one specific production at n_q and n_d are the same, and n_q and n_d are pre-terminal nodes, then $CTF(n_q, n_d) = 1$.
3. Otherwise, if the productions at n_q and n_d are the same, and n_q and n_d are not pre-terminal nodes, then $CTF(n_q, n_d) = \prod_{j=1}^{nc(n_q)}[1+CTF(n_q^{ch(j)}, n_d^{ch(j)})]$ where $nc(n_q)$ is the number of children of n_q and $n_q^{ch(j)}$ is the j-th child of the node n_q.

In the calculation of CTF, it is quite straight-forward for the first two cases. For the third case, CTF is defined recursively. Note that to get a common tree fragment rooted at n_q and n_d, we can take the production at n_q and n_d, together with either simply taking the non-terminal at the child, or taking any one of the common tree fragments at the child, for each child of n_q and n_d. Thus, there are $(1 + CTF(n_q^{ch(j)}, n_d^{ch(j)}))$ choices for the j-th child. Putting them together, we can see that CTF can effectively compute the number of common tree fragments rooted at n_q and n_d.

Calculating POS Order Similarity. To compute the POS order similarity, we first define POS tags list and longest common sub-POS sequence (LCS sequence) between two parse-key trees.

Definition 8 (POS tags list). *Given a parse-key tree, the POS tags list of the parse-key tree is the list of its pre-terminal nodes' labels.*

Definition 9 (LCS sequence). *Given two parse-key trees, the longest common sub-POS sequence (LCS sequence) between the two parse-key trees is the longest common subsequence between their POS tags lists.*

Consider the parse-key tree in Fig. 2(b), the POS tags list of this parse-key tree is {"NN", "SYM", "PRP", "VBD"}. The LCS sequence between a parse-key tree with POS tags list {"NN", "SYM", "PRP", "VBD"} and another parse-key tree with POS tags list {"VBD", "JJ", "NN", "PRP"} is {"NN", "PRP"}.

Given two parse-key trees T_q and T_d, assuming LS is their LCS sequence, and their POS tags list are L_q and L_d, respectively. $P_{L_q}(s)$ is the position of the POS tag s in L_q, and $P_{L_d}(s)$ is the position of the POS tag s in L_d. The order similarity of s in LS is defined as:

$$Sim_{order}(s) = \frac{1}{|P_{L_q}(s) - P_{L_d}(s)| + 1} \tag{1}$$

where $|P_{L_q}(s) - P_{L_d}(s)|$ is the position distance of s between L_q and L_d. For example, the position distance of "NN" between $L_q = \{$"NN", "SYM", "PRP", "VBD"$\}$ and $L_d = \{$"VBD", "JJ", "NN", "PRP"$\}$ is $|P_{L_q}(\text{"NN"}) - P_{L_d}(\text{"NN"})| = 2$, where $P_{L_q}(\text{"NN"}) = 1$, $P_{L_d}(\text{"NN"}) = 3$.

The POS order similarity $Sim_{POSorder}$ between T_q and T_d is calculated as the summation of order similarity of all elements in their LCS sequence divided by the longer length of L_q and L_d. Given two parse-key trees T_q and T_d, their POS order similarity is defined as:

$$Sim_{POSorder}(T_q, T_d) = \frac{1}{max(|L_q|, |L_d|)} \sum_{s \in LS} Sim_{order}(s) \tag{2}$$

where $max(|L_q|, |L_d|)$ is the longer length of lists L_q and L_d.

Parse-Key Tree Similarity. In order to compute the similarity score between the parse-key trees T_q and T_d, we normalize the range of the structural similarity and POS order similarity to [0, 1] using unity-based normalization[1] method.

Given the parse-key trees T_q of query Q_q and T_d of question Q_d in the database. Let $Sim'_1(T_q, T_d)$ and $Sim'_2(T_q, T_d)$ be normalized $Sim_{structural}(T_q, T_d)$ and $Sim_{POSorder}(T_q, T_d)$, respectively. The parse-key tree similarity is the combined score of structural similarity and POS order similarity. The parse-key tree similarity between Q_q and Q_d is defined as:

$$Sim(T_q, T_d) = k_1 Sim'_1(T_q, T_d) + k_2 Sim'_2(T_q, T_d) \tag{3}$$

where k_1 and k_2 are weighting factors.

3.3 Ranking

After computing the parse-key tree similarity, we rank the questions according to their parse-key tree similarity scores and return the ranked questions to the user. Noted that, if the query contains correct answer to the MCQ question, we will replace the blank with the correct answer. Then we will parse the updated

[1] https://en.wikipedia.org/wiki/Normalization_(statistics).

question. Parsing the updated question may improve the retrieval accuracy. In this paper, we only consider the case that the user do not know the correct answer. Since the input query and the database questions that are parsed by the Stanford parse contains blank, we may get incorrect parser trees. However, since we parse both the query and the questions in database with the sentence with blank, the relevant query and questions still have similar parse-key trees.

4 Performance Evaluation

In this section, we discuss the performance evaluation of the proposed approach.

4.1 Experimental Setup

In the experiments, we use a total of 4,580 English grammar MCQ questions as the dataset for performance evaluation. The size of the training and test sets were 180 questions and 4,400 question respectively. The questions are gathered from primary school leaving examination (PSLE) and Gaokao (NCEE). PSLE is an annual national examination in Singapore administered by the Ministry of Education and taken by all students near the end of their sixth year in primary school before moving on to secondary school. Gaokao is an academic examination held annually in China, and is a prerequisite for entrance into almost all higher education institutions at the undergraduate level. We randomly split the test questions into two sets: 100 questions will be served as test queries, while the remaining 4,300 questions will be served as database questions for query retrieval. Relevant database questions for each query are manually annotated.

For evaluation, we use the following two metrics:

- Mean Average Precision[2] at rank K (MAP@K): It measures the mean of the average precision scores for each question query and is calculated as: $MAP@K = \frac{1}{N_q}\sum_{q=1}^{N_q}\sum_{i=1}^{K} P(q,i)/relevant(q)$, where N_q is the number of question queries, $rel(i)$ is an indicator function equaling 1 if the question at rank i is a relevant question, zero otherwise, $P(q,i)$ means the percentage of relevant questions ranked at top i positions of query q, $relevant(q)$ is the number of relevant questions of query q.
- Mean Reciprocal Rank[3] (MRR): It measures the average of the reciprocal ranks of results for a sample of question queries and is calculated as: $MRR = \frac{1}{N_q}\sum_{q=1}^{N_q}\frac{1}{rank_q}$, where N_q is the number of question queries and $rank_q$ is the ranked position of the first relevant question for the query q.

In the experiments, we measure the performance of the methods using the metrics MAP@1, MAP@3, MAP@5 and MRR.

---

[2] https://www.kaggle.com/wiki/MeanAveragePrecision.
[3] https://en.wikipedia.org/wiki/Mean_reciprocal_rank.

4.2 Parameter Tuning and Learning

Firstly, we find the optimal values for the parameters M and N which are used to construct parse-key tree as discussed in Sect. 3.1. For this purpose, we study each value of M and N from the ranges of $[-5, 0]$ and $[0, 5]$ respectively. Our approach achieves the best performance when $M = -1$ and $N = 2$. Secondly, we learn the optimal values for the parameters k_1 and k_2 which are used in Eq. (3). For this purpose, we apply the ridge regression technique [6] as follows. The training set conclude 30 question queries. Each query has five most relevant questions in the database ranked from 1 to 5. For each question, we estimate its similarity score as $(1 - \frac{r-1}{5})$, where r is the rank of this question. We then use Eq. (3) to learn the best combination of the parameters using the ridge regression algorithm. The results for the learning method are $k_1 = 0.25$ and $k_2 = 0.67$ for Eq. (3).

4.3 Methods Used for Performance Comparison

In the experiments, apart from evaluating our proposed approach, we also compare our proposed approach with the following classical text and sentence retrieval methods:

- BM25 [9]: This is the text retrieval method, which is based on statistical analysis of term occurrences in the text.
- Collins and Duffy [5]: This is the method based on syntactic parse tree and the original tree kernel function for counting common sub-trees between syntactic trees.
- Carmel et al. [3]: This method considers both statistical features and syntactic features.
- Maxwell and Croft [7]: This is the retrieval model based on the term ranking algorithm, PhRank.

4.4 Performance Results

Table 2 shows the performance of structural similarity, POS order similarity and the combined similarity of the proposed approach. As shown in Table 2, the use of both structural similarity and POS order similarity has improved the performance by more than 16.3% in MAP@3 and 14.5% in MRR compared with using structural similarity or POS order similarity alone. Structural similarity evaluates the structural information while the POS order similarity evaluates word ordering information. Both similarity measures are useful for English grammar question retrieval.

Table 3 shows the performance comparison of our proposed approach against other classical text and sentence retrieval methods. We can observe that our proposed approach has improved the performance by 37.0% in MAP@3 and 32.3% in MRR when compared with BM25. One intuitive explanation is that the purpose of grammar question retrieval is to find questions with most similar grammatical structure and usage, and text retrieval based methods are not very effective for this task. When compared with other methods such as Collins and Duffy, our proposed approach has improved the performance by 30.9% in MAP@3 and 27.7% in MRR. It shows that our proposed syntactic parse-key tree approach is more effective than other classical text and sentence retrieval in retrieving relevant grammar questions with similar grammatical focus.

Table 2. Performance results for the proposed approach

	MAP@1	MAP@3	MAP@5	MRR
Structural similarity	54.2	59.4	58.2	64.6
POS order similarity	50.0	55.9	54.9	61.2
Structural similarity + POS order similarity	70.8	75.7	71.7	79.1

Table 3. Performance comparison with other methods

	MAP@1	MAP@3	MAP@5	MRR
BM25	36.0	38.7	41.5	46.8
Collins and Duffy	41.7	44.8	44.8	51.4
Carmel et al.	20.8	25.0	31.3	35.8
Maxwell and Croft	31.8	33.7	34.4	43.2
Our approach	70.8	75.7	71.7	79.1

5 Conclusion

In this paper, we have proposed an effective syntactic parse-key tree based approach for English grammar questions retrieval. The proposed parse-key tree is able to capture the grammatical usage of the question query and database questions according to their blank or answer position, and the questions are ranked based on the parse-key similarity between the question query and database questions. The performance results have shown that our proposed approach has significantly outperformed other classical text and sentence retrieval methods such as BM25 and other syntactic tree based methods for grammar question retrieval.

Acknowledgement. The work is supported by the Research Innovation Program for College Graduates of Jiangsu Province (Grant No. KYLX15_0076), and National Natural Science Foundation of China (Grant No. 61271204).

References

1. Augustinus, L., Vandeghinste, V., Van Eynde, F.: Example-based treebank querying. In: LREC, pp. 3161–3167. Citeseer (2012)

2. Bendersky, M., Croft, W.B.: Modeling higher-order term dependencies in information retrieval using query hypergraphs. In: Proceedings of the 35th International ACM SIGIR Conference on Research and Development in Information Retrieval, pp. 941–950. ACM (2012)
3. Carmel, D., Mejer, A., Pinter, Y., Szpektor, I.: Improving term weighting for community question answering search using syntactic analysis. In: Proceedings of the 23rd ACM International Conference on Conference on Information and Knowledge Management, pp. 351–360. ACM (2014)
4. Chinkina, M., Kannan, M., Meurers, D.: Online information retrieval for language learning. In: ACL 2016, p. 7 (2016)
5. Collins, M., Duffy, N.: Convolution kernels for natural language. In: Advances in Neural Information Processing Systems, pp. 625–632 (2001)
6. Hastie, T., Tibshirani, R., Friedman, J.: The Elements of Statistical Learning, 2nd edn. Springer, New York (2009)
7. Maxwell, K.T., Croft, W.B.: Compact query term selection using topically related text. In: Proceedings of the 36th International ACM SIGIR Conference on Research and Development in Information Retrieval, pp. 583–592 (2013)
8. Moschitti, A.: Efficient convolution kernels for dependency and constituent syntactic trees. In: Fürnkranz, J., Scheffer, T., Spiliopoulou, M. (eds.) ECML 2006. LNCS, vol. 4212, pp. 318–329. Springer, Heidelberg (2006). doi:10.1007/11871842_32
9. Robertson, S., Zaragoza, H.: The Probabilistic Relevance Framework: BM25 and Beyond. Now Publishers Inc., Hanover (2009)
10. Robertson, S.E., Walker, S., Beaulieu, M., Gatford, M., Payne, A.: Okapi at TREC-4. NIST Special Publication SP, pp. 73–96 (1996)
11. Schubotz, M., Grigorev, A., Leich, M., Cohl, H.S., Meuschke, N., Gipp, B., Youssef, A.S., Markl, V.: Semantification of identifiers in mathematics for better math information retrieval. Energy **2**(5), 10 (2016)
12. Tymoshenko, K., Moschitti, A.: Assessing the impact of syntactic and semantic structures for answer passages reranking. In: Proceedings of the 24th ACM International on Conference on Information and Knowledge Management, pp. 1451–1460. ACM (2015)
13. Wang, K., Ming, Z., Chua, T.S.: A syntactic tree matching approach to finding similar questions in community-based QA services. In: Proceedings of the 32nd International ACM SIGIR Conference on Research and Development in Information Retrieval, pp. 187–194. ACM (2009)
14. Wang, Y., Wu, S., Li, D., Mehrabi, S., Liu, H.: A part-of-speech term weighting scheme for biomedical information retrieval. J. Biomed. Inform. **63**, 379–389 (2016)
15. Zhang, W., Ming, Z., Zhang, Y., Liu, T., Chua, T.S.: Exploring key concept paraphrasing based on pivot language translation for question retrieval. In: AAAI, pp. 410–416 (2015)
16. Zhu, M., Zhang, Y., Chen, W., Zhang, M., Zhu, J.: Fast and accurate shift-reduce constituent parsing. In: ACL, pp. 434–443 (2013)

A Discriminative Possibilistic Approach for Query Translation Disambiguation

Wiem Ben Romdhane[1], Bilel Elayeb[1,2(✉)], and Narjès Bellamine Ben Saoud[1]

[1] RIADI Research Laboratory, ENSI Manouba University, Manouba, Tunisia
br.wiem@yahoo.fr, Bilel.Elayeb@riadi.rnu.tn, Narjes.Bellamine@ensi.rnu.tn
[2] Emirates College of Technology, P.O. Box: 41009 Abu Dhabi, United Arab Emirates

Abstract. We propose, assess and compare in this paper a new discriminative possibilistic query translation (QT) disambiguation approach using both a bilingual dictionary and a parallel text corpus in order to overcome some drawbacks of the dictionary-based techniques. In this approach, the translation relevance of a given source query term is modeled by two measures: the possible relevance allows rejecting irrelevant translations, whereas the necessary relevance makes it possible to reinforce the translations not eliminated by the possibility. We experiment this new approach using the French-English parallel text corpus *Europarl* and the *CLEF-2003* French-English CLIR test collection. Our experiments highlighted the performance of our new discriminative possibilistic approach compared to both the probabilistic and the probability-to-possibility transformation-based approaches, especially for short queries and using different assessment metrics.

Keywords: Cross-Language information retrieval (CLIR) · Query translation disambiguation · Probabilistic model · Possibilistic model · Relevance

1 Introduction

Nowadays, the number of online non-English documents on the Internet is continuously increased, which requires the availability of high-performance cross-language information retrieval (CLIR) systems satisfying the Internet users' needs. Query translation (QT) techniques are the main research task in the domain of CLIR [12]. Besides, the usefulness of the simple dictionary-based translation approaches in QT has been improved due to the availability of machine readable bilingual dictionaries for several languages. However, these approaches are lacked by many major challenges such as: (i) the translation disambiguation problem known as the difficulty to choose the correct translation corresponding to each source query term among all the possible translations existing in the dictionary; and (ii) the poor coverage of the available dictionaries suffering from the missing of many translations corresponding to new terminologies. Nevertheless, many research works in the literature [20, 22, 25] are dedicated to manually or automatically collect larger lexical resources in order to

F. Frasincar et al. (Eds.): NLDB 2017, LNCS 10260, pp. 366–379, 2017.
DOI: 10.1007/978-3-319-59569-6_45

increase the coverage of these dictionaries. Moreover, translation ambiguity can decrease IR effectiveness. In order to overcome this limit, some approaches have used a phrase dictionary to firstly select noun phrases in the source query and secondly translate them as units.

We propose, assess and compare in this paper a new discriminative possibilistic QT approach dedicated to solve the problem of QT ambiguity using both a bilingual dictionary and a parallel text corpus in order to overcome some drawbacks of the dictionary-based QT techniques. In this approach, the relevance of a source query term translation is modeled by two measures: The possible relevance allows rejecting irrelevant translations, whereas the necessary relevance makes it possible to reinforce the translations not eliminated by the possibility. We compare this new approach to both the probabilistic and the probability-to-possibility transformation-based approaches [11], in which we start by identifying noun phrases (NPs) using the *Stanford Parser*[1] and translating them as units using translation patterns and a language model. Then, remaining source query terms are translated using a probabilistic word-by-word translation technique. Indeed, the suitable translation of each source query term or NP has a tendency to co-occur in the target language documents unlike unsuitable ones. Besides, additional words and their translations are automatically generated from a parallel bilingual corpus in order to increase the coverage of the bilingual dictionary. We assessed our approach using the French-English parallel text corpus *Europarl*[2] and the *CLEF-2003* French-English CLIR test collection. Our results confirmed the performance of our new discriminative possibilistic approach compared to both the probabilistic and the probability-to-possibility transformation-based approaches [11], principally for short queries and using various evaluation scenarios and metrics.

This paper is organized as follows. We present in Sect. 2 related works in the field of QT and discuss the solutions aiming at solving the problem of translation ambiguity. In Sect. 3, we recall the necessary of possibility theory. The new discriminative possibilistic QT approach is given in Sect. 4. Section 5 details our experimentations, expose and discuss a comparative study between QT approaches. Section 6 concludes our work in this paper and suggests some perspectives for future research.

2 Related Work

Since the early 1990's, many researchers (e.g. [19]) showed that the usefulness of a manually translating phrases have performed better results in CLIR effectiveness than a word-by-word dictionary-based translation. Moreover, CLIR performance was increased by [6] when they used their phrase dictionary generated from a set of parallel sentences in French and English. In the same way, Ballesteros and Croft [2] confirmed that translations of multi-word concepts as phrases are more perfect than word-by-word translations. Indeed, phrases translations were achieved using information existing in phrase and word usage available in the Collins machine readable dictionary.

---

[1] http://nlp.stanford.edu/software/lex-parser.shtml.

[2] http://www.statmt.org/europarl/.

Unfortunately, it is hard to find or build an exhaustive phrase dictionary in CLIR since we have until now many missing phrases in these available lexicons. Therefore, it is not easy to select all missing phrases in the queries and suitably translate them. Actually, many unfamiliar phrases suffer from the problem of their identification and translation since they cannot be identified in any dictionaries. Hence, the problem of the lexicon coverage is one of the limits of this approach since we cannot know until now: How can one build an exhaustive phrase dictionary?

On the other hand, many authors have tackled the problem of translation ambiguity using word sense disambiguation (WSD) techniques. For example, Hull [18] used structured queries for disambiguation in QT task. Besides, co-occurrence statistics from corpora are used by Ballesteros and Croft [13] in order to decrease translation ambiguity in CLIR. Then, many disambiguation strategies are suggested and evaluated by Hiemstra and Jong [61] in CLIR tasks. Later, a technique-based statistical term similarity for word sense disambiguation was suggested and tested by [1] in order to enhance CLIR effectiveness. Even if the difficulty of translation ambiguity was significantly decreased, Xu and Weischedel [24] showed that it is not evident to accomplish perfect enhancement in CLIR performance. Recently, Lefever and Hoste [21] have argued the advantage of moving from traditional monolingual WSD task into a cross-lingual one. In fact, this new technique, namely "Cross-Lingual WSD" (CLWSD) has been involved in CLIR since SemEval-2010 and SemEval-2013 competitions. The participant in these exercises confirmed that CLIR effectiveness has been enhanced due to the new CLWSD technique which significantly resolves the problem of translation ambiguity.

QT techniques require training and matching models in order to compute a score of relevance (or similarities) between source query terms/phrases and their possible translations. Existing QT approaches in the literature are based on poor, uncertain and imprecise data, while possibility theory is naturally dedicated to this type of applications, since it takes into account of the imprecision and uncertainty at the same time and it makes it possible to express ignorance. However, the main challenge of our approach is that the context used in the translation disambiguation process of a given source query term can be also ambiguous. Consequently, we consider this phenomenon as a case of imprecision. That's why we are inspired from the possibility theory which naturally applies to this kind of imperfection. By cons, the probability theory is not suitable to deal with such type of data. Besides, and given that the possibility theory is the best framework suitable for imprecision treatment, we have taken advantage of possibility distributions in order to solve the problem of translation ambiguity in CLIR task. Recently, we have proposed and tested in [11] a possibilistic QT approach derived from the probabilistic one using a probability-to-possibility transformation as a mean to introduce further tolerance in QT process. This approach has achieved a statistically significant improvement compared to the probabilistic one using both long and short queries.

3 Possibility Theory

We briefly present in the following sections the basic elements of possibility theory such as the possibility distribution (cf. Sect. 3.1), the possibility and necessity measures (cf. Sect. 3.2) and the possibilistic networks (cf. Sect. 3.3). More details and discussions about possibility theory are available in [7–10].

3.1 Possibility Distribution

The fundamental element of the possibility theory is the *possibility distribution*. Given the universe of discourse $\Omega = \{\omega_1, \omega_2, \ldots, \omega_n\}$, we symbolised by π the basic concept corresponding to a function which associates to each element $\omega_i \in \Omega$ a value from a bounded and linearly ordered valuation set (L, <). Moreover, the *possibility degree* is defined as the value in which our knowledge on the real world is encoded. Indeed, this scale has two interpretations: (i) when the handled values reflect only an ordering between the different states of the world, it is the *qualitative* setting which can be applied using the *min* operator; and (ii) when the handled values have a real sense, it is the *quantitative* setting which can be applied using the *product* operator. Flexibility is modelled by allowing providing a possibility degree from the interval [0, 1]. We note that $\pi(\omega_i) = 1$ means that it is fully possible that ω_i is the real world, and $\pi(\omega_i) = 0$ means that it is impossible that ω_i is the real world. The possibility theory provides different significant exacting cases of knowledge as the following: (i) *Complete knowledge* ($\exists\ \omega_i \in \Omega$, $\pi(\omega_i) = 1$ *and* $\forall \omega_j \neq \omega_i$, $\pi(\omega_j) = 0$); (ii) *Partial ignorance* ($\forall\ \omega_i \in A \subseteq \Omega$, $\pi(\omega_i) = 1$, $\forall \omega_i \notin A$, $\pi(\omega_i) = 0$; when A is not a singleton); and (iii) *Total ignorance:* all values in Ω are possible ($\forall\ \omega_i \in \Omega$, $\pi(\omega_i) = 1$).

3.2 Possibility and Necessity Measures

The two dual measures in which a possibility distribution π on Ω enables events to be qualified in terms of their *plausibility* and their *certainty* are respectively known as the *Possibility* (Π) and the *Necessity* (N) [7]. Given a possibility distribution π on the universe of discourse Ω, the corresponding possibility and necessity measures of any event $A \subseteq 2^{\Omega}$ are respectively determined by the Eqs. (1) and (2):

$$\prod(A) = \max_{w \in A} \pi(w) \tag{1}$$

$$N(A) = \min_{w \notin A}(1 - \pi(w)) = 1 - \prod(\overline{A}) \tag{2}$$

In fact, $\Pi(A)$ provides an assessment similar to a degree of *non-emptiness* of the intersection of the fuzzy set having π as membership function with the classical subset A. Thus, $\Pi(A)$ measures at which level A is *consistent* with our knowledge represented by π. While, $N(A)$ assesses at which level A is *certainly* inferred by our knowledge represented by π; since it is a degree of inclusion of the fuzzy set corresponding to π into the subset A.

3.3 Possibilistic Networks (PN)

The numerical and graphical components are the main characteristic of a directed possibilistic network on a variable set *V*. These two components are defined as follow: (i) the distinct links in the graph are quantified via the *numerical component*. Indeed, it represents conditional possibility matrix of every node given the context of its parents. (ii) The *graphical component* is a directed acyclic graph (DAG). The DAG enables representing conditional dependency between dependent or independent variables. Every link denotes a dependency between two variables and every node in the graph denotes a domain variable. The graph structure encodes independence relation sets between nodes. Moreover, these possibility distributions should respect the normalization feature [4]. For each variable *V*:

- If *V* is a root node and *Dom(V)* the domain of *V*, the prior possibility of *V* should satisfy:

$$max_{v \in Dom(V)} \Pi(v) = 1 \tag{3}$$

- If *V* is not a root node, the conditional distribution of *V* in the context of its parents denoted U_V should satisfy:

$$max_{v \in Dom(V)} \Pi(v|u_V) = 1; \; u_V \in Dom(U_V) \tag{4}$$

Where: *Dom*(*V*): domain of *V*; U_V: value of parents of *V*; *Dom*(U_V): domain of parent set of *V*.

We suggest in this paper a new possibilistic approach for QT disambiguation based on possibilistic network (cf. Sect. 4). We link in this network the possible translations (T_i) to the terms of a source query $SQ = (t_1, t_2, \ldots, t_p)$, which represents its context. In this case: $v_i = t_i$; $u_V = T_i$; $Dom(V) = \{t_1, t_2, \ldots, t_p\}$; and $Dom(U_V) = \{T_1, T_2, \ldots, T_N\}$.

We provide in Sect. 4.2 an illustrative example including detailed calculus. The possibilistic graph which associated conditional possibility distribution is based on the product operator. The product-based possibilistic graph (*PPG*), is generally comfortable for the numerical setting where possibility measures represent numerical values in [0, 1]. The possibility distribution of product-based possibilistic networks (π_p) obtained by the associated chain class is calculated via Eq. (5):

$$\pi_p(V_1, V_2, \cdots, V_N) = \prod_{i=1}^{N} \Pi(V_i|U_{V_i}) \tag{5}$$

4 The Discriminative Possibilistic QT Approach

We present in Sect. 4.1 the formulae for calculating the Degree of Possibilistic Relevance (DPR) and an illustrative example with a detailed calculus in Sect. 4.2.

4.1 The Degree of Possibilistic Relevance (DPR)

Let us consider the source query (*SQ*) enclosing *P* terms and denoted as: $SQ = (t_1, t_2, \ldots, t_P)$. We assume that *SQ* includes only one ambiguous term having several possible translations. We note the Degree of Possibilistic Relevance of a translation T_j given *SQ* by $DPR(T_j|SQ)$. We have taken advantage of a possibilistic matching model of information retrieval (IR) used in [5, 12–16] in order to assess the relevance of a translation T_j given a source query *SQ*. In the case of IR, the matching score is calculated between a query and a document. However, in case of QT disambiguation, we model the relevance of a translation given a source query using double measures: The *possible* relevance and the *necessary* relevance. The irrelevant translations are rejected due to the possible relevance, while the relevance of the remaining translations, which have not been rejected by the possibility, is reinforced due to the necessary relevance.

Figure 1 presents our possibilistic network which links the word translation T_j to the terms of a given source query $SQ = (t_1, t_2, \ldots, t_P)$. The output of the QT disambiguation process is the target query $TQ = (T_1, T_2, \ldots, T_P)$. The later will be useful to retrieve a set of relevant documents on the target language.

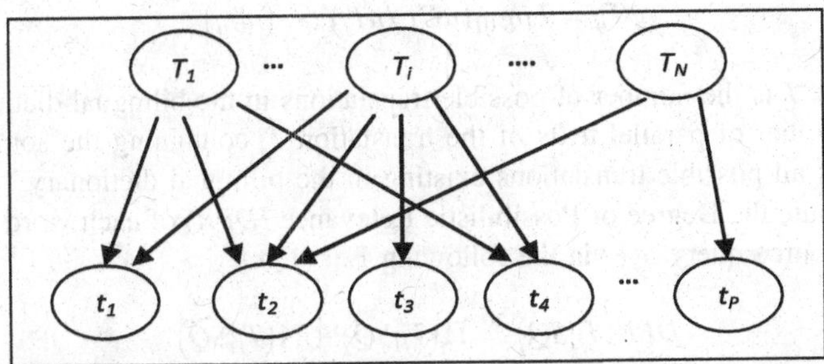

Fig. 1. Possibilistic network of the QT disambiguation approach

Giving the source query *SQ*, the relevance of every word translation T_j is computed as the following:

Analogically to the IR matching model proposed in [46–49], the possibility $\Pi(T_j|SQ)$ is proportional to:

$$\Pi'(T_j|SQ) = \Pi(t_1|T_j) * \ldots * \Pi(t_P|T_j) = nft_{1j} * \ldots * nft_{Pj} \tag{6}$$

Where:

- $nft_{ij} = tf_{ij}/max(tf_{kj})$: the normalized frequency of the source term t_i in the parallel text of the translation T_j.
- tf_{ij} is the number of occurrence of the source term t_i in the parallel text of the translation T_j divided by the number of terms in the parallel text of the translation T_j.

We compute the necessity to restore a relevant translation T_j given the source query SQ, denoted $N(T_j|SQ)$, as the following:

$$\mathrm{N}(T_j|SQ) = 1 - \Pi(\neg T_j|SQ) \quad (7)$$

Where:

$$\Pi(\neg T_j|SQ) = (\Pi(SQ|\neg T_j) * \Pi(\neg T_j))/\Pi(SQ) \quad (8)$$

At the same way $\Pi(\neg T_j| SQ)$ is proportional to:

$$\Pi'(\neg T_j|SQ) = \Pi(t_1|\neg T_j) * \ldots * \Pi(t_P|\neg T_j) \quad (9)$$

This numerator can be expressed as the following:

$$\Pi'(\neg T_j|SQ) = (1 - \phi T_{1j}) * \ldots * (1 - \phi T_{Pj}) \quad (10)$$

Where:

$$\phi T_{ij} = Log_{10}(nCT/nT_j) * (nft_{ij}) \quad (11)$$

Where: nCT is the number of possible translations in the bilingual dictionary. But, nT_j is the number of parallel texts of the translation T_j containing the source term t_i. This includes all possible translations existing in the bilingual dictionary.

We compute the Degree of Possibilistic Relevance (DPR) of each word translation T_j giving a source query SQ via the following Eq. (12):

$$DPR(T_j|SQ) = \Pi(T_j|SQ) + \mathrm{N}(T_j|SQ) \quad (12)$$

Finally, the suitable translations are those which have a high score of $DPR(T_j|SQ)$.

4.2 Illustrative Example

We provide here a numerical calculation example for reasons of brevity. But, we have already detailed in [11] some data/corpus-based examples in which we have showed the difference between the probabilistic and the possibilistic QT approaches.

Let us consider the source query $SQ = (W, t_2, t_4, t_5, t_7)$, which contains only one polysemous source query term W in order to simplify the calculus in this example. We assume that W has two possible translations T_1 and T_2 in the bilingual dictionary. We suppose also that the parallel text of T_1 is indexed by the three terms $\{t_1, t_2, t_3, t_4\}$ and the parallel text of T_2 is indexed by $\{t_1, t_4, t_5, t_6, t_7\}$. We have:

$\Pi(T_1|SQ) = nf_{(W,\ T1)} * nf_{(t2,\ T1)} * nf_{(t4,\ T1)} * nf_{(t5,\ T1)} * nf_{(t7,\ T1)} = 0*(1/4)*(1/4)*0*0 = 0$. Where: $nf_{(W,\ T1)}$ is the normalized frequency of W in the parallel text of the first translation T_1.

$\Pi(T_2|\ SQ) = nf_{(W,\ T2)} * nf_{(t2,\ T2)} * nf_{(t4,\ T2)} * nf_{(t5,\ T2)} * nf_{(t7,\ T2)} = 0*0*(1/5)*(1/5)*(1/5) = 0$. We have frequently $\Pi(T_j|\ SQ) = 0$; except if all the words of the source query exist in the index of the parallel text of the translation.

On the other hand, we have not null values of $N(T_j|\ SQ)$:

$N(T_1|\ SQ) = 1- ((1 - \phi(T_1, W)) * (1 - \phi(T_1, t_2)) * (1 - \phi(T_1, t_4)) * (1 - \phi(T_1, t_5) * (1 - \phi(T_1, t_7)))$; $nf_{(T1,\ W)} = 0$, so $\phi(T_1, W) = 0$; $\phi(T_1, t_2) = log_{10}(2/1)*(1/4) = 0{,}075$; $\phi(T_1, t_4) = log_{10}(2/2)*(1/4) = 0$; $\phi(T_1, t_5) = 0$; $\phi(T_1, t_7) = 0$. So: $N(T_1|\ SQ) = 1 - ((1 -0) * (1-0.075) * (1-0) * (1-0) * (1-0)) = 1- (1* 0.925* 1* 1*1) = 0.075$. Thus, $DPR(T_1|\ SQ) = 0.075$. $N(T_2|SQ) = 1- ((1 - \phi(T_2, W))* (1 - \phi(T_2, t_2))* (1 - \phi(T_2, t_4)) * (1 - \phi(T_2, t_5) * (1 - \phi(T_2, t_7)))$. Where: $\phi(T_2, W) = 0$ because $nf(T_2, W) = 0$; $\phi(T_2, t_2) = 0$; $\phi(T_2, t_4) = log_{10}(2/2)*(1/5) = 0$; $\phi(T_2, t_5) = log_{10}(2/1)*(1/5) = 0.06$; $\phi(T_2, t_7) = log_{10}(2/1)*(1/5) = 0.06$. So: $N(T_2|SQ) = 1 - ((1-0)* (1-0)* (1-0)*(1-0.06)*(1-0.06)) = 1 - (1* 1*1*0.94* 0.94) = 1 - 0.8836 = 0.1164$. Thus, $DPR(T_2|SQ) = 0.1164 > DPR(T_1|SQ) = 0.075$.

We notice that the source query SQ is more relevant for T_2 than T_1; because it encloses three terms (t_4, t_5, t_7) of the index of the parallel text of T_2 and only two terms (t_2, t_4) of the index of the parallel text of T_1.

5 Experiments and Discussion

We assess, compare and discuss in this section the discriminative possibilistic approach for QT disambiguation. Indeed, we suggest various evaluation scenarios and metrics using the CLEF-2003 standard CLIR test collection. We compare the performance and the efficiency of the discriminative approach to both the most known efficient probabilistic and the probability-to-possibility transformation-based ones [11]. Moreover, our evaluation is performed according to the TREC protocol. We used the IR matching model OKAPI-BM25 existing in *Terrier*[3] platform in order to retrieve English relevant document. We are focused on performance metrics such as *Recall* and *Precision*, mostly used in the evaluation of CLIR tools. The evaluation assumes that there is an ideal set the system is supposed to search. This ideal set is useful to define these two metrics as follows. The recall is the percentage of documents in the ideal set that were retrieved by the system, while the precision is the percentage of documents retrieved by the system, which are also in the ideal set. Moreover, we used the precision (Y-axis) over 11 points of recall in the X-axis (0.0, 0.1,…, 1.0) to draw all recall-precision curves.

Besides, we evaluated these approaches using both the Mean Average Precision (*MAP*) and the exact precision (*R-Precision*). The latter is defined as the precision at rank *R*; where *R* is the total number of relevant documents, while the MAP is the mean of the average precision scores for each query. The Equations of calculating the *MAP* and the *R-Precision* are given in [11]. We compute also the improvement percentage between two variations of the model variables. This percentage is obtained in generally for two variables *A* and *B* measuring the percentage of *C* as $\%C = [(B - A)/A]*100$. Our 54 test queries enclose 717 French words having 2324 possible English

[3] http://terrier.org/.

translations in the bilingual dictionary. Indeed, we firstly generate our bilingual dictionary from the *Europarl* parallel corpus using all French words with their possible translations existing in this corpus in order to enlarge our lexicon coverage. Then, we have benefited from the online intelligent speller and grammar checker *Reverso*[4] in order to check this dictionary. Finally, the free online Google translate[5] has been used to enrich and check this bilingual dictionary.

Firstly, we provide in Fig. 2 the Recall-Precision curves comparing monolingual (English queries provided by CLEF-2003), discriminative, probabilistic and probability-to-possibility transformation-based (possibilistic) runs using the *title* part of the source queries as input data to our CLIR tool described in [11]. Secondly, we provide the precision values at different top documents P@5, P@10,…, P@1000, the *MAP* and the *R-Precision*. For example, the precision in point 5, namely P@5, is the ratio of relevant documents among the top 5 returned documents. The goal of the following experiments and discussion is to show and assess our contributions compared to these competitors QT disambiguation approaches mainly investigated and tested in [11].

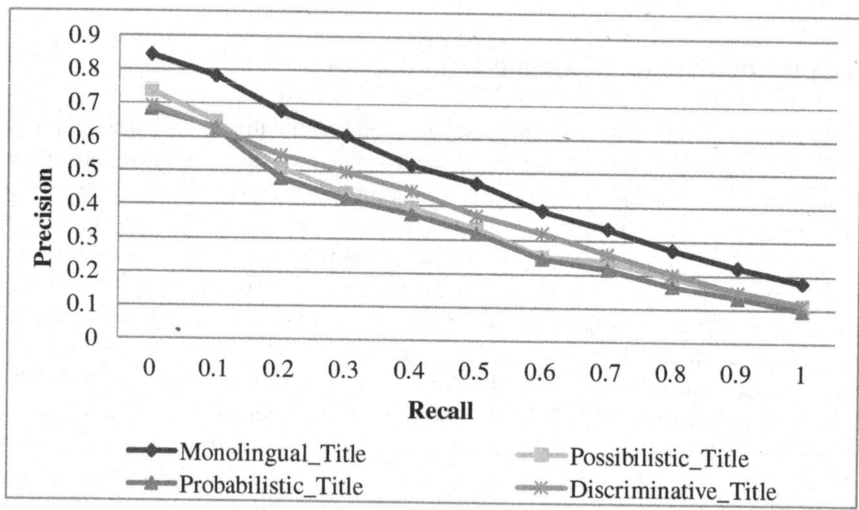

Fig. 2. Recall-Precision curves comparing monolingual, discriminative, probabilistic and probability-to-possibility transformation-based (possibilistic) runs

If we focus only on the *title* part of the query, the context is limited to a few numbers of terms in which the identification of the NP is not frequent in this case. Therefore, the discriminative possibilistic approach significantly outperforms both the probabilistic and the probability-to-possibility transformation-based (possibilistic)

---

[4] http://www.reverso.net/spell-checker/english-spelling-grammar/.

[5] https://translate.google.fr/?hl=fr.

approaches; except in some low-levels points of recall (0 and 0.1). Unfortunately, the monolingual run is still outperformed these approaches in all points of recall.

On the other hand, and in order to further confirm our conclusions made above, we provide a comparative study between the monolingual, the discriminative, the possibilistic and the probabilistic runs using the precision at different top documents, the *MAP* and the *R-Precision* metrics (cf. Fig. 3). It is trivial that the precision decreases when the number of returned documents increases. Moreover, short queries using only *title* are more efficient for the discriminative approach for all top returned documents; except for some rare cases such as P@100 and P@1000 where the number of returned documents is important, which increases the noise in the retrieved results. Unfortunately, the monolingual run is normally upper bound of CLIR performance in all our experiments, because we don't involve in our tests any query expansion step before and/or after the translation process and no close phrases/words have enriched the source and/or the target queries before returning search results.

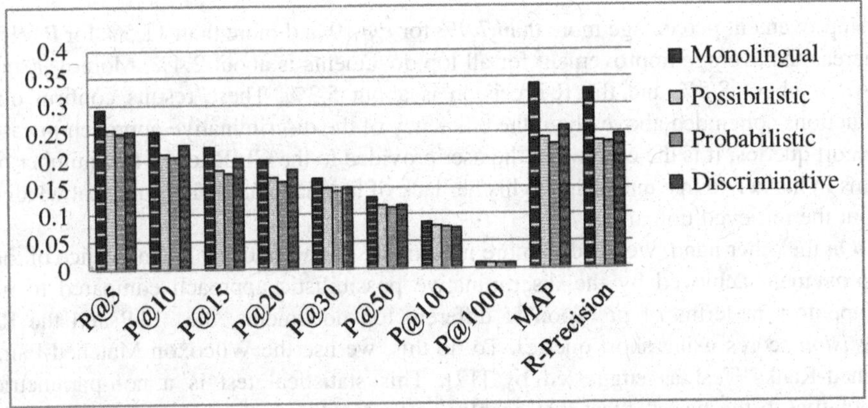

Fig. 3. Results using the precision at different top documents, MAP and R-Precision

We remark that the discriminative approach outperformed both of them in terms of the *MAP* and the *R-Precision*. In fact, these two metrics confirm again that short query using *title* is still suitable for the discriminative approach compared to its two competitors QT techniques. We present in Table 1 the improvement percentage of the discriminative approach compared to both the probabilistic and the probability-to-possibility transformation-based approaches using the precision at different top documents, the *MAP* and the *R-Precision*. Firstly, and compared to the probabilistic, the discriminative approach has performed a significant improvement in terms of precision of documents returned to the top of list using the *title* of the source query. For example, we have registered an improvement percentage more than 15% for P@15 and almost 14% for P@20, while the average improvement for all top documents is about 6%. Besides, if we focus on the *MAP* metric, the improvement of the MAP is about 14.4% and about 6% for the R-Precision metric. Secondly, and compared to the probability-to-possibility transformation-based approach, the discriminative achieved

Table 1. The improvement percentage of the discriminative compared to both the probabilistic and the probability-to-possibility transformation-based approaches

Precision metrics	% improvement Discriminative *vs.* Probabilistic	% improvement Discriminative *vs.* Possibilistic
P@5	1.53	−1.45
P@10	10.8	7.91
P@15	15.52	11.57
P@20	13.86	8.83
P@30	4.75	0.81
P@50	4.01	0
P@100	−2.88	−5.59
P@1000	0	−2.91
MAP	14.4	8.54
R-Precision	6.14	5.27

an improvement percentage more than 7.9% for P@10 and more than 11.5% for P@15, whereas the average improvement for all top documents is about 2.4%. Moreover, the MAP is about 8.5% and the R-Precision is about 5.3%. These results confirm our deductions concluded above about the efficiency of the discriminative approach in case of short queries. It is the case when the user provided to the CLIR tool a few number of terms in his/her source query due to his/her lack of language or his/her limit knowledge about the retrieved domain.

On the other hand, we need to more investigate on the statistical significance of the improvement achieved by the discriminative possibilistic approach compared to its competitors in terms of precision at different top documents, the *MAP* and the *R-Precision* scores using short queries. To do this, we use the Wilcoxon Matched-Pairs Signed-Ranks Test as suggested by [17]. This statistical test is a non-parametric alternative to the paired *t*-test that enables us to decide whether the improvement by method 1 over method 2 is significant. Indeed, the *t*-test computes a *p*-value based on the performance data of both methods 1 and 2. The improvement is more significant for the smaller *p*-value. Generally, the improvement is statistically significant if the *p*-value is small enough (p-value < 0.05).

The improvement of the discriminative possibilistic approach compared to the probabilistic one is statistically significant (p-value $= 0.010793 < 0.05$), while it is not statistically significant (p-value $= 0.085831 > 0.05$) compared to the probability-to-possibility transformation-based approach. Globally, these tests confirms again the performance of our discriminative possibilistic approach in the disambiguation of short queries using *title* compared to both the known efficient probabilistic and to the probability-to-possibility transformation-based approaches using different assessment metrics. Finally, and in order to provide an objective evaluation of our approach, we are limited in our empirical comparative study to these two approaches (probabilistic and possibilistic); because the other state-of-the-art QT techniques detailed in Sect. 2 are assessed using both different linguistic resources (dictionary and parallel corpora) and different CLIR test collection for different pair of languages.

6 Conclusion and Future Work

The translations' ambiguities in a QT process are considered as cases of imprecision since many possible translations are available for each ambiguous source query term. The disambiguation process consists of using the context of the source query which can be also ambiguous. Consequently, we propose in this paper a new discriminative possibilistic approach for QT disambiguation dedicated to improve the dictionary-based QT ones. This new technique has taken advantage of both a parallel text corpus and a bilingual dictionary in order to overcome some weaknesses of the-state-of-the-art QT approaches. Indeed, we have modelled the relevance of possible translations within two measures: the possible relevance allows eliminating irrelevant translations, whereas the necessary relevance makes it possible to reinforce the translations not rejected by the possibility. We assessed and compared the discriminative possibilistic approach using the French-English parallel text corpus *Europarl* and the CLEF-2003 French-English CLIR test collection. Our experiments highlighted the performance of our new discriminative possibilistic approach compared to both the known efficient probabilistic and the probability-to-possibility transformation-based approaches [11] using different assessment metrics. Indeed, the improvement of the discriminative approach compared to the probabilistic one is statistically significant in terms of precision at different top documents, the MAP and the R-Precision.

In spite of its significant efficiency in translating short queries, the discriminative possibilistic approach suffers from some weaknesses in case of specific domain queries. Consequently, the identification of the suitable translations requires a domain-specific translation [23] and a language model. Nevertheless, combining a language model with a domain-specific translation and their integration in the discriminative approach are not easy tasks. Moreover, the evaluation processes of our approach should be done in real contexts by allowing the users to contribute in its assessment. It is also relevant to assess the impact of QT disambiguation on CLIR efficiency before and/or after query expansion process using our recent techniques in [3, 13, 15].

References

1. Adriani, M.: Using statistical term similarity for sense disambiguation in cross-language information retrieval. Inf. Retr. **2**(1), 67–78 (2000)
2. Ballesteros, L., Croft, W.B.: Resolving ambiguity for cross-language retrieval. In: Proceedings of ACM-SIGIR, pp. 64–71 (1998)
3. Ben Khiroun, O., Elayeb, B., Bounhas, I., Evrard, F., Bellamine Ben Saoud, N.: Improving query expansion by automatic query disambiguation in intelligent information retrieval. In: Proceedings of ICAART 2014, pp. 153–160 (2014)
4. Benferhat, S., Dubois, D., Garcia, L., Prade, H.: Possibilistic logic bases and possibilistic graphs. In: Proceedings of the UAI 1999, pp. 57–64 (1999)
5. Boughanem, M., Brini, A., Dubois, D.: Possibilistic networks for information retrieval. Int. J. Approx. Reason. **50**(7), 957–968 (2009)

6. Davis, M.W., Ogden, W.C.: QUILT: implementing a large-scale cross-language text retrieval system. In: Proceedings of ACM-SIGIR, pp. 92–98 (1997)
7. Dubois, D., Prade, H.: Possibility theory: qualitative and quantitative aspects. In: Gabbay, D. M., Smets, P. (eds.) Quantified Representation of Uncertainty and Imprecision, Handbook of Defeasible Reasoning and Uncertainty Management Systems, vol. 1, pp. 169–226. Klower Academic Publishers, Netherlands (1998)
8. Dubois, D., Prade, H.: An overview of ordinal and numerical approaches to causal diagnostic problem solving, abductive reasoning and learning. In: Gabbay, D.M., Kruse, R. (eds.) Handbooks of Defeasible Reasoning and Uncertainty Management Systems, Drums Handbooks, vol. 4, pp. 231–280 (2000)
9. Dubois, D., Prade, H.: Représentations formelles de l'incertain et de l'imprécis, Concepts et méthodes pour l'aide à la décision - outils de modélisation. In: Bouyssou, D., Dubois, D., Pirlot, M., Prade, H. (eds.) vol. 2, pp. 99–137 (2006)
10. Dubois, D., Prade, H.: Formal representations of uncertainty. In: Bouyssou, D., Dubois, D., Pirlot, M., Prade, H. (eds.) Decision-Making Process, ISTE, pp. 85–156. Wiley, London and USA (2009)
11. Elayeb, B., Ben Romdhane, W., Bellamine Ben Saoud, N.: Towards a new possibilistic query translation tool for cross-language information retrieval. Multimedia Tools Appl. (2017). doi:10.1007/s11042-017-4398-2
12. Elayeb, B., Bounhas, I.: Arabic cross-language information retrieval: a review. ACM Trans. Asian Low-Resour. Lang. Inf. Process. **15**(3), Article 18, 44 (2016)
13. Elayeb, B., Bounhas, I., Khiroun, O.B., Bellamine Ben Saoud, N.: Combining semantic query disambiguation and expansion to improve intelligent information retrieval. In: Duval, B., Herik, J., Loiseau, S., Filipe, J. (eds.) ICAART 2014. LNCS, vol. 8946, pp. 280–295. Springer, Cham (2015). doi:10.1007/978-3-319-25210-0_17
14. Elayeb, B., Bounhas, I., Ben Khiroun, O., Evrard, F., Bellamine Ben Saoud, N.: Towards a possibilistic information retrieval system using semantic query expansion. Int. J. Intell. Inf. Technol. **7**(4), 1–25 (2011)
15. Elayeb, B., Bounhas, I., Ben Khiroun, O., Evrard, F., Bellamine Ben Saoud, N.: A comparative study between possibilistic and probabilistic approaches for monolingual word sense disambiguation. Knowl. Inf. Syst. **44**(1), 91–126 (2015)
16. Elayeb, B., Evrard, F., Zaghdoud, M., Ben Ahmed, M.: Towards an intelligent possibilistic web information retrieval using multiagent system. Interact. Technol. Smart Educ. Spec. Iss.: New Learn. Support Syst. **6**(1), 40–59 (2009)
17. Hull, D.A.: Using statistical testing in the evaluation of retrieval experiments. In: Proceedings of ACM-SIGIR, pp. 329–338 (1993)
18. Hull, D.A.: Using structured queries for disambiguation in cross-language information retrieval. In: Hull, D., Oard, D. (eds.) Proceedings of the AAAI Symposium on Cross-Language Text and Speech Retrieval, California, USA, pp. 84–98 (1997)
19. Hull, D.A., Grefenstette, G.: Querying across languages: a dictionary-based approach to multilingual information retrieval. In: Proceedings of ACM-SIGIR, pp. 46–57 (1996)
20. Kowk, K.L.: Exploiting a Chinese-English bilingual wordlist for English-Chinese cross-language information retrieval. In: Proceedings of the 5th International Workshop on Information Retrieval with Asian Languages, Hong Kong, pp. 173–179. ACM Press (2000)
21. Lefever, E., Hoste, V.: SemEval-2013 Task 10: cross-lingual word sense disambiguation. In: Proceedings of SemEval 2013, Atlanta, Georgia, pp. 158–166 (2013)
22. Nie, J.Y., Simard, M., Isabelle, P., Durand, R.: Cross-language information retrieval based on parallel texts and automatic mining of parallel texts from the web. In: Proceedings of ACM-SIGIR, pp. 74–81 (1999)

23. Ture, F., Boschee, E.: Learning to translate: a query-specific combination approach for cross-lingual information retrieval. In: Proceedings of EMNLP, pp. 589–599 (2014)
24. Xu, J., Weischedel, R.: Cross-lingual information retrieval using hidden markov models. In: Proceedings of the 2000 Joint SIGDAT Conference, pp. 95–103 (2000)
25. Xu, J., Fraser, A., Weischedel, R.: TREC 2001: cross-lingual retrieval at BBN. Proceedings of the TREC **2001**, 68–77 (2002)

Building TALAA-AFAQ, a Corpus of Arabic FActoid Question-Answers for a Question Answering System

Asma Aouichat(✉) and Ahmed Guessoum

Laboratory for Research in Artificial Intelligence (LRIA),
University of Sciences and Technology Houari Boumediene, Algiers, Algeria
{aaouichat,aguessoum}@usthb.dz

Abstract. In this paper, we describe the development of TALAA-AFAQ, a Corpus of Arabic Factoid Question Answers that is developed to be used in the training modules of an Arabic Question Answering System (AQAS). The process of building our corpus consists of five steps, in which we extract syntactic, semantic features and other information. In addition, we extract a set of answer patterns for each question from the web. The corpus contains 2002 question answer pairs. Out of these, 618 question-answer pairs have their answer-patterns. The corpus is divided into four main classes and 34 finer categories. All answer patterns and features have been validated by experts on Arabic. To the best of our knowledge, this is the first corpus of Arabic Factoid Question Answers which is specifically built to support the development of Arabic QASs (AQAS).

Keywords: Factoid questions · Answer patterns · Arabic question-answer corpus

1 Introduction

The interaction of a user with the World Wide Web is most useful when the user gets short and precise answers to his/her questions. Question-Answering Systems (QAS) come to satisfy this need. An important challenge facing the development of good Arabic Question-Answering Systems (AQASs) is the absence of Arabic Answer Patterns and Arabic Question-Answer corpora.

We present in this paper a corpus that has been developed to support Arabic QASs. TALAA-AFAQ, a corpus of Arabic FActoid Question-answers consists of a collection of question-answer pairs that we have classified into main classes and finer categories; we have also vocalized the questions (i.e. added the Arabic diacritics to the letters); and extracted a set of lexical, syntactic, and semantic features. In addition, we have included a set of answer patterns for each question. To the best of our knowledge, this is the first Arabic corpus that includes very rich information that supports the various facets of Arabic QASs. This makes TALAA-AFAQ a rich corpus for this purpose.

F. Frasincar et al. (Eds.): NLDB 2017, LNCS 10260, pp. 380–386, 2017.
DOI: 10.1007/978-3-319-59569-6_46

In the remainder of this paper, Sect. 2 introduces research related to the development of corpora for QA systems. Section 3 describes TALAA-AFAQ, in which we describe in detail the building and validation of our corpus. In Sect. 4, we present different interfaces that we have developed to help the users handle the corpus as well as contribute to its enrichment. Section 5 presents statistics related to the corpus and, to conclude, we discuss in Sect. 6 possible applications as well as some challenges that can be addressed as future work.

2 Related Work

2.1 Question-Answer Corpora for Non-arabic Languages

We have found various works on the development of corpora for QASs, especially for English. The learning process proposed in [5] for QASs consists of inspecting a collection of answered questions and characterizing the relation between a question and its answer through a statistical model. To serve as a collection of answered questions, they assembled two types of data sets: 1,800 pairs from Usenet FAQ documents and 5,145 from customer service call-center dialogues. [1] developed a QAS that was trained on a collection of about 30 000 question-answer pairs obtained from more than 270 Frequently Asked Question (FAQ) files on various topics in the FAQFinder project [4]. In [10] the authors built a large training corpus consisting of QA pairs (for non-factoid questions) with a broad lexical coverage. The authors reported a total collection of roughly 1 million QA pairs. TrainQA [11] describes the development of an English corpus of factoid TREC-like QA pairs. The corpus consists of more than 70,000 samples, each containing a question, its question type, an exact answer to the question, the different context levels (sentence, paragraph and document) where the answer occurs inside a document, and a label indicating whether the answer is correct (a positive sample) or not (a negative sample).

2.2 Arabic Question-Answer Corpora

Research in the field of Arabic QA systems is carried out here and there but one of the serious challenges facing it is the absence of sizeable Arabic corpora. It turns out indeed that the development of Arabic QA corpora is less bright than for other languages. We have found two such QA corpora which are presented in the remainder of this section. Unfortunately, and to the best of our knowledge, no Arabic corpus already exists which contains answer patterns and which can thus support the automatic generation of answer patterns for Arabic QASs. This explains why we have decided to develop a corpus of question-answer patterns from scratch. [12] presented a list of 50 definition questions (DefArabicQA), a set of 50 files containing snippets collected from Wikipedia and a set of 50 files containing snippets from the Google search engine. [9] presented work on Arabic question-answering by means of instance-based learning from a FAQ corpus. They described a way of accessing Arabic information using a Chatbot. Documents containing Frequently Asked Questions were used to build a small corpus of 412 Arabic QA pairs covering 5 domains.

3 TALAA-AFAQ: A Corpus of Arabic FActoid Question-Answers

With the aim of facing the acute need for QAS corpora, we have designed TALAA-AFAQ in such a way that it can be used in different modules in Question Answering Systems. For this reason, we have built a corpus that contains for each question the right classification, the set of features for each question; the named entities, keywords, synsets and headword in the question; and the question POS-tags and question chunks. The development of our corpus was done in two stages: (1) Building of TALAA-AFAQ, (2) Validation of this corpus.

3.1 Building of the Corpus of Arabic FActoid Question-Answers

In order for the techniques that are used to develop QASs to build robust systems with good performance, the availability of validated corpora is required. This is why we have put a lot of effort into building an Arabic factoid question-answer corpus. The methodology applied to develop this corpus is detailed in this study as follow:

Step 1: Collection of Question-Answer Pairs. We have first collected a set of simple Arabic factoid question-answer pairs, that ask for specific information, while ensuring that the question should be grammatically correct and has only one correct Answer which is a Named Entity or a numeric value. This step has used various resources: the QA4MRE@CLEF corpus [3,8], the set of TREC and CLEF Arabic questions which was made available by Lahsen Abouenour and Paolo Rosso[1], in addition to Question-answer pairs collected from the web, and others generated from various texts.

Step 2: Classification of the Questions. In the spirit of the model proposed in [7], we have manually classified our corpus manually classified into 4 main classes: Name, Location, Time, and Quantity. For each class, we specify the finer category of the question (34 refined categories) as shown in Table 1.

Step 3: Extraction of Answer Patterns. The aim behind extracting a set of answer patterns from the question-answer pairs is to use them for the training of the QAS. The process starts by generating a query through the extraction of the set of keywords from the question, and these get added to the answer part. Then the query is sent to the web and a list of snippets is returned the 20 of which will be selected. The process continues by filtering each document in the list and selecting the paragraphs which contains the answer. From each paragraph, only the sentences that contain the answer entity will be returned as the selected set of patterns for the question-answer pair.

[1] http://users.dsic.upv.es/grupos/nle/?file=kop4.php.

Step 4: Vocalization of the Questions. The vocalization (i.e. addition of diacritics to the Arabic letters) helps in the annotation and chunking process. It was performed using the Mishkal Arabic Text Vocalization tool[2] and then validated by Arabic language experts.

Step 5: Feature Extraction. In this step, we extracted syntactic and semantic features from each question in the corpus. These consist in the set of named entities in the question using [2], the set of keywords and their Synsets, the head which represents the question focus, and the Part-Of-Speech tags and question chunks which were generated using the AMIRA tool for Arabic Processing [6].

3.2 Validation of TALAA-AFAQ

The main steps in the process of building TALAA-AFAQ have been validated via an online web interface which was developed to assist in this task (Fig. 1). The users are asked to validate the generated answer patterns, the vocalized questions and the set of extracted features.

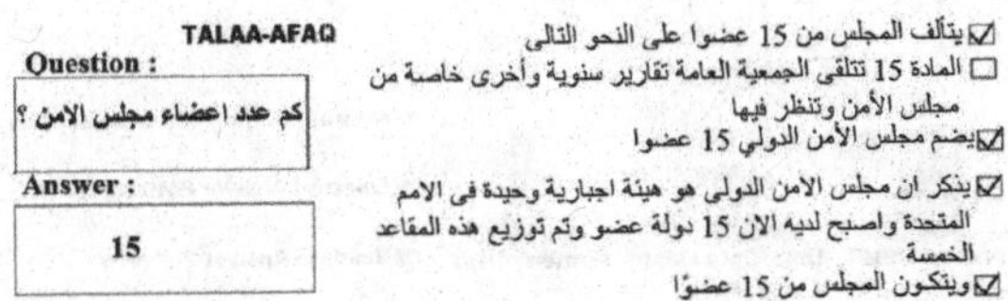

Fig. 1. Web interface for the validation of the answer patterns

4 Corpus Access and Usage

The TALAA-AFAQ can be queried via a developed online web interface. Through this interface, the users can download our corpus or enrich it online. In addition, the interface allows the validation of extracted features and the evaluation of the selected answer patterns for each pair of question-answers in the corpus. We hope to be able to get the research communitys contribution to the enrichment and boosting of TALAA-AFAQ.

5 Corpus Statistics

As mentioned above, the TALAA-AFAQ corpus consists of 2002 question-answer pairs subdivided into in four mains classes (Name, Quantity, Date/Time, Location), each of which is subdivided into finer categories that contain questions

[2] http://tahadz.com/mishkal/.

Table 1. Number of questions in each finer category

Main classes	Finer categories
Numeric(420)	Speed(2), Age(26), Average(2), Count(276), Power(2), Weight(11), Distance(45), Duration(23), Money(18), Percent(8), Temperature(6)
Name(926)	Group(11), Individual(899), Club(26)
Location(323)	Address(13), Location Boundaries(4), Continent(9), River(1), Country(121), Gulf(3), Island(4), Mountain(2), Sea(2), Ocean(2), Place(22), Planet(1), Quran Location(2), State(137)
Time/Date(321)	Date(81), Day(1), Month(6), Period(28), Year(204)

that ask for finer types of entities. The number of questions per finer category is as given in Table 1.

The numbers of question-answer pairs which have answer patterns are shows in Fig. 2. In addition, the number of validated and non-validated answer patterns for each main class.

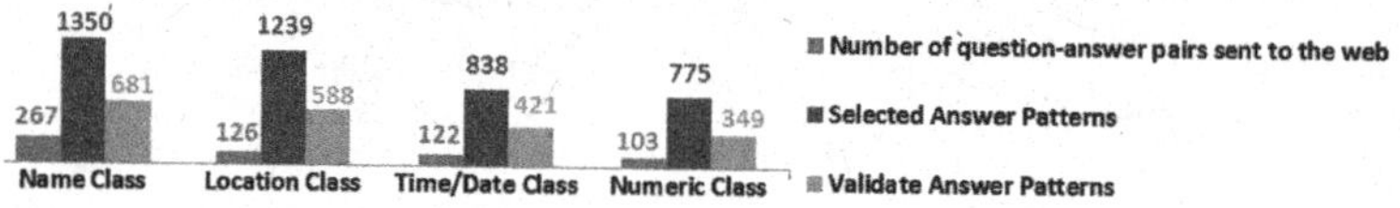

Fig. 2. Number of question-answer pairs sent/or not to the web along with the number of validated and non-validated answer patterns per QA main class

Figure 3 shows one instance of question-answer pair with all validated information, presented as a package in TAALA-AFAQ:

```
<Package id_pack="12">
 <MainClass>NAME</MainClass> <FineClass>Individual</FineClass> <source>Manual Collection</source>
<question>من هو ملك الاردن ؟</question><VocalizeQst>مَن هُو مَلِكُ الأَرْدُن ؟</VocalizeQst><answer>الحسين بن طلال</answer>
<Features>
      <NE>الاردن</NE><Head>ملك </Head><KWD>ملك , الاردن </KWD><Synset>رئيس , قائد </Synset>
      <chunking>WHNP من/WP NP هو/PRP_MS3 NP ملك/NN NP الاردن/DET_NNP ؟/PUNC</chunking>
      <posTagging>من/WP هو/PRP_MS3 ملك@@@NN الاردن/DET_NNP ؟/PUNC</posTagging>
</Features>
 <Patterns>
<pattern N="0" weight="2" source="http://ar.wikipedia.org/wiki/...">زوجة ملك الأردن الحسين بن طلال الثالثة</pattern>
<pattern N="1" weight="2" source="http://mawdoo3.com/...">الملك حسين بن طلال هو ملك المملكة الهاشمية الأردنية</pattern>
<pattern N="2" weight="3" source="http://www.aljazeera.net/...">تربع الحسين بن طلال على عرش المملكة الأردنية الهاشمية أكثر من 47 عاما
</Patterns>
```

Fig. 3. Example of a (Question-Answer) package in TALAA-AFAQ

6 Conclusion and Future Work

In this paper, we have described the development of TALAA-AFAQ, a corpus that is intended to help on many tasks in Arabic QAS. Our corpus consists of 2002 question-answer pairs collected from various resources. The corpus was classified into 4 main classes and 34 finer categories; after that, we extract set of answer patterns of 618 question-answer pairs, from the web. It was enriched by the vocalization of the questions and a set of lexical, syntactic and semantic features. To make the TALAA-AFAQ corpus available to the research community and to boost its development, a web application with an easy-to-use interface has been developed to allow language experts to enrich the corpus and go through the process of validation of QA patterns. We believe that TALAA-AFAQ is much needed by the community working on Arabic QASs.

References

1. Agichtein, E., Lawrence, S., Gravano, L.: Learning search engine specific query transformations for question answering. In: Proceedings of the 10th International Conference on World Wide Web, pp. 169–178. ACM (2001)
2. Benajiba, Y., Diab, M., Rosso, P.: Arabic named entity recognition using optimized feature sets. In: Proceedings of the Conference on Empirical Methods in Natural Language Processing, pp. 284–293. Association for Computational Linguistics (2008)
3. Bhaskar, P., Pakray, P., Banerjee, S., Banerjee, S., Bandyopadhyay, S., Gelbukh, A.F.: Question answering system for QA4MRE@CLEF 2012. In: CLEF (Online Working Notes/Labs/Workshop) (2012)
4. Burke, R.D., Hammond, K.J., Kulyukin, V., Lytinen, S.L., Tomuro, N., Schoenberg, S.: Question answering from frequently asked question files: experiences with the FAQ finder system. AI Mag. **18**(2), 57 (1997)
5. Cohn, A.B.R.C.D., Mittal, D.F.V.: Bridging the lexical chasm: statistical approaches to answer-finding. In: Proceedings of the Annual International ACM-SIGIR Conference on Research and Development in Information Retrieval, p. 192. ACM Press (2000)
6. Diab, M.: Second generation AMIRA tools for Arabic processing: fast and robust tokenization, POS tagging, and base phrase chunking. In: 2nd International Conference on Arabic Language Resources and Tools (2009)
7. Li, X., Roth, D.: Learning question classifiers: the role of semantic information. Nat. Lang. Eng. **12**(03), 229–249 (2006)
8. Peñas, A., Hovy, E.H., Forner, P., Rodrigo, Á., Sutcliffe, R.F., Forascu, C., Sporleder, C.: Overview of QA4MRE@CLEF 2011: question answering for machine reading evaluation. In: CLEF (Notebook Papers/Labs/Workshop), pp. 1–20 (2011)
9. Shawar, B.A., Atwell, E.: Arabic question-answering via instance based learning from an FAQ corpus. In: Proceedings of the CL 2009 International Conference on Corpus Linguistics. UCREL (2009)

10. Soricut, R., Brill, E.: Automatic question answering using the web: beyond the factoid. Inf. Retrieval **9**(2), 191–206 (2006)
11. Tomás, D., Vicedo, J.L., Bisbal, E., Moreno, L.: Trainqa: a training corpus for corpus-based question answering systems. Polibits **40**, 5–11 (2009)
12. Trigui, O., Belguith, H., Rosso, P.: Defarabicqa: Arabic definition question answering system. In: Workshop on Language Resources and Human Language Technologies for Semitic Languages, 7th LREC, Valletta, Malta, pp. 40–45 (2010)

Detecting Non-covered Questions in Frequently Asked Questions Collections

Mladen Karan(✉) and Jan Šnajder

Text Analysis and Knowledge Engineering Lab,
Faculty of Electrical Engineering and Computing,
University of Zagreb, Unska 3, 10000 Zagreb, Croatia
{mladen.karan,jan.snajder}@fer.hr

Abstract. Frequently asked questions (FAQ) collections are a popular and effective way of representing information, and FAQ retrieval systems provide a natural-language interface to such collections. An important aspect of efficient and trustworthy FAQ retrieval is to maintain a low fall-out rate by detecting non-covered questions. In this paper we address the task of detecting non-covered questions. We experiment with threshold-based methods as well as unsupervised one-class and supervised binary classifiers, considering tf-idf and word embeddings text representations. Experiments, carried out on a domain-specific FAQ collection, indicate that a cluster-based model with query paraphrases outperforms threshold-based, one-class, and binary classifiers.

Keywords: FAQ retrieval · Novelty detection · Question answering

1 Introduction

Frequently asked question (FAQ) collections are document collections comprised of edited question-answer pairs (henceforth: FAQ-pairs). FAQ collections offer an effective and intuitive way of presenting information to the users. FAQ are popular with large-scale sevice providers, and are typically domain-specific.

While the task of FAQ retrieval has received considerable attention, not much work has been done on the task of detecting when a user's query is *not* covered by a FAQ collection. This task is not trivial and it is of particular importance for FAQ retrieval: as FAQ collections are of limited coverage, there is a chance of retrieving a non-relevant FAQ-pair, leading to a high fall-out rate (probability of false alarms). A high fall-out rate reduces the retrieval effectiveness and inevitably erodes the users' trust in the retrieval system.

In this work we address the task of detecting when a user query is not covered by a FAQ collection. More specifically, the system must classify a user's query as *covered* or *not-covered*. We see three benefits of solving this task. First is the reduction of fall-out rates, increasing user's trust in the system. Secondly, reliable detection of covered user's queries could be used to reduce the workload on customer support services, as only the non-covered queries would have to be forwarded to

F. Frasincar et al. (Eds.): NLDB 2017, LNCS 10260, pp. 387–390, 2017.
DOI: 10.1007/978-3-319-59569-6_47

human agents. Thirdly, it would allow for more efficient maintenance and updating of the FAQ collection. We tackle the task using several methods with varying degree of supervision. We demonstrate the difficulty of the task and – although our results are preliminary – identify the most promising methods for solving it.

2 Related Work

One of the first works to tackle FAQ retrieval was the FAQFinder system [1]. The system presented in [2] leverages additional metadata associated with FAQ-pairs. Considerable improvements were obtained using supervised machine learning with similarity-based features [3] and network-based representations [4].

To the best of our knowledge, this is the first work to explicitly focus on the detection of non-covered questions in FAQ collections, rather than having it as one component of a larger system. From a machine learning perspective, this task is related to the well-studied problem of novelty detection. One of the most successful algorithms for novelty detection is the one-class SVM [5]. For an overview of novelty detection methods, the reader is referred to [6].

3 Retrieval Models

We frame the task as follows: given a user's query q_{new}, the system should classify it as either *covered* or *not-covered.* We experiment with two groups of models.

Retrieval-based models. This is a baseline approach in which an information retrieval model is first used to retrieve a ranked list of potentially relevant FAQ-pairs, after which the query q_{new} is classified as covered if the score of the top ranked document is above a threshold t. To this end, we rely on the classic BM25 model, as well as a standard tf-idf-weighted vector space retrieval model. We optimize the threshold t on a small validation set.

Cluster-Based Models. In this approach we assume that we have access to a set of queries, $Q = \{q_1, \ldots, q_N\}$, that we know are covered by the FAQ collection. Moreover, we assume that we know which of the given queries address the same information need. Thus, the queries can be grouped into clusters, $\{C_1, \ldots, C_M\}$, where all queries from the same cluster C_i represent different wordings (paraphrases) of the same information need. The number of clusters corresponds to the number of distinct information needs covered by the FAQ collection. The advantage of such a setup is that we can now model every information need covered by the FAQ collection using a cluster of queries. To determine whether a new query is covered, our procedure finds the query that is most similar to q_{new}. If this similarity is above a threshold t, the query is classified as *covered,* otherwise it is classified as *non-covered.* More formally, q_{new} is classified as *covered* iff $\max_i \{sim(q_{new}, C_i)\} \geq t$. Same as for the retrieval-based models, t is optimized on a validation set. In a realistic scenario, we cannot expect to have available the paraphrased queries pertaining to the same information need. However, these can be easily produced by rephrasing the question parts of FAQ-pairs already

Table 1. Classification performance of all models (averages of 10 measurements).

Model	P	R	F1
BM25	0.635	0.902	0.738
VS	0.635	0.896	0.737
Cos	0.741	0.874	**0.794**
SVMdist	0.588	**0.994**	0.733
SVMvote	0.821	0.416	0.551
BSVMdist	0.882	0.613	0.714
BSVMvote	**0.894**	0.606	0.718

present in the collection. We argue that for FAQ collections typically used by large-scale service providers, whose size is typically a few hundred questions, it is feasible to produce paraphrases for the entire collection. We expect models that leverage this additional information to perform better than the baselines, justifying additional annotation effort. As the vector representation of text for all models, we experiment with *PARAGRAM* vectors described in [7], since they outperformed standard tf-idf weighted vectors in preliminary experiments. We investigate several ways to implement the $sim(q_{new}, C_i)$ function:

Cos – similarity is the an aggregation of cosine similarities of q_{new} and $q_i \in C_i$. We experiment with *min*, *max*, *mean* as the aggregation function;
SVMdist – for each cluster, we train a one-class SVM [5] with *covered* as the positive class. The kernel type and kernel parameters are optimized on the validation set. The similarity is the distance between q_i and the separating hyperplane for the SVM corresponding to C_i (if q_{new} is deeper inside the positive side of the separating hyperplane, then the similarity is higher);
SVMvote – one-class SVM models are trained in the same way as for the SVMdist model. The similarity is defined as 1 if C_i classified q_{new} as a positive example and 0 otherwise. Threshold t is set to 0.5. With these modifications, SVMdist degenerates into a voting scheme, i.e., q_{new} will be classified as *covered* if at least one of the SVM models classifies it as belonging to its cluster;
BSVMdist – same as SVMdist but with binary SVM models, considering all examples outside of C_i as negative. Class imbalance problems are handled by oversampling the positive class;
BSVMvote – the same scheme that transforms SVMdist to SVMvote is used to transform BSVMdist into BSVMvote.

4 Experiments

To evaluate the models, we use FAQIR, a domain-specific FAQ retrieval collection compiled by [8]. To make the evaluation more realistic, we modified the dataset as follows. First, we removed from the dataset all FAQ-pairs that are not relevant for any of the queries. The rationale for doing so is that FAQ collections are generally compiled specifically for the popular queries that are repeated often. This step left us with 779 FAQ pairs. Furthermore, to simulate the absence of questions from the FAQ collection, we randomly chose 25 out of the 50 queries and removed all FAQ-pairs relevant for these queries from the collection.

We evaluate the models using nested cross-validation with 5 inner and 10 outer folds. Results are given in Table 1. We observe that the best clustering-based models outperform retrieval-based baselines. The *SVMdist* model achieves exceptionally high recall, the *BSVMdist* model achieves good precision, while the *Cos* model achieves the best trade-off in terms of the F1-score.

5 Conclusion

We addressed the task of detecting non-covered questions in domain-specific frequently asked question (FAQ) collections. The best results were obtained using a cluster-based model with word embedding representations of query paraphrases. On our dataset, this model considerably outperforms all other considered models. We note that this model relies on manually compiled query paraphrases, however we argue that the increased performance justifies the low effort required for paraphrase compilation. These preliminary results provide a basis for further experiments on detecting non-covered FAQ questions. An immediate direction for future work is more extensive experimentation with different word representations and similarity functions across several different data sets.

References

1. Burke, R.D., Hammond, K.J., Kulyukin, V., Lytinen, S.L., Tomuro, N., Schoenberg, S.: Question answering from frequently asked question files: experiences with the FAQ finder system. AI Mag. **18**(2), 57 (1997)
2. Sneiders, E.: Automated FAQ answering with question-specific knowledge representation for web self-service. In: 2nd Conference on Human System Interactions 2009, HSI 2009, pp. 298–305. IEEE (2009)
3. Surdeanu, M., Ciaramita, M., Zaragoza, H.: Learning to rank answers to non-factoid questions from web collections. Comput. Linguist. **37**(2), 351–383 (2011)
4. Feng, M., Xiang, B., Glass, M.R., Wang, L., Zhou, B.: Applying deep learning to answer selection: a study and an open task. In: 2015 IEEE Workshop on Automatic Speech Recognition and Understanding (ASRU), pp. 813–820. IEEE (2015)
5. Schölkopf, B., Platt, J.C., Shawe-Taylor, J., Smola, A.J., Williamson, R.C.: Estimating the support of a high-dimensional distribution. Neural Comput. **13**(7), 1443–1471 (2001)
6. Pimentel, M.A., Clifton, D.A., Clifton, L., Tarassenko, L.: A review of novelty detection. Signal Process. **99**, 215–249 (2014)
7. Wieting, J., Bansal, M., Gimpel, K., Livescu, K., Roth, D.: From paraphrase database to compositional paraphrase model and back. Trans. Assoc. Comput. Linguist. **3**, 345–358 (2015)
8. Karan, M., Šnajder, J.: FAQIR – a frequently asked questions retrieval test collection. In: Sojka, P., Horák, A., Kopeček, I., Pala, K. (eds.) TSD 2016. LNCS, vol. 9924, pp. 74–81. Springer, Cham (2016). doi:10.1007/978-3-319-45510-5_9

Semantics-Based Models and Applications

Vector Space Representation of Concepts Using Wikipedia Graph Structure

Armin Sajadi(✉), Evangelos E. Milios, and Vlado Keselj

Faculty of Computer Science, Dalhousie University, Halifax, NS B3H 4R2, Canada
{sajadi,eem,vlado}@cs.dal.ca

Abstract. We introduce a vector space representation of concepts using Wikipedia graph structure to calculate *semantic relatedness*. The proposed method starts from the neighborhood graph of a concept as the primary form and transfers this graph into a vector space to obtain the final representation. The proposed method achieves state of the art results on various relatedness datasets.

Combining the vector space representation with standard *coherence model*, we show that the proposed relatedness method performs successfully in Word Sense Disambiguation (WSD). We then suggest a different formulation for coherence to demonstrate that, in a short enough sentence, there is one *key entity* that can help disambiguate every other entity. Using this finding, we provide a vector space based method that can outperform the standard coherence model in a significantly shorter computation time.

Keywords: Semantic relatedness · Entity representation · Word Sense Disambiguation · Graph methods

1 Introduction

Semantic Relatedness is a real valued function defined over a set of concept-pairs that can reflect any possible taxonomic or non-taxonomic relation between them. This measure can be extracted from either unstructured corpora or lexical resources, each with their own pros and cons [1]. Regarding knowledge based methods, Wikipedia is gaining popularity due to its broad coverage of concepts and named entities in different domains; previous research shows that it can perform close to or even better than human curated domain specific ontologies and corpora [29]. Wikipedia graph structure provides a rich source for many graph based Natural Language Processing (NLP) methods and has been used extensively in text analysis. Our research is motivated by this graph structure, and investigates efficient and effective ways to represent a concept using this structure for calculating semantic relatedness. Relying on vector representation is not necessary for semantic relatedness calculation, but it can provide a large repository of methods and techniques, referred to by Vector Space Model (VSM).

The proposed method is in fact a compromise between two extremes: one is to use only in-coming or out-going links of a concept to represent it [20], and the

F. Frasincar et al. (Eds.): NLDB 2017, LNCS 10260, pp. 393–405, 2017.
DOI: 10.1007/978-3-319-59569-6_48

other is to use the whole Wikipedia graph to extract the representation [2,31]. While the former keeps the task simple, it does not take advantage of the full network structure, and the latter makes the task so complex that it is practically intractable. We conjecture that using the neighborhood of a vertex benefits the representation compared to merely in (out)-links, and also that using vertices further away does not contribute to the representation, and may even decrease the quality. We demonstrate the quality of the representations in both semantic relatedness and word sense disambiguation.

To evaluate in WSD, we start from standard *coherence model* formulated in Integer Programming to provide a fair comparison with the most popular relatedness method in WSD, i.e., WLM [20]. Then, based on our observations, we conjecture that in a short sentence, there is one *key entity* that suffices to disambiguate other entities. Using this assumption, we first simplify the *coherence* definition and provide a quadratic time algorithm that can confirm our conjecture experimentally. Using this finding, we provide a simple and linear time complexity algorithm that can benefit from vector space calculations and achieve superior results compared to the coherence model, but with a dramatically lower cost.

2 Related Work

Relatedness from Wikipedia. Semantic relatedness approaches are categorized as distributional or knowledge based. The broad coverage of domain specific terminologies and named entities in Wikipedia has made it a highly popular knowledge source in recent years. A wide range of approaches have been used to calculate semantic relatedness from Wikipedia, including adaptations of ontology based methods (WikiRelate [26]), distributional (Kore [11], CPRel [12]), graph-based (Wikipedia Link Measure (WLM)) [20], HITS-Sim [29]) or hybrid (WikiWalk [31]). To the best of our knowledge, WLM is the most popular method in different applications of Wikipedia, such as Named Entity Recognition [4,27].

A more recent graph based approach is a Personalized PageRank (PPR) based method (UKB) [2] which was previously shown to be the state of the art for WordNet [1], but was not very successful on Wikipedia (WikiWalk)[31]. UKB achieved this improvement over WikiWalk by using only reciprocal links. The main idea of the PPR based methods is to run Personalized PageRank on the whole graph, but customized for a given concept. Being interesting from theoretical point of view, it has some limitations in realistic applications: first, using the whole link structure of Wikipedia is practically impossible; second, most of the non-popular entities of Wikipedia do not have a considerable number of reciprocal links. Another similar graph based method, HITS-Sim [29] ranks the vertices in the neighborhood. Despite achieving good results, at the end it works only by using a mixture of list similarity metrics and combining different similarities from different neighborhoods. As a result, it fails to provide any representation, which limits its applicability to different tasks. Several distributional methods have been proposed for utilizing the text of Wikipedia, such as representing a concept using the anchor texts (CPRel [12]) or the keywords (Kore [11]) in the page associated with it. More recent techniques are mainly focused on applications of word2vec [18] on the Wikipedia text to represent the concepts [30].

Word Sense Disambiguation (WSD). WSD is a classic NLP task with a wide range of approaches. In the context of Wikipedia, it is defined as a subtask of a more general one, Named Entity Linking, that is linking mentions of entities in the text to a knowledge base. While using semantic relatedness is not necessary for the task [16], most entity linking systems benefit from it [4,27]. In this context, relatedness is usually referred to by semantic *coherence* and can be incorporated in a variety of ways in the disambiguation, for example as a link weight in a subgraph mining algorithm [11], but mostly as a feature fed to a classifier [4,27]. Most of the mentioned methods use WLM as a popular relatedness method, although there exist some other tailored relatedness for this task, such as Kore [11].

3 Concept Representation

We start from preprocessing Wikipedia hyperlink structure and create the graph $G(V, E)$ following the guidelines of [29]. Given a vertex v, the concept is represented in the space of *Wikipedia graph vertices*. This is done in two steps, (1) we extract the closed neighborhood graph for v, $G_v = (V_v, E_v)$ with adjacency matrix $\mathbf{A}_v$. (2) embed G_v in a vector space defined by the Wikipedia graph vertices. Five different methods are evaluated to embed the graph into vector space: Spectral embedding (Fiedler's vector) [6], HITS [14], Centrality (Katz) [13] and PageRank [22] (and Reverse PageRank [10]). All these methods return a normalized vector of assigned values to each node in V_v. This vector is then augmented by letting the value of vertices not in V_v to zero. This leads to the embedding of G_v, hence the representation of v, denoted by $\mathcal{R}(v)$. Among all the vectorizing methods, we only explain the winner, which is *Reverse PageRank* (rvsPageRank). Having the vector representations of two concepts, u and v, semantic relatedness is defined to be the cosine similarity of the two vectors, denoted by $\mathcal{R}(u) \cdot \mathcal{R}(v)$.

We typically could use the whole neighborhood, or using only *in* or *out* neighborhoods as defined in [29]. We chose to embed both neighborhoods separately and then calculate the average vector. This way we can compare the importance of each neighborhood as well. The results reported in this paper are obtained by the average vector, unless otherwise stated.

3.1 (Reverse) PageRank

PageRank [22] is a link analysis algorithm primarily used to rank search engine results. It is defined as a process in which starting from a random vertex, a random walker with probability α is moving to a random neighbor, or with probability $1 - \alpha$ jumps to a random vertex. The values are the limiting probabilities of finding the walker on each vertex. Let $\mathbf{D}_{n \times n}$ be the diagonal matrix with the out-degree of each vertex on the diagonal. If we set $\mathbf{W} = \mathbf{A}^T\mathbf{D}^{-1}$, then the PageRank vector, initialized with $\mathbf{1}/n$, where $\mathbf{1}$ is a vector of length n, can be obtained from $\boldsymbol{pr}_{t+1} = (1-\alpha)\frac{1}{n}\mathbf{1} + \alpha\mathbf{W}\boldsymbol{pr}_t$.

Reverse PageRank can be obtained from PageRank simply by inverting the directions of the edges of the Graph. We had various motivations to analyze rvsPageRank and it showed to be the most successful embedding: (i) HITS results showed that hub-score were outperforming authority scores on out-neighborhood, and rvsPageRank calculates the hub scores similar to HITS [8], (ii) It has a higher convergence rate and more potential to be locally approximated [3] (iii) A Wikipedia page is defined and explained by its outgoing rather than incoming links and in such cases, reversing the links makes more sense to get the importance of the page in a network, similar to the case of calculating trust [10].

4 Word Sense Disambiguation (WSD)

In this section we formulate the WSD problem as an optimization that merely is focused on the quality of the concept representations. We do this by ignoring other aspects of the problem, such as the effect of non-mention words, prior distributions of entities or null-mentions.

For every entity e, there exist one or more string representations, a.k.a *mentions* of e, and vice versa. This forms a many-to-many relationship from mentions to entities. By ignoring non-mention phrases in the text, i.e., phrases that cannot possibly refer to any entity, we can represent a sentence S by a list of mentions $\mathcal{M} = [m_1, \ldots, m_n]$. Each mention m_i can have k_i potential senses or candidates: $\mathcal{C}_i = \{c_i^1, \ldots, c_i^{k_i}\}$ and $\mathcal{C} = \bigcup_i \mathcal{C}_i$ is the set of all candidates. The goal is to find $\mathcal{E} = [e_1, \ldots, e_n]$ where e_i is the "*correct*" entity to which mention m_i refers, using "*only*" the semantic relatedness between the concepts.

4.1 Coherence Modeling Using Integer Programming (IP)

While there can be many different ways to measure the coherence of a sentence, the most popular one is defined by the sum of all mutual semantic relatedness of the entities of a sentence [15,27]. Let $r(\cdot,\cdot)$ be the relatedness function and $\hat{\mathcal{E}} = [\hat{e}_1, \ldots, \hat{e}_n]$ be a solution, i.e., each m_i is resolved to $\hat{e}_i$, then the problem is to find the $\mathcal{E}^*$ that maximizes the coherence:

$$\mathcal{E}^* = \underset{\hat{\mathcal{E}} \in (\mathcal{C}_1 \times \cdots \times \mathcal{C}_n)}{\arg\max} \sum_{i<j} r(\hat{e}_i, \hat{e}_j) \tag{1}$$

Finding optimal solution for Eq. 1 is NP-complete, hence, we use the approach taken by [15] to solve the NP-complete problem directly by formulating it as an *Integer Programming (IP)*:

Let s_i^k denote whether or not c_i^k is selected, $s_{i,j}^{k,l}$ denote if both c_i^k and c_j^l are selected and $r_{i,j}^{k,l} = r(c_i^k, c_j^l)$. We can formulate the disambiguation problem as a Binary IP problem

$$\text{Maximize} \sum_{i<j} s_{i,j}^{k,l} r_{i,j}^{k,l} \text{ for } 1 \leq i,j \leq n, 1 \leq k \leq k_i, 1 \leq l \leq k_j$$

$$\text{subject to: } s_i^k \in \{0,1\} \text{ and } s_{i,j}^{k,l} \in \{0,1\}$$

$$\forall i \sum_k s_i^k = 1$$

$$\forall i,j,k,l : s_{i,j}^{k,l} < s_i^k \text{ and } s_{i,j}^{k,l} < s_j^l \tag{2}$$

Given a sentence S, an IP is built and solved to find the correct senses for each mention using COIN-OR Branch and Cut Solution (CBC) [17]. Arbitrary sized sentences are chunked and fed to the solver to keep the problem tractable.

4.2 Key Entity Modeling

Plato Entity Linker [16] conjectures that, for each mention, there is usually one context word that suffices to disambiguate it. Using this assumption, they provide a probabilistic model, referred to as *selective context model.* Motivated by this, we advance the idea and conjecture that, given a short sentence, there exists one entity, referred to as "*key entity*" in this paper, that can help disambiguating every other one. With the key entity denoted by e^*, this assumption will lead to a different formulation for coherence:

$$(e^*, \mathcal{E}^*) = \underset{\substack{\epsilon \in \mathcal{C} \\ \hat{\mathcal{E}} \in (\mathcal{C}_1 \times \cdots \times \mathcal{C}_n)}}{\arg\max} \sum_{i=1}^{n} r(\epsilon, \hat{e}_i) \tag{3}$$

Unlike Eq. 1, there is a quadratic time solution for this optimization. We first assign to each entity $\epsilon_i \in \mathcal{C}$ a best candidate list $\mathcal{B}_i = [b_i^1, ..., b_i^n]$ where b_i^j is the best candidate for m_j assuming ϵ_i be the key entity, i.e., the most similar entity to ϵ_i in $\mathcal{C}_j$. Next, we find the $\mathcal{B}_i$ with maximum coherence w.r.t its corresponding key, ϵ_i:

$$\text{Step 1: } \forall \epsilon_i \in \mathcal{C}, \mathcal{B}_i = \left[\underset{t \in \mathcal{C}_j}{\arg\max}\, r(\epsilon_i, t) \mid \forall j \leq n \right] \tag{4}$$

$$\text{Step 2: } \mathcal{E}^* = \underset{\mathcal{B}_i}{\arg\max} \sum_{t \in \mathcal{B}_i} r(\epsilon_i, t)$$

both steps have $O(|\mathcal{C}|^2)$ complexity. Our experiments demonstrate the effectiveness of this method, hence, the existence of such *key entity.*

4.3 VSM Key Entity Recognition

While solving Eq. 3 is computationally faster, the improvement is not dramatic. Key entity model, similar to IP, needs to calculate $|\mathcal{C}|^2$ similarities which can be very expensive even with fast relatedness methods. Both our embedding and

WLM have $n \log n$ complexity with n being the number of neighbors (and assuming that the embeddings are computed offline), and moreover, the big size of Wikipedia and hardware limitations leads to I/O delay in accessing those neighbors, making the whole process expensive. But fortunately the insight that this approach gives is promising. Inspired by the existence of this key entity, we aim to guess it by benefiting from the vector representations. The idea is to assume the key entity to be the one that can be resolved with the highest *certainty*, defined as follows. We extend the definition of $\mathcal{R}(\cdot)$ to mentions, and define the *representation of a mention* m, $\mathcal{R}(m)$, to be the average of its candidate representations, and the *context vector w.r.t mention* m, $\hat{\mathcal{R}}_m$, to be the average of other mention representations in the sentence.

$$\text{Let } \mathcal{R}(m_i) = \frac{1}{|\mathcal{C}_i|} \sum_{t \in \mathcal{C}_i} \mathcal{R}(t) \text{ and } \hat{\mathcal{R}}(m_i) = \frac{1}{n-1} \sum_{m_j \in \mathcal{M} \setminus m_i} \mathcal{R}(m_j) \quad (5)$$

And let's assume that for each mention m_i, k_i^1 and k_i^2 be the best and second best candidates w.r.t its context vector:

$$k_i^1 = \arg\max_{t \in \mathcal{C}_i} \mathcal{R}(t) \cdot \hat{\mathcal{R}}(m_i) \text{ and } k_i^2 = \arg\max_{t \in \mathcal{C}_i \setminus \{k_i^1\}} \mathcal{R}(t) \cdot \hat{\mathcal{R}}(m_i) \quad (6)$$

We assume that the difference between the similarities of k_i^1 and k_i^2 to the context representation of m_i, $\hat{\mathcal{R}}(m_i)$, is a good indicator of how *certain* we are in resolving m_i to the entity k_i^1. Therefore, we define the key entity k^* to be the one that has the largest margin with its closest competitor:

$$k^* = k_i^1 \text{ where } i = \arg\max_{i \leq n} \left\{ \frac{\mathcal{R}(k_i^1) \cdot \hat{\mathcal{R}}(m_i) - \mathcal{R}(k_i^2) \cdot \hat{\mathcal{R}}(m_i)}{\mathcal{R}(k_i^2) \cdot \hat{\mathcal{R}}(m_i)} \right\} \quad (7)$$

Once k^* is found, the disambiguated entities $\mathcal{E}^*$, are those with maximum cosine similarity to $\mathcal{R}(k^*)$.

$$\mathcal{E}^* = \left[\arg\max_{t \in \mathcal{C}_i} \mathcal{R}(t) \cdot \mathcal{R}(k^*) \mid i = 1 \ldots n \right] \quad (8)$$

Our VSM based key entity recognition method has a linear complexity in terms of the number of candidates $|\mathcal{C}|$ and also calculates only $2|\mathcal{C}|$ similarities. Surprisingly, the experiments demonstrate that this method, despite its suboptimality in terms of coherence, can outperform previous models in terms of precision. This is not a contradiction: coherence is a measure to predict precision, but does not imply it.

5 Experiments

5.1 Experiment 1: Semantic Relatedness

As pointed out by [29], Wikipedia does not cover general domain words as well as a general lexicon such as WordNet, while its main advantage is in domain specific vocabularies and entities. We evaluate all methods on both general and domain specific datasets, but emphasize that due to large number of non-covered or low quality pages for the general domain, the comparisons on the domain specific datasets (the right side of Table 1) are more meaningful.

Relatedness datasets typically are lists of word pairs along with their relatedness associated by experts. In the general domain we use three datasets, Miller and Charles (MC) [19] (28 pairs), Rubenstein and Goodenough (RG) [28](65 pairs) and the WordSimilarity353 collection [7] disambiguated to Wikipedia [21](318 pairs). For domain specific datasets we focus on the biomedical domain that has high quality datasets and are mapped to Wikipedia concepts [29], namely *Pedersen* (29 pairs) [25], *Mayo benchmark* (101 pairs) [24], *UMN Similarity benchmarks* (587 pairs) [23] and *UMN Relatedness benchmarks* (566 pairs) [23]. We also evaluate on a dataset specifically curated for Wikipedia relatedness, Kore-relatedness [11]. Kore-relatedness has a different structure and the task is to sort a list of concepts with respect to relatedness to a given concept.

Baselines. Among graph based methods, we use WLM, UKB, HITS-Sim and two graph similarity metrics. We reimplemented WLM and for UKB, we used the provided source code[1]. Among distributional methods, we choose the most recent approaches, CPRel, Kore and the word2vec embedding method [18]. Concepts are often more than one single word and this affects word2vec performance, hence we try two different approaches. First, we use the original method for phrase detection [18], to which we refer by $word2vec_1$, and then we use the embeddings from [30], to which we refer by $word2vec_2$. The latter goes through a preprocessing that uses the link structure of Wikipedia and unifies different entity mentions by replacing them with the entities they are linked to (we our best result was obtained with dimensionality set to 300).

Vectorizing the two graphs is not the only way to compare them, because there exist a few (pure) graph similarity metrics. In our case, the two graphs are both induced sub-graphs from Wikipedia and therefore, vertex overlap would result in edge overlap to some extent, referred to by Graph-Overlap (or simply *overlap* in the tables). A better approach is to use a variation of Normalized Graph Edit Distance (NGED) [9] to compare the graphs. NGED, similar to edit distance in strings, tries to convert one graph to another by means of a few operations (vertex/edge insertion/deletion/substitution) with different costs for each operation. The problem is NP-complete in general. In our case edge substitution is never the case (they are induced subgraphs from the same graph). We let vertex substitution cost be ∞ for two vertices that have different labels and every other cost to 1, and derive a simple version of NGED:

$$NGED(G_1, G_2) = \frac{|V_1 \bigtriangleup V_2| + |E_1 \bigtriangleup E_2|}{|V_1 \cup V_2| + |E_1 \cup E_2|} \tag{9}$$

[1] http://ixa2.si.ehu.es/ukb/.

Table 1. Comparison between Wikipedia based methods: correlation across measures and ground truth. *: automatic phrase detection, †: manual concept resolution using anchor texts

	General datasets			Wikipedia Datasets				
Method	MC	RG	WS353	KORE-DS	Ped	Mayo	UMN-sim	UMN-rel
Size	28	65	318	400	29	101	566	587
cprel	.83	.79	.64					
kore (method)				.67				
$word2vec_1^*$	.85	.77	.62	0	.35	.17	.17	.12
$word2vec_2^\dagger$	.81	.78	.63	.53	.66	.29	.30	.38
WLM	.86	.82	.68	.68	.67	.49	.58	.5
UKB	.87	**.87**	.7	.66	**.82**	.39	.55	.51
HITS-Sim	.88	.81	.71	.67	.71	.52	.59	.52
overlap	.86	.8	.69	.63	.64	.44	.54	.44
NGED	.86	.79	.66	.6	.70	.48	.56	.5
Fiedler	.72	.7	.55	.52	.80	.5	.49	.44
Katz	.75	.73	.55	.62	.63	.52	.45	.37
HITS auth	.85	.72	.67	.56	.59	.49	.47	.41
HITS hub	.86	.77	.69	.62	.62	.52	.56	.51
PageRank	.8	.69	.61	.54	.16	.12	.22	.15
rvsPageRank	**.90**	.82	**.72**	**.72**	.69	**.56**	**.62**	**.57**

where $\triangle$ is the *symmetric difference* of the two sets. We did not perform any parameter tuning and used popular default values for the constants, i.e., $\alpha = 0.005$ for Katz and $\alpha = 0.85$ for PageRank.[2]

Relatedness Performance. The results provided in Table 1 show that neighborhood embedding methods are mostly successful. More specifically, rvsPageRank stands out among all and obtains the most promising results. The only exception is UKB on RG and Pedersen, which are relatively small datasets compared to the rest and moreover, UKB is more than 40 times slower than our method (1.74 s per concept for rvsPageRank versus 78 s for UKB).

Which Neighborhood Matters? We compare in- and out-neighborhoods in Table 2 and we observe that, as preferred, out-neighborhood can benefit more from the embedding and generate promising results. Preferring out-neighborhood results from having a significantly lower upper-bound and a lower variance (vertices having too many or too few neighbours) on the size: in the version of Wikipedia we experimented with, the maximum number of outgoing

[2] We use Wikipedia 20160305 dump for relatedness.

links is less than 3000, while the maximum in-link is almost one million. This results in a more robust, and much faster embedding on the out-neighbourhood.

From the table we can also see that the main advantage of rvsPageRank is its ability to embed out-neighborhood while PageRank performs very poorly, as expected. We also tried reciprocal links, as conjectured by [2], which did not work in our case (not reported in the paper due to lack of space), mainly because there is a much lower number of them and many of the concepts do not have any. While it needs to be noted that the main advantage of word2vec and generally distributional methods is their ability to represent non-concept words, they underperform when dealing with concepts, mostly due to the rarity of many concepts in the Wikipedia text, while on the other hand the graph is rich: many concepts are not mentioned in the text of Wikipedia, while they play a role in the graph structure via their links to other pages and categories.

Off-the-Shelf Usage: Publicly Available Embeddings. PageRank can be calculated using power iteration and can converge in a reasonable time. Table 2 summarizes some performance statistics about the method. While on-the-fly performance is acceptable (1.74 s, compared to 78 s for UKB), real-time performance can be achieved by calculating the embeddings offline. All the pre-embeddings, the source code for calculating the embeddings and the evaluated datasets, along with a web-service to facilitate the incorporation are available from the project website under MIT license[3]. Experiments are performed on a 32×2.0 GHz core computer with 256 GB of RAM.

5.2 Experiment 2: Word Sense Disambiguation

We evaluate our proposed method as well as graph *overlap*, WLM and *word2vec*$_2$ on five different datasets: AQUAINT [21] (50 documents from news), MSNB [5] (20 news document) and Kore [11] (50 human curated hard sentences). We use two large scale datasets: (a) CoNLL annotated by [11] that consists of 1393

Table 2. Graph comparison (with no-embedding) vs embedding on different kinds of subgraphs.

	Graph stats		Method	KORE rel	Ped	Mayo	UMN sim	UMN rel
IN	Size	1440	*overlap*	.62	.62	.46	.58	.5
	Sparsity	.87	NGED	.61	**.72**	.49	.59	.53
	T (on the fly)	1.74 (s)	PageRank	.68	.67	.52	.59	.53
	T (pre-embedding)	008 (s)	rvsPageRank	.64	.67	**.58**	.59	.53
OUT	Size	302	*overlap*	.61	.61	.43	.49	.4
	Sparsity	.78	NGED	.62	.64	.48	.51	.44
	Time (s) (on the fly)	.22	PageRank	.28	-.08	.02	.14	.06
	Time (s) (pre-embedding)	.001	rvsPageRank	.71	.65	.53	.59	.53
Both*	Cols 4-8 form Table 1		rvsPageRank	**.72**	.69	.56	**.62**	**.57**

[3] http://cgm6.research.cs.dal.ca/~sajadi/wikisim/.

articles and (b) the first 5000 article of Wikipedia (Wiki dataset). Because entities are not necessarily linked throughout the whole article, we only choose the opening paragraphs which tend to have a higher quality[4]. We experiment with candidate lists of size 5, 10 and 15 (any number beyond 15 was not feasible with our hardware), the list always contains the correct entity. Sentences are chunked and each chunk consists up to 5 mentions.

Standard Coherence: Evaluation of Our Relatedness Method. We plug different relatedness methods into IP (Eq. 2) and solve the equation to find the entities. Macro average precisions is reported over the five datasets and different candidate numbers, shown in Table 3. Our embedding based method outperforms other methods in most of the datasets and this trend stays the same with the increase of the number of candidates.

Table 3. Integer programming results for WSD: macro average precision for WSD methods across different candidate numbers and datasets

Can#	Method	MSNBC	AQUAINT	Kore	Conll	Wikipedia
5	overlap	.82	.64	.74	.68	.64
	WLM	.83	.69	.78	.67	.62
	word2vec$_2$	.84	.62	.81	.69	.63
	rvsPageRank	**.86**	**.72**	**.86**	**.73**	**.67**
10	overlap	.78	.55	.68	.59	.58
	WLM	.78	.59	**.76**	.58	.55
	word2vec$_2$	.79	.53	.74	.63	.57
	rvsPageRank	**.82**	**.64**	.75	**.66**	**.59**
15	overlap	.76	.51	.62	.52	.53
	WLM	.76	.55	**.72**	.54	.49
	word2vec$_2$	.77	.49	.65	.57	**.56**
	rvsPageRank	**.80**	**.59**	**.72**	**.61**	.54

The Proposed Key Entity Recognition Vs Standard Coherence Model. The idea that there exist only one entity that can disambiguate the rest as well as full coherence model (Eq. 3), is supported by the results in Table 4. The results for our proposed VSM key entity recognition method are shown in the same table. The model can be very successful despite its simplicity. The main strength point of the model is its speed, summarized in Fig. 1 (log scale). As we see, a better performance with a dramatic speedup (more than 50×) provides more evidence for the quality of the embeddings.

[4] The dataset is publicly available on the project website.

Table 4. comparison (MAP) of * standard Coherence, † key entity Modeling and, ‡ VSM based key entity recognition.

Can#	Method	MS-NBC	AQU-AINT	Kore	CO-NLL	Wiki
5	ILP*	.87	.71	.86	.73	.74
	key†	.87	.70	.87	.73	.75
	key-vsm*	.87	.70	.89	.81	.79
10	ILP	.82	.64	.77	.67	.65
	key	.82	.61	.79	.67	.68
	key-vsm	.82	.64	.77	.76	.71
15	ILP	.80	.59	.75	.63	.61
	key	.80	.56	.73	.62	.66
	key-vsm	.81	.59	.75	.73	.67

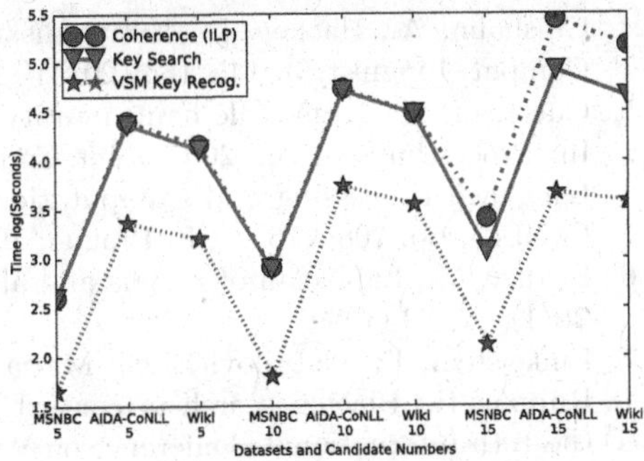

Fig. 1. log-lin of time spent for 3 largest datasets

6 Conclusion

We presented a vector space representation for Wikipedia concepts that performs better in semantic relatedness and also word sense disambiguation. The representation is constructed by vector space embedding of the neighborhood graph of the concept. We demonstrate that our method can outperform similar methods on various relatedness datasets. We also evaluated the method in a word sense disambiguation task by using a standard coherence modeled based on Integer Programming (IP) and demonstrated that it performs better than the other methods used in this task. Moreover, by reformulating coherence, we demonstrated that there is often one *key entity* in a sentence that can help disambiguating the rest of the entities. This finding led to a very fast yet more accurate method that we refer to as *VSM key entity recognition*. We make available the concept embeddings for public use so that they can be simply incorporated in any NLP relatedness task with minimum overhead.

Acknowledgments. This research was funded by the Natural Sciences and Engineering Research Council of Canada (NSERC), the Boeing Company, and Mitacs. We would also like to thank Jeannette C.M. Janssen for comments that greatly improved the manuscript.

References

1. Agirre, E., Alfonseca, E., Hall, K., Kravalova, J., Paşca, M., Soroa, A.: A study on similarity and relatedness using distributional and wordnet-based approaches. In: North American Chapter of the Association for Computational Linguistics, NAACL 2009, pp. 19–27. Association for Computational Linguistics, Stroudsburg (2009)
2. Agirre, E., Barrena, A., Soroa, A.: Studying the wikipedia hyperlink graph for relatedness and disambiguation. CoRR abs/1503.01655 (2015)
3. Bar-Yossef, Z., Mashiach, L.T.: Local approximation of pagerank and reverse pagerank. In: Proceedings of the 17th ACM Conference on Information and Knowledge Management, CIKM 2008, New York, NY, USA, pp. 279–288 (2008)

4. Chisholm, A., Hachey, B.: Entity disambiguation with web links. Trans. Assoc. Comput. Linguist. **3**, 145–156 (2015)
5. Cucerzan, S.: Large-scale named entity disambiguation based on Wikipedia data. In: Proceedings of the 2007 Joint Conference on Empirical Methods in Natural Language Processing and Computational Natural Language Learning (EMNLP-CoNLL), pp. 708–716. ACL, Prague, June 2007
6. Fiedler, M.: Laplacian of graphs and algebraic connectivity. Banach Center Publ. **25**(1), 57–70 (1989)
7. Finkelstein, L., Gabrilovich, E., Matias, Y., Rivlin, E., Solan, Z., Wolfman, G., Ruppin, E.: Placing search in context: the concept revisited. In: Proceedings of the 10th International Conference on World Wide Web, WWW 2001, pp. 406–414. ACM (2001
8. Fogaras, D.: Where to start browsing the web? In: Böhme, T., Heyer, G., Unger, H. (eds.) IICS 2003. LNCS, vol. 2877, pp. 65–79. Springer, Heidelberg (2003). doi:10.1007/978-3-540-39884-4_6
9. Gao, X., Xiao, B., Tao, D., Li, X.: A survey of graph edit distance. Pattern Anal. Appl. **13**(1), 113–129 (2010)
10. Gyöngyi, Z., Garcia-Molina, H., Pedersen, J.: Combating web spam with trustrank. In: Proceedings of the Thirtieth International Conference on Very Large Data Bases, VLDB 2004, vol. 30. pp. 576–587. VLDB Endowment (2004)
11. Hoffart, J., Seufert, S., Nguyen, D.B., Theobald, M., Weikum, G.: Kore: Keyphrase overlap relatedness for entity disambiguation. In: Proceedings of the 21st ACM International Conference on Information and Knowledge Management, CIKM 2012, New York, NY, USA, pp. 545–554 (2012)
12. Jabeen, S., Gao, X., Andreae, P.: CPRel: semantic relatedness computation using wikipedia based context profiles. Res. Comput. Sci. **70**, 55–66 (2013)
13. Katz, L.: A new status index derived from sociometric analysis. Psychometrika **18**(1), 39–43 (1953)
14. Kleinberg, J.M.: Authoritative sources in a hyperlinked environment. J. ACM (JACM) **46**(5), 604–632 (1999)
15. Kulkarni, S., Singh, A., Ramakrishnan, G., Chakrabarti, S.: Collective annotation of wikipedia entities in web text. In: Proceedings of the 15th ACM SIGKDD International Conference on Knowledge Discovery and Data Mining, KDD 2009, New York, NY, USA, pp. 457–466 (2009)
16. Lazic, N., Subramanya, A., Ringgaard, M., Pereira, F.: Plato: a selective context model for entity resolution. Trans. Assoc. Comput. Linguist. **3**, 503–515 (2015)
17. Lougee-Heimer, R.: The common optimization interface for operations research: promoting open-source software in the operations research community. IBM J. Res. Dev. **47**(1), 57–66 (2003)
18. Mikolov, T., Sutskever, I., Chen, K., Corrado, G.S., Dean, J.: Distributed representations of words and phrases and their compositionality. In: Advances in Neural Information Processing Systems (NIPS), pp. 3111–3119 (2013)
19. Miller, G.A., Charles, W.G.: Contextual correlates of semantic similarity. Lang. Cogn. Process. **6**(1), 1–28 (1991)
20. Milne, D., Witten, I.H.: An effective, low-cost measure of semantic relatedness obtained from wikipedia links. In: Proceedings of AAAI 2008 (2008)
21. Milne, D., Witten, I.H.: Learning to link with wikipedia. In: Proceedings of the 17th ACM Conference on Information and Knowledge Management, CIKM 2008, New York, NY, USA, pp. 509–518 (2008)

22. Page, L., Brin, S., Motwani, R., Winograd, T.: The pagerank citation ranking: bringing order to the web. Technical report 1999-66, Stanford InfoLab, November 1999
23. Pakhomov, S., McInnes, B., Adam, T., Liu, Y., Pedersen, T., Melton, G.B.: Semantic similarity and relatedness between clinical terms: an experimental study. AMIA Ann. Symp. Proc. **2010**, 572–576 (2010)
24. Pakhomov, S.V.S., Pedersen, T., McInnes, B., Melton, G.B., Ruggieri, A., Chute, C.G.: Towards a framework for developing semantic relatedness reference standards. J. Biomed. Inform. **44**(2), 251–265 (2011)
25. Pedersen, T., Pakhomov, S.V., Patwardhan, S., Chute, C.G.: Measures of semantic similarity and relatedness in the biomedical domain. J. Biomed. Inform. **40**(3), 288–299 (2007)
26. Ponzetto, S.P., Strube, M.: Knowledge derived from wikipedia for computing semantic relatedness. J. Artif. Intell. Res. (JAIR) **30**, 181–212 (2007)
27. Ratinov, L., Roth, D., Downey, D., Anderson, M.: Local and global algorithms for disambiguation to wikipedia. In: Proceedings of the 49th Annual Meeting of the Association for Computational Linguistics: Human Language Technologies, HLT 2011, vol. 1, pp. 1375–1384. Association for Computational Linguistics, Stroudsburg (2011)
28. Rubenstein, H., Goodenough, J.B.: Contextual correlates of synonymy. Commun. ACM **8**(10), 627–633 (1965)
29. Sajadi, A., Milios, E.E., Kešelj, V., Janssen, J.C.M.: Domain-specific semantic relatedness from wikipedia structure: a case study in biomedical text. In: Gelbukh, A. (ed.) CICLing 2015. LNCS, vol. 9041, pp. 347–360. Springer, Cham (2015). doi:10.1007/978-3-319-18111-0_26
30. Sherkat, E., Milios, E.: Vector embedding of wikipedia concepts and entities. ArXiv e-prints, February 2017
31. Yeh, E., Ramage, D., Manning, C.D., Agirre, E., Soroa, A.: Wikiwalk: random walks on wikipedia for semantic relatedness. In: Proceedings of the 2009 Workshop on Graph-based Methods for Natural Language Processing, TextGraphs-4, pp. 41–49. Association for Computational Linguistics, Stroudsburg (2009)

Composite Semantic Relation Classification

Siamak Barzegar[1(✉)], Andre Freitas[2], Siegfried Handschuh[2], and Brian Davis[1]

[1] Insight Centre for Data Analytics, National University of Ireland, Galway, Ireland
{siamak.barzegar,brian.davis}@insight-centre.org
[2] Digital Libraries and Web Information Systems,
University of Passau, Passau, Germany
{andre.freitas,siegfried.handschuh}@uni-passau.de

Abstract. Different semantic interpretation tasks such as text entailment and question answering require the classification of semantic relations between terms or entities within text. However, in most cases it is not possible to assign a direct semantic relation between entities/terms. This paper proposes an approach for composite semantic relation classification, extending the traditional semantic relation classification task. Different from existing approaches, which use machine learning models built over lexical and distributional word vector features, the proposed model uses the combination of a large commonsense knowledge base of binary relations, a distributional navigational algorithm and sequence classification to provide a solution for the composite semantic relation classification problem.

Keywords: Semantic relation · Distributional semantic · Deep learning · Classification

1 Introduction

Capturing the semantic relationship between two concepts is a fundamental operation for many semantic interpretation tasks. This is a task which humans perform rapidly and reliably by using their linguistic and commonsense knowledge about entities and relations. Natural language processing systems which aspire to reach the goal of producing meaningful representations of text must be equipped to identify and learn semantic relations in the documents they process.

The automatic recognition of semantic relations has many applications such as information extraction, document summarization, machine translation, or the construction of thesauri and semantic networks. It can also facilitate auxiliary tasks such as word sense disambiguation, language modeling, paraphrasing, and recognizing textual entailment [5].

However it is not always possible to establish a direct semantic relation given two entity mentions in text. In the Semeval 2010 Task 8 test collection [5] for example 17.39 % of the semantic relations mapped within sentences were assigned with the label *"OTHER"*, meaning that they could not be mapped to the set of

F. Frasincar et al. (Eds.): NLDB 2017, LNCS 10260, pp. 406–417, 2017.
DOI: 10.1007/978-3-319-59569-6_49

9 direct semantic relations[1]. In many cases, the semantic relations between two entities can only be expressed by a composition of two or more operations. This work aims at improving the description and the formalization of the semantic relation classification task by introducing the concept of composite semantic relation classification, in which the relations between entities can be expressed using the composition of one or more relations.

This paper is organized as follows: Sect. 2 describes the semantic relation classification problem and the related work followed by the proposed composite semantic relation classification (Sect. 3), Sect. 4 describes the existing baseline models; while Sect. 5 describes the experimental setup and analyses the results, providing a comparative analysis between the proposed model and the baselines. Finally, Sect. 6 provides the conclusion.

2 Composite Semantic Relation Classification

2.1 Semantic Relation Classification

Semantic relation classification is the task of classifying the underlying abstract semantic relations between target entities (terms) present in texts [10]. The goal of relation classification is defined as follows: given a sentence S with the pairs of annotated target nominals e_1 and e_2, the relation classification system aims to classify the relations between e_1 and e_2 in given texts within the pre-defined relation set [5]. For instance, the relation between the nominal **burst** and **pressure** in the following example sentence is interpreted as **Cause-Effect** (e_2, e_1).

The $< e_1 >$ *burst* $< /e_1 >$ has been caused by water hammer $< e_2 >$ *pressure* $< /e_2 >$.

2.2 Existing Approaches for Semantic Relation Classification

Different approaches have been explored for relation classification, including unsupervised relation discovery and supervised classification. Existing literature have proposed various features to identify the relations between entities using different methods.

Recently, Neural network-based approaches have achieved significant improvement over traditional methods based on either human-designed features [10]. However, existing neural networks for relation classification are usually based on shallow architectures (e.g., one-layer convolutional neural networks or recurrent networks). In exploring the potential representation space at different abstraction levels, they may fail to perform [15].

The performance of supervised approaches strongly depends on the quality of the designed features [17]. With the recent improvement in Deep Neural

[1] Cause-Effect, Instrument-Agency, Product-Producer, Content-Container, Entity-Origin, Entity-Destination, Component-Whole, Member-Collection, Communication-Topic.

Network (DNN), many researchers are experimenting with unsupervised methods for automatic feature learning. [16] introduce gated recurrent networks, in particular, Long short-term memory (LSTM), to relation classification. [17] use Convolutional Neural Network (CNNs). Additionally, [11] replace the common Softmax loss function with a ranking loss in their CNN model. [14] design a negative sampling method based on CNNs. From the viewpoint of model ensembling, [8] combine CNNs and recursive networks along the Shortest Dependency Path (SDP), while [9] incorporate CNNs with Recurrent Neural Networks (RNNs).

Additionally, much effort has been invested in relational learning methods that can scale to large knowledge bases. The best performing neural-embedding models are Socher(NTN)[12] and Bordes models (TransE and TATEC) [2,4].

3 From Single to Composite Relation Classification

3.1 Introduction

The goal of this work is to propose an approach for semantic relation classification using one or more relations between term mentions/entities.

"The $< e_1 >$ *child* $< /e_1 >$ was carefully wrapped and bound into the $< e_2 >$ *cradle* $< /e_2 >$ by means of a cord."

In this example, the relationship between *Child* and *Cradle* cannot be directly expressed by one of the nine abstract semantic relations from the set described in [5].

However, looking into a commonsense KB (in this case, ConceptNet V5.4) we can see the following set of composite relations between these elements:

$< e_1 >$ *child* $< /e_1 >$ *createdby* $\circ$ *causes* $\circ$ *atlocation* $< e_2 >$ *cradle* $< /e_2 >$

As you increase the number of edges that you can include in the set of semantic relations compositions (the size of the semantic relationship path), there is a dramatic increase in the number of paths which connect the two entities. For example, for the words *Child* and *Cradle* there are 15 paths of size 2, 1079 paths of size 3 and 95380 paths of size 4. Additionally, as the path size grows many non-relevant relationships (less meaningful relations) will be included.

The challenge in *composite semantic relation classification* is to provide a classification method that provides the most meaningful set of relations for the context at hand. This task can be challenging because, as previously mentioned, a simple KB lookup based approach would provide all semantic associations at hand.

To achieve this goal we propose an approach which combines *sequence machine learning models*, *distributional semantic models* and *commonsense relations knowledge bases* to provide an accurate method for composite semantic relation classification.

The proposed model (Fig. 1) relies on the combination of the following approaches:

i Use existing structured commonsense KBs define an initial set of semantic relation compositions.
ii Use a pre-filtering method based on the Distributional Navigational Algorithm (DNA) as proposed by [3]
iii Use sequence-based Neural Network based model to quantify the sequence probabilities of the semantic relation compositions. We call this model Neural Concept/Relation Model, in analogy to a Language Model.

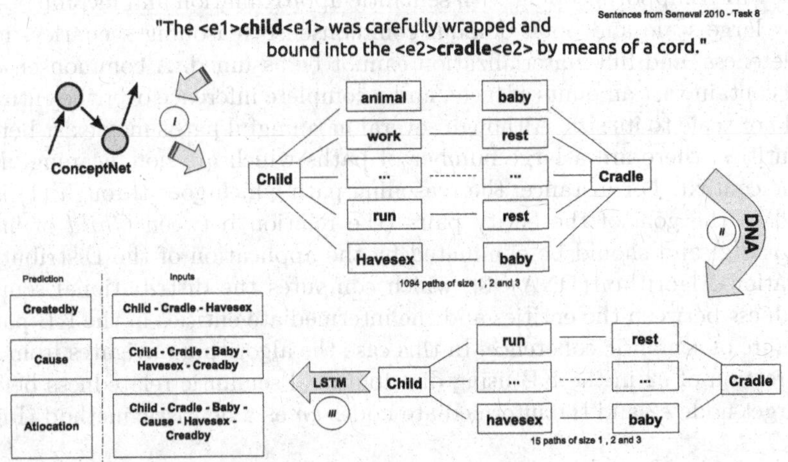

Fig. 1. Depiction of the proposed model relies on the combination of the our three approaches

3.2 Commonsense KB Lookup

The first step consists in the use of a large commonsense knowledge base for providing a reference for a sequence of semantic relations. ConceptNet is a semantic network built from existing linguistic resources and crowd-sourced. It is built from nodes representing words or short phrases of natural language, and labeled abstract relationships between them.

1094 paths were extracted from ConceptNet with two given entities (e.g. *child* and *cradle*) with no corresponding semantic relation from the Semeval 2010 Task 8 test collection (Fig. 1(i)). Examples of paths are:

- **child/canbe/baby/atlocation/cradle**
- child/isa/animal/hasa/baby/atlocation/cradle
- child/hasproperty/work/causesdesire/rest/synonym/cradle
- child/instanceof/person/desires/baby/atlocation/cradle
- child/desireof/run/causesdesire/rest/synonym/cradle
- **child/createdby/havesex/causes/baby/atlocation/cradle**

3.3 Distributional Navigational Algorithm (DNA)

The Distributional Navigational Algorithm (DNA) consists of an approach which uses distributional semantic models as a relevance-based heuristic for selecting relevant facts attached to a contextual query. The approach focuses on addressing the following problems: (i) providing a semantic selection mechanism for facts which are relevant and meaningful in a particular reasoning & querying context and (ii) allowing coping with information incompleteness in a huge KBs.

In [3] DSMs are used as a complementary semantic layer to the relational model, which supports coping with semantic approximation and incompleteness.

For large-scale and open domain commonsense reasoning scenarios, model completeness, and full materialization cannot be assumed. A commonsense KB would contain vast amounts of facts, and a complete inference over the entire KB would not scale to its size. Although several meaningful paths may exist between two entities, there are a large number of paths which are not meaningful in a specific context. For instance, the reasoning path which goes through (1) is not related to the goal of the entity pairs (the relation between *Child* of human and *Cradle*) and should be eliminated by the application of the Distributional Navigation Algorithm (DNA) [3], which computes the distributional semantic relatedness between the entities and the intermediate entities in the KB path as a measure of semantic coherence. In this case the algorithm navigates from $e1$ in the direction of $e2$ in the KB using distributional semantic relatedness between the target node $e2$ and the intermediate nodes en as a heuristic method (Fig. 2).

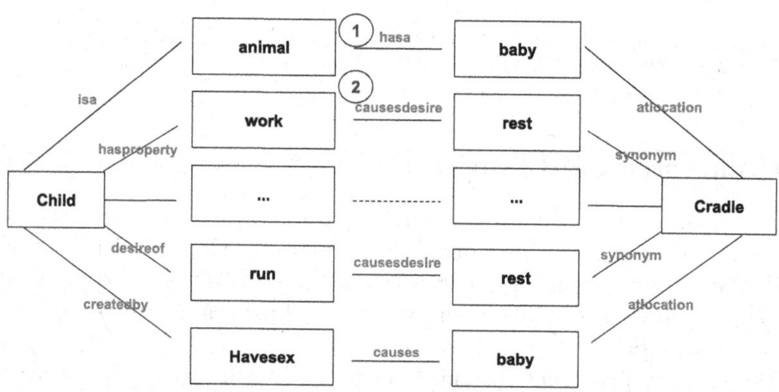

Fig. 2. Selection of meaningful paths

3.4 Neural Entity/Relation Model

The Distributional Navigational Algorithm provides a pre-filtering of the relations maximizing the semantic relatedness coherence. This can be complemented by a predictive model which takes into account the likelihood of a sequence of relations, i.e. the likelihood of a composition sequence. The goal is to systematically compute the sequence of probabilities of a relation composition, in a similar fashion to a language model. For this purpose we use a Long short-term memory (LSTM) recurrent neural network architecture (Fig. 3) [6].

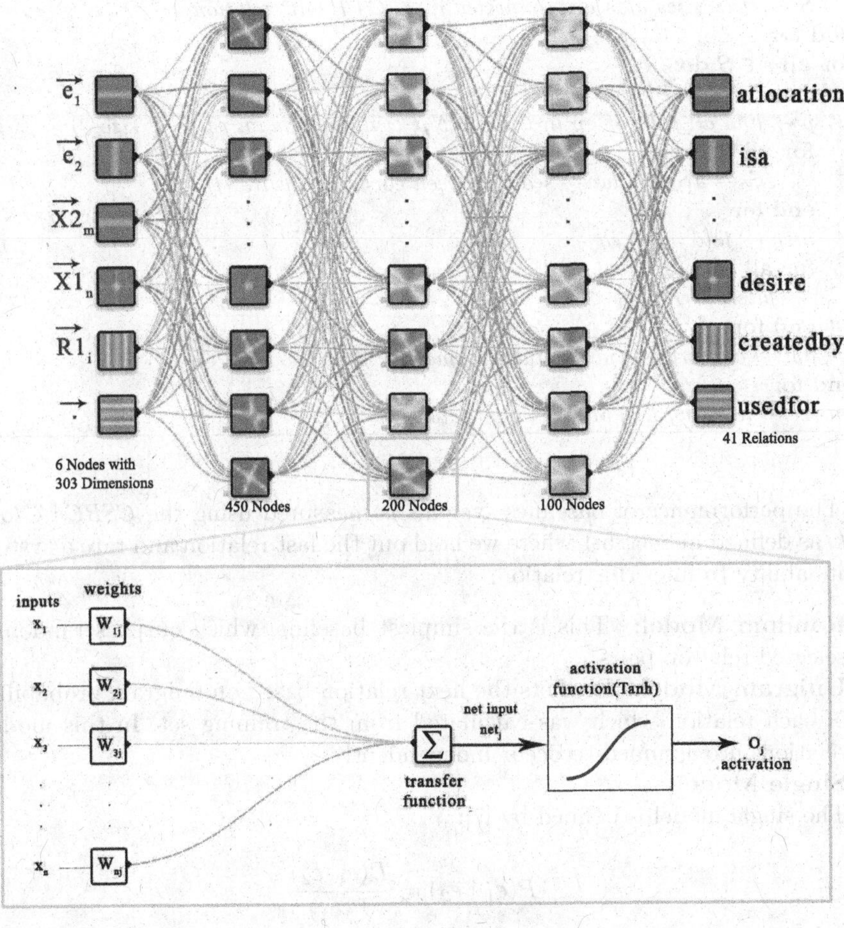

Fig. 3. The LSTM-CSRC architecture

4 Baseline Models

As baselines we use bigram language models which define the conditional probabilities between a sequence of semantic relations r_2 after entities r_1, i.e. $P(r_1 \mid r_2)$.

Algorithm 1. Composite Semantic Relation Classification

```
I : sentences of semeval 2010-Task 8 dataset
O : predefined entity pairs (e1, e2)
W : words in I
R : related relations of w
for all s ∈ I do:
    S ← If entities of s are connected in a OTHER relation
end for
for all s ∈ S do:
    ep ← predefined entity pairs of s
    p ← find all path of ep in ConceptNet (with maximum paths of size 3)
    for all i ∈ p do:
        sq_i ← avg similarity score between each word pairs [1]
    end for
    msq ← find max sq
    for all i ∈ p do:
        filter i If sq_i < msq - msq/2
    end for
    dw ← convert s into suitable format for deep learning
end for
model ← learning LSTM with dw dataset
```

The performance of baselines systems is measured using the *CSRC*[2] *Cloze task*, as defined in Sect. 5.1 where we hold out the last relation and rate a system by its ability to infer this relation.

- **Random Model:** This is the simplest baseline, which outputs randomly selected relation pairs.
- **Unigram Model:** Predicts the next relation based on unigram probability of each relation which was calculated from the training set. In this model, relations are assumed to occur independently.
- **Single Model:**
  The single model is defined by [7]:

$$P(e_1 \mid e_2) = \frac{P(e_1, e_2)}{P(e_1)} \tag{1}$$

where $P(e_1 \mid e_2)$ is the probability of seeing a_1 and a_2, in order. Let A be an ordered list of relations, $|A|$ is the length of A, For $i = 1, .., |A|$, define a_i to be the ith element of A. We rank candidate relations r by maximizing F(r,a), defined as

$$F(r, a) = \sum_{n-1}^{i} logP(r \mid a_i) \tag{2}$$

With conditional probabilities $P(e_1 \mid e_2)$ calculated using (1).

[2] Composite Semantic Relation Classification.

- **Random Forest:** is an ensemble learning method for classification and other tasks, that operate by constructing a multitude of decision trees at training time and outputting the class that is the mode of the classes. Random decision forests correct for decision trees' habit of overfitting to their training set.

5 Experimental Evaluation

5.1 Training and Test Dataset

The evaluation dataset was generated by collecting all pairs of entity mentions in the Semeval 2010 task 8 [5] which had no attached semantic relation classification (i.e. which contained the relation label *"OTHER"*).

For all entities with unassigned relation labels, we did a *Conceptnet* lookup [13], where we generated all paths from sizes 1, 2 and 3 (number of relations) occurring between both entities(e_1 and e_2) and their relations (R).

For example:

$\mathbf{e1} - R1_i - \mathbf{e2}$
$\mathbf{e1} - R1_i - \mathbf{X1}_n - R2_j - \mathbf{e2}$
$\mathbf{e1} - R1_i - \mathbf{X1}_n - R2_j - \mathbf{X2}_m - R3_k - \mathbf{e2}$

where X contains the intermediate entities between the target entity mentions **e1** and **e2**.

In next step, the Distributional Navigational Algorithm (DNA) is applied over the entity paths [3]. In the final step of generating training & test datasets, the best paths are selected manually out of filtered path sets.

From 602 entity pairs assigned to the *"OTHER"* relation label in Semeval, we found 27,415 paths between 405 entity pairs in ConceptNet. With the Distributional Navigation Algorithm (DNA), meaningless paths were eliminated, and after filtering, we have 2,514 paths for 405 entity-pairs.

Overall we have 41 relations and 964 entities. All paths were converted into the following format which will be input into the neural network: $\mathbf{e}_1 - R1_i - \mathbf{X1}_n - R2_j - \mathbf{X2}_m - R3_k - \mathbf{e}_2$ (Table 1).

Table 1. Training data-set for CSRC model

Input	Classification
$\mathbf{e}_1$ $\mathbf{e}_2$ $\mathbf{X1}_n$	$\mathbf{R1}_i$
$\mathbf{e}_1$ $\mathbf{e}_2$ $\mathbf{X2}_m$ $\mathbf{X1}_n$ $\mathbf{R1}_i$	$\mathbf{R2}_i$
$\mathbf{e}_1$ $\mathbf{e}_2$ $\mathbf{X2}_m$ $\mathbf{R2}_i$ $\mathbf{X1}_n$ $\mathbf{R1}_i$	$\mathbf{R3}_i$

We provide statistics for the generated datasets in the Tables 2 and 3. In Table 3 our dataset is divided into a training set and a test set with scale (75 – 25 %), also we used 25 % of the training set for cross-validation, 3120 examples for training, 551 for validation and 1124 for testing. Table 2 shows statistics for test dataset of baseline models.

Table 2. Number of different length in the test dataset for baseline models

Test dataset	# Length 2	# Length 4	# Length 6
Baselines	245	391	432

Table 3. Dataset for LSTM model

Dataset	# Train	# Dev	# Test
CSRC	3120	551	1124

5.2 Results

To achieve the classification goal, we generated a LTSM model for the composite relation classification task. In our experiments, a batch size 25, and epoch 50 was generated. An embedding layer using Word2Vec pre-trained vectors was used.

In our experiment, we optimized the hyperparameters of the LSTM model. After several experiments, the best model is generated with:

- Inputs length and dimension are 6 and 303, respectively.
- Three hidden layers with 450, 200 and 100 nodes and $Tanh$ activation,
- Dropout technique (0.5),
- *Adam* optimizer.

We experimented our LSTM model with three different pre-training embedding word vector models:

- Word2Vec (Google News) with 300 dimensions
- Word2Vec (Wikipedia 2016) with 30 dimensions
- No pre-training word embedding

The accuracy for the configuration above after 50 epochs is shown in the table below (Table 4).

Table 4. Validation accuracy

CRSC	W2V Google_News	W2V Wikipedia	No pre training
Accuracy	0.4208	0.3841	0.2196

Table 5 contains the Precision, Recall, F1-Score and Accuracy. Between the evaluated models, the LSTM-CSRC achieved the highest F1 Score and Accuracy. The Single model achieved the second highest accuracy 0.3793 followed by Random forest model 0.3299. The LSTM approach provides an improvement of 9.86 % on accuracy over the baselines, and 11.31 % improvement on the F1-score. Random Forest achieved the highest precision, while LSTM-CSRC achieved the highest recall.

Table 5. Evaluation results on baseline models and our approach, with four metrics

Method	Recall	Precision	F1 score	Accuracy
Random	0.0160	0.0220	0.0144	0.0234
Unigram	0.0270	0.0043	0.0074	0.1606
Single	0.2613	0.2944	0.2502	0.3793
Random forest	0.2476	**0.3663**	0.2766	0.3299
LSTM-CSRC	**0.3073**	0.3281	**0.3119**	**0.4208**

Table 6. The extracted information from Confusion Matrix - Part 1

Relation	# Correct predicted	# Correct predicted rate	Relation	# Correct predicted	# Correct predicted rate
notisa	2	1	memberof	1	0.5
atlocation	172	0.67	hasa	24	0.393
notdesires	6	0.666	hassubevent	12	0.378
similar	5	0.625	partof	16	0.374
desires	36	0.593	haspropertry	12	0.375
hasprerequest	23	0.547	sysnonym	54	0.312
causesdesire	17	0.548	derivedfrom	20	0.307
isa	147	0.492	etymologically derivedfrom	6	0.3
antonym	68	0.492	capableof	13	0.26
instandof	46	0.479	motivationbygoal	3	0.25
usedfor	47	0.475	receivsection	5	0.238
desireof	5	0.5	createdby	4	0.2
hascontext	2	0.5	madeof	3	0.16
haslastsubevent	2	0.5	causes	3	0.15
nothasa	1	0.5	genre	1	0.11

The extracted information from confusion matrix show in Tables 6 and 7. At table 6 *'Correctly Predicted'* column indicates the proportion of relations are predicted correctly, and *'Correct Prediction Rate'* column indicates the rate of correct predicted. For instance, our model predicts the relation *notisa* 100 % correct.

Table 7 shows the relations which are wrongly predicted (*'Wrongly Predicted'* columns).

Based on the results, the most incorrectly predicted relation is '*isa*', which accounts for a large proportion of relations of the dataset (around 150 out of 550). In the second place is '*atlocation*' relation (172 out of 550). The third place is the '*antonym*' relation. On the other hand, some relations which are correctly unpredicted, can be treated as semantically equivalent to their prediction, where

Table 7. The extracted information from Confusion Matrix - Part 2

Relation	# Correctly predicted	Rate	Wrong relation 1	# False predicted for relation 1	Wrong relation 2	# False Predicted for relation 2	Wrong relation 3	# False predicted for relation 3
atlocation	172	0.67	antonym	20	Usedfor	17		
desire	36	0.593	isa	6	Capableof	6	Usedfor	5
hasprerequest	23	0.547	sysnonymy	4	antonym	3	atlocation	2
causesdesire	17	0.548	usedfor	7				
isa	147	0.492	atlocation	26	antonym	22	instanceof	22
antonym	68	0.492	isa	17	atlocation	9		
instandof	46	0.479	isa	27	atlocation	8		
usedfor	47	0.475	atlocation	26	isa	18		
hasa	24	0.393	antonym	11	usedfor	6		
hassubevent	12	0.378	causes	5	antonym	4		
partof	16	0.374	synonym	12	antonym	3	hasproperty	3
haspropertry	12	0.375	isa	8				
sysnonym	54	0.312	isa	31	hasproperty	17	atlocation	12
derivedfrom	20	0.307	isa	10	sysnonym	8	etymologically-derivedfrom	8
etymologically-derivedfrom	6	0.3	derivedfrom	6				
capableof	13	0.26	usedfor	13	isa	7		
motivatedbygoal	3	0.25	causes	3	hassubevent	2		
receivsection	5	0.238	atlocation	9	usedfor	3		
createdby	4	0.2	antonym	6	isa	5		
madeof	3	0.16	isa	7	antonym	3	hsaa	2
causes	3	0.15	causesdesire	6	hassubevent	4	derivedfrom	3

the assignment is dependent on a modelling decision. The same situation occurs for '*etymologicallyderivedfrom*' and '*derivedfrom*' relations.

Another issue is the low number of certain relations expressed int he dataset.

6 Conclusion

In this paper we introduced the task of composite semantic relation classification. The paper proposes a composite semantic relation classification model which combines *commonsense KB lookup*, a *distributional semantic based filter* and the application of a *sequence machine learning model* to address the task. The proposed LSTM model outperformed existing baselines with regard to f1-score, accuracy and recall. Future work will focus on increasing the volume of the training set for under-represented relations.

References

1. Barzegar, S., Sales, J.E., Freitas, A., Handschuh, S., Davis, B.: Dinfra: a one stop shop for computing multilingual semantic relatedness. In: Proceedings of the 38th International ACM SIGIR Conference on Research and Development in Information Retrieval, pp. 1027–1028. ACM (2015)

2. Bordes, A., Usunier, N., Garcia-Duran, A., Weston, J., Yakhnenko, O.: Translating embeddings for modeling multi-relational data. In: Advances in Neural Information Processing Systems, pp. 2787–2795 (2013)
3. Freitas, A., da Silva, J.C.P., Curry, E., Buitelaar, P.: A distributional semantics approach for selective reasoning on commonsense graph knowledge bases. In: Métais, E., Roche, M., Teisseire, M. (eds.) NLDB 2014. LNCS, vol. 8455, pp. 21–32. Springer, Cham (2004)
4. Garcia-Duran, A., Bordes, A., Usunier, N., Grandvalet, Y.: Combining two and three-way embedding models for link prediction in knowledge bases. J. Artif. Intell. Res. **55**, 715–742 (2016)
5. Hendrickx, I., Kim, S.N., Kozareva, Z., Nakov, P., Ó Séaghdha, D., Padó, S., Pennacchiotti, M., Romano, L., Szpakowicz, S.: Semeval-2010 task 8: multi-way classification of semantic relations between pairs of nominals. In: Proceedings of the Workshop on Semantic Evaluations: Recent Achievements and Future Directions, pp. 94–99. Association for Computational Linguistics (2009)
6. Hochreiter, S., Schmidhuber, J.: Long short-term memory. Neural Comput. **9**(8), 1735–1780 (1997)
7. Jans, B., Bethard, S., Vulić, I., Moens, M.F.: Skip n-grams and ranking functions for predicting script events. In: Proceedings of the 13th Conference of the European Chapter of the Association for Computational Linguistics, pp. 336–344. Association for Computational Linguistics (2012)
8. Liu, Y., Wei, F., Li, S., Ji, H., Zhou, M., Wang, H.: A dependency-based neural network for relation classification (2015). arXiv:1507.04646
9. Nguyen, T.H., Grishman, R.: Combining neural networks and log-linear models to improve relation extraction (2015). arXiv:1511.05926
10. Qin, P., Xu, W., Guo, J.: An empirical convolutional neural network approach for semantic relation classification. Neurocomputing **190**, 1–9 (2016)
11. dos Santos, C.N., Xiang, B., Zhou, B.: Classifying relations by ranking with convolutional neural networks. In: Proceedings of the 53rd Annual Meeting of the Association for Computational Linguistics and the 7th International Joint Conference on Natural Language Processing, vol. 1, pp. 626–634 (2015)
12. Socher, R., Chen, D., Manning, C.D., Ng, A.: Reasoning with neural tensor networks for knowledge base completion. In: Advances in Neural Information Processing Systems, pp. 926–934 (2013)
13. Speer, R., Havasi, C.: Representing general relational knowledge in conceptnet 5. In: LREC, pp. 3679–3686 (2012)
14. Xu, K., Feng, Y., Huang, S., Zhao, D.: Semantic relation classification via convolutional neural networks with simple negative sampling (2015). arXiv:1506.07650
15. Xu, Y., Jia, R., Mou, L., Li, G., Chen, Y., Lu, Y., Jin, Z.: Improved relation classification by deep recurrent neural networks with data augmentation (2016). arXiv:1601.03651
16. Xu, Y., Mou, L., Li, G., Chen, Y., Peng, H., Jin, Z.: Classifying relations via long short term memory networks along shortest dependency paths. In: Proceedings of Conference on Empirical Methods in Natural Language Processing (to appear) (2015)
17. Zeng, D., Liu, K., Lai, S., Zhou, G., Zhao, J., et al.: Relation classification via convolutional deep neural network. In: COLING, pp. 2335–2344 (2014)

Vector Embedding of Wikipedia Concepts and Entities

Ehsan Sherkat(✉) and Evangelos E. Milios

Faculty of Computer Science, Dalhousie University, Halifax, Canada
ehsansherkat@dal.ca, eem@cs.dal.ca

Abstract. Using deep learning for different machine learning tasks such as word embedding has recently gained a lot of researchers' attention. Word embedding is the task of mapping words or phrases to a low dimensional numerical vector. In this paper, we use deep learning to embed Wikipedia concepts and entities. The English version of Wikipedia contains more than five million pages, which suggest its capability to cover many English entities, phrases, and concepts. Each Wikipedia page is considered as a concept. Some concepts correspond to entities, such as a person's name, an organization or a place. Contrary to word embedding, Wikipedia concepts embedding is not ambiguous, so there are different vectors for concepts with similar surface form but different mentions. We proposed several approaches and evaluated their performance based on Concept Analogy and Concept Similarity tasks. The results show that proposed approaches have the performance comparable and in some cases even higher than the state-of-the-art methods.

Keywords: Wikipedia · Concept embedding · Vector representation

1 Introduction

Recently, many researchers [10, 13] showed the capabilities of deep learning for natural language processing tasks such as word embedding. Word embedding is the task of representing each term with a low-dimensional (typically less than 1000) numerical vector. Distributed representation of words showed better performance than traditional approaches for tasks such as word analogy [10]. Some words are Entities, i.e. name of an organization, Person, Movie, etc. On the other hand, some terms and phrases have a page or definition in a knowledge base such as Wikipedia, which are called concepts. For example, there is a page in Wikipedia for Data Mining or Computer Science concepts. Both concepts and entities are valuable resources for getting semantic and better making sense of a text. In this paper, we used deep learning to represent Wikipedia concepts and entities with numerical vectors. We make the following contributions:

- Wide coverage of words and concepts: about 1.7 million Wikipedia concepts and nearly 2 million English words were embedded in this research, which is

F. Frasincar et al. (Eds.): NLDB 2017, LNCS 10260, pp. 418–428, 2017.
DOI: 10.1007/978-3-319-59569-6_50

one of the highest numbers of embedded concepts that currently exists, to the best of our knowledge. The concept and words vectors are also publicly available for research purposes[1]. We also used one of the latest versions of the Wikipedia English dump to learn word embedding. Over time, each term may appear in different contexts, and as a result, it may have different embeddings so this is why we used one of the recent versions of Wikipedia.

Table 1. Top similar terms to "amazon" based on Word2Vec and GloVe.

Word2Vec	itunes	www.play.com	cli	adobe_acrobat	amiga	canada
GloVe	www.amazon.com	Rainforest	Amazonian	Kindle	Jungle	Deforestation

- Unambiguous word embedding: Existing word embedding approaches suffer from the problem of ambiguity. For example, top nine similar terms to 'Amazon' based on pre-trained Google's vectors in Word2Vec [10] and GloVe [13] models are in Table 1. Word2Vec and GloVe are the two first pioneer approaches for word embedding. In a document, 'Amazon' may refer to the name of a jungle and not the name of a company. In the process of embedding, all different meanings of the word 'Amazon' are embedded in a single vector. Producing distinct embedding for each sense of the ambiguous terms could lead to better representation of documents. One way to achieve this is using unambiguous resources such as Wikipedia and learning the embedding separately for each entity and concept.
- We compared the quality versus the size of the corpus on the quality of trained vectors. We demonstrated that much smaller corpora with more accurate textual content is better than very large text corpora with less accuracy in the content for the concept and phrase embedding.
- We studied the impact of fine-tuning weights of network by pre-trained word vectors from very large text corpora in tasks of Phrase Analogy and Phrase Similarity. Fine-tuning is the task of initializing the weights of the network by pre-trained vectors instead of random initialization.
- Proposing different approaches for Wikipedia concept embedding and comparing results with the state-of-the-art methods on the standard datasets.

2 Related Works

Word2Vec and GloVe are two pioneer approaches for word embedding. Recently, other methods have been introduced that try to improve both the performance and quality of the word embedding [3] by using multilingual correlation. A method based on Word2Vec is proposed by Mikolov et al. for phrase embedding. [10]. In the first step, they find the words that appear more frequently together than separately, and then they replace them with a single token. Finally, the

[1] https://github.com/ehsansherkat/ConVec.

vector for phrases is learned in the same way as single word embedding. One of the features of this approach is that both words and phrases are in the same vector space.

Graph embedding methods [1] using Deep Neural Networks are similar to the goals of this paper. Graph representation has been used for information management in many real world problems. Extracting deep information from these graphs is important and challenging. One solution is using graph embedding methods. The word embedding methods use linear sequences of words to learn a word representation. For graph embedding, the first step is converting the graph structure to an extensive collection of linear sequences. Perozzi presented a uniform sampling method named Truncated Random Walk for converting the graph structure to a linear sequences [14]. In the second step, a word embedding method such as Word2Vec is used to learn the representation for each graph vertex. Wikipedia can also be represented by a graph, and the links are the inter citation between Wikipedia's pages, called anchors.

Sajadi et al. [16] presented a graph embedding method for Wikipedia using a similarity inspired by the HITS algorithm [7]. The output of this approach for each Wikipedia concept is a fixed length list of similar Wikipedia pages and their similarity score, which represents the dimension name of the corresponding Wikipedia concepts. The difference between this method and deep learning based methods is that each dimension of a concept embedding is meaningful and understandable by the human.

Milne and Witten [12] proposed a Wikipedia concept similarity index based on in-links and out-links of a page. In their similarity method, two Wikipedia pages are more similar to each other if they share more common in- and out-links. This method is used to compare the result of the Concept Similarity task with the proposed approaches.

The idea of using Anchor texts inside Wikipedia for learning phrase vectors is being used in some other research [17,18] as well. In this research, we proposed different methods to use anchor texts and evaluated the results in standard tasks. We also compared the performance of the proposed methods with top notch methods.

3 Distributed Representation of Concepts

From this point on, we describe how we trained our word embedding. At first we describe the steps for preparing the Wikipedia dataset and then describe different methods we used to train words and concepts vectors.

Preparing Wikipedia dataset: In this research, the Wikipedia English text from the Wikipedia dump on May 01, 2016 is used. In the first step, we developed a toolkit[2] using several open source Python libraries (described in Appendix A) to extract all pages in English Wikipedia, and as a result 16,527,332 pages were

[2] https://github.com/ehsansherkat/ConVec.

extracted. Not all of these pages are valuable, so we pruned the list using several rules (check Appendix B for more information).

As a result of pruning, 5,001,168 unique Wikipedia pages, pointed to by the anchors, were extracted. For the next step, the plain text of all these pages was extracted in such a way that anchors belonging to the pruned list of Wikipedia pages were replaced (using developed toolkit) with their Wikipedia page ID (the redirects were also handled), and for other anchors, their surface form was substituted. We merged the plain text of all pages in a single text file in which each line is a clean text of a Wikipedia page. This dataset contains 2.1B tokens.

ConVec: The Wikipedia dataset obtained as a result of previous steps was used for training a Skip-gram model [10] with negative sampling instead of hierarchical softmax. We called this approach ConVec. The Skip-gram model is a type of Artificial Neural Network, which contains three layers: input, projection, and output. Each word in the dataset is inputted to this network, and the output is a prediction of the surrounding words within a fixed window size. We used a window size of 10 because we been able to get higher accuracy based on this window size. Skip-gram has been shown to give a better result in comparison to the Bag of Words (CBOW) model [10]. CBOW gets the surrounding words of a word and tries to predict the word (the reverse of the Skip-gram model).

As a result of running the Skip-gram model on the Wikipedia dataset, we got 3,274,884 unique word embeddings, of which 1,707,205 are Wikipedia concepts. Words and Anchors with a frequency of appearance in Wikipedia pages less than five are not considered. The procedure of training both words and concepts in the same time, results in that concepts and words belonging to the same vector space. This feature enables not only finding similar concepts to a concept but also finding similar words to that concept.

ConVec Fine-Tuned: In image processing approaches, it is customary to fine-tune the weights of a neural network with pre-trained vectors over a large dataset. Fine-tuning is the task of initializing the weights of the network by pre-trained vectors instead of random initialization. We tried to investigate the impact of fine-tuning the weights for textual datasets as well. In this case, we tried to fine-tune the vectors with GloVe 6B dataset trained on Wikipedia and Gigaword datasets [13]. The weights of the skip-gram model initialized with GloVe 6B pre-trained word vectors and then the training continued with the Wikipedia dataset prepared in the previous step. We called the concept vectors trained based on this method ConVec Fine-Tuned.

ConVec Heuristic: We hypothesize that the quality of concept vectors can improve with the size of training data. The sample data is the anchor text inside each Wikipedia page. Based on this assumption, we experimented with a heuristic to increase the number of anchor texts in each Wikipedia page. It is a Wikipedia policy that there is no self-link (anchor) in a page. It means that no page links to itself. On the other hand, it is common that the title of the page is repeated inside the page. The heuristic is to convert all exact mentions of the title of a Wikipedia page to anchor text with a link to that page. By using this heuristic, 18,301,475 new anchors were added to the Wikipedia dataset. This method is called ConVec Heuristic.

ConVec Only-Anchors: The other experiment is to study the importance and role of the not anchored words in Wikipedia pages in improving the quality of phrase embeddings. In that case, all the text in a page, except anchor texts were removed and then the same Skip-gram model with negative sampling and the window size of 10 is used to learn phrase embeddings. This approach (ConVec Only-Anchors) is similar to ConVec except that the corpus only contains anchor texts.

An approach called Doc2Vec was introduced by Mikolov et al. [8] for Document embedding. In this embedding, the vector representation is for the entire document instead of a single term or a phrase. Based on the vector embeddings of two documents, one can check their similarity by comparing their vector similarity (e.g. using Cosine distance). We tried to embed a whole Wikipedia page (concept) with its content using Doc2Vec and then consider the resulting vector as the concept vector. The results of this experiment were far worse than the other approaches so we decided not to compare it with other methods. The reason is mostly related to the length of Wikipedia pages. As the size of a document increases, the Doc2Vec approach for document embedding results in a lower performance.

4 Evaluation

Phrase Analogy and Phrase Similarity tasks are used to evaluate the different embedding of Wikipedia concepts. In the following, detailed results of this comparison are provided.

Phrase Analogy Task: To evaluate the quality of the concept vectors, we used the phrase analogy dataset in [10] which contains 3,218 questions. The Phrase analogy task involves questions like "*Word1* is to *Word2* as *Word3* is to *Word4*". The last word (Word4) is the missing word. Each approach is allowed to suggest the one and only one word for the missing word (Word4). The accuracy is calculated based on the number of correct answers. In word embedding the answer is finding the closest word vector to the Eq. 1. V is the vector representation of the corresponding Word.

$$V_{Word2} - V_{Word1} + V_{Word3} = V_{Word4} \tag{1}$$

V is the vector representation of the corresponding Word. The cosine similarity is used for majoring the similarity between vectors on each side of the above equation.

In order to calculate the accuracy in the Phrase Analogy, all four words of a question should be present in the dataset. If a word is missing from a question, the question is not included in the accuracy calculation. Based on this assumption, the accuracy is calculated using Eq. 2.

$$Accuracy = \frac{\#CorrectAnswers}{\#QuestionsWithPhrasesInsideApproachVectorsList} \tag{2}$$

Table 2. Comparing the results of three different versions of ConVec (trained on Wikipedia 2.1B tokens) with Google Freebase pre-trained vectors over the Google-100B-tokens news dataset in the Phrase Analogy task. The Accuracy (All) shows the coverage and performance of each approach for answering questions. The accuracy for common questions (Accuracy (Commons)) is for fair comparison of each approach. #phrases shows the number of top frequent words of each approach that are used to calculate the accuracy. #found is the number of questions where all 4 words are present in the approach dictionary.

Embedding name	#phrases	Accuracy (All)		Accuracy (Commons)	
		#found	Accuracy	#found	Accuracy
Google Freebase	Top 30,000	1048	55.7%	89	52.8%
	Top 300,000	1536	47.0%	800	48.5%
	Top 3,000,000	1838	42.1%	1203	42.7%
ConVec	Top 30,000	202	81.7%	89	82.0%
	Top 300,000	1702	68.0%	800	72.1%
	Top 3,000,000	2238	56.4%	1203	61.1%
ConVec (Fine-Tuned)	Top 30,000	202	80.7%	89	79.8%
	Top 300,000	1702	68.3%	800	73.0%
	Top 3,000,000	2238	56.8%	1203	63.6%
ConVec (Heuristic)	Top 30,000	242	81.4%	89	80.9%
	Top 300,000	1804	65.6%	800	68.9%
	Top 3,000,000	2960	46.6%	1203	58.7%

We compared the quality of three different versions of ConVec with Google Freebase[3] phrase vectors pre-trained over the Google-100B-token news dataset. The Skip-gram model with negative sampling is used to train the vectors in Google Freebase. The vectors in this dataset have 1000 dimensions in length. For preparing the embedding for phrases, the authors used a statistical approach to find words that appear more together than separately and then considered them as a single token. In the next step, they replaced these tokens with their corresponding freebase ID. Freebase is a knowledge base containing millions of entities and concepts, mostly extracted from Wikipedia pages.

In order to have a fair comparison, we reported the accuracy of each approach in two ways in Table 2. The first accuracy is to compare the coverage and performance of each approach over all the questions in the test dataset (Accuracy All). Based on the training corpus and the frequency of each word vector inside the corpus, each approach is able to answer a different subset of questions from the list of all questions inside the phrase analogy dataset. An approach can answer a question if all four words of a question are present in the dataset. For example, the ConVec base model is able to answer 2,328 questions out of 3,218 questions of the phrase analogy dataset for the top 3,000,000 phrases. The

[3] https://code.google.com/archive/p/word2vec.

second accuracy is to compare the methods over only common questions (Accuracy commons). Common questions are the subset of questions where all four approaches in Table 2 are able to answer them.

Each approach tries to answer as much as possible the 3,218 questions inside the Phrase Analogy dataset in *Accuracy-for-All* scenario. For the top 30,000 frequent phrases, Google Freebase was able to answer more questions, but for the top 3,000,000 frequent phrases ConVec was able to answer more questions with higher accuracy. Fine-tuning of the vectors does not have impact on the coverage of ConVec; this is why the #found is similar to the base model. We used the Wikipedia ID of a page instead of its surface name. The heuristic version of ConVec has more coverage to answering questions in comparison with the base ConVec model. The accuracy of the heuristic ConVec is somehow similar to the base ConVec for the top 300,000 phrases, but it will drop down for the top 3,000,000. It seems that this approach is efficient to increase the coverage without significantly sacrificing the accuracy, but probably it needs to be more conservative by adding more regulations and restrictions in the process of adding new anchor texts.

Only common questions between each method are used to compare the *Accuracy-for-Commons* scenario. The results in the last column of Table 2 show that the fine-tuning of vectors does not have a significant impact on the quality of the vectors embedding. The result of the ConVec Heuristic for the common questions, argues that this heuristic does not have a significant impact on the quality of the base ConVec model and it just improved the coverage (added more concepts to the list of concept vectors). The most important message of the third column of Table 2 is that even a very small dataset (Wikipedia 2.1 B tokens) can produce good vectors embedding in comparison with the Google freebase dataset (100B tokens) and consequently, the quality of the training corpus is more important than its size.

Phrase Similarity Task: The next experiment is evaluating vector quality in the Phrase similarity datasets (Check Table 3). In these datasets, each row consists of two words with their relatedness assigned by a human. The Spearman's correlation is used for comparing the result of different approaches with the human evaluated results. These datasets contain words and not the Wikipedia concepts. We replaced all the words in these datasets with their corresponding Wikipedia pages if their surface form and the Wikipedia concept match. We used the simple but effective most frequent sense disambiguation method to disambiguate words that may correspond to several Wikipedia concepts. This method of assigning words to concepts is not error prone but this error is considered for all approaches.

Wikipedia Miner [12] is a well-known approach to find the similarity between two Wikipedia pages based on their input and output links. Results show that our approach for learning concepts embedding can embed the Wikipedia link structure properly since its results are similar to the structural based similarity approach of Wikipedia Miner (See Table 3). The average correlation for the heuristic based approach is less than the other approaches, but the average of

Table 3. Comparing the results in Phrase Similarity dataset. Rho is Spearman's correlation to the human evaluators. !Found is the number of pairs not found in each approach dataset. The average scores are weighted average score of the approach for each of the datasets. The weights are number of found pairs for each dataset.

Datasets		Wikipedia Miner		Google Freebase		ConVec		ConVec (Heuristic)	
# Dataset Name	#Pairs	!Found	Rho	!Found	Rho	!Found	Rho	!Found	Rho
1 WS-REL [4]	251	114	0.6564	87	0.3227	104	0.5594	57	0.5566
2 SIMLEX [6]	961	513	0.2166	369	0.1159	504	0.3406	357	0.2152
3 WS-SIM [4]	200	83	0.7505	58	0.4646	81	0.7524	41	0.6101
4 RW [9]	1182	874	0.2714	959	0.1777	753	0.2678	469	0.2161
5 WS-ALL [4]	349	142	0.6567	116	0.4071	136	0.6348	74	0.5945
6 RG [15]	62	35	0.7922	14	0.3188	36	0.6411	25	0.5894
7 MC [11]	28	15	0.7675	9	0.3336	16	0.2727	12	0.4706
8 MTurk [5]	283	155	0.6558	123	0.5132	128	0.5591	52	0.5337
- Average	414	241	0.4402	217	0.2693	219	0.4391	136	0.3612

Table 4. Comparing the results in the Phrase Similarity datasets for the common entries between all approaches. Rho is Spearmans's correlation.

Datasets			Wikipedia miner	HitSim	ConVec	ConVec (Heuristic)	ConVec (Only anchors)
#	Dataset name	#Pairs	Rho	Rho	Rho	Rho	Rho
1	WS-REL	130	0.6662	0.5330	0.6022	0.6193	0.6515
2	SIMLEX	406	0.2405	0.3221	0.3011	0.3087	0.2503
3	WS-MAN [4]	224	0.6762	0.6854	0.6331	0.6371	0.6554
4	WS-411 [4]	314	0.7311	0.7131	0.7126	0.7136	0.7308
5	WS-SIM	108	0.7538	0.6968	0.7492	0.7527	0.7596
6	RWD	268	0.3072	0.2906	0.1989	0.1864	0.1443
7	WS-ALL	192	0.6656	0.6290	0.6372	0.6482	0.6733
8	RG	20	0.7654	0.7805	0.6647	0.7338	0.6301
9	MC	9	0.3667	0.5667	0.2667	0.2167	0.2833
10	MTurk	122	0.6627	0.5175	0.6438	0.6453	0.6432
-	Average	179	0.5333	0.5216	0.5114	0.5152	0.5054

not-found entries in this approach is much less than in the others. It shows that using the heuristic can increase the coverage of the Wikipedia concepts.

To have a fair comparison between different approaches, we extracted all common entries of all datasets and then re-calculated the correlation (Table 4). We also compared the results with another structural based similarity approach called HitSim [16]. The comparable result of our approach to structural based methods is another proof that we could embed the Wikipedia link structure properly. The result of the heuristic based approach is slightly better than our base model. This shows that without sacrificing the accuracy, we could increase the coverage. This means that with the proposed heuristic, we have a vector representation of more Wikipedia pages.

Results for the only anchors version of ConVec (see the last column of Table 4) show that in some datasets this approach is better than other approaches, but the average result is less than the other approaches. This shows it is better to learn Wikipedia's concepts vector in the context of other words (words that are not anchored) and as a result to have the same vector space for both concepts and words.

5 Conclusion

In this paper, several approaches for embedding Wikipedia concepts are introduced. We demonstrated the higher importance of the quality of the corpus than its quantity (size) and argued the idea of the larger corpus will not always lead to better word embedding. Although the proposed approaches only use inter Wikipedia links (anchors), they have a performance as good as or even higher than the state of the arts approaches for Concept Analogy and Concept Similarity tasks. Contrary to word embedding, Wikipedia concepts embedding is not ambiguous, so there is a different vector for concepts with similar surface forms but different mentions. This feature is important for many NLP tasks such as Named Entity Recognition, Text Similarity, and Document Clustering or Classification. In the future, we plan to use multiple resources such as Infoboxes, multilingual version of a Wikipedia page, Categories and syntactical features of a page to improve the quality of Wikipedia concepts embedding.

A Appendix: Python Libraries

The following libraries are used to extract and prepare the Wikipedia corpus:

- Wikiextractor: www.github.com/attardi/wikiextractor
- Mwparserfromhell: www.github.com/earwig/mwparserfromhell
- Wikipedia 1.4.0: www.pypi.python.org/pypi/wikipedia

The following libraries are used for Word2Vec and Doc2Vec implementation and evaluation:

- Gensim: www.pypi.python.org/pypi/gensim
- Eval-word-vectors [2]: www.github.com/mfaruqui/eval-word-vectors

B Appendix: Pruning Wikipedia Pages

List of rules that are used to prune useless pages from Wikipedia corpus:

- Having <ns0:redirect>tag in their XML file.
- There is ‘Category:’ in the first part of age name.

- There is 'File:' in the first part of page name.
- There is 'Template:' in the first part of page name.
- Anchors having '(disambiguation)' in their page name. Anchors having 'may refer to:' or 'may also refer to' in their text file.
- There is 'Portal:' in the first part of page name.
- There is 'Draft:' in the first part of page name.
- There is 'MediaWiki:' in the first part of page name.
- There is 'List of' in the first part of the page name.
- There is 'Wikipedia:' in the first part of page name.
- There is 'TimedText:' in the first part of page name.
- There is 'Help:' in the first part of page name.
- There is 'Book:' in the first part of page name.
- There is 'Module:' in the first part of page name.
- There is 'Topic:' in the first part of page name.

References

1. Cao, S., Lu, W., Xu, Q.: Deep neural networks for learning graph representations. In: Proceedings of the Thirtieth AAAI Conference on Artificial Intelligence, pp. 1145–1152. AAAI Press (2016)
2. Faruqui, M., Dyer, C.: Community evaluation and exchange of word vectors at wordvectors.org. In: Proceedings of ACL: System Demonstrations (2014)
3. Faruqui, M., Dyer, C.: Improving vector space word representations using multilingual correlation. In: Association for Computational Linguistics (2014)
4. Finkelstein, L., Gabrilovich, E., Matias, Y., Rivlin, E., Solan, Z., Wolfman, G., Ruppin, E.: Placing search in context: the concept revisited. In: Proceedings of the 10th International Conference on World Wide Web, WWW 2001, pp. 406–414. ACM, New York (2001)
5. Halawi, G., Dror, G., Gabrilovich, E., Koren, Y.: Large-scale learning of word relatedness with constraints. In: Proceedings of the 18th ACM SIGKDD International Conference on Knowledge Discovery and Data Mining, pp. 1406–1414. ACM (2012)
6. Hill, F., Reichart, R., Korhonen, A.: Simlex-999: evaluating semantic models with (genuine) similarity estimation. Comput. Linguist. **41**, 665–695 (2016)
7. Kleinberg, J.M.: Authoritative sources in a hyperlinked environment. J. ACM (JACM) **46**(5), 604–632 (1999)
8. Le, Q.V., Mikolov, T.: Distributed representations of sentences and documents. In: ICML, vol. 14, pp. 1188–1196 (2014)
9. Luong, T., Socher, R., Manning, C.D.: Better word representations with recursive neural networks for morphology. In: CoNLL, pp. 104–113 (2013)
10. Mikolov, T., Sutskever, I., Chen, K., Corrado, G.S., Dean, J.: Distributed representations of words and phrases and their compositionality. In: Advances in Neural Information Processing Systems, pp. 3111–3119 (2013)
11. Miller, G.A., Charles, W.G.: Contextual correlates of semantic similarity. Lang. Cogn. Process. **6**(1), 1–28 (1991)
12. Milne, D., Witten, I.H.: An open-source toolkit for mining Wikipedia. J. Artif. Intell. **194**, 222–239 (2013). Elsevier
13. Pennington, J., Socher, R., Manning, C.D.: Glove: global vectors for word representation. In: EMNLP, vol. 14, pp. 1532–1543 (2014)

14. Perozzi, B., Al-Rfou, R., Skiena, S.: DeepWalk: online learning of social representations. In: Proceedings of the 20th ACM SIGKDD International Conference on Knowledge Discovery and Data Mining, pp. 701–710. ACM (2014)
15. Radovanović, M., Nanopoulos, A., Ivanović, M.: Hubs in space: popular nearest neighbors in high-dimensional data. J. Mach. Learn. Res. **11**, 2487–2531 (2010)
16. Sajadi, A., Milios, E.E., Kešelj, V., Janssen, J.C.M.: Domain-specific semantic relatedness from wikipedia structure: a case study in biomedical text. In: Gelbukh, A. (ed.) CICLing 2015. LNCS, vol. 9041, pp. 347–360. Springer, Cham (2015). doi:10.1007/978-3-319-18111-0_26
17. Tsai, C.-T., Roth, D.: Cross-lingual wikification using multilingual embeddings. In: Proceedings of NAACL-HLT, pp. 589–598 (2016)
18. Camacho-Collados, J., Pilehvar, M.T., Navigli, R.: Nasari: integrating explicit knowledge and corpus statistics for a multilingual representation of concepts and entities. J. Artif. Intell. **2240**, 36–64. Elsevier (2016)

TEKNO: Preparing Legacy Technical Documents for Semantic Information Systems

Sebastian Furth[1(✉)], Maximilian Schirm[1,2], Volker Belli[1], and Joachim Baumeister[1,2]

[1] denkbares GmbH, Friedrich-Bergius-Ring 15, 97076 Würzburg, Germany
{sf,ms,vb,jb}@denkbares.com

[2] Institute of Computer Science, University of Würzburg, Am Hubland, 97074 Würzburg, Germany

Abstract. Today, service information for technical devices (machines, plants, factories) is stored in large information systems. In case of a problem-situation with the artefact, usually a service technician needs these systems to access relevant information resources in a precise and quick manner. However, semantic information systems demand the resources to be semantically prepared. For new resources, semantic descriptions can be easily created during the authoring process. However, the efficient semantification of legacy documentation is practically unsolved. This paper presents a semi-automated approach to the semantic preparation of legacy documentation in the technical domain. The knowledge-intensive method implements the document structure recovery process that is necessary for a further semantic integration into the system. We claim that the approach is simple and intuitive but yields sufficient results.

Keywords: Document structure recovery · Semantic information systems · Technical documentation

1 Introduction

Semantic information systems in the technical domain proved to be industrially successful in the past years. The meta-data of the information resources are represented by ontologies, thus facilitating better search, navigation, and composition of information resources [3]. In industry, there typically exist large corpora of legacy documentation mostly stored as PDF documents. Obviously, a standard PDF document is not suitable for the integration into a semantic information system, since the partitioning of information resources and the availability of describing meta-data is typically not existent – we call this situation the *legacy gap*. For the integration into a (semantic) information system the transformation of legacy data into a more meaningful format becomes necessary. Such a format has to describe (1) atomic information units and (2) semantic annotations (representing the topic/subject). In this paper, we introduce a knowledge-intensive

F. Frasincar et al. (Eds.): NLDB 2017, LNCS 10260, pp. 429–434, 2017.
DOI: 10.1007/978-3-319-59569-6_51

approach to recover information units from legacy technical documentation. For a thorough description of the subsequent semantic annotation of recovered information units please refer to previous work [2].

We first will refine the general document structure recovery process for technical documentation in Sect. 2. Here, we introduce set-covering models as a classic knowledge representation for handling uncertain classification knowledge and we show the application of this representation to the structure recovery process. A case study and a practical implementation demonstrate the applicability of the approach in Sect. 3. The paper is concluded in Sect. 4.

2 Structure Recovery for Technical Documents

2.1 Methodology and Distinction

Multiple prior works surveyed the topic of document structure recovery (mainly on scientific articles), for example see Mao et al. [6]. While the basic methodology of (1) identifying contiguous text blocks, (2) classifying these text blocks and (3) 'post-processing' these classified text blocks is similar, the presented approach introduces novel aspects that especially improve the recovery of structures in technical documents. Formally defined: Given a document first find contiguous blocks of text b, such that document $D = \cup b$; then, for each contiguous block of text $b \in D$ find a logical class C that correctly represents its semantics. Similar to scientific articles technical documentation usually follows special (corporate) style guides. In contrast to scholarly works, however, the number of classification targets, is much higher; around 40 [5] in scholarly texts versus more than 400 structures [9] in technical documents. This induces higher error susceptibility and semantic ambiguity. Another shortcoming of existing solutions (based on rules or machine learning algorithms) is that they can be hardly applied by domain experts/technical writers. Thus, the application of existing approaches for structure recovery is in most cases not practically applicable for technical documents. Therefore, the presented approach adapts the idea of exploiting formatting information but operates on a knowledge representation that (a) appears more natural for domain experts and (b) is more flexible with respect to inconsistencies and similarities of and between document structures, see Sect. 2.2.

2.2 Knowledge Representation

Document Structure Ontology. The goal of the presented approach is the decomposition of a document into its logical structures for the subsequent use in semantic information systems. Hence, the fundamental knowledge representation is an ontology describing structures that might occur in technical documents and relations between these structures. Document structures that shall be recognized during the recovery process are modeled as classes, which are instantiated for concrete text blocks after the classification process. The underlying idea of such ontologies is the description of structures that can occur in a certain relation with other structures in a document.

Excursus: Set-Covering Models. The presented approach uses Set-Covering Models [1,7] to explicitly represent syntactic knowledge about the document structure. In the following we give a brief introduction into the key concepts, for more details we refer to the original works. In contrast to rules, Set-Covering Models allow for an independent modeling and the inherently support of uncertainty. The key idea of set-covering models is the definition of set-covering relations of the following form:

Definition 1. *If a class is assigned, then the parameters (attributes)* $A_1, ..., A_n$ *are usually observed with corresponding values* $v_1, ..., v_n$.

A set covering relation is formally defined as $r = C \rightarrow A : v$ where $A : v$ denotes a feature and C a target class. In this paper a target class is derived from an ontology describing document structures (see Sect. 2.2). A single set-covering relation expresses that a class covers a feature.

In the following we give some basic definitions. We define Ω_C as the universal set of all classes. The universe of all possible parameters (attributes) is defined as set Ω_A where each parameter A has a range of values $dom(A)$. The universe of all possible values is defined by $\Omega_V = \cup_{A \in \Omega_A} dom(A)$. From the universe of all parameters and all values we define the set of all features as $\Omega_F = \{A : v \,|\, A \in \Omega_A, v \in dom(A)\}$. Then Ω_R denotes the universal set of all set-covering relations. A set-covering model is then defined as $R \subseteq \Omega_R$.

An observation is defined as a subset $\mathcal{F}_O \subset \Omega_F$ of all possible features. A subset $\mathcal{H} \subseteq \Omega_C$ of classes is defined as hypothesis. A hypothesis $\mathcal{H} = \{C_1, ..., C_n\}$ can be handled as a conjunction of classes $C_1 \wedge ... \wedge C_n$ which shall explain the given observation $\mathcal{F}_O$. During the classification the goal is to find the best matching hypothesis $\mathcal{H}$ that explains all observed features. A hypothesis $\mathcal{H}$ explains all observed features, if all features are covered by at least one class $C \in \mathcal{H}$.

Quality measures are employed for the evaluation of a hypothesis. These quality measures are functions that compute the difference between the observed features $\mathcal{F}_O$ and expected features $\mathcal{F}_{\mathcal{H}} = \cup_{C \in \mathcal{H}} \mathcal{F}_C$, where $\mathcal{F}_C$ corresponds to the features of class C.

Textual Parameters for Set-Covering Models (Classifying Style Sheets). In the specific implementation of set-covering models for the classification of text blocks the universal set of all classes Ω_C corresponds to the set of structures that shall be recovered from a legacy document, e.g. section headers on different levels, paragraphs, and many more. The universes of all possible parameters Ω_A and associated values Ω_V correspond to features of text blocks and their value ranges respectively. These features can consider different aspects of the text, e.g. alignment (left, middle, right) font and formatting information (font name, bold, italics etc.), statistical features (density, frequencies etc.) or the text itself. In this context, a set-covering relation is defined as a relation between a document structure (e.g. section header) and a textual feature (e.g. alignment) including its corresponding value (e.g. left). For a document structure typically multiple set-covering relations exist. We refer to the grouped set-covering relations for a single document structure as *Classifying Style Sheets* (in analogy to the well-known Cascading Style Sheets [4]).

2.3 Classification

Set-Covering-based Classification. Once the Classifying Style Sheets have been created, the subsequent classification of complete documents using set-covering models is very simple: Given a set of observed features, i.e., parameter-value pairs, a hypothesize-and-test strategy [8] is employed. Text blocks are classified as follows: First the textual parameters and values (observed features) are extracted from an unclassified text block. Then, a hypothesis is generated, i.e., a set of possibly matching classes. Given a set-covering model the covering degree between the observed features from the text block and the hypothesis is computed. Hypotheses with a covering degree exceeding a certain threshold are assigned as possible classes to the text block, i.e., in this phase a text block might have multiple classes assigned (ensuring a high recall).

A single class assignment for an individual text block is defined as triple $t = \{b, \mathcal{H}, q\}$ with the text block in focus b, the corresponding hypothesis $\mathcal{H}$ and a quality score q. For each individual text block multiple class assignments can exist, they are grouped in a set $g_b = \{t_1, ..., t_n\}$. All grouped class assignments define the classification result $\Gamma = \{g_{b_1}, ..., g_{b_m}\}$.

Class Disambiguation (Ontology-Based Optimization of Global Coherence). A classification Γ is assumed to have a high recall but might contain multiple class assignments for single text blocks, due to the uncertainty considerations that where integrated in the underlying set-covering model. We compute a globally optimized classification result Γ^* being a classification result $\Gamma^{'}$ with a single class assignment t for each text block b by solving the following equation:

$$\Gamma^* = argmax\ \Gamma^{'} \sum_{g_b}[\phi(t) + \theta(\Gamma^{'})]$$

Where $\phi(\cdot)$ denotes a local optimization function for a class assignment of a text block and function $\theta(\cdot)$ ensuring that the document structure constraints are not violated for a classification result $\Gamma^{'}$, i.e., by computing a bonus or penalty on basis of the information contained in the document structure ontology.

3 Implementation Remarks and Case Study

Although Classifying Style Sheets are assumed to have a catchy knowledge representation, their creation remains a cumbersome task when operating without tool support. We therefore created the visual knowledge acquisition tool TEKNO[1]

[1] TEKNO: TEchnical KNowledge Ontology.

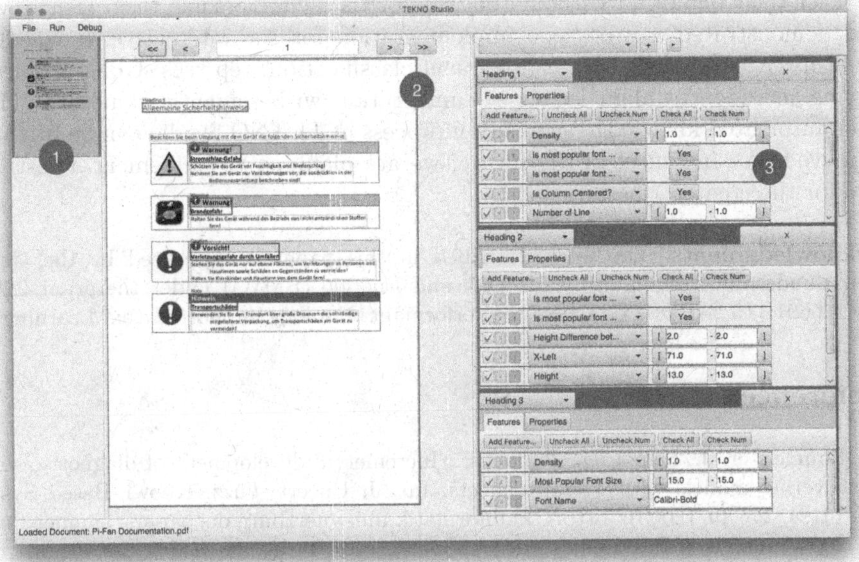

Fig. 1. TEKNO Studio: tool support for interactive knowledge acquisition

Studio. TEKNO Studio (see Fig. 1) consists of three fundamental views, a sidebar (1–1) with thumbnails of considered documents, the main view (1–2) for the selection of text blocks and the model view (1–3) for creating, modifying or deleting Classifying Style Sheets and associated set-covering relations. We successfully applied the TEKNO approach and the knowledge acquisition tool TEKNO Studio in several industrial projects. However, the underlying corpora of technical documentation are not publicly available and can not be published. Therefore, we also evaluated the approach against a PDF version of the "Pi-Fan" data set [10]. The Pi-Fan corpus comprises multilingual technical documentation for fictive table fans and has been created for benchmarking content management and content delivery systems. In the training phase we created classifying style sheets for the most important structures with 7 covering relations on average. We classified single text blocks using the classifying style sheets created during the training phase and achieved 95,52% precision and 83,11% recall.

4 Conclusion

Structure recovery is one of the fundamental steps in a semantics-aware information environment. In this paper we introduced a novel approach to the semi-automated structure recovery of technical documents. The approach is based on set-covering models that we have adapted to the special needs of the structure recovery problem of technical documents. The employed set-covering models are an intuitive knowledge representation for building annotation systems, however their definition without tool support is a cumbersome task. Hence, we also demonstrated a prototype implementation for the interactive knowledge acquisition. We showed how a subsequent classification step uses strong-problem solving methods to align legacy documentation with semantic structure. The semi-automated knowledge acquisition process in TEKNO Studio can be further improved. For instance, in the future, we are planning to implement a testing tool for the created classifications.

Acknowledgments. The work described in this paper is supported by the German Bundesministerium für Wirtschaft und Energie (BMWi) under the grant ZIM ZF4170601BZ5 "APOSTL: Accessible Performant Ontology Supported Text Learning".

References

1. Baumeister, J., Seipel, D., Puppe, F.: Incremental development of diagnostic set-covering models with therapy effects. Int. J. Uncert. Fuzz. Knowl.-Based Syst. **11**(2), 25–49 (2003). http://ki.informatik.uni-wuerzburg.de/papers/baumeister/2003-baumeister-SCM-ijufks.pdf
2. Furth, S., Baumeister, J.: Semantification of Large Corpora of Technical Documentation. IGI Global (2016). http://www.igi-global.com/book/enterprise-big-data-engineering-analytics/145468
3. Guha, R., McCool, R., Miller, E.: Semantic search. In: Proceedings of the 12th International Conference on World Wide Web, pp. 700–709. ACM (2003)
4. Lie, H.W., Bos, B., Lilley, C., Jacobs, I.: Cascading style sheets. WWW Consortium, September 1996 (2005)
5. Luong, M.T., Nguyen, T.D., Kan, M.Y.: Logical structure recovery in scholarly articles with rich document features. In: Multimedia Storage and Retrieval Innovations for Digital Library Systems, vol. 270 (2012)
6. Mao, S., Rosenfeld, A., Kanungo, T.: Document structure analysis algorithms: a literature survey. In: Electronic Imaging 2003, pp. 197–207. International Society for Optics and Photonics (2003)
7. Reggia, J.: Computer-assisted medical decision making. In: Schwartz (ed.) Applications of Computers in Medicine, pp. 198–213. IEEE (1982)
8. Schreiber, G., Akkermans, H., Anjewierden, A., de Hoog, R., Shadbolt, N., de Velde, W.V., Wielinga, B.: Knowledge Engineering and Management - The CommonKADS Methodology, 2nd edn. MIT Press, Cambridge (2001)
9. Walsh, N., Muellner, L.: DocBook: The Definitive Guide, vol. 1. O'Reilly Media Inc., Sebastopol (1999)
10. Ziegler, W.: Content Management und Content Delivery. Powered by PI-Class. Tagungsband zur tekom Jahrestagung (2015)

Improving Document Classification Effectiveness Using Knowledge Exploited by Ontologies

Zenun Kastrati(✉) and Sule Yildirim Yayilgan

Information Technology and Electrical Engineering,
Norwegian University of Technology and Science, Gjøvik, Norway
{zenun.kastrati,sule.yayilgan}@ntnu.no

Abstract. In this paper, we propose a new document classification model which utilizes background knowledge gathered by ontologies for document representation. A document is represented using a set of ontology concepts that are acquired by exact matching technique and through identification and extraction of new terms which can be semantically related to these concepts. In addition, a new concept weighting scheme composed of concept relevance and importance is employed by the model to compute weight of concepts. We conducted experiments to test the model and the obtained results showed that a considerable improvement of classification performance is achieved by using our proposed model.

Keywords: Document classification · Domain ontologies · SEMCON · iCVS

1 Introduction

Ontology-based document classification utilizes ontologies as a means to exploit content meaning of documents which are typically represented as vectors of features. These vectors are composed of concepts acquired from ontologies, and concepts weight indicated by frequency of occurrences of the concept in the document. Concepts gathered from an ontology are associated with a document using an exact matching technique. The idea behind this technique is searching only concept labels that explicitly occur in a document.

Background knowledge exploited by ontologies is extensively used for enriching documents representation with semantics, particularly documents from medical domain. The work presented by Camous et al. [1] is an example where Medical Subject Headings (MeSH) ontology is used to enrich with semantics the existing MeSH based representation of documents. New concepts are identified and acquired in documents using semantic similarity measure computed by counting number of relations between concepts in the MeSH hierarchy. The authors in [2] presented a similar approach to Camous et al. but they employed a different measure, namely content based cosine similarity measure for extraction of the domain concepts. Sy et al. [3] presented another similar approach and they developed an ontology-based system called OBIRS to enrich document representation with semantics using MeSH ontology.

F. Frasincar et al. (Eds.): NLDB 2017, LNCS 10260, pp. 435–438, 2017.
DOI: 10.1007/978-3-319-59569-6_52

Even though the existing approaches use background knowledge derived by ontologies for enriching document representation, they however have some drawbacks. Firstly, they focus on searching only the presence of concept labels thereby limiting the capability of capturing and exploiting the whole conceptualization involved in user information and content meaning. Secondly, the concept weight is computed by considering only the concept relevance and does not take into account the importance of the concept.

These drawbacks are addressed in this paper by proposing a new document classification model supervised by domain ontologies. The proposed model relies on background knowledge derived by domain ontologies for document representation. It associates the document with a set of concepts using the exact matching technique and also through identification and acquiring new terms which can be semantically related to the concepts of ontologies. We achieve this by employing SEMCON [4], which is an objective metric developed for enriching domain ontologies with new concepts by combining context and semantic of terms occurring in a document. Weight of concepts are computed using concept weighting technique described in [5]. This weighting technique computes the weight of a concept using both, the relevance and the importance of the concept.

The model is tested running experiments on a real ontology and a data set and the results achieved by experiments show that the classification performance is improved using our proposed model.

2 Proposed Classification Model

The proposed model presented in this paper is a supervised learning model and it utilizes background knowledge exploited by ontologies as a means for enriching document representation. The model, illustrated in Fig. 1, consists of two phases: training and testing.

The training phase departs from a set of documents which are labelled manually into appropriate categories by an expert of the domain. These documents are simply represented as plain text and there is no semantics associated with them at this point.

Next step of the training phase is incorporation of semantics into documents. The semantics is embedded using the matching technique which relies on matching the terms in the document with the relevant concepts in the domain ontology. Term to concept mapping is achieved using SEMCON metric. It maps a term to a concept by the exact matching which searches only the concepts (concept labels) that explicitly occur in a document, and through identification and extraction of semantically associated terms.

The exact matching performed by SEMCON is a straightforward process. There maybe single label concepts, i.e. *grant*, in a domain ontology as well as compound label concepts i.e. *project_funding*. To acquire single label concepts, SEMCON searches only those terms from the document for which an exact term exists in the ontology, while to acquire compound label concepts, it searches those terms in the document which are present as part of a concept in the ontology.

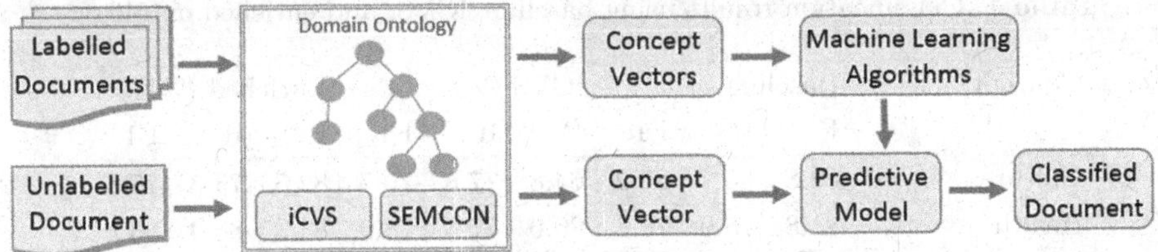

Fig. 1. Proposed classification model

Identification and extraction of new terms that are related with the concepts of the domain ontology is a more complex process accomplished by SEMCON than the exact matching. To achieve this, it primarily computes an observation matrix which is composed of three statistical features, namely, term frequency, term font type, and term font size. Observation matrix is then used as input to derive the contextual information computed by using the cosine measure. In addition to the contextual information, SEMCON embeds the semantics by computing a WordNet based semantic similarity score.

Once we embed the semantics into documents, we then build the category semantics by aggregating the semantics of all documents which belong to the same category. By doing this, the classification system can replicate the way an expert categorizes the documents into appropriate categories. This way, each category is represented as a vector composed of two components: concepts of the domain ontology and concepts weights.

Concept weight is computed using the concept weighting technique described in [5]. This technique defines the weight of a concept as the quantity of information given by the presence of that concept in a document and it is computed by the relevance of the concept and the importance of the concept. Relevance of a concept is defined by the number of occurrences of that concept in the document, while concept importance is defined as the number of relations a concept has to other concepts and it is computed using one of the Markov-based algorithms employed into the ontology graph.

The final step of the training phase is to employ one of the machine learning algorithms to train the classifier and to create a predictive model which can be used for classifying a new unlabelled document into an appropriate category.

The testing phase of the model deals with new unlabelled documents. Each document that has to be classified is primarily represented as a concept vector. Such representation of the document is done by using the same steps described above in the training phase. Finally, a document goes through the predictive model built by the machine learning algorithms and it is being classified into the appropriate category.

To demonstrate the applicability of our proposed model we conducted experiments using three different scenarios: (1) baseline ontology, (2) improved concept vector space model (iCVS), and (3) enriched ontology. Decision Tree is used as a classifier and the INFUSE dataset consisting of 467 documents is used for training and testing the classifier. The result obtained for each category and the weighted average results of the dataset are shown in Table 1.

Table 1. Classification results using baseline, iCVS, and enriched ontology

Concept	Baseline (%)			iCVS (%)			Enriched (%)		
	P	R	F1	P	R	F1	P	R	F1
Culture	63.8	66.7	65.2	64.8	77.8	70.7	82.5	73.3	77.6
Health	81.8	75.0	78.3	80.0	77.8	78.9	83.3	83.3	83.3
Music	50.0	16.7	25.0	50.0	16.7	25.0	100	16.7	28.6
Society	62.0	75.6	68.1	69.8	73.2	71.4	71.1	92.7	80.9
Sportssociety	50.0	33.3	40.0	66.7	33.3	44.4	70.0	58.3	63.6
Weighted avg.	**66.1**	**66.4**	**65.5**	**69.1**	**70.0**	**68.8**	**79.2**	**77.9**	**76.7**

As can be seen from the results given in Table 1, an improvement of classification accuracy is achieved when it is performed using iCVS, and the enriched ontology, respectively. This improvement can be reflected by the F1 measure which is increased from 65.5% to 68.8% when iCVS is being employed. Moreover, a substantial improvement of classification performance, from 65.5% to 76.7%, is achieved using the enriched ontology.

3 Conclusion and Future Work

An ontology-based classification model for classifying text documents from the funding domain is presented in this paper. The model represents a document as a concept vector whose components are a set of ontology concepts acquired using SEMCON model, and concepts weights computed using an enhanced concept weighting scheme.

In future work we plan to test our model on larger datasets and ontologies.

References

1. Camous, F., Blott, S., Smeaton, A.F.: Ontology-based MEDLINE document classification. In: Hochreiter, S., Wagner, R. (eds.) BIRD 2007. LNCS, vol. 4414, pp. 439–452. Springer, Heidelberg (2007). doi:10.1007/978-3-540-71233-6_34
2. Dinh, D., Tamine, L.: Biomedical concept extraction based on combining the content-based and word order similarities. In: ACM Symposium on Applied Computing, pp. 1159–1163 (2011)
3. Sy, M.-F., Ranwez, S., Montmain, J., Regnault, A., Crampes, M., Ranwez, V.: User centered and ontology based information retrieval system for life sciences. BMC Bioinform. **13**(1) (2012)
4. Kastrati, Z., Imran, A., Yayilgan, S.: SEMCON - a semantic and contextual objective metric for enriching domain ontology concepts. Int. J. Semant. Web Inf. Syst. **12**(2), 1–24 (2016)
5. Kastrati, Z., Imran, A., Yayilgan, S.Y.: An improved concept vector space model for ontology based classification. In: 11th International Conference on Signal Image Technology & Internet Systems, pp. 240–245 (2015)

Text Summarization

Document Aboutness via Sophisticated Syntactic and Semantic Features

Marco Ponza(✉), Paolo Ferragina, and Francesco Piccinno

Dipartimento di Informatica, University of Pisa, Pisa, Italy
{marco.ponza,paolo.ferragina,francesco.piccinno}@di.unipi.it

Abstract. The *document aboutness* problem asks for creating a succinct representation of a document's subject matter via keywords, sentences or entities drawn from a Knowledge Base. In this paper we propose an approach to solve this problem which improves the known solutions over all known datasets [4,19]. It is based on a wide and detailed experimental study of syntactic and semantic features drawn from the input document thanks to the use of some IR/NLP tools. To encourage and support reproducible experimental results on this task, we will make accessible our system via a public API: this is the first, and best performing, tool publicly available for the document aboutness problem.

1 Introduction

In Information Retrieval (IR), *document aboutness* is the problem that asks for creating a succinct representation of a document's subject matter by detecting in its text *salient* keywords, named entities, concepts, snippets or sentences [12]. It is not surprising then that document aboutness is become a fundamental task on which several IR tools hing upon to improve their performance, such as contextual ads-matching systems [16], exploratory search [1], document similarity [5], classification, clustering and web search ranking [6].

The first solutions to the document aboutness problem were based on the extraction of salient *lexical elements* from the input text such as keywords, terms and sentences (aka *keyphrases*) by means of several heuristics [8,10]. But unfortunately the use of keyphrases showed four well-known limitations (e.g. see [7]): (i) their interpretation is left to the reader (aka, *interpretation errors*); (ii) words that appear frequently in the input text often induce the selection of not-salient keyphrases (aka, *over-generation errors*); (iii) infrequent keyphrases go undetected (aka, *infrequency errors*); and (iv) by working at a pure lexical level the keyphrase-based systems are unable to detect the semantic equivalence between two keyphrases (aka, *redundancy errors*).

Given these issues, some researchers [4,19] tried very recently to introduce some "semantics" into the aboutness representation of a document by taking

This work has been supported in part by the EU H2020 Program under the scheme "INFRAIA-1-2014-2015: Research Infrastructures" grant agreement #654024 "SoBigData: Social Mining & Big Data Ecosystem".

F. Frasincar et al. (Eds.): NLDB 2017, LNCS 10260, pp. 441–453, 2017.
DOI: 10.1007/978-3-319-59569-6_53

advantage of the advances in the design of entity annotators (see e.g. [21] and references therein). The idea is to represent the document aboutness via well-defined entities drawn from a Knowledge Base (e.g. Wikipedia, Wikidata, Freebase, etc.) which are unambiguous and, moreover, can exploit the structure of the graph underling those KBs in order to implement new extraction algorithms and more powerful document representations, such as the ones introduced in [11,18]. These approaches are called *entity-salience* extractors and their best implementations are given by the CMU-GOOGLE's system [4] and the SEL system [19].

The CMU-GOOGLE's system [4] uses a proprietary entity annotator to extract entities from the input text and a binary classifier based on very few simple features to distinguish between salient and non-salient entities. Authors of [4] have shown that their system significantly outperforms a trivial baseline model, via some experiments executed over the large and well known New York Times' dataset, and concluded that: *"There is likely significant room for improvement, [...]. Perhaps features more directly linked to Wikipedia, as in related work on keyword extraction, can provide more focused background information"*.

Last year Trani *et al.* [19] proposed the SEL system that hinges on a supervised two-step algorithm comprehensively addressing both entity linking (to Wikipedia's articles) and entity-salience scoring. The first step is based on a classifier aimed at identifying a set of candidate entities that are likely to be mentioned in the document, thus maximizing the precision without hindering its recall; the second step is based on a regression model that aims at choosing and scoring the candidate entities actually occurring in the document. Unfortunately SEL was compared only against *pure* entity annotators (such as the old TAGME, 2010), which are not designed for salience detection; moreover, their experiments were run only over a new dataset (i.e. Wikinews), much smaller than NYT, and dismissed a comparison against the CMU-GOOGLE's system.

The net result is that the literature offers two entity-salience solutions whose software are not available to the public and whose published performance are incomparable. In our paper we continue the study of the document aboutness problem and address the issues left open in the previous papers by proposing an entity-salience algorithm, called SWAT, that offers three main novelties: (i) it carefully orchestrates state-of-the-art tools, publicly available in IR and NLP literature, to extract several new features from the syntactic and the semantic elements of the input document; (ii) it builds a binary classifier based on those features that achieves improved micro and macro F1-performance over both available datasets, namely New York Times and Wikinews, thus showing that SWAT is the state-of-the art for the document aboutness problem via the first throughout comparison among all known systems; and (iii) it will be released to the scientific community (unlike [4] which deploys proprietary modules and unlike [19] which is not publicly available) thus allowing its use as a module of other IR tools or the reproduction of our experiments, possibly on other datasets.

Technically speaking, the algorithmic structure of SWAT is based on several novel features which are extracted from the input document by means of three main IR/NLP tools: (i) CoreNLP [9], the most well-known NLP framework to analyze the grammatical structure of sentences, that will be used to extract the morphological information coming from the dependency trees built over the sentences of the input document; (ii) Wat [15], one of the best publicly available entity annotators [21], that will be used to build an entity graph which differs in structure and use from the ones introduced in [4,19]; (iii) TextRank [10], the popular document summarizer which returns a powerful keyphrase score for each sentence of the input document. The final set of extracted features expands significantly the ones investigated in the previous papers [4,19], and leads a binary classifier to achieve improved detection performance of the salient entities present in the input document.

The performance of Swat will be assessed via a large experimental test executed over the two datasets mentioned above (i.e. NYT and Wikinews) and involving both the Cmu-Google's system and Sel, plus few other solutions that will allow us to dig into the contributions and specialties of the various features we introduce. This will constitute the second contribution of this paper which will offer, for the first time in the literature, a throughout comparison among the best known tools for the document aboutness problem.

This experimental comparison will show that Swat raises the known state-of-the-art performance in terms of F1 up to about 10% (absolute) over Cmu-Google's system and up to 5% (absolute) over Sel's system in either of the two experimented datasets. These results will be complemented with a throughout study of the contribution of each feature (old and new ones) and an evaluation of the performance of known systems in dealing with documents where salient information is not necessarily biased to the beginning. In this setting, we will show that the improvement of Swat wrt to Cmu-Google's system over the largest dataset NYT gets up to 9% in micro-F1.

In summary, the main contributions of the paper are the following ones:

- We design and implement Swat, an effective entity-salience system that identifies the aboutness of a document via novel algorithms that extract a rich set of syntactic (sentences' ranking, dependency trees, etc.), and semantic (computed via a new graph representation of entities and several centrality measures) features.
- We are the first ones to offer a thoughtful comparison among all known entity-salience systems (i.e. Swat, Sel and the Cmu-Google's system, plus several other baselines) over two available datasets: namely, New York Times (provided by [4]) and Wikinews (provided by [19]).
- This comparison shows that Swat improves the F1 performance of the Cmu-Google's system [4] and Sel [19] consistently over both datasets. Precisely the improvement is up to about 10% (absolute) over Cmu-Google's system and up to 5% (absolute) over Sel's system.
- These figures are accompanied by a thoughtful feature and error analysis showing that the new features are crucial to achieve those improved performance, they are flexible in detecting salient entities independently of their

position in the input document, and generalize better than other systems to new datasets when NYT is used for training.

- In order to encourage and support reproducible research, we release SWAT as a public API which actually implements the full annotation-and-salience pipeline thus allowing its easy plugging in other IR tools.

2 Related Work

Known solutions to document aboutness are based on two main algorithmic approaches: the first and classic one, known as keyphrase extraction [7], represents the aboutness of an input document via some of its lexical elements such as words labeled with specific POS-tags [8,10], n-grams [20], or words which belong to a fixed dictionary of terms [13] or identified as proper nouns [6]. The candidate keyphrases are then filtered via supervised or unsupervised approaches [6,13]. Limitations of this approach have been discussed in the previous Section.

The more recent and powerful approach, known as *entity salience*, captures the aboutness of an input document by its *semantic elements* represented via entities drawn from a KB, such as Freebase or Wikipedia. The detection of entities in texts is a well studied problem for which several effective solutions are known (see e.g. [21] and refs therein); on the other hand, the task of assigning a *salience score* to those entities is still in its infancy and just two solutions are known: the first one denoted as CMU-GOOGLE's system [4] is based on few simple features tested over the large and well known New York Times' dataset [17], and the second one denoted as SEL [19] deploys a more extended set of features tested just over the small Wikinews dataset.

Hence the literature offers two systems which have been not compared to each other, are not available to the public for reproducing their experimental results or for deploying them in other IR tools, and are incomparable in the published figures. SWAT and the large set of experiments performed in this paper will address those issues.

3 Our Proposal: Swat

SWAT is a novel entity-salience system that aims at identifying the semantic focus of a document via a pipeline of three main stages: document enrichment, feature generation and entity-salience classification.

Stage 1: Document Enrichment. This stage aims at enriching the input document d with a set of semantic, morphological and syntactic information generated by orchestrating three IR/NLP tools, as follows:

1. CORENLP [9] tokenizes the input document d, assigns a part-of-speech-tag to each token, generates dependency trees, identifies proper nouns and finally generates the co-reference chains.

2. WAT [15] enriches d with a set of annotations (m, e), where m is a sequence of words (called, *mentions*) and e is an entity (i.e. Wikipedia page) that disambiguates the mention m. WAT assigns to each annotation two scores: (i) the *commonness* score, that represents the probability that m is disambiguated by e in Wikipedia, and (ii) a *coherence* score (denoted by ρ), which represents the semantic coherence between the annotation and its context in d. SWAT uses WAT in two ways: first to annotate the mentions which are the proper nouns identified by CORENLP; second to generate an *entity graph* in which nodes are the annotated entities and edges are weighted with the relatedness between the edge-connected entities (see next).
3. TEXTRANK [10] scores and ranks the sentences of d via a random walk over a complete graph in which nodes are sentences and edge-weights are computed as a function of the normalized number of common tokens between the connected sentences.

Stage 2: Feature Generation. The second stage deploys the enriched document representation above to map each entity annotation (m, e) into a rich set of features. We remark one of the key novelties of SWAT: we manage the pair mention-entity (i.e. annotation) instead of the individual entities because we wish to exploit at the best both syntactic and semantic features, as we will detail in the next pages. Different from [19], where a mention can have more than one relevant entity, we rely on *unambiguous* annotations: this allows us to directly identify each mention with one unique entity and to model it with a feature space which is unique within the document where the entity appears.

Stage 3: Entity-salience Classification. The goal of this third and last stage is to classify entities into salient and non salient given the features computed in the previous stage. For this we deploy the efficient and highly scalable *eXtreme Gradient Boosting* (XGBOOST) suitable for handling sparse data [3] and trained as will be detailed in Sect. 4.

3.1 More on Feature Generation (Stage 2)

Let us dig into the algorithms deployed to map each annotation (m, e) detected in d onto the rich set of features we designed for this task. It is clear that our feature space spans well-known features (i.e. frequency- and position-based) as well as novel features (i.e. summarization-, annotation-, relatedness- and dependency-based). For the sake of space, we comment only the new features introduced in SWAT and refer the reader to a web page[1] for the full list of them.

Position-based Features: *spread* and *bucketed-freq*. These features are derived from the position of an entity e within the document d, in terms of tokens or sentences. For token-level features (indicated with t) we consider the index of the first token of the mention of e, normalized by the number of tokens of d; whereas for sentence-level features (indicated with s) we consider the index

[1] pages.di.unipi.it/ponza/research/aboutness.

of the sentences where the entity e is annotated, normalized by the number of sentences of d. The key idea underlying those set of features is to take into account the distribution of the entity mentions within the document in order to predict their salience score; this feature naturally improves the $1st\text{-}loc(e, d)$ feature introduced in [4] thus making more robust SWAT wrt the distribution of salient entities, as shown in Sect. 5.

Summarization-based Features: *TextRank-stats*. Our intuition behind these features is that summarization algorithms assign high scores to sentences that contain salient information and thus possibly contain salient entities. So we computed, for each entity e, some statistical measures derived from the scores assigned by TEXTRANK [10] to the sentences where a mention of e occurs.

Linguistic-based Features: *dep-.** Our intuition behind these features is to exploit the grammatical structure of sentences in order to generate features which rely on the relation between entities given the dependency trees of their occurring sentences. Unlike [4], where dependency trees are used to extract only the head of a mention, we combine frequency, position and summarization information with dependency relations generated by the CORENLP's dependency parser. Moreover, we take into account only the mentions m of e that have at least one token dependent of a specific dependency relation, limited to those ones where salient entities appear more frequently in the training set: they were preposition-in, adjective modifier, possessive, noun compound modifier and subject dependency relations. The investigation of the usage of other dependency relations is left to future work.

Relatedness-based Features: *rel-.** These features are introduced to capture how much an entity e is related to all other entities in the input document d, with the intuition that if an entity is salient then its topic shouldn't be a *singleton* in d. In this context we use the Jaccard-relatedness function described in [15], since its deployment in the disambiguation phase allows WAT to reach the highest performance over different datasets [21]. We introduce two classes of features: (i) the ones computed via several centrality algorithms (i.e. Degree, PageRank, Betweeness, Katz, HITS, Closeness and Harmonic [2]) applied over the entity graph described in Stage 1 of the SWAT algorithm; (ii) the ones computing proper statistics over the Jaccard-relatedness scores concerning with some entity e and the other entities in d.

Other known features. For the sake of completeness, Sect. 5 will experiment also with the whole feature set proposed in [4] in order to investigate the relevance of these features wrt our novel proposals. We remark that our extended set of features supersedes the ones introduced in [19] in terms of ensemble of computed statistics, for the use of annotations (instead of just entities), and for the use of the entity-relatedness not only to compute the graph but also to evaluate the coherence between entities. So our experimental evaluation of the features set will implicitly consider also those ones.

4 Experimental Setup

4.1 Datasets

New York Times. The annotated version of this dataset for the document aboutness problem was introduced in [4]. It consists of annotated news drawn from 20 years of the New York Times newspaper (see also [17]). It is worth to point out that the numbers reported in [4] are slightly different from the ones we derived by downloading this dataset: authors informed us that this is due to the way they have exported annotations in the final release. Such a difference will impact onto the F1-performance of their system, as reported in [4], for about −0.5% in absolute micro-F1.[2] We will take these figures into account in the rest of this section when comparing SWAT with the CMU-GOOGLE's system.

Since the entity annotator used in [4] is not publicly available (and this was used to derive the ground truth of the NYT dataset), we kept only those entities which have been generated by SWAT and the CMU-GOOGLE's system. The final figures are the following: the news in the training + validation set are $99,348 = 79,462 + 19,886$, and are 9577 in the test set; these news contain a total of 1276742 entities in the training + validation set (i.e. $1021952 + 254790$) and 119714 entities in the test set. Overall the dataset contains 108925 news, with an average number of 975 tokens per news, more than 3 million mentions and 1396456 entities, of which 14.7% are labeled as salient.

Wikinews. This dataset was introduced in [19]. It consists of a sample of news published by Wikinews from November 2004 to June 2014 and annotated with Wikipedia entities by the Wikinews community. This dataset is significantly smaller than NYT in all means: number of documents (365 news), their lengths (an average of 297 tokens per document) and number of annotations (a total of 4747 manual annotated entities, of which 10% are labeled as salient). Nevertheless, we will consider it in our experiments because it has some remarkable features wrt NYT: the ground-truth generation of the salient entities was more careful being based on human-assigned scores rather than being derived in a rule-based way, and because salient entities are both proper nouns (as in NYT) and common nouns (unlike NYT).

As far as the dataset subdivision and evaluation process are concerned, we used the following methodology. For the NYT, we use the same training + testing splitting as defined by [4], using as validation set a portion of the training set (20%). For Wikinews we deploy the evaluation procedure described by [19], namely the averaged macro-F1 of a 5-fold cross-validation.

4.2 Tools

Baselines. We implemented four baselines. The first one is the same baseline introduced in [4], it classifies an entity as salient if it appears in the first sentence of the input document. The other three baselines are new and try to better

[2] Thanks to the authors of [4] for pointing this out to us.

investigate the individual power of some novel features adopted by our SWAT. More precisely, the second baseline extends the previous one by adding the check whether the ρ-score (capturing entity coherence) is greater than a fixed threshold. This will be called the ρ-baseline. The third (resp. fourth) baseline classifies an entity as salient if its maximum TEXTRANK (resp. Rel-PageRank) score is greater than a fixed threshold.

Cmu-Google's System and our re-implementation. This system uses a proprietary entity annotator which links proper nouns to Freebase entities. The ntity-salience classification works by deploying a small number of standard text-based features, based on position and frequency, and a graph-based centrality score. We decided to implement the CMU-GOOGLE's system from scratch, because it is not available [4], by substituting the proprietary modules with open-source tools. So we used WAT as entity annotator [15] and a state-of-the-art logistic regressor as classifier (shortly, LR [14]). This (re-)implementation achieves very close performance to the original system (see Table 1) and thus it is useful to obtain a fair comparison over the Wikinews dataset (where the CMU-GOOGLE's system has not been experimented).

Sel. A supervised system that uses a machine learning regressor to detect salient entities via a set of features that is larger than the ones used in CMU-GOOGLE's system (see our comments in Sect. 3.1). In the following, since this system is not available to the public, we will report in our Tables its performance figures published [19].

Configuration of Swat and Baselines. We experimented upon two configuration settings, according with the characteristics of the ground-truth datasets. For NYT, where the ground truth was generated by assuming that salient entities can be mentioned in the text only as proper nouns, we configured SWAT and the baselines to annotate only proper nouns detected by CORENLP, whereas for Wikinews, where the ground truth comes with no assumptions, we tested two versions of our systems: one detecting only proper nouns, the other detecting both proper and common nouns.

4.3 Experimental Results

Experimental figures on the two datasets are reported in Tables 1 and 2, where we denote by CMU-GOOGLE-ours our implementation of the system in [4]. This system is only slightly worse than the original one, which could depend both on the differences in the NYT dataset commented above and in the deployment of open-source modules which are possibly different from the proprietary ones. In any case the performance is so close to what claimed in [4], and in footnote 2, that our implementation will be used to derive the performance of CMU-GOOGLE over the Wikinews dataset too.

We notice that both TEXTRANK and Rel-PageRank baselines obtain the lowest micro- and macro-F1 performance over NYT and Wikinews. This figure is probably due to the characteristics of the datasets: the salient information in news is typically confined to initial positions, so those systems are drastically penalized by ignoring positional information. This statement is further supported by the results of Positional and Positional-ρ baselines: they are trivial but yet achieve better performance.

Table 1. Performance on the New York Times' dataset.

System	Micro			Macro		
	P	R	F1	P	R	F1
Positional baseline	59.1	38.6	46.7	39.0	32.7	33.0
Positional-ρ baseline	61.9	36.9	46.2	38.5	31.0	32.0
TextRank	27.0	58.8	37.0	30.0	48.6	33.4
Rel-PageRank	20.3	62.5	30.6	21.3	**55.3**	28.0
CMU-GOOGLE [4]	60.5	**63.5**	62.0	n.a.	n.a.	n.a.
CMU-GOOGLE-ours	58.8	62.6	60.7	47.6	50.5	46.1
SWAT	**62.2**	63.0	**62.6**	**50.0**	50.7	**47.6**

Results on New York Times' dataset. We notice that the new syntactic and semantic features introduced in SWAT allow our system to outperform CMU-GOOGLE-ours by 1.9% in micro-F1 and by 1.5% in macro-F1; the improvement against the original CMU-GOOGLE's system is +1.1% in micro-F1 (see footnote 2). This contribution is particularly significant because of the size of NYT.

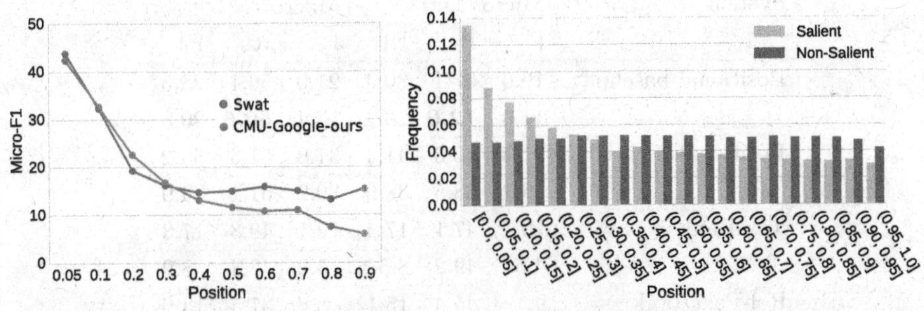

Fig. 1. On the left: micro-F1 performance through first token positions: point (x, y) indicates that the micro-F1 is y for all salient entities whose position is larger than x. On the right: The histograms plot the frequency distribution of salient versus non-salient entities according to their positions in the documents.

In order to shed more light on the previous experimental results we investigated how much the difference in performance of the top-systems depends on the distribution of the salient entities in the input documents. We already commented about this issue when discussing the poor performance of the baselines

TextRank and Rel-PageRank, here we dig more into it and derive an estimate on the *flexibility* of the known systems: thus addressing a question posed in [4]. Figure 1(right) shows the distribution of the salient and non-salient entities within the NYT dataset. As expected most of the salient entities are concentrated at the beginning of the news but, surprisingly, there is a significant number of them occurring at the end of news too. This motivated us to investigate the performance of Swat and Cmu-Google as a function of the position of the salient entities.[3] Figure 1(left) shows this comparison: both systems are highly effective on the classification of salient entities mentioned at the beginning of the document, but their behavior differs significantly when salient entities are mentioned at the documents' end: in this case, Swat does not overfit upon the positional feature and, indeed, obtains a high improvement wrt Cmu-Google-ours which is up to 9% in micro-F1. As a consequence we can state that Swat is more flexible wrt salient-entities' position than Cmu-Google, so that it could be used consistently over those documents where salient information are not necessarily mentioned at the beginning.

Results on Wikinews. On this dataset the improvement of Swat against the state-of-the-art is even more significant than in NYT: it is about 4.8% in macro-F1 wrt Sel and it is about 10% in micro-F1 wrt Cmu-Google-ours (remind that Cmu-Google is not available).

Table 2. Performance on the Wikinews dataset. For each system we report the score obtained by the system configured to annotate either only proper nouns (top) or both proper and common nouns (down).

System	Micro			Macro		
	P	R	F1	P	R	F1
Positional baseline	19.6	67.1	30.4	21.0	56.1	28.5
	11.9	**72.0**	20.4	13.4	**60.6**	20.8
Positional-ρ baseline	31.5	60.3	41.4	31.8	51.3	36.2
	29.2	58.5	38.9	30.2	51.1	34.9
TextRank	10.7	47.1	17.4	12.1	40.8	17.3
	4.6	49.2	8.5	5.2	42.4	8.9
Rel-PageRank	9.1	45.4	15.1	8.8	37.5	13.6
	9.0	35.6	14.4	9.2	28.9	12.2
Cmu-Google-ours	37.6	57.1	45.3	35.7	48.6	38.0
	33.0	58.2	42.1	34.1	50.5	37.6
Sel [19]	n.a.	n.a.	n.a.	42.0	51.0	43.0
Swat	**54.7**	56.9	**55.6**	45.9	56.3	47.5
	49.3	63.6	55.3	**47.3**	55.2	**47.8**

[3] Remind that Sel's implementation is not available.

The second question we experimentally investigated is about the *generalization ability* of the feature set of SWAT: so we trained it over NYT and tested it over Wikinews. In Table 3 we consider two variants of SWAT: SWAT-NYT, the system trained over NYT and directly used over Wikinews and SWAT-NYT-prob, the system whose regressor was trained over NYT but whose classifier is tuned over Wikinews by maximizing the macro-F1 over the training folds (as done by [19]).

According with Table 3, SWAT-NYT obtains performance lower than the systems trained over Wikinews (as expected), such as SWAT and SEL, but the difference is small and the system turns actually to be better than CMU-GOOGLE-ours by +2.2% in macro-F1. The tuning on Wikinews by SWAT-NYT-prob allows to achieve better performance in macro-F1 than both CMU-GOOGLE-ours and SEL, respectively by 6.8% and 1.8%, but yet SWAT (trained over Wikinews) is still better. These figures show that the features introduced by SWAT are flexible enough to work over news, independently from their source and without overfitting the large single-source training data (e.g. NYT).

Table 3. Generalization ability of SWAT. For each system we report the score obtained by the system configured to annotate either only proper nouns (top) or both proper and common nouns (down).

System	Micro			Macro		
	P	R	F1	P	R	F1
SWAT-NYT	33.3	68.5	44.8	34.6	58.1	40.2
	24.7	73.8	36.9	28.0	63.4	36.2
SWAT-NYT-prob	46.2	60.0	52.1	44.4	51.9	44.8
	42.7	59.5	49.6	41.8	51.9	42.9

5 Feature and Error Analysis

A crucial step in our experiments was to analyze the impact on SWAT's performance of the many and variegated features introduced in this paper. This study was driven by the importance score assigned to each feature by XGBOOST, which captures the number of times that feature splits the data across all decision trees.

Let us jointly discuss the most important features emerged from incremental feature additions experimented on both datasets (see Fig. 2). Through this analysis we aim to shed the light onto the understanding of the key elements needed for the aboutness' identification. We notice that the most important features depends on four common elements: (i) *position* (e.g. title or the beginning of the document), (ii) frequency (e.g. *head-count*), (iii) the "quality" of the entity annotation (e.g. ρ- and *commonness*-based features) and (iv) the relationships between entities (*relatedness*-based features). On the other hand, several other features based on TEXTRANK and Dependency Relations appear between 20–50

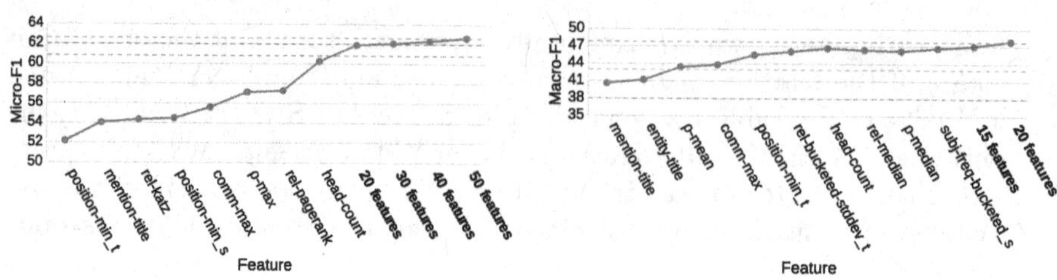

Fig. 2. Incremental feature addition on NYT (on the left) and on Wikinews (on the right) according to the feature ranking provided by XGBoost. The red, green, yellow and blue dashed lines report the performance of Cmu-Google, Cmu-Google-ours, Sel and Swat (with all features), respectively. (Color figure online)

and 10–20 positions for NYT and Wikinews, respectively. In spite of their marginal role, they allow Swat to refine its predictions and eventually get the top performance claimed in Tables 1 and 2.

In order to gain some insights on Swat's performance and possible improvements, we analyzed its erroneous predictions by drawing a subset of 80 (40 + 40) documents from the NYT and Wikinews datasets. The most significant result here is to prove what argued by [7]: namely that the deployment of semantic knowledge (i.e. entities) into the identification of document aboutness eliminates some errors that originally afflicted keyphrase extraction algorithms. However, we notice that false-negative errors (i.e. entities classified as non-salient, despite being salient) are mainly due to the position-based features which frequently induce to miss a salient entity because it is not at the beginning of the news. On the other hand, a large percentage of the analyzed news of NYT (∼35%) and Wikinews (∼40%) contain false-positive errors which are ground-truth errors: in these cases Swat correctly identifies the salience of an entity, but the ground truth does not label it as salient and so it is unfortunately counted as an error in our Tables!

This analysis suggests that Swat's performance may be actually higher than what we claimed before and a better ground-truth dataset should be devised. In future work we aim to improve the quality of the NYT dataset (which is the largest one and which allows Swat to generalize the task also when tested on news of different sources), by (i) augmenting its annotations with common nouns (which are fundamental in the understanding of the aboutness of documents) and (ii) by labeling its ground-truth via a crowdsourcing task.

6 Future Work

For the contributions of this paper we refer the reader to the introduction. Here we comment on two research hints spurring by the extensive experiments we have conducted over the NYT and Wikinews datasets: (i) scaling up to the mining of large datasets, such as NYT, needs faster entity annotators (the current annotation by Wat needed about 20 days!); (ii) a recent trend in document analysis is deploying deep neural networks (e.g. word2vec) to extract powerful word-distributional features which should be checked for effectiveness also in the entity-salience's context. These directions will be the topic of our future research.

References

1. Anick, P.: Using terminological feedback for web search refinement: a log-based study. In: SIGIR, pp. 88–95 (2003)
2. Boldi, P., Vigna, S.: Axioms for centrality. Internet Math. **10**, 222–262 (2014)
3. Chen, T., Guestrin, C.: XGBoost: a scalable tree boosting system. In: SIGKDD, pp. 785–794 (2016)
4. Dunietz, J., Gillick, D.: A new entity salience task with millions of training examples. In: EACL, p. 205 (2014)
5. Gabrilovich, E., Markovitch, S.: Computing semantic relatedness using wikipedia-based explicit semantic analysis. In: IJCAI, pp. 1606–1611 (2007)
6. Gamon, M., Yano, T., Song, X., Apacible, J., Pantel, P.: Identifying salient entities in web pages. In: CIKM, pp. 2375–2380 (2013)
7. Hasan, K.S., Ng, V.: Automatic keyphrase extraction. A survey of the (state of the) art. In: ACL, pp. 1262–1273 (2014)
8. Liu, Z., Huang, W., Zheng, Y., Sun, M.: Automatic keyphrase extraction via topic decomposition. In: EMNLP, pp. 366–376 (2010)
9. Manning, C.D., et al.: The stanford CoreNLP toolkit. In: ACL, pp. 55–60 (2014)
10. Mihalcea, R., Tarau, P.: TextRank. Bringing order into texts. In: EMNLP (2004)
11. Ni, Y., et al.: Semantic documents relatedness using concept graph representation. In: WSDM, pp. 635–644 (2016)
12. Bruza, P.D., Huibers, T.W.C.: A study of aboutness in information retrieval. Artif. Intell. Rev. **10**, 381–407 (1996)
13. Paranjpe, D.: Learning document aboutness from implicit user feedback and document structure. In: CIKM, pp. 365–374 (2009)
14. Pedregosa, F., et al.: Scikit-learn: machine learning in python. J. Mach. Learn. Res. **12**, 2825–2830 (2011)
15. Piccinno, F., Ferragina, P.: From TagMe to WAT: a new entity annotator. In: ERD Workshop, Hosted by SIGIR, pp. 55–62 (2014)
16. Radlinski, F., et al.: Optimizing relevance and revenue in ad search: a query substitution approach. In: SIGIR, pp. 403–410 (2008)
17. Sandhaus, E.: The New York Times Annotated Corpus. LCM, Philadelphia (2008)
18. Scaiella, U., Ferragina, P., Marino, A., Ciaramita, M.: Topical clustering of search results. In: WSDM, pp. 223–232 (2012)
19. Trani, S., et al.: SEL: a unified algorithm for entity linking and saliency detection. In: DocEng, pp. 85–94 (2016)
20. Turney, P.D.: Learning algorithms for keyphrase extraction. Inf. Retriev. **2**, 303–336 (2000)
21. Usbeck, R., et al.: GERBIL: general entity annotator benchmarking framework. In: WWW, pp. 303–336 (2015)

Summarizing Web Documents Using Sequence Labeling with User-Generated Content and Third-Party Sources

Minh-Tien Nguyen[1,2(✉)], Duc-Vu Tran[1], Chien-Xuan Tran[1], and Minh-Le Nguyen[1]

[1] Japan Advanced Institute of Science and Technology (JAIST), 1-1 Asahidai, Nomi, Ishikawa 923-1292, Japan
{tiennm,vu.tran,chien-tran,nguyenml}@jaist.ac.jp

[2] Hung Yen University of Technology and Education (UTEHY), Hung Yen, Vietnam

Abstract. This paper presents *SoCRFSum*, a summary model which integrates user-generated content as comments and third-party sources such as relevant articles of a Web document to generate a high-quality summarization. The summarization was formulated as a sequence labeling problem, which exploits the support of external information to model sentences and comments. After modeling, Conditional Random Fields were adopted for sentence selection. *SoCRFSum* was validated on a dataset collected from Yahoo News. Promising results indicate that by integrating the user-generated and third-party information, our method obtains improvements of ROUGE-scores over state-of-the-art baselines.

Keywords: Data mining · Document summarization · Social context summarization · Sequence labeling

1 Introduction

Online news providers, e.g. Yahoo News[1] interact with readers by providing a Web interface where readers can write their comments corresponding to an event collected from an original Web page. For example, after reading the Boston bombing event mentioned in an article, users can directly write their comments (user-generated content) on the interface of Yahoo News. In the meantime, by searching the title of the article using a search engine, we can retrieve relevant Web documents (third-party sources), which have two characteristics: (i) they have an implicit relation with the original document and (ii) they also include the event content in a variation. The user-generated content and third-party sources, one form of social information [1,5,9,14,17,22,24,26], cover important aspects of a Web document. This observation inspires a challenging summary task, which exploits the user-generated content and third-party sources of a Web document to support sentences for generating a summarization.

[1] http://news.yahoo.com.

F. Frasincar et al. (Eds.): NLDB 2017, LNCS 10260, pp. 454–467, 2017.
DOI: 10.1007/978-3-319-59569-6_54

Extractive summarization methods usually formulate sentence selection as a binary classification task [11,21,26], in which they mark summary sentences by a label. These methods, however, only consider internal document information, e.g. sentences while ignoring its social information. How to elegantly formulate sentence-comment relation and how to effectively generate high-quality summaries by exploiting the social information are challenging questions.

Social content summarization has been previously studied by various approaches based on different kinds of social information such as hyperlinks [1], click-though data [22], user-generated content [8,9,14,17,24,26]. Yang et al. [26] proposed a dual wing factor graph model for incorporating tweets into the summarization and used Support Vector Machines (SVM) and Conditional Random Fields (CRF) as preliminary steps in calculating the weight of edges for building the graph. Wei and Gao [24] used a learning to ranking approach with a set of features trained by RankBoost for news highlight extraction. In contrast, Gao et al. [8] proposed a cross-collection topic-aspect modeling (cc-TAM) as a preliminary step to generate a bipartite graph, which was used by a co-ranking method to select sentences and tweets for multi-document summarization. Wei and Gao [25] proposed a variation of LexRank, which used auxiliary tweets for building a heterogeneous graph random walk (HGRW) to summarize single documents. Nguyen and Nguyen [17,18] presented SoRTESum, a ranking method using a set of recognizing textual entailment (RTE) features for single-document summarization. These methods, however, exist two issues: (i) ignoring the support from third-party sources which can be seen as a global information and (ii) eliminating sequential aspect which is the nature of the summarization.

Our objective is to automatically extract summary sentences and comments of a Web document by incorporating its user-generated content and third-party sources. This paper makes four main contributions:

- It denotes the relation of sentences and comments in a mutual reinforcement fashion, which exploits both local and social information.
- It proposes sophisticated features which integrate the social information into the summary process.
- It conducts a careful investigation to evaluate feature contribution, which benefits the summarization in selecting appropriate features.
- It presents a unified summary framework which exploits user-generated content and third-party sources for producing the summarzation.

We next introduce our idea and data preparation for the summarization, then we describe the process of SoCRFSum. After generating the summary, we show compared results over baselines with discussions and deep analysis. We finish by drawing important conclusions.

2 Summarization with User-Generated Content and Third-Party Sources

2.1 Basic Idea

We formulate the summarization in the form of sequence labeling, which integrates the user-generated content and third-party sources of a Web document. Such information represents supporting features, which help to enrich the information of each sentence or comment. For example, in Fig. 1, when modeling a sentence, a set of comment features (the red line) and third-party features (the purple line) from relevant documents are exploited to support local features. Similarly, social features from sentences (the blue line) and third-party features are also utilized to support local features of each comment. In this view, we also consider information from sentences as the social features of comments. After modeling, a dual CRF-based [12] summarization model is trained to select sentences and comments as the summarization.

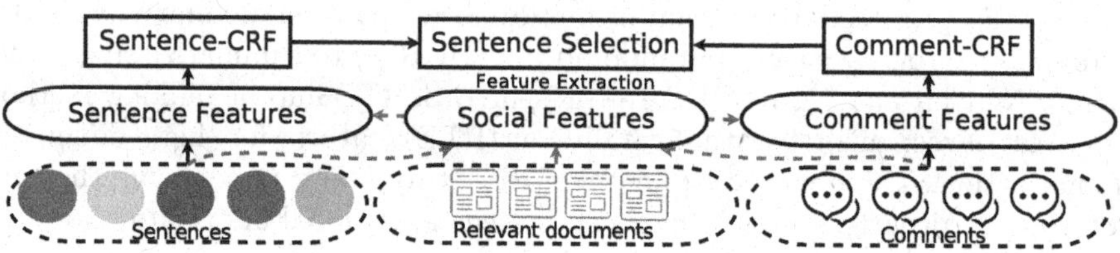

Fig. 1. The overview of SoCRFSum. (Color figure online)

Our approach is different from [8,17,20,21,23–25] in two aspects: (i) exploiting both the information from users and relevant documents and (ii) formulating the summarization as a sequence labeling task.

2.2 Data Preparation

Since DUC (2001, 2002 and 2004)[2] lacks social information, we used a standard dataset for social context summarization named SoLSCSum from [19]. The SoLSCSum [19] is an English dataset collected from Yahoo News[3]. It contains 157 news articles along with 3,462 sentences, 5,858 gold-standard references, and 25,633 comments, which were manually annotated. To create third-party sources, we manually retrieved 1,570 related documents by selecting top 10 Web pages, which appear on the search result page of Google[4] by searching the title of each document. Unnecessary information, e.g. HTML tags was removed to obtain raw texts. We kept the order of the relevant documents.

[2] http://duc.nist.gov/data.html.
[3] https://www.yahoo.com/news/.
[4] https://www.google.com.

2.3 Summarization by SoCRFSum

Basic Model with Local Information: As mentioned, our goal is to build a sequence model for the summarization. To do that, we followed the model with basis features stated in [21]. The basic features include sentence position, sentence length (the number of tokens with stopword removal), log-likelihood, thematic words, indicator words (count the number of indicator words using a dictionary), uppercase words, Cosine similarity with previous and next N ($N = 1, 2, 3$) sentences, LSA and HIT score. The remaining sections describe our new features used to improve the performance of the summary model.

New Local Features: We define a set of new features[5], which represent inherent information of each sentence. They capture the similarity of a sentence (or comment) with a title, informativeness, and topical covering aspect.

- Common Word: counts common words of the title and a sentence.
- Stop Word: counts the number of stop words in a sentence or comment.
- Local LDA Score: bases on a hypothesis that a summary sentence or comment usually contains salient information represented in the form of topics. We trained two topic models for sentences and comments by using Latent Dirichlet Allocation (LDA[6]) [2] ($k = 100$, $\alpha = \beta = 0.01$ with 1000 iterations). Given a document d with its comments, we formed sentences and comments into d_S and d_C, two smaller documents. For each d_S (or d_C), LDA infers to obtain top five topics, which have the highest topic distribution with d_S (or d_C). With each topic, we select top five topical words, which have the highest weights. As the result, each d_S (or d_C) has 25 topical words. Given a set of topical words $TW = \{w_1, ..., w_k\}$, Eq. (1) defines the local LDA score of a sentence:

$$local\text{-}lda\text{-}score(s_i) = \frac{\sum_{j=1}^{k} weight(w_j)}{n} \text{ if } w_j \in s_i \tag{1}$$

  where: $weight()$ returns the word weight of w_j (normalized in [0, 1]) in s_i; n is the number of words in s_i after removing stop words.

Social Context Integration: We consider the user-generated content, e.g. comments and third-party sources, e.g. relevant news articles returned by a search engine as the social context of a Wed document d. In this view, the content of a document is not only mentioned in comments but also described in other Web pages from different news providers. We generated 13 new features, in which each feature covers the characteristic of a summary sentence or comment, that may match with the gold-standard references.

User-generated Features: cover semantic similarity, topic, and textual entailment aspect of a sentence-comment pair.

[5] We remove stopwords when modeling all features.

[6] http://mallet.cs.umass.edu.

- Maximal W2V Score: This feature captures the generation behavior of readers, in which they generate comments based on sentences in a variation form. For example, a sentence and comment containing word *"police"* and *"cops"* can be considered to be similar. Equation (2) defines this feature:

$$w2v\text{-}score(s_i) = \max\left(\overset{m}{\underset{j=1}{sentSim}}(s_i, c_j)\right) \tag{2}$$

where: m is the number of comments, $sentSim()$ returns semantic similarity of s_i and c_j and is calculated by Eq. (3):

$$sentSim(s_i, c_j) = \frac{\sum_{w_i}^{N_s} \sum_{w_j}^{N_c} w2v(w_i, w_j)}{N_s + N_c} \tag{3}$$

where: N_s and N_c are the number of words in s_i and c_i; $w2vSim()$ returns the similarity of two words computed by *Word2Vec* [15].
- Auxiliary LDA Score: states that the content of a summary sentence should also appear in comments represented by topics. This feature is similar to *Local LDA Score* but topics and topical words were inferred from comments.
- Maximal Lexical Similarity: denotes the lexical similarity of a sentence and auxiliary comments, in which the content of a summary sentence should appear in several comments. We exploited similarity measures in [17] for modeling this feature. Equation (4) presents the lexical similarity aspect:

$$rte\text{-}lex(s_i) = \max\left(\overset{m}{\underset{j=1}{lexSim}}(s_i, c_j)\right) \tag{4}$$

where: m is the number of comments; $lexSim()$ returns the lexical similarity of s_i and c_j and is computed by Eq. (5):

$$lexSim(s_i, c_j) = \frac{1}{|F|} \sum_{n=1}^{|F|} f_n(s_i, c_j) \tag{5}$$

where: F contains lexical features [17]; $f_n()$ is a similarity function computed by each nth feature.
- Maximal Distance Similarity: This feature shares observation with the lexical feature but using distance aspect. It was calculated by the same mechanism in Eq. (4), but using distance features [17]. By adding two new similarity features, we cover the entailment aspect between a sentence and comment.

Third-party Features: An event in an original document is also mentioned in relevant Web documents from different news providers. We define the relation of the original and its related documents D as an implication because all the documents are created independently without the presence of social users. We only apply these features to the relevant documents instead of comments due to the implicit relation. The features capture social voting, social distance, and the appearance of frequent words of a sentence in the related documents D.

- Voting: bases on a hypothesis that the relevant documents should include salient terms in a summary sentence. Given a sentence s_i in the original document d, the voting in Eq. (6) counts Cosine similarity (greater than a threshold) with all sentences in the relevant documents.

$$n\_vote(s_i) = \frac{\sum_{j=1}^{m} cos(s_i, t_j)}{N_S} \quad (6)$$

where: m is total sentences in the relevant documents and N_S is the number of sentences in d.
- Cluster Distance: states that a summary sentence should be close to clusters represented by the relevant documents, in which each of them is a cluster. Given a sentence s_i and a relevant document $rd_j \in D$ represented by a set of frequent terms, Eq. (7) denotes this feature.

$$c\text{-}dist(s_i, D) = \frac{\sum_{j=1}^{N_D} eucDist(s_i, rd_j)}{N_D} \quad (7)$$

where: $eucDist()$ returns Euclidean distance of s_i and rd_j using bag-of-words model, N_D is the number of relevant documents.
- Sentence-third-party Term Frequency: bases on a hypothesis that a sentence containing frequent words appearing in both of the original document and third-party sources is more important than other ones. Given a sentence s_i in d and N_{SD} is total sentences in D, Eq. (8) defines this feature.

$$stp\text{-}TF(s_i) = \frac{\sum_{j=1}^{|s_i|} TF(w_j) \times IDF(w_j)}{|s_i|} \quad (8)$$

$$TF(w_j) = \text{the frequency of } w_j \text{ in } d \quad (9)$$

$$IDF(w_j) = log(\frac{N_{SD}}{DF(w_j)}) \quad (10)$$

where: $DF(w_j)$ is the number of sentences in D containing w_j.
- Frequent-Terms Probability: The remaining features base on an assumption that the summarization should include the most frequent words if they appear frequently in the relevant documents. We first collected a set of frequent terms from the raw texts of D. If frequency of a term is greater than a certain threshold, it was considered to be frequent. Given a frequent term set $FT = \{w_1, ..., w_t\}$ and the original document d, we included three probability features: the average probability of frequent terms (aFrqScore), frequent term sum score (frqScore), and relative frequent term sum score (rFrqScore) [23]. Equations (11), (13) and (14) present these feature.

$$aFrqScore(s_i) = \frac{\sum_{w \in s_i} p(w)}{|w \in s_i|} \quad (11)$$

where: $w \in FT$.

$$p(w) = \frac{count(w)}{|w \in d|} \quad (12)$$

where: $count(w)$ is the frequency of w in d, and $|w \in d|$ is total number of frequent words in d.

$$frqScore(s_i) = \sum_{w \in s_i} p(w) \tag{13}$$

$$rFrqScore(s_i) = \frac{\sum_{w \in s_i} p(w)}{|s_i|} \tag{14}$$

Note that we also applied the features to model comments in the same mechanism. After modeling, two CRF-based models were separately trained for generating the summarization.

Summarization: We employed Viterbi[7] algorithm for decoding to generate the summarization. In decoding, if the number of sentences and comments labeled by 1 is larger than m, we select top m sentences and comments[8]; otherwise, we select all of them as the summarization.

3 Results and Discussion

3.1 Experimental Setup

Comments with fewer than five tokens were removed. 10-fold cross-validation was used with $m = 6$ as the same setting in [19]. Summaries were stemmed[9].

Word2Vec was derived by using SkipGram model[10] [15], dimension = 300, data from Google 1 billion words. Language models for learning to rank (L2R) baseline are uni-gram and bi-gram taken from KenLM[11]. The threshold of term frequency used for Eqs. (11), (13) and (14) is 0.65 when modeling sentences and 0.35 when modeling comments.

3.2 Baselines

- **SentenceLead:** chooses the first m sentences as the summarization [16].
- **LexRank**[12]: was proposed by [6]. We employed LexRank with tokenization and stemming[13].
- **SVM:** was proposed by [4] and used in [19,26]. We adopted SVM[14] by using RBF kernel with feature scaling in $[-1, 1]$; comments were weighted by 85% as the suggestion in [19] by using features in [26].

[7] https://en.wikipedia.org/wiki/Viterbi_algorithm.
[8] We do this because baselines also pick up top m sentences.
[9] http://snowball.tartarus.org/algorithms/porter/stemmer.html.
[10] https://code.google.com/p/word2vec/.
[11] https://kheafield.com/code/kenlm/.
[12] https://code.google.com/p/louie-nlp/source/browse/trunk/louie-ml/src/main/java/org/louie/ml/lexrank/?r=10.
[13] http://nlp.stanford.edu/software/corenlp.shtml.
[14] http://www.csie.ntu.edu.tw/~cjlin/libsvm/.

- **SoRTESum:** was proposed by [17] using a set of similarity features. This method contains two model: using inter information (SoRTESum Inter Wing) and dual wing information (SoRTESum Dual Wing).
- **CRF**: was used in [21] for single document summarization. We used basic features in [21] to train two summary models for sentences and comments.

3.3 Evaluation Method

Gold-standard references (labeled by 1) were used for evaluation by using F-1 ROUGE-N[15] (N = 1, 2) [13].

3.4 Results

We report the summary performance of all methods in term of F-1 ROUGE-scores. The results in Tables 1 and 2 indicate that SoCRFSum clearly outperforms the baselines except for LexRank in ROUGE-1 on the comment side, i.e. 0.232 vs. 0.244. In sentence selection, our method slightly surpasses CRF with the basic features, e.g. 0.426 vs. 0.413 in ROUGE-1. It is understandable that the basic features in [21] are efficient to capture sequence aspect in documents. On the other hand, our method obtains significant improvements compared to CRF in comment extraction, e.g. 0.232 vs. 0.074. This is because the sequence aspect does not exist in comments; therefore, basic features, e.g. Cosine ($N = 1, 2, 3$) score are inefficient for covering summary comments. In this sense, our proposed features boot the summary performance.

In document summarization, SoCRFSum significantly outperforms SVM because our method exploits the sequence aspect and new features from additional sources. Our method achieves sufficiently improvements compared to other baselines because it exploits the support from both user-generated content and third-party sources. For example, there is a big gap between our approach and

Table 1. Sentence selection performance; * is supervised methods; **bold** is the best, *italic* is second best; methods with *S* use social information.

Method	ROUGE-1			ROUGE-2		
	Avg-P	Avg-R	Avg-F	Avg-P	Avg-R	Avg-F
SentenceLead	0.749	0.242	0.365	0.635	0.216	0.322
LexRank	0.671	0.217	0.328	0.517	0.171	0.258
SVM*	0.712	0.185	0.293	0.573	0.151	0.239
SoRTESum Inter Wing (S)	0.705	0.239	0.357	0.582	0.201	0.298
SoRTESum Dual Wing (S)	0.721	0.242	0.362	0.593	0.203	0.302
CRF*	0.925	0.266	*0.413*	0.864	0.253	*0.391*
SoCRFSum* (S)	0.939	0.275	**0.426**	0.882	0.264	**0.407**

15 http://kavita-ganesan.com/content/rouge-2.0-documentation.

Table 2. Comment summarization, SentenceLead was not used.

Method	ROUGE-1			ROUGE-2		
	Avg-P	Avg-R	Avg-F	Avg-P	Avg-R	Avg-F
LexRank	0.541	0.157	**0.244**	0.360	0.087	*0.140*
SVM*	0.507	0.082	0.141	0.296	0.042	0.073
SoRTESum Inter Wing (S)	0.523	0.153	*0.237*	0.341	0.084	0.134
SoRTESum Dual Wing (S)	0.518	0.129	0.206	0.339	0.068	0.113
CRF*	0.639	0.039	0.074	0.539	0.033	0.062
SoCRFSum* (S)	0.870	0.134	0.232	0.767	0.121	**0.209**

SoRTESum even though SoRTESum also integrates social information. The comparison is consistent in comment extraction. However, in some cases, our method is limited due to the sequence aspect in comments. For example, LexRank and SoRTESum Inter Wing slightly surpass our method in ROUGE-1, e.g. 0.237 vs. 0.232, but in ROUGE-2, our method is the best.

We compared our model to state-of-the-art methods reported in [19] for social context summarization. Table 3 indicates that our method performs significantly better than other methods except for ROUGE-1 in comment extraction. As mentioned, the lack of sequence aspect in comments challenges our approach. The results of L2R CCF and SVM Ranking suggest that formulating sentence extraction by learning to rank benefits the summarization. HRGW achieves competitive results due to the integration of social information. The results of cc-TAM are quite poor because it is used for multi-document summarization while the dataset in [19] is for single document summarization.

Table 3. Comparison results; *: supervised learning methods.

Method	Document		Comment	
	ROUGE-1	ROUGE-2	ROUGE-1	ROUGE-2
HGRW [25]	0.377	*0.321*	*0.248*	0.145
cc-TAM [8]	0.321	0.268	0.166	0.088
L2R* CCF [24]	0.363	*0.321*	0.217	0.111
SVM Ranking* [19]	*0.420*	0.317	**0.365**	*0.154*
SoCRFSum*	**0.426**	**0.407**	0.232	**0.209**

3.5 Feature Contribution

We investigated feature contribution by the minus ROUGE-scores of SoCRFSum using all and $n-1$ features (leave-one-out-test). Table 4 shows that in document summarization, most of the features positively affect our model. Our proposed

Table 4. Feature contribution, **bold**: new basic and *italic*: basic features.

Basic Feature	Document		Comment		User-generated Feature	Document		Comment		Third-party Feature	Document		Comment	
	R-1	R-2	R-1	R-2		R-1	R-2	R-1	R-2		R-1	R-2	R-2	R-2
Position	5x10-3	0.001	-0.034	-0.001	**In title**	9x10-3	0.003	-0.002	-0.002	Voting	0.002	0.003	8x10-3	0.003
Length	-0.003	-0.003	-0.005	-0.004	**#Stop words**	0.001	0.005	-0.015	-0.014	c-distance	0.001	0.002	0.035	0.028
Log-LH	-3x10-3	1x10-3	0.006	0.007	Local LDA	3x10-3	0.001	-2x10-3	-3x10-3	stp-TF	-0.001	-5x10-5	0.005	0.006
Them-word	7x10-3	7x10-3	-5x10-3	6x10-3	Aux LDA	3x10-3	0.001	-2x10-3	-3x10-3	A-Frq-Score	9x10-3	0.001	0.002	0.001
Upp-word	-8x10-3	-0.004	-0.013	-0.015	Max Cosine	6x10-5	-3x10-6	0.004	0.003	Frq-Score	1x10-3	-3x10-3	0.003	0.003
Cosine (N-1)	0.001	0.002	0.018	0.015	Max-dist RTE	3x10-3	0.001	0.007	0.007	R-Frq-Score	-3x10-3	7x10-3	0.004	0.003
Cosine (N-2)	-0.001	8x10-3	7x10-3	-6x10-3	Max-lex RTE	3x10-6	0.002	0.004	0.004	—	—	—	—	—
Cosine (N-3)	5x10-3	0.001	0.004	0.004	Max-aux W2V	3x10-3	0.001	0.007	0.007	*Cosine (N+2)*	0.002	0.002	0.004	0.002
Cosine (N+1)	-0.001	-7x10-3	0.009	0.006	—	—	—	—	—	*Cosine (N+3)*	-0.001	1x10-3	0.004	0.004
Ind-word	0.003	0.004	-0.010	-0.007	*LSA score*	0.001	0.002	-0.003	-3x10-3	*HIT score*	3x10-3	0.001	0.007	0.007

features contribute to the model except for *stp-TF* and relative frequent term score (R-Frq-Score). In comment extraction, most of new features are positive except for *in title*, *#Stop words*, *local and aux LDA* compared to basic features, which most of them are negative. This observation explains the results in Tables 1 and 2. Interestingly, *#Stop words* is positive in sentence selection but is negative in comment extraction because comments are less formal than sentences. Also, *sentence position* and *in title* are inefficient for comments.

We also observed the contribution of feature groups by running our method with each separate group. Figure 2 indicates that in both document and comment extraction, the usage of all features benefits the summarization. In sentence selection, the model with the basic or user-generated features outputs similar performance, but in comment extraction, basic features are inefficient due to the lack of sequence aspect. Interestingly, in the both cases, the model with third-party features performs comparably to SoCRFSum with all features because many Web pages contain salient keywords in the summary sentences.

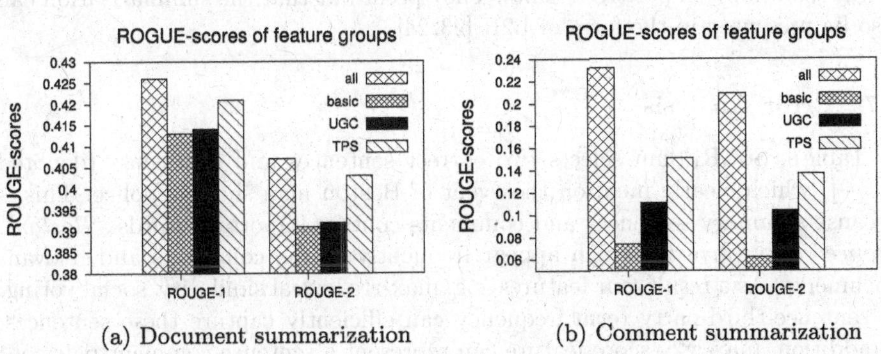

(a) Document summarization (b) Comment summarization

Fig. 2. The contribution of feature groups; *UGC* denotes user-generated content features; *TPS* presents third-party-sources features.

3.6 Summarization with L2R Methods

We observed the contribution of our features with learning to rank (L2R) methods by running three L2R methods: RankBoost [7], RankNet [3] implemented in RankLib[16], and SVM Ranking[17] [10] with default settings.

Table 5. The performance of L2R methods with our features; methods with NF combine the old and new features.

System	Document		Comment	
	ROUGE-1	ROUGE-2	ROUGE-1	ROUGE-2
RankBoost	**0.417**	0.342	0.283	0.153
RankBoost (NF)	0.414	**0.344**	**0.285**	**0.158**
RankNet	0.388	0.317	0.219	0.120
RankNet (NF)	**0.389**	**0.318**	0.219	0.120
SVMRank	0.414	**0.345**	0.341	0.168
SVMRank (NF)	**0.421**	0.337	**0.379**	**0.175**

The results in Table 5 (NF means that an L2R method uses new features) show that our features contribute to improve the summary performance, especially with SVM Ranking. The improvement in comment extraction is larger than sentence selection. However, it is slightly increased compared to Tables 1 and 2. This is because our features may be appropriate for sequence labeling rather than L2R. The results in Tables 5 and 3 are consistent, in which L2R methods obtain competitive results. They point out that the summarization can also be presented in the form of L2R [23,24].

3.7 Error Analysis

In Table 6, SoCRFSum selects two correct sentences and comments (denoted by [+]) which clearly mention the event of Boston man shot by police. This is because summary sentences and comments contain important words *"Boston"*, *"police"* and *"arrest"*, which appear frequently in the comments and relevant documents. As a result, our features, e.g. max-rte lexical similarity, social voting, or sentence-third-party term frequency can efficiently capture these sentences. In addition, max-w2v score feature can represent a sentence-comment pair containing words *"police"* and *"arrest"* by using semantic similarity. This leads to the improvements in Tables 1 and 2.

On the other hand, non-summary sentences (denoted by [−]), e.g. S3 and C3 also including salient keywords challenge our method. For example, C3 contains *"police"* and *"gun"*; therefore, our features are inefficient in this case. In

[16] http://people.cs.umass.edu/~vdang/ranklib.html.

[17] https://www.cs.cornell.edu/people/tj/svm_light/svm_rank.html.

Table 6. A summary example of 121th document. Three extracted sentences and comments are shown in stead of six ones due to space limitation

Summary	
Sentences	Comments
[+]S1: The 26-year-old man, identified as Usaamah Rahim, brandished a knife and advanced on officers working with the Joint Terrorism Task Force who initially tried to retreat before opening fire, Boston Police Superintendent William Evans told reporters	[+]C1: "Boston Police and State Police made an arrest this evening in Everett"
[+]S2: "The FBI and the Boston Police did everything they could to get this individual to drop his knife," Evans said	[+]C2: This looks like the police are looking for an acceptable reason to shot and kill people
[+]S3: Law enforcement officials are gathered on a residential street in Everett, Massachusetts	[+]C3: It makes it sound like the police, armed with guns, were frightened nearly beyond control

addition, the similar sentence length of S3 and C3 also challenges our method. However, these sentences are still relevant to the event. SoCRFSum generates C1 which perfectly reflects the content of the document. C2 and C3 show the guess of readers after reading the document. These comments support sentences to provide a perspective viewpoint on the event.

4 Conclusion

This paper presents a summary model named *SoCRFSum* to address social context summarization. The model regards a document as a sequence of sentences and learns to generate a label sequence of sentences and comments. Our work is the first to combine both user-generated content from readers and relevant Web documents in a unified model, which operates in a mutual reinforcement fashion for modeling sentences or comments. We conclude that: (i) sequence labeling with the support of additional information improves the summarization over state-of-the-art baselines and (ii) our features and proposed model are efficient for summarizing single Web documents.

For future directions, an obvious next step is to examine how the model generalizes to other domains and text genres. More sophisticated features should be considered to address the sequence problem in comments.

Acknowledgments. This work was supported by JSPS KAKENHI Grant number JP15K16048, JSPS KAKENHI Grant Number JP15K12094, and JST CREST Grant Number JPMJCR1513, Japan.

References

1. Amitay, E., Paris, C.: Automatically summarising web sites: is there a way around it? In: CIKM, pp. 173–179 (2000)
2. Blei, D.M., Ng, A.Y., Jordan, M.I.: Latent dirichlet allocation. J. Mach. Learn. Res. **3**, 993–1022 (2003)
3. Burges, C., Shaked, T., Renshaw, E., Lazier, A., Deeds, M., Hamilton, N., Hullender, G.: Learning to rank using gradient descent. In: ICML, pp. 89–96 (2005)
4. Cortes, C., Vapnik, V.: Support-vector networks. Mach. Learn. **20**(3), 273–297 (1995)
5. Delort, J.Y., Bouchon-Meunier, B., Rifqi, M.: Enhanced web document summarization using hyperlinks. In: Hypertext, pp. 208–215 (2003)
6. Erkan, G., Radev, D.R.: Lexrank: Graph-based lexical centrality as salience in text summarization. J. Artif. Intell. Res. **22**, 457–479 (2004)
7. Freund, Y., Lyeryer, R.D., Schapire, R.E., Singer, Y.: An efficient boosting algorithm for combining preferences. J. Mach. Learn. Res. **4**, 933–969 (2003)
8. Gao, W., Li, P., Darwish, K.: Joint topic modeling for event summarization across news and social media streams. In: CIKM, pp. 1173–1182 (2012)
9. Hu, M., Sun, A., Lim, E.P.: Comments-oriented document summarization: understanding document with readers' feedback. In: SIGIR, pp. 291–298 (2008)
10. Joachims, T.: Training linear svms in linear time. In: KDD, pp. 217–226 (2006)
11. Kupiec, J., Pedersen, J., Chen, F.: A trainable document summarizer. In: SIGIR, pp. 68–73 (1995)
12. Lafferty, J., McCallum, A., Pereira, F.: Conditional random fields: probabilistic models for segmenting and labeling sequence data. In: ICML, pp. 282–289 (2001)
13. Lin, C.Y., Hovy, E.: Automatic evaluation of summaries using n-gram co-occurrence statistics. In: HLT-NAACL, vol. 1, pp. 71–78 (2003)
14. Lu, Y., Zhai, C., Sundaresan, N.: Rated aspect summarization of short comments. In: WWW, pp. 131–140 (2009)
15. Mikolov, T., Sutskever, I., Chen, K., Corrado, G., Dean, J.: Distributed representations of words and phrases and their compositionality. In: NIPS, pp. 3111–3119 (2013)
16. Nenkova, A.: Automatic text summarization of newswire: lessons learned from the document understanding conference. In: AAAI, pp. 1436–1441 (2005)
17. Nguyen, M.-T., Nguyen, M.-L.: SoRTESum: a social context framework for single-document summarization. In: Ferro, N., Crestani, F., Moens, M.-F., Mothe, J., Silvestri, F., Nunzio, G.M., Hauff, C., Silvello, G. (eds.) ECIR 2016. LNCS, vol. 9626, pp. 3–14. Springer, Cham (2016). doi:10.1007/978-3-319-30671-1_1
18. Nguyen, M.T., Nguyen, M.L.: Intra-relation or inter-relation?: exploiting social information for web document summarization. Expert Syst. Appl. **76**, 71–84 (2017)
19. Nguyen, M.T., Tran, C.X., Tran, D.V., Nguyen, M.L.: Solscsum: a linked sentence-comment dataset for social context summarization. In: CIKM, pp. 2409–2412 (2016)
20. Nguyen, M.T., Tran, D.V., Tran, C.X., Nguyen, M.L.: Learning to summarize web documents using social information. In: ICTAI, pp. 619–626 (2016)
21. Shen, D., Sun, J.T., Li, H., Yang, Q., Chen, Z.: Document summarization using conditional random fields. In: IJCAI, pp. 2862–2867 (2007)
22. Sun, J.T., Shen, D., Zeng, H.J., Yang, Q., Lu, Y., Chen, Z.: Web-page summarization using clickthrough data. In: SIGIR, pp. 194–201 (2005)

23. Svore, K.M., Vanderwende, L., Burges, C.J.: Enhancing single-document summarization by combining ranknet and third-party sources. In: EMNLP-CoNLL, pp. 448–457 (2007)
24. Wei, Z., Gao, W.: Utilizing microblogs for automatic news highlights extraction. In: COLING, pp. 872–883 (2014)
25. Wei, Z., Gao, W.: Gibberish, assistant, or master?: using tweets linking to news for extractive single-document summarization. In: SIGIR, pp. 1003–1006 (2015)
26. Yang, Z., Cai, K., Tang, J., Zhang, L., Su, Z., Li, J.: Social context summarization. In: SIGIR, pp. 255–264 (2011)

"What Does My Classifier Learn?" A Visual Approach to Understanding Natural Language Text Classifiers

Jonas Paul Winkler(✉) and Andreas Vogelsang

Daimler Center for Automotive IT Innovations, Technische Universität Berlin, Berlin, Germany
{jonas.winkler,andreas.vogelsang}@tu-berlin.de

Abstract. Neural Networks have been utilized to solve various tasks such as image recognition, text classification, and machine translation and have achieved exceptional results in many of these tasks. However, understanding the inner workings of neural networks and explaining why a certain output is produced are no trivial tasks. Especially when dealing with text classification problems, an approach to explain network decisions may greatly increase the acceptance of neural network supported tools. In this paper, we present an approach to visualize reasons why a classification outcome is produced by convolutional neural networks by tracing back decisions made by the network. The approach is applied to various text classification problems, including our own requirements engineering related classification problem. We argue that by providing these explanations in neural network supported tools, users will use such tools with more confidence and also may allow the tool to do certain tasks automatically.

Keywords: Visual feedback · Neural networks · Artificial intelligence · Machine learning · Natural language processing · Explanations · Requirements engineering

1 Introduction

Artificial Neural Networks have become powerful tools for performing a wide variety of tasks such as image classification, text classification, and speech recognition. Within the natural language processing community, neural networks have been used to tackle various tasks such as machine translation, sentiment analysis, authorship attribution, and also more fundamental tasks such as part-of-speech tagging, chunking, and named entity recognition [4]. More recently, convolutional neural networks that were almost exclusively used for image processing tasks were also adapted to solve natural language processing tasks [5].

However, neural networks usually do not explain why certain decisions are made. Especially when incorporating a trained neural network in a tool with heavy user interaction, users may need to understand why the network produced

F. Frasincar et al. (Eds.): NLDB 2017, LNCS 10260, pp. 468–479, 2017.
DOI: 10.1007/978-3-319-59569-6_55

certain results in order to make better decisions. If such an explanation is not provided, users may be frustrated because they do not understand the reasons behind some decisions and consequently do not profit from the tool. In order to provide such explanations, additional techniques are required.

In this paper, we propose a technique to trace back decisions made by convolutional neural networks and provide visual feedback to explain these decisions. The basic idea is to identify which parts of the network contributed the most to a decision and to further identify the corresponding words in the input sentence. We use that information to highlight certain parts within the input sentence.

The remainder of this paper is structured as follows. Our approach for computing *Document Influence Matrices* and creating visual representations is presented in Sect. 3. In Sect. 4, we evaluate our approach on three different datasets. We describe how we apply our approach on a specific use case in Sect. 5. Section 6 concludes.

2 Related Research

Understanding neural networks and providing explanations for network decisions is a well-established area of research. Early approaches use fuzzy logic and create rules from trained networks, ultimately explaining how input neurons relate to output neurons [2,3]. In contrast to these works, our approach operates on individual classification results, similar to what has been presented in [1,8]. These methods usually exploit the weights of a trained network to compute an explanation gradient. These gradients may then be used to identify individual inputs as particularly important.

Application of this type of approach to image classification tasks are presented in [10,11]. Here, the authors visualize intermediate networks layers to understand what the network has learned.

Within the natural language processing community, approaches to explain natural language classifiers exist as well. In [6], the authors visualize network structures to show the impact of salient words on the classification outcome.

3 Document Influence Matrices

In this section, we present our approach to compute *Document Influence Matrices*, which contain information about how strongly each word in an input document contributes to a decision made by a convolutional neural network. These matrices may then be used to create visual representations, which highlight individual words that contributed most to the classification outcome.

3.1 Classifying Text Using CNNs

This section describes the operations performed by convolutional neural networks as proposed by [5]. The architecture of the network is displayed in Fig. 1.

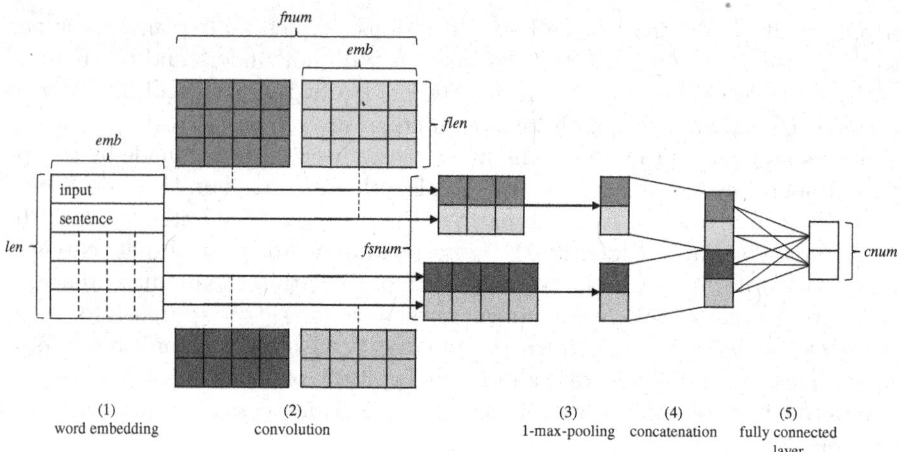

Fig. 1. Network architecture as proposed by [5] (Color figure online)

(1) **Word embedding.** The first step is to transform documents into numerical representations. This is done by using the word2vec [7] word embedding technique. Word2vec maps individual words to vectors $v \in \mathbb{R}^{emb}$, where *emb* is the number of dimensions used for the word embedding. The word vectors are obtained by training the word2vec model on a corpus. Furthermore, each input document may be transformed into a matrix $s \in \mathbb{R}^{len,emb}$, where *len* is the length of the input document.

(2) **Convolution.** Next, a convolution operation applies filters to the input document matrix. A filter is a matrix $f \in \mathbb{R}^{flen,emb}$ of trainable weights, where *flen* is the length of the filter. A filter set is a rank-3 tensor $fs \in \mathbb{R}^{fnum,flen,emb}$ and contains *fnum* filters of the same length. Multiple sets of filters with varying filter lengths may be used. In Fig. 1, two sets of filters (blue and red) with filter length 3 and 2 are illustrated. A filter set is applied to a document matrix by moving each filter as a sliding window over the matrix, producing a single value at each position resulting in a matrix $v^{(1)} \in \mathbb{R}^{fnum,len+1-flen}$:

$$v_{i,j}^{(1)} = \sigma\left(\left(\sum_{k=1}^{flen}\sum_{l=1}^{emb} fs_{i,k,l} \cdot s_{j+k-1,l}\right) + b_i\right) \quad (1)$$

In this equation, σ is an arbitrary activation function, such as *sigmoid* or *rectified linear units* and $b \in \mathbb{R}^{fnum}$ holds a trainable bias for each filter.

(3) **1-max-pooling.** 1-max-pooling reduces $v^{(1)}$ from the previous step to a vector $v^{(2)} \in \mathbb{R}^{fnum}$ by selecting the maximum value of each filter:

$$v_i^{(2)} = \max\left(v_{i,1}^{(1)}, v_{i,2}^{(1)}, ..., v_{i,len+1-flen}^{(1)}\right) \quad (2)$$

(4) **Concatenation.** The computations described in step 2 and 3 are performed once for each filter set, resulting in multiple matrices $v^{(2,i)}$. Given *fsnum* filter

sets, these are concatenated to form a feature vector $v^{(3)} \in \mathbb{R}^{fsnum \cdot fnum}$:

$$v^{(3)} = v^{(2,1)} \| v^{(2,2)} \| ... \| v^{(2,fsnum)} \tag{3}$$

(5) **Fully connected layer.** This feature vector is used as the input for a fully connected layer, in which values from the feature vector are associated with the output classes. Given *cnum* output classes, the output $v^{(4)} \in \mathbb{R}^{cnum}$ of this layer is computed as follows:

$$v_i^{(4)} = \left(\sum_{j=1}^{fsnum \cdot fnum} w_{j,i} \cdot v_j^{(3)} \right) + b_i \tag{4}$$

In this equation, $w \in \mathbb{R}^{fsnum \cdot fnum, cnum}$ is a matrix of trainable weights and $b \in \mathbb{R}^{cnum}$ is a vector of trainable biases.

Finally, the values computed for the output classes are transformed into true probabilities by applying the *softmax* function.

After the network is trained on a training dataset, its filters have learned to identify output classes based on the presence or absence of certain words and word groups. For any given input document, the network yields probabilities for all classes, indicating which class the input document belongs to.

3.2 Computing Document Influence Matrices

A Document Influence Matrix is a matrix $DIM \in \mathbb{R}^{len, cnum}$. Each value $DIM_{i,c}$ indicates how strongly the word at position i influences the network to classify the document as class c. A high value at $DIM_{i,c}$ means that the word at position i strongly suggests the classification of the document as class c, whereas a value close to 0 means that there is no correlation between the word and the class.

To compute a Document Influence Matrix for a particular input document, we analyze the output of the network and trace the decisions made by the network at each layer back to its input. This is done by consecutively computing intermediate influence matrices (IIM) at each major step.

(1) **Examining the network output.** When the network has reliably classified a document as a particular class, the output of the network for this true class will be close to 1, whereas the outputs for the other classes will be close to 0. The definition of the *softmax* function implies that the output of the fully connected layer for the true class is much higher than any of the outputs for the false classes.

(2) **Tracing back fully connected layers.** Let us examine Eq. 4 for computing the output of a fully connected layer in more detail. It may also be written as follows:

$$v_i^{(4)} = w_{1,i} \cdot v_1^{(3)} + w_{2,i} \cdot v_2^{(3)} + ... + w_{m,i} \cdot v_m^{(3)} + b_i \tag{5}$$

Since the result of this equation for the true class is much higher than the result for any of the other classes, it must have more $w_{j,i} \cdot v_j$ summands

with high values. Therefore, a $w_{j,i} \cdot v_j$ summand with a high value has a strong influence towards classifying an input document as a particular class, whereas a $w_{j,i} \cdot v_j$ summand with a negative value has a strong influence against classifying an input document as a particular class.
Furthermore, each $w_{j,i} \cdot v_j$ summand may be associated with one particular input neuron of the layer. The influence of one particular input neuron on a certain class is thus defined by the sum of all related $w_{j,i} \cdot v_j$ summands. The matrix $IIM^{(fcl)} \in \mathbb{R}^{inum,cnum}$ for a fully connected layer with *inum* input neurons and *onum* output neurons is computed as follows:

$$IIM^{(fcl)}_{i,c} = \sum_{j=1}^{onum} IIM_{j,c} \cdot w_{i,j} \cdot v_i \tag{6}$$

(3) **Tracing back concatenation.** In Sect. 3.1, step 4, multiple feature vectors are concatenated to form a single feature vector. To trace back the concatenation operation, the previous IIM is sliced into multiple pieces, resulting in *fsnum* matrices $IIM^{(concat,fsnum)} \in \mathbb{R}^{fnum,cnum}$:

$$IIM^{(concat,n)}_{i,c} = IIM_{(n-1)\cdot fnum+i,c} \tag{7}$$

Each of these matrices is traced back further individually.
(4) **Tracing back 1-max-pooling.** 1-max-pooling is used to select the highest out of several values resulting from the application of one particular filter everywhere in the input document. Only this highest value has impact on the classification outcome and thus receives all influence. The rank-3 tensor $IIM^{(1max)} \in \mathbb{R}^{fnum,len+1-flen,cnum}$ is computed as follows:

$$IIM^{(1max)}_{i,j,c} = \begin{cases} IIM_{j,c} & v^{(1)}_{i,j} = v^{(2)}_{j} \\ 0 & \text{otherwise} \end{cases} \tag{8}$$

(5) **Tracing back convolutional layers.** Tracing back convolutional layers follows the same principles as tracing back fully connected layers. The rank-3 tensor $IIM^{(conv)} \in \mathbb{R}^{len,emb,cnum}$ is computed as follows:

$$IIM^{(conv)}_{i,j,c} = \sum_{k=1}^{fnum} \sum_{l=1}^{len+1-flen} IIM_{k,l,c} \cdot s_{i,j} \cdot \begin{cases} fs_{k,i+1-l,j} & i+1-l \in [1, flen] \\ 0 & \text{otherwise} \end{cases} \tag{9}$$

(6) **Putting it all together.** So far we have defined operations for computing IIMs for each operation of the neural network. A DIM may be computed using the following procedure:
1. Define an initial influence matrix $IM \in \mathbb{R}^{cnum,cnum}$ where $IM_{c,c} = out_c$ for each class c. All other fields are zero. Given the output of the last layer of the network, this matrix states that each output has influence on its respective class only.
2. Compute Intermediate Influence Matrices according to the architecture of the network. At the concatenation step, continue individually for every split.

3. Perform element-wise summation of all $IIM^{(conv)}$ matrices:

$$IIM^{(sum)} = \sum_{i=1}^{fsnum} IIM^{(conv,i)} \tag{10}$$

   The matrix $IIM^{(sum)}$ holds influence values of all word2wec components of each word of the input document on each of the output classes.
4. Reduce the matrix $IIM^{(sum)}$ to a matrix $DIM \in \mathbb{R}^{len,cnum}$:

$$DIM_{i,c} = \sum_{j=1}^{emb} IIM^{(sum)}_{i,j,c} \tag{11}$$

   This matrix finally contains individual influence values of each word on each output class.

3.3 Creating a Visual Representation from Document Influence Matrices

A visual representation of a Document Influence Matrix may be created by following these steps:

1. Normalize the matrix so that all of its values are within the range $[0, 1]$.
2. Select a distinct color for each class.
3. For each word in the document, select the highest value from the normalized matrix, select the color of the class corresponding to this value, use the value as the colors transparency, and use that color as the background for the word.

Table 1 shows examples from the datasets used in our experiments.

4 Experiments and Results

To prove the effectiveness of our approach, we conducted two different experiments on multiple datasets.

The datasets used in these experiments are listed in Table 2. The *Requirements* dataset contains natural language requirements written in German and taken from multiple requirement specification documents describing automotive components and systems, such as wiper control, outside lighting, etc. It also contains an equal number of *Information* objects (e.g. examples, informal descriptions, and references). More information on this dataset is given in Sect. 5.

The *Question* dataset[1] contains short natural language questions asking for different kinds of answers, such as locations, numeric answers (dates, numbers), persons, entities, descriptions, and abbreviations. The task is to detect what kind of information a question asks for.

The *Movie Reviews* dataset[2] consists of single line movie reviews. These are either positive or negative.

[1] http://cogcomp.cs.illinois.edu/Data/QA/QC/.

[2] https://www.cs.cornell.edu/people/pabo/movie-review-data/.

Table 1. Examples

Dataset	Requirements[2]
Classes	requirement information
requirement	the duration until the switch is recognized as hanging must be a configurable parameter .
information	the component conditionally drives an external fan . this fan is required for active ventilation of the headlight .
Dataset	Questions
Classes	description numeric human entity abbreviation location
description	why did the chicken cross the road ?
numeric	how long does it take sunlight to reach earth ?
human	which of the following people is not associated with andy warhol ?
Dataset	Movie Reviews
Classes	positive negative
positive	both a successful adaptation and an enjoyable film in its own right .
negative	just a bunch of good actors flailing around in a caper that's neither original nor terribly funny .
negative	... unbearably lame .
positive	it's a minor comedy that tries to balance sweetness with coarseness , while it paints a sad picture of the singles scene .

Table 2. Datasets

Dataset	Classes	Train examples	Test examples	Classification accuracy
Requirements	2	1854	206	84.95 %
Questions	6	4906	546	83.70 %
Movie Reviews	2	9595	1067	73.29 %

4.1 Analyzing Most Often Highlighted Words

The goal of our first experiment is to prove that our approach is capable of finding and highlighting relevant words within input documents. Since our approach assigns high influence values to important words and low influence values to unimportant words, aggregating highly influential words per class should yield lists of words commonly used to describe individuals of a particular class.

We computed Document Influence Matrices for all examples in the test set of each dataset. Then, for each individual word used in the dataset, we aggregated the total influence of that word across all Document Influence Matrices per class. This results in lists of words per class and their influence on that class (i.e. how often are they highlighted in the test set). The words were sorted descending by their accumulated influence.

Table 3. Requirements dataset: most often highlighted words

Class	Most often highlighted words
Requirement	must, of, must (plural), contractor, be, shall, may, client, that, shall (plural), active, to, supply voltage, a, agreed, must (old German spelling)
Information	described, can (plural), two, can, the, defined, requirements, in, only, included, description, vehicle, so, require, deliver, specification

Table 4. Questions dataset: most often highlighted words

Class	Most often highlighted words
Abbreviation	stand, does, abbreviation, mean, is, for, an, number, beer, fame, term
Description	how, what, is, do, are, the, does, why, a, origin, did, of, difference, mean
Entity	what, the, name, was, is, of, a, fear, are, for, does, did, to, do, color
Human	who, what, was, name, the, of, and, actor, company, school, tv
Location	where, country, city, can, capital, the, was, state, are, what, does, in, of
Numeric	how, many, when, did, does, was, year, long, the, do, average, is, of

Table 3 shows the results for the *Requirements* dataset. Words commonly used to write requirements such as *must* and *shall* and their various German variations (i.e. "The system shall ..." and "The contractor must ensure that ...") are highlighted most frequently, which is exactly what we expected. A commonly used information-type sentence in our dataset is a reference to another document (i.e. "further requirements are *specified* in ...") and as such, the word *specified* is highlighted very often. The other words are not particularly significant. Furthermore, many sentences not containing certain requirement keywords are information, although it is hard to specifically tell why exactly a sentence is an information based on its words.

The results for the *Questions* dataset are displayed in Table 4. Most of the classes can be identified very easy based on certain combinations of question words and pronouns. Questions starting with "how many" are most likely asking for numeric answers, "who was" is a strong indicator for a question asking for a human's name, and sentences containing "in which city" usually ask for a specific location. The results in the table show that these terms are indeed the most frequently highlighted.

Table 5 contains the most often highlighted words for the *Movie Reviews* dataset. The list of positive words contains expected words such as *best*, *worth*, *fun*, *good* and *funny*, but also words that we would not associate with positive reviews at all (e.g. *that*, *is*, *of*, etc.). It seems that these words are often used in phrasings with a positive sentiment. The word *but* is highlighted most in negative reviews since it is often used when something is criticized (e.g., "The plot was okay, *but* ..."). Also, different negative words such as *bad*, *doesn't*, *no*, and *isn't* appear in this list since these are often used to express negative sentiment.

Table 5. Movie Reviews dataset: most often highlighted words

Class	Most often highlighted words
Positive	that, is, of, a, has, film, us, with, best, makes, an, worth, performances, it's, fun, who, good, documentary, funny
Negative	but, too, and, more, bad, no, so, movie, in, or, doesn't, just, only, about, the, there's, i, are, isn't

4.2 Measuring the Quality of the Visual Representations

We have conducted an empirical study to assess the quality of the visual representations created by our approach in more detail.

For each example in the test sets, we manually decided which words should be most important for deciding the class and then compared our expectation to the actual visual representation. Each example is then assigned one of the following quality categories:

- **Perfect match.** Our approach highlighted exactly all words that we considered to be important. No additional and unexpected words are highlighted.
- **Partial match.** Only some of the words we considered to be important are highlighted. No additional and unexpected words are highlighted.
- **Mixed match.** The visual representation highlights some or all of the expected words. Additionally, some words, which we considered to be irrelevant, are also highlighted.
- **Mismatch.** The visual representation did not highlight any expected words.

After conducting this evaluation on all three datasets, we accumulated the count of perfect, partial, mixed, and mismatches in total. In order to better understand the results, we also separately accumulated the counts on correctly/incorrectly classified examples and on examples with prediction probabilities greater/less than 95%. The results are displayed in Fig. 2.

On the *Requirements* dataset, 57% of the examples are highlighted according to our expectations. On 16% of the examples, the visual representations are not useful at all. On the visual representations of the remaining 27% of the examples either not all expected words are highlighted or some unexpected words are highlighted as well.

The separated results on correctly and incorrectly classified examples reveals that our approach naturally fails to provide reasonable visual representations for incorrectly classified examples. Contrariwise, for almost all (94%) correctly classified examples, the visual representation contained all or at least some relevant words. Inspecting the prediction probabilities also reveals an interesting correlation: The visual representation of an example with a high prediction probability is more likely to be correct than the visual representation of an example with a low prediction probability.

Within the *Question* dataset, about 59% of all examples are accurately highlighted. 11% of the examples are partially highlighted, whereas within the remaining 30%, irrelevant words are highlighted. Just as with the *Requirements*

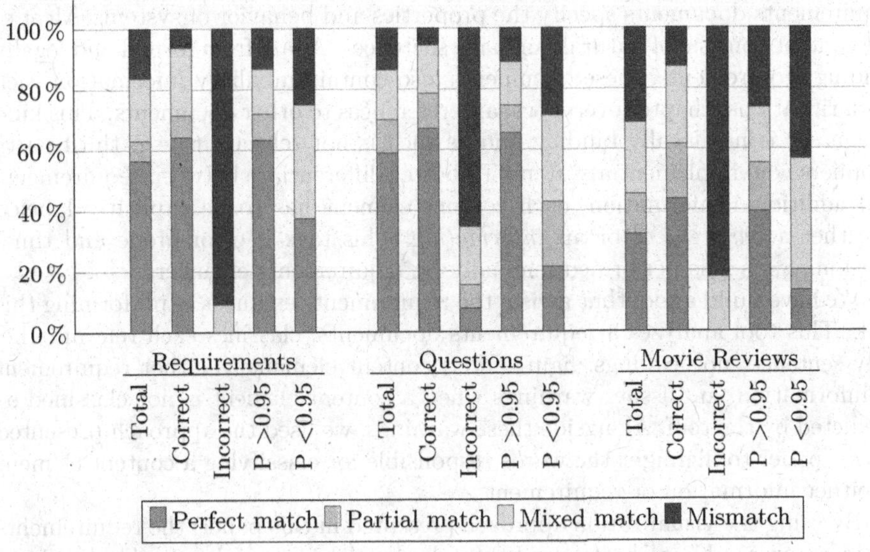

Fig. 2. Relation between important words and words highlighted by the approach.

dataset, the overall quality of the visual representations on correctly classified examples and examples with high prediction probabilities is much higher than the overall quality on incorrectly classified examples and examples with low prediction probabilities.

Results on the *Movie Reviews* dataset are considerably worse than the results on the other two datasets. Only 32% of the examples had completely correct visual representations. In 69% of all cases, at lease some relevant words are highlighted. In 55% of all examples, irrelevant words are highlighted as well. We suspect that this is due to the lower accuracy of the model compared with the other two models and due to the higher complexity of the classification task.

Based on the individual results for these three datasets, we made the following general observations:

- The overall quality of the visual representations strongly correlates with the performance of the trained model. The higher the accuracy of the model on the test set, the better the overall quality, i.e. more relevant and less irrelevant words are highlighted.
- The quality of an individual examples' visual representation correlates with the probability on the predicted class. Higher probabilities usually lead to visual representations closer to what we expected.

5 Application to Natural Language Requirements Classification

We have applied the approach presented in our previous works [9] in an industrial setting to automatically classify natural language requirements, which are written down in requirements specification of automotive systems. These requirements documents specify the properties and behavior of systems. Most of the content consists of natural language sentences. Apart from formal and legally binding requirements, these documents also contain auxiliary information such as clarifications, chapter overviews, and references to other documents. This kind of content is not legally binding and as such is not relevant to e.g. third party suppliers who implement a system. To better differentiate between requirements and additional information, each content element has to be explicitly labeled as either a *requirement* or an *information*. This task is error-prone and time-consuming, as it is performed manually by requirements engineers.

We have build a tool that assists the requirements engineer in performing this task. This tool analyzes a requirements documents, classifies each relevant (i.e. only sentence, no headings, figures etc.) content element as either requirement or information, and issues warnings when a content element is not classified as predicted by the tool. Alongside these warnings, we used the approach presented in this paper to highlight the words responsible for classifying a content element as either information or requirement.

By using the visualization approach presented in this paper, the requirements engineers were able to better understand why the tool made specific decisions. If a user does not understand the classification outcome, the user is pinpointed to phrases or individual words that contribute to the outcome. The user can interpret these results and react to them in several ways:

- The user recognizes that the chosen phrasing may not be suitable for the kind of content the user wants to express. Therefore, the user may revise the sentence and thus increase the quality of the specification.
- The user recognizes that rules for classifying content items are used inconsistently between requirements engineers. Therefore, the user initiates a discussion for specific phrases or formulations w.r.t. their classification.
- The user recognizes that the tool has learned something wrong or that the learned decision procedure does not match the current classification rules (which may change over time). Therefore, the user marks this result as a false positive. The neural network may adapt to this decision and keep up to date (c.f. active learning).

6 Conclusions and Future Work

In this paper, we have presented an approach to create visual representations for natural language sentences, which explain classifier decisions by highlighting particularly important words. As shown in our evaluation, these visual representations are accurate as long as the underlying model is accurate.

As we integrated our approach in our requirement classification tool, we have received very positive feedback from industry experts. We argue that an approach to explain network classification decisions to users increases both usability and acceptance of a tool. A visual approach as presented in this paper is sufficient although any other approach may work as well.

In the future, we plan to conduct a more extensive field study on a large user base to better understand the qualities and limitations of our approach.

References

1. Baehrens, D., Schroeter, T., Harmeling, S., Kawanabe, M., Hansen, K., Müller, K.R.: How to explain individual classification decisions. J. Mach. Learn. Res. **11**, 1803–1831 (2010)
2. Benítez, J.M., Castro, J.L., Requena, I.: Are artificial neural networks black boxes? IEEE Trans. Neural Netw. **8**(5), 1156–1164 (1997)
3. Castro, J.L., Mantas, C.J., Benítez, J.M.: Interpretation of artificial neural networks by means of fuzzy rules. IEEE Trans. Neural Netw. **13**(1), 101–116 (2002)
4. Collobert, R., Weston, J., Bottou, L., Karlen, M., Kavukcuoglu, K., Kuksa, P.: Natural language processing (almost) from scratch. J. Mach. Learn. Res. **12**, 2493–2537 (2011)
5. Kim, Y.: Convolutional neural networks for sentence classification. In: Proceedings of the 2014 Conference on Empirical Methods in Natural Language Processing (EMNLP), pp. 1746–1751 (2014)
6. Li, J., Chen, X., Hovy, E., Jurafsky, D.: Visualizing and understanding neural models in NLP. In: Proceedings of NAACL-HLT, pp. 681–691. Association for Computational Linguistics, San Diego, California (2016)
7. Mikolov, T., Chen, K., Corrado, G., Dean, J.: Efficient estimation of word representations in vector space. arXiv preprint arXiv:1301.3781 (2013)
8. Ribeiro, M.T., Singh, S., Guestrin, C.: "Why should i trust you?" explaining the predictions of any classifier. In: Proceedings of the 22nd ACM SIGKDD International Conference on Knowledge Discovery and Data Mining, pp. 1135–1144. ACM, New York (2016)
9. Winkler, J.P., Vogelsang, A.: Automatic classification of requirements based on convolutional neural networks. In: 3rd IEEE International Workshop on Artificial Intelligence for Requirements Engineering (AIRE) (2016)
10. Yosinski, J., Clune, J., Nguyen, A.M., Fuchs, T., Lipson, H.: Understanding neural networks through deep visualization. In: Deep Learning Workshop, 31st International Conference on Machine Learning (2015)
11. Zeiler, M.D., Fergus, R.: Visualizing and understanding convolutional networks. In: Fleet, D., Pajdla, T., Schiele, B., Tuytelaars, T. (eds.) ECCV 2014. LNCS, vol. 8689, pp. 818–833. Springer, Cham (2014). doi:10.1007/978-3-319-10590-1_53

Gated Neural Network for Sentence Compression Using Linguistic Knowledge

Yang Zhao[1,2(✉)], Hajime Senuma[1,2], Xiaoyu Shen[3], and Akiko Aizawa[1,2(✉)]

[1] The University of Tokyo, 7-3-1 Hongo, Bunkyo-ku, Tokyo, Japan
zhao@is.s.u-tokyo.ac.jp

[2] National Institute of Informatics, 2-1-2 Hitotsubashi, Chiyoda-ku, Tokyo, Japan
{senuma,aizawa}@nii.ac.jp

[3] Spoken Language System, Saarland University, Saarbrücken, Germany
xshen@lsv.uni-saarland.de

Abstract. Previous works have recognized that linguistic features such as part of speech and dependency labels are helpful for sentence compression that aims to simplify a text while leaving its underlying meaning. In this work, we introduce a gating mechanism and propose a gated neural network that selectively exploits linguistic knowledge for deletion-based sentence compression. Experimental results on two popular datasets show that the proposed gated neural network equipped with selectively fused linguistic features leads to better compressions upon both automatic metric and human evaluation, compared with a previous competitive compression system. We also investigate the gating mechanism through visualization analysis.

Keywords: Sentence compression · Neural network · Gating mechanism · Linguistic knowledge

1 Introduction

Sentence compression is an important task in text simplification that aims to simplify a text while remaining leaving its underlying meaning. In this technique, the grammar and structure of sentences are compressed to generate more concise sentences, which contributes ideally to improving the automatic summarization and statistical machine translation [1]. In recent years, most of the sentence compression systems have been deletion-based; the compressions consist of subsequent tokens of the original sequence [1,5,10,12,13]. For example, if an input sentence, as the Fig. 1 shows, is, *A man suffered a serious head injury after an early morning car crash today.*, an appropriate compression would be *A man suffered a serious head injury after an car crash.* In such a way, compression is generated by keeping and dropping tokens in the original input.

To avoid introducing grammatical mistakes in the compressions, previous works have usually relied on syntactic information or syntactic features as signals [2,5,10,13], or directly pruned dependency or constituency trees [1,7,12]

F. Frasincar et al. (Eds.): NLDB 2017, LNCS 10260, pp. 480–491, 2017.
DOI: 10.1007/978-3-319-59569-6_56

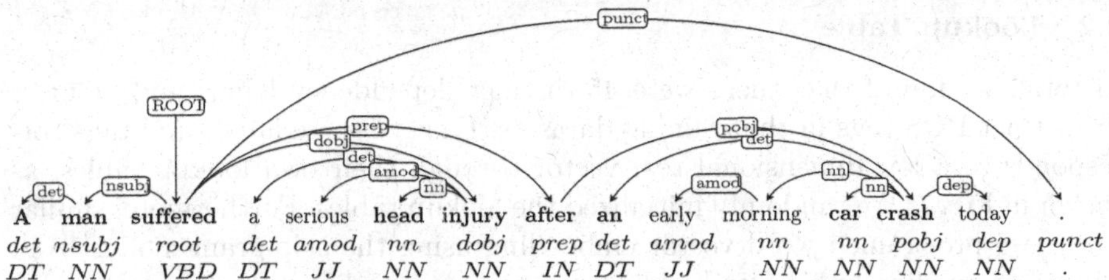

Fig. 1. Dependency parsing result of the example sentence from Google dataset, which lies in the first row. Bold words refer to the compression, the second row consists of dependency labels for each word, while the third row consists of part-of-speech tags for each word.

to generate compressions. Recently, much attention has been given to neural-networks-based approaches that does not require labor-intensive feature designs. Filippova et al. [8], for the first time, applied LSTM to sentence compression; Klerke et al. [11] further leveraged eye-movement information in multi-tasking through LSTMs and achieved encouraging performance. In this work, we propose linguistic knowledge based gated neural networks capable of selectively utilizing these linguistic features to make prediction. We will detail it later in Sect. 2. In short, our contributions are two-fold:

- Incorporate linguistic knowledge into recurrent neural networks to make better use of syntactic information for sentence compression.
- Propose a gating mechanism for sentence compression to selectively exploit linguistic features and achieve competitive results on the downstream datasets. A visualization analysis of the gating mechanism is also conducted.

2 Models

2.1 Linguistic Knowledge

In this work, two kinds of linguistic features are considered, dependency labels and part-of-speech (POS) tags. We firstly parse[1] the input sentences and yield the dependency labels as well as POS tags for each word. Figure 1 gives an example; each node (word) in a dependency tree would have a unique parent node except for the root node for which we assign the "ROOT" label. We take the modified relations labels between target word and its parent as the dependency labels. Likewise, we label each word in sentences with POS tags using parser.

[1] We use Parsey McParseface, one of the state-of-the-art English parsers released by Google https://github.com/tensorflow/models/tree/master/syntaxnet.

2.2 Lookup Table

In total, we found that there were 45 distinct dependency labels and at most 38 distinct POS tags in the training datasets. Each of these labels and tags corresponds to a low-dimensional real vector through their own lookup tables, as shown in Fig. 2. We randomly initialized the lookup tables. Furthermore, similar to [8], we pre-trained word vector embedding using the skip-gram model[2] [14]. Therefore, we finally have embedding, dependency, and POS lookup tables. By virtue of these lookup tables, each word corresponds to three feature representations whose concatenation is taken as the input of neural networks.

2.3 Linguistic Knowledge Based Recurrent Neural Network (LK-RNN)

The recurrent neural network (RNN) [6] is able to model sequences with arbitrary length and bi-directional RNN is even more powerful, capable of capturing both forward and backward information. Formally, the hidden layer h_i^1 in the forward direction and the hidden layer h_i^2 in the backward direction are

$$h_i^1 = tanh(W_1 x_i + U_1 h_{i-1}^1 + b_1),$$

$$h_i^2 = tanh(W_2 x_i + U_2 h_{i+1}^2 + b_2),$$

where W_1, U_1, b_1 and W_2, U_2, b_2 are model parameters. As shown in Fig. 2, we obtain $h_i^{12} = [h_i^1; h_i^2]$ for the i-th word in input sentences. Here, [ ] means the concatenation operation of vectors. We take the concatenation of feature representations as input to a two layer bi-directional RNN (two bi- RNN units) followed by a fully connected layer. The output layer is a SoftMax classifier that predicts label 1 if a word is to be retained in the compression or label 0 if a word is to be dropped.

2.4 Linguistic Knowledge Based Gated Neural Network (LK-GNN)

On the top of LK-RNN, we add a gated neural network (GNN) unit between the bi-directional RNN and Softmax layer, as shown in Fig. 2. The added GNN is capable of fusing each feature to yield a combination in the first place.

$$r_1 = sigmoid(W_3[h_i^{12}; x_i^{emb}] + b_3)$$

$$r_2 = sigmoid(W_4[h_i^{12}; x_i^{dep}] + b_4)$$

$$r_3 = sigmoid(W_5[h_i^{12}; x_i^{pos}] + b_5)$$

Here, the contextual information, h_i^{12}, can be seen as a conditioning signal for gates. Similar to candidate activation in a GRU unit [3], the combination of three feature inputs, h_i^r, is yielded through element-wise multiplication $\odot$.

$$h_i^r = r_1 \odot x_i^{emb} + r_2 \odot x_i^{dep} + r_3 \odot x_i^{pos}$$

[2] https://code.google.com/p/word2vec/.

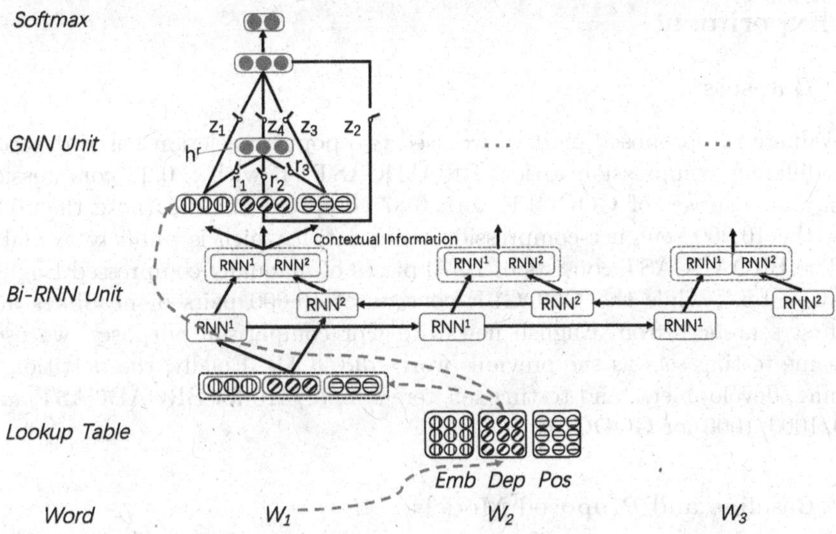

Fig. 2. Graphical illustration of gated neural network. Emb, Dep, and Pos respectively stand for word embedding, dependency, and part-of-speech lookup tables.

Then, update gates z_1, z_2, z_3 and z_4 are used to yield linear interpolation between three feature inputs and their combination, h_i^z.

$$z_1 = exp(W_6[h_i^{12}; x_i^{emb}] + b_6)$$

$$z_2 = exp(W_7[h_i^{12}; x_i^{dep}] + b_7)$$

$$z_3 = exp(W_8[h_i^{12}; x_i^{pos}] + b_8)$$

$$z_4 = exp(W_9[h_i^{12}; h_i^r] + b_9)$$

Each z_i is normalized by their sum $\sum_i z_i$. Finally,

$$h_i^z = z_1 \odot x_{emb} + z_2 \odot x_{dep} + z_3 \odot x_{pos} + z_4 \odot h_i^r$$

Here, h_i^z is fed into the SoftMax layer to make a prediction. x^{emb}, x^{dep}, x^{pos}, W_i, b_i (i ranges from 1 to 9), U_1, U_2 and W_{10}, b_{10} (for the SoftMax layer) are parameters to be learned during training. Models are trained to minimize a cross-entropy loss function, with a l_2 regularization term.

$$L(\theta) = -\sum_{w \in S} \sum_{i=1}^{C} P_i^{'} logP_i + \frac{\lambda}{2} \parallel \theta \parallel^2,$$

where θ is the set of model parameters, w refers to a word, S refers to a sentence, C is the number of classes (here, C = 2) and P_i is the predicted probability. $P_i^{'}$ has a 1-of-K coding scheme where k equals the number of classes, and the dimension corresponding to the ground truth is 1, with all others being 0. λ is the regularization hyper-parameter.

3 Experiment

3.1 Datasets

To evaluate the proposed models, we used two popular deletion based datasets with different compression ratios, BROADCAST [4] with a 0.27 compression ratio, and a subset of GOOGLE with 0.87 compression ratio (note that 0.87 is for the 10,000 sentence-compression pairs data), which is publicly available [8]. The BROADCAST consists of 1,370 pieces of manually compressed English newswire text, while the GOOGLE consists of 10,000 pairs of headlines and the first sentences from English newswire. For comparison purposes, we used the same testing sets as the previous works did [8,11]. Finally, the partition of training, development, and testing set were 882/78/410 for BROADCAST, and 8000/1000/1000 for GOOGLE.

3.2 Baseline and Proposed Models

LSTM [9] has shown promises in lots of NLP tasks due to its ability to overcome the vanishing gradient problem and thus retain long-distance dependency. Klerke et al. [11] applied three-layer bi-LSTM to the sentence compression problem. As such, we implemented this three-layer bi-LSTM as the baseline. Furthermore, we also implemented a sequence-to-sequence (seq2seq) framework whose both encoder and decoder are both LSTM, since LSTM network shows promising performance in a variety of NLP tasks. As for parameters setting, the dimension of each input feature was set to 50. The number of dimensions of hidden layers were 150 in the case of GOOGLE, for BROADCAST, these dimensions were halved due to the relatively small size of the training corpus.

The models were trained by using stochastic gradient descent and regularization hyper-parameter λ equals 10^{-4}. The iterations stopped when the accuracy on the development set did not increase any more for a while. All of the experiments were conducted using a deep learning framework, Theano (version 0.8.2). The datasets and codes are publicly available on github [3].

4 Evaluation and Analysis

4.1 Automatic Evaluation

Token-level F_1 score results are presented in Table 1. We observed that both proposed models lead to improvements over the baseline, three-layer bi-LSTM, and across two datasets, suggesting that the introduction of linguistic knowledge did help the models to exploit syntactic information to determine which of the words should be kept or dropped.

Among the others, LK-GNN significantly outperformed the previous state of the art [11], and also showed better performance than LK-RNN (although not

[3] https://github.com/Dodo-Cho/NLDB-2017.

Table 1. F_1 Results for BROADCAST dataset with three annotators and GOOGLE dataset. †, ‡, and ◇ respectively stand for significant difference with 0.95 confidence between two results in the same column. Best results are in bold font.

Model	BROADCAST1	BROADCAST2	BROADCAST3	GOOGLE
Seq2seq (LSTM)	72.44†‡	79.16†‡	66.88†‡	74.83†‡
Baseline	73.91†‡	79.92†‡	68.30†‡	79.90†‡
Klerke et al. (16)	75.19	**82.17**	70.12◇	80.97◇
Our LK-RNN	75.76†	82.09†	71.71†	82.32†
Our LK-GNN	**76.41‡**	82.00‡	**72.34** ‡◇	**82.73**‡◇

significantly). We speculate that this may be because the gating-mechanism-based RNN selectively fuses and exploits features according to different target words and adaptively captures the long-distance relations by virtue of integrating the linguistic knowledge, rather than just capturing sequential relations in the LSTM baseline. It is worth pointing out that while the huge dataset of sentence compressions in [8] is not available to us, we achieved competitive results by using 10,000 sentence-compression pairs (less than 0.5%) instead of 2 million pairs.

To further observe how much of a contribution each linguistic feature makes, we conducted experiments with different combinations of the features as the Table 2 shows. The results show that the combination of all features performed the best, suggesting that all of the features do contribute to the final prediction. Also, adding dependency labels seems to bring a few improvements over the model with word embedding only, while not significantly. This is also true for the part-of-speech feature. These results imply that the dependency label feature and part of speech feature are relatively independent, which is consistent with the fact: a dependency parse connects words according to their dependency relationships, while a constituency parse aims to use sub-phrases in text to form a tree.

Table 2. F_1 Results for BROADCAST and GOOGLE dataset. "Emb" means using the word embedding feature only; "Emb + Dep" means using both word embedding and dependency label as features; "Emb + Pos" means using word embedding and part-of-speech tags as features; "All features" is the our LK-RNN model that uses all the word embedding, dependency label, and part-of-speech tags.

Feature	BROADCAST1	BROADCAST2	BROADCAST3	GOOGLE
Emb	74.01	80.41	70.88	80.67
Emb + Dep	74.11	81.55	71.41	81.86
Emb + Pos	74.65	81.61	71.24	81.48
All features	75.76	82.09	71.71	82.32

4.2 Human Evaluation

We conducted a human evaluation in which the compressions (of the first 200 sentences in the GOOGLE dataset) generated by LK-GNN and the baseline method were shown to two native English speakers. We asked them to rate them in terms of grammatical correctness without showing the original sentences. Then, they were to assign one label out of GNN, BASELINE, BOTH, NEITHER to each pair of sentences, according to the criteria above. Here, GNN means that the compression generated by LK-GNN was better. BASELINE means that the compression generated by the baseline was better. BOTH means that the compressions generated by the two models were the same or nearly the same, and NEITHER means that neither made sense or neither was complete. The results, which are summarized in Fig. 3, show that, on average, in 45% of cases (90/200), the proposed LK-GNN was better than the baseline in terms of syntactically correctness, while in 22.5% of cases (45/200), the baseline performed better. Also, we observed that, in 20% of cases (40/200), the two models performed nearly equally. Both failed in only 12.5% of cases (25/200) where both fail. To assess the inter-assessor agreements, we computed Cohenś unweighted κ [18]. The computed unweighted κ was 0.485, reaching a moderate agreement level [4]. We therefore conclude that the linguistic knowledge supervised neural network is more likely to generate more grammatically correct sentences that make sense.

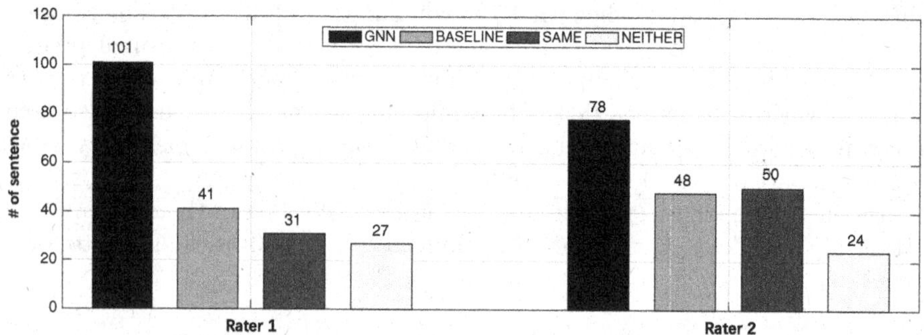

Fig. 3. Human evaluation results of two native English raters. The number on top of each bar means the number of sentences.

For further analysis, we investigated the examples listed in Table 3, which shows that by incorporating syntactic information, gated neural networks performed well in some cases such as in compressing less important phrases (such as G_2^g and G_1^b) or clauses such as (G_2^b), but failed in some ways (such as G_2^g and B_3^b) compared with the baseline model. We are aware of this problem of the

[4] Landis and Koch [17] characterize κ values < 0 as no agreement, 0–0.20 as slight, 0.21–0.40 as fair, 0.41–0.60 as moderate, 0.61–0.80 as substantial, and 0.81–1 as almost perfect agreement.

Table 3. Examples for original sentences (O) and compressions. B and G respectively stand for compression generated by baseline model and proposed LK-GNN. Best one of each set is in bold font. First half of examples are from GOOGLE, while the second half of examples are from BROADCAST.

O_1^g:	A woman accused of beating her poodle puppy to death and then burying it in her backyard was allowed to go free Thursday
B_1^g:	A woman accused of beating her poodle puppy to death
G_1^g:	**A woman accused of beating her puppy to death was allowed to go free**
O_2^g:	A man who was shot in the head in front of his teammates as he walked off a soccer pitch knew his life was in danger, an inquest heard
B_2^g:	A man who was shot off a knew life was
G_2^g:	**A man who was shot knew his life was in danger**
O_3^g:	BWV group middle east has confirmed that the new bmw 5 series will go on sale in the middle east in september
B_3^g:	**New BWV 5 series will go on sale**
G_3^g:	The new BWV 5 series will go on sale east
O_1^b:	Against this background, it is somewhat surprising that EPA would, on its own initiative, undertake a major new program as part of its brownfields action agenda
B_1^b:	would, on its own initiative, undertake a major new program as part of its brownfields action agenda
G_1^b:	**It is surprising EPA would on initiative, undertake a major new program as part of its brownfields action agenda**
O_2^b:	I think we have heard from a very small minority, and unfortunately, they're bullies
B_2^b:	think we have heard from a very small minority, and unfortunately, they're bullies
G_2^b:	**We have heard from a minority and, they're bullies**
O_3^b:	He has a plan where you go, what to do, what to talk about
B_3^b:	**He has a plan where you go, what to do, what to talk about**
G_3^b:	He has a plan where what to do, what to talk about

quality of compressions generated by our method not always being satisfactory, which we believe could be improved by applying a natural language generator to our present compression results. We leave this as the future work.

4.3 Visualization of Gating Mechanism

To further investigate how the gating mechanism adaptively makes use of different linguistic features, we visualized the gates z_1, z_2, z_3 and z_4 using a color gradient map. Each gate was actually a vector and each dimension of this vector corresponds to a real value between 0.0 and 1.0. Gates were normalized by their sum, thus satisfying $\boldsymbol{z_1} + \boldsymbol{z_2} + \boldsymbol{z_3} + \boldsymbol{z_4} = \mathbf{1}$. All gates depended on the contextual information h_i^{12} of the current word. On top on that, $\boldsymbol{z_1}$ is further depended on word embedding; $\boldsymbol{z_2}$ is further depended on dependency label embedding; $\boldsymbol{z_3}$ is further depended on part of speech embedding; $\boldsymbol{z_4}$ is further depended on the fused embedding of word, dependency label, and part of speech embedding. Similar to the GRU unit [3], each gate was thought to be able to control the flow of information and we accordingly assume that the bigger the value of a gate is, the more information flow could go through that gate. For instance, if the dependency gate $\boldsymbol{z_2}$ had a bigger value on each of its dimensions, it would mean that the dependency label embeddings made more of a contribution to the final prediction. Furthermore, since each gate is a vector, for simplicity, we average all dimensions of a gate vector and took its mean as the representative to draw the color gradient map. Thus, each gate vector was turned into a real value (scalar) between 0.0 and 1.0.

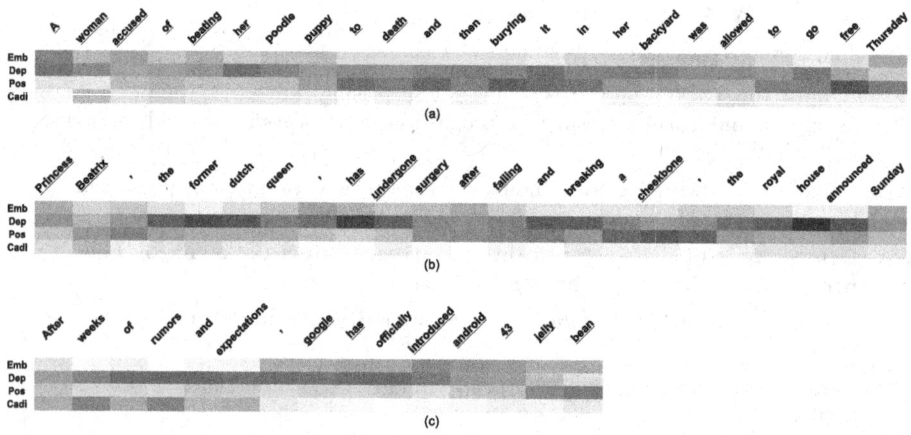

Fig. 4. *Emb*, *Dep*, *Pos*, and *Cadi* respectively refers to z_1, z_2, z_3 and z_4 of our proposed LK-GNN model (Sect. 2.4). The darker each gate is, the more information that flows through each gate; the lighter each gate is, the less information flows through each gate. Words kept by LK-GNN are underlined.

Figure 4 show three example sentences processed by our LK-GNN model: (a), (b), and (c). *Emb*, *Dep*, *Pos*, and *Cadi* respectively refer to word embedding gate $\boldsymbol{z_1}$, dependency label embedding gate $\boldsymbol{z_2}$, part of speech embedding gate $\boldsymbol{z_3}$, and fused embedding gate $\boldsymbol{z_4}$. The darke the corresponding box gets, the more information that flows through the gate; the less the information that flows through the gate, the lighter the box gets. In all example sentences, dependency gate $\boldsymbol{z_2}$ allows more information to go through it, suggesting that dependency information may play an important role in the decision to keep (words with an underline) or drop (word without underline), we did not do statistical significance tests though. To be more specific, for case (b) and (c), the words modified by (*nsubj*, *root*, and *dobj*) were respectively (*Beatrix*, *undergone*, *surgery*) and (*google*, *introduced*, *bean*), which can be viewed as the core of those sentences. This implies that the model learned that these dependency labels are crucial for sentence compression by having more information flow go through that gate. On the other hand, word *free* in (a) made more use of the part-of-speech gate to decide whether it should be kept or not. This means that the proposed model seemed to consider different feature sources to make the best prediction. However, a further and more exact explanation would require more experiments in future.

As a matter of fact, the gating mechanism and attention mechanism share a lot in common. For instance, they both allocate different weights to different information sources, allowing neural network models to focus on the information important to the prediction. However, it is worth pointing out the difference between both. The attention mechanism was originally developed to solve the word alignment problem in neural machine translation. To condition words in a decoder on more relevant hidden states in an encoder, attention weights are used to be as relevant coefficients for each hidden states in the encoder. Its weight is usually a scalar (0-dimensional tensor) in many works such as [20], while it could be a vector (1-dimensional tensor) in a few works such as [21]. In contrast, a gate is a vector capable of dynamically controlling the neural network architecture in that gates seem to change the direction in which the information flow goes by opening or closing the gates. Here, element-wise product operation plays an important role. More importantly, due to the introduction of gates, the neural network has both control information (gate) and data information (such as a neural network layer), which make it a bit different from the commonly used McCulloch-Pitts neural network [22]. Our experimental results also show that through the neural network learning (training), a gate, as a controller of information, is capable of conditioning the prediction on different information sources (inputs), achieving a dynamic network architecture in a sense.

5 Related Works

There are two research lines regarding deletion-based sentence compression. The first one relies on linguistic knowledge such as syntactic information or syntactic features as signals [2,5,10,13]. These linguistic features function as an indicator for compression. In another, [1,7,12] generate compressions directly by pruning dependency or constituency trees. Among others, [16] incorporates linguistic knowledge into a compression model, which is similar to ours. Instead of dropping or keeping words on the word level, they focus on operating on nodes in syntactic trees, yielding better sentence quality.

Another research line is based on neural network methods due to the advances in computational power and data amount. Such kind of methods rely on big labeled data to automatically extract features, with promising results. In 2015, Filippova et al. [8], for the first time, applied LSTM to sentence compression in a sequence-to-sequence learning fashion. They constructed over 2 million sentence-compression pairs and yielded encouraging results. In 2016, [15] represented a neural network architecture for deletion-based sentence compression using over 2.3 million instances as [8] did. They represented word with word embedding, dependency labels, as well as part of speech tags, and sliding a window left-to-right to make decisions on the basis of the local context. However, neither of their large deletion-based sentence compression datasets are publicly available. On the other hand, in the same year, Klerke et al. [11] leveraged eye-movement information as external knowledge in a multi-task learning fashion to achieve comparable performance. Their work implies that external knowledge usually helps in the case of small training datasets. We follow this fashion and take it as a sequence labeling task. While the previous works such as [15,19] also exploit dependency labels and part-of-speech tags, our work is different from them in two ways. Firstly, we represent a neural network architecture that is able to selectively make use of different feature sources. Secondly, we further investigate the gating mechanism through visualization analysis.

6 Conclusion and Future Work

In this work, we proposed a linguistic-knowledge-based gated neural network (LK-GNN) for deletion-based sentence compression. Two kinds of syntactic knowledge are considered, namely, the dependency labels and part-of-speech tags. Experimental results on two popular sentence compression datasets showed that the proposed LK-GNN yielded comparable or better performance in terms of F_1 score and was able to generate more readable sentences. Furthermore, visualization of the gating mechanism suggests that the proposed model seems to be able to selectively employ different features to make the best prediction. In the future, we will consider more semantic features such as combinatory categorical grammar tags or dependency minimal recursion semantics relations to enrich our feature extractions. Also, since our proposed framework is easy to extend to other sequence labeling tasks, we plan to apply it to other relevant NLP tasks.

Acknowledgments. This work was supported by JSPS KAKENHI Grant Numbers 15H02754, 16H02865. We also thank anonymous reviewers for their careful reading and helpful suggestions.

References

1. Berg-Kirkpatrick, T., Gillick, D., Klein, D.: Jointly learning to extract and compress. In: Proceedings of the 49th Annual Meeting of the Association for Computational Linguistics: Human Language Technologies, vol. 1, pp. 481–490 (2011)
2. Bingel, J., Søgaard, A.: Text simplification as tree labeling. In: The 54th Annual Meeting of the Association for Computational Linguistics, pp. 337–343 (2016)
3. Cho, K., van Merriënboer, B., Bahdanau, D., Bengio, Y.: On the properties of neural machine translation: encoder-decoder approaches. In: Syntax, Semantics and Structure in Statistical Translation, pp. 103–111 (2014)
4. Clarke, J., Lapata, M.: Constraint-based sentence compression an integer programming approach. In: Proceedings of the COLING/ACL on Main Conference Poster Sessions, pp. 144–151 (2006)

5. Clarke, J., Lapata, M.: Global inference for sentence compression: an integer linear programming approach. J. Artif. Intell. Res. **31**, 399–429 (2008)
6. Elman, J.L.: Finding structure in time. Cogn. Sci. **14**(2), 179–211 (1990)
7. Filippova, K., Altun, Y.: Overcoming the lack of parallel data in sentence compression. In: EMNLP, pp. 1481–1491 (2013)
8. Filippova, K., Alfonseca, E., Colmenares, C., Kaiser, L., Vinyals, O.: Sentence compression by deletion with LSTMs. In: EMNLP, pp. 360–368 (2015)
9. Gers, F.A., Schmidhuber, J., Cummins, F.: Learning to forget: continual prediction with LSTM. Neural Comput. **12**(10), 2451–2471 (2000)
10. Jing, H.: Sentence reduction for automatic text summarization. In: Proceedings of the sixth Conference on Applied Natural Language Processing, pp. 310–315 (2000)
11. Klerke, S., Goldberg, Y., Søgaard, A.: Improving sentence compression by learning to predict gaze. In: Proceedings of NAACL-HLT 2016, pp. 1528–1533 (2016)
12. Knight, K., Marcu, D.: Statistics-based summarization-step one: sentence compression. In: AAAI/IAAI, pp. 703–710 (2000)
13. McDonald, R.T.: Discriminative sentence compression with soft syntactic evidence. In: EACL, pp. 297–304 (2006)
14. Mikolov, T., Sutskever, I., Chen, K., Corrado, G.S., Dean, J.: Distributed representations of words and phrases and their compositionality. In: Advances in Neural Information Processing Systems, pp. 3111–3119 (2013)
15. Andor, D., Alberti, C., Weiss, D., Severyn, A., Presta, A., Ganchev, K., Petrov, S., Collins, M.: Globally normalized transition-based neural networks (2013). arXiv:1603.06042
16. Li, C., Liu, Y., Liu, F., Zhao, L., Weng, F.: Improving multi-documents summarization by sentence compression based on expanded constituent parse trees. In: EMNLP, pp. 691–701 (2014)
17. Richard Landis, J., Koch, G.G.: The measurement of observer agreement for categorical data. Biometrics **33**, 159–174 (1977)
18. Cohen, J.: A coefficient of agreement for nominal scales. Educ. Psychol. Measur. **20**(1), 37–46 (1960)
19. Chen, D., Manning, C.D.: A fast and accurate dependency parser using neural networks. In: EMNLP, pp. 740–750 (2014)
20. Bahdanau, D., Cho, K., Bengio, Y.: Neural machine translation by jointly learning to align and translate (2014). arXiv:1409.0473
21. Zeng, W., Luo, W., Fidler, S., Urtasun, R.: Efficient summarization with read-again and copy mechanism (2016). arXiv:1611.03382
22. McCulloch, W.S., Pitts, W.: A logical calculus of the ideas immanent in nervous activity. Bull. Math. Biophys. **5**(4), 115–133 (1943)

A Study on Flexibility in Natural Language Generation Through a Statistical Approach to Story Generation

Marta Vicente(✉), Cristina Barros, and Elena Lloret

Department of Software and Computing Systems,
University of Alicante, Alicante, Spain
{mvicente,cbarros,elloret}@dlsi.ua.es

Abstract. This paper presents a novel statistical Natural Language Generation (NLG) approach relying on language models (Positional and Factored Language Models). To prove and validate our approach, we carried out a series of experiments in the scenario of story generation. Through the different configurations tested, our NLG approach is able to produce either a regeneration in the form of a summary of the original story, or a recreation of one story, i.e., a new story based on the entities and actions that the original narration conveys, showing its flexibility to produce different types of stories. The results obtained and the subsequent analysis of the generated stories shows that the macroplanning addressed in this manner is a key step in the process of NLG, improving the quality of the story generated, and decreasing the error rate with respect to not including this stage.

Keywords: Natural language generation · Macroplanning · Content selection · Surface realisation · Story generation

1 Context and Motivation

Macroplanning (i.e., what to say) and surface realisation (i.e., how to say it) are two key stages in the process of Natural Language Generation (NLG). Research in the area usually addresses each of them separately due to their different challenges and goals, with the macroplanning part mostly fixed a priori or manually determined. This results in ad-hoc NLG systems, barely adaptable for being used in several contexts with different communicative goals.

Advancing towards the development of more flexible NLG systems, the main objective of our research is the analysis, design, and evaluation of a novel method able to automatically produce a text according to some genre constraints. Specifically, our current work is focused on the possibility to learn about the presence, relevance or distribution of different kind of elements (i.e., lexical fverbs,

This research work has been partially funded by the Generalitat Valenciana, by the grant ACIF/2016/501, and the Spanish Government through the projects PROMETEOII/2014/001, TIN2015-65100-R, and TIN2015-65136-C2-2-R.

F. Frasincar et al. (Eds.): NLDB 2017, LNCS 10260, pp. 492–498, 2017.
DOI: 10.1007/978-3-319-59569-6_57

nouns,...) as well as their linguistic realisation, in the context of narrative text, in particular, stories for children. We conduct a preliminary analysis into how the approach performs on two tasks: (i) regeneration of stories in the form of an abstractive summary, and (ii) recreation of a story, that consists of generating a new story taking into account the same structure and vocabulary of another.

Previous work in narrative and storytelling have been addressed for regenerating stories from graphs of intentions [5] or differentiating levels of narrative simultaneously (discourse/story planning) [11]. Nevertheless, in the first case the graph has to be populated by humans and in the second one, certain information is required to start with, as a set of action types or the goal conditions. The novelty of our proposal lays on the use of language models to learn dynamically the document plans from plain text, so the required content is first extracted and then provided to the surface realisation stage, where sentences are generated from the information also obtained through language models. In this manner, more flexible systems may be produced.

2 Statistical Approach Based on Language Models

Figure 1 depicts our proposed NLG approach. At the end of the process, information for each position and word remains stored *-matrix of scores*(MS). The relevant content will appear as an intermediate representation, the document plan (DP), that would work as guidance from the macroplanning to the surface realisation stage, where Factored Language Models (FLM) will be used, following an overgeneration and ranking strategy (o&r) to select for the story the best sentence from a set of candidate generated sentences.

2.1 Positional Language Models for Macroplanning

Usually based on bag-of-words approaches, language models have represented text as a set of elements with little or no consideration for their location along the document. Positional Language Models (PLM) can overcome such issue generating a model for each position of the text, on the basis of term propagation.

It is possible to calculate a score for each term at every position of a text, by means of a propagation function *f(k,j)* that rewards term repetition and closeness

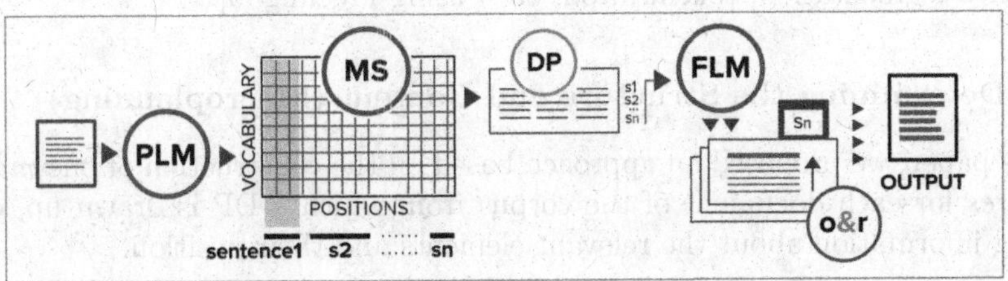

Fig. 1. Overview of our statistical generation process.

of the appearance. In this sense, for any position in the text k, it is calculated a a model that assigns a value to each term of the vocabulary V, $P(w|k)$:

$$P(w \mid k) = \frac{\sum_{j=1}^{|D|} c(w,j) \times f(k,j)}{\sum_{w' \in V} c(w',k)} \tag{1}$$

where $c(w,j) \in [0,1]$, and indicates the presence of term w in the position j, and $|D|$ refers to the length of the document. Therefore, information about both location and relevance of the term w in place k can be processed in order to elicit knowledge that improves the content selection and structuring, which are in fact the essential elements that define macroplanning.

2.2 Factored Language Models for Surface Realisation

FLMs are an extension of language models proposed in [1], which have been successfully employed in NLG [7,8]. The main objective of a FLM is to create a statistical model $P(f|f_1,\ldots,f_N)$ where the prediction of a feature f is based on N parents $\{f_1,\ldots,f_N\}$. In this model, a word is viewed as a vector of k factors such that $w \equiv \{f^1, f^2, \ldots, f^K\}$. These factors can be any lexical, syntactic or semantic features such as lemmas or stems.

Differently from previous NLG approaches, FLMs are used in our approach to generate text based on the information given by the macroplanning stage, applying over-generation and ranking techniques. For each line specified in the DP a set of candidate sentences is generated according to the grammar.

Then, these candidate sentences are ranked by their probability in order to select only one, following the approach suggested in [2]. The selected sentence is then inflected using a rule-based system developed for this purpose. This generation process is repeated for each sentence specification within the DP.

3 Experimental Scenario: Story Generation

A corpus of 67 English children stories extracted from *Bedtime Stories*[1] was used for the experiments. To enrich and complete the experimentation, it was enlarged for some stages of the process, with other fairy tales corpora (825 documents in total). All the documents were pre-processed at different linguistic analyses (sentence segmentation, tokenisation, etc.) using Freeling [9].

3.1 Determining the Structure and Content (Macroplanning)

In this paper, we proposed an approach based on the construction of one *matrix of scores* for each document of the corpus from which a DP is drawn up, containing information about the relevant elements and their position.

[1] https://freestoriesforkids.com/.

Computing the Matrix of Scores. The first step for filling the MS is to elaborate a *matrix of importance* (MI), a bi-dimensional collection of values with one row per word of the vocabulary and as many columns as positions in the text. MI[w,j] is equal to one if the term w appears in the position j, zero otherwise. For the current experiments, the decision was to generate very basic structures, simple verbal and noun phrases that could contain nouns and adjectives. Therefore, only lemmas of these categories would shape the set of terms of interest and, thus, the vocabulary. Afterwards, the proximity-based count is calculated using a propagation function. Several functions can be used here but, following previous work [4,6], we used the Gaussian Kernel:

$$f(k,j) = e^{\frac{-(k-j)^2}{2\sigma}} \tag{2}$$

In Eq. 2, the parameter σ is responsible for the spread of kernel curves and represents the semantic scope of a term. Some experiments, later explained, were conducted to finally set its value in 25.

At this stage, MS[w,k], which is equivalent to $P(w|k)$ in equation (1), can be computed for a term w in the position j, through the aggregation of the Gaussian value for each position of the same term in different places of the text: $\sum_{j=1}^{|D|} c(w,j) \times f(k,j)$.

Generating the Document Plan. The scores in the MS serve to create the DP. In this first attempt, values are retrieved respecting certain partitions or sections, constituted by the set of positions (sub-matrix of MS) conforming each sentence. Since our purpose was to recreate or to regenerate a story, this allows to keep the same number of sentences in both stories, the initial and the final one. From each sub-matrix, it is possible to distinguish those terms with higher values. Among them, for each sentence to be generated, the same amount of words of the three categories accepted (verb, noun, adjective) is selected into the DP. This number is constrained by one preset very simple grammar, so the length of generated sentences will range between 5 and 7 words. For this experiment, 5 words per category are transferred into the DP.

At this point, we were able to experiment with several values for σ, being finally empirically determined (25) after analysing results for a set of values (25, 75, 100, 175). It was observed that upper values led to a lower variety of elements in the DP and, thus, to poorer outcomes.

3.2 Surface Realisation

For surface realisation, several FLMs were used. On the one hand, a FLM using the whole corpora was trained, in order to enrich the vocabulary to perform the generation of a new story with original content. On the other hand, a single FLM for each of the stories within the 67 English children tales was trained too. This duality led to the possibility of producing two types of texts: (i) an abstractive summary (*regeneration task*) , and (ii) a new story based on the same vocabulary and elements of a particular tale (*recreation task*).

Additionally, a *baseline* method was defined: during the generation, the information extracted from the title of the original stories was employed instead of the information given by the DP, i.e., no macroplanning stage is used.

4 Evaluation and Discussion

As a quality indicator, the word variation was measured both in all the outputs and the source stories (i.e., the original ones). To obtain this value, we consider the ratio between the total number of words and the number of different words in such set (unique words). The higher the value, the richer the variety and the better the output. Results are shown in Table 1.

Table 1. Results for the regeneration and recreation task (%)

	Regeneration task			Recreation task		
	Baseline (no DP)	Macro-planning	Originals	Baseline (no DP)	Macro-planning	Originals
General variation	54.34	34.61	61.06	59.49	34.43	61.06
Verb V	40.80	18.15	61.74	64.23	26.09	61.74
Noun V	55.49	40.02	55.49	55.94	36.96	55.49
Adjective V	73.97	42.64	78.83	59.08	39.79	78.83
ROUGE-1 R	47.00	52.00	–	–	–	–

Furthermore, Rouge metric [3] was employed for the *regeneration task* to compare the regenerated stories (i.e., summary) with the original ones. The recall measure for unigrams is reported, showing the results improvement when the macroplanning stage is used. This indicates that the macroplanning is providing the appropriate information about what elements to incorporate into the story.

In all the cases, regarding variety, the values for the original stories are higher, but as well the length of the documents, since they are not limited by the grammar applied. The *baselines*, i.e., the approach without the macroplanning stage, present more variety than those generated from the data in the DP. This is because introducing the DP implies a restriction in the choices the model can make and furthermore, because it is possible that words with high value in the MS appear in consecutive lines when the surface realisation looks for relevant terms there, which clarifies these results.

Additionally, the generated sentences (i.e., with both configurations) were evaluated with the TER [10] metric, comparing them with the original story from the corpus. In this respect, the results obtained using macroplanning improve against those obtained for the baseline, specifically, showing an increase of 3.81% for *recreation* and 5.74% for *regeneration*.

4.1 Error Analysis

A manual analysis of the results revealed several limitations. Regarding the verbs within the generated stories, there is a high number of repetitions of the most commonly used verbs in English (e.g., *to be, to have*), which leads to a low verb variability problem in some of the stories (lowest rates in Table 1).

Moreover, the election of a simple grammar for our first attempt has advantages but clear limitations too, from the inability to create negative or interrogative sentences to the restriction regarding the extent for a richer vocabulary, or the enlargement of types of elements (adverbs, pronouns, etc.).

5 Conclusion and Future Work

This paper presents a novel NLG approach that integrates the stages of macroplanning and surface realisation. Macroplanning employs PLMs to locate and extract the elements of interest shaping the document plan. From there, realisation is made through FLMs trained both from the whole corpora and from each tale itself, which gives way to two different tasks: recreation and regeneration of the original texts. The preliminary results obtained are very promising, opening an interesting research line.

In the future, we plan to increase the set of elements of interest for the macroplanning (e.g., synonymy relations), as well as analyse how different configurations for the PLMs (kernel selection, sigma parameter) may influence on the document plan. Regarding surface realisation, we plan to improve the approach, especially for other languages.

References

1. Bilmes, J.A., Kirchhoff, K.: Factored language models and generalized parallel backoff. In: Companion Volume of the Proceedings of HLT-NAACL, pp. 4–6 (2003)
2. Isard, A., Brockmann, C., Oberlander, J.: Individuality and alignment in generated dialogues. In: Proceedings of the INLG Conference, pp. 25–32. ACL (2006)
3. Lin, C.Y.: Rouge: A package for automatic evaluation of summaries. In: Text Summarization Branches Out: Proceedings, pp. 74–81. ACL (2004)
4. Liu, S.H., Chen, K.Y., Chen, B., Wang, H.M., Yen, H.C., Hsu, W.L.: Positional language modeling for extractive broadcast news speech summarization. In: INTERSPEECH, pp. 2729–2733 (2015)
5. Lukin, S.M., Reed, L.I., Walker, M.A.: Generating sentence planning variations for story telling. In: 16th SIGDIAL, p. 188 (2015)
6. Lv, Y., Zhai, C.: Positional language models for information retrieval. In: Proceedings of the 32nd International ACM SIGIR, pp. 299–306. ACM (2009)
7. Mairesse, F., Young, S.: Stochastic language generation in dialogue using factored language models. Comput. Linguist. **40**(4), 763–799 (2014)
8. Novais, E.M., Paraboni, I.: Portuguese text generation using factored language models. J. Braz. Comput. Soc. **19**(2), 135–146 (2012)
9. Padró, L., Stanilovsky, E.: Freeling 3.0: towards wider multilinguality. In: Proceedings of LREC 2012. European Language Resources Association (2012)

10. Snover, M., Dorr, B., Schwartz, R., Micciulla, L., Makhoul, J.: A study of translation edit rate with targeted human annotation. In: Proceedings of AMTA, pp. 223–231 (2006)
11. Winer, D.R., Young, R.M.: Discourse-driven narrative generation with bipartite planning. In: Proceedings of the 9th INLG Conference, pp. 11–20 (2016)

Author Index